ALSO BY GREGORY ORFALEA

The Man Who Guarded the Bomb:
Stories

Angeleno Days:
An Arab American Writer on Family, Place, and Politics

The Arab Americans:
A History

Messengers of the Lost Battalion:
The Heroic 551st and the Turning of the Tide
at the Battle of the Bulge

The Capital of Solitude

Before the Flames:
A Quest for the History of Arab Americans

Edited by Gregory Orfalea

with Barbara Rosewicz:
Up All Night:
Practical Wisdom from Mothers and Fathers

with Sharif Elmusa:
Grape Leaves:
A Century of Arab-American Poetry

JOURNEY
TO THE SUN

JUNÍPERO SERRA'S DREAM
and the FOUNDING *of* CALIFORNIA

GREGORY ORFALEA

SCRIBNER

New York   London   Toronto   Sydney   New Delhi

SCRIBNER
A Division of Simon & Schuster, Inc.
1230 Avenue of the Americas
New York, NY 10020

First Scribner hardcover edition January 2014

For information about special discounts for bulk purchases,
please contact Simon & Schuster Special Sales at 1-866-506-1949
or business@simonandschuster.com.

The Simon & Schuster Speakers Bureau can bring authors to your live event.
For more information or to book an event, contact the Simon & Schuster Speakers Bureau
at 1-866-248-3049 or visit our website at www.simonspeakers.com.

Jacket design by Marlyn Dantes and Tal Goretsky
Jacket photograph by Mark Schoen

Manufactured in the United States of America

1   3   5   7   9   10   8   6   4   2

Library of Congress Control Number: 2013040181

ISBN 978-1-4516-4272-8
ISBN 978-1-4516-4275-9 (ebook)

To
Sister Mary Mark Schoenstein, O.P.

And in memory of
Father John Columba Fogarty, O. Carm.

CONTENTS

CONTENTS

PART THREE

THE FIRST NINE CALIFORNIA MISSIONS

PART FOUR

IN THE SHADOW OF SERRA

JOURNEY TO THE SUN

Anna Seile's map of "The Americas: A New Description,"
with outsized dagger-shaped California as island, 1663.

PROLOGUE

Who is God's companion?
    Junípero Serra might have contemplated this thought on the road in the Salinas Valley of California, where in 1771 he met an Indian woman who offered him "a present." When he asked her name, she murmured *Soledad,* Spanish for "solitude." Or at least that is what he heard: "I was astonished, and turning to my companions said, 'Here, gentlemen, you have María de la Soledad.'" He gave her glass beads for seeds; she nodded. As "the name stuck to the place," Serra made a note to found a mission in that desolate, treeless spot. Soledad later became the most hard-luck mission of all those that were built on the coast.

Serra had undergone plenty of solitude, the *soledad* of the trail, the one that surrounded your neck like water at night, a *soledad* to conquer by singing Matins before first light. Not English or American solitude, which celebrated being on one's own, without others; Spanish *soledad,* which longed for them.

Serra was not about *soledad*; neither were the Franciscan fathers. He'd swallowed his fill of it as a boy, losing two sisters and a brother, working the quiet fields of Petra, his home village on the Spanish island of Mallorca. But his father's leather hand was always on his shoulder, and later his confreres' *abrazos*; even those strangers in the confessional cut *soledad* with their pain. Serra respected the solitude Christ felt in the garden that last night of his life when the apostles slept. But Serra wasn't Simon of the Desert, standing on his pillar alone. He loved community, loved performing marriages. He traveled as much as he could in a pair or group, because outside the mission walls lay a solitude so vast only the sun could disperse it.

Now the dew was on the leaf, the earth shorn briefly of dust. Dark and lovely and cool. The sun began its climb of the Santa Lucia Mountains, casting them in gray outline. As his mule snorted, taking him north in the

1

early morning, the sun regarded Serra; he dared not look back. The sun warm on his forehead, rising over the crown of the forest, now arched in his mind above the Tramuntana range of his old island and its olive groves to the sea, the Mediterranean waded into the Pacific, the sun wrapping the world in its arms.

Who was God's companion?

He was.

For a second, he looked at the sun; God put a white spot in his eye.

PART ONE

SERRA BEFORE CALIFORNIA

Nicolas Sanson's map of "The Isle of California" and "New" Mexico, 1657.

CHAPTER ONE

ISLAND SON

I, the one who hugs you,
I am not alone!
—GABRIELA MISTRAL

Sancturi de Cura on Mount Randa, Mallorca.

$\mathcal{A}$t the darkest point of night, the point at which the light begins to grow, Miquel José Serre was born at 1 A.M. by the flickering of an olive oil lamp on November 24, 1713, in the little farming village of Petra, slightly east of dead center of the island of Mallorca, one of three Balearic Islands off the coast of Spain in the northwest Mediterranean. His father, Antonio, put a sprig of laurel on the door, indicating the baby was a boy; a myrtle branch would have meant a girl. Petra was a village of two thousand then, and it is barely larger today.

With a population of about seventy thousand, Mallorca had a climate of dry heat and white light. But it was no resort. In the eighteenth century, the island traffic consisted of horse and mule carts and men hoisting shovels. The nineteenth-century writer George Sand, visiting Mallorca to care for the sickly Frédéric Chopin, called the Mallorcan peasant "a gentle, kind creature, with peaceful habits . . . he has no love of evil and knowledge of good . . . you can no more hate him than you could an ox or a sheep, for he is close to the savage whose soul is lulled in animal innocence."

With its whiff of Gallic superiority, this perception missed a key element: community. Peasant farmers in the Petra area who tended sheep, olive and almond groves, and citrus trees lived not in isolated huts in the field, but in town in seamlessly attached Santanyí sandstone homes situated along narrow, labyrinthine streets. They lived in close proximity, hearing each other's coughs and moans and prayers through the clay walls and screenless windows. Though in our world these conditions would be taken as a sign of poverty, the peasant farming village community of eighteenth-century Spain was hardly downtrodden. People worked hard and were proud of it. Mallorcan peasant homes were sturdily made—clay, stone, tiled, or wattled roofs—and when little Miguel (the Castilian spelling of the Mallorquín "Miquel") put his head out the window of his second-story bedroom he stared right across the narrow street at his double, a boyhood friend who put his own head out the window, and the signals of boys' and girls' heads and their calls down the street brought them to work in the field, to play, and to attend Mass on Sunday.

Serra's comfort with and affection for close-knit village life was in his blood. He was benignly crushed together with his neighbors because his parents, Antonio Serra and Margarita Ferrer, had been so crushed. Natives of Petra, their families have been traced there as far back as 1577, though the direct lineage of Serra runs out by 1839. His father was baptized Antonio Nadal Serre on Christmas Day 1675. "Serre" is the strictly Mallorquín version of the word "saw." In fact, a workman's saw is on the Serra family's coat of arms.

There is more than a little evidence that the boy who would grow up to be among the leaders of the first group of white men to walk into and stay in today's California had Jewish blood. His paternal grandmother was named Juana Abraham. Abraham also could be a Europeanization of the Muslim name Ibrahim, so it is possible that he could have been of Arab extraction. Or both, since most Jews in Spain were Sephardic and traced their roots across North Africa back to Palestine. Also, as the Arabs spent five hundred years ruling Spain, clinging most tenaciously to little Mallorca until it was given up in 1229 (with shrewd allowance by James I of Aragon that Muslims "retain some of their own civil and religious institutions"), it's not far-fetched to posit that his grandmother's Old Testament (and Koranic) surname made Serra part Jew and part Arab.

The Inquisition, though diminished in its scope by Serra's time, was not entirely abolished in Spain until the early nineteenth century, and had examined in its obsessive and murderous fervor several families in the sixteenth century named Serra. There is more than a little evidence that some of Serra's ancestors through his father's line were inspected (and suspected) as *cuetas*, that is, Mallorcan Catholics who had converted from Judaism—and perhaps Islam. (One historian also speculated that Serra descended in part from the love life of a freed fourteenth-century Moorish slave on Mallorca.) Serra himself—and his parents—had little, if any, consciousness of being descendants of Arabs or *cuetas*, but it would be surprising if Serra was not aware that the name had echoes attached to it, especially through his paternal grandmother. His strong and early fervor for Catholicism had an edge of the anxious assertiveness of the convert, or more accurately and suspiciously, the *conversos,* those who converted under pressure of persecution. In short, Serra may have had to prove himself more Catholic than the Catholic, which could be one explanation—though only one—for his later missionary zeal.

The hardihood of Miguel Serra's mother, Margarita Ferrer, can be divined by the etymology of her surname. Ferrer derives from *fierro*, or iron; it suggests ironworkers in her past (or blacksmiths, *herreros*). Margarita had married Antonio Serra in Petra at St. Peter's Church on August 7, 1707. She was twenty-nine, he was thirty-one. They had two children, a boy, Miguel, and a daughter, Juana. But both lives were quickly snuffed out.

The Miguel Serra we know today was named after a deceased sibling, as was his younger sister, Juana. Serra was a sickly boy, probably an asthmatic, thin and short even by Mallorcan standards. Aware that he was essentially a replacement child, born six years into his parents' marriage, he must have had an acute sense of mortality, "the preciousness of life." There is some speculation that the early losses of children in their infancy may have inclined Antonio and Margarita toward becoming a secular monk and nun—people operating outside the monastery in civil society known as tertiaries, or third order, of Franciscans. These losses almost certainly frightened them enough to do something with the "new" Miguel that was unusual for most Mallorcan families: he was baptized on the day of his birth rather than several days later, as was customary, as if daring the devil—or God—to take yet another child.

A procession of relatives and neighbors carrying laurel sprigs made their way to St. Peter's, men in Moorish wool trousers, women dressed in long skirts, fringed shawls, and nunlike wimples, the midwife carrying the infant. The priest, Bartolomé Llado, poured water from a "silvered" shell over the baby's forehead and blessed him as he was held by his god-mother, Sebastiana Serra, Antonio's sister, over the octagonal Santanyí sandstone font.

The majesty and shadow of the Arab Muslims in Spain flickers across Junípero Serra's life from his earliest days as Miguel. Apparently, an obses-sion with how to deal with the Moor inside and out made a short entry at Serra's baptism. When the midwife handed the infant Miguel to his mother, Margarita kissed him, probably for the first time. Why? Because it was Mallorcan custom to call the newborn "a little Moor" (*un moret*), withholding a kiss until he was rescued from unknown misery by Chris-tian baptism. Moorishness was thus conflated on the island with original sin. The priest was thanked for his troubles with a basket of pears, and at the Serra home the celebrants were treated to cookies called *paciencies*, which were—as are pastries throughout the Arab world—touched with anise, that seed essential to licorice and goodwill.

The year Serra was born—1713—was also the bitter end of the com-plicated War of the Spanish Succession. The Hapsburg monarchy that descended from Ferdinand and Isabella had literally died out with Charles II, known as the Bewitched, who keeled over on November 1, 1700, childless. Just before Serra's birth (and during the time of the crib deaths of his older sister and brother), Catalonia and Mallorca were pulled in great pain between two forces contending to rule Spain after the Bewitched: those of Philip of Anjou (France) and those of Charles of Austria, who had a Hapsburg coalition of England, Germany (with rem-nants of the Holy Roman Empire), and Holland.

The French were the largest immigrant group in Spain, "a very vis-ible presence" with "economic dominance," thus "Francophobia had deep roots in Spain." In 1705, at the beginning of the War of the Spanish Succession, Frenchmen passing through Saragossa were beaten and mur-dered. The upper and middle classes sided with the Bourbons in the war, but the blue-collar and farm workers sided with the Hapsburgs. This did not later dispose the son of the soil Serra toward Philip of Anjou, whose climactic 1713 attack on Barcelona killed 9,700 citizens making a heroic but futile defense of their city, to which the Hapsburgs gave no relief. In the end, the Catalonians were alone against Philip. Serra was born the very year the city across the water from his island was smothered.

• • •

The death of their first two children thrust Antonio's and Margarita's already faithful lives into a spiritual zeal that made them usher their new precious son to Petra's Franciscan friary, San Bernardino, at the earliest possible moment for his education. His mother was particularly protective of Miguel and "did not allow any contact with anyone who could tamper with her children's innocence." Margarita sternly ensured that no "hair on the tongue" (*no trahe pelos en la lingua*)—gossip—would mar his young spirit. His schooling began with trips to friends they had made among the friars, and by the age of six or seven became more formalized in a classroom.

For a precious three years, little Miguel had had the rule of the roost and the undivided affections of his parents. Then on January 28, 1716, his sister, Juana María, was born. Juana was to be an important figure in his early life, his one surviving sibling, and the only one to carry the Serra family's blood forward with her own three children—one of whom died, one of whom became a priest, and one of whom produced a priest through a child, thus halting the Serra family forever at the altar. Five years after his dear Juana, Serra's second sister (Martina María) was born, but Martina also died young. Three out of five siblings dead: it was a family sown in a bitter field, with love precious as gold.

Miguel was, presumably, especially close to his father, working with him in the orchards and fields from an early age. Like other children of his time and place, he probably awoke early at the *casa solariega* (ancestral home) at 6 Calle Barracar, before light, just as his mother and father did, as farms all over the world do not wait for light. Juana, his sister, probably arose and dressed before him, helping her mother knead dough for bread. As the Serras lived under the same roof with farm animals, Juana went to the cow in the front room of the house, bringing the candle close, feeling the warm udder, squeezing the withered teats. The land was often dry, and the island was in constant search for methods to catch the little rain that fell. But Juana squirted enough milk steaming in the chilled pail that her mother said to her, "*Bon día, gratias*"—naming the day in Catalán with a wisp of that French *bon*. Serra awoke to the smell of bread put in the bake oven out back near the pig wallow. Juana fetched it through chickens trembling out of the coop, where she took up a few warm, damp eggs.

Gradually, the sky grew blue—first so dark as to be indistinguishable from the sea, then cobalt, then royal as the Blessed Mother's robes. Little Miguel hitched the mule for his father, and climbed aboard, his father holding the rein in one hand, a shovel over his shoulder in the other. They would spend the morning picking olives—winter olives, as they grew three-quarters ripe, the exact moment of the picking—between November and March. If it was January or February, they picked by the light of the white-blossoming almond trees, the *amatllers*. Miguel grew up thinking the earth itself was full of light, especially after the Epiphany on January 6, a beauty so strong it hurt the eyes. He climbed the olive trees with his sack attached to his belt and began to denude them. He picked olives by the light of incipient almonds, picked until his frail brown arms began to ache.

Mallorcan olives are small and green and have a slightly bitter taste. In Serra's time they were the top export of the island—averaging 75 percent of Mallorca's trade—most in the form of olive oil. The oil went north—to Marseilles, Amsterdam, London, even Hamburg, where it was used less for eating than to fill oilcans that lubricated the gears of the textile mills. In Marseilles, Mallorcan olive oil was made into soap.

After a day's harvest, the Serra family would join the olive growers of the area surrounding Petra and add their harvest to full burlap sacks that would be hauled by mule train about forty miles west—nearly the island's girth—over the chief mountain range, the Sierra de Tramuntana, to the northwestern port town of Soller. There ground the great circles of stone, the oil presses. Little Miguel may have accompanied this olive train with his father. Today there is a tunnel through the mountain; then there was no way to get the olives to press without mounting the steep rise on mule or on foot.

Returning to Calle Barracar, both Antonio and son Miguel would knock before entering and say, "*Ave María Puríssima*" (Hail Mary, Most Pure), and either Margarita or Juana would answer, "*Cancebuda sens pecat*" (Conceived without sin). This homage to the Immaculate Conception of Christ's mother, Mary—so particular to Mallorcans—is practiced even today.

Later, in summer, the work switched to harvesting wheat, carob, and the almond trees, whose bright flowers had grown husks to be picked and shucked, the white nuts stripped of their brown skin to make oil exported to the South and Central American colonies for medicinal balms and facial cosmetics. The almond had been brought to the island by the ancient Romans. (After the colonies received independence, Mallorcan almonds were shipped to Spain and Europe or kept locally for a sweet additive to milk, ice cream, and nougats.)

But until March, the olives consumed them. As the morning sun rose over the cross at the top of Ermita de Bon Any, little Miguel may have broken from his olive picking and walked up the steep hill to the shrine of Our Lady of the Good Year to ring the noon bells. *Ermitas*, or shrines, were all over Mallorca, and most remain. No hilltop was without an *ermita* or *santuari* (a monastery). Within a year of its construction in 1609, abundant rain fell on Mallorca, and thus the shrine was named Nuestra Señora de Bon Any—prayers were for a "good year," meaning rain. Serra grew up with the 1663 bell of that miraculous shrine at the highest point of his gaze. He made his way to the breathtaking view, probably gulping for breath. Already winded by the toil in the olive groves, he walked the half mile to Bon Any up a steep dirt path. He would walk the asthma out of himself. If his lungs felt like two iron weights, he would walk.

At the top, looking out on the island, he might pray for family, animals, or fruit, then consume a lunch of orange-red Mallorcan sausage on bread, a slip of cheese. Climbing up the olivewood steps to the belfry, Miguel might ring the twelve bells that recalled not just the middle of the day, but the Twelve Apostles—"Peter, Andrew, James, John" (the first four).

At the top of Nuestra Señora de Bon Any, Miguel was 1,289 feet above sea level. The view from the belfry could take away what little breath he had left and lift him out of his wheezing body. Blue spangled in three directions: to the north Miguel saw the crescent Bay of Alcudia, which the Romans had entered two thousand years before to retake Iberia from Carthage. With apostles to the east—"Philip, Bartholemew, Matthew, Thomas"—the Santuari de Sant Salvador pointed to heaven just before the open Mediterranean. To the south and southwest, the far-off old Roman capital of Palma sparkled before the eye, lost in blue that stretched all the way to Algeria. The only direction blocked of a view of the sea was straight west—"James, Jude, Simon, and Judas Iscariot"—the Tramuntana Mountains. How he must have longed to see over that wall, to expand on the glimpse he got once a year near the olive press.

If he was coming down Bon Any or from the fields on an important feast day, he went to visit his godparents, Sebastiana Serra and Bartholmé Fiol, and kissed their hands with the traditional reverence Mallorcan children had and still have for godparents.

In the afternoons, Miguel went to school at the friary of the magnificent Franciscan church of St. Bernardine, perhaps the finest on the island outside Palma. Finished in 1677 and named for the fifteenth-century comforter of plague victims who denounced the fratricidal wars of Italian princes, San Bernardino was a place of deep mystery and wonder. Its Moorish steeple was gilded in gold and Baroque in style, its main altar unfolding to ten side altars, five on each side of the church. Each of these sub-altars had its own story with paintings of the saints, such as San Juan Capistrano, whose foot crushes the head of a Turk.

The only two academic subjects referred to by Serra's first biographer and former student Francisco Palou (in discussing Serra's boyhood instruction from the friars of San Bernardino) are Latin and "plain chanting." But Serra certainly had lessons from among the sixteen Franciscan friars in religion, writing, mathematics, and reading. It seems likely that as a boy Serra read the lives of the saints, particularly Franciscan figures such as Raymond Lull, St. Bernardine of Siena, and St. Francis of Assisi. He may have even read a novel popular for two centuries in Spain called *The Labors of the Very Brave Knight Esplandián* (1510), whose knight hero ventures bravely to an island called California.

But the missionaries were the ones who truly captured his imagination. Raymond Lull has been called "the greatest of medieval missionaries," and perhaps the greatest Christian missionary between St. Paul in the first century and the late eighteenth century's Baptist-gone-to-India William Carey. As a Mallorcan, Lull had a special appeal to the young Miguel. Lull wrote—by hand, of course—over 250 books, some multilayered and complex, many with a strong emphasis on human love as a mirror of the divine (*The Tree of Love*; *The Book of the Lover and the Beloved*). He was fascinated, if not obsessed, with the Muslim world (perhaps out of guilt—when his black Muslim slave teacher of Arabic cursed a Christian for a racial slur, Lull had the slave imprisoned, where he committed suicide). Lull preached for much of his life, though not all of it, a "peaceful Crusade," believing that salvation was to be won in people's hearts and not on the battlefield with mace and longbow. Fluent in Arabic and well versed in the Sufi poets, Lull founded in 1276 what may have been the first (post-Muslim occupation) college in Spain for the study of Arabic, at Miramar in Mallorca. Thirteen Franciscan friars enrolled.

Born in Palma, Mallorca, in 1232—just three years after the Muslim leadership had abandoned the island—in his twenties Lull lived the dissolute life of a rich man's spoiled kid—drinking, whoring; he hardly saw the inside of a church. He married and had two children but was regularly unfaithful. Though brilliant like Augustine, Lull was more of a poet (and mathematician). At thirty, removing himself to Mount Randa, he was casually writing a love poem to one of his paramours when he had a vision of Christ on the Cross. He fought off the vision, but it kept returning—three more times. Terrified at first, Lull realized that perhaps his life was about to change—and should. Soon after these disturbing visitations, he read the life of St. Francis, who had insisted on going directly to the Muslim caliph in Egypt to settle the problems between Islam and Christianity nonviolently. That Lull, a Mallorcan, had done virtually the same thing, except to Tunisia, stirred the heart of his fellow Mallorcan.

The Glow of Love. This is what Lull sought between antagonists—quixotically, perhaps, but not without deep grounding in his newfound Christianity. He writes in the *Book of Contemplation*: "Men are wont, O Lord, to die from old age, the failure of natural warmth and excess of cold; but . . . Thy servant . . . would rather die in the glow of love."

Nevertheless, Lull's rationalist mysticism came under the fire of two popes; the Inquisition condemned dozens of his teachings. At eighty, Lull quietly gained five high-ranking converts in Tunis, but when he went shouting the Trinity creed in the town square in Bugia, east of Algiers, he was stoned and mortally wounded, dying before reaching Mallorca and realizing thereby what one writer saw as the Franciscans' "mania for martyrdom."

Young Serra would not have had that mania, at least not yet. But he was deeply moved by Christ's Passion. At San Bernardino, Serra would not have encountered Lull's abstruse theology; that would have been later, in seminary at Palma. But he certainly would have been fascinated by Lull's audacious love, a love that made him cross the waters to the Other. That Other had ruled over Mallorca and all of Spain; at its height had held Islam, Judaism, and Christianity in a rare balance in Andalusia; and was now a short boat ride south across the water. That Other had also magnetized his greatest hero.

St. Francis, who died two years before Lull's birth but whose myth was growing exponentially in Lull's time, also profoundly influenced young Miguel. In his schoolbooks, so much about the man who founded the Franciscans appealed to him: the fact that Francis was part French and loved Troubadour poetry; the fact that, as G. K. Chesterton would say centuries later, he "never, all his life, exactly understood what money was"; that he had "all his life a great liking for people who had been put hopelessly in the wrong"; that Francis was forever being pulled like a "deep tide driving out to uncharted seas of charity"; that he kept up his fellow prisoners' spirits in captivity; his boldness and dramatic nature; his instinct for "creative monuments of peace"; his absolute conviction that poverty leads to interior richness. Francis's clarion call was to be a *jongleur de Dieu*, or (Chesterton again) "the court fool of the King of Paradise"—and this wild man of God absolutely captivated the demure farmer's son.

Serra's eyes could light up reading about St. Francis's voyage to Egypt to convert the Sultan al-Kamil as his forces stood outside Damietta, under siege of the Crusade. St. Francis must have baffled the Muslim leader. He ordered the friars served a good meal ending with a kind of lemony sherbet made "from the icy mountains of Lebanon."

"It was, of course, simply the idea that it is better to create Christians than to destroy Moslems," wrote Chesterton about this extraordinary encounter. Francis spoke about Christ's poverty, suffering, and return from the dead—themes that appealed deeply to Kamil, given his predicament. But when Francis offered to step into a fire to show that his God would protect him, the sultan, astonished, declined the contest. His subsequent offer of a truce and a return of Jerusalem to the Christians was inspired by this portentous meeting with the saint, who was allowed safe passage back to the Christian lines. But a squabble between King Jean of France and the cardinal on the spot foreclosed the truce. Francis withdrew. His peace mission ended with Kamil's forces routed, beheaded, and dumped summarily outside the sultan's camp.

How much of this story did Miguel Serra take away? And what lessons would he have learned? His beloved Francis—who praised Brother Sun and Sister Moon in his "Canticle of the Sun"—had failed in his peace mission to Islam, done in, in fact, by his own Christians. Better an enemy who listens than a friend who doesn't?

What must have struck him most in the St. Francis story was the stigmata. Francis had returned from North Africa disconsolate about his failed mission, only to behold his followers in Italy availing themselves of a large manor in Bologna and living something of the good life. He railed against them as stridently as did Christ the Temple moneylenders, and he soon left for a mountain called Alverno. There a great mystery happened; when Francis came down from the mountain he was bleeding from holes in five places—in his hands, his feet, and his chest, just as Christ had on the cross. It was the first known stigmata in the history of the Church.

The farmer's boy on peaceful Mallorca had more than a vague sense of the meaning of such a branding. There was, he learned, something holy in suffering.

During his schooling at San Bernardino in Petra, perhaps the most important thing Miguel Serra did was not study, but sing. He had a strong, mellifluous, deep voice, and the friars sensed his gift early, inviting him to join them when they sang the Divine Office on feast days.

Song surrounded the island at the May wheat harvest, with *trilladors*, men who harnessed mules to a cylindrical stone, cracking the wheat as they followed the animals and trilling. Song was crucial, too, to the most important holy day of the year then as now in Latino countries, Tres Reyes, or the Feast of the Three Kings or Wise Men on January 6, also known as the Epiphany. Tres Reyes is deemed more important—and certainly more magisterial and mysterious—than Christmas. It was accompanied in Mallorca by great theater. Children filled their shoes with long carob pods, then placed the shoes on window sills or balconies, in supplication to the Wise Men, who would replace the pods with gifts. In Petra on January 5, the three men would come galloping into town in glittering saddles and colorful clothes as if they were kings from the far reaches of the world (at least one would be Muslim, not so far off). *Dimoni*, or devil figures, would lurk around them, symbolizing what the kings had to overcome to view the Creator in swaddling clothes.

On January 6, a great morning Mass was said at St. Peter's, where not only Communion but fresh hot bread (*pan de promesa*, the bread of promise) brought by the villagers was given to each congregant, who in Serra's childhood were often made hungry by drought. The actor kings came to the altar with a real lamb to give the infant figure in the manger, played by one of the better-behaved babies. And then a "young boy with a bell-like voice" would sing the *sibila*, a solemn, but hopeful reminder of the end of the world at the commemoration of its Christian beginning. Perhaps Serra was one with that bell inside.

At the end of Mass, a basket of sweets and meat pies, the *cucaña* (*piñata* in Mexico), suspended by colorful ribbons across the church, was cut down with a sword and children such as Miguel would come running to scoop up the rewards, modern equivalents of the Wise Men's gifts.

Did Miguel throw his candy at someone? We do not have a boyhood ne'er-do-well or coming-of-age story of Miguel "Junípero" Serra. We do not have a story of transgression, such as Augustine's stolen pears. We don't even have a story of brash goodness in his teen years, such as Francis of Assisi's throwing off his fine clothes to a beggar. What we do know is that on return from school or church, his parents would give him the common blessing, "May God make a saint of you" (*Deu te faci un sant*). Another common prayer in the form of song was known as the *Alabado*, perhaps the most widespread song from the early days in Hispanic America, which originated among the Franciscan missionaries of Mallorca and no doubt was sung in Petra at San Bernardino by little Miguel himself. It derived, too, from a common greeting the young Serra heard every day on Mallorca, "*Alabado sea Dios*" (Praise to God).

But there was something else Miguel Serra must have heard even before he spied it through the arched colonnades of San Bernardino. It was a short whip with metal tailings, commonly used by monks in the eighteenth century. The muffled cry of a friar drew him, as if he might help him in his suffering. But what he saw would have confused him. The priest did not want help. He may later have explained he was trying to be like Christ, to help expiate the sins of the world. It did not make sense to the boy Serra, such blood drops on stone. But sacrifice, the kind of backbreaking work his father was introducing him to in the almond groves, did.

The boy probably recoiled from the *disciplina*, as it was called. It was too cruel for the world he knew in Mallorca, even one of such hard work, because there was serenity in Sunday afternoons, togetherness. There were the *amatllers*. Their light. Christ did not whip himself. He was whipped by the soldiers who made fun of him, who drew lots for him, who pressed thorn bushes into his head.

Serra was an unusually intelligent boy. Everyone could see it—his father and mother, his sister, Juana, his godparents, the friars at San Bernardino. And though like any teenager he had his questions, no doubt most were held down. But some days, such as one scaling the hard high road up the Tramuntana with his father's pack train of olives, they could visit him mutely: *Why did you create the world in the first place? Why did the boy I am named for die before I breathed?* Above Soller at last, Miguel Serra would have seen the sun's ladder on the water leading west. It shimmered silver. It roiled his eyes. When he closed them, the darkness behind his lids bloomed. Sunspots. Opening them, the water was illuminated like a manuscript. Like all Mallorcans, he read it.

From that vision, Miguel and his father would come back with the mules without olives, their burden lightened. As they slowly moved through the light of the almond trees, Miguel might forget his questions. The world was too beautiful for answers.

CHAPTER TWO

THE CALL

I consecrate you, God, because you love so much
Because you never smile; because your heart
Must all the time give you great pain.
—CÉSAR VALLEJO

Soller, site of the old Mallorca olive press
over the Tramuntana massif.

What calls a boy to the priesthood? Unlike today, celibacy was, for the most part, accepted by eighteenth-century Mallorcans; priestly status and its requirements were revered. Palou, whom Serra would meet as a seminarian in Palma, tells us that as soon as his parents apprehended their boy's "holy vocation" they whisked him to the city of Palma.

But how did Miguel's parents "realize" his "holy vocation"? Was it something he said or had done? Was it what some have called "an itch that longs to be scratched"? One acclaimed poet thought that when common fishermen "put everything down to walk away" to follow Christ as the Twelve Apostles, *that* was the most miraculous thing of all.

For fifteen-year-old Miguel Serra, it may have been nothing particularly inspiring. In eighteenth-century Europe, the calling was more likely poverty itself. The priesthood was a position of esteem to the rural poor, and particularly so on Mallorca. A sizable portion of the people on the island were in religious orders, either as priests, nuns, monks, or tertiaries, or were working closely with them. To be a priest was to elevate oneself up the social and even political ladder, as no ruler and his lieutenants could operate without significant consultation with, if not outright blessing from, the clergy. Priests may have taken vows of poverty, chastity, and obedience, but they never took one against power.

So what Antonio and Margarita Serra "realized" about their precocious, fervent son may have had more to do with what they knew about their own predicament. They were farmers. They were going nowhere beyond beautiful, poor Petra and its hard soil. Their one chance at ascension was through this frail boy given to them after two infant deaths. The friars at San Bernardino may have felt something similar. Send this one to Palma. Send this one to the Great Outer World.

Palma, which in 1728 had a population of roughly thirty-five thousand (perhaps half that of the island), was seventeen times the size of Petra. To the young Serra, it was an imposing, walled metropolis. If Mallorca is shaped like a horsehead, Palma is where the bit catches the back of the mouth. And it caught him. The skinny, short boy of fifteen studied under the canon (perhaps Don Antonio Figuera) at the cathedral for a year. La Seu, as the cathedral is called in Catalán, was built over a mosque shortly after James I of Aragon retook the island from the Muslims in 1229. It dominates the skyline of Palma, "the finest example of Mediterranean Gothic architecture" due in part to its "sensations of light . . . in comparison with the shadows" of other, darker Gothic churches across the continent. If the teenage Serra hiked to the Bellver Castle—also of thirteenth-century vintage, with a sweeping view of the Bay of Palma—he would have seen how the southern sun coming out of Africa stuns La Seu as it sits astride the bay like a galleon. "The sun could kiss it at all hours of the day," wrote a Spanish artist. "The Cathedral of Palma is an island in the heart of an island." The rose window, with 1,236 pieces of glass radiating from a red center to blue to yellow at the corona, flooded all three naves of La Seu with rose afire.

Moving from his study with the canon in one of the chambers of the cathedral into the central nave bathed in roseate light would have pulled Serra into the center of the rose, where the great Christian mystics lived. He must have experienced some fundamental shift, as within six months after turning sixteen, he applied to enter the Franciscan order. He was turned down. He seemed too young and "rather sickly," according to Palou. But there may have been another reason: up until the seventeenth century—for over a hundred years—if you had the surname "Serre," you came into the crosshairs of the Inquisition. Add this to his grandmother's surname Abraham, and it spelled fear of the *cueta*.

Just before he turned seventeen, Serra tried again; this time he passed muster. On September 14, 1730, he was given the Franciscan gray wool habit (gray for the ashes of mortality) and the signature rope cincture by the provincial for Mallorca, Antonio Perelló Moragues. He would cling to it for fifty-four years, until it was threadbare halfway around the world.

Almost as if snared, Miguel Serra was taken out of the rose light of La Seu, and for a year outside the city of Palma he studied as a novice at the Convento de Santa María de los Angeles de Jesús. Set in a wooded upland, the Convent of Jesus (its shortened, Anglicized name) was "in all its parts consonant with . . . poverty," its much smaller Gothic church topped with a Middle Eastern–like pyramid. There was a view of the mountains to the north and the towers of the Palma cathedral to the south. Serra was sent there because the Franciscans were trying to see if the new entrant to the order could take its ascetic rigors before pronouncing solemn vows of self-denial a year hence.

It meant long swaths of spiritual reading, prayers, silence. No one was allowed to visit him; he could not write letters; letters that came were thrown away. At midnight, Serra was roused from sleep by his master, Antonio Corrio, to sing out the Compline in Gregorian chant. He had less godward tasks to do daily, such as sweep the floors, take out chamber pots full of excrement and urine to trenches in the woods, prepare the meals. But he came up literally short on one of the higher duties at Mass—turning the sizable sheepskin pages of the choir book with their large print and musical notes for the choir. In a word, he was too short to reach it. Serra was probably less than five feet at this point. He confessed to Palou, "When I was a novice I was always sickly and very small of body, so small I could not reach the choir rack." He did serve Mass in other ways—answering the Latin of the priest, filling the cruets with wine and water, handing the priest the purificator, a white linen cloth on which the crumbs of Christ fell and with which the priest wiped his hands and mouth of the holy.

A year later, he puckishly conceded that a little miracle had occurred: "After making the vows I began to grow in strength and health and succeeded in reaching a medium stature." It was hardly a growth spurt; Serra as a man was five foot two. But for him, that two-inch miracle was enough to convince him he had made the right choice. He echoed an Egyptian Jew who lived in the century before Christ: "All good things came to me with the coming of this."

During his year of novitiate outside Palma in the dark grove, Miguel Serra read voraciously, a habit from early school days with the Franciscans in his native Petra. The same year two Spanish Franciscans were beatified— that is, made Blessed by the pope—almost four centuries after their martydoms. They were Brother Peter Duenas and Father John of Cetina. In 1397, the two had gone to the southern tip of Spain to evangelize the last remaining Moors of the peninsula, in Granada. They were promptly captured and beheaded. Peter Duenas was only nineteen, less than two years older than Serra at the time of beatification. Duenas's grisly end may have shaken the novice; more likely, it moved him in the throes of his early zeal for Christ to thoughts of flinging himself away to far-off lands.

For Franciscans at the inception of their order, the far-off lands were those inhabited by Arabs. Serra read deeper into the mystical life of Raymond Lull (dead in Algeria) and, of course, St. Francis of Assisi (turned away empty-handed in Egypt and heartbroken as his own Crusaders raced to the slaughter). More and more, the Moors held a fascination for him as an Other, one he saw in arches all over Mallorca, and an Other lurking inside his own frail body, if not soul.

Slowly the Moor and the Indian, to whom Franciscans had been ministering in the New World for two centuries, elided in his vision of the "perfect" kind of imperfection—those who embodied fertile ground for Christ's message of love and salvation. The recent beatifications of those trying to convert the Arabs (forget that the Arabs contained among them the earliest of all Christians, as did the Jews) echoed the canonization, when he was only thirteen, of a missionary to Peru, Francis Solano. A great celebration at the Bernardine monastery in Petra in 1726 marked the first naming of a saint in Serra's young life. Born in Granada in 1549 (not long after that last bastion of the Moors fell), Francis Solano had a practice, when his Franciscan novices did wrong, of blaming himself. He used a natural *disciplina,* throwing himself through patches of cactus. Solano also ministered to the plague-stricken in Granada in 1583, many of them *conversos*, and even broke out with the buboes himself. But it was Solano's mission to Peru and the Incas that fascinated Miguel Serra the most. In 1589, caught in a bad storm off the coast of Peru, Solano's ship broke in two, drowning several blacks he had refused to leave when others abandoned ship. A gifted sermonist, Solano railed against the corruption of the new Spanish aristocracy.

Francis Solano's attitude toward Blacks and Indians was "wonderful," noted Father Agusti Boadus Llavat, chief Franciscan archivist in Barcelona. "He worked against slave traders."

Though Serra did not speak in tongues or effect miracles by it, as Solano was said to have done, he had a beautiful singing voice, an echo of Solano's mastery of the lute.

Chief among Serra's other favorite saints were Augustine and Teresa of Avila—though for very different reasons. With Teresa, it was her long bout with sickness that emboldened suffering, something that the asthmatic Serra understood. With Augustine, the attraction was, as it had been for over a thousand years, vicarious sex. Augustine to pubescent Catholic boys of Serra's generation was what "The Miller's Tale" was to Chaucer's contemporaries or *Tropic of Cancer* would be to Henry Miller's in the twentieth century. Some intrepid Spanish seminarians of the era may have traded guffaws over the bawdier lyrics of the Roman poet Catullus or saucier passages in the vernacular of Cervantes. But for most, Augustine was it.

In the *Confessions*, Augustine scoffs that a celibate life would never be his. He famously loved, took a long-term mistress, and had a child out of wedlock. A Manichaean (who believed evil and good were equally strong in the world, led by an equally powerful God and Devil) and master rhetorician, Augustine's pride—and sexual proclivities—kept him outside Christianity throughout his twenties into his early thirties. His mother, Monica—for whom Santa Monica in California is named and whose statue stands at the western terminus of Wilshire Boulevard in front of the Pacific Ocean—prayed for years for the turn of his soul, to no apparent effect. She even tried to set him up with a young bride to anchor his passions, but that didn't work. Augustine understood that God existed, but it brought him no pleasure and no desire to join the Christian throng: "I was too weak to find my joy in you. I prated as if I was well-instructed, but I did not know enough to seek your way in Christ our Savior." The climax of Augustine's long spiritual ordeal comprises "one of the greatest pages in the entire psychology of religion." It's the moment he retreats to the umbrella of a fig tree, breaking into tears, sobbing, "How long? How long? Tomorrow and tomorrow? Why not now?" And then he hears the strangely simple, yet immortal Latin injunction, *Tolle. Lege.* "Pick it up. Read it." It was a "voice of a boy or a girl, I know not which" coming from a nearby house in Milan where he had been teaching. To Augustine, it was nothing short of a divine directive, for he went into the house where he had been fitfully reading the Bible, opened it up randomly, stabbed his finger in a frenzy that landed on a passage of St. Paul and read it: "Let us walk becomingly as in the day, not in revelry and drunkenness, not in debauchery and wantonness, not in strife and jealousy. But put on the Lord Jesus Christ, and as for the flesh, take no thought of its lusts." Similar to St. Anthony, Augustine was stunned: "There was infused in my heart something like the light of full certainty and all the gloom of doubt vanished." For Augustine, this conversion was directly related to a major turn away from "the flesh."

As far as we know or can even divine, Serra didn't experience a conversion of this sort. No doubt, with his love of the sun, the injunction just before the Pauline passage he stabbed may have hit him harder: "Lay aside the works of darkness, and put on the armor of light." Just as Augustine gathered new Christians around him to guard him from despair when his mother suddenly died, Serra may have felt the call to the Franciscan community as a way out of nagging loneliness at the center of his island—and his parents' hearts.

While at the Convent of Jesus outside Palma, Miguel Serra took up the reading of the immensely popular fourteenth-century classic, *The Little Flowers of St. Francis* (or *Fioretti*). The unknown author, who lived a generation after St. Francis in or near Assisi, had essentially taken down the most outlandish and inspiring of stories about Francis and the band of brothers he gathered around him. Serra could have taken his name from Brother Angelo, once a fearsome knight who kept his proud bearing as a friar. Leone would have been a dramatic name to adopt. Brother Leone's astonished discovery of the stigmata on Francis's feet, tearing off bandages to see the blood gushing from the wounds of Christ on his own companion, was enough to make the brother swoon that "he will be destroyed by the power of this love." Instead, on the eve of his more formal profession of vows on the road to the priesthood, Miguel Serra chose Junípero, known as "the clown of God."

It was a strange choice, as there wasn't a clownish bone in little Miguel's serious body. Even as he grew to manhood, and taught philosophy at the university in Palma, his own sense of humor had a decidedly stinging quality, like that of brilliant academicians. So who was this Brother Juniper who served as his namesake?

Certainly he was, in the best sense of the word, crazy. His antics included cutting off silver bells from the altar cloth at the main Franciscan monastery and giving them away to a beggar woman, walking half naked in the marketplace with a bundle of clothes on his head, going silent for six months, and cooking a meal for the friars he thought would last a fortnight all in one giant pot. Juniper threw in several live chickens without plucking them, and dozens of eggs in their shells. Repelled, the friars rebuked Juniper for wasting so much food. Juniper answered humbly, smiling ear to ear, that he was just trying to save time. Then he prostrated himself, begging them to cut out his eyes and then hang him, before he walked merrily away.

Once, when entering Rome to an admiring and growing throng who knew of his closeness to Francis, Brother Juniper spotted two children seesawing on what appears to have been a crude sawhorse. Brother Juniper gently moved one off, took his place on the plank, and began seesawing with the other. The crowd laughed and clapped. But Juniper didn't get off or wave. He was totally entranced and kept doing it long after the crowd and even the child left. The emblematic story of Brother Juniper, however, concerns the pig's foot.

One day a friar, racked by a painful illness, was asked by Juniper if there was anything he could get him to ease his pain.

"Oh, for a tasty pig's foot!" the friar said.

Brother Juniper did not waste time. He grabbed a butcher's knife from the priests' kitchen, took off to a local wooded area where some pigs were foraging, and promptly cut off a foot. He ran back with the bloody stump, cooked it, salted it, and gave it to the fellow monk in his agony, who "ate it with avidity," to Junípero's delight.

The swineherd, however, was not impressed. He'd seen the apparently mindless butchery and ran to tell the lord of the estate, who soon followed the bloody trail to the Franciscan monastery and gave Francis a piece of his mind. For Francis, whose love of justice was acute, this was one prank too many. Apologizing, Juniper "flung himself on the man's neck and embraced him," an inspired Groucho. The lord was so moved he gave the entire pig to the monks, who had themselves one fine ham roast.

"Would to God, my brethren, that I had a forest of such Junipers!" Francis sighed. No surprise there is neither date nor place of birth for Brother Juniper; such people seem to have lit down from the empyrean. It was a blithe spirit young Serra hoped to call on.

And so after a year of his novitiate, on September 15, 1731, kneeling before the Franciscan provincial Antonio Perelló Moragues, Miguel Serra took the spiritual name of Junípero just before reciting vows of poverty, chastity, and obedience to the Franciscan order. An editor of Palou's writings about Serra ventures that it was Brother Juniper's "ready wit and epigrammatic speech" that appealed to Serra, but Brother Juniper's "wit" was, if anything, burlesque, and his speech seems to have been marked not by epigram so much as utter guilelessness. At the end of his university philosophy lectures, Serra would typically praise the Trinity, Blessed Mother Mary, and then several saints, the last of whom was always Brother Juniper. He even carved a Brother Juniper woodblock to print holy cards as gifts. This "clown of God," to him, was "the greatest exemplar of holy simplicity." So it was simplicity he admired the most, "the Gift to be Simple," as the Quakers memorably sang in the part of the New World that was least Spanish. The year Serra took his vows on Mallorca, half a world away Benjamin Franklin founded the first public library in the British colonies in Philadelphia. A year later, George Washington would be born.

Serra was not simple. In fact, he had none of the guilelessness of Brother Juniper, or that radical humility, and in his adult life he would chastise himself often in print and in front of others for harboring "pride" in his heart of hearts. In short, Brother Juniper was everything Serra was not. Perhaps he was forcing on himself an identity he longed for, but that continually escaped him—an Other, an innocent he would search for his whole life.

Serra was nearly eighteen years old when he took Moragues's hands at the Convent of Jesus, and with a vision of blue surrounding him forever, he said in a raw voice, his eyes tearing from the incense, "I, Fray Junípero Serra, vow and promise to Almighty God, to the Blessed Virgin Mary, to Blessed Father Francis, to all the saints, and to you, Father, to observe the whole span of my life the rule of the Friars Minor confirmed by his Holiness, Pope Honorius III, by living in obedience, without property, and in chastity."

In addition, an extra vow—peculiar to Mallorcan Franciscans—was spoken by Serra, to propagate the dogma not yet accepted by Rome, that is, that Christ's mother, Mary, was "conceived without original sin from the first moment of her existence." This put Mary almost on the same level as Christ; if not God herself, she was the mother of God and quite simply—perfect. To Catholics, only Christ and Mary were born spotless, with no bent even in the smallest way toward evil. Serra's lifelong devotion to Mary and her Immaculate Conception was sealed. For a man fated to live among men, it was more than the normal nod toward the feminine. It was as solemn a vow as his priesthood.

On December 18, 1731, Serra completed his philosophy course with a flourish, scripting his conclusion like a funnel (or chalice) on his scroll, saluting "all the citizens of heaven" (including "the most special patron of my heart"—Bernardine of Siena), adding with a wry note: "Just as we finish the small logic, so [too] the great by the grace of God." At the tip of the funnel he wrote boldly in a banner, "Friar Junípero Serra of the Minor Order, faithfully writing." Touching the banner was a heart with five wounds (*cinco llagas*), Francis's stigmata; but also a hint: faithful writing involved suffering.

Did the Franciscans have a special mark that attracted Serra above other monastic orders tracing themselves all the way back to St. Anthony of Egypt in the third century? He could have signed up with the Benedictines, one of the oldest orders, founded on Monte Cassino in 529 by a monk who stressed manual labor; the Carmelites, begun in 1206, may have been too brooding and mystical; but the famously bright Jesuits founded by Ignatius Loyola in 1534 may have appealed, if not the Dominicans started by Francis's own friend, Dominic, in 1216, who reached their height with the great theologian and doctor of the church Thomas Aquinas and their nadir with the Inquisition's Torquemada. However, though it may have been a close call philosophically with the "teaching order" Dominicans, Serra picked the Franciscans because the Franciscans picked him. They were his teachers in Petra at the Convent of St. Bernardine; they whisked him to their own in Palma. Serra loved stories of sacred brashness and humility, and St. Francis's life spoke directly to him, as did Brother Juniper's. They also appealed to his flair for the dramatic. The Franciscans' zesty answer to the call to "set sail" in your life as a missionary tugged at an island person to whom the sea was ever-present and insistent. What may have cinched the deal: only one order was given protectorate of the Holy Places in Palestine, especially Jerusalem—the Franciscans. It is still so today.

Berkeley theologian Kenan Osborne reflects that Serra may have been attracted to three Franciscan predilections: the centrality of Jesus; the closeness to nature (the sun and moon as brother and sister); and the primacy of the Gospel ("Franciscans are attracted to the Gospel in almost a mystical way—not the way of Thomas Aquinas"). There is also the matter of Francis's wariness of the mighty: "Franciscans were not interested in Catholic power. They loved a poor life in a small building." Llavat adds, "The Franciscans are the most sympathetic to women and the poor of all the orders. It's a political view, but true."

Serra moved back to Palma, a changing if not changed young man. He was now a Franciscan, but not yet a priest. He couldn't be one until he was twenty-four. That required six more years of college-level study, primarily in theology and philosophy. By November 1731, he had turned eighteen and was already launched in his cloistered college life. Each day before and after classes, he sang Matins and Vespers in the great Gothic church of San Francisco, "after the cathedral, Majorca's prize ecclesiastical structure," built in 1232, just when Mallorca was reconquered by James I of Aragon from the Muslims. In tandem with the laying of the original Convento de San Francisco cornerstone, the Franciscans had entered Mallorca from Italy only five years after the death of St. Francis. Though it was moved in 1278 farther inland from what may have been a mosquito-infested swamp, a place of sewage, or a hospice for poor souls infected with bubonic plague, the church of San Francisco was about as close as you could come in the eighteenth century to being one with Francis in Assisi in the thirteenth century. One imagines Serra walked in the stone silence; slowly the sun ignited flame in the 114 Gothic arches of San Francisco's arcade. Arches flickered within arches. It must have set Junípero's mind spinning, the visual accompaniment to the choir music he had just sung bouncing off the trefoil arches, the carp moving under the lily pads of the fountain, God at the gills.

It was all alive. The stone, the water, the arches, the light. It was a four-square heaven. How could he increase such a thing?

Was his breathing heavy when he slid into the church itself? San Francisco's thick mahogany, its twenty-three subaltars, glowed greenish in the candlelight. Everything holy was holding: the sixteenth-century statue of Nuestra Señora de Los Angeles holding the baby Jesus, himself holding the globe of the world; the thirteenth-century triptych of St. Ursula held in a boat bound for England with eleven thousand virgins, holding on to their heads, soon to be cut off; Raymond Lull's crypt holding Serra's hero; the 1611 mural of a giant holding an earthen glass, about to strike a blow to Lull, whose brow and beard hold the light, the Glow of Love. Did Junípero ask himself: *And what will you hold*?

On the winter solstice, December 21, 1731—the darkest day of the year—Serra left Palma to visit Santa Margarita just north of his hometown of Petra. There he bent his small head to the barber's clippers, and the haircut he received was not stylish; a bowl-like opening was carved on top of his head, leaving a "monastic crown" of hair ringing his forehead and circling back above his ears to the base of his brain. It was the tonsure, Roman style. Tradition had it begun by St. Peter, as an imitation of Christ's crown of thorns.

Serra took the opportunity to visit his parents and Juana, who was now fifteen and thinking of getting married. He let them call him Miguel, the name that was no longer his. He probably slept in a modest plank bed at home that did *not* have a square halo in the headboard (as is there today), though that image would have fit Serra. He went to Christmas Mass with his family at St. Peter's in Petra. He visited with the friars who had first taught him at San Bernardino. And in early January 1732, he returned to Palma in a horse cart, his newly bald pate stinging with cold, his breath visible. As he traveled, the sun grew stronger, burning off the fog. All around in the green pastures, almond trees, those *amatllers* of his childhood, festooned with blossomed light.

Back in Palma, Serra's studies continued. His entering class at the Convento de San Francisco had thirty-three students, many seminarians like him, but also lay students from across the island. Among his studies were logic, dialectics, metaphysics, cosmology; by 1735, he was studying a moral theology course devoted to "Conscience," with Buenaventura Amoros. That same year Serra grew entranced by Pedro Vaquer's intense, mystical course, "Habitual Grace."

Serra constructed a deft model of the universe with movable paper discs of the various planets in orbit. However, Serra placed not the sun but the earth in the center of things, Ptolemy-style. (Good farmer's son that he was, he drew a tiny cow munching meadow grass on the central figure of the earth.) Was Serra rejecting Copernicus? Some think so; it may also have been an assignment. One Franciscan theologian wasn't convinced this school project was determinative: "Serra was not medieval; some scholars who say so are anti-Catholic."

In addition to study in Raymond Lull, St. Francis, Aquinas, Augustine, and the other doctors of the church, seminarian Serra began to discover on his own the writings of María de Agreda, one of the most unusual figures the Catholic Church has ever known. Sor María was born in Agreda, Spain, in 1602, and though quite beautiful—"handsome of face, very fair of color, with a slight rosy tinge and large black eyes"—she became a Conceptionist nun at sixteen. Her visionary geography, *Face of the Earth,* which drew on an Arab cosmographer known as Alphraganus, reflected a Franciscan "amazement in the face of beauty and immensity of Creation." Her fellow sisters would testify that they watched Sor María levitating in ecstatic prayer, as had Teresa of Avila.

But what really drew Serra to María de Agreda was her claim that she bilocated, that is, she regularly visited the New World without ever leaving her hometown in Spain. Whether she flew there or just vanished and reappeared, she said she got there, apparently arriving in the region known today as New Mexico. In 1629, fifty Jumano Indians approached the first priests arriving in Isleta, requesting baptism. The priests were astonished. How do you know about this, they asked. They responded they had been directed by a "Lady in Blue," as María was soon to be known. They identified her from the painting of another Conceptionist nun, remarking on her blue cape, except that "their" nun was younger and more beautiful. María de Agreda was twenty-seven at the time and, though she had never left her hometown, she described in great detail the leader of the Jumano Indians who arrived that day for baptism.

Whether it was her early enrapt witness of a play by Lope de Vega or being forced by her parents to an "exceedingly straight and narrow path" of daily contemplative prayer, Sor María certainly developed a highly imaginative mind, if not wings, later expressing puzzlement as to how it actually happened, wondering if an angel "went for me." She also wrote an unusual, abstruse, and yet ecstatic four-volume novelistic meditation on the life of Mary, Christ's mother, *The Mystical City of God*. In it, María intensely reflects on the life of the Blessed Mother, but she also speaks closely and mystically of a concern Serra expressed from his early days—Why Creation? Why did God start all this in the first place? What need had he, if he already had everything? Aquinas could tell us how— the First Cause Uncaused. It was logical. But Aquinas did not address why, though he hinted at the insistence of his giving nature. María de Agreda said she held "in my lukewarm heart" two things "in wonder and inflame it unto annihilation." The first was "the inclination and urgent desire" of God "to communicate his Divinity and the treasures of His grace." The other was the "unspeakable and incomprehensible immensity of the good gifts." She argued that God had to create by his nature and infinity: "It is much more natural that He communicate gifts and graces, than that fire should ascend, or the stone should gravitate towards its center, or that the sun should diffuse its light." To María, God not only created; he *was* creation.

This kind of thinking—not to mention her claims of flying off to the New World—brought María under examination of the Inquisition as a witch, if not a pantheist. The descendant of Jewish *conversos*, she none-theless escaped her accusers, and her magnum opus has since been pub-lished all over the world in many languages.

His mind perhaps filled with Sor María and her flights west, Serra walked the streets of Palma on Sunday afternoons after Mass, some of his only free moments in the week. He walked the Old Quarter, called Medina Mayurka by the Muslims, and entered the old Arab baths, just to see the tiny aperture in the peak of the ceiling. He may have imagined that the body could be cleansed but the spirit still caked, still wanting to go through that blazing hole to its origin. If he went down to the sea past the fishmongers throwing their sardines into tubs, did he smile at the children along the quay, the drunken boatman with his missing teeth, the sun a communion above Africa?

As if insisting that he was, indeed, a Mallorcan, Serra ended notes for his last college class on June 23, 1737, "Fray Junípero Serre" in a funnel-like flourish, using the old Mallorquín spelling of his last name. "Today I finished my studies," he wrote flatly. That last class, fittingly enough, was on "Angels" as treated by Raymond Lull. He was ready to fly as a priest.

But priests are not angels; their wings may even be heavier than others' as they take on not only their own frailties but those of all humankind in the confessional. Added to the weight of Serra's final acceptance of Holy Orders, the sacrament that consecrates a priest in the Catholic Church, is the fact that the date of Serra's ordination is not clear. Geiger calls it "an unsolved mystery concerning the most important event of his life." He surmises that while most of his fellows who entered seminary with him received Holy Orders on May 31, 1737, Serra had not yet achieved the minimal age of twenty-four. So it appears he had to wait until at least his birthday in November, and most likely was consecrated without them.

There is another possibility. Recently uncovered Spanish documents "put away under lock and key in a closet" and translated for the first time reveal that Serra himself was disciplined by the Inquisition. On January 27, 1738, either in a sermon or one of his last seminary papers, Serra had included ardent assertions of Mary's Immaculate Conception and graphic descriptions of Christ's Passion. The Holy Tribunal in the person of Antonio Salas ordered such references stricken or curtailed and the documents themselves turned over, "collected with discretion in the least noisy way."

Serra was not given faculties to hear confessions until February 1739. That's a long period after Geiger's estimate of a November 1737 solo ordination. And it shows how far Serra would go to buck orthodoxy for what he believed.

But somewhere between winter 1737 and winter 1739, it happened. Prostrate on the cold sandstone cobbles of Convento de San Francisco, Serra heard the Lord knocking his rib cage, even as his knees stung against the floor. Nose to Brother Stone, maybe he thought: *Thank you, hard pillow.* The bishop's incensor above him shook in its brass chains; the smoke made him want to sneeze. Brother Sneeze. Hurting stone.

He was made a priest alone.

CHAPTER THREE

A PROFESSOR, WANTING

To fall into a habit is to begin to cease to be.
—MIGUEL DE UNAMUNO

Convento de San Francisco, Palma, Mallorca,
Serra's pulpit as a young priest.

*T*here was probably never a more bookish conquistador than Junípero Serra, and perhaps it is appropriate that he has been called "the last of the conquistadors." Not only would he be the last Spaniard to enter the untouched territories of the native peoples of North America, he would take to them the mind-set of someone used to speaking with young people about great theological, philosophical, and historical topics, who himself was college-educated and a college professor. But from the start, Serra was a priest and teacher uncomfortable with election. After two quiet years hearing confessions and preaching around the island, the young priest became a librarian at the Convento de San Francisco. He said an Epiphany Mass on January 6, 1740, in Algaida, staring up with his leg of mutton afterward at Mount Randa, where Raymond Lull had lived as a hermit five centuries earlier. There Lull had "read" the runes on the *mata escrita* (a common bush on the mountain) that became his masterwork, *Ars Magna*.

Even when on January 9, 1740, at the age of twenty-seven, Serra was officially commissioned to teach at San Francisco, he preferred that his students refer to him and to each other as *los condiscípulos* (fellow students), though almost certainly they called him *Padre*. However, the affectionate greeting of *mi condiscípulo!* (with its echo of the original disciples of Christ) stuck with Serra and his first fateful students after they became priests themselves, "even on another continent, and until their last members died."

Seventeen-year-old Francisco Palou and nineteen-year-old Juan Crespí, two students in Serra's first class of twenty-eight, would remain with him for life. Both followed him to the New World, Palou becoming Serra's first biographer.

Unlike Serra, who was a child of the interior, Palou and Crespí were born and raised in Mallorca's chief port, Palma, and had known each other since childhood. They ran down Palma's sunstruck, windy streets to the peal not only of iron and bronze church bells, but the brass bells of ships harboring. As Palou later put it, "We grew up together as children and studied together almost from our ABCs until we finished theology."

Crespí seems not to have been the best student. He had problems with memorization, composition, and sentence structure. Rather generously, Geiger ventures that Crespí "made up in industry what he lacked in retentiveness." A grinder, full of energy, always in motion, Crespí may not have been an entirely bad companion. Teachers can be drawn to students who make charming mistakes, and Crespí, whose strong Catalán-Balearic accent endeared him to that proud Mallorcan Serra, had made plenty, to the point that one scholar thought he suffered mild retardation.

The blue-eyed, black-haired, voluble Crespí—who wrote with a flurry of exclamation points that Serra, one by one, removed—recalled the Brother Juniper that Junípero himself wanted to be. He took to his seminary studies a "dove-like candor," according to Palou. Nicknamed *Beato* (blessed one) by childhood friends, Crespí evidently made the taciturn Serra smile from that first class in Palma through the coldest days in Carmel.

Palou, taller than both Serra and Crespí, was the youngest of the trio, and was drawn to Serra from the start, startled by the deep voice that came from his small body. Serra's intense elucidations of Aristotle's philosophy, not to mention the difficult Duns Scotus (the medieval philosopher) and the mystical webs of María de Agreda, had Palou stuck to his teacher long after they left the classroom. Each seemed to know what the other was thinking before he said it; they grew to a "mutual love," said Palou, greater than blood relatives. "I was the object of his very special affection," Palou admitted.

Interestingly, we don't know anything about the content of Serra's first philosophy "Class Extraordinaire" from Palou or Crespí, or any of the sixty students who attended Serra's classes over the next three years at the lectern of the Convento de San Franciso. With one exception.

Francisco Noguera's 808 pages of notes on Serra span his entire three years at San Francisco and rest in the San Felipe Library in Palma. Unlike his fervent confreres, whose paper trails disappeared on the way to or in the New World, Noguera stayed put on Mallorca, where his papers stayed, too. The lectures he dutifully took down—many in Latin—contain close studies of logic and are filled with comments on Aristotle, Aquinas, Augustine, Raymond Lull, and particularly Duns Scotus.

Serra welcomed his first class: "My most beloved students, the long-awaited and much desired day has dawned for us on which we begin the labors of the three forthcoming years in the exercise of philosophy's dialectics." Quickly it became apparent three things dominated Serra's philosophical concerns: "mental light," a fear of the Lord, and devotion to Blessed Mother Mary. He urged his students to see no contradictions in the worlds of science, philosophy, and theology, echoing the beginning of John's Gospel: "Walk in that light worthily that you may be sons of Him who is Light itself and in Whom there is no darkness." John's reference to Christ as "the Word" appealed to Serra, who wanted students to sense the power of language to echo the Creator, as well as conquer evil. You not only are what you say; you are *by saying*. At the same time, like Augustine, Serra would come to know the limits of mere rhetoric.

Fear of the Lord was "the beginning of wisdom" and evil and sin the antithesis of wisdom. Serra's sense of the physicality of sin—that sin was a bodily thing, hence, no doubt, sexual—was probably taken from Augustine, whose sense of the snares of concupiscence—plain old desire—was acute, having himself given in to it for so long outside of marriage. In this view abstinence and sensuality are not opposite; in fact, they may be related (as are promiscuity and the dulling of sensuality). Romantic poetry, certainly in its Germanic root with the myth of Tristan and Isolde—required separation, if not distance: Tristan lies with Isolde, but only after putting a sword between them. For Serra, the primary owner of a philosophy that combined art and love was none other than Duns Scotus, who taught that love "adds beauty beyond the natural goodness" and that "the divine ear . . . takes delight at the beautiful harmony of the music of human love and goodness." In short, a good act is a work of art, and vice versa: "In Scotus, there is something performative about a good act. Every morally good act is unique, as is a person."

Serra recommended María de Agreda's obsession with the Immaculate Conception of Jesus' mother, Mary: "Devotion to her as a Scotist I commend to you as other Scotists, and by means of it God will aid you in all things to prosper." Also, as a Scotist, Serra hoped his students had become distinct souls: "To Scotus, God did not create human beings, but individuals with names. Individualism is very big in Scotus." Finally, at the end of three years' study, Serra said good-bye. "I am no longer your professor, but your humble servant," and told them to "sing out" those lines of Virgil: "Jove will soon dispose to future good/Our past and present woes." Serra favored those who plowed their darkness into the soil for a better harvest.

And yet, Serra's attaching himself so forcefully to María de Agreda's "spotlessness" may indicate a fear of spots—that is, evil. We don't know where this fear comes from, as it seems that as a child and young man Serra wasn't exposed to it. The rampancy of infant mortality in his own family and throughout the island—spots? Perhaps the dispiriting decline of the Spanish Empire qualified for a sort of evil, or the Inquisition itself, which evidenced for Serra both evil and mercy.

For a time in his late twenties and early thirties, Serra examined book manuscripts waiting for the Church's imprimatur to see if they conformed to Church doctrine. As such, he served occasionally as a *comisario*, or an auxiliary commissioner of the Inquisitional office, on Mallorca. By then (the 1740s), the Inquisition was long past its terrifying heights 250 years before (the bloodiest days in Spain of the Grand Inquisitor Torquemada were from its inception in 1480 to 1530). Inquisition historian Henry Kamen estimated two thousand people were killed under the Inquisition in its most feverish years before 1530. Here the elision of Others—Moor, Jew, and Indian—Old World to not-so-New World was hardly positive.

In 1700–1746, the twilight years of the miserable institution (certainly the blackest chapter in the history of the Catholic Church), no one was executed on Mallorca by the Inquisition, and eleven who were brought to trial were released with penances. This is not to exonerate the murderers because their crimes had decreased dramatically by the eighteenth century; this is to say that Serra as a boy and as a young priest before he left Mallorca for the New World could not have witnessed anyone burned at the stake or otherwise killed by the Inquisition on his native island.

Still, historian Steven Hackel is rather inquisitional: "Was [Serra] aware of the ability of the Inquisition to destroy people in the pursuit of religious orthodoxy? Certainly. Was he aware of the fate of Mallorca's Jews and crypto-Jews? Certainly." Maybe. Maybe not. But even if he was, it is still a leap to say he approved—especially this late in the decline of the Inquisition—of its worst crimes. Everything about his philosophical affinities with Raymond Lull and St. Francis—who both insisted on "peaceful" missions to the Moors—as well as the emphasis on mercy and the beauty of good acts in the teachings of Duns Scotus indicates that the blind fury and vengeance of the Inquisition would have had rather the opposite effect on Serra.

Serra knew, of course, that Mallorca had an old Jewish community. The Convento de San Francisco—Serra's residence for eighteen years before leaving—was near the Jewish quarter of Palma, where St. Eulalia's was an active *converso* parish. A synagogue once stood near the Convent of Jesus on the outskirts of the city where Serra took his vows. After a 1652 plague took the lives of up to 20 percent of Mallorca's population, the island's financial fortunes climbed upward, and some 1,500 Jews and *marranos* (*conversos*) "formed the backbone of Palma's commercial class." It was not long before "these people found themselves targeted." Hounded by Inquisitional authorities, hundreds were rounded up in 1679, suspected of faking their Christianity, though the subtext was probably of a more mundane nature: resentment over their prosperity. The seizure of property, according to historian Henry Kamen, was among the worst in the history of the Inquisition and, according to one anthropologist, the "medieval Catholicism" that dominated the countryside didn't help matters.

In Serra's time a terrifying painting hung at the Church of Santo Domingo that depicted a group of Jews in different stages of abased judgment, including wearing the *sabenitos* cap.

While Serra's role with the Inquisition in Mallorca was tangential, it was still a troubling one. It is not clear whether he was assigned the task of thumbing through manuscripts that conformed to Catholic doctrine and those that did not, or if he chose the task. One theologian felt "Serra was chosen because of his superior education on a very small island." In 1742, when he was teaching at the seminary and working on his doctorate in theology at the Lullian University in Palma, he could not have been in a position to decline such a task, being under a vow of obedience. He could have also taken it as an opportunity to assume greater responsibility in the Church and tamp down any lingering doubts about his own murky lineage. Serra's affection for two places where such obsession about lineage could be thrown off, Andalusia and California—the former lost, the latter not yet discovered—points to his affinity for land where such strict lines were not feared or even drawn.

Serra's affinities for the tolerance embodied by Andalusia soon become obvious in sermons in which he pointedly refers to acceptance of Muslims by the Christian king of Aragon, Alfonso I. Serra's own multifaith blood, as well as the peaceful missions of two of his strongest heroes, St. Francis and Raymond Lull, to the Muslims of North Africa, would also have inclined him toward, if not equality, coexistence of faiths. He had to have felt conflicted that the Inquisition, even in its twilight days, followed perhaps the longest, most culturally rich experience in religious tolerance in history, when Muslims, Christians, and Jews enjoyed three hundred years of relative tranquillity in Andalusia (from roughly 756 and the fall of Córdoba to Abd al-Rahman to 1082, when Alfonso VI of Castile seized Toledo, upsetting the balance severely). The mystery of its very name—al-Andalus in Arabic—evokes wonder: lux in Latin and the luz in Spanish shimmer with light.

At the hub of Andalusia at the beginning of the tenth century was the astonishing city of Córdoba. The Great Mosque of Córdoba, begun by Abdulrahman I in 785 and completed in the tenth century, "recapitulates the artistic history of Spain in a way that no other structure can possibly do." The writer was being literal; many of its original 1,200 pillars (only eighty still exist) were not just copies, but original Roman, Byzantine, Visigoth, and Carthaginian pillars from lands spanning North Africa to Constantinople. The vertiginous effect of these flickering columns of the ancient and medieval worlds is captured beautifully by Mexican novelist Carlos Fuentes:

> The mosque offers the sensation of walking through a centerless vision of the infinite, where God and man can be imagined ceaselessly searching for each other in a cool labyrinth, each depending on the other to continue the unfinished task of creation. The forest of stone pillars seems to be changing constantly. . . . Indeed, all things have to be reimagined at this, one of the most marvelous and stimulating buildings in the world.

Andalusia was not perfect; as Yale professor María Rosa Menocal notes, what golden age is? Jews and Christians were watched over by Muslims as *dhimmi,* or "people of the book," the "protected ones," but they had to pay a special tax. Historian Richard Fletcher speaks of "hygienic apartheid" in the baths (nine hundred in Córdoba alone), where Jews, Muslims, and Christians had their own days for bathing. Still, Andalusia was the apex of that dream of communion between the three great monotheisms that so animated St. Francis, to some extent Raymond Lull, and perhaps Serra himself. Its advances in the economic, architectural, scientific, artistic, intellectual, and spiritual realms were unprecedented. Muslim gold flowed into Christian lands and built many of the medieval castles in Spain. The great Arab love of textiles created five thousand looms, weaving multicolored, spangled cloths of silk, linen, wool, and cotton hardly seen in Spain before, except among nobles. Methods of irrigation unknown to Europeans brought gardens to flower and orchards of oranges and lemons Europe had never tasted on its own soil.

What was done with water alone was astounding, both beautiful and practical. The Muslim practice of *wudu,* or bathing of the feet before prayer, was especially poignant for people who originated in a desert and for whom water was gold. The result was the inclusion of the tiled fountain and its hypnotic spray that adorned every courtyard in mosque or manor.

The caliph's library at Córdoba had 400,000 volumes, in contrast to the largest library in all of Christian Europe outside Spain, which had no more than four hundred. Catalogues alone formed forty-four volumes, and that wasn't even the only library; there were sixty-nine others. Clearly, Andalusians were not just people of the Book; they were in love with books, a romance buttressed by the new paper factory near Valencia, itself a product of Muslim ingenuity and northern wood.

Intellectually, Paris exploded with interest in the Averroes (Ibn Rushd) version of Aristotle, a renaissance before the Renaissance, which reconciled two often opposed disciplines: theology and the philosophy of science. This "double truth," as Fuentes calls it, "became one of the hallmarks of modern thought." Twinned with the Arab Averroes, the esteemed Jewish doctor and scholar Maimonides wrote in Arabic and reconciled Judaism with Greek philosophy. Both Cordobans, Averroes and Maimonides were two great arches of the same aqueduct.

Not all historians see Andalusia as a pinnacle of human history. Fletcher calls it "a myth of the modern liberal imagination," asserting that "thoroughly dismissive attitudes to Christians and Jews may be found in the Arabic literature of al-Andalus." Yet even during Andalusia's steep descent from tolerance (under the Almoravids and Almohads), in 1246 the mother of Ferdinand III—the king of Castile and vanguard of the

Reconquista—was laid in her coffin with her head on a magenta pillow embroidered with holy sayings in Arabic calligraphy.

The logical extension of the eclipse of Andalusia from its multicultural heights was the Crusades, launched by Pope Urban II in 1095 from his perch in France. Soon both Jews and Arabs were in hiding, if not retreat, throughout Spain. The chimera of social purity—especially seductive in hard times—seems to be one of society's greatest temptations, and it was, once again, a great tragedy that Andalusia's flowering trellis of communities of faith and race ended in a stripping of that flower for a dream of a pure garden. The drive for fanatical purity that was the Crusades reached its worst moment in the Inquisition in Spain. Launched in 1480, it was the polar opposite of the entrepreneurial and intellectual culture of Andalusia or the spirit of Christianity itself. Though hardly seen this way at the time by its proponents, it was in fact the anti-Christ.

The first Inquisition in Europe actually had nothing to do with Jews or Arabs, but with Christians of a different bent, the Cathars of southern France. In the twelfth century, Pope Lucius III declared an inquisition against those who held the Albigensian heresy (for the town of Albi near Toulouse). These people, also called Cathars, believed in two gods—one ruled the physical world and one ruled the spirit. The Cathars were the first free lovers, though the "free" they lived had a good deal more distance and propriety in it than the "free" we live. You usually don't strum a ballad on a lute while in bed.

The Spaniards took the Albigensian inquisition to new lows. The Spanish Inquisition was established by Ferdinand and Isabella, the married monarchs of Spain. It was a document that underwrote a political lunge, nothing less. Under cover of religious fervor was greed for land and power. The Catholic Church, already battling Moors in the Holy Land, was a natural instrument for this purpose. Ferdinand and Isabella united Aragon and Castile, respectively. Protecting their lands from potential "fifth columns" of people whose religion they suspected as compromising their allegiance to the Crown was, besides the land itself, a second reason for the Inquisition. Lastly, and perhaps the most cogent of all, was money. The Jews and the Arabs owned a lot of land and property, and they had the most money. As early as 1484, a woman from Ciudad Real, Catalina de Zamora, was brought to trial after mouthing something too close for comfort: "This Inquisition that the fathers are carrying out is as much for taking property from the *conversos* as for defending the faith." Some estimate ten million ducats were seized in the first forty years of the Inquisition. A common saying in the vernacular in Spain at the time was "The goods are the heretics."

Just before the final expulsion of Arabs, all Jews were ordered expelled from Andalusia in 1483. Some witnesses thought hundreds of thousands left, but Inquisition historian Henry Kamen puts the figure much lower—about 50 percent of Spain's eighty thousand Jews left, some to Italy, more to North Africa and other reaches of the Ottoman Empire, as well as the New World. By 1530 (again, the high-, or low-, water mark of the Inquisition), two thousand people had been killed by decree of Suprema tribunals, the vast majority of whom were Jews. Kamen estimates five thousand killed in total (including also *moriscos*, heretics, and even bigamists) under the three-hundred-year reign of Spanish terror.

Most of the eighteenth century saw a great decline in Inquisition activity; the ideas of the Enlightenment—Locke, Rousseau, Voltaire—about the rights of man and egalitarianism inevitably spread into Spain, such that previously submerged critiques of the Inquisition began to be published and widely read as early as 1759. About the time of Serra's scrutinizing manuscripts for the Suprema (the 1740s), "The Holy Office had come to be a species of commission for book censorship, nothing more." The list of foreign authors banned is a stellar one, including Ovid, William of Ockham, Rabelais, Erasmus, Dante, and Thomas More (known as Tomás Moro), who, as much a speak-truth-to-power advocate as Serra would become, also favored Duns Scotus in his teaching. Thomas More was not the only censored writer of the Inquisition who would later be declared a saint. Still, most of the great Spanish authors' run-ins with the Inquisition were as cursory as they were inevitable. Only one line was deleted from Cervantes's *Don Quixote*; the work of the poet Luis de Góngora was repeatedly inspected, but only minor parts removed. Censorship, according to Kamen, although "imposing in theory was unimpressive in practice." In 1774, explorer, scientist, and anthropologist Alejandro Malaspina openly taught Royal Navy officers in Cádiz several works banned by the Inquisition: "The ban apparently stimulated rather than discouraged Iberian readers."

That is the climate under which Junípero Serra took up book manuscripts. It was dolorous duty and probably recognized as futile, if not foolish.

As quiet as Serra's life seemed to be shaping up, life in Mallorca was not. As the eighteenth century moved to its midpoint, the fiercely independent Spanish island was rocked by epidemics, drought, an increasingly lawless clamp on its draftable young men, heavy taxation by authorities in Castile, and the deaths of many island leaders, as well as the hated king of Spain, Philip V (who was replaced by someone even more hated, Ferdinand VI). Life in Palma seemed a heart-shaking series of funeral processions, afflictions of nature, and manic parades of military victory over Muslims in North Africa.

On March 13, 1739, while Serra was tending to his library, the governor of Mallorca died. On the hour every hour for a day and night, the great eleven-ton bell N'Eloi rang out from the cathedral playing "Na Barbara," an old dolorous melody in honor of St. Barbara. It took thirteen bell ringers to move the 1389-vintage iron monster N'Eloi. In grim duet with the cathedral, a cannon was shot on the hour into the harbor. A week later, on March 21, Serra found himself in a sandstone wall-to-wall funeral procession to La Seu, representing the Convento de San Francisco, along with two bronze artillery pieces, eight braying mules kicking up their black cloths, two companies of huffing soldiers, priests and friars from the Dominicans, Jesuits, Franciscans murmuring Latin, twelve torches, the coffin lined with black velvet trimmed in gold that contained Don Patricio Laules himself, dead in his blue uniform with red clasps, and finally four horses stained with blood.

Despite this, Serra moved upward. While teaching seminarians at Convento de San Francisco he studied for his doctoral degree at the Lullian University, established in 1673 in honor of Mallorca's own Raymond Lull. An easy seven-minute walk from his lodgings at San Francisco, the Lullian University was one block up from the cathedral at the juncture of Calle San Roque and Estudio General, narrowing in the oldest place in Palma.

On August 5, 1741, the year before Serra received his doctorate in theology, something happened with two ardent hearts on the island that set all tongues wagging.

The lieutenant of the Oran Regiment—the Mallorcan unit that had conquered the Algerian city of that name for the Spanish Crown nine years before, to raucous fiestas and parades lasting through the summer—ran away with a nun. They rushed "out through the gutter under the king's orchard to the sea," the nun in man's dress, stealing away in a French boat (it had to be French) two hundred miles south across the sea to Cartagena on the mainland. The plot wasn't quite *Anna Karenina*, but it was close. The unlikely lovers certainly had their devil's bargain—five passionate weeks in the hot port. But if Lieutenant Manuel Bustillo thought the Moors were a tough match in Oran, he had not yet met the bishop of Palma, who hunted the couple down with a naval party in a three-sailed *jabeque* complete with cannon on September 15, bringing Don Manuel in irons back to Palma. Sister Isabel was literally gotten to a nunnery—her own—sentenced to four years inside its walls and a dubiously enforced silence for the rest of her life.

On May 4, 1742, around the time Serra bent his head to receive the doctoral regalia over his red robe in the great cathedral, its huge rose window ablaze, Manuel Bustillo bent his head into the dip of a chopping block. The condemned man, an engineer, had helped carve out a slot for the blade in the wood block that was previously used to cut cheese. He was brought out atop a mule covered in black, beating his chest with a cross he gripped nervously, calling out with dry mouth for God's forgiveness. No one knows if Serra was there, but the nun's affair with the lieutenant was the talk of the island for ten months. The handsome Bustillo appears to have been greatly admired, even loved ("a noble gentleman"), and his long incarceration caused diarist Nicolás Ferrer to speculate "that the people would try and free him," with as much as ten thousand pounds sterling (or *libras*) offered for his release.

When the sun dropped into the sea, the sea wind was not strong enough to obliterate the sound of the blade coming down, "shooting the head three feet away."

Not long before, a Moor who killed a priest had had his hand chopped off and hooked on the Guixeria Gate; and now the gentle lieutenant's head was rolling in sand toward the port, its blood pouring out. These were hardly celebrations of the Intellect.

In 1744, just as Fra Junípero ascended (unanimously) the Scotist Chair in Philosophy at the Lullian University, a plague swept over the island "like a flame." Over ten thousand people died, as many as thirty a day, and they died quickly—five days from symptoms to death. Resistant to just about every kind of treatment, from fierce sweats, to purgatives, to bleeding, the plague left the village of St. Eugenia east of Palma practically empty; one piece of property there changed owners eight times in twenty days. The epidemic lasted into March of the following year.

Thus Serra began his five-year-long stint in one of the most honored chairs as a university professor, battling with the sublime as wailing, stinking flesh, and open sores erupted through the city. He was beloved by students, and presided at or oversaw in committee over a hundred final examinations for the bachelor's and doctoral degrees in theology. Sadly, but tellingly, Junípero left little record of his university career, and hardly ever referred to it later. According to Palou, Serra's eloquence, not just in class, but in giving sermons throughout the island on feast days, was becoming legendary. He was much sought after—by village congregations and religious orders as much as the university community. This common touch was not common for a Lullian professor.

Serra's excellence did what it can do in the academy: spawn jealousy. In April 1744, Dr. Miquel Ramonell, a fellow professor, stood up and castigated Serra in cryptic language as he was overseeing three-day theology exams: "He [Ramonell] protested and does now protest to the said Father Junípero Serra, *catedrático* [head of a department], that in this examination as well as in future ones, the precedence he seeks to obtain cannot serve him in any way by prepossession nor can the said Father Junípero maintain any possessory right thereto." It's not certain what such gobbledygook meant, but what we know for sure is that after the incident Serra's name moved from fourth from the last on the list of examiners to fourth from the top, just above Ramonell's. Clearly, Serra had been favored over Ramonell as a master of exams.

At some point in 1744, probably as the leader of a week's retreat, Serra gave a series of four sermons to the Claretian Sisters in their Convento de Santa Clara. Serra's closeness to women was evident in his bond with his only living sibling, Juana, and his respect for holy women, such as María de Agreda and the Blessed Mother herself. (Serra also grew up at a time when the handiwork of women caused textile exports from Mallorca to triple.) The four sermons to the Claretian nuns are the only ones we have of hundreds, if not thousands, Serra gave on his home island in Spain, in Mexico, and ultimately in California. And yet, perhaps due to their complex mix of Latin and Mallorquín Spanish—not to mention their challenging, even strange theology—they were not translated until 1989. If Serra gave these four homilies to the nuns *before* Professor Ramonell's tempest in a teapot at the university, one can imagine Serra's spirit undergoing a severe deflation, moving, as it would have, from the sublime to the ridiculous. If the homilies occurred after the silly accusations, Serra may have launched into them with great spiritual gusto and gratitude, leaving Ramonell's envy, in a sense, in his wake.

Likewise, the sermons—steeped in God's mercy and love—came to the Claretians at a needy time. Like everyone else, they must have been appalled by the Bustillo-Isabel affair—more by the nun's punishment of complete silence, perhaps, than her love of the lieutenant. Circulating in the new undercurrents of the Enlightenment, the poetry of Sor Juana, the brilliant Mexican nun—"I suffer in loving and being loved"—was at its height of popularity in Spain, and the Claretians would have understood its erotic tensions. On the other hand, they may also have been privy to stories about the extremely misogynistic, if not crazy, Father Barcia, who at the end of the seventeenth century tried to lock up all the women in Mexico City in a convent completely blocked from any exit to or entrance of men. Predictably, most of those caught in this bizarre padre's net were prostitutes, actresses, and tightrope walkers—in short, women who had no protection. Their men set siege to the convent, freeing the ladies, who ran off "telling the good father if this was heaven they preferred hell." Barcia went completely insane, trying to kill himself by jamming suppositories of holy water up his rear end.

That was the Age of the Baroque in extremis, the sacred and profane so entangled as to strangle each other. Knowing of these pulls on the faith of the Claretians, Serra had to steer a difficult course between their call to love God and their need to love man. Both could be fearful. Serra, then thirty-three, Christ's age when he was crucified, had his own magnetism.

Serra plowed four deep furrows of spiritual ground he felt could help the nuns face the miseries piling up on Mallorca. In that, of course, he was certainly plowing the dark territory of his own fears. The four subjects, probably taken up on four separate days, were: listening for God's voice; the lightness of his yoke or Law; the meaning of suffering; and finally, and almost symphonically, God's boundless mercy.

The sermons are punctuated by exclamations at critical moments of revelation: "Christians!" Not Catholics, mind you. Not Sisters. *Christians*— that is, all those seeking the meaning of that strange man among men named Christ. The sermons are an unusual combination of the incantatory and epistemological. They contain both song and logic, reverie and close intellectual inspection. They are filled with allusions to the Old and New Testaments, many saints, philosophers such as Aristotle; they also revel in luminous anecdotes that have a touch of the wry. Finally, for a friar supposedly caught up, as is sometimes claimed, in the Counter-Reformation, there is a surprising absence of fire and brimstone.

The first sermon—about God's quiet voice—paradoxically begins with an exclamation: "What a difference between a harsh, strict and terrible temper, and a good, loving, sweet and gentle disposition!" For a priest with fifty-two nuns and nine novices staring up at him to commence not with theology but with psychology was daring.

Serra straightaway launches into a political anecdote, not about Alfonso VI of Castile, who leveled the Moors at Toledo and brought down Andalusia, but Alfonso I of Aragon, whose rules (*fueros*) in 1119 governing Christianized Arabs (*mudejars*) of Tudela were refreshingly humane: "The Mudejars were to be governed by an official of their own choosing according to the conventions of Islamic law 'as in the time of the Moors.' They were permitted freedom of worship. They were guaranteed possession of their property, freedom of movement, freedom to buy and sell." Serra admitted to the nuns that "some of the grandees thought his indulgence was too great. His answer to them was: 'I prefer to win over many with my mercy than to lose some . . . with severity and harshness.'" Serra was an exacting student of Spanish—and Andalusian—political history, even before he unwrapped his considerable theological erudition. His selection also demonstrates two important aspects of his personality: he knew how to play to his audience; and second, he was not a fundamentalist Christian. In reality, his life was lived in the trench between the Counter-Reformation and the Enlightenment, both chronologically and spiritually, being pulled sometimes back, sometimes forward, often caught in the perilous, fertile middle.

Throughout the first sermon (and indeed all four), Psalm 33 repeatedly echoes its sensual refrain: *Gustate et videte quoniam suavis est Dominus* ("O taste and see how gentle is the Lord"). Serra insisted, "To anyone who has tasted the gentleness of the Lord even once, all pleasures and delights of this life are anything but that. They are boring." He compared the Lord's kindness to "the sweet nectar of a mother's breast." In speaking to a cloistered female audience, Serra knew what he was doing—he converted God into a woman. Serra speaks directly to the nuns' emotions: "I ask you to reflect a moment on what goes on in your heart." He makes of the shape of the heart an original metaphor: "The heart you will find upside down, because the Supreme Creator shaped it like a pyramid." (The nuns had to have smiled.) "The widest side is on top, with the greatest surface to receive the influence of heaven, and the vertex is at the bottom with its smaller surfaces to which the things of this life could cling. But you find your heart crowded by the terrestrial, rather than the sublime!"

He quotes Isaiah: "Listen to your heart (*Redite ad cor*)." He also says the "sweet voice" of God will counteract "the voices that the enemy uses to twist you more and more," whose voice will try to act godlike in its dark facsimile.

Turning from the auditory, sensual subject of God's voices, in his second sermon Serra took on a more abstract topic: the Law. But right off, he cited St. Matthew: "His yoke is easy, his burden is light" (*Jugum meum suave est, et onus meum leve*, 11:30). It's highly doubtful that Serra sang this out the way Handel scripted it, but it is intriguing that the *Messiah* was first performed in 1742, two years before Serra spoke to the Claretians, and that Handel ended the entire joyful first movement of his greatest work—perhaps the most beloved of all classical symphonies—with Matthew's reassuring words. The German composer on an island (England) and the Spanish preacher on an island were on the same page.

Serra often invokes St. Gregory the Great, the first monk to become pope (in the sixth century), though he fled into the forest when his election was announced; Gregory, who probably originated Gregorian chant, ministered widely from England to Constantinople, a great doctor of Church unity and, as well, protector of Jews. Serra used Gregory to show the nuns that over time following the Law makes what seems a narrow road become "wide and soft." He quotes St. Jerome, "There is nothing easier than to love." Still, Serra picks up one of the thorniest questions, one he admits many popes have taken up "time and again"—why evil? "Why did God punish the sin of our first parents, one that seems of such little gravity?" Serra asks, referring to Adam and Eve plucking fruit from the forbidden tree. To evoke "eternal banishment from Paradise and all the miseries they suffered and we suffer for a mere bite of a given tree's fruit"? Such punishment, he implies, is absurd.

Serra defers to Augustine's "clever" argument here: "The smaller you consider our first parents' sin, the larger you make their fault." God put one tree off limits (the Tree of the Knowledge of Good and Evil), and, as we know, that apple shined a bit too much, even with a big worm around it. With a million trees, it should have been easy to keep hands off one. But it wasn't. The sin of pride (if not curiosity) seems at the root of all ethical problems, not to mention evil in the world.

How is the Law intrinsic? For Serra, as for St. Paul, "What I command you is on your lips and in your heart." In essence, he was telling the nuns, you know what is right; it's hardwired into a human being's brain. It's called a conscience, an innate instinct to good. Serra counts 613 precepts in Hebraic Law: "Ours, as you know, only counts 10, and really, only one, that is, to love." Here Serra was conflating the Two Great Commandments, as Christ saw them—to love the Lord with everything you've got, and your neighbor as yourself. One might call this a gorgeous fundamentalism—it's all love. And Serra is even more radical than Christ himself in asserting it.

Oddly, Serra ended his second sermon with a most unusual, blood-curdling thought, especially after all the rhetoric about love. He addresses a topic intrinsically revolting, but even more so for the women before him: killing children as "sacrifice." Serra gave historical examples of the Carthaginians (three hundred children killed in a day), the Romans (one-tenth of their children in a year); ancient Mexico (twenty thousand hearts eaten in a year).

"If these barbarians could kill their children because such cruel gods ordered it, will it be so hard to observe the Law given by a God so good and gentle?" Serra asks, bolstering the nuns.

His third sermon deals with suffering. Why do we suffer? Why would a perfect God make such an imperfect world? These are timeless theological questions that Serra must have thought about from his childhood days when his father and mother could bury themselves in their hands, sobbing, over the deaths of three infants. And yet, for a sermon about suffering, Serra began playfully, even teasingly.

"I'd like a bell to ring out before I start today, because I come to make a public announcement," he said with a laugh. "Start congratulating yourselves!"

The nuns must have moved nervously in their pews, large black olive-wood rosaries clattering.

"What I have to announce to you today, is the high ransom of a coin which will make you all rich!"

Some hesitant smiles?

"This coin is suffering."

That had to put the smiles away.

"This coin is so valuable you can buy glory in heaven."

One imagines a nun or two thinking: *Another man telling us to shut up and suffer!*

"Taste and see the goodness of God. Softly he scourges his children." *Suavis in filiorum flagellatione.*

Serra could have stopped there and left the nuns pretty worked up, softly scourged. But he plowed on, into a decidedly unusual interpretation of the story of Lazarus. Serra asks the question: "Why didn't Christ hurry over to cure him?" Instead he waited four days after his death to pay the corpse a visit, giving the sisters four more days to mourn. Is God a sadist? the nuns must have wondered. Serra quoted St. Aloysius: "The tribulations of this life are the most remarkable gifts of God and there is no more certain sign of his favor or love." In brief, Serra was underscoring a central fact of Christianity, and in particular, Catholicism, one honored more in the breach than in practice: suffering ennobles. Serra asks rhetorically, "How could it be kindness to punish and to grieve?" Serra offers Psalm 91:15, "I am with him in troubles; I will deliver and glorify him."

We are made human by pressure and pain. And more than human: Christ-like. "True happiness," Serra calls this third step to glory, "is in suffering, patiently, the labors of this life."

Serra's view of love-in-the-punishment is arresting. He asked the nuns, "How can the tender love of a father towards his son fit with the fact of punishing and afflicting him?" The answer: what characterizes a true father is "this harmony between love and severity." That this disposed Serra himself to corporal punishment is shown in his quoting of Paul's Letter to the Hebrews: "The Lord troubles the one He loves; but he whips the one He receives as a son." But where does one draw the line between what is necessary discipline and sadism? Serra comes up with a most unusual metaphor: God as a "lily that fights among the thorns." A fighting lily! An attempt, at least metaphorically, to soften the blow.

If suffering is an indication of God's love, the converse is the fate of Cain, who literally got away with murder: "He was so evil he was not worthy to be punished."

Oxymorons of faith! Singing paradoxes! Serra tells the story of a hermit who had a long way to walk to get his water. He considered moving his hermitage closer to the spring: "One day while he was going back burdened with his jug, he heard a voice calling one, two, three, four. He stopped, looked around, saw nobody, and kept walking. But the voice continued counting five, six, seven, eight, and said, 'I am an angel sent by God to count the steps you take so that none is left without reward.' The hermit moved his hermitage, indeed, *further* from the fountain!"

The fourth and last sermon followed from the third—God's boundless mercy, "the fourth step on the mystic stairway." Why is God merciful? "Because he knows the fragility of the mud with which we were formed." He knows what he made, and he knows it was—or became—frail. Forgiving, to Serra, is God's "most characteristic feature," a direct function of his greater love (to Scotus) and something he applies "with greater intensity than any other virtue." Thus Serra warns against suicide, the ultimate despair ("There is nothing more horrible and unworthy") because it turns away from inexhaustible mercy.

Serra reassured the nuns about the fate of the amorous fleeing nun Isabel, personifying the Creator, "He is sort of anxious when He is not forgiving." Mercy came, he noted, when "The Lord fell in love with light" (Psalm 144). To St. Gregory the Great, God's mercy was an "ever-flowing fountain," to St. John Chrysostom, "an immense sea." He even invokes that pagan philosopher Aristotle: "Oh infinite sea, since we cannot embrace you, embrace us!"

To Serra, God has "a repugnancy to punish," pointing to the Genesis flood and the "apology" of the rainbow. Aware of the nuns' skepticism, Serra told a most unusual story, of a monk who prayed, perhaps at first by mistake, *Miserere tui, Deus* (Forgive yourself, God), after which a sweet, flowery odor filled his cell. His superior walked by and noticed the perfumelike smell and asked the monk what he was doing: "He answered that he was so miserable that he only knew this prayer: *Miserere tui, Deus.*" The superior corrected him and told him to say the normal prayer, *Miserere mei* (Forgive me). But after the monk obeyed, the flowery odor disappeared. So the surprised superior ordered him to pray his original mistake, and "the heavenly fragrance" returned.

Serra concluded, "It seems that the Lord wanted us to see how it pleases Him to forgive and how little is necessary to reach his divine mercy." But perhaps what Serra really meant was: God's mercy is so great he even forgives himself, and what is even more unorthodox—he *should* do so, given the misery that fills his generous creation.

After this marathon series of sermons to the nuns of St. Clare, Serra was in demand more than ever. He was paid around one or two dollars for some, often in Italian and French currency (lira and sous). He fanned out across the island, walking through a grove of twenty-five windmills (which the Arabs had brought to the island) to speak at a church fashioned from a mosque in Felanitx to the east, then north to the villages of Manacor, Algaida, Montiuri, Inca, and Alaro, and finally to Bunyola, up against the high western mountain wall alongside Our Lady of Snows. He had to marvel in his island spiral at how Mallorca irrupts from its flat plain to unlikely peaks, climbing to rest at these risen hermitages, sanctuaries, and caves, as if the Mallorcan earth wanted God more. Down in the towns, he tried to address the people's suffering in drought and plague as he had with the nuns—it was a secret blessing from God. In the 1740s he preached five times in his hometown of Petra and at six nunneries in Palma; among his favorite subjects were the Immaculate Conception (four times), Corpus Christi (four times), Christ's suffering the crown of thorns (three times), and on the *Via Crucis* (Way of the Cross—twice). He favored the feast days of St. Anthony, Mary's assumption in heaven, Nuestra Señora de Los Angeles (August 2), and Mary Magdalene. All of those sermons of his island forays are lost.

On March 10, 1746, snow fell on the island. Even light snow was a rare occurrence, but this was an inundation by any standard; in two days, one witness thought the snow was as high as eight feet. It broke the limbs of the gnarled fig and olive trees, and froze the budding blossoms of the peach and almond trees. The delicate white of the *amatllers* was smothered by a hard white. It snowed into April, into Easter, canceling or abbreviating the Easter processions. The snowfall didn't stop until June, destroying grass, limiting the harvest of cow and sheep milk, and therefore meat production. For much of the year, the island population ate virtually no meat. The snow and icing of brooks and rivers wrecked the fishing, as well; salted fish—as much a hallmark of Mallorcan cuisine as olives—was not to be found anywhere. Most tragically, rather than soaking into the ground, the meltwater from this snow ran off to the sea. The drought continued. Wheat was brought in from Minorca, a smaller island just east of Mallorca, and the mainland, if it didn't rot on the docks for lack of a ship or get stolen by pirates.

As a coda to such punishment, on April 28, one of the most beloved priests on the island, José de Villaluengo, a Capuchin Franciscan, died. It's almost certain Serra attended his funeral. The diarist Nicolás Ferrer wrote, "God wanted to take him so soon so that he would not see the disgraces we would continue to experience on our island." He lauded the deceased as "so candid and humble that he was more like an angel than a man; everything he said came from the heart." Then on July 9, 1746, the king died after forty-five years on the throne, "suddenly, with no priest holding his hand." Philip V, the former Bourbon duke of Anjou, had been the only Spanish king Serra had known.

Ferdinand VI, the new king, "added new burdens," including fourteen thousand libras (or pounds sterling) straight to the king, new taxes for tools and tobacco. The new king also kindly offered indulgences for days off in Purgatory, at a required fee of thirty thousand libras.

If all this wasn't enough, on January 31, 1747, over 1,400 young men were seized by the military and impressed into service in one of the new king's adventures in Naples. If they couldn't be found, their fathers or employers were grabbed instead. The new military commander, who refused all petitions from mothers for their hijacked sons, was compared to the murderous Roman emperor Diocletian, and Mallorca to Babylon: "I heard of people whose children were slaves in Algeria who considered themselves lucky, suffering in Moors' land preferable to inhuman capture in their own Christian lands."

"It was the saddest day in the history of Mallorca," said Nicolás Ferrer.

The commander's soldiers must have brought it all home to Serra through a visit at the Convento de San Francisco before his theology class at Lullian. Could Serra have escaped a demand to hand in his roster of students? Could he have avoided soldiers, swords in their hands, flinging open the classroom door, pulling the few students not in hiding out into the street? Doubtful. The seized included some seminarians whose hair, cut in a tonsure, clearly identified them as religious.

During Lent in 1747, Serra himself came under direct attack. While giving a sermon at the church in Selva up toward the mountains, "an obsessed or hysterical woman" confronted him, standing up in the crowd and screaming, "Keep on yelling, keep on yelling, Father! You won't live to see Easter." That must have made his throat swell, his body grow hot in the wool of his order; for the moment, he was disordered and may have felt like disrobing, as had St. Francis the night of his death. But this was no stigmata; this was a wide-eyed Mallorcan, perhaps missing a tooth, telling him to shut the hell up. Was she pushed down the Selva church's forty steps? Perhaps she was schizophrenic, a century and a half before it was determined to be a medical condition. He may have addressed the drought in his sermon or St. Saturnine himself on his feast day, who lost his head for the faith. It was hard to keep his own head. Was he really going to die before Easter in the Old World? He tried to make light of the incident to Palou in a letter: "I expect to finish this Lent because the father of lies has made noises abroad that I shall not finish it." Serra made it to Easter, but he was shaken.

In February 1748, Serra's esteemed predecessor at the university, the philosophy professor Antonio Perelló, died at seventy-five. Serra (with an associate) was asked for an "approval" of the eulogy given by Father Pedro Riera. Though jointly written, Serra's fingerprints are all over the commentary and constitute a kind of second eulogy. The gloss on Riera is a gem. At first, Serra almost refused to do it, citing Virgil facing Dido of Carthage, "Our heart spontaneously cried out, as did the poet . . . *Do you wish to renew that unspeakable sorrow?*"

Serra talks about Riera's "phoenix," but Serra himself needed to be a phoenix. Mallorca was increasingly in ashes. On July 17, 1748, the marshal of the Holy Office Tribunal of the Inquisition, Gaspar de Puigdorfila y Villalonga, died suddenly at forty-six. Fighting broke out between priests and servants of the deceased over who owned several dozen funeral torches. On September 23, Serra's likely first teacher in Palma, the canon at the cathedral, Antonio Figuera, died at seventy-seven. It seemed to the university professor that much of his childhood and early manhood had died around him. That same month, so great was the antipathy of the islanders against the Crown, in order to protect them a royal order forbidding judges to go out of their own homes or entertain anyone was issued.

The year 1748 marked the worst suffering of the three-year drought on Mallorca, and Serra's sermons around the island were almost entirely preceded by blessings of the fields and chanting processions for rain. Whole wheat bread was forbidden to anyone but the sick, and a doctor's prescription was needed to get it. Barley was normally fed to cattle, but if used now, the offender was fined four hundred libras. People were arrested for making a doughnut or pastry. What little flour there was had to be rationed, and any baker who baked bread outside the ration was condemned to death. Great crowds of beggars filled Palma. On March 17, ships sailing for wheat were stopped in the harbor by a heavy wind and Serra took part in a chanting procession from the general hospital where many lay dying of malnutrition. This time they were praying not for rain but for ceasing of the wind. Children died of hunger and autopsies revealed their stomachs were crammed with inedible carob pods, grass, and dirt. Two days later, near Santa Clara, the commander of the Mallorca

Guard was stoned by a mob and guards around a Palma bakery were attacked and beaten.

Those who could afford to left the island. Serra could sense this emptying in the meanness of the streets, in the empty desks at the university. On February 1, 750 more men were seized for the warships; this time many were married, with one even being plucked on his wedding day from the church; another conscript was a seminarian.

In such a calamity, it would not be unusual for a Mallorcan peasant to collapse on a statue, praying while holding its hand. No doubt Serra, increasingly aware of how useless was high learning in such a time, would have been touched seeing such a man holding on to a statue, his head dropping, arching his shoulders as if on an invisible cross.

Meanwhile, a rumor started among the Franciscans that someone wanted to go to the New World. A professor of philosophy at the Lullian University, Rafael Verger, told Palou he had heard the rumor and was thinking of going himself. Palou, newly ordained and not yet embarked on a teaching assignment that he was slated to begin in 1750, was thinking the same. Palou thought the original rumor was started by Serra himself.

In the fall of 1748, Serra called Palou to his gloomy room at San Francisco. Palou told his mentor that he had begun to be consumed with the idea of going to the New World to minister to the gentiles (Serra's preferred nomenclature for the Indians over the more commonly used "pagans" or "barbarians"). There were many rumors about that others felt the same way. Tears sprang to Serra's eyes.

"Francisco, the rumor is true," Serra revealed. "I am the one who is anxious to make this long journey. My grief has been that there was no one to go with me as a companion, though I am not deterred." Serra mentioned praying to Francis Solano, the apostle of Peru, and the Blessed Mother "to touch the heart of someone who might go with me."

"Since you found out the news without knowing who was planning it, and I feel such a great drawing to you, it is, without a doubt, God's will," Serra breathed out. For the moment, Serra asked Palou to continue with novenas for guidance, but in secret.

Soon Serra wrote to the priest in Madrid in charge of all missions to the Indies, Matías de Velasco, asking for permission for himself and Palou to be missionaries. The die was cast. But the first response was not encouraging. The two outposts in New Spain seeking recruits—in Queretaro and Mexico City—had already filled their quotas (thirty and thirty-three friars, respectively). Serra and Palou would essentially be put on a waiting list. Palou suggested that some of the hesitation was due to what he called a presumption about Mallorcans' supposed "instability of character." The origin of the stereotype is uncertain; it could have been anything from the special *fueros* (laws) applied to Mallorcans during the *Reconquista* that they could trade with the Muslims of North Africa due to their chronic droughts, to current civil unrest over the famine, to the islanders' legendary independence.

Strangely enough, it may have been their own success that spawned this stereotype. A native Mallorcan, Antonio Llinas, had gone to New Spain (which essentially covered all Spain's holdings in North America, the Caribbean, and the Philippines), and established the College of Santa Cruz in Querétaro in 1683. He established other such colleges throughout Spain, but only in Mallorca did his superiors balk, finding their own young priests "too inconstant and fickle in character to become model missionaries." Apparently, there was a high dropout rate among Mallorcan missionaries before their ten years was up. In any case, the lack of a missionary college on Mallorca led Serra and Palou to look to mainland Spain for bona fides to the New World.

Their plans on hold, Serra gave the highly esteemed annual sermon on January 25, 1749, in honor of the feast day of Blessed Raymond Lull, the namesake of the university. Chosen by a panel of his peers for the honor, Professor Serra mounted the high pulpit in the dark, gold-leafed church of San Francisco near the crypt of Raymond Lull, complete with relics. A great pageantry had followed him into the church of all the professors and administrators of the university and their colorful regalia, the beadle and his mace, the bishop and governor of the island, the aldermen of the city, the nobles, blowing trumpets, thumping drums.

Whatever Serra said, his words were like rain. But they died to history. Palou asserted, "All who heard him were in admiration. When he finished the sermon, I heard a retired professor [a *Jubilado*] who himself was very famous . . . and in no way partial to the preacher, say: 'This sermon should be printed in letters of gold." It *was* printed, as records of printing fees show. But in gold or not, it was lost. No copy of it outlasted the closing of the university in 1823 or the ravages of the Spanish Civil War and its aftermath, in which Generalissimo Franco took revenge on Catalonia by destroying many of its historical records.

Serra would almost certainly have quoted Raymond Lull himself: "As the needle naturally turns to the north when it is touched by the magnet, so is it fitting, O Lord, that Thy servant should turn to love." Serra could have explained Scotus as Mary Beth Ingham does: "Indeed, this God [to Scotus] is not best encountered by thinking or speculating about the divine nature: not a God of theory at all. This is a personal God encountered by and in the activity of loving and selfless generosity: a God of *praxis.*" Finally, with an eye to a West none could yet see, Serra may have quoted María de Agreda writing to the friars in New Mexico, "I see what I have been and what I am, and fear what I may become to be. Thou hast lighted up, most high King, my understanding and inflamed my will."

Despite his rising station at the university, Serra must have been anxious to learn the outcome of his request to be sent to the New World. In the midst of the severe spring drought and people dropping from famine and plague, Antonio Llinas, now an old man, returned from his missions in the New World to say masses at St. Eulalia Church praying for rain. Father Serra conferred with him in secret about his hidden desire to leave his current life. In February, Serra held his last public examinations for the higher degrees. Lent began early that year (February 19) and when he was invited to baptize and confirm townspeople of his native Petra, he leapt at the opportunity, sensing, perhaps, it could be his last. Meanwhile, as yet unknown to him, five friars on the dock at Cádiz froze up, quitting the voyage "on account of their fear of the sea which they had never seen." This opened up room for even "inconstant" seaworthy Mallorcans, namely, Palou and Serra. Suspiciously, the official letters from Cádiz authorizing travel to the New World as missionaries didn't arrive; as Palou put it drily, they "were lost between the doorway [to San Francisco] and my cell." Whoever had tried to kill the call of the two priests to mission would have been guilty of excommunication.

Fortunately, the Cádiz officials, alarmed that in a month no response had come from Mallorca, sent letters again. This time they arrived at San Francisco by special messenger exactly on Palm Sunday. Palou received them just as he was about to go out to bless the palms for the procession. He left immediately by horse-drawn cart for Petra. When he handed the letters to Serra, Palou reported, "His joy and happiness was greater than if he had received a call to be a Bishop."

Yet Serra tarried in Petra. He knew the leave-taking of a lifetime was coming and he thought to stave it off. Holy Tuesday of Easter Week arrived, with the traditional procession from his old parish of St. Peter's up the steep hill to Bon Any, the shrine whose bells he had rung so briskly as a boy, the place where he had first glimpsed the sea. Following two men hoisting a statue of St. Joseph, the townspeople followed their favorite son Junípero Serra for what would be his last Mass in his hometown. Holding fast to his secret, Serra clutched the church's supposed relic of the godfather of Christ. The crowd chanting the Litany of All Saints moved up the steep path. They passed through paintings on poles of the fourteen Stations of the Cross, from Christ's scourging all the way to being laid dead in his mother's arms.

At the Offertory, or beginning, of the Mass, Serra joined the congregation in singing the "Joys of Our Lady of the Good Year": "Give us a good day and a good year, O Lady!" Serra called out for rain, *Lluvia! Lluvia!* Outside after Mass, the good people of Petra shared the few Easter *frits de pasco* and *empanadas* they could spare in the miserable drought. Serra looked at the faces in the crowd he had known as a boy; they, like him, were grown. He was thirty-six, almost too old to be thinking of leaving to go anywhere, much less across two seas and an ocean.

He must have faced his parents, and told them he had a new assignment. Perhaps his father, Antonio, now seventy-four, bent his whitened head, then looked up and out over the fields where the few surviving almonds were small and green in their husks. Did his seventy-two-year-old mother, Margarita, tear up and hold him? If so, their son must have thought: *I cannot tell them where I am going. I cannot look them in the eye. If I do, I will never leave.*

Geiger insists that "Neither the conditions of the times nor dissatisfaction with his employments had anything to do with Serra's decision to become a missionary," and he points out Palou's quoting Serra on the matter: "I have no other motive but to revive in my soul those intense longings which I have had since my novitiate when I read the lives of the saints. These longings had become somewhat deadened because of the preoccupation I had with studies."

But these two biographers were both Franciscan priests and were putting the purest motive possible on the largest decision of Serra's life. Serra himself may have been doing so. We can say now that as he rode his mule the seven-hour, twenty-five-mile ride back to Palma, the pastures that had been so green in his youth were now dry and crisp underfoot of the mule, and the sheep once so thick with wool were thin and their wool patchy. If he looked carefully at the fava beans they were infested with maggots. If he tried to imagine the sanctified white of the *amatllers*, all he would have seen now across the fields were naked trees whose leaves had not greened but curled. The olives, always small on Mallorca, were now smaller than a rat's eye, and the almonds wormy.

Back in Palma, he gave one last sermon at San Francisco on April 10, 1749, chanting with the parish for *"Lluvia! Lluvia!"* It was a wonder there was even enough altar wine to turn to Christ's blood.

Underneath all his excitement to leave loomed a great heartbreak that his home island was in the throes of death. He saw it in the red-rimmed eyes of the starving, the throngs of beggars, the violence over crumbs, the plague-ridden cemeteries, his classrooms emptying of students sent to fight senseless wars.

On April 13, the Sunday after Easter, Serra and Palou said good-bye to their fellow friars at San Francisco. Serra made a public confession of his faults. He then knelt to kiss the feet of the priests and brothers who had known him for many if not all of these seventeen years in Palma. Among them was Juan Pol, his first professor of philosophy, who was deeply moved at Serra's humility.

One last time Serra walked the church at the Convento de San Francisco near Raymond Lull's remains. Maybe it was then that he pried open the crypt, or took advantage of someone else doing the honors, because on the boat he would carry pieces of Lull's bones in back of a large cross he would sleep with for the rest of his life. Perhaps at this time, too, he saw a peasant praying again, holding on to Nuestra Señora de Los Angeles, leaning in his sorrow.

"May their souls rest in peace, for I will never see them again."

So wrote Francisco Noguera on April 13, 1749, shortly after Serra's and Palou's departure by sea from Palma that day. "I was a friend of both," Noguera scratched in the past tense, as if he had just signed their death warrant.

The English cargo ship was bound for Málaga. Noguera may have been one of those who accompanied them to the docks, even onto the ship. Serra may have handed him his personal 1608-vintage Bible, a mammoth 1,170-page tome too large to haul across the seas. There, just before anchor was weighed, last *abrazos* with their compatriots clasped, Serra turned to Palou and said:

"Let us stop these titles of respect and superiority from now on. No more 'Master' and 'Your Reverence.' We are now equals completely."

Palou put his hand on his heart, shaking his head. Even the cherished *condiscípulos* was subordinated to their simple first names.

"I call you Francisco; call me Junípero."

The small group of friars and other well-wishers walked off the ship bobbing in the harbor. Noguera went home and consigned those departed in writing to the deep.

Beyond the wake of the ship, the lights of Palma glittered and disappeared. Serra would never return.

CHAPTER FOUR

TO THE SPANISH MAINLAND

. . . Forgetting how many go forth looking for wool and come back shorn?
(His niece to Don Quixote)
—MIGUEL DE CERVANTES

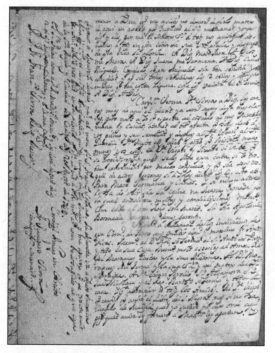

The last leaf of Serra's good-bye letter
to his parents from Cádiz, 1749.

*T*he "packet boat," as Palou called it (*paquebote*), was under English
flag and probably sailing from Minorca (wrested from Spain by
England in the 1713 Treaty of Utrecht that ended the War of the Spanish
Succession). Called "the workhorse" of passenger and mail service of the

western Mediterranean to the Atlantic coasts of Spain, Portugal, France, and England, the packet boat was built to withstand rough seas and carry about one thousand tons, so it was not sleek, but "full-bodied and somewhat tubby." These vessels were of substantial size, about 170 feet long and 35 feet wide.

The packet boats took their names from their captains, who were called "packet rats," for their somewhat nefarious character. Some had done time for petty thievery, others enjoyed their grog overmuch, and some were escaping irate husbands (or wives). Some held all three distinctions. A few days out of Palma on the high seas going south, someone approached Serra in his berth and pointed a knife at his throat.

It was the English packet boat captain, "furious," according to Palou, probably under the influence of whiskey, and fond neither of Catholicism nor clerics. The man is as nameless to history as his boat, but "during the two weeks which the voyage lasted till we reached Málaga he did not leave us in peace." Unable to speak Spanish, his English useless, whenever he saw the two friars saying the prayers of their Divine Office, tipping back and forth with the pitch of the sea, he would clamber down the gunwales and fly into a rage, sputtering bad Portuguese. The captain pulled a small Bible from his shoulder satchel and quoted a particularly contentious part of the New Testament. To Palou, he was nothing short of a "stiff-necked heretic" with a "murderous design."

At first Serra tried to avoid the incensed captain rasping out a language neither of them knew well. He bent with Palou under the yardarms, balanced himself on the gunwales, took spray from the sea; the captain followed them stern to bow. In the back of the packet boat they were caught in the heretic's net, his Bible in one hand, his index finger lifted high from the other, a sly smile on his leathery face. *Try that one on for size, mates!*

We don't know the texts the captain cited for argument, only that the largest storm was not on the sea, but "arose on deck." No doubt the English salty dog had in his wobbling hands a King James Bible, authorized about a century before (1611), nine-tenths of it taken whole from the first widely disseminated Bible in English (translated from the Latin of St. Jerome) by William Tyndale in 1526. An Oxford scholar who devoted his whole life to this translation, Tyndale had the misfortune to incur the wrath of Henry VIII, who had him exiled to Antwerp, then strangled and burned at the stake in Brussels, about the time (1536) that Henry was blasting the Spaniards for the Inquisition.

What was the English sea captain's theological beef with the Catholic Church? Palou gives no hint, except to say that he became so enraged with Serra "on several occasions" that "he threatened to throw us into the sea and to sail away for London." Serra had a deft response: "Our king will demand indemnity from your king and you will pay with your head." This threat must have inspired another swig or two. The captain, certainly no theologian, misquoted or only partially quoted the passages he was so angry about; too, they had to be quoting from different Bibles. "Our Father Junípero," says Palou, as if this were a debate tournament rolling with the waves, "cited the text which he had misinterpreted to sustain his opinion, and then he would quote another text which completely upset the man's arguments." The befuddled captain took another look at his "musty Bible" and retreated with an *argumentum ad miseracordiam*, insisting "the page must be torn out." It would have been funny, if it weren't for his threats to drown them. Or the knife.

One of the earliest abrasions for Protestants the century before Henry VIII's serial uxoricide was the doctrine of transubstantiation, which held that the priest at Catholic Mass changed the bread and wine into the actual body and blood of Christ. There may be no more important doctrine for Catholics—and one that is impossible to prove by any logic or science. John Wyclif, an Oxford don at loggerheads with Rome (he had pleaded unsuccessfully for a lessening of England's papal taxes), "regarded the doctrine as a clerical deception." The early Swiss Protestant Ulrich Zwingli won over the entire city of Zurich by a clever comparison of Old Testament semantics (*"Hoc est enim pactum meum"*—For this is my agreement—in Genesis 17:10), with the Gospel of Mark's plain-spoken *"Hoc est enim corpus meum"* (For this is my body). Like many Protestants, Zwingli suggested that the bread and wine were as symbolic as Jonah spending time in the belly of a whale. Perhaps the captain saw transubstantiation as even worse: *"He's got a loaf of bread . . . and calls it his body. He swigs some wine, mates! And then the aw-dass-ity to tell 'em to drink 'is blood! Wot say, padre? 'At's cannibals to my ears."*

In truth, Serra probably knew there was not much wiggle room to explain transubstantiation to anyone, much less an irritated sea captain from England. Aquinas himself relied on Aristotle's distinction of "substance" and "accidents" to explain the seemingly impossible transformation. That is, the bread of the host and wine in the chalice were mere accidents, an outward appearance. But the "substance" of both, in the priestly blessing at Mass, was indeed Christ's body and blood. Such a thing was hard for even sober theologians to grasp, not to mention the naked eyes, and it sent Aquinas into all sorts of bizarre convolutions to explain what should be done if poison is put in consecrated wine, a fly drops in, or a priest vomits his own Communion.

Serra could have quoted John 22:19: "Do this in remembrance of me" and let the captain meditate on Christ's own insistence on commemoration. Catholic theologians, as well as Protestants, have often cited this passage as a possible explanation for the inexplicable. Another theological favorite is John's evocation of Christ's self-metaphorizing: "I am the Bread of Life. He who comes to me shall not hunger and he who believes in me shall not thirst" (6:35). Yet what to make of Christ's insistence shortly after this metaphor that is anything but metaphoric: "Amen, amen, I say to you, unless you eat the flesh of the Son of Man and drink his blood, you shall not have life in you" (6:54)? These bald injunctions disturb us today as much as they did the original disciples, who were said to "murmur" to each other, "This is a hard saying. Who can listen to it?" (6:61). The sea captain surely didn't.

At the end of its first session, the Council of Trent in 1551 made the definition of transubstantiation that endures in Catholicism to this day, though soon after one author counted two hundred different interpretations of transubstantiation, including Martin Luther's "sacramental union" of Christ entering Communion as a spirit.

The sea captain may have had it easier taunting Serra about the avarice of Spanish rulers, pointing to the flood of gold and silver coming into Spain from the New World and Spanish ostentation, quoting St. Luke that it's tougher for the rich to get to heaven than to pass a camel through the eye of a needle. Serra would have fended him off, noting that in Aramaic, a needle's eye was one of the archways into Jerusalem. And for saving, it wasn't for us to judge, "all things are possible with God" (Mark 10:27).

Finally, the captain may have surpassed "heretic" status to out-and-out scorn for Christ himself, laughing at how Christ seems to subvert the Fourth Commandment to "Honor thy father and thy mother," and even the Fifth Commandment against murder, citing that difficult Matthew passage: "Do not think that I have come to send peace upon the earth; I have come to bring a sword, not peace. For I have come to set a man at variance with his father, and a daughter with her mother" (10:34–35). Theologians see Christ in this passage as basically suggesting—if you believe in me, expect to come into conflict with the world, expect a spiritual battle. But Serra still could not have answered this one quickly.

"'My yoke is easy, and my burden is light,'" Serra may have concluded with one of his favorite wisdoms, before slipping perhaps on the scum of cod and losing his Bible.

What probably undergirded our sea captain's anger—more immediately compelling than Christ's body in Communion or a gospel's meaning or the demon rum—was the recently concluded War of Jenkins' Ear between

England and Spain. It wouldn't be far-fetched to imagine the captain had fought in it, or knew people killed in it, and for him to heap *that* blame on top of the Spanish friars in the guise of the Bible.

The origins of the war could be found in Spain's loss of the island of Minorca to the British, which gave England a sizable foothold into trade to the Spanish Americas. The British secured a thirty-year contract, the *asiento*, to sell slaves and five hundred tons of goods at ports in New Spain. But the Spanish never trusted the English to hold to the trade limits, and after several skirmishes at sea, the 1729 Treaty of Seville allowed the Spaniards to board British vessels and inspect them to see if the *asiento* was being abused. This enflamed the British sea captains. In 1731, the commander of a Spanish coast guard ship ran alongside the British brig *Rebecca*, climbed up a rope ladder, and promptly cut off the ear of the brig's captain, Robert Jenkins. Seven years later, Jenkins gave a dramatic retelling of the incendiary incident to Parliament, and within a year of that, the War of Jenkins' Ear began, about the time Serra became a priest.

Whatever the explanations for that fateful night on his sea voyage to Málaga, the captain "with every intention, apparently, of taking his life," raised the knife above Serra, who himself slowly raised up in his berth, putting his hand gently at the knife tip. The captain suddenly came to his senses, backed away, and stumbled to his quarters, passing out on his bed, sick with drink. But Serra was now wide awake. His voice seemed strangely "full of joy," to Palou; his mentor even cracked one of his wry jokes, suggesting if not careful they might be thrown overboard.

"Stay awake, Francisco. Otherwise we'll certainly find the gold and silver we're searching for before we ever get to Málaga."

Palou breathed out, the more fearful of the two, noting later that God intended for Junípero "a more prolonged martyrdom."

Terrified or transfixed, the two priests came out on deck and stared out at the moon over the black sea. The threatened knifing had lanced an inner boil; they were not confronted again by the packet rat at the helm. Serra confessed to Palou, "I comfort myself that I never provoked him to argument or even conversation. That would have been useless. But in conscience I thought I ought to answer as a Catholic."

The trip to Málaga took two weeks. Given that the distance from Palma to the southern port is about 675 nautical miles, that's roughly forty-eight miles a day. Today a ship can make that trip in about twenty-four hours; even by eighteenth-century standards, the packet captain was poking along.

Anxious to leave the walls of their endless monastery and its creaking and moaning, Serra and Palou didn't need a dictionary to rejoice when the lookout yelled in English from the crow's nest on the mainsail, "Land ahoy!" They must have put down their brevaries, picked up their habits, and made it to the boat's rail.

They beheld the tallest steeple in the port, the 276-foot-high north tower of Santa Iglesia Catedral Basílica de la Encarnación. Outside of the cathedral of Seville, it was the highest man-made structure in Andalusia.

As they entered the horseshoe harbor, Málaga's ancient past grew before them. At the foot of the brick-and-limestone Moorish fortress, the Alcazaba, the semicircle seats of the first-century BC Roman theater shimmered, and tall palms reached up the hill. Higher yet, in back of the town, a Moorish castle straddled Mount Gibralfaro. The Moors were leading Serra to the New World.

Their time in Málaga was brief. Greeted by Juan Jurado, the superior of the Franciscan convent of St. Luis, they walked down the wharf; the smell of tuna and cod spilling from the fishing boats into large wooden trays onshore quickened their bellies.

The two Mallorcans insisted on walking through the city streets. They talked animatedly with Father Juan, himself a former professor, their feet perhaps cherishing terra firma. Málaga was one of the oldest continually inhabited cities in the world, founded in 770 BC by Phoenicians as *Malaka*, its name transformed under the Arabs to *Malaqah*, in tribute to the salted fish for which the city was famous (from *malah*, Arabic for salt). They passed through the marketplace, filled with lemons and oranges, grapes and almonds. Serra may have spotted a few early pomegranates.

It was two weeks after Easter, around Pentecost, and Serra would have jerked his head to see a spontaneous *seata*, a solo flamenco inspired by the moment, the flames of the spirit going from head to dancing toe, surrounded by a circle of clappers.

The Mallorcan pair stayed about a week in Málaga before, on May 2 or 3, they boarded a smaller coastal trawler (a *xebec*) that would take them on a five-day trip southwest through the Strait of Gibraltar, turning then northwest. Once again, they waved to confreres getting smaller and smaller as they went out of the harbor. But shore was not as far this time. This time they hugged the coastline and could see the buff-colored crags from out at sea ripple in the heat, the palms shaking their heads. They headed toward Columbus's port, Cádiz. The wind was warm.

Did Serra and Palou hear the cackling of the Barbary macaques on Gibraltar? Approaching the funnel out of Europe, they were certainly in awe of the Rock. It jutted nearly 1,400 feet above the Strait, a massive hunk of Jurassic limestone like the brow of a god in exile. In fact, the ancient Greeks had identified Gibraltar as one of the two Pillars of Hercules (or Heracles) created by the son of Zeus, twinned with the outcropping of land across the water in North Africa (today's Almina). Geologically, North Africa and Europe had been joined at the hip until a great flood divided the two continents by nine miles 5.3 million years ago, during an interglacial period of warming. It was also on Gibraltar that those ancestors of man, the Neanderthals, had made their last camps twenty-four thousand years earlier.

The two friars may not have heard the strange monkeys, the only monkeys in all of Europe, gathered on that Rock. The ocean sent their little *xebec* up and down, spray booming over the gunwales. The Strait of Gibraltar is the turbulent nexus of currents from the Atlantic clashing with those from the saltier Mediterranean. The friars may not have seen dark things moving over the rock, but if they fought off seasickness (as at least Palou did) and the ship slid into a trough of calm, they could have looked up to see the Rock girded in olive trees, pines, and a flower found nowhere else in Europe—the white candytuft.

On May 7, the *xebec* approached the great harbor of Cádiz, their last stop in the Old World and the place from which the conquistadors had been sailing westward for two and a half centuries, since Columbus's second voyage in 1493. The two friars knew they were latecomers to wonder, with all the anxious fervor that implies. Serra and Palou's 125-mile voyage from Málaga was over, as was their life in the Old World. Here, at the prow of the ship called *Europe*, they would linger for over three months before setting out forever across the Atlantic.

It was a long last look. As far back as 1104 BC, the city of Gadir (meaning "walled stronghold") had been precariously built by the Phoenicians on a strand protected by a high sea wall nearly its entire length north to south, later reinforced by the conquering Carthaginians (it was Hannibal's chief base for his assault on Europe). The Spaniards later made sure all approaching ships got a good look at the cannon-lined ramparts of the Fortress of Candelaria, built on the sea wall. Serra must have marked each of those iron barrels and the 160 towers behind the sea wall, many of them used by merchants trying to spy their wares—or pirates—coming in on the galleons and packet boats. The first impression of Cádiz was hardness, protection, suspicion facing all that great wealth moving back to Spain and all who followed it stealthily across the Atlantic.

As the Franciscans debarked, they marveled at the number of ships and wharves, far more than Málaga, inlets and slips on both sides of the peninsula. It was not unusual to have eight hundred ships in the deep-water port, flags of many nations flying from the yardarms and castle keeps.

Once again, they gave their stiff legs a walk. Quickly they discovered Cádiz was not quite carefree Málaga. It was a frenzied stew, a Babel of languages rioting in their ears: French, Portuguese, Spanish accented a half dozen ways, Flemish, English, Gaelic (the Irish had a thriving expatriate community in Cádiz, and still do), German, Italian, Arabic. Sailors clutching their caps, twisting scarves; officers in cockade hats and brass-buckled navy coats; stevedores hauling crates of sherry, port, rum, and sacks of beans and rice; wheat by oxcart; missionaries of many orders, rosary crosses swaying at the hip; wives greeting their husbands long at sea; concubines with their lovers sashaying down the wharves; pickpockets snatching their dinner; dogs yelping. A priest who sailed out of Cádiz the same year as Serra described the extraordinary human melee of the Old World's last stop: "In this city, we began to understand what is meant by the confusion of the world." He recommended those who followed him "caution . . . accommodating oneself to the exigencies of a motley population without sacrificing religious moderation," meaning grog shacks in the tightly packed streets and houses with lace-graced ladies who never sleep. Seaports are seaports, after all; they teem with the sexual ardor of those long pent-up coming in and those fearful of their lives going out. And this was no normal seaport. It was the launch across a major ocean to Terra Incognita, or partly Cognita. And it was the first precarious unwrapping of what became the largest heist of stolen goods in human history. Stability and Cádiz were incompatible.

Serra and Palou finally found their way to the Franciscan house named exactly as their home in Mallorca—Convento de San Francisco. Soon they were told that there were three extra spaces in the ship that still needed to be filled. Worried their departure would be delayed, Serra suggested Fathers Rafael Verger, Juan Crespí, and Guillermo Vicens, who grew up in Petra.

With the vacancies resolved, the new recruits for the Mexico mission were led to the Spanish government's Board of Trade in downtown Cádiz. Each Franciscan was interviewed extensively; clearly Spain was keeping close watch on its priestly emissaries. Serra was described in the official document of the voyage as "a lector of theology, native of Petra in the Diocese of Mallorca, thirty-five years old, of medium height, swarthy, dark eyes and hair, scant beard." (Interesting—the root of the Spanish word for "swarthy"—*moreno*—is *moro*, or a Moor.) Except for his age, Palou was found to be almost identical to his companion: "a lector of philosophy, native of Palma, twenty-six years old, of medium height, swarthy, dark eyes and hair," lacking only Serra's "scant beard." Rafael Verger, a native of Santanyí on Mallorca, but the same age as Palou and also a philosophy professor, had a different shade of skin: "fair complexion, face pock-mocked, somewhat florid." He also had Serra's "scant beard." Juan Crespí had the honor of having his name misspelled ("Chrispin"); the Palma native was two years older (twenty-eight) than Palou and Verger, "short of stature, sallow skin but somewhat florid complexion . . . and dark hair." Crespí's "blue eyes" stood out. It soon became clear to Serra—if it hadn't already—that he wasn't going to the New World solely for God. The pecuniary tie was knotted right at the start of his journey. The Spanish Board of Trade had authorized Serra and Palou a per diem income of seven reales a day for their journey from Palma to Cádiz (eight reales was the famous "piece of eight," equal to one Spanish silver dollar, or peso). The board had computed Palma to Cádiz at a distance of 309 leagues (roughly eight hundred miles). After prayers and their initial meal, veteran missionary Pedro Pérez de Mezquía plopped a bag of thirty-nine pieces of eight into Serra's proud Mallorcan hands.

Yes, it was over thirty pieces of silver. Serra knew what that was: the exact amount it took to sell Christ, not something to long meditate.

Had Serra fingered one of the silver coins, he would have read around its circumference in abbreviated Latin, "Philip V, by the Grace of God, King of the Spains and the Indies." This was silver unearthed by Indian slaves from the mines at Potosí, Bolivia. The coin had been minted in 1731 in Mexico. On the front side, the Pillars of Hercules—through which Serra had just sailed at Gibraltar—bracketed the two hemispheres of the globe over which the Spanish crown hung, with the Latin inscription, *Utraque Unum*—Both Are One. Flipping it over, the coin's imprint of arms showed Castile, León, and Granada, with an escutcheon of Anjou, France.

Serra knew the "special relationship" between the Church and Spain regarding the conquest of the New World had been cemented early on, within two decades of Columbus's discoveries. In 1508, Pope Julius II issued a bull, *Universalis ecclesiae*, in which the king of Spain was made the vicar of the pope in the so-called *real patronato*, in exchange for supplying missionaries all they needed—including a salary, food, soldiers, even beads—to spread Christianity among the native residents of the new lands. Christ had said no one could serve two masters; he had explicitly also insisted, in political matters, "Render unto Caesar the things that are Caesar's and unto God the things that are God's" (Matthew 22:21). Serra knew in his heart which master trumped the other. But his pocket now jangled. Franciscan pockets were not supposed to do that.

He had also read—few missionaries could have been unaware of it—of the early outrage in Cuba of the Dominican Bartolomé de Las Casas: "The *cacique* [Hatuey, the chief] . . . asked the Franciscan friar if Christians all went to Heaven. When told that they did, he said he would prefer to go to Hell. Such is the fame and honor that God and our Faith have earned through the Christians who have gone out to the Indies." Serra would have been doubly embarrassed that the man on the spot for the Church in that early moment (1513) was a Franciscan, not to mention Las Casas's witness to this scene: "Suddenly, without cause and without warning, and in my presence, the devil inhabited the Christians and spurred them to attack the Indians—men, women, and children—who were sitting there before us. In the massacre that followed the Spaniards put to the sword more than three thousand souls. I saw such terrible cruelties done there as I had never seen before nor thought to see."

Two hundred years had passed; the Enlightenment was helping Spain progress beyond the "Black Legend" of its first conquistadors in the Caribbean, Mexico, and Peru. Official proclamations by the Council of the Indies of a more tolerant Indian policy would help Serra. But still, those masters existed side by side; in fact, they were yoked. Serra deeply wanted to take the higher road, what he understood to be the Christian road, at its best.

The Convento de San Francisco could not fit all the newly approved missionaries gathering from around Spain, and many were farmed out to churches across the bay in the Spanish mainland or even to secular hotels and private homes. The freedom of movement these friars enjoyed "was a condition that commissaries did not like but . . . were forced to tolerate."

Whether or not Serra was one of the lucky liberated, he loved a good walk, and no doubt after singing Matins and saying Mass strolled through the streets of Cádiz to fill out official documents at government offices or while away the time before Vespers, at times with Fathers Palou and the newly arrived Verger, but on occasion alone. Though he marveled at the many saints' relics gathered from monasteries around Spain in the Baroque-style Church of Santiago, he would have been downcast at the charred ruins of the old Cádiz Cathedral. Built in 1260, just after the *Reconquista*, the cathedral had been burned to the ground in 1596, during one of many English attacks on this chief harbor of the once invincible Spanish fleet.

The downward arc of Spain's fortunes and the age of the city were everywhere visible in the peninsula's narrow streets, even as Serra was jostled at the elbow by people haggling for copperware and bread, fruit and cloth. Cádiz was the oldest continually inhabited city in Spain, and probably in all of Western Europe. The ancient history of which he had been so proud in Mallorca found an even deeper mark in Cádiz, but by now such a thing had to have pained Serra. Was Serra tired of the Old World? Weighed down by his knowledge that the semicircle stone seats of the Roman theater, second only to Pompeii's in size, had been slave-hauled by order of the Roman emperor Lucius Cornelius Balbus?

Farther on, Serra may have spied the *puterías*, whose popularity in Spain he knew of, especially the renowned large brothel across the sea from Mallorca in Valencia, where "there is a whole quarter of the city where they can ply their trade in complete freedom. The women are dirt cheap compared with the excessively high prices of other merchandise." An apostolic notary and constable at the time wrote, "The public *putería* is so common in Spain that on entering a town, many people go there before going to church." Serra probably ascertained this fact of life—the famed Valencia brothel, and those on his own island—from the confessional. On the wrought iron balconies the prostitutes laughed and waved to men below. If they wore silk, the only late silk for Serra would have been the pink chasuble of *Gaudete* Sunday in Lent, that brief joy in the middle of sorrow.

Ah, the air was like white peaches in Cádiz! It was that hour when the body is glad to be done of its day, the senses filled. And perhaps on an iron balcony, a *tusona*, a blonde, appeared and leaned. She would move anyone, of any vow. There were priests who would go up there, and undoubtedly confessed to it to fellow priests such as Junípero Serra.

Walking down such a street, where would Serra's gaze have been? Palou started a myth of coolness: "When he was in the presence of women he was always serious and modest in his glance and his speech." Fitch stretched this further: "Women never saw the warmer, gracious side of his character," painting Serra as "habitually unsmiling, even stern" with them. But there is plenty of evidence to the contrary—from his love for his sister, Juana, to his playfulness with the Claretian nuns.

Passing the *puterías*, Serra may have meditated that the first person to whom Christ reveals the most important fact of his entire life on earth—that he has walked out of a grave, that he is the first human being ever to conquer death—is not Peter, whom he picked to lead his Church, not John, the beloved, not even his own mother, Mary. No, it was Magdalene, the prostitute, once held by seven devils, declared fit by the religious authorities of the time only for a stoning. Christ calls her, with obvious affection, "Mary" (John 20:16). And what about the Samaritan woman bending down to draw water from the well? The first person—perhaps the only one—to whom Christ directly admits he is the Messiah. His own rebuke of the dumbstruck disciples, to whom the woman is fallen,

JOURNEY TO THE SUN

at best, is typically subtle and striking: "I have food to eat of which you do not know" (John 4:26–33). As tongue-stilling as God's answer to Job.

The Franciscan who had now left home for good was the kind of man who would see in the *tusona*'s eyes not lust, but hopelessness. And his eyes might sting, watering, looking downward, thinking that Christ did love Magdalene, the woman at the well, and she who dipped her hair in ointment to rub his feet, to the shock of his Pharisee host: "Thou givest me no kiss, but she from the moment she entered has not ceased to kiss my feet. . . . Wherefore I say to thee, her sins, many as they are, shall be forgiven her, because she has loved much" (Luke 7:45, 47).

But there was something else in the Cádiz air, tawny and smoky, something that could draw a man, a priest, a king away from the *puterías*. Some blocks up stood the gigantic Royal Tobacco Factory, built only twenty years before, still expanding, men hauling the dark gold leaves from the New World into the storage vaults for curing, a building destined to be the second largest in Spain (behind the Escorial near Madrid). Passing, Serra, who loved snuff, would have to have inhaled with pleasure.

On August 20, 1749—a week before he set sail on the past for good—Junípero Serra folded a piece of thin paper the color of hot chocolate, took up a quill, dipped it in ink by a candle in Cádiz, and wrote the letter of his life. It was one he had avoided for four months since leaving Mallorca. It was his good-bye letter to his parents.

Maynard Geiger called it "the magna carta of Serra's apostulate." It is certainly one of the most emotional and personal of the letters that have survived. It is also the only surviving letter of his first thirty-five years—in short, his entire life in Spain.

The physical letter itself has several noteworthy aspects. Though it has four pages, they are not separate but rather the result of folding one sheet of ten-inch-by-twenty-eight-inch paper, making the four leaves five inches by seven inches. Paper was expensive then, and all the space on this sheet is utilized. The last two pages, in fact, are crammed with sideways writing in Serra's sizable left margin; clearly, he had so much to say he did not want to stop. The original of this unique pre-voyage letter rests in the Capuchin Monastery in Barcelona, Spain, perhaps one of the last he ever wrote in Mallorquín Catalán. Most importantly, Serra did not address this letter to his parents, though it was meant for them. He seemed to need to deflect the pain of permanent separation to an interlocutor, a young Franciscan priest with his last name, probably a distant cousin, Francesch Serra.

The letter unfolds in three parts, in three different tones. Here is the first:

66

Jesus, Mary, Joseph!

Dearest friend in Christ Jesus, Father Francesch Serra:

I am writing this letter in farewell, while we are getting ready to leave the city of Cádiz and embark for Mexico. The actual departure day is unknown to me, but the trunks containing our baggage are locked and strapped, and they say that after two, three, or possibly four days, our ship called Villasota, will sail. We had thought it would be sooner, as I wrote; it was to be around St. Bonaventure's day, but it has been put off until now.

Friend of my heart: At this moment, words fail me, trying to express my feelings, as I bid you farewell, nor can I properly ask again the favor of your consoling my parents who, I do not doubt, need it in their suffering. I wish I could share with them the great joy that fills my heart. Surely then they would encourage me to move forward and never turn back. May they be advised that the actual work and practice of an Apostolic Preacher is the greatest calling which they could have wished for me.

Since they are advanced in years, ask them to recall that life is uncertain and, in fact, short. If they compare it with eternity, they will clearly realize that it is only an instant. If this is true, it will be most pleasing to God not to emphasize the little help that I could be to them in this life. Better that they should strive to merit from our Lord, that if we never again see each other in this life, we will be joined forever in eternal glory.

Tell them that I shall always feel the loss of not being able to be near them, to console them as before, but since first things are first, the first thing to do is to fulfill the will of God. It was for the love of God that I was forced to leave them and if I, for the love of God and with the aid of His grace, had the strength of will to do so, may I suggest that they, too, for the love of God, be content despite being deprived of my company.

Tell them to heed the advice of their confessor in this matter. They will realize then in all truth that God has come into their home. In holy patience and resignation, bending to God's holy will, they will save their souls, and in so doing, attain eternal life.

Let them attribute what they now lament to no one but God, our Lord. They will find how sweet is His yoke, and that He will convert their current sorrow into happiness. Now is not the time to muse or worry over the unanswered things of this life, but rather be conformed entirely to the will of God, striving to prepare themselves for a happy death, which is the most important thing in this life. For if we reach that goal, it matters little if we lose all the rest. But if we do not reach it, nothing else will have mattered.

Let my parents rejoice that they have a son who is a priest, though bad and sinful, who daily in the holy sacrifice of the Mass prays for them with all the fervor of his soul and on many days says Mass for them alone, that the Lord may help them; that they may not lack their daily bread; that He may give them patience in their trials, resignation to His holy will, peace and union with everyone, courage to fight the temptations of the evil one, and last of all, when it is God's will, a calm death in His holy grace. If I, by the grace of God, succeed in becoming a good religious, my prayers will become more potent, and they, in turn, will reap the benefit.

As soon as Serra veers into the meat of the subject, he loses language: "Words fail me." He understands his parents need consolation, "who, I do not doubt, need it in their suffering." But this is as close as he comes to admitting what he has done: left them with no word or explanation. The outstanding aspect of this first part of the letter is how purposely distanced it is—through the sieve of the namesake priest, the cousin. He places that famous notion, "to move forward and never turn back" on his parents' shoulders. Three times in one paragraph he repeats, as if kicking himself—and by implication, them—"for the love of God." Admitting "I shall always feel the loss of not being able to be near them," his insistence on "first things first" seems formulaic, as well as the almost churlish "may I suggest that they . . . be content despite being deprived of my company." Still, as Serra progresses he begins to open up, calling himself "a bad and sinful" priest, even admitting that there are "unanswered things of this life." This vulnerability helps him, paradoxically, stumble on a strong, unusual realization. For Serra, a "happy death," which he prays for his parents, is "the most important thing in this life."

The second part of the Cádiz good-bye letter shows Serra gaining the courage to speak directly to his loved ones:

The same I say to my beloved sister in Christ, Juana, and to my brother-in-law, Miquel. Let them not be concerned about me now, but rather let them commend me to God that I may be a good priest and a holy minister of God. In this, we are all very interested and this alone matters. I recall the occasion when my father was so ill that extreme unction was administered to him. I, being a religious, was at home at the time, and thinking that he was going to die, we two being alone, he said to me, "My son, let me embolden you to be a good religious of your Father, St. Francis."

Now, dear father, be assured that those words are as fresh in this very moment as when they came from your lips. Realize, too, that in order to become a good religious, I have set out on this journey. So do not be distressed when I am carrying out your will, which is also the will of God. The same goes for my mother, who has never ceased to commend me to God so that I may be a good religious. Therefore, dear mother, if perhaps God set me in this course as a result of your prayers, be content with what God disposes and facing all obstacles, say: "Blessed be God. May His holy will be done."

And Juana, my sister, knows that not so long ago she was at death's door when the Lord, through merits and intercession of Mary Most Holy, restored her to perfect health. Had she died, she would not be concerned one way or the other whether I was in Mallorca or not. Better she should give thanks to God for whatever He does, because what He does fits. Moreover, it may be quite true that the Lord gave her good health precisely so that she might be able to be the consolation of our good, aged parents now that I have had to depart. Let us give praise to God who loves us all, that He keeps us close to Him.

My brother-in-law Miquel and my sister Juana, I sincerely entreat you as I entreated you before to live together in great peace and harmony; show respect for, to bear with, and to console our old parents; and to take most diligent care in raising your children. I encourage all to be conscientious in attending church, in going to confession and receiving Communion frequently, in making the Stations of the Cross, in short, in striving in every way to be a good Christian. I have every confidence that since you have not forgotten to pray for me for God's help before, you will not fail to do so in the future. Thus while we continue to supplicate God for one another—I for them, and they for me—the same Lord will aid us in this life by giving us His holy grace, and after this life, glory.

Serra enfolds his closest family members in a kind of holy conspiracy to send him abroad (all the while dodging his own immediate caregiver responsibilities). If their faith has brought the family to parting, and that is good, then it follows that they should intensify efforts to model Christ in their lives. Finally, in the last third of the letter, the dam breaks:

Goodbye, my father! Goodbye, my mother! Goodbye, Juana, my dear sister! Goodbye, brother-in-law Miquel! Take good care of little Miquel and see to it that he becomes a good Christian and student, and that the two girls grow up as good Christians and have confidence in God that their uncle may yet do some worthy, helpful thing for them. Goodbye! Goodbye!

Most dear confrere, Father Serra, goodbye. From now on my letters to you, as I have said before, shall be less frequent. Please be faithful in consoling my parents, sister, and brother-in-law. You first, then to Father Vicar, Father Guardian and Father Master, I confide: "All you are my letter." If they feel comfortable and for greater consolation, let Father Vicar and Father Master be present when this letter is read. But not in the presence of anyone other than those four: father, mother, sister, and brother-in-law. If anyone else is to hear it, then let it be my cousin Juana, their neighbor, and give her my most cordial regards. Also our cousin Roig, her husband. My aunt Apolonia, Baronada, Hurxa, and other relatives.

Remember me to everyone of that community of Petra, omitting none, but special regards to Fray Antonio Vives. Remember me to Doctor Fiol, his brother Antonio, his father, and family. Remember me especially to Rafael Moragues Costa and his wife. To Doctor Moragues, his brother, and his wife; also to Doctor Serralta. To Señor Vicari Perelló, Señor Alzamora, Señor Juan Nicolau and to councilman Bartholomé, his brother, and the entire household. In short, to all my friends.

Tell Father Vicar who was hoping that the book of Señor Negro would be returned, that in case it does not come from Madrid before I leave, I shall ask the Fornaris when they return to Mallorca to take it with them. Ask him, too, to spread devotion to my saint, St. Francis Solanus [Solano]. The enclosed letter is for Mado Maxica, who lives near the convent. It is from her son Sebastian, who has come back from the Indies. It appears all is well with him.

Finally, may the Lord bring us together in heaven, and for now, may He guard your Reverence for many more years. This I pray, from this house of the Holy Mission in this city of Cádiz, August 20, 1749.

Father Palou sends Your Reverence repeated regards and kindly give the regards of both of us to Señor Guillermo Roca and the members of his household.

> *Your cordial friend in Christ,*
> *Fray Junípero Serra*
> *most unworthy priest . . . FM*

A close examination of the letter's script shows that Serra seemed to downgrade himself. He first wrote "Unworthy priest" (*indigno*) but changed his mind. The superlative, "Most unworthy" (*indigníssimo*), appears inserted. Perhaps Serra now knew what he had done: cut himself off forever from everyone he loved. He also knew, after all the theological sugarcoating, he had subordinated their needs to his. If he spends much of the letter trying to prove the worthiness of his mission—and to persuade his parents not to be saddened as they had prayed for such a thing—he signs off knowing he has dealt them, and perhaps himself, a mortal blow. It may be signature Serra humility, but it seems more. Clearly, he was listing every person he had ever loved, and many he probably only liked, in his good-byes. It is a cascade of farewells, almost as if number could decrease guilt. He doesn't want to end. His sentences break down. His eloquence deserts him. One imagines him breaking into tears (at the bottom of the last page there are two blurred spots).

Why was Serra so certain he wasn't returning to Spain? Most conquistadors came back. Cortés returned twice, and even had time for a foray against the Moors before he died in Seville. Columbus returned four times, dying in Valladolid. Many religious also came home to Spain; Las Casas returned to advocate ferociously for the Indian, dying in Madrid. On the other hand, Serra's own self-proclaimed "favorite," St. Francis Solano, died in the company of Indians he served in Peru.

Other than Solano (who left at forty), Serra was on the older side for a missionary. His thirty-five years would be closer to fifty today. Serra knew his actuarial odds for returning were poor; his parents, in any case, were in their seventies, his father having already escaped death once—and his sister, too. What was the use in waiting around for everyone and everything to die, with the hunger in his heart still burning?

His decision to leave, born of a careful assessment of the desiccation of life on Mallorca—the university snobbery, the plagues and famines, the endless feeding of the dying Spanish war machine—as well as something irrational that came from the depths of his soul—didn't make it any easier. As Geiger put it plaintively, "he had run away from home," tacking on "for God's sake." But Serra had left many suffering in his wake; his August 20 letter is testimony to that. Now he faced the open Atlantic and lands most Spaniards knew nothing about, and one coast, one he had had his inner eye on, no European had ever settled and only a handful had even seen. For this, he had truly come out of his skin.

About European history prior to the discovery of the Indies, Carlos Fuentes shrewdly observes, "You went westward to Spain and there you stopped."

But Serra wasn't stopping. In truth, Serra was dying to the old life, and he did so willingly. But the whole weight of what he was losing came down on him as he faced the Atlantic: "Going west there was nothing except fear, the unknown, not 'our sea' but the Sea of Mystery, Mare Ignotum." As Christ himself to the desert, he would go into a desert of blue.

He was leaving behind everything dear to him—his family, friends, students, most of his Mallorcan confreres and superiors. All would be dead to him. Where he was going, almost no one but a few companion Mallorcans would know his language. The Atlantic Ocean was, to the Arabs, the Sea of Darkness. And yet, what a challenge! To find out what man is in the rudest circumstances, to form a new community from these basic elements, a community of God. Of course, the circumstances were not so rude; the American Indian had culture, and beliefs, and governance. But from Serra's perspective—that of Christianity—the Indian was something of a spiritual tabula rasa. To a man enflamed with Christ, despairing of his own world, and to some extent, himself, that was intoxicating. Far on the horizon of the West, there was the last strand of innocence. His faith, rising out of the water, as it had when he was young.

CHAPTER FIVE

THE SEA OF DARKNESS

The ship of the soul . . .
with rudder broken, yardarms snapped,
kissing each grain of sand
with every splinter.
—SOR JUANA INÉS DE LA CRUZ

The retreat of the Spanish Armada, 1588.

On August 30, 1749, Junípero Serra left Spain forever. His boat, the *Villasota*, left the port of Cádiz with twenty Franciscans and seven Dominicans in tow, under the captainship of Juan Manuel de Bonilla. The priests stowed their brevaries, Bibles, snuff, and hidden packets of chocolate in their sailors' sleeping cuts below, and shook out their habits. Except for the vision of the Canary Islands one week out of port, they would see nothing but an infinite, dizzying cobalt blue for nearly two months. Land was heaven. More than a few wondered if they would ever reach it, especially when their water began to run out.

"The shortage of water was our greatest trial," Serra later wrote. Within a few weeks, serious rationing began; at its worst the priests and everyone else onboard were restricted (save, presumably, the hard-working captain and his mates) to what amounted to two jiggers (or three ounces) of water a day. Serra called it "so small it came to one glass about the size of those used in the dining room at Petra" and even these were not properly filled, but were "a good finger's breadth short of the top. . . . I was so thirsty that I would not have hesitated to drink from the dirtiest puddle in the road—or anything."

One month out, in the middle of that pitch-dark Atlantic Ocean, the relative calm gave way to a storm. It was the night before and day of St. Michael's Feast (September 29)—Serra's original feast day for his birth name, Miguel. That night, winds lashed the *Villasota*. Serra careened in his berth and got up. He may have clutched a volume of María de Agreda to his chest, staggered up the moaning stairs to the deck, and cried out to the Lord God. Wind flogged the mainsail. Perhaps Serra saw the captain's helm wheeling without him. That would have sparked a wild prayer, drenched the Agreda, and thrown Serra to the gunwales. Palou and the others may have been brought to their knees in the hold, where Serra would have had to have practically swum to fall in.

In the early morning, the sea calmed, they slept the sleep of the dead.

After the storms of the Middle Atlantic and the calming of the seas, Serra took to reading the one book other than the Bible he had brought, the mystic Spanish nun María de Agreda's *The Mystical City of God*. He might have wondered, however, about her contrasting the life of those who take a vow of chastity to those buffeted by the sexual passions: "By this vow the religious live as in a secure port, while other souls navigate and are tossed about in the storms of a dangerous sea." Serra and his fellow Franciscans and Dominicans had been tossed in a literal sea, and chastity hadn't much helped.

Still, after reading about "spacious fields of virtue" and that "on such spacious grounds can a nun recreate and enjoy herself; and only when she fails in this enjoyment, does she begin to feel narrow confinement in this, the greatest freedom," Serra could see over the railing of the *Villasota* a spacious blue field unlike anything he had ever seen. Blue in all directions. Sapped by little food and less water, a head filled with such a vision would become dizzy. Was this heaven? Were they sailing not on earth, but the sky? And by Agreda's analogy, the confinement of their boat (and priesthood) lost in such vastness a key to infinite joy?

María de Agreda went further: "Rise up to the height of the knowledge and love of God, where there are no limits or confines to hold thee, and where thou canst live in unbounded liberty. From that eminence thou wilt see how small, vile, and despicable is all that is created, and how much too narrow it is to hold thy soul." In such a moment, it's doubtful Serra would have found anything in creation "despicable." But his soul? It was as unbounded as the sea.

Perhaps, filled with a gorgeous thought, he stood to share it with his fellows, and found them, not asleep as Christ found his apostles in the Garden of Gethsemane, but huddled, complaining about lack of water, the stale biscuits, the taste of mold.

"Talk less; save saliva," Serra spoke sharply to the grumblers.

It would be fifty days of little talking before the voyagers would see land. Plenty of time for prayers and contemplation, for the healing of their knees scraped on the old wood of the hold while praying in a storm. Serra knew from geography there was more sea than land in the world. Was all that blue the love of God for the earth, the basin of his tears?

On more than one of those fifty borderless sunsets, Serra would have seen a ladder thrown down on the water, its silver rungs reaching toward their little ship, pulling it west. To Serra, such a sight might have meant what St. Bonaventure meant—the restoration of the ladder to God man broke in Eden. Serra had glimpsed that ladder as a boy from the heights of Bon Any and the Tramuntana. Was this how María de Agreda got to the New World and the Indians of New Mexico? Was this the ladder she climbed, without ever moving from Spain? But Junípero Serra was not so blessed. His bag of bones was packed into a ship. This was no bilocation. Mallorca was gone, gone forever.

"I was made to see such wonders, that the greatness of them took away my speech," Agreda had said. When Serra was through reading, he closed the book, and saved saliva.

The contemplations of an evening were answered by one of the sailors, who happened to be a Mallorcan and approached the padres with a little extra water for their breakfast. "Whether he saved some for his own rations, or maybe he stood well with the cook, I do not know," Serra wrote. "Most probably he deprived himself. In any case, he was a godsend to Palou and myself."

This small refreshment from a man far from home reoccurred in the last days of the journey, just when Serra's patience was giving out. He redoubled his efforts to hear confessions and say daily Mass, as he had for the whole two months of the journey, setting a small wooden table out, the hosts and altar wine swaying with the sea.

On October 18, 1749—the Feast of St. Luke—the horizon grew thicker.

"*La tierra!*" the castle-keep yelled out, and soon no one was saving saliva, everyone was pointing and shouting. After almost two months at sea, the *Villasota* entered the inner harbor of the islet of San Juan, Puerto Rico (now Old San Juan, a small island at the mouth of the larger one).

Puerto Rico may have mirrored Mallorca, but San Juan mirrored Cádiz: both port cities were shaped like arrows shot out to sea. Cádiz was aimed at North America, San Juan at Florida and Mexico. And like so many of the conquistadors, the man who discovered Puerto Rico (in 1508), Ponce de León, had fought the Moors in their final expulsion from Granada. With no more Arabs to fight, he had joined Columbus's second voyage in 1493 and found plenty of Taíno Indians to destroy in Hispaniola, when the Caribes weren't eating them. Ultimately, his vanity got the better of him; although historians tend to put more emphasis on his search for gold, Ponce de León led an expedition from Puerto Rico to Florida searching for waters to bathe in that might give his aging body longevity, the proverbial Fountain of Youth. Instead what he got was an arrow in the thigh from the Calusa Indians around Florida's Port Charlotte. It was poisoned from sap of the manchineel tree. He died soon after (1521), his bones interred in the San José Church on the fortress island, which Serra passed entering San Juan Harbor.

The sea of heaven receded.

Though a city of over a half million today, in the eighteenth century, San Juan was a small town of four thousand in about a square mile, hardly larger than Serra's native Petra. It was a little grid clustered at the tip of the arrow of six streets running east–west and seven streets north–south. The houses of the prosperous Spaniards were made of stone topped with tile, some with *azoteas,* flat roofs with gardens. Lush papaya and banana trees lined the streets and ducks, chickens, and dogs wandered freely. According to Geiger, drinking and cooking water was collected from the abundant Caribbean rain by roof cisterns. The homes were earthquake-proof, at least for the time, as they were limited to one story because of the hurricanes and earthquakes the island suffered. Black and Indian slaves, Spaniards, Englishmen, some French, all mixed together to make "what may be considered a new race," a mestizo and mulatto population that greeted the newly arrived Franciscans and Dominicans. As no priests had come to the island in nine years, and none was there in residence, the people were anxious for the ceremonies of their faith, wilted over time in the humidity.

Serra's first clash with authority in the New World, though minor, took shape quickly on hearing of the Puerto Ricans' spiritual hungers. Directed by his superior, Manuel Cardona, to lead the Rosary and sing the *Tota Pulchra* that first night in San Juan from the pulpit at La Concepción, Serra—according to Palou—surprised the crowd (and Cardona), announcing that the visiting friars the very next day would "begin a mission for as long as our ship remains in port." In short, Serra had gone over Cardona's head, leaving "the rest of the missionaries thunderstruck." The friars were exhausted from their months-long journey and had had no preparation for leading such an intensive spiritual exercise for a population they knew nothing about. The crowd left in an animated buzz. Cardona "had not thought of such a thing" and "asked our good Father why he had done it."

Serra responded, "What words of greater consolation could I give these poor Islanders than to announce a mission during our stay?" Palou relates that then Cardona "rejoiced." (Serra himself wrote in a letter two months later that he announced the mission on the second day, not the first, "in accordance with the (Father) President's orders." If this was an early example of covering your backside, even Palou—who normally is almost idolatrous of Serra—did not fall for it.

What is a mission, exactly, in the Catholic Church? It is a dawn-to-dark "retreat" from normal work and day activities for those who participate, and it is usually led by a priest or group of priests, giving motivational sermons, or *feverinos*. For Serra to declare it, with or without orders, was no small thing for people who hadn't seen a priest in nine years. It was an early warning shot of his zeal. Geiger called it plainly "an assault, or spiritual attack upon the people's hearts."

The friars fanned out across the island, announcing the mission as true as any carnival barker, calling out, singing hymns, holding up signs. The crowd that came was three times the size of the chapel at La Concepción, and so all were led in a procession of "simply great commotion" (Serra's words) to the cathedral.

Cardona and Serra gave the finale sermons on alternating nights, all twenty priests hearing confessions virtually nonstop, starting at three in the morning, lasting all afternoon and going through till midnight. Palou thought the entire town confessed. That would have meant two hundred confessions per priest. As it seems the mission went on nearly the entire two weeks they were in San Juan, that meant about twenty confessions a day per confessor. No doubt penances lightened considerably toward midnight.

Though it appeared that the mission was a great success, Serra did not spare himself. His oratory, a source of his fame in Mallorca to his own troublesome pride, was not up to that of Father Cardona: "There was such a contrast between our preaching, as much difference as between straw and gold, snow and fire, night and day. Every evening that Father President preached, the audience was so shaken with tears, lamentations and beatings of the breast . . . the church resounded with their shouts and cries. Still weeping, they made their way back to their homes." But after Serra concluded his sermons, "not a sigh was heard although I preached on the most terrifying subjects and used my voice to its fullest extent."

He confessed to his cousin back home that perhaps he lacked "interior fire," being "unable to find the right words to move the hearts of my audience."

Was this Serra's signature humility in a bow to his superior, Father Cardona? Or was it rather worry that a gift had deserted him? Clearly, what had served him so well on his native island of Mallorca was not doing so in his first test in the New World, in Puerto Rico. It's possible his Mallorcan accent and dialect may not have helped. But of course Serra was not referring to clarity of diction; he was pointing out fire in the belly, and in that the older man had more and hotter.

What had worked so well back home with university students and Mallorcan villagers who knew him as a child would have to be abandoned. He was dealing with a whole different people, whose needs were different, whose ears were different, and indeed, when he got to the Indians of Mexico and California, whose tongues were completely different. Eloquence would have to be abandoned at the door. He would have to find another way.

In the evenings after the missions, San Juan went dark. There was no olive oil for lamps, the staple of light in Spain. At most, a stray candle illuminated a mother's face, a father's forearm, the cradle of a child. It was not the first time Serra would feel out of the world as he had known it.

Shorn of eloquence, if nothing else "during his first hours on American soil he was demonstrating his selfless industry." Serra had grown up a farmer's son, working the soil with his father. He was a very hard worker. And, when he needed to be, he was inventive. For his initiative in San Juan, he and all the priests were showered with gifts in thanks for the mission, among them: "chocolate, pipe tobacco, snuff and lemonade," luxuries for monastic priests. It eased the fact that the captain of the *Villasota* had gone back on his promise to provision the friars in Puerto Rico. Stepping on shore with nothing, they held a mission, and ended up with a cornucopia.

Soon this good-pay-for-good-work idyll ended. On October 31, 1749, the *Villasota* left Puerto Rico for Mexico. Almost immediately, the boat snagged on boulders in the harbor's shallow water (two fathoms or less, Serra wrote—about ten feet) and looked to be grounded for good. The captain shot off cannon, and nearly everyone with a boat raced out to rescue the ship, the religious first. Food came for the shaken passengers; beds were set up in the patio of La Concepción. The priests returned the favor, saying the Rosary, hearing yet more confessions (was the captain among them, confessing the harbor tides and currents had grounded him?).

By midnight it was November 1, All Saints Day, but also the Day of the Dead across the water in Mexico, a syncretic mixture of Aztec and Catholic rites honoring those gone to the afterlife. Serra makes no note of it, but it is likely that he and his fellow friars heard *Santería* practices peculiar to Puerto Rico on this feast day, a musical combination of West African (Yoruba), Caribbean Indian, and Catholic bowings to dead relatives. Orisha spirits disguised as Catholic saints; people sleeping on their loved ones' graves; drums; women wearing a flower on their dresses pinned to the exact spot on the body that signified the relative lost. Serra would have marveled at all these, and perhaps been troubled by them. (If nearby Haiti's drums and flutes on the Day of the Dead, which featured a skeleton figure with top hat, smoking a cigar, a glass of rum in his grip, crept into San Juan that night, Serra surely would have gone to bed stunned.)

After morning Mass on All Saints Day, when their boat was towed off the rocks and into deeper water, the fathers reembarked for a voyage "disproportionately long, like the first,"—a full month (and about two thousand miles) to Veracruz, on the Gulf of Mexico. They had been well stocked by San Juan with food and water; however, satiation must equate with wordlessness. Neither Serra nor Palou left any comment on that meandering last leg of their three-month journey from Spain, now through reefs, shoals, and islands of the Caribbean.

But there was plenty to say when on December 2 they spotted the mainland of North America for the first time, and almost died.

As if punished for daring to think their journey finished, the *Villasota* was abruptly hit by a hard northern storm, which drove the ship away from Veracruz in heavy rain toward the Yucatán Peninsula. The storm flayed the ship for two days and nights. Seawater flooded on deck. The bilge pumps failed, the boat's hold began to spring leaks, and, according to Serra, badly battered, "the mainmast continued in use only by a miracle." In the storm, to Palou, "we gave ourselves up for lost and thought there was nothing else to do but to prepare for death."

But Serra somehow had the presence of mind to pull the twenty Franciscans bound for Mexico City and the seven Dominicans bound for Oaxaca together to beg for a miracle. He wrote:

Quid resolvendum? Ought we not to make some promise to call down on us the Lord's mercy? We decided that each should write on a piece of paper the name of his favorite saint, without telling anyone else. After putting the names in a bowl and invoking the Holy Spirit, we recited the prayer of All Saints to know by drawing lots who would be our special patron.

There were Serra and the twenty-six other priests scrambling in water up to their ankles, if not their shins, ripping swatches of paper not completely wet, grabbing and dipping pens in ink, all the while swaying in the rain and the erupted sea like drenched penguins. Palou's praise for Serra's calm in such a scene is not a typical exaggeration.

Serra himself chose St. Francis Solano, the apostle of Peru he loved. Palou chose St. Michael the Archangel, Serra's own patron saint. The only other selected saint whom we know of is that of Father Juan Ferrer of Valencia—St. Barbara. It was her feast day—December 4. Whether Ferrer knew it or not, it was a smart choice; almost 150 years before, Sebastián Vizcaíno had singled St. Barbara out for help with a storm off the coast of California—just before her feast day—and it had worked.

Sure enough, St. Barbara's name was the name pulled from the bowl on the *Villasota* and everyone cried out, "Long live St. Barbara!" The effect: "the storm ceased immediately." For Serra and Vizcaíno, a calming lightning struck twice, if not in the same place exactly, in the same circumstance—approaching the New World—with the same woman on or just before her feast day. Whether she was real or not didn't matter. The sea was calmed, a southerly wind blew, and soon the *Villasota* cast anchor in Veracruz, its mainsail destroyed, holes in the hull large enough to ride a horse through. The friars were convinced they had witnessed a miracle.

The only one of all the twenty-seven priests aboard by his own assertion never to have gotten seasick the entire three months, Serra later wrote, "I hardly knew I was at sea. And that is a fact."

On December 6, 1749, Serra landed at Villa Rica de la Vera Cruz (the Rich Town of the True Cross), as Cortés had named his first encampment of tents on the beach 230 years before, the first step in the founding of New Spain (and the destruction of most of the natives of central Mexico). The next day, December 7, one day before the Feast of the Immaculate Conception—still not at that time sanctioned as a holy day that required attendance at Mass, but a cause he fervently supported—Junípero Serra said his own first Mass on the North American continent.

By Palou's own account, Serra gave an astounding sermon, running back with meticulous detail through the ninety-nine days of their voyage; it was "of such perfection and eloquence that he produced wonderment in them all [his fellow friars]." Unfortunately, if the sermon was written down, it has been lost.

As he knelt at his cot that night in the Franciscan monastery, with that signature foursquare colonnade surrounding a garden with a fountain at the center, Serra would have had to have felt strangely at home. A look out the small window in the adobe walls would have shown, at sundown, the smoke of olive oil lamps rising, threading through the last light. And perhaps in that smoke, Serra felt a shudder of ghosts.

Almost from the moment of his landing and naming Veracruz over two centuries before, Hernán Cortés lived, moved, and conquered by one falsehood after another. His whole mission to the land of the Mexica (or Aztecs) appears a renegade one; according to Bartolomé de Las Casas, the great priest-critic of the early Spanish conquest, Cortés had been told specifically not to set out by his superior on Cuba, Diego Velázquez, who later ordered Cortés arrested in Trinidad. Setting up his tents on the Mexican shore, he craftily sent a letter to King Carlos V in Spain, utilizing an obscure law that would allow a group of Spaniards to found a municipality anywhere that need only report directly to the king (thus bypassing Velázquez). It worked, and Veracruz was born. Cortés was greeted by the Aztec messenger Teudile, who, in an odd gesture of respect, wetted his lips, touched the ground, put dirt into his mouth and swallowed it; he then presented Cortés with gifts, not only gold objects to be worn, featherware, and jewels, but also "straws dipped in his own blood." Las Casas thought the exchanges Cortés made—a chair, some beads, and a purple cap—were received for what they were: "shit."

When he heard about the landing, the great Mexica leader Montezuma was stunned. He sacrificed two captives, drank their blood, and threw blood on the messengers. "He has appeared! He has come back!" he cried out, knowing that the return of the Aztec god Quetzalcoatl (with whom he identified Cortés) he could not violently oppose, meaning the overthrow of his rule and indeed, his world, was at hand. Referring to the Spaniards' use of helmets and horses, Teudile described them as having "iron on their heads" and "when they mounted their deer, they were roof-high." By year's end, Tenochtitlán, the island capital of the Mexica, would lie in ruins, and forty thousand Mexica would be killed, including Montezuma. Cortés blamed the massacre on his native "auxiliaries" run wild. Soon the landmass of what today is Mexico was in Spanish hands.

Did Serra pray for a better way before snuffing his olive oil lamp that first night in Veracruz? The oil from thousands of olives in the wake of forty thousand lost, plundered souls, went out.

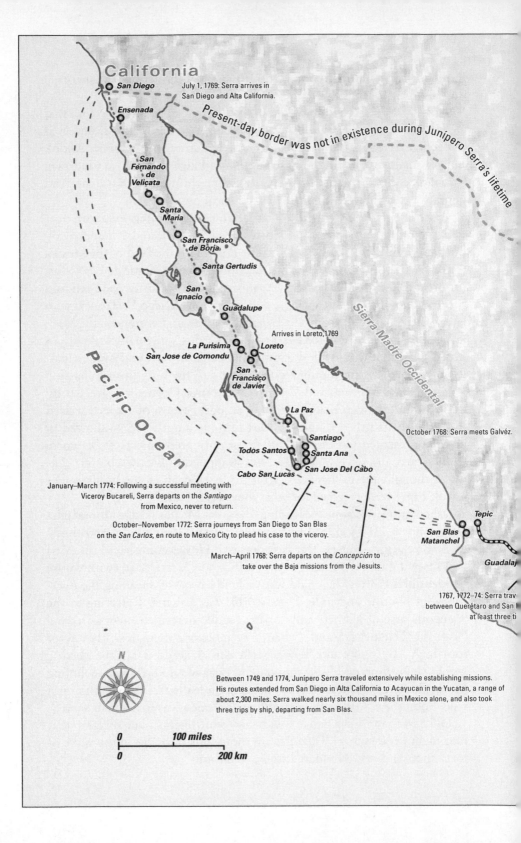

California

San Diego — July 1, 1769: Serra arrives in San Diego and Alta California.

Ensenada

Present-day border was not in existence during Junípero Serra's lifetime

San Fernando de Velicata

Santa Maria

San Francisco de Borja

Santa Gertudis

San Ignacio

Guadalupe

La Purisima
San Jose de Comondu

Loreto — Arrives in Loreto, 1769

San Francisco de Javier

Sierra Madre Occidental

Pacific Ocean

La Paz

Santiago

Todos Santos

Santa Ana

Cabo San Lucas

San Jose Del Cabo

October 1768: Serra meets Galvéz.

January–March 1774: Following a successful meeting with Viceroy Bucareli, Serra departs on the *Santiago* from Mexico, never to return.

October–November 1772: Serra journeys from San Diego to San Blas on the *San Carlos*, en route to Mexico City to plead his case to the viceroy.

March–April 1768: Serra departs on the *Concepción* to take over the Baja missions from the Jesuits.

Tepic

San Blas
Matanchel

Guadalaj

1767, 1772–74: Serra trav between Querétaro and San at least three ti

N

Between 1749 and 1774, Junípero Serra traveled extensively while establishing missions. His routes extended from San Diego in Alta California to Acayucan in the Yucatan, a range of about 2,300 miles. Serra walked nearly six thousand miles in Mexico alone, and also took three trips by ship, departing from San Blas.

0   100 miles
0   200 km

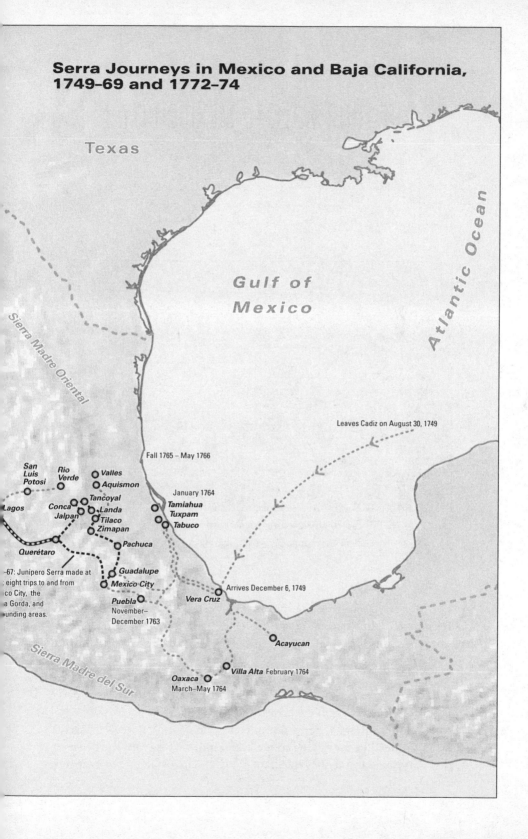

Serra Journeys in Mexico and Baja California, 1749–69 and 1772–74

Texas

Gulf of Mexico

Atlantic Ocean

Sierra Madre Oriental

Sierra Madre del Sur

Leaves Cadiz on August 30, 1749

Fall 1765 – May 1766

San Luis Potosi

Rio Verde

Valles

Aquismon

January 1764

Tamiahua
Tuxpam
Tabuco

Lagos

Conca
Jalpan

Tancoyal
Landa
Tilaco
Zimapan

Querétaro

Pachuca

–67: Junípero Serra made at
eight trips to and from
co City, the
a Gorda, and
unding areas.

Guadalupe

Mexico City

Puebla
November–
December 1763

Vera Cruz

Arrives December 6, 1749

Acayucan

Villa Alta February 1764

Oaxaca
March–May 1764

CHAPTER SIX

THE LONG WALK TO MEXICO CITY

Joy for the living is sorrow for the dead.
—OCTAVIO PAZ

The famed Mexico City Zócalo, or Plaza Mayor,
where Serra met Viceroy Bucareli in 1773.

Shortly after landing in the mosquito-infested swamps of Veracruz, Francisco Palou became deathly ill, and though neither Serra nor Palou named the illness in their writings, given what we know about Veracruz it was probably malaria or yellow fever. The low-lying area around Veracruz had one of the richest varieties of wildlife in the Western Hemisphere, and was especially infested with insects. Palou was probably literally bitten by the New World bug.

If he was discouraged, Serra doesn't say, but within a week of arriving he announced he was going to walk 250 miles west from the coast to Mexico City, the capital of New Spain. This journey started the exaggerated legend of Serra walking everywhere he went in the Americas. The path was strewn with jaguars, coatis, and ocelots (all now endangered), as well as rivers loaded with alligators. A day before he began his walk to the capital, Serra wrote to a friar who remained in Mallorca that they'd meet again "if not in this world, at any rate in heaven." Then he was off, leaving Palou behind to recuperate.

The walking legend derives, at least in part, from Franciscan rules, written by St. Francis in 1223 and underwritten by Pope Honorius III, which required friars to avoid horseback riding—often a sign of wealth, social status, if not knavery—with only two exceptions: "manifest necessity or infirmity." Serra set off on December 15 wearing sandals and accompanied only by a nameless priest from Andalusia. They began their long walk with copies of the Bible, breviaries, and their trust in God, what Palou referred to as "the best passport." (Serra probably had María de Agreda's work in his bag, too.) They were going to spend their first Christmas in the New World either in small Indian and mestizo towns or in the wild.

After a long first day out under call of parrots and crows, the two reached a river, probably the Antigua, right outside old Veracruz. The river swelled unexpectedly (the rainy season in Mexico ends in October) and they were afraid they weren't going to reach the other bank before dark, as they were urged to do. While praying the *Benedicta*, they saw a shadow moving across the river.

"Hail, Holy Mary!" Serra called out, as if the object of their prayer, the Blessed Mother herself, was lighting down. "Is that a Christian?"

"Yes! What do you want?"

"*Dónde está el vado?*" the two travelers cried.

"*Vienes!*" the voice yelled back. He called out to them to walk a ways along the bank till he told them to stop. It was a distance before they spotted rocks in moonlight.

"*Allá!*" the voice cried, acknowledging the ford.

Soon a "well-dressed Spaniard, very attentive" (according to Palou) was ushering the two tired walkers, their gray robes wet and clinging to their knees, to his farmhouse, another healthy walk under the moon. They were excited to meet such a man from the Old World. He cooked for them a good dinner and gave them beds for the night. The next morning they awoke to cold noses and, walking to say Mass in the small town close by, they stepped around icy ruts. Palou makes it clear Serra told him "they must surely have perished" in subfreezing weather without the stranger. Why was the man out so late at night by the river? Serra had asked before they left.

"Business," the Spaniard replied.

And although the travelers demurred so as "not to further show their curiosity," if the man had had a clandestine liaison that night with some mestiza in an outbuilding, it wouldn't have been the first time a sinner saved a good man.

This second day, they set out on the dirt path leading 4,681 feet up to Jalapa in the Sierra Madre, where there was a pass through the mountains. The steepening path became exhausting under a sun that turned the ice of the night before to puddles. But before nightfall, they encountered a second guardian stranger—this time a man astride a horse.

"Your Reverences must be tired and thirsty." The rider bent with two fruits in his hand. "Here, take these pomegranates. They will refresh you."

Pomegranate trees, with their small pointed leaves, typically fruit in September; three months later, these pomegranates may not have been the freshest. But Serra and his companion clutched them with gratitude, plunging their fingernails into the hard reddish rind. The magenta jewels squirted juice over their gray habits and they laughed. Serra wondered later—and mentioned it many times in the pulpit—if those two anonymous benefactors his first arduous days in North America were one and the same man, inspired by St. Joseph or even St. Joseph himself. They bedded down for the night in care of yet another generous man—a farmer.

For the third day of their long walk, the farmer gave them a loaf of bread, but in true Franciscan fashion, when they encountered a beggar on the road, they gave their loaf to him. Soon, they became dizzy from the heat and hunger, and collapsed against a tree. Once more, just when they needed it, a rider galloped by, saw them, came back, broke a loaf of his own bread in two and gave each friar half. At first "they dared not eat it because . . . it seemed to be made only of Indian corn, raw and not well-kneaded." But soon the power of famishment won over, and on tasting the bread they discovered it was delicious, having an "unusually savory quality as if mixed with cheese." These four intercessions of food and lodging helped deliver Serra and his companion to Mexico City in one piece, serving to him evidence of God's ever tender and watchful eye.

But the devil would have his say before they finally slept.

Somewhere on their journey—perhaps in the desert between the volcanoes of Orizaba and Malinche (named after Cortés's Indian mistress)—Serra was bitten on the foot by what appears to have been a spider. His foot itched and swelled badly. At a farmhouse where Serra and his companion spent the night Serra could not stop scratching the bite. In the morning, his foot was streaked with dried blood; he decided for the only day of his journey to rest.

If Serra were bitten in the desert, it was probably by a six-eyed sand spider, or it could have been the brown recluse spider (also known as the violin spider, or fiddler, for its elongated legs and quick balling-up movements when surprised) at one of the farmhouses between Veracruz and Jalapa. This particular spider has venom that, though not life-threatening, can cause wounds that take months or even years to heal. Serra's necrotizing ulcer evidently became infected and stayed infected from the dirt or bacteria of the road, destroying the soft tissue on his foot and running up his calf.

The two made their way in increasingly cold weather and winter light. Except for those first three nights, records do not show that they found any more farmhouses on the other eleven days of the walk. It is likely that they spent nights out in the weather curled up under leaves—if they could find any.

They would have had to pass by the magnificent, snow-dipped neck of the giant Orizaba volcano, visible all the way from Veracruz to Mexico City. Orizaba stands like a rock-solid urn of ice in the hot plain. Serra regarded its white peak through palm fronds—a unity of opposites that must have recalled his childhood visions of snow and palm staring at the high wall of the Tramuntana on Mallorca. Orizaba is 18,491 feet above sea level, the highest mountain in Mexico, and nothing in the contiguous United States is higher.

With a painful, festering foot to blame, Serra trod in slow awe through Mexico's Valley of Volcanoes, famous not just for the lava but for the hot blood spilled on this path—Mexica, Tlaxcalan, and Spanish. The Olmecs, even earlier than the Aztecs, had regularly journeyed to the top of Orizaba, which they believed had been created by an Eagle God, to beg his mercy not to erupt. Their anti-lava rituals went on for days. Olmec descendants, the Aztecs, sacrificed youths and ate their hearts, not just to help lift the sun, but to keep the lid on the Valley of Volcanoes. It was a dangerous place, de facto—on the ground and in the psyche.

At Jalapa, Serra would have encountered descendants of the tribe that kept Cortés and his men from being swallowed alive by the Aztecs. The Totonacs had served as guides, interpreters, and porters for the invading army.

Serra may have spent Christmas across the desert from the mountain chain that held the Malinche volcano, in Xocotla, a village where Bernal Díaz del Castillo estimated he saw 100,000 skulls. This was the land of the Tlaxcalans, the last Nahuatl-speaking Indian tribe not to be subdued by Montezuma. Though they, too, were avid cannibals, the Tlaxcalans hated the Aztecs for the high taxes they demanded—often in the form of youths for blood sacrifice (evidently if they were going to kill the young, they preferred doing it themselves). These were the people Cortés allied with to storm Tenochtitlán, the Aztec capital; they added six thousand to his puny army of five hundred. Truly it was an alliance with the devil, and Cortés soon knew it. He also knew that without the Tlaxcalans he would have been finished, his heart devoured and his head stuck on a pike.

The next possible site for Serra's first New World Christmas was the town of Tlaxcala, close to the Malinche volcano (14,636 feet), but at a lower altitude (7,336 feet). If Serra stopped to welcome the Prince of Peace in Tlaxcala, he would have done so over the bones of the natives who, with vastly superior forces, couldn't break the five-hundred-man Spanish rectangle of Cortés with its muskets and cannons. Spain lost only forty-five men there, as well as a horse whose head was slashed off its body by the broadsword of a Tlaxcalan warrior, who had never seen one before.

The defeat of Tlaxcala and the union of their forces with his was the turning point of Cortés's conquest of Mexico. "Order and politeness everywhere in the streets," wrote Cortés. "The people as intelligent as Moslems."

But the small mestizo population in a mountain town Serra would have encountered was not enveloped in the stench of blood or incense. They exhaled plain cold breath, selling chickens, lamb's wool vests, and parrots, probably happy to direct him to the local church. He may have cried out at Mass, *Pacem in terra!* Good will to men!" and the Tlaxcalan descendants resounded, "Amen!" their ears pierced with knitted cotton earrings that hung alongside their cheeks.

The last possible first Mexican Christmas site for Serra would have been Cholula. If this were the spot, he would have knelt in front of a Mexican manger at the Church of Nuestra Señora de los Remedios. Built on top of the old Aztec temple, it would have been the bloodiest of the three spots. Cholula was part of Montezuma's confederacy; it was not, like Tlaxcala, peripheral. In October 1519, when Cortés attacked without provocation, being fearful perhaps of Cholulan ambush or Tlaxcalans' treachery, he let his auxiliaries loose. It only took five hours for them to kill three thousand Cholulans and ethnic-cleanse the rest of the city. It was Cortés's first major massacre, aided by the fact that Cholula was, in Aztec mythology, the home of Quetzalcoatl. The Cholulans gave little resistance to their miserable demise.

"*Misere nobis*," Serra may have called out, begging for mercy 230 years after the deed.

• • •

Ultimately, Serra and his priest friend may have had to share Christmas out in the open, between towns, hearing wolf calls and nuzzling close in the cold. In any case, the two of them walked into Mexico City the last night of the year, December 31, 1749, limping with joy up the steps of the heart of Mexican Catholicism—the Shrine of Our Lady of Guadalupe, built four years before Serra was born (1709).

"Why do you fret?" the apparition told the Indian Juan Diego that starry night on the hill of Tepeyac in 1531. "Am I not your mother?"

Serra must have felt the watermark of his own mother's kiss, so far off, imprinted on his tired chest. On New Year's Eve Serra celebrated not with brandy, dancing, or sex, but in prayer, kneeling to the Blessed Mother ablaze, her two-centuries-old image with tumbling roses still imprinted on Juan Diego's peasant tunic.

The next morning, he lit the candles of the altar, and with permission from the shrine's pastor, said Mass, with more thanks given to the small, amazed crowd gathered at dawn.

After Mass, Serra looked out on the sad, sprawling city of one hundred thousand, the laboring twin of what would become Los Angeles. On the skyline behind Mexico City were the snow-capped volcanoes Popocatepetl ("El Popo") and Iztaccihuatl, their craters rimmed with gold. Then the two companions were off on foot the last stretch to the Franciscan College of San Fernando—thirteen miles on the other side of town. On the approach to the Zocalo, one of the largest town squares in the world, they discovered that Mexico City was a city of broken roads dipped over landfill of the once proud lake surrounding the capital of the Aztecs. They walked along the main thoroughfare of the capital city— Calle de Tacuba-Hidalgo—once a main causeway over the lake down which Cortés fled from Tenochtitlán during what was called the Battle of the Sad Night (*La Noche Triste*): June 30, 1519, one day after Montezuma's death at the hand of his own people by stoning. The Aztecs had finally seen through Cortés; after turning on Montezuma, the brunt of their wrath came down on the pretender-god Spaniard, as the Mexica chased him down the very road Serra now walked (then called Tlacopan). Half of Cortés's 1,600 men (inflated by auxiliaries) were killed fleeing to Tlaxcala. In a year, they would return to destroy Aztec civilization forever.

Along an old Mexica aqueduct, under the red stone *tezontle* buildings, past the Quemadero where the Jews and witches, homosexuals, and others had been trapped by the Spanish Inquisition, past the spot of the worst Spanish losses on *La Noche Triste* and the temple at San Hipólito, converted in Serra's time to an insane asylum close by the College of San Fernando, Serra and his companion finally arrived. Palou and his fellow Mallorcans ran out to greet him. (Sick, Palou had left on horseback and beaten his teacher to the spot.)

The missionary colleges were the brainchild of Father Antonio Llinas, an old man in retirement when Serra had met him in Mallorca. Diego de Alcántara, San Fernando's first president, spotted the diminutive, limping, but smiling Junípero Serra, and exclaimed, as had St. Francis to his own protégé: "Would that we had a whole forest of junipers such as this one!"

"Our Seraphic Patriarch [St. Francis] did not ask for this sort," Serra said after bowing his head and embracing his superior, "but for others much different."

Father Diego may have laughed, leading Serra to his quarters. Assigned to the man in charge of initiates, the thirty-seven-year-old priest felt it was just what he needed. In many ways, Serra was starting all over, beginning his life's true work, which was to minister not to those who agreed with him about God, but to those who couldn't disagree more.

But Serra went further and actually asked to live with the novitiates, something that was against Franciscan rules. He was quickly rebuked. "Your reverence will live in the cell assigned to you just like all the rest, and you will be permitted to attend only the special exercises of the novitiates," said Father Bernardo Pumeda.

Serra took the snub without comment. It wasn't much of a loss, anyway, as there was only one novitiate, Estevan Herrera, and he was ordained as a priest in two months, leaving the novitiate at the time of Serra's life at San Fernando empty. Still, Geiger seems dumbfounded at Serra's forgetfulness, or willingness to overleap custom: "It is rather surprising that Serra did not recall [the rules]. His humility was admirable but his zeal had to be tempered within reasonable limits of the law." It would not be the last time Serra's zeal needed tempering.

On April 2, Serra was pleased to welcome to San Fernando the second group of friars from Spain, which included his old student Juan Crespí and other fellow Mallorcans Rafael Verger and Guillermo Vicens, who grew up with Serra in Petra. One of this group, José Santiestevan, was fated to be martyred by the Comanches in Texas. Combined with Serra's first wave of Franciscans from Spain, this was to be a historic, seminal group in many ways, ultimately including three mission field presidents (Serra, Palou, and Juan Ramos de Lora).

Except for five priests who left within six months of Serra's arrival for moral, constitutional, health, or other reasons, the friars had signed up for a ten-year hitch, at the expense of the king of Spain. Those who stayed at the college were obliged to spend half the year giving on-the-spot missions in towns across Mexico. Others used the college as home base for longer missionary assignments. For Serra, life at San Fernando for six months before his assignment was a blissful experience. The place reminded him of tiny Petra's sandstone narrow streets, and the small-town cloister fostered close friendships. He liked that this particular group of friars included the intrepid, those who would go out on a limb to explore a new world.

For a few months, Serra reveled in the habits of San Fernando. He rose at midnight to sing Matins and Lauds for two hours, and went back to sleep to wake up at dawn. Four more prayerful chants would follow in the day—Prime, Terce, Sext, and Nones. Singing for an aggregate four hours daily, the ritual was designed to make the throat sore, the heart raw, and the soul as open as a manor's gate. It was to bring God's love closer to home; if the Aztecs felt the gods had to be satiated with blood, Serra felt God had to be pummeled with song.

Breakfast was a noisy one where tortillas and *huevos rancheros* were likely served on feast days, and a roll and hot chocolate on all others. Morning classes covered Indian customs and languages, mystical theology, Christian pedagogy in missions, new songs. After lunch and a siesta, a class on moral theology followed vespers. At 5:30 P.M., there was Compline, a litany, another hour of meditation, and prayer before the Blessed Sacrament in a monstrance, a silver-plated gold vessel spiked as if a sunburst around the consecrated host in a small round window, all of which the priest could not touch with his bare hands but had to enfold in a humeral veil over his shoulders. Dinner was served at seven—perhaps some shredded pork on a good evening, some chiles, potatoes, and jicama root—after which the *Tota Pulchra* rang its praise for Mary's "complete beauty" from satisfied, tired, quietly belching souls. Saturdays the friars fasted and sang *Salve Regina*. All turned in at eight, and the bell rang for silence. Some probably read; the fathers were in training for the hard life of the frontier—spiritual and physical—and if they couldn't make it, they were gone. The toughness was symbolized by their gray habits—woven by combining rough black and off-white wool, no dye of any kind.

One day in spring 1751, the guardian of San Fernando, the leader of the Franciscan community, Father Ortés de Velasco, told the friars he had a problem with the missions in the Sierra Gorda, a rugged mountain chain about 150 miles north of Mexico City. Franciscans had taken over these missions in 1744 from the Dominicans and Augustinians in the wake of a scorched-earth campaign by General José Escandón against the Jonace and Pame Indians. Trying to win back the trust of the Pames was a difficult task, especially since there wasn't much to win back from the nearly wiped-out tribe. Four missionaries had recently died in the Sierra Gorda, if not violently, probably from exhaustion and broken hearts. The whole project was in danger of collapsing.

"*Ecce ego,*" Serra spoke up first, in Latin. "*Mitte me!*" It was an echo of Isaiah (6:8), "Here I am! Send me!"

Eight others, including Palou, joined Serra in their entreaties, to Velasco's delight. Official papers were drawn with the government and the Church.

On May 30, in an effort to "try out his learning," Velasco gave Serra the assignment of providing the sermon for a public Mass held on one of the most important feast days, the Feast of San Fernando, the Spanish king and saint. The governing text for the sermon Serra chose came from Psalm 44: "My heart overflows with a goodly theme; as I sing my ode to the king, my tongue is nimble." Serra spoke not of the Spanish king, really, or even the saint, but of what constitutes a kingly life, even for the lowest man hauling sticks on a mule. As in Palma for the Lull commemoration, the crowd was ecstatic, and many begged for it to be printed. This would be Serra's first landmark sermon in the New World.

Several clerics in Mexico City as well as back in Mallorca thought Serra was wasting his talents with the illiterate Pames. But Ortés de Velasco knew that Serra hadn't come to the New World for honors: "A university professor with the spirit of a child might be just the leader [the Indians] needed."

Whether Serra, a shrewd operator on the frontier, was childlike is a matter to ponder. When he spoke as Isaiah, "Here I am. Send me!," Velasco and perhaps even Serra himself forgot the rest of the quote. For God replies to Isaiah: "Go and say this to the people: Listen carefully, but you shall not understand! Look intently, but you shall know nothing" (6:9–10).

This parable would prove to be true of the Spanish military, the settlers, the Pames, and just about every Indian tribe Serra would confront and minister to in the New World. They were going to have to lose, lose a lot, before they gained, if they gained, from this new blistering word of God.

CHAPTER SEVEN

NEW WORLD OTHERS

"They are going out there to dance," she said.
He put away his arrow-making things.
—ISHI (YAHI), "THE STORY OF LIZARD"

Ohlone natives in reed canoes, San Francisco Bay.

By 1750, Serra was one of the last in the long line of explorers and missionaries making the exceedingly complex, tragic, and occasionally inspiring contact with the American Indian. Only the Great Plains and Far West Indians had yet to succumb to the colonial regimes, but when the United States was born in 1776, pushing ever westward toward lands conquered by Spain, the die was cast for the proud Cheyenne, Sioux, Comanche, and other tribes of the open central plains of the continent. For the United States, it has never been a proud story, rather one that haunts to this day; for the Indians, it was a cross larger than a Christian's.

And therein lay the challenge for someone like Serra, passionately convinced that Christ offered a better day to any soul of this earth.

It is difficult to absorb, let alone to neatly summarize, two hundred years of the missionary colonization of an entire continent meted out primarily by three seafaring nations with imperial goals—England, France, and Spain. Understanding the evangelization effort over an area at least three thousand miles wide and six thousand miles long (from Panama to the Arctic), containing hundreds of tribes speaking different languages and governed by different faith systems, would be a hopeless task considering even the most unified powers, which these three nations were not. Though all were Christian, the imperial nations were far from homogeneous. In Europe they were still at war, with the New World providing a remote refuge from internecine Christian upheavals of the Inquisition, Protestant Reformation, and the Counter-Reformation, if not the bullion to fuel such conflict.

In this context, Serra was a latecomer who would have to learn from the mistakes of the past missionaries—Franciscans, Jesuits, and Dominicans—who had tried to commingle the Old World with the New. By the time he arrived in central Mexico to work with the Pame Indians, the challenge of alchemizing peace out of all the bloodshed was a daunting one. The relationship with the military on several fronts complicated matters even further. With the evangelical mission in cinders and the Indian population decimated by epidemics and pillaging, Serra had his work cut out for him. He was aided in this effort by a salubrious distinction: "Hispanics made room for the Indian in their society."

It could be said that to the natives of North America, the English were indifferent, if not cruel; the French enamored; and the Spanish enslaving, saving, and joining. The original arrival of the British at Jamestown in 1607 is fringed romantically by *la belle sauvage* Pocohantas pleading for Captain John Smith's life to her father, the chief Powhatan. That was successful, as was her subsequent marriage to the widower John Rolfe, whose tobacco plantations, thanks to some lucrative lessons Indians gave him, soon spanned south and west to what became North Carolina.

There was no Thanksgiving in Jamestown. Powhatan was a powerful, no-nonsense monarch who had banded together thirty tribes in the Powhatan Confederacy (the thirty-first, resisting, was exterminated). The notion of monogamy that the first meek ministers in Virginia croaked had no effect on him; at any one time, Powhatan had a dozen wives and ended up with one hundred in the aggregate. Captain John Smith claims to have witnessed cannibalism, including something he termed "powdered wife." (We are cautioned by anthropologists and recent historians, notably Jake Page, that cannibalism is a sensitive topic to Native Americans primarily because it was used as an epistemological cudgel by invading Europeans when evidence of it beyond the Aztecs is scant.)

It didn't take Powhatan long to figure out what was what with the British. Powhatan's complaint in 1610—"What will avail you to take that perforce [which] you may quietly have with love or to destroy them that provide you with food?"—represents an early existential indictment of the entire Anglo-American experience in the New World.

In 1622, in response to their encroachment, 347 British colonists were killed in a Powhatan Confederacy attack. One of the few Virginian efforts to reach out to the Indians—a plan to build an Indian college—was smothered in the British counterattack. The "last stand" of the Powhatans took place in 1644. Five years later, most of the fourteen thousand Piedmont Indians in Virginia were dead of disease or violence, and the office of the Powhatan Confederacy chief became empty. When the College of William and Mary was established in part for Indians in 1692—the first school of higher education in what became the United States—the few Indians left in Virginia were unlikely to care, and even if they did, would have had trouble getting in. As for Pocahontas, she had long since died in her early twenties, in Kent, England.

We are taught that the "first" Thanksgiving with the Pilgrims and the Wampanoag Indians in the Northeast took place in 1621 at Plymouth, Massachusetts, a year after the Pilgrims landed on that sandy shore that extends into Cape Cod. In fact, for a full century before Plymouth and the founding of the Massachusetts Bay colony, English, Basque, and French whalers and fishermen had plied the waters off Newfoundland, Halifax, and New Brunswick, as well as the mouth of the St. Lawrence River. It's estimated as many as twenty thousand such friendly encounters took place between European and Indian fishermen up to a half century before Plymouth Rock. These initial, historically anonymous touch points between the two civilizations had already opened the door to microbes that would kill the Indians en masse. Some have estimated that 90 percent of the coastal Northeast tribes were done in before the first Thanksgiving flared a coal.

Several other factors, however, would add to a quickly volatile mix between the English and the Indians in the cold Northeast. Upstate New York tribes below Lake Ontario and Lake Erie had long been bickering and warring with each other. The creation of the Iroquois Confederacy (probably early in the century before the arrival of the Pilgrims, and perhaps catalyzed by the appearance of these odd, white fisherman out of the Atlantic) did not halt the fighting so much as redirect it. Unfortunately, mourning became the "Mourning Wars" when the Iroquois Confederacy clashed with the Huron Confederacy, made up of tribes to the north and west. Another element of great disruption was the outbreak of smallpox in 1633, which in a decade cut the population of the Five Nations in half. The spiritual coldness and suspicions of the already isolated Puritans provided a less than promising foundation from which they could reach out to the quickly disassembling Iroquois, "the people of the longhouse." No doubt the longhouse itself, with its families scrunched together on either side of a line of cooking fires, unbroken by screens or walls, spread the dreaded disease no shaman or white man could stop.

Historians have also blamed the quick expulsion, if not disappearance, of the New England Indians on Britain's take-no-prisoners, scorched-earth policies in other realms of its dominion, particularly in Ireland and Scotland. The few attempts of the Puritans to redistribute land to the Massachusetts and Wampanoags would run aground on two essentially different concepts of land and home: "The idea of someone's claiming irrevocable title to the land, distinct from tribal possession, was as absurd as trying to own air or sunlight."

By 1664, when the Dutch sold Manahatta Island to the British, two-thirds of Iroquois villages were composed of refugees, the total native population of the Northeast down to ten thousand amid a British colonial population five times that.

The isolated attempts at Indian conversion by Puritans and other Protestants in New England were hampered by the reluctance of their own condition and fatalistic attitudes of predestination: "Having left Old England because of an unwillingness to compromise on matters of belief and conduct, [the Puritans] were not about to tolerate deviant customs in a setting they controlled. . . . As a persecuted minority fleeing from episcopal interference, they were more interested in establishing security for their own 'tribe' than in extending its benefits to others." And unlike the Spaniards, for whom missionaries long preceded parishes, for the Puritans the parish, once consolidated, cut missionary activity off. (In fairness, though the first English were not coming for souls, as did the Spaniards, they also were not coming for gold.)

Still, a few British attempts to appeal to the refugee Iroquois's notion of a "Great Spirit" (*Manitou*, or godly power, master of breath) were made. Unlike the Powhatans to the south, the Massachusetts and other New England tribes did not foster incest and were not polygamous (though they appeared serially monogamous).

Dubbed "apostle to the Indians," the Puritan minister John Eliot gave a first sermon to natives at Dorchester in 1646. They listened politely to a dissertation on the Old Testament until their sachem Cutchamekin asked if Eliot could explain how exactly thunder, the winds, and the tides worked. That stole Eliot's thunder until some months later, when he had a little more success with a tribe near Newton, though not much, with stories of Christ's sufferings, heaven, and hell. Eliot translated both a Catechism and the Bible itself into Algonkian by 1663. He also wrote the first book banned in America, at least by the British—*The Christian Commonwealth*—which envisioned a British theocracy that would embrace the Indians. Needless to say, this was hardly the cup of tea the newly crowned King Charles II of England was eager to sip.

Puritans and their English supporters were anxious that the Indians "were really learning and internalizing God's truths, not simply memorizing and parroting catch phrases in the manner of the hated Papists." Yet imitation was exactly what the Puritans were about: "For the godly, the upholding of models meant that life was to be derivative [of the Bible], not innovative . . . little value was placed on the act of discovery." Historian Richard Pointer is incisive: "What Puritans asked of natives was not what they asked of themselves, but instead its precise opposite . . . that irony seems to have escaped most colonists . . . In the long run, such distrust of the native neighbors killed the Puritan missionary enterprise . . . for two generations as New Englanders preferred annihilating Indians over evangelizing them."

The doctrine of original sin was to be one of the most difficult for Christian missionaries to inculcate. To Indians, existence was not "fallen." It was just there, to be enjoyed or not, to be despoiled or enhanced with harmonious actions and prayers. There was, of course, sin, or transgression, in the eyes of the Massachusetts and Wampanoag tribes, but its punishment did not await in the hereafter. It was meted out immediately.

Two of the earliest questions John Cotton elicited from the Massachusetts on Martha's Vineyard in the 1660s and 1670s were barely hidden inquiries into arrogance: "If we are so ignorant of God, were Englishmen ever that way, too? And if we all have the same Father, why do we have dissimilar faiths?" Two very tough questions, in the face of which one minister simply threw up his hands "because it was too difficult." Still, by 1674, fourteen of Eliot's "praying Indian" towns scattered across Massachusetts managed to carry on. The 1675 Indian rebellion called King Philip's War, however, destroyed what small progress Eliot had made. The killing of 6 percent of the white population enflamed the Puritans, already a "worrisome people," with racial rage, and before long, loyal Indians were herded into concentration camps. By 1698, only ten Indians of a shrunken Natick community of 180 were going to church (by 1855, only one Indian was left to count).

A few undaunted souls pushed into western Massachusetts, such as Yale University graduate John Sergeant, who baptized 129 Housatonics at Stockbridge and taught them to read and sign in English. His charismatic work was cut short by an early death in 1749. In contrast, the melancholic minister John Brainerd, expelled from Yale, tried his luck farther south, in New Jersey, with a decidedly negative attitude toward the Delawares: "Not one in a thousand of them has the spirit of a man." In the end, however, Brainerd found his "heart was knit to them," despite his self-absorption and depression.

The French and Indian War of 1754—four years after Junípero Serra's entry into the Sierra Gorda of Mexico—settled matters in New England and contestation of the British and French in America for good. The Iroquois sided with the British, the Huron with the French, and the British won. After this carnage takes the life of the heroic character and Iroquois leader Uncas's life—depicted famously in James Fenimore Cooper's *The Last of the Mohicans*—Cooper gives his Indian father, Chingachgook, the last say: "I am a blazed pine, in a clearing of the pale faces."

A codicil to the unhappy spiritual outreach to the Indians of New England is encapsulated in the wandering vocation of the only known native clergyman, a Mohegan named Samson Occom, who ministered to the Oneida. When his mentor, Eleazar Wheelock, turned bitter and closed Occom's school, Moor's Charity (Wheelock called Indians "children" who were inclined to the "lazy, sordid life" before he founded Dartmouth College for whites only), Occom took to the road in Connecticut, where he was given to "bouts of self-pity and alcohol." He held up for a time in Montauk at the east end of Long Island, where he served as a kind of Christian shaman for Indian refugees, giving up his tortured bi-religious ghost in Brothertown, near New York City, in 1784.

The Quakers did somewhat better in Pennsylvania with the Delaware; William Penn was one of the few colonists (or Americans) who actually honored a treaty with Indians. Meanwhile, in 1746, as the seeds of the New World began to sprout in Serra's soul, the colonial government of New Jersey bought all the land of the Delawares for a thousand pounds, hemming the natives in a reservation in the Pine Barrens.

Perhaps the only truly successful evangelists of New England and the Middle Atlantic weren't British, but rather the pacifist German Moravians, who constructed a blacksmith shop in Shamokin, Pennsylvania, for refugee Onondagas. Pastor David Zeisberger, who had had to flee New York during the French and Indian War, joined his flock of Delawares in prison in Philadelphia for sixteen months. Released in 1765, Zeisberger built a brand-new community on the Susquehanna River called Frieden-

shutten, which featured twenty-nine log houses, fruit orchards, vegetable gardens, and butter churns. Together with a nearby settlement at
Gnadenhutten, it survived in relative serenity—exactly the period of Serra's industrious years in the Sierra Gorda—until tragedy struck. In 1782,
ninety Christian Indians, including twenty-seven women and thirty-four
children, were "clubbed, scalped and burned" by suspicious American
settlers, along with some soldiers from Fort Pitt. The Battle of Fallen
Timbers (1794) and Tecumseh's hapless pan-Indian alliance with the British against the rapacious Americans in the War of 1812 essentially ended
Indian life in the American East.

The Americans certainly would outdo even their forebears for brutality. But of the three chief colonial powers in North America, according
to historian Charles Bowden, "it was the English who seemed most arrogant . . . and least concerned to preserve any aspect of native civilization."

The French present a different picture, for the most part. Perhaps it
is no surprise that the least successful of the major powers of Europe in
North America was the most successful in its relations with the Indians.
Their record of intermarriage was second to none in the early decades
(producing the unique Creole and Cajun cultures in Louisiana), though
the Spaniards certainly outpaced them over time. Citizenship, which the
British hardly entertained and the Spanish came to later, was offered as an
incentive by the French fairly early in the contact period.

In 1608, nearly a full century after a tough Jacques Cartier named
the St. Lawrence River, which ran through Quebec and bordered New
York, and a year after the English came to Jamestown, a most unusual
man arrived from France. Samuel Champlain, shrewd as well as compassionate, "stressed the importance of converting the Indians to Christianity, celebrated their intelligence, and validated the Indians as human
beings." Champlain came to his extraordinary humanism not just from
reading and even knowing leaders of the French Enlightenment, but from
childhood experiences with diversity and war. From an early age, as his
biographer David Hackett Fischer recounts, Champlain lived in borderlands and got used to difference and negotiating conflict. The city of his
youth, Saintonge, is located at the crook of France's west coast between
English-influenced Brittany to the north and Spanish-influenced Gas-
cony (with its Basques and Béarnais) to the south. As a young French
soldier, Champlain "witnessed atrocities beyond description" in a land of
near-constant religious strife for half a century, including nine civil wars.
Like Serra, wracked on his Mallorca by plague and wars that snatched
up his students before his own eyes, Champlain sought a way out of
the eternal cycle of violence: "This war weary soldier dreamed of a new

world where people lived at peace with others unlike themselves." Serra, like Champlain, was a man prepared for otherness, an otherness that was in his very blood.

At the time of Champlain, the first French missionaries arrived in New France, reform Franciscans led by Joseph Le Caron in 1615, the Recollets. They ministered to Montagnais and throughout Quebec to the Hurons, but they were turned away, largely out of a refusal to live in Indian villages, isolating themselves. (Dejected, the Franciscans left Canada to be replaced in 1625 by the Jesuit Jean de Brébeuf, who gained respect by learning the Huron language. But Brébeuf met his end in 1649 by horrible torture at the hands of the Hurons' enemies, the Iroquois, who marveled at his refusal to cry out. Brébeuf was canonized in 1930.)

The Jesuits penetrated southward. The Black Robes were led by Jacques Marquette and the trader and trapper Louis Jolliet—who lost all his maps in an overturned canoe—down the upper Mississippi in 1673. The Jesuits gained immeasurable credibility from Indian tribes for traveling with no firearms, and often in very small parties, even alone.

In the wake of Marquette and Jolliet, the French Jesuits ministered to the *pays en haut* (upcountry Midwest), especially the twenty thousand refugees from the intertribal, English-French warfare in the East who gathered up in Green Bay, Wisconsin, crowding the native Menominee and Winnebago. The Jesuits gained ground with tribes shell-shocked by seemingly endless warfare by participating in three standard Indian conflict resolution practices: gift giving, the blessing of tribal (and white-Indian) intermarriage and adoption, and the smoking of the calumet, or peace pipe.

But the Huron were the French's not-so-secret sharers. As great canoeing traders themselves surrounded by the Great Lakes, the Huron were perhaps the perfect match for the river-hiking Jesuits who were plying trade, not war. Christian motifs won favor with the Huron, with whom they shared some cosmology. A supreme, world-engaged "God above" ensconced in the sky (or heaven), angels (or Oki, as the Huron named spirits), songs to Jesus ("Jesus Ahatonia"), prayers for rain, and the very physicality of the Catholic seven sacraments (something the Puritans abhorred) mirroring rites of passage (shamanic rattles and smoke in teenage puberty rites or for the dying were not unlike confirmation or Extreme Unction) made the French and Huron closer. The doctrine of Christian reconciliation found a remarkable (to the Jesuits) counterpart in the Huron practice of requiring the bestowing of thirty gifts to the family of a murdered man by the offender's family (murder of a woman gained forty gifts, either a comment on Huron feminist tendencies, or a terrible goad, depending on how you looked at it). One historian thought Huron life "sensible and confident with few sources of traumatic anxiety."

Still, the Huron were no saints. Prisoners of war were either adopted or executed; they weren't returned. Torture was common for male prisoners, who could run gauntlets between rows of stick- and club-wielding Indians for up to a week.

As always, the least common ground was over sin and salvation, and "universal guilt." Bowden interpreted the Huron's understanding of the Crucifixion: "Christ's atoning death seemed to them inappropriate as it was unnecessary." A lack of abstract nouns in the Algonkian language made inculcation of such Christian notions as expiation, resurrection, transubstantiation, and the like nearly impossible. (They are mysterious enough in French or English.) But the Jesuits were canny. Red was a holy color to the Huron, so the Jesuits painted their crosses red. They won women over by making them *dogiques*, catechists. Knowing the importance of dream interpretation (Jean de Brébeuf thought dreams "the principal God of the Hurons"), a nightmare, the Jesuits humbly pointed out, might be what was in store for us all in hell. Jesuits, however, were not beyond the Machiavellian: they handed out special trading privileges to those who became Christians. By 1648, one in five Hurons was a Christian.

The rigorous education, love of learning, and discipline in the Jesuit spiritual toolbox did not hurt the French *pères*. They had learned through hard experience facing the Protestant Reformation that head-on theological assaults accomplish little and that accommodation often wins out over reactionary attack. In Latin America, one of the most successful of all missionary activities in the New World was the seventeenth- and eighteenth-century Jesuit *reducciones*, thirty Indian missions where Paraguay, Brazil, and Argentina come together (dramatically rendered in the 1986 film *The Mission*).

The French Jesuits were successful in the very lap of English missionary failures. The Abenaki of Maine wore crosses around their necks and even hung wampum belts on Catholic statues. Father Sebastian Rasles spent thirty years with the Abenaki; he confided in a letter to his brother the necessity "to conform to their manners and customs that I might gain their confidence." He also confessed, "As for what concerns me personally, I assure you that I see, that I hear, that I speak only as a savage." The British saw Rasles as an incitement, and in 1724 razed the Abenaki village of Norridgewock, killing the priest and mutilating his body.

The final (and with Montreal, most lasting) French experiment in North America was New Orleans, founded by Pierre Le Moyne d'Iberville in 1699 (after La Salle was killed on the Mississippi by French muti-neers). First, Indians were enslaved to work wheat fields; when most escaped, they were replaced by African slaves. With few French women settlers, intermarriage with blacks and Indians proliferated, producing the beautiful mélange that was Cajun and Creole (and their mouth-watering cuisines). For a time, the French allied militarily with the Choctaws versus the British-backed Chickasaws from the Carolinas, but France never gave Louisiana much priority and soon abandoned the whole effort to the new United States, which ran out what was left of the Indians in the Southeast on the infamous Trail of Tears. What was left in New Orleans? Forty ways of preparing corn, bouillabaisses of lobster, rice, and okra; as one historian reminds us, New Orleans, like any frontier, "was rarely a one-way street; typically, it was an arena of creativity and social innovation on the ground, much of it violent and tragic, but some of it relatively benign."

The Spanish arrived sooner than the British or French, stayed longer and in a much larger area (two continents), and the notion of an Indian's soul was very much alive not only in Spanish ecclesiastical and political cir-cles, but in sexual relations. Miscegenation was less a debate than a fact of life. So persistent despite the original slaughter was Indian life in Mexico, so various were its ways of melding, so voracious its desire for transcen-dence, it's a good question who saved whom in Mexico. For all the inev-itable rebellions, Indian spirituality, abetted by the humble Juan Diego's vision of the Blessed Mother near Mexico City shortly after Cortés's conquest, created an Indian embrace of Christ with fervor equal to the passionate embrace that created the mestizo. To put it crudely, despite the arrogance and atrocity, Indian and Spaniard turned each other on. At least they did in Mexico. Author Richard Rodriguez, whose books acutely examine race, the West, and their complexities, is most perceptive about this: "Race is not such a terrible word for me. . . . [It] encourages me to remember the influence of eroticism on history." That the attrac-tion of Indian and Spaniard was as much a spiritual phenomenon as phys-ical may have been due to the enormous importance and pervasiveness of the life of faith in Spain and Mesoamerica. Whatever their genius, Voltaire and Shakespeare were not Cervantes or Sor Juana.

Intermarriage and concubinage created a new nation neither Indian nor Spaniard, but Mexican. One wonders, as Octavio Paz intimated, if Mexico itself is a creation of two vast solitudes—that of Spain, cut off from the rest of Europe, and that of the Mexica, whose capital, Tenoch-titlán, was surrounded by water—an island on the land (something the California historian Carey McWilliams would call the West Coast many centuries later). In fact, Paz sees the Mexican as inexorably caught in a third solitude, inside the dominant Anglo world of North America: "The history of Mexico is the history of a man seeking his parentage, his origins. . . . He wants to go back beyond the catastrophe he suffered; he wants to be a sun again. . . . Our solitude has the same roots as religious feelings. It is a form of orphanhood, an obscure awareness that we have been torn from the All. . . . Nothing could be further from this feeling than the solitude of the North American. . . . North Americans consider the world to be something that can be perfected, and . . . we consider it something that can be redeemed."

Another key to the uniqueness of their North American colonial settlement is that Spain was the first European country to abolish slavery (in 1542), a direct result of the protests of Bartolomé de Las Casas over the massacres in Cuba and Hispaniola. It is true (and unfortunate) that this applied primarily to Indians, and not blacks. Spain abolished the African slave trade about the same time as Great Britain, 1818, and though the United States abolished slave trading earlier, in 1808, the nation as a whole did not follow New York's lead in abolishing slavery itself (done in 1828) until the conclusion of the Civil War in 1865, several decades after black slaves were free in Spain and Mexico. The early Spanish conscience concerning Indian slavery certainly affected the work of friars like Junípero Serra.

Serra was well aware of his Spanish missionary predecessors to the New World, both Franciscans and Jesuits. Though the former's founding preceded the latter's by three hundred years, their founders had some things in common. Both Giovanni di Bernardone (St. Francis) and Inigo López de Loyola (St. Ignatius) were born into wealth, lived somewhat dissolute lives in their youth, and—most galvanizing—were crippled by war after throwing themselves impetuously into soldiering. Francesco (Bernardone giving way to a name his father chose) followed a roundabout road to faith, but the defining moment was his capture under arms and meditative days as a prisoner of war. Loyola had a leg shattered during a military assault, and the other sufficiently wounded that he was laid up in bed for months. He read the lives of the saints and something began to move inside him.

Francis emerged from prison a changed man. He took on his father (after stealing his cotton to sell for money to rebuild a broken-down church), he took on his town (literally giving the shirt off his back, and a few other items, to a beggar), and soon he was taking on the world. His radical rejection of material possessions was unlike anything the Church had seen; some saw it as more Christ-like than the original apostles themselves. The Franciscans formed a sort of on-the-move hermitage. Francis told his followers that they should possess just about nothing other than one tunic—no shoes, no walking sticks, no money. At first, any book but the Bible was jettisoned, as Francis "regarded knowledge as a form of possession and property and the educated (*doutos*) as an especially formidable section of the powerful." The Franciscans were sort of itinerant laborers; they earned their food by the sweat of their brow and hands. Francis was the ultimate "less is more" philosopher, and he wore his love of God lightly and yet profoundly.

Ignatius Loyola was a more worldly man, and he had no problem with books; in that sense Serra, a scholar and professor of theology, was something of a Jesuit Franciscan. The Society of Jesus was founded on principles Ignatius spun into the *Spiritual Exercises* begun in his convalescence from the war wound. Ignatius paid close attention to how he thought and felt—early phenomenology; such self-consciousness was abhorrent to Francis. Dealing with doubt, what impulses came from God and what from the devil, determining what "signs" (as well as actions) led to the good and right life was the central motif in meditations Ignatius called "discernment of the spirits." Part and parcel of this "discernment" process was the shedding of naïveté, the welcoming of complexity, the intense love of learning, and seeing a problem from various vantages that came to be a hallmark of Jesuit education. Discipline—of the will and mind—shaped the Jesuit love of learning.

According to the perceptive anthropologist Maria Wade, "Ignatius's practice of reading signs, ascertaining their godly origin and value, and foreseeing a future sanctioned by God's will may have differed from Native American shamanic practices in its procedures but not in its goals or results." A treasured story about Ignatius is his insistence that his friars not wander after dinner into the garden or other places, but listen to his latest thoughts on obedience. It sounds a little egotistical, to say the least, but one day while Ignatius read from his notes, the roof collapsed in the garden. Ignatius smiled, indicating those who had obeyed despite themselves had just saved their lives. This disposition fit Native American readings of nature.

Papal approval for the Franciscans (1223) and Jesuits (1539) did not always translate into papal favor. In fact, Franciscan emphasis on poverty and a nonmaterialist lifestyle some took as "an overt indictment of the church." People also saw the Franciscan emphasis on love bending too close to Catharism, the philosophy of the troubadors of southern France. In the wake of Francis's death, fissures among the Franciscans led to many Gray Robes being tried by the Inquisition. Likewise, at one point, Ignatius himself was tried and sentenced by the Inquisition. The list of good, even great, men and women who came under its shadow is not a short one. Tyranny devours its own.

Nevertheless, Spanish Franciscans and Spanish Jesuits led the charge for Christ in the realms of New Spain. They were very different orders who tapped different kinds of people to bring to bear different pedagogies and conversion strategies. The Franciscan emphasis on "gathering no moss" in their spiritual quests, their poverty of spirit and body, and their love of the road appealed especially to hunter-gatherer tribes of Indians; Francis's near animistic love of animals and nature, too, appealed to the native occupants of the land who endowed nature with supernatural powers. The Jesuits' virtuoso experience with innovative teaching methods and relentlessly expansive theology also, in the right hands, brought spiritual bounty and a breakthrough to Indians imbued with natural and understandable skepticism, if not outrage.

Pointer has given us original insights about the vehicle of music: "Multiple generations of later Spanish Catholic missionaries were inspired by New Spain's first friars and took music with them as a tool of evangelism around the world." In turn, during a remarkable—though short—post-Conquest period, the spiritual street opened in two directions. There was a "'Nahuaization' of Christianity." Indeed, in 1570, there were an estimated one thousand Indian church choirs singing the entire Mass. Native instruments such as Nahua trumpets, *vihuelas de areo* (a guitar with a bow), and drums and rattles were often taken into the services, and Christian holy days were adorned with pre-conquest butterfly imagery and quetzal flowers. The *Psalmodia Christiana* (1583) of Bernardino de Sahagún incorporated such elements in ninety-one songs known as *Cantares mexicanos*, after Aztec "ghost songs" praising fallen ancestors. So valued were Indian religious singers in the early days that they were paid better than Indian laborers. Something utterly amazing occurred in all this: "The missionary who is missionized." Unfortunately, this exceptional linking of two cosmologies fell prey to the homogenization of Catholic practices at the Council of Trent (1545–63), the inspection of the Holy Tribunal, and a general flattening of what was liturgically acceptable. Two centuries later, Serra would resuscitate some of this intercultural wonder in the Sierra Gorda and Alta California.

After this florescence in central Mexico, one of the first encounters northward in Florida was Spain's least successful effort. Ponce de León, an original member of Columbus's first colony on Hispaniola, made most of the Indian population old before their time. Though he was run off on his first landing in 1513 at Fort Myers on the Gulf Coast by Florida's Calusa tribe, de León kept at it and was soon enslaving every Indian he could find and handing them over to settlers. Predictably, the Timucuas went from fifty thousand at contact to ten thousand, an 80 percent attrition in only forty years.

Spanish Jesuits tried their hand with surviving Calusa Indians around Charlotte Harbor from 1567 to 1568. Felipe, the Calusa chief, was quite an operator and for a time reversed the evangelical direction, teaching Father Juan Rogel the Calusa view of the "three souls" in a man. For his part, Rogel exacted concessions from Felipe in many areas (idols, shamanic practices, sodomy, killing children at burials, even long hair and black paint on faces), except one: polygamy. On that, the priest conceded and let Felipe have his several wives, declaring, "I see no impediment of the faith of our Lord Jesus Christ in the entire heathendom."

Having exhausted the Calusa, the Spaniards pressed westward in Florida to the northern Gulf Coast, near Tallahassee, where the Apalachees were violently put down, though some converted, perhaps out of desperation. Three Apalachees were found buried with rosaries in their hands.

In the wake of these events, subsequent Jesuit conversion attempts in Florida, from 1697 to 1698, and later in 1743, were doomed. Many of the remnant natives were lost to alcohol and demanded rum, which the Spanish priests flatly refused to give. The Calusa chided them for hypocrisy; why were they drinking wine at Mass? They refused Catholic last rites and burial blessings, preferring their own. As Maria Wade put it baldly, "The Calusa neither mellowed nor melted." At the end of the seventeenth century, the Franciscans thought they might challenge the Jesuit way right in their midst with the Calusa, but their more confrontational methods bore even less fruit than Rogel's Socratic dialogues. The Franciscans did smartly withhold display of gold sacra, such as chalices and ciboriums, not just to appear less arrogant but to avoid tempting thieves. But when Spanish clerics referred to Calusa temples as synagogues or the natives as Mohammedans or heretics, the Calusa threw the terms back in the priests' faces, calling one of their temples "the house of Mahoma." No doubt "use of such terms underscores the extent to which stereotypes of the Inquisition had permeated." Faced with Franciscan failure to read what their refusal of the Jesuits meant, the Calusas literally pissed on the Gray Robes, rubbing feces into the priests' faces, stripping them naked, and leaving them destitute in the Florida Keys, where they were picked up by a Spanish ship.

Spain moved outward in the Southeast, a trail of blood and chimera. Hernando de Soto, who made a fortune sacking the Incas in Peru as Pizarro's deputy, landed in Tampa Bay ten years after Pedro Menendez (who founded St. Augustine in 1565) with seven hundred men, including blacksmiths to forge, among other things, chains for the ankles of Indians. De Soto literally threw Indian chiefs "to the dogs" searching for his "New Andalusia," perhaps as far north as Cape Hatteras. In 1541, in a vicious battle near Mobile, Alabama, the Tuscaloosa nearly overran the Spaniards. De Soto died the next year, thrown into the Mississippi by his own troops, who feared angry Indians would mangle his corpse.

By 1763, the Spanish abandoned Florida entirely, taking eighty-nine Apalachees from St. Augustine as indentured servants to Cuba. The Timucans, Guales, and the rest of the Apalachees were left with no prayers, only smallpox. One historian spoke of the great "silence" that enveloped the Southeast, one that called up comparisons to the Black Death that killed off half of Europe's people. A silence, one has to believe, broken by moans and whimpers of the dying in the Land of Flowers.

Consider the devastation. This pox swelled with fluid, then pus. When lesions burst, whole parts of subcutaneous skin fell off. At least 30 percent of smallpox victims died within two weeks of the appearance of the lesions. There was no cure.

Whole worlds fell apart. Fields went untended, animals and children unfed. Mass graves were common. Historian Barbara Tuchman highlighted how smallpox could affect the mind-set of a people: "The sense of a vanishing future created a kind of dementia and despair." Creeks and Seminoles filtered into the empty spaces of the Southeast. They, too, would soon be driven off the land or greatly diminished.

New Spain had a somewhat more lasting—though mixed—experience on its northern periphery in what we call today the American Southwest. The success of friars—and steadfastness of the Pueblo Indians—combined to make modern New Mexico and Arizona the most lasting example of Indian culture in the United States. But the beginnings were not auspicious. The first explorers there were fired by tales of the Seven Cities of Cibola or Quivira, places teeming with silver and gold, largely the invention of one gifted storyteller, the North African slave known as Estebán the Moor (or Estevanico). He was probably the first Muslim and Arab in America. Cabeza de Vaca, who had been shipwrecked with Estebán the Moor, later wrote a notable memoir of life among the Indians, perhaps the earliest such testimony we have by a white man: the *Account*, in which he joined forces with the Dominican friar Las Casas in warning about Spanish depredations on Indian life, "All these people, in order to be attracted to becoming Christians and subjects of your Imperial Majesty, need to be treated well."

In 1539, Coronado followed on the path of Fray Marcos de Niza up the border between Arizona and New Mexico, silverstruck. What he found was a lot of saguaro cacti and sand. And the Zuni, who promptly drew a line with cornmeal in that sand at Hawikeh and told Coronado to go no farther. In one hour, he slaughtered them. Returning to Mexico, he was indicted, but never convicted.

One does not need much imagination to realize these geographic thrusts by essentially delusional men did not make for easy living. The unsavory Juan de Oñate, the spoiled son of a rich mining family in Mexico, brought seven Franciscan friars and two lay brothers into the El Paso area and explored the "la Jornada del Muerto" or "badlands" north of it. But after a run-in with the Acoma on a four-hundred-foot mesa in which twelve of his men were killed, including his nephew, Oñate took a harsh revenge. Over eight hundred Acoma Indians fell to the Spaniards in 1598; every Acoma man over twenty-five had a foot cut off before going into slavery. No surprise that four hundred years later, a statue of Oñate in Española, New Mexico, had its bronze foot sliced off during a statewide commemoration of the Franciscan arrival.

In such a hot, arid place, and in the wake of the unscrupulous, the friars themselves had to be especially resilient and dedicated. One such was Eusebio Kino, an Italian Jesuit who came in with the Spanish to preach to the Pimas in Arizona in the late 1680s. Smartly, Kino did not inveigh against native witchcraft, nor did he isolate shamans or even rebuke drunkenness. He threw himself into some native rituals and storytelling, all the while discussing what Christ said and did, and he loved to compare theological notes with the Pima *caciques*. In short, as one historian put it, "[Kino] was, in the Jesuit manner, a good manager."

Nevertheless, by 1670, the number of Pueblo Indian towns was halved and the population down to a mere seventeen thousand, almost a 90 percent drop. In addition to smallpox, the natives of the Southwest fought anthrax, perhaps brought in by Spanish sheep.

In 1680, the Pueblo Revolt was unleashed, the most successful uprising by natives in the entire history of the United States. Among the Navajo resentments had been simmering for some time. Some Franciscans, evil-obsessed and harsher than Kino, pushed hard to close down native ceremonies, breaking and burning dancing masks. They called kivas "mosques." The natives noted that teaching Christ's benevolence was not bringing better harvests, peace, or health. After the torture in prison of forty-seven Pueblo medicine men by the Spanish governor in 1675, one seething Tewa shaman named Popé, when released, went on to organize the uprising.

The Pueblo Revolt spread over a wide area of New Mexico, from Albuquerque all the way north to Taos. About 380 Spaniards—15 percent of the settler population—were killed; churches were set aflame; altars and crosses were smeared with feces. At least one priest, Juan Pío, was murdered. Surviving settlers flooded into Santa Fe's plaza; under siege for two weeks, residents, loyalist Isleta Indians, and a thousand Spanish soldiers were allowed to pass out of town to El Paso. These refugees ended up founding nearby Juárez.

It's no exaggeration to say that Spain's increasingly desperate empire was built on the backs of the New World Indian. New Spain's exports of silver constituted at least half its shipments to the mother country for two hundred years; in the peak year of 1595, 95 percent of Mexican exports to Spain was silver bullion: "American silver came to play a crucial role not only in Hapsburg foreign policy but also in early modern European development." In short, Spain's wars, in no small part due to its superior fleet and its ambitious trade with Asia, were a vortex fed by Indian-mined silver. In 1658, in the area just south of Texas, Jumano and Babine Indians appealed to the padres for a mission pueblo near Saltillo where they could escape the abusive *encomenderos* (colonists given land and Indian laborers). Moved by their desperation, the Franciscan Juan Larios, who lived in close habit to St. Francis himself, with no permanent abode and begging for food, offered love and care to the Indians.

In 1712, Lieutenant Manuel Mendoza reported to civil and ecclesiastic authorities several troubling things: natives were killed in the "cast nets" of the mine and farm owners; natives were buried right under the hooves of horses and cows in their corrals; marauding soldiers were paid in Indian slaves; some mothers, terrified of being rounded up to go into labor camps, committed infanticide. Two years later, the Franciscan Vicente Santa María told the Crown that the creation of pueblos (*congregas*) was nothing but a farce, a collection point for Indian slavery, and that the land sold to the *encomenderos* was valued not by its fertility but by the number of Indians packaged with it. The Christian aspect to all this was virtually invisible.

In answer to mounting complaints from the colonies led, in fact, by the Church, the Spanish king himself decried "those pernicious abuses" and insisted that if landowners wanted Indian labor "for no motive whatsoever can they avail themselves of them . . . except that it be voluntary in them, and they pay them their wages." In 1715, King Philip V issued new provisions to the Laws of the Indies that were in some cases sweeping reforms, often micromanaged in the finest detail. Tlaxcalans were eligible for a 227-square-foot house; other Indians got a 151-square-foot house (such favors did not endear the Tlaxcalans to other tribes). Work in field or mine was to be paid two reales daily, with food; or three reales without food (women as domestics were paid, as they always have been, less—one real a day). A kind of ombudsman position, *protector de indios*, who had to be an Indian himself, was created. Indians were given the right to sue; land and water rights in Indian pueblos could not be sold.

For the first time, Spanish law tried to rein in disciplinary whippings, a most disturbing aspect of Spanish-Indian relations. No whippings were allowed except for "grave crimes." Ethnic cleansing of Indians would incur ten years in prison and (if the offender were lower-class) two hundred lashes, as well. If, however, an Indian labored outside the pueblo, corporal punishment was allowed.

Texas has always been a story unto itself, as any Texan will tell you, at least since the Battle of the Alamo (Mission San Antonio de Valero's nickname), the place of the legendary 1836 massacre of white settlers and frontiersmen. Shortly afterward, however, Texas, never securely held by Spain, wrested itself independent from Mexico at the Battle of San Jacinto. Prior to that, Texas was just the northern sector of Coahuila Province, whose capital was not Austin but rather Saltillo, south of the Río Grande.

Serious colonization did not happen until Spain realized the French were pushing west from Louisiana. Missions around the Red River Valley dividing present-day Texas from Oklahoma failed. One mission, San Miguel de Linares de los Adaes, fared reasonably well, as it had the luck of construction just over the Sabine River into Louisiana, a kind of no-man's-land between Spanish, French, and Hasinai. Some descendants of the Adai community persist today. Though for a time the San Antonio missions prospered, by 1788 only 290 natives were left at the five missions, not enough to run them.

Most Texas missions had built high walls from the late 1720s on to protect them from the great warrior tribes, the Comanches and Apaches, who showed their displeasure at the arrival of the Marqués de Aguayo with soldiers (his immediate target was the French) by wielding arrow shafts with flapping red rags and thrusting them into the earth.

As Serra entered the Sierra Gorda in central Mexico in 1750, he may have had in his mind's eye such threatening arrows.

CHAPTER EIGHT

THE FAT MOUNTAINS

Is it wind and dust? I think someone is coming.
—INYO-KUTAVERE, MOJAVE INDIAN

Letter written by Serra during his Sierra Gorda period, 1755.

The Sierra Gorda (Fat Mountains) are so called because, with the exception of a ten-thousand-foot peak at Pinal de Amoles, most of the mountains are less than half that height and spread out as far as the eye can see in all directions.

The mountains might be fat, but the people were lean, hardy, and poor—among the poorest even today in all of Mexico, far removed from much of the world. And in 1750, they were disoriented by recent physical and spiritual onslaughts from a people they hardly knew or understood. Serra was called to balance them and try to win them over to a life that was largely foreign. It was not an easy first crucible for a missionary, but it is the life he had wanted from his earliest days as a teaching priest on Mallorca.

On June 1, 1750, Serra embarked upon the labyrinthian road, setting out from the College of San Fernando in Mexico City on foot, with Francisco Palou at his side. They were headed north into the Sierra Gorda, the 250-mile central section of the massive Sierra Madre Oriental mountain range that runs north–south from the slender waist of Mexico at the Gulf of Mexico all the way to Texas. Accompanying them were several Pame Indians who had already converted through the intermittent efforts by Augustinian, Dominican, and earlier Franciscan monks over the past half century. The Pames led the relief party of soldiers and pack animals laden with provisions and water to Jalpan, which, with a population of two thousand, was the largest town in the mountains. The sixteen-day journey aggravated Serra's foot wound severely.

We do not know the exact route Serra took. There were two possibilities. He could have chosen the flatter, longer route northwest through Querétaro (population ten thousand), where he would have encountered the *arboles de la cruz*, known as the miraculous cross trees, growing in back of the Santa Cruz church. If Serra took the eastern route into the mountains, he would have passed through the site of Juan Diego's vision of the Blessed Mother at Guadalupe. In either case, a miraculous site would have helped lighten his second swollen-footed walk in Mexico.

Serra's eight years in the Sierra Gorda are document-poor. But we do know that seven friars traveled with him into the Sierra Gorda in 1750, including Palou and Crespí, his Mallorcan ex-students. On either route, the Serra party would have passed significant mines. The northwestern route, through more mountains, proceeds first through the blindingly white, rock-studded plain at Vizarrón, with its massive marble quarry. Alternately, on the northeastern route the missionaries would have come face-to-face with one of their chief antagonists—the great silver mine at Pachuca (one of the largest in the world and still producing today). There Serra got his first look at his flock, and it was not a reassuring one: the surviving Pames and Jonaces, scorched-faced, dead tired, and covered in silver dust. Many were virtual slaves.

The road tilted slowly, inexorably. For a view of heaven, Serra and his compatriots were going to have to feel their legs fall off. This was the gorge of the Río Extoraz, which they had to cross by a cable rope bridge, before the dizzying journey around escarpments, switching back and forth uphill, thinking they had made a crest, before a slight incline and then another crest. And another. The endless Sierra Gorda. At night, they cooked their modest meals of chiles, rice, and beans, or relished a chicken from a mountain Indian.

At Pinal de Amoles, ten thousand feet up, they looked back. All mountain. They looked forward. Mountain. Soon the sound of rushing water made them veer from the path. It was the Río Escanela. Their Pame guide would have known of three sizable waterfalls in the area; the Cascada El Chuveje was the closest to the road—only a half hour's walk down into a gorge. It would have been hard for the fathers to resist a natural shower. The Río Escanela stepped down in a broad, clear water staircase. The heat of day would have made them squat, dip their hands down to drink, and throw water in their faces, flecking their gray robes dark.

Soon they faced it: the tallest waterfall in central Mexico, one hundred feet high, dropping like white rope you could climb to the Creator. Could they have resisted taking their sandals off, putting their feet into the icy pool, watching the fall break on the high rock, listening to that roar of snowmelt? If not, they could have lost their own fears or disdain of the poor naked body and shed their habits and become, for a moment, Indian in the Cascada El Chuveje, themselves in the fall, with the fall, of the fall. And for once not assuming sin, just the clean cloth of their skin.

On June 16, 1750, Serra and his party reached Jalpan (from Xalpam, a Nahuatl word meaning "over the sand of the mountain"), the chief mountain town; it didn't take long to realize he had quite a calamity on his hands. Though nominally there were a thousand Pame Indians registered at the six-year-old mission church, none of them had been to the sacraments for years. Serra walked into what had become a defeat not only for the Indians but for José de Escandón himself, who had moved on to Nuevo Santander, a region northeast on the Gulf of Mexico (today's South Texas and the Mexican state of Tamaulipas).

José de Escandón was an Indian fighter on the order of an Andrew Jackson. Not as ruthless, perhaps, but Escandón was nevertheless dubbed by some in Mexico "the exterminator."

Born in Sota de la Marina, Spain, in 1700—in what had been known as the Santander Province—Escandón came to the New World as a fifteen-year-old, fighting as a youthful horseman in the War of the Spanish Succession when the English came snooping along the Yucatán coast. Promoted to lieutenant, he soon became known for his steely determination and was sent to fight the Apaches in Texas; meeting with little success, he returned to Querétaro, around which he put down at least four Indian revolts. His exploits got him promoted to colonel. In Querétaro, he kept a large burnished orange stucco home with wrought iron bars facing the street, preferring to treat the Indians "as friends, with a soft hand, and as enemies with implacable rigor." Too often the rigor left little for the soft hand to do.

The "father of the lower Río Grande," Escandón is primarily known to history as the Spaniard who "pacified" Nuevo Santander. However, Escandón was relieved in 1767, accused on thirty-eight counts of violating Spanish law.

Both in the Sierra Gorda and in Nuevo Santander, Escandón had the advantage—at least as the Crown saw it—of being rich, and therefore saving the state the expense of the campaigns to break the backs of the most recalcitrant Indians at the north-central and northern peripheries of New Spain. Escandón had made a fortune with a textile mill he had established in Querétaro, where he bought and sold slaves. He was lionized by members of the Spanish elite. One historian called him "a capable and fair-minded military leader and administrator." In fact, the Franciscans hated him for usurping their protective authority over the Indian, while others gave him credit for enforcing a "radical experiment—one that Spain never repeated in America." That is, he forbade the padres congregating Indians into missions isolated from settlers; they would attach more, in his vision, to landholders as cheap labor than in the spiritual hothouse of the mission. In a word, Escandón espoused free-market capitalism.

Throughout the eighteenth century, as the winds of Enlightenment gained speed, the debate between the missionaries and the Spanish authorities on what to do with the Indians intensified, the Franciscans seeking to protect them while some Spanish authorities criticized the friars for abusing their privileges, infantilizing the Indians, and walling them off from economic and social reality. Each side accused the other of abusing the Indian, the friars indicting the landowners and their vicious *encomiendas* of near slave labor, and the secular officials asserting that the priests were keeping the Indians against their will in the missions. Ironically, the Indian was often caught, if not rubbed out, in the middle of this ongoing argument. Meanwhile, one of the richest men in Spain and the viceroy's legal counsel, the Marqués de Altimira, urged Escandón to fight a war "of fire and blood," convinced that "If only one [Indian] remained alive, it will be enough to upset all."

Such a clarion, needless to say, was hardly enlightened. There is little doubt that, at least where the elusive, cave-dwelling Jonace are concerned, Escandón's campaign (1735–43) was nearly genocidal. As for the more passive crop-tending Pames, after having witnessed the slaughter of the Jonaces, for the most part they submitted.

The Franciscans were not happy with what was going on in the Sierra Gorda in the 1740s. In 1742, they "denounced the use of Jonace people as involuntary laborers on the haciendas of two regional officials." Serra's predecessor, Pedro Pérez de Mezquía, didn't help matters when he instituted an onerous series of "Rules and Regulations for Spiritual Direction" that included the natives "without exception" kissing the priest's hand on roll call. Needless to say, this humiliating practice didn't get far with the Pames. Epidemics of smallpox, drought, the general depression of a people witness to mass killings of their cousins and subject to war themselves, soon made the kissing of hands scarce.

This was the scene that Serra's relief mission in 1750 confronted. Since 1744, the population of the five missions had decreased by 30 percent (to 2,600), and almost half the Pame couples were childless; orphans were rampant. Serra seems to have realized right off that if things were going to turn around, he would need to do two things: improve on Mezquia's stiff rulings by learning the Pames' language, and then literally get down on his knees in front of the people. He wasn't asking them to kiss him; he was going to wipe their feet.

Quickly Serra chose the local Pame Indian governor (presumably appointed by Escandón), Balthasar Coronel, as his language teacher. Though he thought he didn't learn fast enough, Serra took a gift for languages to preaching in the Oto-Manguean language of the Pame, alternating Spanish prayers with those in the Pame tongue. He carried his grammar and vocabulary notebook everywhere, a treasure that appears to have been lost.

Three liturgical practices Serra performed in dramatic fashion, a methodology that became his signature: his own confession, the Stations of the Cross, and the imitation of Christ washing the disciples' feet at the Last Supper. Clearly, he wanted to appeal to the Indians' sense of faith as ritual, especially physical ritual. As Maynard Geiger put it simply, "To persuasion he added example."

One of those early days in the mountains, on a feast day, Serra blessed himself walking into the little worship structure—hardly a church, more a longhouse like that of the Iroquois (which he set to replacing with an extraordinarily beautiful structure). He was with Palou. The Pames on the small wooden benches may have stood, probably curious to see what the two would do rather than showing deference. They went straight up to the altar, where stood a confessional made of wood. Palou walked into the middle compartment and drew a curtain. Serra went up to the little window, perhaps thatched or covered with some sort of screen. He stood, as confessionals in that era were made for the sinner to confess standing. And Serra began to confess his sins. It was a public confession. Perhaps it began with a Pame language version of "Bless me, Father, for I have sinned." But the rest would have been Mallorquín to a Mallorcan, and not understandable to the Indians. This was in keeping with Church practices guarding the secrecy of confession. Not even a murderer's confession can be made public by a priest.

Still, no one confesses like that, in front of the crowd, then or now. Somehow, Serra's sorrow over doing wrong was communicated to the crowd.

Pride, cursing over a leg wound, lust in Cádiz, anger in Selva, doubt (no sin really, for we'd all be confessing it half the day); Serra went over his sin—whatever it may have been—like a man sampling cloth.

The Pames stirred. They saw Serra drop to his knees after his confession and put his face in his hands. They must have been touched, for soon they were putting their own faces in their hands. And the church slowly began to fill.

What would the Pames have begun to confess? Again, "interchanges between priest and penitent were supposed to be secret, and hence transcription of them are absent." Recent discovery, however, by an especially perceptive scholar who has looked closely at a rarely inspected private manuscript of a seventeenth-century priest who ministered in central Mexico to the surviving descendants of the Aztecs (or Mexica), found something revealing. He was the Spanish Jesuit Horacio Carochi, "the greatest colonial grammarian of Nahuatl," according to the discoverer and translator of the text, Los Angeles educator Barry Sell.

The confessions, faithfully recorded by Carochi shortly before the time of the publication of his *Grammar of the Mexican Language* (1645), were used as teaching aids for young priests learning Nahuatl and ministering to Indians. The portrait that emerges is of timeless small-town foibles (in this case, Tepotzotlán, outside Mexico City) of fighting, drunkenness, and adultery. But there are also striking admissions of despair, such as an Aztec woman's outburst of suicidal thoughts after an abortion: "Let me find a river or maybe a mountain where I can hurl myself down on some volcanic rocks. . . . Let me become food there for coyotes and buzzards. . . . Let my Lord God efface and kill. . . . Perhaps our Lord God has forgotten me." If Serra was made aware of such happenings, he would have emphasized, as he did to the Claretian nuns on Mallorca, God's infinite mercy.

In addition to illuminating the power of confession, Serra's celebration of Christmas made the event come to life. At his first Christmas with the Pames, he orchestrated a mystery play, distributing parts to young Indians for Mary, Joseph, even Christ (who could be an infant wrapped in a white cotton blanket or child dressed up in cutaway coat looking more like a butler than the savior). The celebration continued until New Year's Eve and a midnight Mass, thus "reproducing the great Mystery with great vividness," according to Palou. "In this way, he was able to instruct them and win their affection."

More impressive to the Pames, perhaps, was Serra himself shouldering a cross. The Sierra Gorda was a potential Calvary in every direction, a veritable surfeit of suffering. And so, that first year with the Pames, he picked a hill outside town and constructed, with the help of the Indians, Jalpan's own Calvary. After they'd hoisted the stripped pine trunk on top of Serra, the Indians stood back, thinking, perhaps, he was either holy or crazy. The first time Palou saw this, he was dumbstruck. The cross was "so large and heavy that I, stronger and younger though I was, could not lift it." But Serra always had had nearly superhuman endurance, despite his size and history of asthma.

There is something even more compelling about Serra's shouldering of a literal cross. One of his favorite theologians was St. Bonaventure, who had a mystical understanding of Christ's suffering on the cross. "Whoever loves this death can see God," the thirteenth-century mystic states plainly in his masterwork, *The Soul's Journey to God.* "On the Cross the whole Trinity cries out to you," Bonaventure insists. Christ's taking on human form to save humanity from its violent selfishness reached its apex on the cross, which is, of course, the very embodiment of the "Greater love hath no man" message—sacrificing one's very life for another, what soldiers do on the battlefield, a brother diving into a turgid sea to rescue a sister, a daughter who puts aside her own life to be beside a stricken mother. Bonaventure's emphasis—and this spoke deeply to the professor in Serra—was that an ecstatic union with Christ's selflessness on the cross cannot be achieved by intellectual pursuits: "For Christ goes away when the mind attempts to behold this wisdom through intellectual eyes, since it is not the intellect that can go there, but the heart . . . for the heart reaches down into the depths of Christ." Unity with Christ's "greater love" brings us to a paradoxical mystery: "the radiance of darkness . . . yet the soul is supremely flooded with light." In short, "Bonaventure illuminates love as the metaphysical foundation of the journey to God." This journey is boosted immeasurably by going right through the unimaginable suffering of the Crucifixion.

But what might have won the Pames over and above Serra's bearing that heavy trunk of a cross or the food the padres provided during the worst drought any of them would have ever witnessed was the ritual of Holy Thursday: the washing of the feet. Serra went to the elderly of the Pame. He put his hand on the shoulder of what appeared to be the eldest members of the community, asking around for *los viejos.* Soon he gathered the undoubtedly bemused white-haired women and men onto the altar of the old, makeshift chapel. There he had brought practically every chair he could find, twelve in all, and gestured that all should sit. An Indian boy filled a clay jug with water from the creek and warmed it on a fire before bringing it to Father Serra with a cloth. Serra then did something that shocked the onlookers. He sat on the floor beneath the oldest man, took his old, smelly feet out of his sandals, and began to wash them with the warm water. The old man must have smiled. Who wouldn't? Serra did this eleven more times, to each old person he had gathered.

Other dramatic Holy Week features Serra created involved Indians placing a newly carved, life-size statue with thatched hair and hinged arms of the slain Christ in a casket, which was then lifted on top of the altar. For a Feast of Corpus Christi procession, Serra had the Pames build flowering arches and four little altars as a resting place for Christ's body along the way; at each, an Indian boy would recite a poem, two in Spanish, two in Pame, which "caused devotion in everyone and softened their hearts." Musicologist Craig Russell comments on this procession: "Serra's deliberate use of Pame, in particular, reveals his attitude regarding worship to be largely inclusive and practical, as opposed to elitist or inflexible."

On the Feast of the Immaculate Conception (another Serra and Franciscan favorite), there was a novena and singing, especially about the joy of Mary. Entering the church in procession, the early Christian *Tota Pulchra* was sung in Spanish and Pame. The Indians apparently sang about Mary "with great solemnity, producing in all who heard it the greatest tenderness," including that stirring line, "Your clothing is white as snow and your face is like the sun."

One of the reasons for that "tenderness" may have been that the Pames revered their own mother sun goddess, Cachum. They prayed to her for rain, good crops, health, victory in war, and a good wife, though "there is no mention of the women praying for suitable husbands." Carved in nearly clear marble (*tecale*), the Cachum bust of Jalpan had been snatched away from the marauding soldiers of Escandón by an old man, probably a shaman, to a mountaintop cave, a place where the Pames buried and revered their dead chiefs.

When soldiers discovered this place sacred to the Pame, they tried to burn it down. "For Godsake, and for our most holy Mother, light it up!" the sergeant ordered, but three or four attempts would not make the holy hut burn. It did ignite, finally, "with a disgusting odor." But Serra thought enough of it that, when some Christianized Pames presented the singed Cachum to him, far from destroying it or throwing it away, he took it as a good luck trophy on a 1752 journey to Mexico City and presented it to the guardian Pumeda at the College of San Fernando for its archives.

• • •

Cachum may have welcomed Serra to the Fat Mountains, but within a year of his arrival, Serra found the welcome of now General Escandón wearing very thin. Before leaving for Nuevo Santander, Escandón had set aside lands for soldiers and for the mission and its Indians in Jalpan. But for two years, he told the guardian, Ortés de Velasco, soldiers complained to him that the missions were handing land back to the Indians, land the soldiers themselves—including those who were actively "reducing" Indians—wanted. Escandón's attitude toward the Indians, despite his insistence that he sought harmony between them and the settlers, can't be mistaken; he called them "lazy, free, and barbarous."

Escandón had other bones to pick with the Franciscans. Placing seven families "as a roadblock against fugitive Indians" a few miles from the Tancoyol mission hadn't sat well with the priests there, who probably suspected them of being squatters siphoning off more Indian land. Escandón fumed that he'd written Serra several times, without answer.

Within a week of receipt of Escandón's fiery letter, Ortés de Velasco stepped down as guardian, Bernardo Pumeda ascended to the position, and Serra, after first refusing it, accepted the title of president of the mountain missions. Now Serra was in the direct bead of Escandón. Cannily, Serra nudged Pumeda, who in a June 29 letter took on Escandón directly with his own barely hidden anger: "You are bound by a strict conscientious obligation and in justice to favor, defend, and protect these Indians because of their great poverty, even though it should be necessary to sustain a financial loss to your own income."

Escandón, taken aback by this lecture, nevertheless seemed "more hurt than angry." In a detailed retort, he tries to set the record straight, claiming Pumeda was getting "news in the apparently distorted manner . . . a common occurrence when such distances are involved," concealing his distaste for Serra. He had every intention of returning the fugitive Pames—rounding fugitives up had been his job for six years, he says. But they had their claims, too: mission food was bad, labor onerous, punishments too severe.

There's some irony and straight out contradiction here, for both Escandón and Serra. If, for example, Escandón actually was the revolutionary thinker for which he wanted to be taken, favoring Indian life outside the missions, why was he willingly bringing fugitives back? If he were indeed for free-market capitalism, why was he proposing settling Indian land with newcomers who had fought the Indians? That's pure social engineering. As for Serra, if he was not forcing Indians into the missions, why was he taking roll at Sunday Masses and punishing them for leaving? In any event, not that many Pames stayed: "They . . . lived in their own homes, many of which were located at some distance of the mission compound." Still, Pames were becoming apprenticed to master craftsmen, learning trades, and getting paid. And mission Indians in the Sierra Gorda (whether on-site or "parishioners") increased significantly under Serra, though numbers declined after he left.

Before Pumeda answered Escandón's complaints about the missions, Escandón announced a jarring initiative. About six miles east of Jalpan in the Tancama Valley, he had just launched a settlement of twenty-three Spanish soldiers and their families (something he had been planning for seven years). Soon enough Escandón would know that the Tancama project was opposed by everybody: the Indians of Jalpan, the Franciscans, the College of San Fernando, and, finally, the Spanish governmental authority. A legal battle over authority in Indian policy ensued. The Laws of the Indies forbade Spanish settlement in mission lands, and the Indians made it clear they would take up arms against the soldier-settlers to retain their ever-diminishing lands. In this matter, "Serra sided with the Indians."

After receiving testimony from San Fernando, missionaries, and Indians, a viceroy commission's ruling—probably written by Serra—came down on December 14, 1751: Escandón's Tancama colony was null and void. Some settlers spoke of the "impious" Franciscans.

And they continued to scheme. In a word, the settlers refused to budge, pressuring the Indians to protest to the viceroy and Escandón that at the mission they were essentially being starved, abused physically by beatings, and forced to act as pack animals for trips to the Gulf of Mexico. Apparently the Indians, some inured to mission life, some not, were wise to the Machiavellian settlers and resisted this lobbying effort. Still the matter dragged on. Finally, on January 27, 1753, the settlers were formally evicted, the commission having agreed to their resettlement from Tancama to Saucillo, a relatively flat and arable plain between Landa and Tancoyol. By February, the settlers were ensconced in Saucillo. The four-year battle of Tancama was over.

In late summer 1752, Serra traveled to Mexico City for supplies but also, it seems, to lodge serious complaints with Inquisition officials about another matter entirely, one he thought darkly supernatural. Serra had "several grave indications" about people in and around the Jalpan area "who are addicted to the most detestable and horrible crimes of sorcery, witchcraft and devil worship." He even claimed they were "flying through the air at night in the habit of meeting in a cave on a hill near a ranch called El Saucillo."

Serra pointed out sacrifice to goatlike devils. But what's more fascinating than Serra's fear of witches and devils—a common enough Christian obsession at the time—is that three times he insists to his superiors that the problem is not the Indians, but the rather crazy, if not possessed, Spaniards, whom he calls the *gente de razón* ("people of reason"). Three times he pointedly says the guilty are "not Indians," as if staving off a stereotype of the infidel that, presumably, the Holy Tribunal would have had. He actually warns against the Spaniards contaminating the Indians, rather than vice versa: "If such evil is not attacked the horrible corruption will spread among the poor neophytes who are in our charge."

Possessing "accusations which appear to be bona fide concerning the matter," Serra was not shy about naming names: he accused Melchora de los Reyes Acosta ("a married mulattress") and "a very clever Mexican woman" named Cayetana, who had a mulatto husband and who confessed and was already under arrest. We may question just what Serra was trying to convey by revealing mixed bloods in the matter, while defending the Indians—which part of the mixture was reprehensible? In any event, within a day the tribunal gave Serra powers as inquisitor for all of New Spain that he undoubtedly turned to his advantage with the settlers. What, if anything, became of the so-called devil worshippers? The record does not say.

Armed with one hundred nails, carpentry tools, and a new set of María de Agreda books, Serra returned to Jalpan from Mexico City ready to construct an inspiring church. He was energized enough, it seems, to also outfit himself with a new *saylete*, a light fabric garment worn under the habit, for his old one was in shreds. At 693 pesos, the *saylete* cost sixty times as much as a similar tunic he purchased three years later for ten pesos. It was a splurge (unless a misprint). Serra had to sense his newfound power.

Indeed the facade of the church at Jalpan is bold, a phantasmagoria of imagery, both Christian and Pame, a stunning example of the Spanish Baroque. Beginning in late 1752 and finishing six years later, Serra built the church in a frenzy, utilizing Pames as laborers, painters, sculptors, and possibly as designers. (The price was certainly low, however; Serra brought back from the capital Indian work fees barely higher than what he was paying for hay for the mules—316 versus 314 pesos. At the same time, he paid 393 pesos for clothes for the Indians.) It seems likely that he brought an architect and an expert mason back to the mountains, but being given to practicing what he preached, Serra threw himself into the work, hauling the cement, boards, and water for the workers, wearing sandals the natives called *apats nipis*. In the evenings, he pulled out something else he had purchased in Mexico City to cut the solitude of the mountains: a shiny violin.

Leering monkeys, bats, eagles, snakes, grapes, pineapples, and vines, along with saints and crosses and scrolls, all twined together in Serra's mind for the church at Jalpan. In fact, so outlandish is Jalpan's facade—a style replicated at the other four mountain missions—some have suggested Serra was later transferred out of the Sierra Gorda because the fronts of his churches were overly sensual and stimulating.

Mission Santiago de Jalpan's facade is not stone or adobe but *argamasa*, a remarkably enduring mixture of sand, lime, eggshell, mud, and a thick substance from the nopal cactus—exactly the material used to shape the temples of the Aztecs, further encouraging us to see the hand of the Pame Indians in its construction. This natural cement has been uncannily resistant to rain over the years. Above the main door at the entry a large arc radiates upward in a scallop shell motif, a symbol of St. James—Santiago Matamoros (James the Moorslayer), the patron saint of Spain. Some have suggested the use of scallops in several of the Sierra Gorda missions is not only sacred but also profane imagery—a touch of the seafaring Mallorcan drawing the sea into the mountains. Above the entry, halfway up the facade, two arms cross over the cross of Christ so that the arms indicating Christ and St. Francis of Assisi are "crucified" together—a Franciscan symbol of the stigmata of Francis.

On either side of the entry to Jalpan church are two three-foot statues of Saints Peter and Paul, the "pillars" of the early Church. Just above them in the next register, flanked by paired pilasters, St. Dominic and St. Francis appear (a peace symbol for Dominicans and Franciscans), with the Blessed Mother higher up in two forms, one as Our Lady of Guadalupe and the other as Our Lady of the Pillar. In short, the design emphasized the double tradition of Mexico and Spain. And on either side of the entry the fierce Hapsburg—and Indian—symbol of the two-headed eagle with a long snake clamped by both beaks that appears on the flag of Mexico greets visitors. The gentleness of the eagle heads has led the art historian Richard Perry to opine that the bird may originally have been meant as the Christian pelican, a symbol of atonement and great sacrifice, as the pelican is said to feed its young by piercing its own breast for blood. In this reading, what the Spanish architect—or Serra himself—may have sketched could have morphed from pelican to eagle. A double-headed eagle to the Pames revealed the virility of the Sun God. In either case, power over evil both Christian and Indian. Everything about the Serra facade at Jalpan is double: doctors of the church, heads of missionary traditions, two kinds of Mary, two heads to the eagle (in two sets). If there was one God, as Serra was, of course, convinced, he also knew, like Noah, there should be room for two of everything, including his new parishioners' way of seeing God. Love is not a solo art.

The monkeylike figures, a friar sculpted in an Indian-like loincloth, the two naked gargoyles with staffs, and the two bats on top of the facade hanging over all this beauty like a dark reminder can be seen as the holy surrealism of Serra 250 years before his fellow Catalán Salvador Dalí made the technique famous throughout the world. Many of the motifs of Santiago de Jalpan were replicated not only in the Sierra Gorda of Mexico but also decades later in California.

We must presume the trauma the Pames had already sustained wouldn't have disappeared quickly. Nevertheless, Serra was making progress with the Indians, turning back sections of their own land to farm and plant—pumpkins, corn, beans—and throwing in a pig or two, a cow, or yoke of oxen. Women made mats of palm and sisal ropes to sell in the mining camps of Zimapán in exchange for cotton, which in turn they wove for clothes. In 1756, as the church in Jalpan was nearing completion (1758), Serra's first confessor in the New World, Bernardo Pumeda, visited. Pumeda marveled at Serra traipsing about, mud on his habit. "A key element of Franciscan life," Father Kenan Osborne tells us, "is getting your hands dirty with good cheer." At one point, twenty Pames were carrying a particularly heavy beam. They were all taller than Serra, but in order to help support them, he threw his habit up on his shoulder, doubling and tripling it to make up the space between beam and the shoulders of the taller Indians.

At some moment in those vigorous years in the Sierra Gorda, perhaps toward the end, as they were sitting on the church steps at night, Serra turned to his companion, Juan Ramos de Lora, who would go on to fame as a bishop and founder of a university in Venezuela, and said, "We are not safe here." The two went into the friary, Lora deeply troubled. Sure enough, they discovered the next day someone had planned to kill the muddy-robed Mallorcan.

Neither Palou nor Geiger say who was planning the murder attempt, though Palou notes that they uncovered the plot "with certainty." Though one might suspect the Pames, the plotter seems more likely to have been a Spanish settler.

The whole dilemma of how to protect the Indian from Spanish encroachment even as he himself was encroaching, though spiritually, was beginning to sprout its nettles in Serra's soul. As Geiger notes, there's no doubting where Serra stood over the issue of Tancama: with the

Pames. He knew the Indians' anxiety over the potential of the mission to be more of an internment than haven, and the lands the missionaries turned back to them were critical to gain trust. Tancama had challenged this forcibly. It had finally died down. But he had to know the issue was far from dead.

Sometime during this period, Serra must have received word that his mother, Margarita, had died in Mallorca and was buried on Christmas Day 1754. She was seventy-seven. (Serra's father, Antonio, had died at seventy-eight a year and a half earlier, on May 5, 1753.) Margarita's will shows two things: she was intensely attentive to spiritual ritual and detail, and she was poor. What little she had (five sous) was going to the local priest. She demanded that the wax candles for her funeral be inspected by her heirs, and that five rituals be performed over her body. She wanted thirteen Masses said for her soul: five at St. Peter's parish in Petra, five at her La Purisima crypt at San Bernardino, and the last three wherever her heirs wished. Serra must have offered up one, once he found out, halfway around the world in Jalpan, though his parents' bodies were long under marble.

Whatever the Tancama cross weighed, the loss of his mother and father had to have weighed more. Vexed, certainly heartbroken, Serra nevertheless did not acknowledge in print, as far as we know, the deaths of his parents.

Meanwhile, the four other mission churches in the Sierra Gorda began to take shape under Serra's detailed plans, if not his actual eye. The smallest of the five missions—at Conca (*kon-kank*, "with myself" in Pame) a few miles up the road northwest of Jalpan—was the second to begin construction, in 1754, though it was completed before Jalpan in 1758. Father José Antonio de Murguía supervised the creation of Conca's facade, speaking of the triumph of good over evil, with a militant St. Michael the Archangel wielding his sword over a winged devil he seems to be kicking over the peak of the church itself. Some have seen the prevalence of Michael in the Sierra churches as secretly evoking Tlaloc, the Aztec god of rain, and others have caught indigenous faces in the angels. One commentator has seen Conca's faith fantasy as "movement-enfused, gravity-defying." Lighthouse finials top two angled columns that reinforce the facade, and carved on them are a rabbit and that two-headed eagle again, "proof of the syncretism that took place between the two cultures [and] the use of native labor, since these figures represent the important indigenous deities of the Sun and Moon."

Serra's close, younger friend, Father Juan Crespí, who had crossed the

Atlantic a few months after him and caught up with him at San Fernando in Mexico City, took over the Tilaco community and began construction of its church in 1754, at the same time as Conca, though it was not finished until after Serra had left the mountains (in 1762). A Christian lion in the facade is paired with the Indians' hairless dog, Xolla. But Tilaco's outstanding feature is the sea. Images of the sea are everywhere on it and have caused more than one art historian to think Crespí was recalling (and not just for himself but all the Mallorcan friars in the mountains) his island youth. Four young mermaids, hardly sacred to Catholics, hold up four pillars, while they stabilize on their fishy tails. Plaster replicas of conch and nautilus shells decorate the scalloped arch of the entry to the church. There are even a few 3-D surrealistic mussels in the mouths of the scallops. And washing over the entire facade is the color blue, an extremely rare pigment for outdoor buildings until the nineteenth century, perhaps painted for 1,090 pesos by a rather expensive *pintor* Serra had sent from Mexico City.

Construction on the last two missions that Serra planned began after he had left the mountains and taken up residence in San Fernando in Mexico City—at Tancoyol (1761, completed 1767) and Landa (1760, completed 1768), though there is evidence he revisited the Sierra Gorda. Each has its Serra stamp. Tancoyol (after the Huasteca, *coyoles*, or "source of wild dates") is the farthest away from Jalpan, about sixty miles to the northeast, nearly at a dead end in the verdant Zoyapilca Valley. The road to Tancoyol has the most prehistoric feel to it, through meadows filled with sunflowers, agaves in rock, yuccas flared with the sun, eagles and hawks circling above. Serra must have walked transfixed to Tancoyol; the valley descends into a deep gorge, and as you walk downward, the cliffs rise with pole cacti, tall green sentries without arms. Everywhere there are *lluvia de oro* (gold rain) trees, carobs, mimosas, before the road dead-ends. There, greeting all, is the singular feature of the facade of Tancoyol church: St. Francis receiving the stigmata from an airborne, winged Christ-on-cross who seems to shoot the wounds in red lines into Francis.

Tancoyol is dramatic and the tallest of the five missions, with four rather than three registers in the facade, topped by a step-down gable with "Turk's cap" finials. The sense of the Holy Land is impressed with the Cistercian Cross of Jerusalem and the Dominican Cross of Calatrava with its four quadrants in fleurs-de-lis based on a Moor-fighting order at the top register, along with eight Moorish arches behind the altar inside. Both Peter and Paul statues on the lowest register near the entry were beheaded post-construction, the result of armed battles during the Mexican Revolution and later the reforms under Benito Juárez. The heads are purposely not restored.

Landa, the last of the five missions, completed by Fathers Palou, Miguel de la Campa, and others, has been called the most ornate, its red wash, from cinnabar, the deepest of all. Landa (meaning swampy, *lamba*, in Chichimecan) is anything but still; it appears to be moving, its registers rippling with arches. There is no mistaking Serra's touch here. Two of his great spiritual mentors are carved in bas-relief, sitting at their desks flanking the church entry: Duns Scotus, the philosopher who saw art as a medium to God; and María de Agreda, the Spanish mystic whose books Serra carried everywhere in the New World. They look like they're chatting. This is a shrine not just to saints, but to thinkers and writers. A close look at María's figure shows everything rippling: her nun's habit, the desk itself, her chair.

Life went on in the serene mountains beyond the political joustings with Escandón, the actual crafting and building of the churches, the sowing in the field. In addition to all else, Serra was a parish priest at Jalpan, the first parish for a former professor, and he learned the typical daily rituals of a pastor day by day: baptisms, funerals, novenas for the sick, weddings. On April 7, 1756, he assisted in burial rites at Tilaco for a Pame Indian named, oddly enough, Francisco Escandón, perhaps burying with him the misery brought by his namesake. But it was the prospective wedding of a recent widow, Rita Márquez of Jalpan, to one Manuel Durán that provides a unique glimpse into life in those mountains folded away from the world in the eighteenth century. These come from letters I discovered in 2011 that had been kept in San Pedro Escanela farmhouses for centuries.

On June 8, 1755, Serra wrote Father Joseph Campos that he was having trouble figuring out whether Rita and Manuel should be married at all. There were possible "impediments." First, Rita had recently been widowed under somewhat shady circumstances. Then there was testimony from three witnesses ("they are in my presence") denouncing the would-be couple for particularly racy sexual activities. These denouncers were Rita's sister-in-law (Rita Reyes), Augustín Pérez, and Catholina Varron. All three claimed they saw the prospective groom, Manuel, "in flagrante" with his betrothed's own sister (María Josefina Márquez). A fourth, unnamed witness was shocked to report seeing that the bride-to-be "had carnal knowledge" with Manuel's brothers—Felipe and Antonio. If nothing else, Rita Márquez certainly kept it in the family. In fact, this fourth witness had seen the ménage à trois fleeing, perhaps partially clothed ("in crimine") from a place in Tres Lagunas where her own husband, when alive, had stayed. Left unsaid is whether or not the Durán brothers, all taken with Rita, may have done in her unlucky husband, Don Manuel Reyes, whose sister appears to have been one of the accusers.

The reader may have no more luck deconstructing this soap opera than Serra did; he threw the whole thing onto Campos's good and perhaps expedient judgment: "So, Reverend, you will do anything you think is convenient. My best regards to my brothers Molina and Palou. There is nothing else new in the present and rain has not come."

But the matter does not seem to have calmed down. Several letters appear to have been filed with accusations, denials, more vehement accusations. Finally, on October 6, 1755, Palou himself weighed in that the principal accuser, Rita Reyes, the dead man's sister, "swore to God and the Holy Cross that she had not said anything out of malice, but to fulfill her obligation and conscience." Palou has more details from Reyes. After Rita Márquez's sister María Josefina Márquez invited her to the mission of Ahuacatlán, during eight days there "under some *sapote* trees in the same house Manuel and Josefina lived as if they were married, holding hands one afternoon and going to the same bed." But Palou's not much clearer on what to do: "I can't do the diligence because I don't know the denouncers. I am waiting, hour upon hour, for my Junípero, who some days ago had to put up in Conca Mission due to rivers rising."

The rivers rose; lovers entwined as vines on a mission facade. And rivers receded. It seems rather doubtful Rita Márquez and Manual Durán were the best candidates for monogamy at this point. Meanwhile birds gathered to Moorish arches, nooks in the roof tiles, where they cooed, comfortable in clay. Doves and pigeons and swallows and even a hawk or two continued to land on the new peaks of the Sierra Gorda. Steeples and high crosses draw birds. And if he doubted a moment or even a week of God's grace, Serra heard the cooing, and looked up. There was a high note, a change, in the air.

CHAPTER NINE

LOST

Perhaps because the light needs to find its way!
—GHASSAN ZAQTAN

Don Mathias Josef Cortabarría's will with signature,
Antequera (Oaxaca), 1764.

Serra could have stayed in his lost horizon in the Sierra Gorda the rest of his life. It was not an idyll, but it was improvement. His work among the Pames had gone better than anyone could have expected. In the course of eight years, he had built and stabilized this rather unlikely community in the midst of death and despair. Five new churches stood in gorgeous harmony with the mountains, the fields were fertile with corn, squash, and grape vines, and the Pame women were humming at their looms. Serra had managed a little miracle, weaving the faiths of two people together so that, although one was dominant, the other was not completely squashed, retaining at least a vestige of its quietly evocative presence. He had also managed to advocate successfully for the Pames against rapacious settlers and the man who scorched the mountains.

He could have kept going, but in 1758, Serra was recalled to Mexico City and told by his superiors to prepare to go to Texas. At the northern periphery of the Spanish Empire in the New World he was to face, head-on, one of the most resistant of Indian tribes on the continent—the Apaches. Moreover, Serra was being sent to the exact mission site of a recent Indian massacre of ten people, including two Franciscan priests who had been Serra's companions at San Fernando.

Although initially Serra was overjoyed—he could be a martyr!—he didn't know what he was getting into, what one historian called "a stunning defeat—the worst inflicted on the Spanish in the New World."

As it happens, Spain's mission walls were built higher and higher as they crept north of the Río Grande. Apache raids were endemic; the mobile, horse-striding Apaches were hardly the sedentary Pames. They took no interest whatsoever in the quiet, set life of a mission, or in changing their centuries-old customs. Furthermore, they had both the means and the spirit to repel the overstretched Spaniards.

So it was quite a surprise, when, in 1749, exactly the year Serra first set foot on the continent at Veracruz, Apaches trotted on horseback into San Antonio and announced they would like to enter the embattled mission, render the threat null, and subject themselves to Spanish authority. To "somewhat flabbergasted padres," the Apaches went ever further: they suggested that the Franciscans build a mission deep in their territory, on the San Saba River (near the current city of Menard, Texas). To the friars, this was nothing short of a "mystical dream," and though civil authorities were skeptical, in 1756 a wealthy patron from Querétaro rose to the challenge. Don Pedro Romero de Terreros insisted that his own cousin, Father Alonso Giraldo de Terreros of the College of Santa Cruz in Querétaro, lead the effort.

Just after Christmas 1756, four priests and one hundred soldiers marched into the area under the command of Colonel Diego Ortiz Parilla, a veteran of Apache wars in New Mexico, and deeply skeptical of the San Saba project. On April 18, 1757, the priests took up duty on the south bank of the river; the military garrisoned themselves on the north bank in a presidio. There was only one problem. The Apaches had disappeared.

In fact, the Spanish had been duped. The Apaches had drawn them into their territory with a secret goal: to force Spain to support them in a war against their bitter enemies, who were riding farther south from

Colorado every day—the Comanches, whom the Apaches referred to as *norteños*, those pressing in from the north. Three priests abandoned the project. In their place came a reluctant Miguel Molina, joining the bewildered Terreros and José Santiestevan. They were guarded by five soldiers.

Spring 1758 brought not only rain and wildflowers, but Comanches under a full moon (what Texans still call a "Comanche Moon").

On the morning of March 16, 1758, just after Terreros gave the final blessing at Mass to his tiny congregation, two thousand Comanches with some Wichita allies thundered to the walls of the mission in a storm of dust, clutching feathered lances, bows, arrow quivers at the shoulder, and some with muskets, all painted in scarlet and black. Informed of their arrival, Santiestevan, who was about to say Mass himself, took off his purple Lent chasuble—in fact, all of the vestments that identified him as a priest—knelt in what amounted to underclothes at the altar, and prayed.

Terreros and Molina played for time, going outside the gate of the mission with gifts, which the Comanches accepted "with sardonic smiles." For a moment, as Serra himself later wrote, "playing that comedy," the Comanches spied into the compound. The gate opened for Alonso Terreros and a soldier, both astride the last horse left, hoping to get word to the presidio of an impending attack. Both were shot off the horse and tumbled down. The Comanches buried a lance in Terreros's chest and chopped off his head. Santiestevan, too, was decapitated, his body cut to pieces and found days later under an ash pile. The Comanches tossed the forlorn head back and forth as if it were a ball.

Statues in the chapel were smashed, soldiers and cattle shot and killed; for three days the Indians gorged themselves on the provisions in the storehouse. Though shot in the arm, Molina and a few others ran from one outbuilding to another, finally taking refuge in the chapel as it burned. Molina pulled a waxen "Agnus Dei" (probably a medal of the Lamb of God) off his neck and threw it on the fires, which "suddenly extinguished as if a river had been thrown upon them." Parilla, for the most part, stood down. On the first night of the Comanches' revelry, Molina crawled out of a window of the wrecked chapel, ran between bonfires, slipped into a river, and floated downstream under that Comanche moon. In three days traveling only by night, he made it to the presidio "bleeding and fainting for lack of food."

The reaction of the Spanish settlers and political leaders "amounted to a sort of wholesale panic on the northern frontier of New Spain." Barricaded in their forts, the people of San Antonio let two thousand head of cattle wander off into the prairie because no one would guard them. In Mexico City, the viceroy, the marquis of Las Amarillas, informed of the massacre on April 7, sent three urgent orders to governors in the north to give relief to San Saba, but no one budged.

Despite all this, the man who had initiated the whole miserable project, the silver magnate Pedro Romero de Terreros, insisted that San Saba be "retaken," an odd concept inasmuch as the Indians had left it blowing in the wind. He managed with his blind exuberance to twist the arm of the viceroy, who, on August 4, 1758, asked the Franciscans for four new missionaries to resurrect San Saba. Two were already in Texas; but the other two—Junípero Serra and Francisco Palou—were recalled from the Sierra Gorda, where they had been giving exemplary service, and told to prepare to leave for the charred ruins.

Serra—nervous, excited, expectant—arrived at San Fernando in Mexico City on September 26. But for some reason Don Pedro did not approve of him and Palou for the mission. The irritated guardian José García palmed the matter off on his subordinate, a veteran of Texas and the Sierra Gorda, Pedro Pérez de Mezquía. On March 28, 1759, Pérez de Mezquía regaled the silver magnate with the talents and achievements of Serra ("a professor *de prima* at the University of Majorca") and Palou ("a disciple of the first, a lector of philosophy")—and what they were able to accomplish in Sierra Gorda, stressing their religious fervor and their ability to win over the Indians and nurture the community.

On September 29, 1758, Serra wrote one of his rare soul-searching letters to his nephew back home on Mallorca, Miguel Ribot, who had just been ordained a Capuchin priest. He admits that his constant moving about had prevented him from answering Miguel's good news for a whole year, but that he was headed to the Apaches four hundred leagues away.

Serra gives a graphic description of Santiestevan's and Terreros's martyrdom that spring. He makes a reference to something "miraculous" (and strangely missing from both Palou's and Geiger's biographies), observed when the relief party finally arrived six days after the massacre: "They noticed that the mortal remains of Father Fray Joseph [Santiestevan] gave off a sweet-smelling odor from the wounds still dripping with fresh blood. His head, not far away from his body, was found in the same condition." In this reference to the sweet smell of the martyr's wounds Serra echoes the wonder of the early followers of St. Francis, who smelled something similarly sweet when the thirteenth-century saint was riddled with the five wounds of Christ. Repellent as it sounds, Serra ascribed the odor of bloody stumps to the realm of mystery.

Serra went further, referring to what were probably Molina's impressions of what happened after they buried Santiestevan:

On the spot, a gigantic stalk of maize sprang up, the plant you call there with truth—Indian corn. A marvel—or so it seems to be—signifying this: the grain of wheat that lay dead in the ground is a promise of much fruit in the harvest of souls of these miserable ones. And so may it turn out to be. Amen!

From three planting parables in the Gospel of Matthew (13:5, 37–38), Serra took a pinch of the sower, a speck of the wheat among the weeds, and some crushed mustard, but unlike the Lord himself, he added a new element: the blood of his own Spanish friend. A cynic might see the Indians triumphant in that sprung cornstalk; Serra saw their souls grown tall in Christ. That is why the massacre was not a tragedy to him, but life-giving in the sacrifice of a good man, two good men, actually, nothing less than Christ's own story told on the plains of Texas. The chance to give up his body, not to mention his soul, in service at San Saba "for so great an enterprise" Serra asserts to his nephew is an honor, but one that made him "quite conscious of my uselessness and lukewarmness." With the transfer to Texas pending but not confirmed, it's no surprise Serra felt in limbo. But he cautioned his nephew to remember to "say in the sincerity of your heart: *servi inutiles sumus*. [We are useless servants]" and that "stars fell from heaven."

In August 1759, a full year after the San Saba massacre, the largest Spanish operation ever sent to punish Indians, led by Colonel Ortiz Parilla, was totally bungled. Ortiz Parilla attacked the first settlement he saw, killing seventy-five Tonkawas, who actually hated the Comanches. When he did happen upon a huge encampment of several thousand Comanches, Wichitas, Osages, and Red River Caddoans, he abandoned all his provisions and fled; that was the "stunning defeat," Spain's worst on the continent. Spain never again took on the Comanches in battle in Texas, and the missionary advance into Texas stopped cold. Serra was spared.

Serra stayed in Mexico for nineteen years, truly his great worldly education. After the difficult but positive mission building in the Sierra Gorda, he became an itinerant preacher wandering in some of the most remote, poor areas of southern Mexico, touching Yucatán and close to Guatemala. It was there that Serra would enter the heart of darkness.

Just prior to this assignment, Serra's new work began, deceptively, with a period of calm, in the cloister of the College of San Fernando, in the middle of the continent's largest metropolis, Mexico City. Like St. Francis himself and the order he founded, Serra oscillated between love of the road and love of the cloister. For now, he sank into the adobe walls and tried to forget himself, his ambitions, and the painful frontiers in the heart. He ate little—almost no meat, a virtual vegetarian—and what little he ate he finished before the other friars, taking up a book to read. Food gave him no pleasure: "Some of his confreres thought he lacked a sense of taste."

His sleeping patterns were similarly spare. Most of the friars got about eight hours sleep (from 8 PM to midnight, and then 2:15 to 5:30 AM, plus a siesta after lunch). Serra rarely slept after midnight. He said midnight prayers with everyone, and then continued praying while everyone slept. He got about four hours of sleep a night, plus a one-hour siesta. To add to this dizzying austerity, Serra was known to wear under his gray Franciscan robes a rough burlap inner garment and possibly one stitched with pieces of wire.

For five years (1758–63), he rarely went out, except to hear the confessions of the Poor Clares and other nuns: "He had the reputation of being a sympathetic confessor and a source of balm and comfort to scrupulous souls." It speaks to the trust authority had in him and his comfort with the opposite sex, something his critics neglected to acknowledge.

Serra was always voted high in the leadership of San Fernando by his fellows, but rarely at the highest and never selected at the helm. This may have something to do with his hard-to-follow habits. Men elect those like them—worldly men, men they can relate to. Those who hold people to a higher standard—by painful practice, however inspiring—often end up in second place. In the words of John Vaughn, leader of the Serra Cause, an informal group in the United States advocating sainthood, "Serra was not safe." This relatively quiet period in Serra's life was broken from within by a slowly building pressure, one that, three centuries since his birth, is still hard to name.

During this second half of his life in Mexico, Serra was witness to and deeply involved in three violent deaths. It's probable all three were suicides, one certainly. This violence occurred either in front of him or on the spot where he had just been, as if he had thrown down the gauntlet to a sinner. Each involved confession. He was implicated in all three, dramatically so. Neither Palou nor Geiger, who treat these incidents briefly, offers one word about what effect they had on Serra. Undoubtedly traumatizing, however, their cumulative effect could have produced Serra's darkest moment to that point in his life.

Toward the end of his contemplative period at San Fernando (1761–62?), Serra held a mission in Mexico City, perhaps at San Fernando itself, though the actual place is unknown. At a peak moment in a sermon—perhaps about Christ's own scourging by Roman soldiers the night before his death—Serra suddenly bared his shoulders, took out a chain, and started beating his back "so violently that the entire congregation broke into tears." A man, nameless in history, lifted himself off his knees, stumbled over some congregants in the pews, walked up to the nave, ascended into the altar's sanctuary, snatched the iron chain out of Serra's hand, and cried out: "I am the sinner ungrateful to God who ought to do penance for my many sins—not Father, who is a saint," beating himself until he fell unconscious and soon died. Serra gave him not Communion, but Last Rites.

Three questions arise from this shocking event: Was self-flagellation unusual for Serra's time? How exactly did the man die? And lastly, what was the effect not just on the audience that probably watched the grisly outcome (at least at first) as rapt as any Romans over the lions, but also on his community and on Serra himself?

The practice of self-flagellation has its origins in the whippings Christ endured just prior to the Crucifixion, and in such bibical texts as "If anyone wishes to come after me, let him deny himself and take up his cross daily and follow me" (Luke 9:23), though there are certainly other ways to deny oneself, and no man or woman faces life without multiple crosses that need no *disciplina* to test one's spiritual or physical endurance to the maximum. Nevertheless, the practice seems to have emerged after the fourth century and the rise of monasticism. Later proponents of self-flagellation, such as France's St. John Vianney, the nineteenth-century patron saint of parish priests, had this advice for a grumpy curate who found his parishioners cold and his own faith sterile: "Have you fasted? Taken the discipline? Slept on boards? Until you have done these things, you have no right to complain." Even the current advocate for Serra sainthood admitted using the *disciplina* in novitiate sixty years ago. According to Palou, Serra practiced two other kinds of mortification of the flesh during sermons: holding a crucifix in one hand and beating his chest with a stone with the other; and, in order to invoke what could happen to a soul with no repentance (i.e., hell), lighting four wicks on the edge of a taper and passing them over his bare chest, burning himself or appearing to.

According to Palou, Serra was taken aback by the ostentatious display of wealth he saw in Mexico City, and the women dressed in gold embroidery drinking their hot chocolate during Mass bothered him. Mexico City, after all, was a wealthy place, with bars of silver streaming into it from Pachuca, Zacatecas, and other mining towns; that precious metal, in turn, was propping up an increasingly overstretched and insolvent Spanish Empire. It is possible that Serra was trying to get the audience's attention by beating or burning himself in the hope of awakening the souls of debauched, complacent, or materialistic onlookers to an awareness of the spirit. In the process, the soul would be transformed to "the fourth degree of love" when "the soul descends below herself . . . because of the neighbor." But surely Serra could never have counted on someone taking him so literally that he would throw his own life away on the spot.

And how did the man die? Geiger ventures by heart attack (figuring he was highly emotional) rather than blood loss or hypovolemia, which throws the body into severe shock. But whether he gave himself 250 lashes (which killed a man in Britain at the time), or even thirty-nine (the Mosaic Law limit), it's hard to imagine Serra or anyone in the church in Mexico City watching the man pummel himself that long without intervening.

In 1780, the Franciscan leadership at San Fernando reined in such behavior during missions and in the missions: "The pulpit was not to become a theatre stage." Apparently, playing tricks with a crucifix was becoming troublesome, as the guardian at San Fernando and his cohorts warned against holding a crucifix as if it were a sword. Serra's hinged, mechanical life-size Christ-on-cross was also problematic. Such theatricality was now officially condemned as "irreverent, silly, indiscreet, and indecent." Serra's self-flagellation in church may not have been, in itself, so strange for the time. A book published in 1777 on the history of flagellation—only a decade after the Mexico City incident—notes that, though the orders were "discreet" in what they promulgated about use of the *disciplina*, Ursuline nuns did it every Friday, the Carmelites twice a week, and the Capuchin Franciscans once a day. The crowd may not have been totally scandalized by the man running up to beat himself in public, as the rich and powerful sometimes voluntarily underwent public scourging to expiate wrong, among them England's King Henry II after the assassination of his friend, Archbishop Thomas à Becket.

Still, the sight of both penitents, Serra and the distraught man, meeting on the altar clasping the same chain, must have sent the worshippers that day into utter revulsion, if not a moral tailspin. This is not what should happen in a Catholic church. A penitential method had become a lethal weapon.

Serra's humility was already marked. He signed letters home "most unworthy priest." He was pierced by what Bonaventure called "a sword of compassionate sorrow." He had abandoned all the pretensions of the university life. But suddenly a good example, a zealous example, was not so good. A life was needlessly lost that day on the altar in Mexico City.

"*Domine, non sum dignus*" (Lord, I am not worthy), he must have whispered, kneeling to the empty nave.

Perhaps because of this terrible incident, Serra's superiors sent him away from the capital, farther and farther into the southern hinterlands of Mexico, places where there were more wild animals than men, and the men were nearly wild. Here Serra could shake off the demon eating at his soul—the fear that his goodness was not goodness at all, but punishing evil. The south was the place they hoped his unruly faith might, in even more wildness, be tamed.

In the 1760s, Serra wandered out of San Fernando. The mystifying southern journeys took him down old Indian trails, dusty roads of the Crown, mountain passes in searing sun, sweathouselike jungles, and in a bark on rivers. He covered an estimated 5,500 miles, much on foot, in sandals of two strips of leather, all the while putting up with a bad foot and infected leg skin. It also appears his childhood asthma returned during this wandering period. Yet he kept on.

In September 1763, Bishop Buenaventura Blanco y Helguera of Oaxaca unwittingly prepared the path for Serra's accelerating descent when he asked San Fernando for missionaries to come south and checkmate his city's renowned love of carnival (and debauchery) at the onset of the Easter season the following year. It was to be for Serra a most fateful journey.

The party had some time to kill, six months precisely, before reaching Oaxaca for Lent, which started March 1, 1764. Thus they set out to spring missions on various bishops and towns with little or no time to give advance notice. The first of these was in Puebla, founded in 1531 by one of Mexico's famed "Twelve Apostles"—Padre Toribio Motolinía. One of the most outspoken allies of Bartolomé de Las Casas in his vehement critique of early bloody Spanish suppressions of the Indians, Motolinía gained credibility with the indigenous population of Puebla due to his extreme sensitivity to native customs and faith patterns. He seems to have made good use of connections with the New Testament story of the gifts of the Magi to the newly born Christ. (Following a star to revelation was good Aztec sky gazing.)

Anthropologist Louise Burkhart is insightful about a late-sixteenth-century play about the Wise Men written in Nahuatl, at least in part by a surviving Aztec: "The drama turns the tables on the ethnicity of the principal characters in such a way that Herod comes off seeming like a rude and duplicitous Spaniard and the three Magi-like noble and courteous pre-Conquest lords. . . . So Herod is, in a sense, Cortés as well as Moteuczoma."

Motolinía, the first Franciscan to comment on the convergence of Nahua and Christian customs, observed that the practice of swearing by "the earth goddess" or gods in general in Aztec courts made a similar swearing on the Bible an easy transfer, and it's likely he had Indians in Puebla juridical disputes take oaths in the name of their own gods and "not those of the Christian religion, [so] that they would state the truth."

From Motolinía's Puebla, Serra and his cohorts headed east and north-east toward the Gulf of Mexico. There, for the first time in his missionary life, like the Jesuit Jacques Marquette a century before up north, Serra entered a river by canoe. Which river he entered is a matter of dispute. Serra called it Río de Los Mijes, which doesn't appear on any maps, then or now, but it seems likely it was the Papaloapan River, at least in the beginning, of Yucatán.

In Acayucan, the furthest south and east Serra ever got in Mexico, the Franciscan preached to a small community of some four hundred families, though he considered it "a very large town" for the remote area. It's not clear why Serra chose this off-the-beaten-path place, but it was there that something happened that would haunt him for years to come.

Greeting Serra and his companions at Acayucan was the painful out-cry of an Indian leader flogged for some "misdeed" (Geiger's word) at the very entrance to the town church. "I was witness to the fact," Serra declared years later. The Indian he called "a governor" and the overseer of the punishment "the alcalde mayor." This is a strange thing, as the governor would have been of higher rank than the mayor, which could mean either that Serra got the titles switched, or that the "misdeed" was a severe and probably public one, perhaps adultery discovered in public, serial drunkenness, or long-term embezzlement. He may also have mistreated Indians and been flogged by an Indian himself. There would have been few Spaniards in such a remote town.

After that stark moment, Serra and his confreres proceeded south and west down the Río de Lana, under cackle of macaws, toucans with beaks shaped like machetes, quetzal birds iridescent green in the lazy sun. It was a world festooned with sound, which grew as the foliage thickened. The snip of dragonflies, bees ahum, wasps and flies piercing the carcass of a dead tapir, the screech of kingfishers, the lute of canaries, and rasp of parrots, their eyes permanently circled and startled. Orchids sang, wild white lilies put out their tongues, birds of paradise nodded their spiky heads, bougainvillea crawled over the cottonwoods.

If the views and sounds were pleasurable, the canoes were not. They were dugouts and hard on the back and legs. No doubt Serra had Indians of the region along—Mijes or Zapotecs or Mixtecs—but all would have to have been given a paddle, especially through rapids. Priests stroked with Indians, and soon the river made them one sweating pull.

That pain was good. But there were other discomforts: "the excessive heat, the annoyance of flies, and the danger of alligators, without being able to disembark from the canoe." Palou said they faced "tigers and lions and snakes," but there are no tigers in the Americas (rather jaguars), and the lions would have been cougars. As for the ten-foot-long, sixty-pound boa constrictors, they are a nocturnal animal; chances are any Serra tripped over were half asleep in their weeklong engorgement of a crushed animal. The only real animal that came close to Serra in those eight days was probably a crocodile nudging the canoes, more in a traffic jam than hostility. Another annoyance was the mosquitoes, which bit the Franciscans raw when they stopped in lagoons. The river narrowed. Finally the Franciscans debarked near Villa Alta de San Ildefonso in the mountains, where they rested, put cooling clear salve from the agave plant on their mosquito sores, and then gave a weeklong mission, sending word to the bishop of Oaxaca that they would soon arrive. He sent back a crafty note that he was going to let them take the town by surprise with no formal welcoming, "a spiritual *coup d'état*," to catch Oaxacans before their indulgence in carnival when drunks could shoot people, men ran into the alleys with women they weren't married to, and Indians devoured hallucinogenic plants.

Walking to Antequera (the eighteenth-century name for Oaxaca) from Villa Alta, the threat didn't come from wildlife. The road was honeycombed with caves where thieves hid out and several merchants and at least one priest had been robbed and killed. So Serra took a freshly cut mountain road that led slightly south of Oaxaca through Santo Domingo Xagacia, Tlacolula, and the ancient Zapotec ruins of Mitla with their infinitesimal glass tiles fit without mortar.

The Franciscans then entered the Dominican stronghold of Oaxaca, a "fair and beautiful city to behold," according to the seventeenth-century English Dominican Thomas Gage. On the first day of Lent, March 1, they fanned out in pairs to three places of the provincial City of Light, probably in front of three of the most impressive churches in Mexico: the cathedral itself, Iglesia de Santo Domingo, and La Soledad. They tacked up a schedule of Masses, meditative sermons, and confessions on trees, springing an impromptu sermon on the joys of heaven or the terrors of hell. Speaking of Christ's love and how to live it, the "spiritual assault" had begun. Workers crushing the cochineal beetle for the distinctive crimson dye on Oaxacan fabrics looked up from their benches.

Oaxaca, even in the eighteenth century, was a place of relaxation and pleasure, with the mildest climate in Mexico; no surprise Cortés claimed his largest private tract of land there for himself. But the earth stretched in this place and buildings and faiths often fell to quakes. Other troubles brewed in paradise. Two years previous, in 1762, just as wheat was being harvested, the mayors (*alcáldes*) exhibited "cruelty dealing with indigenous workers" that caused a priest in Mitla to protest vehemently to the viceroy himself, embroiling Blanco and putting him at odds with the government. The year before Serra's arrival, an epidemic of smallpox spread throughout the central valley, "causing significant deaths." The province of Villa Alta—which Serra had just visited—had its Indian population cut by over 90 percent in a century, mostly by disease, to 20,800.

Trying to resuscitate the city's spiritual life was not a small challenge to Serra. Blanco gave him a secondary responsibility of creating a retreat for the Oaxaca diocesan priests, indicating their own dispirit at a time of epidemic, earthquake, and repression of Indians. Serra began most of his own mission preaching in the cathedral, itself a testimony to resurrection. The grand structure originally built within twenty years of Cortés's conquest (in the 1540s) had taken two hits from nature—the massive 1696 earthquake that practically destroyed it, and a second serious quake in 1714 that took down half-rebuilt walls. In 1733, it was finally rededicated, with a gloriously Baroque facade even more intricate than the ones Serra designed in the Sierra Gorda. Foliage and radiant lines fill every square inch around a dozen statues, like the ruins at Mitla, "creating a shimmering tapestry of exotic filigree in the sharp southern sun." Right over the entrance was a sight that lifted Serra's own spirits: the Assumption of the Blessed Mother into heaven, a dramatic scene of the Apostles looking up as God's mother rises bodily upward, all of it cut in stone by the master Oaxacan sculptor Tomás de Sigüenza. It gave an "authentic feeling of spiritual uplift," especially to someone as close to worshipping the Mother of God as God herself as Serra.

On one of the days leading up to Easter (April 22), Serra opened the screen of his confessional to the shadow of a woman. She was young, and her scarf did not hide her beauty. What she said made Serra sit up.

The woman, wiping her face of tears with the scarf, her voice cracking, told him she had been having an affair with a married man since she was fourteen. She was now twenty-eight, so the affair had been going on half her life. She said the man was well known in Antequera, in fact, a *regidor perpetual*, an alderman, a member of the city council appointed for life by the king of Spain. With a wife back in Spain and seven children, the man had been carrying on a double life for many years, and it appears the woman may have served as his second wife, or at least mistress of his house. It seems likely she was accepted in Oaxacan society and perhaps few knew the unusual origins or status of their love.

Based on municipal records in Oaxaca, she was probably María Contreras y Burgoa. Transfixed by Serra's (or one of the other missionary's) sermons, and overcome by "great grief," she was determined "to leave such a dangerous relationship and companion."

Before Serra could give her absolution and move on to the next peni-tent, María told Serra of the danger she was facing; the *regidor* had threat-ened to kill himself or her if she left him. That revelation put Serra in more than a spiritually discomforting situation; these were life-and-death considerations. He felt compelled to find a safe place for her.

And he did. Somehow Serra got María Contreras out of the *regidor*'s mansion and into the home of "a devout woman, one of the leading per-sons of the city, who received her with pleasure."

While the name of the devout woman is lost to history, the married man was almost certainly Mathías Cortabarría, whose life story neither Palou nor Geiger would divulge, even if they knew it. He was born in Spain in the north-central Basque region of Guipuzcoa in the town of Villa de Oñate, the son of Joachím de Cortabarría and María Sarmiento Mijangos y Guzmán. When he was a teenager, he was injured in an acci-dent that left him in serious pain. He had four sons and three daughters, probably with his wife, Josefa Agüero (though it is possible some were by María Contreras). Josefa came with a dowry of four thousand pesos, and she liked nice things, as she had six thousand pesos' worth of jewelry and clothes. His brother, Don José Cortabarría, was a priest. Why and when Mathías came to New Spain is uncertain, but in 1750, the year he began his illicit affair, records show he covered the loan or the fees of a María Contreras y Burgoa to the tune of one thousand pesos paid to the Convent of Santa Catalina Sena in Oaxaca. María was a recent widow of Alonzo de los Reyes. (She was fourteen at the time, not an unusual age for marriage in eighteenth-century Mexico, though losing her spouse that quickly must have been traumatic—and impoverishing—enough to thrust her to a convent.)

In any case, when Mathias Cortabarría realized María Contreras had left him, he tried to abduct her from the older woman's home, but failed. Despairing, he grabbed a thick rope, walked in what must have been a feverish trance to the place of her hideout, threw the rope up to the iron bars of her window, and hanged himself, "delivering his soul to the demons." The date of Cortabarría's death is listed as April 5, though he probably hung dead through the night; the next morning "the body of the miserable creature was found hanging from the bars." That day, as if the God of both Zapotecs and Christians were in a choleric fit as to what to do with the man, "the city was shaken by a great earthquake which frightened everyone."

The pressures on Cortabarría were significant. He had lost his lover of fourteen years who functioned as a real wife. His own priest brother had been telling him for fourteen years that he was living in sin (divorce or even annulments being impossible for Catholics at the time). A new priest had come to town and not only reinforced this opprobrium, but acted like a rival, essentially stealing his woman. Add to that the fact that Cortabarría's *testimonio* (or will) showed him to be, though a man of means and property (worth one hundred thousand pesos), in serious debt to many creditors, an extreme embarrassment to a tax collector. He expresses in the will his doubt as to what to give to whom. The will itself, signed on March 22, two weeks before his death, indicates a rush to judgment—he knew he was going to die, and probably by his own hand. (This also indicates that Serra heard the fateful confession sooner rather than later in the seven weeks of the mission in Antequera, probably in the first two weeks.)

Cortabarría's *testimonio* is deeply sad in parts, and affecting in the circumstance: "I give back to Our Lord God, our Creator and Forgiver, what He has given to me. He knows the infinite price of my precious blood and body on earth." Records state he made a final confession, took Communion, even Last Rites (before he went off to hang himself). Did Serra oblige him, or did his own brother? Would Serra have known the man was going to kill himself, and in a sense, cooperated? If the suicide was publicly acknowledged, Cortabarría would not have been buried in a Catholic cemetery, but the cause of his death is not in his death record, an omission that preserved the burial rights. In fact, because of his position, the body of Don Mathías Cortabarría lay in state in the cathedral for several days and then was buried in the Compañía de Jesus, a cemetery near the *zócalo*.

The public reaction to this tragedy was fierce. Palou admits "a general feeling of horror and alarm," which the earthquake hardly pacified. Cortabarría, apparently, was loved and admired; his right-hand man in the government, Juan de Galardi, quit his post the day his patron took his own life. But "most noticeably affected" was María Contreras, who cut off her long hair, garbed herself in sackcloth, and wandered through Antequera "with loud wails asking pardon for her sins and the unholy life she had lived." She was said to imitate St. Margaret of Cortona, the thirteenth-century patron saint of those unjustly accused. The whole "strange conversion," as Palou called it, caused a flood of conversions, presumably meditating on the fate of "that unfortunate man." The cathedral swelled in the mission's last days.

Serra wouldn't have dismissed the conversions. Astoundingly, Serra's first biographer and close friend passes the whole drama off as one of several "minor incidents" in Serra's life, stopping discussion. Nothing about the family or identity of the suicide, or the ultimate disposition of his lost love, and not a word about Serra's reaction to any of it. Geiger is even more mum than Palou.

The silence on the record in these matters blares more in Oaxaca than in Mexico City, because Palou tells us the whole city of Oaxaca was in shock; most probably knew the story and divined the Franciscan's role in it. Maybe people flocked to the cathedral out of bewilderment as much as guilt. It's a wonder Serra could even carry on for two more weeks of the mission. Was he involved in the funeral or burial? Whoever did so had to completely disregard the traditional shunning of a suicide. How did that go down to a pious man? Could he have appealed to Cortabarría? Did he even try? Or had he left the city councilman to his despair because of something he could hardly speak to himself? One does not have to posit a romantic attachment between Serra and the penitent young woman to sense he was concerned for her, spent time out of the confessional with her, and risked his own life in challenging Cortabarría. Time was short, the emotions in this intense situation were high, and so were the stakes. It would be strange indeed if Serra did not feel something very strong for this woman, and there is nothing else to call such a thing but love.

Serra must have gone through the motions after the death of Cortabarría and the apparent breakdown of María Contreras. For Mass, he entered the cathedral, with its striking "Holy Spirit" dove in the rose window behind the altar darkening. He spoke more slowly than normal at the pulpit, his deep voice ever deeper, quieter, so that people strained to hear him, something that didn't often happen to a man with such a rich voice. During Mass, when he looked up at the magnificent bronze cast of Mary, her arms raised above her head, entreating heaven, could he have conjured the other Mary, María, nearly bald, her hair in patches, her brown eyes now looking out from caverns?

The great Oaxaca cathedral organ, placed strangely up a curvaceous balcony in 1713 (Serra's birth year) halfway down the nave, resounded. It was Carlos Seixas's urgent, anxious *Toccata em re menor*, the music of a Spaniard who died young (thirty-eight) when Serra was still young himself on Mallorca. Such music could have rattled him.

There were other ripple effects from the scandal. Before the year was out, Antequera's mayor was fired for the continued exploitation of the Indian. And soon after that, Archbishop Blanco, who had first invited Serra and the Franciscans to "hurl pious ejaculations . . . like weapons" (Palou's words) at his flock, died suddenly of a heart attack. His replacement, the queen of Spain's own confessor, Bishop Miguel Anselmo Alvarez de Abreu y Valdéz, a brilliant professor of canon law at the University of Seville, had to oversee the expulsion of the Jesuits, of whom he was fond, from Oaxaca, "which worsened his health and took him to his grave." This all happened within two years of Serra's spiritual assault on Oaxaca.

Almost exactly one year after the Cortabarría incident, an unidentified woman was found keeled over dead at the gate of the Virgin of La Defensa chapel, adjacent to the convent of San Francisco, where Serra had stayed. Was she María Contreras?

Serra arrived back at San Fernando in June 1764 exhausted in body and spirit. At this nadir of his spiritual life, he was given back the job as adviser to novices. For about a year, Serra didn't venture outside the cloister. Almost certainly to shake him out of his despair, in fall of 1765 Serra was sent to the Huasteca, a vast area in the dry, flat center of Mexico north of the Sierra Gorda. There he ministered for seven months, reaching Valles, the furthest town north on the Mexican mainland Serra would ever reach, a remote region dominated primarily by Otomi Indians. No mission had been conducted in the area in forty years. Going there was the equivalent of going to cleanse one's soul in the desert, where Christ went after his revelatory day with John the Baptist, and the place he was tempted by the devil three times.

After the first Huasteca mission in an unnamed town, an epidemic broke out and killed sixty people. By the time Serra got to the second town, its inhabitants were up in arms, fearful of the bad fate the Franciscans were bringing and yelling that they turn around and leave. Yet some insisted he stay.

Shortly after he had lifted the cup saying Mass there and then drained it of what was now to him Christ's blood, he collapsed. "Some heavy weight [had] fallen into his stomach as if it were lead," said Palou. Serra's altar wine had been poisoned. Altar servers carried him into the sacristy, where he grabbed his throat, choking. At first he declined an antidote, but after a while took some oil that helped neutralize the poison. When asked why he declined the first offer, he quoted Mark: "And if they shall drink any deadly thing it shall not hurt them" (16:18). And then he explained that since he had just taken Communion, "How could you ask me to take so nauseating a drink after tasting the divine Morsel?"

Who was it out there who wanted his life?

Shaken, barely given a chance to recuperate, Serra was abruptly sent back into the Sierra Gorda, not for pleasure, but to investigate the strange case of a woman in Tancoyol who was accused of making spells and poisoning people. Ordered there as a commissary of the Inquisition, he took leave of his fellows on a mission at Aquismón in May 1766 and traveled alone into the mountains.

Of the three cases Serra worked as a *comisario* for the Tribunal (all in Mexico), two came to nothing. The trail of the 1752 instance of devil worshippers in the Sierra Gorda goes quickly cold. In 1756, he failed to turn up any credible evidence of a possible devil pact by one Antonio Bonifacio, who lived near Jalpan. Serra had been assigned the case, and he seems to have realized its thinness. But there was a third, and this one stuck. The accused's name was María Pasquala de Nava, and she lived in the nearby village of Valle de Maíz. Her accuser was one Dominga de Jesús, who had sought a cure from her as a herbalist for bronchitis, but felt she had been intentionally poisoned nearly to death by Pasquala, who supposedly confessed, though the confession was unsigned and therefore invalid. Nevertheless, Pasquala was in prison when Serra arrived to interrogate her.

After initial questioning, Serra was dubious of the charges brought against her. "That does not seem like an adequate reason for your arrest," he told her, "and for you to be held in prison in irons, and therefore, in accordance with God and your conscience, tell us: Do you think there is another reason?"

Pasquala had told her first interrogator, an army lieutenant, that she was neither a *bruja* (a witch) nor a *hechicera* (purveyor of black magic), though she used herbs for cures. But Serra bore down: "Have you made a pact with or had communication with the Devil?"

María Pasquala must have hesitated before responding, "No, but it's true that *el Demonio* appeared before me several times in the form of a Pames Indian." Pasquala herself was a mulatta.

This statement astounded Serra, but what concerned him most was not the satanic vision, but whether the woman had promised to do evil for him: "Have you made a pact . . . with the same Enemy?"

"No," said the woman. She admitted he'd asked for her soul, for clothing and other support, but she turned him down.

Serra doubled back. "Have you executed any *hechizos* or *brujerías*?"

"No," said María Pasquala.

That, apparently, was that. Serra was satisfied that, whatever harm she had done, stupidly or not with bad medicine, she wasn't involved in a diabolical agreement. Thus he made no referral to the Holy Tribunal. But two days later, nagged perhaps by the unsigned confession in which she had admitted to a demonic pact, he decided one more time to revisit the matter by reading to her the original confession. During the recitation of the rather long document, Serra often halted, saying, "Can you hear me? Do you understand me?" Or: "Did you do that? Did you declare that?" He read the unsettling contents slowly, clearing his throat at times. The document included confessing that the devil had won her soul, commanding her to poison Dominga de Jesús because she was a good singer; that with herbs she "had killed a man . . . as the devil had commanded"; that she had slept with the devil; that he took her to a cave where she sucked the blood of unbaptized children; and that "El Balletón" told her to get a bone out of the cemetery, to stop praying the Rosary, to confess no more than two sins, and to stick Communion under the altar rail.

María suddenly seemed to reverse direction, admitting to everything in her original confession, except for sleeping with the devil and sucking children's blood. She clarified that she stuck Communion under the rail to clear her throat (*hechar flema por la boca*). Pasquala's fate was sealed. She was now not just a self-avowed Satanist, she had admitted murder (though she said she no longer did such things). Serra, however, did not judge her; he sent his finding to Mexico City.

Troubled by these proceedings, wondering what was mania and what was pure evil, Serra met up with Franciscans who had come with him to the Huasteca and were now walking home to Mexico City. It took them a month. During this journey he and his confreres were put up for the night by an old man and his wife and son, poor, but living in a spotlessly clean home. They later recommended the lodging to muleteers, who scoffed that there was no abode anywhere near where the Franciscans had been hosted. Serra was convinced he had had a miraculous encounter with the Holy Family (novelist Willa Cather would make use of it). Following on the Pasquala affair, perhaps the vision, if not hallucination, of good in the Huasteca was one he badly needed.

But what of María Pasquala? On the night of December 11, 1766, judged guilty by the Inquisition "of being a true witch who made a pact with the Devil," she was discovered just outside her cell, at death's door from a "grave accident." She died the next day.

The news of María's death must have crushed Serra's spirit, given how carefully and deliberately he had questioned her. The suicidal deaths in Oaxaca and Mexico City, too, flapped their dark wings inside him. His mission was to elevate souls, not induce further suffering and untimely death. One pictures him flat on the floor of his own cell, as if fallen for the third time, staring at the ceiling, everyone else asleep as he wondered, *What good is the Good if so many are lost?*

CHAPTER TEN

BAJA

Preach the Gospel at all times, and when necessary, use words.
—ST. FRANCIS OF ASSISI

Ruins of San Fernando Velicatá, Serra's one Baja mission.

Between February and July 1767, tacking up notices of a mission ninety miles north of the capital in remote Ixmiquilpan, Serra received word to return to the College of San Fernando at once. His foot was now pure agony; the heat and lack of sustenance for his thin frame made him dizzy. The walk back was slow, but he probably welcomed the return to the cloister. He was tired of the road leading nowhere.

But this was somewhere else indeed, the turning point of his life. At the age of fifty-four, an age by which most people in the eighteenth century were retired if not dead, Junípero Miguel Serra was ordered to what turned out to be his dream work and vocation in his dream place. On his arrival at San Fernando, Father García wasted no time in telling him: *Fray*

Junípero, usted va a California. You are going to California. Serra's initial reaction could have been silence, and a removal of his glasses.

Before him was a vision of finally meeting Indians no one else had met, souls no one else had saved, a land no one else from Europe had really explored and lived in. The tumblers in his mind may already have begun to turn. Ideal communities could spring into being up and down the California coast, heavenly spots, places where he would muster all the energy, learning, and lessons from success and failure he had sustained from life in Mallorca and Mexico's mountains, jungles, and capital city.

But salvation was not the real reason Spain was sending the Franciscans to California. Salvation would be the sheep's clothing. The wolf of conquest was underneath.

As he prepared to cross the Sea of Cortez in 1748, what did Serra, or any other Spaniard at the time, know about this strange, largely mythical land of California?

The first appearance in Spanish writings of the word "California" was, fittingly, a work of the imagination, a novel published in Seville in 1510 about a knight named Esplandián (*Las Sergas de Esplandián*, or *The Labors of the Very Brave Knight Esplandián*). The book was actually a sequel to a four-volume series begun in the 1490s during Columbus's first voyages, highly popular tales of Gulliver-like adventures of a chivalrous knight named Amadis. The Spanish public was captivated by these books—filled as they were with confrontations with everything from Moors to griffins. Their author was a former Moor slayer himself, Garci Rodríguez de Montalvo, who had fought during the final expulsion of the Muslims from Granada and was knighted for his efforts. Soon Montalvo was inflating his exploits in fiction derived from folk stories of the *Reconquista*, as well as tales told by Columbus and other early Spanish voyagers to the Indies west and east. One of Montalvo's most avid readers was none other than Hernan Cortés, the conqueror of Mexico.

The conflation of the Moors and Indians and the rumors of blood lines both Arab and Jewish inside Serra—combined with his spiritual masters' (St. Francis and Raymond Lull) fascination with the Other—would soon come to life halfway around the world. But in the imagination, it had already gathered in this first fictive sputtering of the word "California." The root word of the Golden State's nomenclature lies in the Arabic term *khalifa*, or caliph, ruler in English, as well as the novel's outsized heroine. Montalvo injects plenty of conversion fervor into Esplandián, Amadis's son. The story encounters a place "on the right hand of the Indies [where] there was an island called California . . . very close to the region of Earthly Paradise." This California is populated entirely by black women with gold armor—gold was equated with the dream of California right at its inception—ruled by a queen named Calafia. This rival island to Lesbos—there were no men anywhere on it—sports women of "energetic bodies and courageous, ardent hearts." Things heat up quickly, however, when the women of California hear about the great conflict of the age halfway around the world—Muslims versus Christians. Queen Calafia, for some unstated reason, feels for the Moors—maybe it's their dark skin—and jumps in with her griffins, impressed men, and women warriors against the Christians, though "she did not know what Christians were." But when Calafia ultimately falls for Esplandián in a love-struck scuffle, she tells her ladies to cease and desist. Naturally Calafia converts to Christianity. (At the memorable outset of *Don Quixote*, Cervantes has a petty inquisitor and barber conducting a miniature auto-da-fé of a pile of Quixote's romance books, which have "dried out his brain and lost his sanity," a satire of not just the Inquisition but all chivalric novels in general. The Amadis volumes are spared the fire, but *Esplandián* is tossed in.)

Conversion susceptibility in Esplandián's mythical California must have intrigued Serra. To an island son, California was also Mallorca, a better Mallorca in a better world. He would not be the first or last person in history (or myth—Odysseus!) to leave home in order to find it again.

Serra would probably have read Montalvo and seen California as an island on a map. There were many so drawn. Following reports by the Spanish explorers Juan Rodríguez Cabrillo and Sebastián Vizcaíno, who made brief visits to upper (or "new") California in 1542 and 1602–3, respectively, California was variously pictured: by Anna Seile as a huge dagger-shaped island off the coast of Mexico (1663); like a carob pod with "toes" by French cartographer Nicholas Sanson (1656); and like a bone in George Shelvocke's *A Voyage Round the World* (1726).

The first landing of the Spaniards on the shores of California was the result of a mutiny. In 1533, ordered by Cortés to explore the Pacific Ocean, his cousin Diego de Becerra lost command of his ship—and his life—not long out of port in the Sea of Cortez (or the Gulf of California). The rebel pilot, Fortún Jiménez, guided the vessel to what he thought was an island but was actually the Baja Peninsula, inhabited at the time by seventy thousand Indians. Attempting to land, Jiménez and twenty of his rebel crew were cut down by the astonished natives wielding arrows and clubs.

Reports of loads of pearls in the Indians' canoes stoked the old conquistador himself to make a voyage. But it would turn out not much different from the famous "Lost Colony" of Roanoke established in 1585—fifty years later—in Virginia. Pearl-mad, Cortés reached the southern tip of Baja near present-day La Paz in 1535 and placed a small group of settlers along the bay. After walking around slashing trees with his sword, Cortés created a little ceremony and read from an unrolled parchment proclaiming himself "Governor for His Majesty of those said lands." But the peace of one day did not last. Lacking food and drinking water in the dry terrain and after several attacks by the Indian inhabitants, the first Baja colony (called Santa Cruz by Cortés) withered and was abandoned in one year. It was not restarted for a century and a half.

Spanish appetites, however, were whetted. Serra knew about the 1542 Cabrillo expedition, the first to spot Alta (or Upper) California. Juan Rodríguez Cabrillo, a native of Seville, had been part of the conquest of Cuba. Cabrillo sailed on June 27, 1542, from Navidad on Mexico's west coast and reached the Baja mainland one week later, on July 3. He would have known that the just completed Coronado expedition inland in the areas of today's Arizona and Sonoran provinces of Mexico searching for cities of gold had come up empty, at least of gold. Wallace Stegner has reflected on Coronado's quixotic mission as the watermark for future such infatuations: "The fact is, it [the West] has been as notable for mirages as for the realization of dreams. Illusion and mirage have been built into it since Coronado came seeking the Seven Cities of Cibola in 1540. Coronado's failure was an early, spectacular trial run for other and humbler failures."

Farther north, Cabrillo had come across the finest harbor any Spaniard had yet seen in the New World, San Miguel (today's San Diego). On shore, he gave gifts to three somewhat frightened Indians. But a party of Spaniards trying to fish in a rowboat came under a hail of arrows, which wounded three. Cabrillo welcomed two Indian boys onboard, gave each a shirt, and sent them off. This gesture was met in kind; three adult Indian men risked entering the two-ton Spanish galleon *San Salvador* and tried to explain, by gestures, the root of their concerns. Men they called *Guacamal* were running around, they tried to act out, with crossbows and swords and threw lances: "They indicated that they were afraid because Spaniards were killing many Indians in the region."

After harboring a night in San Pedro (which he called the Bahía de los Fumos, or Bay of Smokes, because of the Indian-controlled fires), another notable California bay, Santa Monica, sheltered its first European. Then Cabrillo sailed to the lush middle coast of Alta California, viewing through his spyglass "an Indian village close to the sea, with large houses like those of New Spain." A navy of native canoes lay in the Santa

Barbara harbor that the Spaniards named Canoe Town (Pueblo de las Canoas).

Refreshed and restocked by the industrious Chumash, sun-soaked by their east–west coastal declination, the little Spanish flotilla followed the coast to its farther western jut, dubbed Point Concepción. Winds forced Cabrillo back south to the Santa Barbara Channel. But he tried north again, and, like many explorers before and after him, Cabrillo got lost in fog, missing the enshrouded entrance to San Francisco Bay. Reversing direction, the fog burned off at Monterey Bay, Cabrillo marveled at its vast crescent and the mountains now at the beginning of winter dusted with snow. He dubbed them the *Sierra Nevada* (or Snowy Mountains—a term that stuck for the higher mountains inland and not the coastal range Cabrillo viewed). Going ashore at San Miguel Island, Cabrillo fell on some jagged rocks and on January 3, 1543, was done in by his own green, smoking, gangrenous leg. No one knows exactly where his bones are interred; no one lives there today, though there is a Cabrillo marker. Thus lay the first documented European "settler" in Upper California until Serra's arrival two centuries later.

Serra would have one more Alta California explorer's notes: those of Sebastián Vizcaíno.

After a series of unsuccessful attempts to chart and secure California by ships coming from the Philippines, in 1602, Vizcaíno was given the nod to retrace Cabrillo's route from New Spain itself with three sizable ships and two hundred sailors. Though he had been a fighter in the conquest of Portugal in 1580, Vizcaíno was a merchant by instinct and profession in Manila and Mexico. At Cabo San Lucas, he stocked up at his own six-year-old general store (named for all its starry hope of reconciliation, Nueva Andalucía). He had licenses in his hand for mining precious metals and pearl diving. When he met natives, he thought them "quite amenable to conversion."

One doubts Vizcaíno asked them, but he did not mince words about what was the attraction—the sight of the Blessed Mother: "They were very friendly to us, and when I showed them the image of Our Lady they were drawn to it and wanted to join us. They were very attentive to the sacrifice of the Mass."

Still, the real import of his encounter was not solely, or even primarily, the Blessed Mother. The natives "are very knowledgeable about silver and gold" and knew exactly where it lay. Thus were riches monetary and spiritual welded at the beginning of the discovery of California.

This scene took place in Monterey Bay with Mass under a large oak by the water. Though warned not to, Vizcaíno went deeper into the country and, with three Carmelite priests aboard (who thought they were going to the Philippines) and bereft of language, he took advantage of the ritualistic symbolism of the Mass, especially of the eating of unleavened bread and the singing. These, more than anything the friars could possibly explain, attracted the first California tribes encountering Vizcaíno's Spaniards. (As a reward to the Carmelites, Vizcaíno named a particularly beautiful stretch of coast dotted with wind-blown cypresses Carmel.)

Earlier, on November 12, 1602, Vizcaíno had landed in San Diego Harbor, declaring it "the best to be found in all the South Sea . . . protected on all sides." He had Mass said there while a hundred Indians "yelling noisily at us" peered down from a hill. Though they brandished bows and arrows, this group of Kumeyaay were less threatening to Vizcaíno than their ancestors had been a half century before to Cabrillo.

Going north, on Santa Catalina Island, Vizcaíno encountered a carved idol, with "two horns, no head, a dog at its feet, and many children painted all around it." It was likely a benign, if not familial, figure, but Vizcaíno took it for an image of the devil and planted a cross and Jesus's name "on the head of the demon," assuring the Indians this was a good, not diabolical, image. But "How much the residents understood or agreed with this theological discourse is not clear."

In the Santa Barbara Channel a violent rainstorm caused all to pray to St. Barbara (it was December 3, one day before her feast day). The intercession worked, the storm abated, and Vizcaíno named the Chumash settlement Santa Barbara. By March 1603, Vizcaíno's ships, decimated by scurvy and bronchial infections, docked in Acapulco.

One of the Carmelites on the Vizcaíno expedition, Antonio de la Ascensión, became an enthusiast from his glimpses of California, convinced it should be an end in itself and not just a watering hole for traders to Asia. "The entire realm of the Californias can be pacified and settled," he wrote in a 1620 report. But though he was not naïve (noting "veteran soldiers skilled in arms and seamanship" should be recruited), Ascensión makes no bones about who should be in charge, and why: "The General, Captains, soldiers, and all others who go on this expedition must be given express orders to hold themselves in strict obedience to and comply with the religious who accompany them." Ascensión insisted, "Without their orders, counsel, or recommendations, no act of war or any other grievance shall be committed against the heathen Indians, even if they might provoke it." This was both a blueprint for peaceful conquest and a warning shot that if the fathers were not in control and the military ascendant "all efforts will fail, and time and money will be wasted."

Ascensión, understanding implicitly the difficulties of evangelizing people whose beliefs were otherwise, underscored how the expedition to California had to take place: "One must live among the Indians with great circumspection, vigilance, precaution and astuteness, but also with a kind and loving watchfulness. They should be treated with love and affection and rewarded with gifts." Guarded love, one might say, a tragically oxymoronic notion.

These reports of Cabrillo, Vizcaíno, and Father Ascensión about California, along with Montalvo's riotous fiction, would have colored Serra's assumptions about the far-off place to which he was inching closer, day by day.

The two chief reasons Spain finally decided to take on California after many a false start and ship lost in fog were political and geopolitical. The first reason had to do with the vacuum of leadership created when the Jesuits were expelled—a vacuum, of course, Spain itself had created. The Jesuits were accused of hoarding wealth, a wild assertion, at least in Baja, where the fifteen Jesuit missions "were set in the midst of one of the most inhospitable and barren territories in the whole realm of New Spain, with rains almost non-existent and natives difficult."

The crisis with the Jesuits had been brewing almost from the day Ignatius Loyola had conceived them in the sixteenth century. Ignatius himself had been pestered by the Inquisition, and that crude experience steeled the rank and file: "no Jesuit . . . ever sat on an inquisitorial tribunal." Jesuit creativity and catholicity in offering free education almost from their inception stimulated interest throughout the lower and middle classes of Europe—and raised eyes among the elite at the arming of the common people with intellectual tools such as the dignity and equality of man, not to mention grammatical knowledge of Romance and Germanic languages. Their anti-cloister, work-in-the-world ethic, while a handy counterpoint to Protestant fury with clerical pretensions, stirred envy: "It was not surprising that the Society soon attracted resentment from friars for what could be regarded as willful selectivity from past disciplines—Jesuits did not always help themselves by their patronizing attitude toward other organizations, an unfortunate side effect of the fact that they were very well trained and mostly very clever."

The secret expulsion declaration of the king of Spain on February 27, 1767, was issued without explanation—not even to the pope. The order was not to be questioned, though many of Spain's highest authorities charged with enforcing it, such as Gaspar de Portolá in Baja, were troubled. Eminent people in other orders also whispered their disagreement, including the Dominican bishop of Oaxaca, who had a heart attack in the wake of the order to expel many of his personal friends. Even Serra, whose questions to Spain's representatives in Baja were met with stone silence, was confounded.

On Christmas Eve that year, the viceroy of New Spain, the Marquis Carlos de Croix, confessed to his brother that the enforced silence he ordered "of this ticklish business" was due to the expulsion's extreme unpopularity: "Everyone is still weeping for them [the Jesuits], at which there is no need for surprise. They were absolute masters of the hearts and consciences of all the inhabitants." He also adds the Jesuit properties, now in the coffers of the Spanish government, were worth "a considerable sum."

The Jesuit stamp on Baja had been recent. In 1697, the great California enthusiast Juan María de Salvatierra established what became mission headquarters for all of California at Loreto (until Carmel replaced it in 1774). Facing a population of fifty thousand natives in Baja, Salvatierra exclaimed, "The word of God sinks into their soul as the rain does the earth," amused so by an October 23 downpour that he called out to his fellow Jesuits as he ran from one tree to another, "It never rains in California!"

The second great stimulus to the drive to California came in a January 23, 1768, dispatch from the minister of state in Madrid, the Marqués de Grimaldi, received by mounted courier as José de Gálvez traveled in carriage from Guadalajara to San Blas. Grimaldi was worried about intelligence from the Spanish ambassador in Moscow: "The Russians on various occasions have made different attempts to facilitate communication with the Americas. . . . They have arrived on the mainland, having made a landing in a place that appeared to be populated by savages whom they fought, resulting in the death of 300 Russians." Grimaldi thought "new expeditions" were in the works "to acquire a new branch of Commerce which they flatter themselves to be very useful despite the great distance in land." The king himself had told Grimaldi to get this message specifically to "the governor appointed to California" (Portolá), via the viceroy, to act with "vigilance and attention . . . in monitoring the attempts which the Russians could make there [in California], frustrating these as much as possible." In short, Spain feared Russia would swallow Alta California before it did.

In fact, Russia never really threatened the West Coast. By the time of Fort Ross's establishment in 1812 north of San Francisco, with its signature windmill, the Spanish Franciscans had been in Upper California for forty years and had founded twenty of their twenty-one missions. If anything, it could be argued Spain's surging presence on the Sun Coast accelerated Russian interest, rather than impeded it, though the interest was more mercenary than military. Russian traders certainly were favored at Spanish mission ports in both Californias, at least by the padres and Indians.

In 1763, Catherine the Great, Russia's ambitious empress, proclaimed her goodwill to the Aleuts of Alaska, only 650 miles east at Unalaska. But the threat of famine was probably a greater incentive than expansion or trade interests. The Russians were already on a remote frontier in Siberia, with long punishing winters and little food. If Siberians were starving, the Russian settlers across the Bering weren't much better off. So desperate was Nikolai Rezanov, the early governor of Russian Alaska's capital at Sitka, to find grain when he pulled into port at San Francisco with a scurvy-ridden crew in 1806, instead of a battle he proposed marriage to María Concepción Argüello, the teenage daughter of the Spanish commander. He also paid three times the going rate (three pesos versus one) for a *fanega* of grain.

In a sense, even China was involved in this "marriage" of Spain and Russia out west. A robe made of sea otter was the prized possession of the Mandarins, and the sea otter fur was considered the finest in the world—dense, extremely soft, longer-haired than the river otter's, and water-resistant. It also had a luminous buff-to-gold color. According to an aficionado of the time, William Sturges, only two things were more attractive in the world than a sea otter: "a beautiful lady and a lovely infant."

But a large cost, as always, was exacted of the natives. The pre-contact population of Aleuts was twenty-five thousand, but Old World diseases derived from Russia killed 80 percent of Aleuts within two generations of Vitus Bering's exploration of North America. By 1811, the annual haul was 8,118 otter pelts, a depletion so severe the Aleuts rose up in rebellion; they were quickly suppressed. The Russians got their grain and pelts, as did the Chinese, and John Jacob Astor—who owned one of the Boston whalers in partnership with the Russians—wound his watch.

There may have been a third reason the Spanish resurrected their presence in Baja. The Jesuit expulsion had stoked the serious uprising of downtrodden Indian mineworkers in Sonora and Guanajuato. José de Gálvez, considered by his biographer "the most able representative of the Spanish Crown in New Spain during the 18th century" was rushed in to put it down. Possessing as much vision as iron fist—a sort of Napoleon figure who took a mile for every bureaucratic inch he was given—Gálvez (and his royal overlords) may have seen in California a way to start anew after the desperate misery of Guanajuato, to which they added a good deal of blood. This motive was aligned with Serra's, whom he would direct into California.

In 1765, faced with a failing economy and effectively broke, Spain made Gálvez visitor-general of public finance in New Spain and sent him on a fateful troubleshooting mission to Mexico City. At the time, defense of New Spain was very weak, and its oversight of trade equally shaky. Spain was losing one million pesos a year from smuggling in New Spain alone, with twelve million lost in all its American possessions. Of thirty-five million pesos' worth of precious metals coming from the New World, only about half was reaching Spain. Quickly, Gálvez brought in more defense forces.

But Gálvez took other measures that were manifestly unpopular, especially raising taxes. In 1767, miners at Zacatecas and Pachuca (mostly Indians) rebelled. Rushed to Guanajuato, Gálvez was guarded by the same troops who were ushering the expelled Jesuits from Mexico City and Puebla. Gálvez wrote Croix a patently misleading note, hoping to fill "the heart of the gentle viceroy with suspicion as to the true nature of the commotions." Gálvez meant the Jesuits themselves, and not their expulsion, and he certainly didn't point out that the masses were angry over the crushing new taxation, as angry as the Boston colonists at the time.

The first major mass disorder occurred on May 10, 1767, at Cerro de San Pedro near San Luis Potosí, where an official reading an order about "vagabonds" was nearly stoned to death by a crowd; he was saved at the last minute by a priest. On August 7, Gálvez hung eleven rioters, putting their heads on pikes. A revolt leader in nearby San Nicolás was drawn and quartered. At San Francisco, forty miles from Potosí, a Jesuit priest, leading the rebellion, was arrested and adjudged by his bishop "insane" (which probably saved his life). Violence spread to Valladolid (now Morelia) and farther west to Uruapan, where the local *alcalde*, Felipe de Neve (who later clashed with Serra as governor of California), was driven out by a mob. Shaking his fist vehemently from a balcony in the thick of the uprising, Gálvez shouted "God always punishes rebellion." When it was over, the Uprising of 1767 left nearly one thousand Indians killed, wounded, or punished.

Gálvez's ruthlessness did not go unquestioned. An observer wrote, "These punishments horrified the entire kingdom, accustomed as it was to see only convicted criminals led to the scaffold," where Gálvez would at times give a speech, affecting a "feigned piety," bursting into tears. But this observer's commentaries over "this peculiar minister" remained anonymous. From the Crown's point of view, Gálvez was a hero. He had, in fact, put down an armed rebellion; the Indians and workers who organized them had demanded at one point not just the restoration of the right to bear arms, but independence and the option to practice their native religion (one can only surmise after the difficult adaptation to Catholicism and reliance on the Jesuit padres the confusion and betrayal Christian Indians must have felt at the expulsion of their pastors). In many ways, the Uprising of 1767 was a bloody rehearsal of the War of Independence from Spain thirty years later.

Call it irony or personal redemption, Gálvez now focused on California.

On July 14, 1767, only dimly aware of the magnitude of the uprisings around New Spain, Junípero Serra and some compatriots could hardly contain their excitement when given a farewell by the guardian at San Fernando, Father José García, who blessed them saying, "You go, beloved Fathers and Brothers, with the blessing of God and Our Holy Father, St. Francis, to work in that mystic vineyard of California." García announced Serra as the new president of missions in that vineyard. Fifteen other Franciscans were chosen to accompany him six hundred miles across the Sea of Cortez, including his fellow Mallorcans Palou and Juan Crespí. They all kissed García's hand in farewell; Serra and the guardian broke down in *un abrazo más fuerte*, knowing "that goodbye was for eternity." A crowd had gathered, shouting *A Dios!* as the Gray Robes mounted their mules and horses, some destined to go "as far as the Golden Gate," though indeed the only thing golden in San Francisco Bay at the time were the pelts of the sea otters and the sun in the eyes of the Miwok.

Serra's group traveled about fifteen to twenty miles a day, faster than normal, pushed by their adrenaline, pulled by the Jesuit vacuum. They were traveling the famed El Camino Real (the King's Highway) beginning in Mexico City and continuing to the coast at San Blas that led across the water to and into California. Briefly, they rested at Santa Cruz in Querétaro, washing and refreshing themselves in water from the old city's magnificent ninety-six-foot-high aqueduct, resting under one of its seventy-four arches. There Serra met the great explorer-friar Francisco Garcés, who would travel the first overland route from New Spain through Arizona to Alta California with Juan Bautista de Anza. Serra's party proceeded through the *bajio* (a place of abundant farms, termed Mexico's breadbasket) and León before stopping for a few days of a mission in Guadalajara, then a town of twenty thousand (and today 1.5 million, Mexico's second largest city). Near an old bridge before the entrance to the city, they passed a mason making a small shrine to the Blessed Mother; he carved the year Serra passed—1767. The friars ascended into the coastal range along the sea, peering down into the great canyons going north (*las barrancas*) before descending quickly through sugarcane fields to Tepic in the foothills of present-day Nayarit. The journey from Mexico City took thirty-nine days; they arrived between August 22 and 24. Serra immediately assigned Fathers Palou and Gastón to a boat carrying Gaspar de Portolá and soldiers across the water to Baja; they sailed on August 24. But fate—and a tornado out on the water—turned them back.

Suddenly the whole effort stalled; to Tepic, the viceroy sent a letter reversing his orders, leaving Palou "astonished at its contents," due to a supposed conflict between the Jalisco and Querétaro friars. Waiting in New Spain, Serra was to find, was an art.

While Serra tried to calm the situation, he was bereft: "The cold facts staring us in the face are—we are out of California, without infidels to convert, and maybe without any missions whatever. . . . We favor the first decision." On November 1, 1767, sent by Serra in the emergency, Palou met with José de Gálvez in Guanajuato (where six hundred rebels, mostly Indians, were in prison; nine were sentenced to death by Gálvez five days later). It's hard to believe Palou wouldn't realize the quaking volcano he sat atop in that moment with the visitor-general, but he was focused on one thing: California. Perhaps Gálvez saw one crack of light in his own darkness, and grasped it. He gave Palou a letter of disapproval of the reversal, saying it was not what the king wanted, and ordered Palou to take it straight to the viceroy in Mexico City. On November 11, saying he had been duped, Croix reversed the reversal.

On March 14, 1768, the Fernandinos boarded the ship *Concepción* at San Blas, a malarial port Serra treasured and years later helped to save from destruction. He was certain he was on a "spiritual expedition of California." In two blue weeks, they crossed the Gulf of California, arriving in Loreto on April 1. The small town of 2,600 was at that time the peninsular capital.

As the Jesuits had found out before the Franciscans, Baja was a vast, dry place—1,100 miles from Cabo San Lucas to Tijuana, its waist narrowing from 130 to forty miles near the midway point. In fact, it was two different topographies; even today maps split at the 28 degree latitude at Scammon's Lagoon, where the Alaska whales mate in winter, and at Mission Santa Gertrudis. Baja California Norte had most of the population then and now (the intertribal conflicts of the south slowly pushed natives to migrate north into its sizable mountain range and along the greener coasts). Tribes were thick around present-day Ensenada, Tijuana, and Mexicali, where 75 percent of the peninsula's population lived. Baja California Sur, however, begins with an agonizing desert at the tip of the northern section running into the south (which Serra was soon to traverse).

When Serra disembarked in Loreto, a few of 120 Guaycura Indians emerged from their mud huts. Sixteen friars sang the "Salve Regina" up from the beach. They were greeted by a pleased Portolá, who had arrived three months before to evacuate the Jesuits. He explained to Serra he had assigned a soldier to guard each of the empty missions in Baja and Serra gave him a list of which Franciscans he had assigned to which mission. Within three days, on April 6, the Franciscans fanned out: Crespí west forty miles to Purísima de Cadegomó, Lasuén 250 miles north to San Borja, Palou only twenty-two miles southwest to San Francisco Javier. Crespí noted the ironies of release, sadly: "For so long we had lived not so much close together as packed together—and now each was going his own way to live in solitude."

Feverish preparations for Upper California began almost immediately. José de Gálvez, following close behind Serra, arrived at San Blas on May 13; in only three days, he held a landmark conference with the ship pilots (and engineer Miguel Costanso) of the *San Carlos* and *San Antonio* (also known as *El Príncipe*) to plan the four-pronged entry into Alta California—two sea voyages and two by land.

By July 5, Gálvez had crossed the Sea of Cortez—after being blown off course to deserted islands and Mazatlán—finally arriving at Cerralvo Island near La Paz. The exhausting trip (forty-two days) had taken over twice as long as it had taken Serra. From Cerralvo, Gálvez sent by small ship an urgent message north to Serra at Loreto that made no bones about his intentions to occupy Monterey in Alta California. So before the end of July 1768, Serra knew he was being invited, quietly, to uncharted land and he accepted enthusiastically, writing back to Gálvez, that he would be the first to volunteer "to erect the holy standard of the cross in Monterey."

On July 12, Gálvez asked all Baja Franciscans for a report on the missions they had taken over, with "documents and the insight I request and need." When he did a bit of his own touring of the southern missions, Gálvez was not pleased with the "absolute state of neglect" he found: "All of them became pitiful deserts, and the wretched Indians debased, living a life of a beast, running through the woods looking for roots and animals through which to live on, and perishing in misery at the hands of hunger." To Gálvez, soldiers administering in the vacuum of the Jesuits, probably half crazy with loneliness, were doing a poor job, keeping shoddy records and worse, stealing from and violating the Indian women. Gálvez told Palou in no uncertain terms to expose the "rascal" soldiers at Mission San Francisco Javier. Some were cashiered. About the bunch he snapped to Serra, "commissioners were born to obey [as soldiers], and not to govern something other than their horses." But in an odd and ultimately tragic reassignment, most of these slipshod if not renegade soldiers were sent to Upper California, a "punishment" that would later haunt Serra.

Typical of his impatient, sweeping style, Gálvez tried to equalize the number of Indians at Baja missions and in doing so accomplished little more than disrupting communities. On the positive side, Gálvez showed great admiration for the Indians around San José del Cabo, who "took to the fields with fervent devotion the image of the patron saint of the Holy Patriarch" to drive off locusts after a year of infestation. He clamped down on "the wild abandon" of card playing and gambling at the missions and carried over his draconian reforms from the Guanuajato experience—nationalizing not just tobacco but also salt, adding a new tax onto Indians in the south, something Serra himself objected to, unsuccessfully. Despite misgivings, Serra kept an avid correspondence going with Gálvez, and the latter responded in kind, genuinely concerned for Serra's perennially ulcerated leg and his capacity to make the journey, insisting "I will never advise Your Reverence to take the journey by sea," though he quickly added, "It's not necessary for Your Reverence to follow my advice"—a concern for health Gálvez soon turned on himself, finding it "necessary to have myself bled." Gálvez quickly planned with Serra the spacing of the Upper California missions. Geiger claims Serra proposed missions be "one day's [horse] journey apart," and that one priest would do; spaced farther, at least two priests would be needed. They chose church supplies from Baja missions; Gálvez gave names to the first three (San Diego, Monterey, San Buenaventura), establishing a tradition that government leaders, not the Church, would name the Upper California missions. Gálvez insisted the Monterey mission be named after San Carlos Borromeo in honor of King Carlos III and the viceroy, Carlos de Croix. Serra was a little taken aback. What about the Franciscans' own founder, St. Francis?

"Let him find the port bearing his name and he will have his mission there," Gálvez is purported to have challenged Serra, goading him to locate the foggy, legendary bay of San Francisco. The visitor-general thought St. Francis should get the second mission. At the same time, Gálvez revealed an uncharacteristically humble side to Serra, asking the father president's critique of his blueprint for life at the missions, for "my labors are sufficiently bad to prevent their author from falling in love with them." He may have even felt Alta California offered a chance at absolution, confessing to Palou, "I second the fervor of such holy designs, as much I desire them in the midst of the confusion that my sins as a profane and wicked man have caused."

Then Gálvez invited Serra south to meet him where there was "stew in abundance and plenty of accomodations." Serra arrived at the mining camp at Santa Ana nine days later, on October 31. It must have been an extraordinary parley, the little man of faith bending his tonsured head to the white-wigged, sky-eyed Spanish patrician from the king's court, each of them barely containing the thrill of their venture, *abrazos* at first sight, each obsessed with the chance for a new life, neither saying a word about expiation for old bloodlettings. Salaries were discussed (seven hundred pesos per missionary from the Jesuits' own funds), while one thousand pesos came from the Crown for the establishment of each mission. (Later, Gálvez agreed to pay Indians six pesos a month for "regular and ordinary tasks" when prompted by an official of Loreto that "*whenever you ask for an Indian, for whatever task, you must give more than the daily ration.*")

Andalusian Captain Vicente Vila had twenty-five soldiers onboard, led by Lieutenant Pedro Fages, when the first ship, the *San Carlos,* sailed from La Paz on January 9, 1769. Also among the crew were engineer and cosmographer Miguel Costanso and "Dr. Crazy," Pedro Prat, who would later flee California in mania. A month later, on February 15, the second San Diego–bound ship, the *San Antonio,* set sail, though directly from Cabo San Lucas, under command of a veteran of the Manila galleon, Juan Pérez, blessed by the same people, its banners and the Spanish flag flapping in the wind. A third boat, the *San José,* shoved off four months later with copious supplies from Loreto on June 16 in order to restock those who made it to San Diego. José de Murguía, who was to be its chaplain, appears to have had a stroke or heart attack just before boarding, and was given Last Rites. Having remained ashore, the good father recovered and had plenty to be thankful for. The *San José* was lost at sea, the victim, perhaps, of the hurricane season that swirls across the Gulf of Mexico and sometimes into the Gulf of California. None of its sailors or cargo or the ship itself was ever found.

Serra thought hard about his assignment of chaplain for the third prong of the expedition to Alta California—an overland party. Despite his closeness to Palou, he bypassed him and picked, to Palou's chagrin (something we may intuit from Palou's later criticism and even seizure of the man's work), the prematurely gray Juan Crespí. Serra had been Crespí's teacher back on Mallorca; he knew the mercurial man's struggles with the language, which included a penchant for superlatives and bald candor. Because of this shrewd pick, however, we are graced with a spirited, closely observed diary record—the most complete one we have of the original journey from Baja all the way to Monterey.

BAJA

On February 26, 1769, Crespí pulled up stakes at his Mission La Purísima Cadegomó and began the six-hundred-mile, two-month-long trek north to San Diego, with only two Indian boys as companions. In a month, Crespí would join the first overland party at Velicatá of Fernando Rivera y Moncada, leader of the military in Baja, who since leaving Loreto in September 1768 had been gathering all the horses and mules the Baja missions could spare for this third prong of the thrust into Alta California.

Crespí's early journal entries are filled with close descriptions of flora, particularly the medicinal jojoba plant ("clad top to bottom in very thorny boughs"), *cirio* trees (so named by the Jesuits, probably boojum trees), palms, and the "very delicious sweet preserve" made of the mescal bush (which he ruefully calls "the wretched heathens' daily bread"). Crespí often complains of the desert cold, as if it were alive; before meeting Rivera and his troops, "I slept out in the open, and the cold at night makes itself thoroughly felt." The solitude was cut after many backbreaking days on the road by reaching Miguel de la Campa at Mission San Ignacio, who gave him "a thousand kindnesses." Out on the trail again he passed, unawares, Scammon's Lagoon, where the blue whales had begun to stir in their mating, before taking their summer journey to the Arctic. Perhaps Crespí heard the boom of their spray.

Three weeks out, a mule collapsed; that night, after enjoying a bitter hot chocolate, and clutching a purple chasuble that had come by horse courier from Father Lasuén for next day's Palm Sunday, Crespí himself collapsed. He had made it 212 miles to the ill-fated Mission de Calamajué, which had been shut down two years before due to bad water.

Leaving the haunted place at midnight (to beat the heat of day), Crespí trudged for two days on a "very bad path" of steep grades and climbs (Serra would call the same foot trail when he passed on it two months later "a tortuous road"). The emptiness stunned Crespí, but he called up a Serra-like dry humor: "there is not a bush in sight or grass enough for a call of nature."

Crespí finally linked up with Captain Rivera and his troops, who emerged from several small tule huts at Velicatá. With twenty-five leatherjacket soldiers, three muleteers, and forty-two Baja Christian Indians, Rivera led their group out, finding La Cieneguilla (Small Swamp) on Good Friday exactly where the Jesuit Wenceslaus Linck had noted it in his journals three years before. The next day, Holy Saturday, they met up with a naked, heavily painted Indian, whom Rivera gave a cigar and who smoked it "with great address," a Spanish version of the peace pipe.

161

As happens out in an extreme wilderness, trees, bushes, and other inanimate objects began to seem animate. Crespí recalled as they were approaching Easter that the jojobas and boojum trees seemed to be accompanying them. Crespí, without knowing it, was becoming Indian; solitude had made the world animistic. Nevertheless, on March 29 he buried his first Indian (of several) on the trail, Luis from Mission San Ignacio. Crespí appears to have dug the grave with his own hands and hoisted a small wooden cross.

Crespí was now deep in the northern part of Baja and the land was changing, greening, moistening. The Spaniards ran into a buck-naked old man accompanying his daughter of about twelve years "covered decently with bunched threads in front and deer hides hanging from the waist behind." Rivera gave her some glass earrings, and by sheepish gesture got her to put them on. Like the girl in Vermeer's painting, "she hung them in her ears immediately with much address," and stared, to smiles and nods.

The next day, March 31, the party happened upon an old-fashioned Indian barbecue, though of mescal plants, in a small village of about ten huts. Frightened, the Indians ran off, leaving the meal smoking. April Fool's Day saw Crespí doing something bizarre—pressing dough with large iron tongs to make unleavened Communion hosts. "Not one of them turned out good enough for saying Mass," he griped.

Seven hundred miles south, while Crespí struggled with his hosts, Junípero Serra embraced Father Palou at Mission San Francisco Javier. "With much sorrow I bade farewell to the said Father, my favorite since our childhood," Serra wrote. Serra walked off as chaplain and diarist of the second land expedition, the fourth prong of Spain's entry into Upper California, led by the Baja governor, Gaspar de Portolá, who was now titular head of the entire operation. Portolá, however, had departed March 9, ahead of Serra, who wanted to complete Easter Week in Loreto (and also to rest his painful leg before the major journey).

"When I saw his wound and the swelling of his foot and leg, I could not hold back my tears," Palou recounted. "I realized how much he was yet to suffer on those rough and painful trails that are known to extend to the frontier, and the others not as yet discovered." Taking advantage of "amiable companionship and the mutual love we bore each other since the year 1740," Palou tried one last time, unsuccessfully, to get Serra to quit the journey: "I begged him to let me go [instead], but he wouldn't allow it." Left to tend to the decrepit Baja missions, Palou betrays some jealousy: "I see myself tied, without being able to run free, as I desire."

Soon a letter arrived from Gálvez, exclaiming, "I greatly rejoice that the Reverend Padre Junípero is going along with the Expedition and I extol his faith and the great confidence he has for his recovery." Serra impressed upon Palou his unshakable will, underscored in his good-bye letter from Cádiz to his parents twenty years before, that they "encourage me to move forward and never turn back."

Still, at the final departure, Palou had to look down: "I saw that in order for him to mount and dismount from his mule, it was necessary for two men to lift him bodily and place him in the saddle." Serra was nearly a cripple.

"*A Dios!*" Serra called out. "Until Monte-Rey, where I trust we shall be reunited to work together in the vineyard of the Lord."

"Until Eternity," Palou said bitterly.

"O you of little faith," Serra chided him, echoing Christ to his apostles. But he added, "That pierces my heart." And then he kicked his mule in the belly and was off in the dust.

About a hundred miles north at Mission Guadalupe where the Indians were practically starving, Serra himself cooked them some *atole*. After this meal, the Indians regaled Serra with "a very tender song" about loving God: "I found great consolation in listening to them." Father Juan Sancho found Serra's mules worse than those that had come through with Captain Rivera and later Portolá, so he gave him fresh animals. He also gave him his own servant, a fifteen-year-old Indian boy, Juan Evangelista Benno, who spoke and read Castilian, to Serra's surprise. Up seventy-five more miles north to Mission San Ignacio, Serra renewed his priestly vows on April 16. Another hundred miles up the road, though he makes no mention of it, he must have encountered the extraordinary Cochimí rock paintings of the Sierra de San Francisco, the best preserved and most important prehistoric art in the Baja Peninsula—preserved from vandalism over the years because they are off road far into the wilderness. Serra's route by horseback or foot went right by them, and he would probably have been told of this ancient artwork dating from 1300 BC to AD 1100 at some 250 sites, discovered by the Jesuit priest Francisco Javier about twenty years before Serra passed through. Rocks are covered with drawings over six feet tall of men (saintly giants), as well as turtles, puma, eagles, sardines, whales, and other animals.

He then pressed on to Mission Santa Gertrudis, where he "kissed the cross" of Father Dionisio Basterra. After Mass, "our eyes filled with tears—and they flow again while I write this." Basterra was not alone; he was "hemmed in by so many Indians." But there was no other Spaniard at Gertrudis, and Basterra, according to Serra, "had fallen into a deep melancholy from loneliness" in one of the most geographically isolated of the Baja missions. No doubt their emotions burst, with Serra saying enigmatically they had "paid, in generous measure, this lawful tribute to nature." Serra stayed longer with Basterra—five days—than at any other stop in Baja.

Serra was so tired he only entered a sentence for each of the next two days—basically "I started out" and "I continued the trip." Though their relationship was later thorny in Upper California, Serra stayed three days with Fermín Lasuén at Mission San Francisco Borja "out of my special love for the splendid minister here." Finally, after enduring the heat and lack of water of *El Caxon* (that "tortuous road" that Crespí had similarly lamented), on May 5, Serra made it to Mission Santa María de Los Angeles, embraced by the governor, Captain Portolá. They were two-thirds up the Baja Peninsula, at the vestibule of San Diego.

By this time, Crespí had reached the ocean near present-day Ensenada, less than a hundred miles south of San Diego, about a month and a half ahead of Serra. There the party splashed their faces, Crespí naming the spot in a flourish, "The Most Holy Cross of the Pools of the Embayment of All Saints," an embellishment of the name on earlier maps: *Ensenada de Todos Santos*. For the first time, Crespí encountered menacing Indians from a thickly populated village who "commenced shouting at us a great deal, seeming by their gestures to be telling us to turn back."

The next day, in a friendly gesture, shouting to Rivera, a villager lifted three arrows out of a fishing net at his waist, placing them on the ground. Rivera believed him, retrieving the bundle and yelling out *"Gracias!"* He had translators call out to the warriors, probably Kumeyaay, to come to the Spanish camp for a visit; they did, exchanging more nets of arrows (and cords "of twisted hairs") for ribbons, beads, and earrings. Two women regaled everyone with "a great speechifying" and were showered with gifts. The Indians added some barbecued sardines to the fest and told Crespí and Portolá about two giant ships that had recently passed alongside going north. The friar and captain nodded, smiling. It had to be the *San Carlos* and the *San Antonio*. However, when the twenty-nine warriors from the previous day appeared, the Spaniards' hosts fled uphill *"hospes in salutato,* as the saying goes," Crespí wryly concluded, that is, "a host only in the greeting."

On May 11, the Rivera land party made it down to the beach and proceeded along the wet firm sand. Crespí's group camped out in a small valley dotted with barrel cactus shaped "like two-fists." A gregarious Indian appeared leading others, beads hanging from his pierced nose, several Indians with hair painted so white Crespí thought they were wigs. The one with the nose beads, having snatched some cowboy spurs and blankets, was soon nicknamed Barrabas, recalling the thief preferred by the crowd in Jerusalem to Christ himself.

On May 13, getting around the typical—and beautiful—outcrops of land that jut into the Pacific Ocean in California, Crespí exulted at the "hardly discernible" sight of the mizzenmasts of the *San Carlos* and the *San Antonio* in the distance: "I cannot tell the happiness and joy we all felt upon seeing the hour arrive of our reaching our so long wished-for San Diego harbor." But then a cloud burst, rain sheeting down, baptizing all.

When the rain stopped, the party marched for six hours under racing clouds, wet to the bone, followed by loads of Indians clutching clubs, their arrows poised, and when they "gained sight of our long wished-for splendid HARBOR OF SAN DIEGO," the party's teeth were knocking on a Communion-less Sunday. Still, they shot off a salvo to hail the ships ahead and received cannon fire in return. No doubt the Indians covered their ears, if not their worries.

Serra was playing catch-up. The very day Crespí's Pentacostal flame was drenched while he made out San Diego in the cold, Serra founded his one and only mission in Baja at Velicatá, called San Fernando. With no incense and only a "stub" of a candle, Serra said its first official Mass with Miguel de la Campa in front of leatherjacket soldiers. Smoke wafted into the makeshift altar from the several-gun salute of the founding, irritating Serra as "the smoke of powder took the place of burning incense." He ventured, "No gentile dared come near, frightened perhaps by so much shooting."

On May 15, Serra had the famous first encounter, and a sensual one, with "new" (nonmissionized) Indians in California, in northern Baja. Hearing they were coming to see him, "I gave praise to the Lord, kissing the ground, and thanking His Majesty for the fact that, after so many years of looking forward to it, He now permitted me to be among the pagans in their own country." Serra's diary makes clear how long California had been on his own mind. More importantly, he says nothing about capturing lands for Spain, but clearly values the encounter of natives *in their own country*, implicitly acknowledging the country is theirs. The irony of being on, if not extending, El Camino Real, the King's Highway, does not disturb him in this moment. He gazes with unmitigated wonder:

> I saw something I could not believe when I had read it, or had been told about it. It was this: they were entirely naked, as Adam in the garden, before sin. So they go, and so they presented themselves to us. We spoke a long time with them, and not for a moment, while they saw us clothed,

could you notice the least sign of shame in them for their own lack of dress. One after the other, I put my hands upon the head of them, in sign of affection. I filled both their hands with dried figs, which they immediately began to eat.

The ten men (and two boys) returned the favor with roasted mescal and four fishes. The lack of shame Serra finds in the Indians about their naked state he answers with his own lack of shame. There is no guilt here, no revulsion, no commanding need to assert dominance or superiority. Only figs, a symbol of sexual fecundity as old as the ancient Greeks. Serra was in Eden. And perhaps, too, in the world of his own childhood on Mallorca. If there was any doubt before, this moment obliterated it: Serra was not in league with the Juan Sepúlvedas of the world who felt the Indian was sub-human, a position Sepúlveda laid out in his famous 1551–52 debates with Bartolomé de Las Casas; he was thoroughly in the camp of Las Casas, the critic of early Spanish colonial violence, and further along in his attitudes toward the humanity of the Indians and their status as equals than many of his own confreres. If anything, he reveals here a wonder that makes us consider that, with Rousseau, the Indian was not only the Spanish equal, he was one giant step up. He was—a key phrase—"before sin." One might ask if he wondered why they even needed saving.

Serra told the Indians through an interpreter that Father de la Campa would look after them, "be their best friend," and that the soldiers "would do them much good and no harm." He cautioned them against stealing and said the good priest would do his best to get them anything they needed, including food and clothing. Soon he named a place of "abundant water" under "a smiling sky" San Juan de Dios, calling May 16, 1769, "a happy day for me because for the first time, we were all together"— that is, he had linked up with the ten-man Portolá party that had left before him. Now Serra was ready for the final leg of his trip three hundred miles north to San Diego, which Crespí had just spotted. Even more enlivening, on May 18, despite a worsening of sores halfway up his leg, Serra welcomed the original Indian party who had so amazed him, now with women and children—forty-four in all—all wanting baptism. He baptized the chief, naturally, Francisco, after the founder of his order, concluding, "May God make him a saint." The whole unlikely moment confirmed in him the experience of blessed María de Agreda, whose *Mystical City of God* he still carried everywhere—that Indians came forward for baptism "at the mere sight of his sons, the Franciscans" as they had in New Mexico in 1631 after having met the bilocated Agreda, an astounding, impossible thing that was as self-evident to Serra now as the appearance of water in a desert. The next day, Serra proclaimed his leg sores much better; his spirits had to be sky-high.

On May 21, the Feast of the Holy Trinity, Serra faced the large group of soldiers, Indians, and muleteers, and gave at Mass "a short exhortation emphasizing the good conduct all should observe on a journey whose principal object is God's greater honor and glory." He and Portolá had a good laugh later in the day when an old Indian man "just as naked as all the rest," quite chipper and nonplussed, and without missing a trick, squatted and defecated right in front of them, "still continuing to speak with us, and he remained just as calm as he was so relieved." Serra was unfazed, asking if the man would like to become a Christian, perhaps figuring he'd never be in a more receptive state, and of course the old fellow agreed and started studying Catechism on the spot. Serra sent him south to Velicatá: "I do not know what outcome it all had; all I know is that the good old man felt happy."

Portolá must have laughed. Portolá was a good man to have at the head of the second land expedition, alongside Serra. He was a fellow Catalán, born in Balaguer in 1717, fifty-two years old, four years younger than Junípero, but with a load of military experience. A bachelor, Portolá was as sensitive as he was dutiful, perhaps one reason at the age of twenty-five he was made guardian of his own father, who had been adjudged insane.

The move north wore on, in "blazing sun that made the journey very painful," Serra admitted. On May 23, he was kept awake by what he thought was a "roaring lion quite close by." It may have been a cougar out of the nearby mountains of San Pedro Mártir. He was beginning to worry that despite the great welcome at Velicatá, Indians were suddenly scarce; spotting them, they fled. On May 26, the Christian Indians with the party roped one of the local Kumeyaay as he ran away. Serra ordered the young man (about twenty), whose name was Axajui, set free, as he was "very frightened and disturbed." Serra put hands on his head, blessed him, recited the Gospel of John, and offered him figs, meat, and tortillas, but Axajui ate little, though he scraped up some earth and said the Spanish word *pinole*. *Pinole* was fetched for him, but he scowled, until more water was added. The excitable man soon confessed to being a spy and that a major attack of four *rancherías* (Indian villages) against the advancing Spanish party was being planned (Portolá's diary entry is more specific: "They were going to lie in ambush to kill the father [Serra] and company").

On May 28, after Portolá ordered two warning shots fired in the air over hostile Indians, Serra noted, "Our Lord sent us other Indians of a more pleasing character." Theater followed threat; during a potluck meal of Indian cooked mescal and Spanish figs and meat, all leaned back to watch a group of Indian actors play "all the parts both of the attacker and the attacked in such a vivid way, and with such address, that it was a pleasant moment of relaxation for us."

Suddenly two native woman approached, the younger, the chief's wife, coming up to Serra, bearing a "great pancake" on her head made of dough and "thick fibers." Serra was embarrassed at first, "anxious not to see them, because I feared they went as naked as the men." He was pleasantly surprised; their breasts and buttocks were "so decently covered that we would feel happy if no greater display of indecency were ever seen among the Christian women of the missions." He betrayed himself immemorially male, however, observing them "talking as rapidly and efficiently as that sex is accustomed to." But when the two ladies left and the chief went on a harangue, Serra regretted "the women's absence."

Coming alongside their village the next day, the expedition was surrounded by natives calling out and yelling in their enthusiasm to be guides, but their loud voices frightened the party's animals, "almost making them bolt." Portolá had to fire shots overhead again to dampen the noise, which it did, but Serra began to worry that the firearms' report was sowing fear: "By such a display, we might leave in their minds some doubt as to our goodwill." That night, Portolá noted the animals were restless as the Indians partied.

On June 1, Serra spotted wild grapes growing along a river, perhaps the San Antonio. The next day, he rejoiced seeing clumps of "the Queen of flowers"—the wild rose of Castile: "While I write this, I have in front of me a cutting from a rose-tree with three roses in full bloom, others opening out, and more than six unpetaled: blessed be He who created them!" The topography was changing, as Crespí had noted before him; to Serra "the thorns and rocks of California have disappeared" and the "enormous mountains" of the Coastal Range were "pure soil."

They were moving closer to the sea; he could feel the damp, smell the salt air; they climbed up slopes to "catch a glimpse of the ocean of the west coast" only to be disappointed at more gulches and hills to climb. Before turning in that night, they happened upon the scattered bones of the Indian Crespí had buried the month before. Evidently, animals (or Indians) had savaged the grave. Serra helped reinter them.

A field of wild roses spread before them June 3, so lush Serra figured "a purveyor of perfume could easily make a fortune." His excitement as they grew closer to San Diego transformed a swamp into a vision of a vineyard "where it would not be difficult to imitate our Father Noah in the planting of vines."

On June 10, at a place called Matiropi, a shaman approached shaking a stick-rattle. At first he would not be coaxed to calm down with food; but when he ate some *pinole*, he threw it up, explaining he had to dance before eating. The Spaniards set one course after another in front of him, and he danced all the more, and when he felt "all fear had left him" he sat down to eat.

The explorer in Serra entered his diary that night, a bit lost. But in a rather shrewd conclusion for someone who was not a professional geographer, he thought a complete water route through the North American continent from sea to sea ending here "an impossible assumption." There was less and less evidence of a "Strait of Anian," the mythical passage that would span the entire continent, each day, and "it is clear that not all the detours in the world by land would ever allow us to cross it."

Now the land itself seemed to be rising up. Serra regarded the coastal range with a combination of awe and dread, "Day by day this country seems to grow bigger and bigger with great walls and fortress-like bastions rising up to defend the west coast." The switchbacks and detours and "gulleys without number" put off their "hope to reach the sea, but it continually escapes us." Water grew scarce. Tempers flared among the muleteers. Without water ("neither for man nor beast," Portolá wrote), nothing could be cooked. An Indian aide to Portolá collapsed and died. On the Feast Day of Saint Anthony (June 13), Serra christened the place San Antonio de los Trabajos "in memory of these trials—or shall we call them blessings?"

Before nightfall the next day, nine Indians deserted the expedition; those who stayed ventured that "being near San Diego, they were afraid they would be forced to stay there without hope of returning to their own missions." Serra was sad but thankful, "May God bless them for the services they have rendered us and the way we will miss them in the future." For those who stayed, he prayed, "May God keep them with us and protect them from all harm." When on June 15 Sergeant Ortega strapped on his leatherjacket, asking Serra for his advice confronting what seemed a Kumeyaay war party, Serra basically said to let them win: "Realizing that this was no time for breaking with the poor Indians, nor was it a matter involving any disgrace, I was all for letting them appear—regretfully however—to be victorious on the field of battle."

More and more, they saw Indian trails; less and less they saw Indians. Nerves among the crew were stretched taut. On June 19, a cook, incensed at a mule in his way, ran a sword up its buttocks and killed it. An angry Portolá fired the cook on the spot, forced him to walk the rest of the way, and fined him forty pesos. Mules were as precious as water, though the few Indians left with the expedition were given the dead beast for a feast. "May it do them good," Serra said.

Finally, at Ensenada they reached the beach and camped "a rifle shot" from the ocean with good sea oats, fresh water in pools, and the wind smiling their faces. It was the Bay of Todos Santos. It was a place both Serra and Crespí thought perfect for a mission, but that was never to be. On June 23, much to their surprise, Serra's expedition was treated to a fiesta of abalone, clams, and fish hosted by Indians of the Ranchería de San Juan (called El Sauza today). Their spirits grew. Dancing went deep into the night. Said Serra, "In fact, all the gentiles have pleased me, but these in particular have won my heart." The Franciscan father found them of "fine stature, deportment, conversation, and gaiety." Clearly, the Indians were physically pleasing to him; he did not hide the fact.

"May God make their souls attractive, too!" Serra exclaimed. "Amen."

Serra picked nits, fleas, and ticks off himself, ruefully commenting that from them, there was no California dispensation. But crowds of Indians were growing and not shying away, "just as if we had been lifelong friends of the closest kind." Serra invited all to come along to San Diego: "May it please God to bring them there, or send them missionaries to lead them to heaven in their own country." Perhaps he realized this was not going to be a simple task, as they were "already given such a wonderful and fruitful country to live in."

Then as now, the rising cliffs along the ocean made their impression. Upon seeing them, Serra noted "a drop so sheer and steep that just to look at it made you shiver." It was necessary to go single-file, to dismount; there was a great deal of "walking, sliding, skidding, and falling." But at the end of it was "a kind of bay where the waves come and break gently." On June 26, they met the largest crowd of Indians they'd seen in all of Baja, who encircled Serra as he sat, one mother placing her baby in his arms, whom he wanted to baptize, but he gave her back: "On all of them I made the Sign of the Cross and had them say, 'Jesus, Mary.' I gave them all I could; I treated them as kindly as I could." The crowd had a "mania for clothes," anything that could "improve their looks," and as they were "sturdy and robust" they hardly needed food. This was a different kind of Indian than those in the parched, bare stretches of lower Baja. They were not in much need; clothes to them were the man (or woman), and several tugged at Serra's gray robe, indicating they'd like to have it, too. Serra joked later, "If I'd given the habit to all who wanted it, there would be by this time a pretty large community of gentile friars." But the most important apparel he made clear: "What I would like to imprint deep in their hearts is this: *Induimini Dominum Jesum Christum*" (Put on the Lord Jesus Christ).

On June 27, Serra lost his eyeglasses to Barrabas, the Indian. For a while, life was a blur. He heard war whoops, feared the worst. But when these villagers made him sit to eat fish sautéed with black spices Serra thought were cloves and pepper, he didn't care if he saw anything. The world was inhale. The world was smell. The world was taste: *O taste and see the goodness of the Lord!* Soon, after half the tribe had tried them on, Serra got his specs back. He spotted an Indian dressed in blue cotton, a complete first, who told them yes, he had gotten the cloth in San Diego from the men in boats. Cloth was so treasured that the men offered both Portolá and Serra women to sleep with in exchange for it, an "intensely sordid" offer to Portolá, though one has to wonder how sordid it would have been if Serra were not around.

On June 28, Sergeant Ortega, scouting ahead, returned grasping letters from Crespí and Father Parron (neither of which has been found), increasing the expedition's excitement and anxiety as it contained troubling news about the sailors and scurvy.

On June 29, in a deep ravine the group came upon "good, sweet water," but they didn't drink it or let the animals drink it: "We did not want to spoil the watering place for the poor gentiles."

The morning of June 30 looked promising, "a wondrous sight" as they crested a hill at dawn of a "measureless plain." But that sight was deceptive; there were countless ravines ahead. Crossing one after the other, Serra began to lose strength and breath: "I summoned up all my courage—because you were no sooner out of one ravine than you were into another, and each was dangerous."

"Is this the last one?" Serra gasped.

"There are plenty more," came the answer, presumably from Ortega.

Nevertheless, "like all things in this world," Serra later wrote, "the gullies came to an end." After several painful, wheezing hours, his lungs burning, they emerged to a beautiful sight—the sea, the blue rippling forever, and they could have easily fallen in it, dizzy, eyes stinging in the salt water. Serra might have taken off his sandals and carried them. Now the sand was perfect, their cut, aching feet tingling in the cold water, avoiding a mussel shell here, a stone there, cracking the pods of kelp with their heels. The next morning, they awoke on a neck of land to see masts above the mist. As the sun burned it off, they walked north, perhaps quaking inside, as in a dream.

Serra's life was about to change forever. So was California, the Indian land, the last virgin land of the continent.

PART TWO

CALIFORNIA BEFORE SERRA

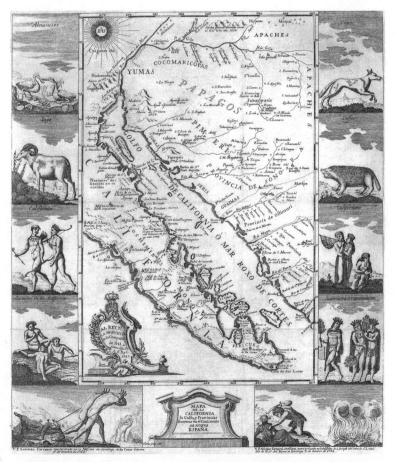

1757 map of Baja California and southern Arizona drawn by the Jesuit
Miguel Venegas, including scenes in the lower corners of the 1734
martyrdom of two Jesuit priests in South Baja.

CHAPTER ELEVEN

WHO THEY WERE, WHAT THEY DID, WHAT THEY BELIEVED

Dancing on the brink of the world.
—COSTANOAN DANCE SONG

The hunt along San Francisco Bay, Ludwig Choris lithograph, *ca.* 1816.

*I*n the summer of 1769 on the Pacific coast of California, time stood still for the last time. As anthropologist Alfred Kroeber has said, "The California Indian did not record the passage of long intervals of time." Of course, tribes noted seasons and had elaborate ceremonies to usher them in, with lunar and solar calendars of various sorts. But "no one knew his own age." Events over a half dozen years back were not calibrated in specific time; most tribes did not have a functioning word for "year," only

175

for season. Thus the California Indian, as with most aboriginal peoples prior to contact with European colonizers, lived in a relatively timeless state. But that was about to change.

With the exception of brief, sporadic encounters with a few European explorers over the previous two hundred years, the Indians of California had lived with no significant disturbance either from the west or from the east beyond the Sierra Nevada for more than ten thousand years, during which time they had been sustained by their own cultures, habits, economies, and beliefs. Theirs was a world of its own—far from perfect, but with parameters and customs they could depend on.

Life for the California Indian before that fateful day in July 1769 in San Diego when Serra and the Spaniards arrived is important to consider if the assessment of Serra's legacy and the history of European settlement in the region is to be judged fairly. The pre-contact Indian life on the West Coast anticipates the extraordinary challenges both Indian and Spaniard had in adapting to each other, especially in the realm of faith, which for Indians involved a painful transformation and for the Christianity-transporting Franciscans upped moral conundrums to new heights. This pre-contact examination also establishes a baseline to determine what was lost—a frightful, if not horrifying amount—not just in culture, lifestyle, and economies, but in life itself. It may also help to identify something rarely discussed (outside early ethnocentric assumptions): what, if anything, may have been gained by Indians, spiritually or otherwise, through the Spanish settlement and, conversely, what spiritual or cultural offerings Indian culture transferred to Europeans and their descendants. Finally, a look back at pre-contact Indian life helps us interpret the conflict within the Spanish authority—the Crown, the military, and the mission—that resulted from at times bitter clashes with the California Indians.

A detailed ethnography of the California Indian is beyond the scope of this biography, but minimizing such matters would make for an incomplete story. Until recent decades the historical portrait of Indians has been largely rendered in rigid designations such as victim, aggressor, or naïf, in rapid movement to vilify, classify, or dismiss. The story has always been much more complex.

Extensive early treatments of pre-contact California Indian life are few. If it wasn't for the Franciscan Gerónimo Boscana's *Chinigchinich*, the 1846 landmark study of the Juaneños of Mission San Juan Capistrano—the first ethnography of California; or Alfred Kroeber, the man who essentially founded the study of anthropology in 1901 at the University of California at Berkeley; or the early-twentieth-century oral history gatherer John Harrington, record of that pre-contact Indian life along the coast would be minimal indeed. It was a largely oral history culture, where stories, songs, and pictographs carried the weight and meaning of experience. There were no documents as we know them (or codices as the Aztecs made). Harrington's ruling metaphor of the whole rescue process ("the house is *afire*, it is *burning*") undergirds with urgency his 1941 injunction to an assistant "to go through the blinding rain, roads or no roads" to "grab these dying languages" for "you will be doing one of the *few* things valuable to the people of the *remote* future" (emphasis Harrington's). Nevertheless, because of these "Big Three" (and many interesting portraits by travelers and explorers—such as the invaluable Serra and Crespí diaries of 1769–70), combined with fascinating, recent archaeological investigations and the development of the whole field of anthropology, a portrait emerges.

At contact in 1769, there were about 225,000 Indians in California (sixty thousand in the coastal area from San Diego to San Francisco, where the Spaniards would soon found missions). There were between five and six hundred largely autonomous tribes or tribelets using seventy-eight mutually unintelligible languages in seven major language groups. These tribes ranged from the Yokuts, who numbered up to seventy thousand and controlled one-ninth of California—and all of the San Joaquin Valley—from Stockton to the Tehachapi Pass just north of present-day Los Angeles; to the Chumash peoples, who numbered twenty-five thousand, but in a relatively densely populated coastal area (including the eight Santa Barbara Channel Islands) with fishing and shellfishing galore, from Paso Robles to Malibu; to the Miwok, whose various sub-tribes honeycombed a lateral area extending from today's Marin County up the coast to Mendocino, then across the middle of the state through Sacramento into the high Sierra Nevada, what became, to their great distress, the American "Gold Country."

With the exception of the Chumash towns along the Santa Barbara Channel, whose thick population made the colonizing Spaniards wary of founding a mission there, most California Indians lived in rather small villages of two hundred to five hundred. Although there were major uprisings against the whites by the Kumeyaay in 1775, the Chumash in 1824, and the Yokuts led by Estanislao in 1828, for the most part the atomization of California Indian tribes in such small settlements across so many different languages and diverse topographies made it hard if not impossible to organize anything like the massive resistance to the white man that occurred with the Plains Indians, or even under a chief like Powhatan in Virginia. Would they have unified more readily if the California Indians had known theirs was among the last regions on the continent entered with settlement by the white man? Would they have been galvanized to a last stand? Unanswerable questions, but tantalizing for a people walled off in beauty.

Across a vast area of the tallest, snowiest mountains outside of the Alaska Range—the Sierra Nevada—with both home tribes and refugees from the coast, across deserts where the Quechan (Yuma) huddled along the Colorado River, down long valleys like the San Joaquin and along rivers such as the Sacramento and Los Angeles (which was not dry then, but provided fish for the Tongva), to the redwood people, the ascetic, melancholic Yurok of the far Northwest coast, or the strong, impressively resistant Kumeyaay of San Diego, Indian culture in California was long-standing, remarkably diverse, and productive in simple and not so simple ways, inhabiting a geography unmatched in its own diversity and beauty. Unlike the Incas or Aztecs, California Indians didn't leave behind glorious pyramid temples, or engage in large-scale ritualistic cannibalism or warfare (the Quechan being an exception). Other than a form of indentured servitude practiced by the Yurok, there was no slavery. Food, game, and fish were plentiful—even the desert had its agave and mesquite. If generally short (life expectancy was roughly thirty-five to forty years, less than the Spaniards, but not much so), life was also relatively good. With such tall mountains to the east, wide deserts to the southeast, the world's largest ocean to the west, and the Siskiyous to the north, the life of the California Indian seemed impregnable.

Though geologically the West Coast is "newer" than the East, Pacific human settlement is much older. Coastal California natives, especially the Chumash of the islands, comprised the oldest habitation in North America; the oldest human remains on the continent, those of the "Arlington Springs Man" (dating to 11,200 BC), were found on Santa Rosa Island.

One of the theories for the extraordinary diversity of languages, cultures, and even physiques of California Indians is that in the Early Period, different tribes migrated into the territory for its salubrious sun, ample fisheries, game, and acorn-bearing oaks. This "fish-trap" theory (first espoused by Kroeber) asserted that once these migrating Indians risked the snowy Siskiyous and Sierras and the blistering Mojave and sampled the plenty along the Pacific, they didn't go back. In a sense, with the average winter temperature of sixty-five degrees, they were happily trapped. The California story is old indeed, as old as cold, or human yearning.

If in early times the California Indian lived in shifting settlements a thousand years before Serra, now they were living in a variety of rather practical, well-made structures of planks, hides, rocks, or earth that protected from wind, rain, or even snow. The Chumash slept in beds (*tep-*

estles) made of heavy wood, higher off the floor, in fact, than ours. Reed mats were used for curtains separating bedroom from the rest of the structure. Smaller beds for children were built below the parents' high bed. The entry to the home could be barred for safety by wood slats or whalebone.

If dress makes the man or woman, it made the California woman more than the man. For the man, dress was no dress; he often went naked (as Serra discovered to his amazement), though he seems to have adapted—from a synthesized shame—a breechclout after contact with the Spaniards. Men were open, relaxed, literally easy in their skin. Father Pedro Font thought the Chumash women "fairly good looking." They were also industrious, hardworking, and inventive. Women wore skirts of buckskin tied with plant fibers, often slit in strips, a form of pleats and clearly useful for dancing. In bad weather, both sexes used a skin blanket, the most prized being that of a sea otter. Everyone, at least in central and northern California, wore moccasins, which extended higher up the calf than those of the Plains Indian. Moccasins were donned for journeys, war, hunting, and food and wood gathering. Around the village, most everyone went barefoot.

While Serra was a figurative "fisher of men," the coastal Indians were true fishermen. So devoted were they to rowing and the sea, the California Indians had the only double-bladed paddle in North America, with the exception of the Inuit. The coastal Indian, like his freeway progeny, liked to move in a hurry. The Southern California canoe, or *tomol*, was a light running vessel made of pine or redwood planks split from driftwood logs and mastered by the great seafarers of California—the Chumash (and island Tongva), whose civilization crowded on the Channel Islands facing all-day saturations of sun on the only east-to-west coastline south of Washington's Olympic Peninsula. The Santa Barbara Chumash drank the sun. Corvettes of their day, *tomols* were decorated with seashells or painted black and red with hematite and cinnabar. These twenty-two-foot canoes were going nonstop; their lightness was aided by the normally calm seas of the channel and Southern California bays. The Yurok and Hupa of the Northwest, however, constructed elegant, heavier canoes out of coastal cedar and redwood. A final canoe type found all over California, though mostly in the rivers and lakes of the central valley and around San Francisco Bay, was the tule canoe, made of tightly twined tule rushes. It was considered too slow for the Olympian crewmen, the Chumash, but it made for a cushioned ride and was favored by the Costanoans, who often used a tall pole to pull it through backwaters, though they, too, favored the double-paddle in deep San Francisco Bay.

Fishing was generous throughout California bays and coastal islands. The Modoc used a serrated bone hook, as well as a purse-seine; the Pomo, Yokuts, and Luiseño used poison; the Chumash filled their catch baskets with broken pieces of cactus; the Yurok, a heavy harpoon that could haul in a sea lion. (Today San Miguel Island has the largest elephant seal rookery in the world.) It was not unusual to see ten men lift a *tomol* off the Santa Barbara beach loaded with tuna, whitefish, bream, sardines, and crab, carrying it to the village for a feast.

Hunts were driven by bows, tall and narrow in the south, shorter and broad in north, where the yew tree provided wood. The Chumash wound theirs with a thong in the middle and three-ply sinew cord, with sinew backing. (Few original California Indian bows have survived the era of guns, and only one harpoon.) Arrows were tipped by obsidian, sharper than flint, and cane was preferred for the shaft. Deer arrows were often tipped with stone.

Interestingly, war arrows often had no head. Stunning and showering an enemy seemed enough choler to expend. This would not have gone down well on the Great Plains with the lethal bowmen of the Comanche, Sioux, and Cheyenne. Needless to say, it was ineffective against Spanish pistols and cannon. Nevertheless, the dignity and industriousness of making arrows—so important to sustenance—was crucial to Indian survival.

When it came to food, the notion that the California Indians were "perhaps the most omnivorous group of tribes on the continent" is sustained by the rich environment, not only of fish and game, but of plants, fruits, and, most widespread, the oak's acorn. The California Indian did not need anyone to teach him how to cook or eat (Serra's and Crespí's savor of cooked mescals underscores this). Theirs wasn't gourmet eating, but good eating, calling on skills of "patience, simplicity, and crude adaptability," as Kroeber put it. One might add inventiveness, considering the uniqueness of acorn processing. Oaks were everywhere: live oak, red oak, white oak. Acorns provided the chief meal, and were pulverized by mortar and pestle, leached in water, mud, or sand to remove the tannic acid until they turned sweet. In addition, the Miwok and Pomo, among others, used pine needles and conifer branches to filter flowing water in their leaching process. Acorn meal was boiled in baskets using hot stones, and the Central Wintun even mixed in red earth to pull out remaining tannin (a process also utilized in Sardinia). A kind of bread dough produced a "pancake" that an Indian chief's wife served to Serra in Baja. All in all, it appears this acorn leaching was unique to the California Indian (the Arizona Yavapai only ate naturally sweet acorns and never learned to transform the bitter to sweet, as had the tribes of the Pacific Coast).

Instead of silos, they carried their food in baskets; weaving was and is a quintessential California Indian art, almost entirely the province of women (the Pomo were the only tribe to allow men to try it). And the Pomo of Mendocino were masters among masters. The Pomos' were also the only Indian baskets that intentionally had at least one break in design; a completely encircled design was thought to bring blindness to the maker. Was this a caution against pride or perfectionism?

Deer, gophers, and rabbits found their way to the hunting net and Pacific hearth. It may have been smoke from a scorching of earth by the Tongva (Gabrielinos) to flush out rabbits that Cabrillo sighted in 1542 when he landed at San Pedro Bay, what he called the Bay of Smokes. Deer were noosed, arrowed, and caught in pits. Lizards, turtles, and rattlesnakes were eaten by the Chukchansi, as well as the Miwok and Salinans. The Yokuts smoked the skunk to death to remove the stink, but the Miwok and Salinans let the skunk alone.

There's plenty of lore, too, in the world of edible insects. One myth had Coyote, in lieu of finding mankind, marrying a louse, who of course gave birth to humanity. The Yokuts had a flea marrying five girls, all of them taking up house in the sky where they became the Pleiades (which, as the Seven Sisters, seems to be missing a flea or two). Still, lice and fleas were hardly a California Indian favorite; the sweathouse was used to kill them, and if that didn't do it, the Mohaves plastered themselves with mud. Nevertheless, grubs of all sorts—bee and wasp larvae, wood beetles—were eaten with delight, especially by children, and maggots and termites in old wood, too. Once called Indian honeydew, the excretions of plant lice, coccids, and others made a sweet find. Only the California Indian could convert blight into a feast: locusts were eaten ground by the ton, fried, roasted, boiled—cooked every possible way. Mono Lake tribes enjoyed a kind of popcorn, *kootsabe*, the larvae of a small fly—and they still do today, as it keeps forever.

Even the desert dwellers of the Mojave found secret sources of sustenance, especially favoring the fruit of the mesquite, "pulpy, sweet and nutritious . . . the staple of the life" to the Cahuilla. Barrows found them harvesting sixty distinct desert plants, trees, and bushes for nutrition and twenty-eight more for medicinal or narcotic purposes. Other delicacies in the dry land included the screwbean (or *tornillo*), which made a kind of molasses and a tasty drink when boiled; a huge plant called "careless weed" (*kit* by the Cahuilla) stored up for use long past picking; the great agave with its mescal heads, baked in pit ovens for tasty eating or boiled (in Mexico) to make an intoxicating drink called *pulque* or *mescal*, a drink the friars fought off in New Spain, to little effect.

Unlike the Aztecs and Incas, gold wasn't on the Californian's mind or under his spade. (If it had been, California would probably have been overrun by Spain two centuries earlier.) At least 131 mines or quarries dug by pre-contact Californians have been found, most controlled by the community. The soft, heat-resistant soapstone (or steatite), rich on Santa Catalina Island, was mined for everything from pots to boil Chumash food to *comals*, or griddlestones, used by the Chumash and Tongva. Obsidian was knapped for arrowheads, knives, or razors. Obsidian Man was mythologized by the Clear Lake Pomo, who explained deposits on Mount Konocti as having been scattered by an early man who, caught in thorny bushes, flailing about to release himself, broke into a thousand pieces. (Earthquakes, too, according to the Kumeyaay, or Southern Diegueño, resulted from a mythological giant blind man rolling over just so while sleeping.)

War was not common in pre-contact California, but conflict was. Tribes or clans clashed often, though revenge was a greater motivator than plunder or terrain. (The Colorado River tribes seem to be the only exception here; the Quechan and Mohave peoples—among the only California tribes who fought en masse—proved capable of harsh attack, not only on each other, but on the Spaniards.) According to Kroeber, most feuds grew out of "the belief that a death had been caused by witchcraft." Such suspicions could linger for years, apparently. Villages could split apart or fracture over petty quarrels, shortages, or suspicions, leading to spontaneous uprooting. But quick wars or raids were mostly economic-based—triggered by trespass of territory, particularly gaming and fishing plots. Torture was practiced by several tribes, including the Gabrielino of Los Angeles and the Maidu of the Sacramento Valley and Sierras near Lake Tahoe. There was no taking of prisoners; men seized in warfare were executed on the spot and sometimes decapitated. Scalping was not uncommon in California, with the scalps exhibited through a village dance, in which women participated. The Yokuts, Maidu, and Pomo (low-lying, wealthy north coast Californians who were also "armorless and shieldless") avoided this ritual, however. The Northwestern tribes neither danced nor took scalps, but rather war-danced before battle, sometimes with the very tribe with whom they had a grudge, thinking the dance might lead to settlement. That didn't happen often. Weapons included the bow and arrow (though, as noted, arrows meant for humans often did not have tips), spears, clubs, slings, and the plain old stone-in-hand. Elk hide armor was rare, found mostly in the extreme north, gleaned in spirit from the Pacific Northwest or Great Basin cultures. Cannibalism, unlike the Aztec or Chippewa, did not occur with the California Indian.

Trade-related issues also precipitated conflict. Bartering, selling, buying, and paying restitution was a way of life for California Indians, who used shell wampum or strings of dentalia shells as currency. In the south, olivella shell discs bored through for strings predominated, strung together by size, beauty, and number. They were often "minted" according to value by natives on Santa Cruz Island and were used for currency by the Chumash and other tribes. For the Yurok, most strings were about two feet long, measuring from thumb to shoulder, eleven to fifteen shells on a string called a *tsik*; for other tribes, smaller strings were measured by a hand's width. Size of shells, for the Yurok, increased a man's fame; a string of very large shells might be enough to buy a wife!

Money was perhaps more important to the Yurok than other California tribes, but possession of large amounts of shell wampum was still the mark of a notable man. Some of the Yurok valuations are fascinating and variations of them, no doubt, obtain for the rest of the area. For example, a large boat cost two twelve-shell strings, a small boat one thirteen-string of smaller shells or three large woodpecker heads (used in dance headdresses). The small boat, in turn, could trade for a blanket of two deerskins sewn together and painted. A entire house could be purchased for three strings, a fishing place for anywhere from one to three strings, depending on its size and amount of fish. (Interesting—a top-notch fishing hole was worth a home, sustenance being more important than cover.) More high-end items included: a white deerskin (ten strings); a high-class wife from a wealthy family (ten strings); restitution for killing a man of standing (fifteen strings), or a common man (ten strings); payment for seducing and impregnating a young woman (five strings); adultery was one to five strings; uttering the name of a dead man (two strings of thirteen shells each) or a rich dead man (three strings).

"The persistence with which the Yurok desire wealth is extraordinary," Kroeber wrote, as men on the way to the sweat lodge were encouraged to imagine money growing on trees.

As political entities, many California tribes were so small (under a hundred members) that Kroeber thought they could not be described as such, especially in contrast to the tribes in the eastern and central United States, which included thousands of individuals speaking the same language with strong solidarity and resistance to others. In California, a village could emerge around a natural drainage area or water source. Most tribes referred to themselves as "people of such and such a place."

It's not hard to see that unless the mission was close to this cherished "spot" and included the close family, the effect was disorienting, to say the least; likewise, such myopia worked against resistance to the mission.

The Yokuts and Chumash had the strongest tribal ties, it seems, along with the militarily cohesive Mohave and Quechan tribes. A hereditary chief predominated, with wealth a major factor, in the south more than the north. The Yurok had rich men of great influence, but no chiefs or political organization to speak of. But as far north as the Miwok, chiefs were important; insults hurled at them from the outside could be a casus belli.

With the exception of tribes east of the Sierras and along the Colorado River, marriage was a pecuniary one-way arrangement—the wife was bought, plain and simple. But in the south it was more a matter of manners than of morals, a custom not unlike a dowry paid by the husband-to-be's family rather than the bride's. If he could afford it, a man, especially a chief, could have more than one wife, so polygamy was, if not encouraged, accepted. The widow married her dead husband's brother, and the widower the dead wife's sister. Vacuums were filled. For the Yurok, "half marriage" was common; if a groom didn't have much wealth, he gave what he could and moved in with the wife's family to pay off the rest in services. But half marriage was also a respectful way of settling a love affair that ended in a child.

And children were children, greatly loved by parents, and given as much, if not more, attention by fathers than mothers. Modoc fathers played with, hugged, and entertained their children. Perhaps the mothers lost some thrill in being expected to give birth every two to four years, enduring a high rate of infant mortality (two out of three died in infancy). Children were prized, given prerogatives early and taught to be self-reliant. If hungry, they were assumed to come at the supper hour. If at an odd hour, they did the cooking. The first loose tooth the child pulled out himself or herself, and tossed toward the setting sun. But children were prized; the Pomo developed a great talent for wickerwork beyond their baskets, and one of their unique displays of it was a canopy of cane for an infant's rocking crib.

The pre-contact California Indians had a rich and varied faith system that contained concepts of grace, reverence, creation story, taboo, superstition, and an afterlife. Tribes practiced ceremonies bringing adolescents to adulthood, often in the form of dance, which in turn with song was a kind of prayer; they had elaborate mourning rites and honored their dead in ways more demonstrative, over longer time, and with seemingly greater devotion than the most advanced societies today.

At the same time, transcendence for the California Indian, and for most aboriginal, if not pre-Christian era, peoples, was rather immanent; that is, a God or gods were contained or at least manifested in the natural world. If they transcended the mortal life, they were never completely untethered from it. Theirs was a pantheistic, animistic world, where nature and animals were revered or feared as part of a whole nexus of spirits, with powers over humanity. And this is no surprise, as a society so immersed in and dependent on the natural world would naturally endow it with great power. The natural world was not fallen, as in Judeo-Christian mythology. It just *was*. And it was everywhere, and not conquerable. Existence was filled with portent and nature not to be overcome—in fact, to do so would have been a great crime, akin to killing a god.

Four basic religious concepts or attitudes of the pre-contact Indian clashed with the Christian civilization he was about to encounter with the arrival of Serra: first, the notion of an enspirited natural world; second, the importance of group identity and responsibility over that of the individual; third, the soul was not fallen or stained by original sin. Though the Indian knew what it meant to suffer—physical pain, ostracism, shame— he did not understand, at first, the notion of expiation, especially of a god himself dying to make everyone better or eligible for everlasting life. Most people could get there without God coming down and subjecting himself to such punishment and ignominy (with the exception of the "Christ-like" Luiseño deity Wiyot). Also, contrary to the saccharine, so-called New Age conversion of everything Indian to the automatically peaceable and benign (a revolting patronization to most Indians), many California tribes prized material wealth as surely as any Roman procurator or American investor. For some tribes religious blessings accompanied material gain, just as the Protestant ethic encouraged wealth as a sign of election. The message the Franciscans brought of Christ—that his kingdom was not really of this world and its material temptations and obsessions, that he was as close to the poor, perhaps closer, as to the rich—was not, at least in the early years, very attractive to most California Indians. It may have become more so as they became poorer and more downtrodden—one of the great ironies of the whole *conquista espiritual*. The notion of Christian love and expiation, separate from passion, was therefore foreign to them, though generosity and pain for a greater good were not. A god primarily of mercy and generosity may have had a significant attraction, as well as (for women) more power.

The fourth and last difference, connected to original sin, was the bone of greatest contention, sex. While the California Indian invested importance in marriage, it was not holy in the Christian sense. It could be dissolved with financial restitution, and accepted—even respected, in rarer manifestations—with homosexuality and bisexuality. And it allowed more than one partner. Many tribes practiced polygamy, enjoyed naked or seminaked dances, and did not consider premarital sex to be sinful, though it might incur a financial levy of some sort, or the earlier mentioned half marriage. Sex was not free; but it was not fallen or evidence of some original contamination. Sex was natural, but was not to be abused or forced.

When he heard creation stories about a flood, the California Indian was more in sync with the Fathers than they probably knew. One of the primal stories of the Tolowa, who lived along the rain-drenched California-Oregon border, speaks of a tidal wave enveloping the earth where the only survivors stand, Noah-like, on Mount Enmai. When the waters recede, they build a new world. The Ohlone of the San Francisco Bay had a similar creation myth that contained the destruction of the world by flood that left only Coyote alive, standing on an island that is today's Mount Diablo. The Cahuilla and Cupeño east of Oceanside speak of the Great Creator as Mukat, who, in a deserted world, begins to be almost overwhelmed by his feelings: "His heart roared/His heart thundered/ Water and mud roared." Lying down "where it was lonely," the world begins. For the Maidu of Sacramento, Earthmaker floats around until he finds a little patch of ground that he proceeds to "stretch out" in four directions, "to the rim of the world."

This is creation by extension, a God who has to create to counteract loneliness and by virtue—as Duns Scotus and Bonaventure felt—of his own nature. And when Earthmaker remarks about his new world, "Good!" we can hear Yahweh nodding about his six days' efforts in Genesis.

Chumash cosmology was developed and taught. It consisted of three worlds: the world above (where the gods and godlike forces of the sky were), below (inhabited by "the angry ones"), and this world, called Shup, under the rule of the powerful sun and cleansing properties of the moon. After death, the Chumash believed the soul traveled west across the Pacific Ocean to the Island of the Dead. Reincarnation was taught by some. On the whole, this cosmology was not so different in its rudiments from the Judeo-Christian, except it didn't have the central figure of Christ.

Instead of a priest, the Indians had a shaman—a figure universal throughout the continent—who functioned not only as a director of spiritual hierophanies, but as a medical doctor. In this function he was both useful and not; when something toxic was ingested, the shaman had a way of sucking the object out or inducing vomiting. He was less effective blowing tobacco smoke over the sick, though a brushing or rubdown of the body couldn't have hurt.

Shamanic potential was detected in the young, mostly boys. Repeated dreams and contact with spirits in nature or ancestral ghosts were taken as an indicator of mysterious power. Their training recalled the severity of the Franciscan novitiate; shamans learned to fast, live abstemiously, and even husband pain or sickness in themselves in order to cure others. In fact, among Shasta tribes the words for "pain" and "spirit" are identical. Animal spirits could be welcomed to enhance the power of the "doctor's dance," the shaman's initiation ceremony. Among some tribes, a last initiation was the ingestion of the hallucinogenic white-trumpeted flower, the datura, which supposedly gave the shaman visions. Adult shamans went on to lead dances and other rituals for healing, celebrating of victory in war, rites of passage for youth, blessings.

California shamans practiced three specialties—shaking in place for rain, tending to snake bites, and projecting prowess by turning into a grizzly bear to take on enemies. But according to Kroeber, the primary task of a California shaman was involved in "the treatment or production of disease," the production being the exercise of power against an enemy, personal or otherwise. A shaman who "lost a patient" to death was subject to death himself. Despite his essentially ambivalent nature, for good or bad, the shaman was at least tolerated and often admired for his *ayelkwi*, or knowledge-power. This sentiment may have been projected, at least initially, to the priest as a shaman with power. Raymond White noted that *ayelkwi* was "omnipresent, imperishable, and immutable" and "above all it is dangerous and difficult to manage." James Sandos took this further: "a prudent Luiseño watched all people carefully and maintained a respectful attitude towards others for fear that the other possessed more formidable *ayelkwi* and could use it to the observer's detriment."

Four religious cults predominated in California, all with accompanying dances: the Kuksu (around the San Francisco Bay north and south and stretching to the northern San Joaquin Valley); the jimsonweed, or Toloache, based on the ingestion of hallucinogenic plants (almost all of coastal southern California, the central San Joaquin, and the extreme northwest corner of the state); wealth dances (exclusively Yurok, in the northwest); and dream singings (along the Colorado River). The Kuksu was unlike anything elsewhere in native America, with the possible exception of the Kachina cult in the Southwest. Kuksu involved boys' initiation through dances that communed with spirits of the dead or even impersonated these departed ones; stabbing, whipping with a bowstring, or ear piercing was involved. Did this self-mutilation make the Franciscans' *disciplina* less strange?

The Toloache cult, including use of datura, or jimsonweed, was most prominent in southern California. This cult undergirded the Chinig-chinich religion, described in detail by Father Boscana of Mission San Juan Capistrano. It had markedly Christian elements. Altars were built to Chinigchinich, painted in the night sky holding up the North Star, hand-prints of humans across his body. But this powerful sky god was pre-ceded by the treacherous death of a charismatic figure, Wiyot, who was born of a virgin made pregnant by lightning. When he found women's legs more attractive than Frog's, old Frog secreted poison from her body into Wiyot's drinking water. Like Christ foreshadowing his Crucifixion, Wiyot knows just what Frog is doing, but allows it to happen, promis-ing he will return to care for his people, though instead of an Easter-like resurrection, Wiyot ends up becoming the Moon. Chinigchinich then follows on, oversees large yearly mourning ceremonies that track the vil-lage dead, as well as Wiyot; such ceremonies were only in Luiseño, the "Latin" of its day. For puberty rites, in a dance hall called the *wamkish*, a teenage woman stripped naked, cupped her breasts, and offered them and herself to any man in the audience. This shocking (to Franciscan sensi-bilities) ritual aside, Indian belief in a hierophanic virgin birth, the use of a kind of sacred "Latin," a sacrificial death (though no real resurrection) made it no surprise that the Luiseño were the most easily converted of the California tribes and gathered into the largest and most successful of the missions, San Luis Rey.

The Chumash, too, were datura cult aficionados, taking the halluci-nogenic plant for everything from luck in hunting to a better love life to contacting the dead. The Chumash, however, didn't have a monotheistic God, such as Chinigchinich. They saw the cosmos caught between two contending powers of a male sun god and a female earth god, who con-trolled wind, rain, and fire. Greek-like, these two played *peón* throughout the cosmos, a kind of shell guessing game using many hands (and bets) replicated today by the Kumeyaay of San Diego. Members of the datura cult were either chosen from birth or because of some singular achieve-ment or skill. A female deity was called Momoy, identified to Chumash around Ventura and Santa Ynéz with datura. This Toloache cult was one of the few religious practices that spanned across tribes.

Unlike on the Great Plains and elsewhere in America, these religious cults in California had no policing or war-arousing function, though their educative (initiating) function was pronounced. In addition to the cults, there were girls' adolescence ceremonies that cut across all tribes pegged to the arrival of menstruation; it was a nervous time for the Indian girl. Her sight could not be met for fear of harm; her eyes were often cov-ered. She couldn't drink cold water; the Luiseños and Gabrielinos actually cooked the girl in a kind of earth oven, though not to expiration, to remove impurities, presumably. Deer-hoof rattles were shaken over her by many tribes, though the Luiseño restricted their use to deer hunts.

California Indians did not see arrival of the white man as a fulfillment of a religious prophecy—unlike Montezuma's wholesale absorption of Cortés's landing. Yet legends and stories imitated, or foretold, the cataclysmic change they were about to witness. On his brief (and fatally wounding) sojourn in the Santa Barbara Channel in 1542, when Cabrillo elicited this response from a Chumash: "they had seen men like the Spaniards before, men who had beards," who could they have been referring to? Coronado? But he was a long way off in Arizona. We know Cortés himself landed on the Isla Cerralvo near La Paz in Baja seven years before, but that was 1,300 miles south. Could Guaycura scouts of southern Baja have made it all the way through the Kumeyaay and Tongva to the Chumash? The sighting of Cabrillo, Sir Francis Drake, or Vizcaíno may have inspired the legendary story of the Kashaya Pomo, California Indians of the north coast around present-day Mendocino. It began: "In the old days, before the white people came . . . there was a boat sailing on the ocean from the south. Because [the people] had never seen a boat, they said, 'Our world must be coming to an end. Couldn't we do something? Let us plan a feast. Let us have a dance.'"

That dance was here. And one dancer was in gray.

PART THREE

THE FIRST NINE CALIFORNIA MISSIONS

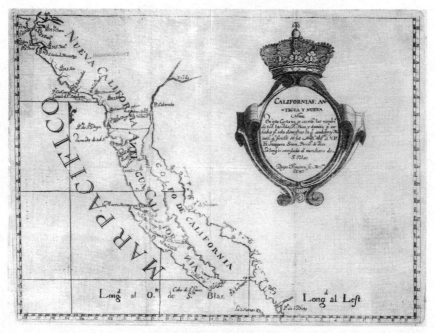

Palou map of *Nueva* or "New" California (above *Antigua*, "Old" California), 1787.

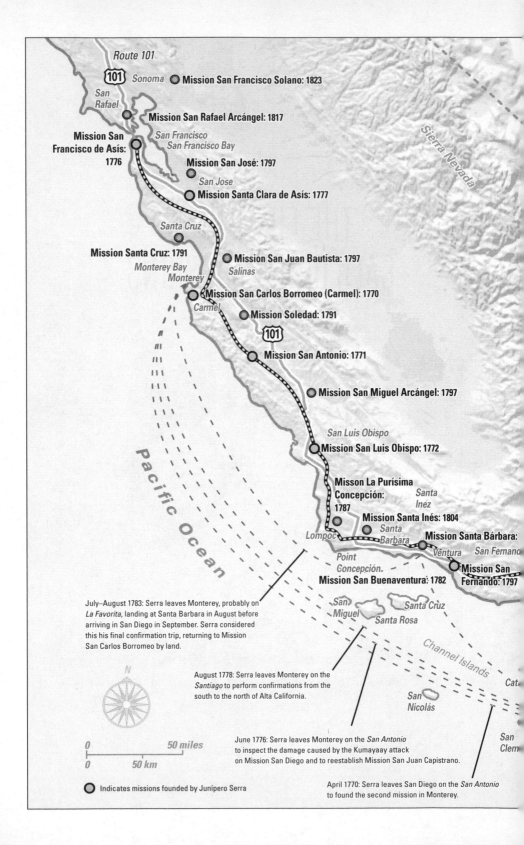

Route 101

🔵 101 Sonoma 🔵 **Mission San Francisco Solano: 1823**

San
Rafael

🔵 **Mission San Rafael Arcángel: 1817**

**Mission San
Francisco de Asís:
1776**

San Francisco
San Francisco Bay

Mission San José: 1797

San Jose

🔵 **Mission Santa Clara de Asís: 1777**

Santa Cruz

Mission Santa Cruz: 1791

Monterey Bay

Monterey

🔵 **Mission San Juan Bautista: 1797**

Salinas

🔵 **Mission San Carlos Borromeo (Carmel): 1770**

Carmel

🔵 **Mission Soledad: 1791**

101

🔵 **Mission San Antonio: 1771**

🔵 **Mission San Miguel Arcángel: 1797**

San Luis Obispo

🔵 **Mission San Luis Obispo: 1772**

**Misson La Purísima
Concepción:**
*Santa
Inez*
1787
🔵 **Mission Santa Inés: 1804**

Santa
Barbara

Lompoc

Mission Santa Bárbara:

Point
Concepción.

Ventura

San Fernand

🔵 **Mission San
Fernando: 1797**

Mission San Buenaventura: 1782

Sierra Nevada

Pacific Ocean

July–August 1783: Serra leaves Monterey, probably on
La Favorita, landing at Santa Barbara in August before
arriving in San Diego in September. Serra considered
this his final confirmation trip, returning to Mission
San Carlos Borromeo by land.

San
Miguel
Santa Cruz
Santa Rosa

Channel Islands

Cat

August 1778: Serra leaves Monterey on the
Santiago to perform confirmations from the
south to the north of Alta California.

San
Nicolás

N

0   50 miles

0   50 km

June 1776: Serra leaves Monterey on the *San Antonio*
to inspect the damage caused by the Kumayaay attack
on Mission San Diego and to reestablish Mission San Juan Capistrano.

San
Clem

🔵 Indicates missions founded by Junípero Serra

April 1770: Serra leaves San Diego on the *San Antonio*
to found the second mission in Monterey.

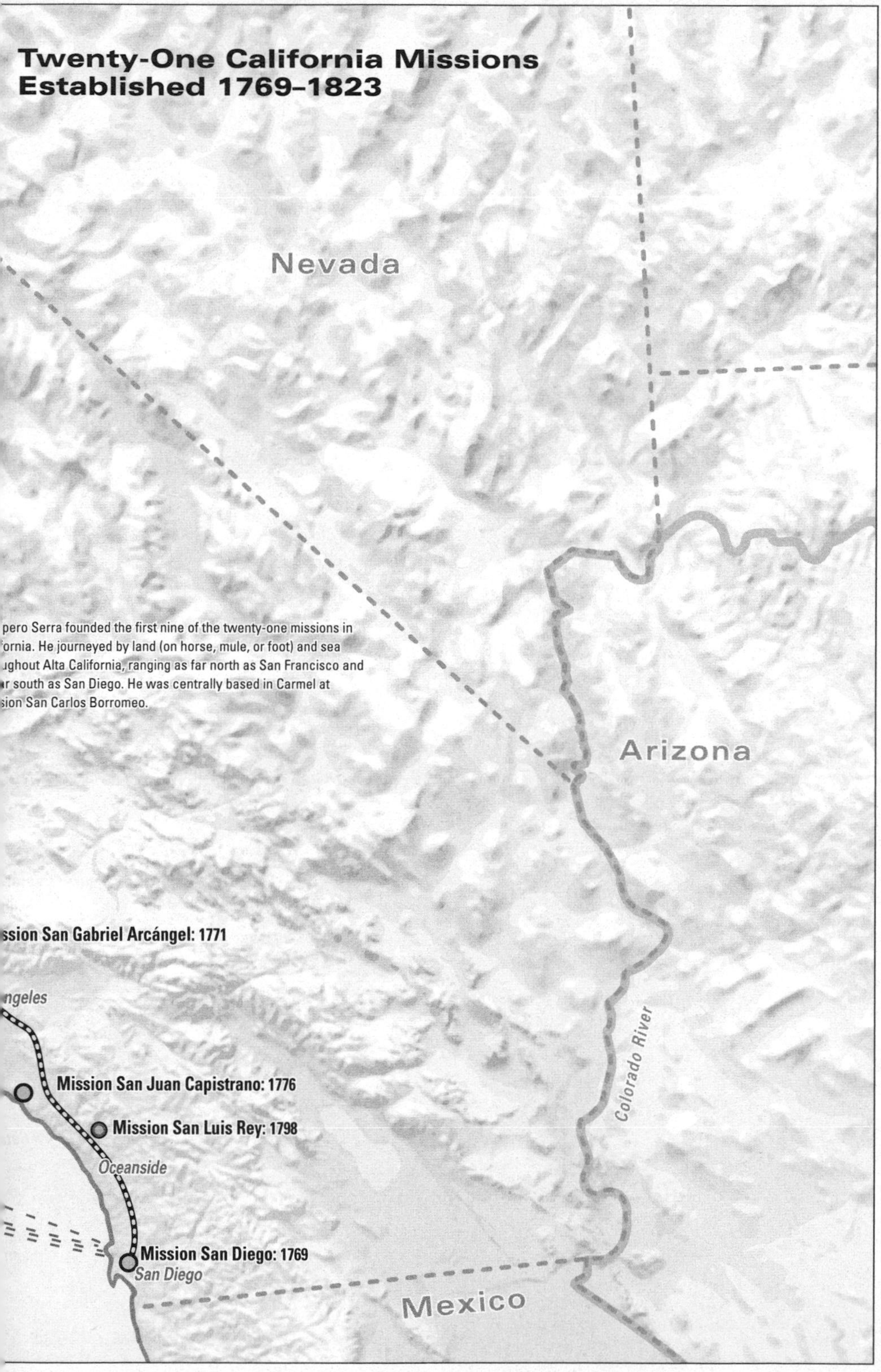

Twenty-One California Missions
Established 1769–1823

Nevada

pero Serra founded the first nine of the twenty-one missions in
ornia. He journeyed by land (on horse, mule, or foot) and sea
ughout Alta California, ranging as far north as San Francisco and
r south as San Diego. He was centrally based in Carmel at
sion San Carlos Borromeo.

Arizona

ssion San Gabriel Arcángel: 1771

ngeles

Mission San Juan Capistrano: 1776

Mission San Luis Rey: 1798

Oceanside

Colorado River

Mission San Diego: 1769
San Diego

Mexico

CHAPTER TWELVE

MISSION SAN DIEGO DE ALCALÁ: THE SOLACE OF UNFORTUNATES

To amass riches—a wealth of sufferings.
—JUNÍPERO SERRA

Earliest photo of Mission San Diego, 1874.

*T*he day the first ship *San Antonio* (or *Príncipe*) set anchor in San Diego Harbor—April 11, 1769—portents in the sky and on earth spoke to the Indians and Franciscans in vastly different ways, a divergence that even four years later neither Serra nor his confreres understood or even perceived. That portentous day, just as runners, out of breath, were trying to explain to their elders at the Kumeyaay village of Cosoy that strange, whale-sized vessels had surfaced in the bay, an earthquake rocked the area, rattling arrows in their quivers, sending the huts of rushes hissing. And this wasn't all. Soon a dark disc moved across the sun and the land itself darkened, even at midday. It was a solar eclipse. The Kumeyaay read these signs gravely. When white-faced, light-haired, bearded men rowed to shore, stumbled up the sandbank, and collapsed from hunger and sickness, the images couldn't have been eerier. The Indians read them as profound indications that the universe did not approve these strange visitors.

Serra, however, read the opposite. In the first lengthy report he sent to the viceroy on the nascent California missions four years later, Serra revealed that he learned of these monumental occurrences nine months after the Spanish ships had arrived from the Indians themselves: "According to the depositions made by the Indians and corroborated by many witnesses, now that we can understand their language, on that day there was an eclipse of the sun and an earthquake, all of which, together with the sight of the ship, which appeared to them far too big to be a whale, as they first supposed, was cause for much amazement. They suspected that there was some great event about to take place." Indeed there was. But in his own reverie, Serra misread the Indians: "On that day, the inanimate creatures of heaven and earth began to preach a most marvelous way to these poor wretched gentiles; the sea also taking its part . . . in proclaiming these wonders." Apparently, the sailors of the *San Antonio* were on deck when the earthquake hit and in the hold for the eclipse, or perhaps they were in such bad shape they wouldn't have known an eclipse from a snowfall. The Indians seem to have told Serra that there was a small tsunami, too. But if "these wonders" were to Serra awe-ful, they were plain awful to the Kumeyaay, and they greatly influenced their initial and subsequent responses to the Spaniards. The Kumeyaay were the most resistant of California Indian tribes, remaining so for half a century. The disconnect between two different mystical interpretations of natural events made for an exceedingly tragic beginning. All this, of course, was set in motion before Serra even arrived.

Serra's joy at first sighting the two ships faded quickly. Up close, the Spanish sailors lay dead or dying of scurvy, sprawled in sea oats or on the naked sand. "The expedition by sea was a disaster," he declared two days later. The *San Carlos*, though it had left earlier than its sister ship, suffered from a grievous miscalculation of latitude. Captain Vicente Vila overshot San Diego by two degrees latitude, halfway up the California coast near San Luis Obispo, where bitter winds thrashed the ship. More significant was a desperate search for fresh water, as the staves of the *San Carlos*'s four water barrels came loose, leaking nearly all the drinking water out into the bilge. The *San Carlos* had stopped along Baja at a place with no water. As happens with scurvy, the sailors got lethargic and weak. Few could man the ship.

After three and a half months at sea for a trip that should have taken half that time, the *San Carlos* had limped into San Diego Harbor, practically a ghost ship. At least twenty-one of its sailors, and several of its twenty-five soldiers, had died at sea of the high fevers and infections that come with scurvy. By the time Serra reached San Diego on July 1, all its sailors except one were dead, as well as most of the soldiers; the cook, four officers, the engineer, and the doctor had barely survived, presumably on the last bad water left. To add to the misery, the crew of the *San Antonio*, which had arrived two weeks earlier (though it had left later) and in decent shape, caught infections from the *San Carlos* crew; eight of the *San Antonio* men had died and many were half delirious on the sand.

As Serra peered under the canopies of palm in the makeshift outdoor hospital, men moaned, their gums spongy and bleeding, their teeth fallen out. Serra blessed their limbs, covered in open sores. He handed out sage gruel given warily by the Kumeyaay for the starving: "It was torture for them when food to cure their illness passed their bleeding gums." He even blessed Captain Juan Pérez of the *San Antonio*, who himself was prostrate on a mat. As Maynard Geiger aptly put it, "San Diego's first institution was not a mission or a pueblo but an infirmary." Or, he might have added, a morgue.

Despite the pall over the rendezvous in San Diego, Serra ended his diary with plainspoken thanks: "God be blessed for everything." He said Mass for all the day after arriving, July 2. Riddled by death as they were, the four prongs of the expedition were now together; "seeing all their parts united into one" gave him joy and resolution. Serra always seemed to have this instinct to rise to adversity; the worse it got, the better he became. He concludes his all-too-rare diary with a lovely phrase; theirs was "the solace of unfortunates."

In fact, the whole expedition was threadbare. Serra himself wrote his superior, Guardian Juan Andrés: "My tunics—well, they are both about falling to pieces." San Diego, too, was "quite cold"—a holdover, no doubt, of the Southland's infamous "June gloom," as well as the winds off Mission Bay. Portolá informed Serra he was ordering Captain Pérez of the *San Antonio*, apparently healthy but strapped for seaworthy mates, to make an emergency trip back to San Blas for food, supplies, and healthy sailors. This was an extremely perilous move, for the third ship, the *San José*, which everyone thought would bring resupply, was nowhere near (and would soon plummet to the bottom of the sea). But Portolá had little choice. The men were dead and dying, and though they had an initial welcome of food from the local Indians, it had withered in the demand for more beads and cloth than the expedition had or was willing to part with. To the Kumeyaay, "This was not only impolite—it was rude." The whole San Diego experiment was on the verge of an early collapse. On July 9, Captain Pérez weighed anchor on the *San Antonio* with only eight of his original twenty-eight sailors and a few others loaned from the *San Carlos*; before he ever got to San Blas, nine crewmen were thrown overboard, dead.

Portolá, sensing doom for San Diego, thought he could salvage something. As a hedge against the Russians, Monterey was the chief goal, and Portolá decided to forge onward toward the elusive northern harbor that had so captivated Vizcaíno in 1602. Combining the two land parties, he took with him seventy-four men, mostly Catalonian soldiers and Baja Indians, including Captain Fernando de Rivera y Moncada and Fathers Crespí (who would continue the diary honors) and Francisco Gómez. But most who marched with Portolá for the first attempt at Monterey were walking wounded, infected by the sailors. Serra sent them hobbling off with a High Mass on July 14 in honor of St. Joseph, the chosen patron of the whole expedition.

Left virtually alone on the San Diego strand with a crippled if not empty *San Carlos*, Serra was undeterred. On July 16, 1769, close to the village of Cosoy, the first mission in California was founded. It was the same day he had founded Velicatá in Baja, the feast day not only of Our Lady of Mount Carmel, but of the major Spanish victory in 1212 over the Moors at Las Navas de Tolosa. It's Palou, not Serra, who opines bombastically that when Serra planted the Holy Cross at San Diego it was "exactly" as at the "great victory over the barbarous Mohammedans . . . driving out all the army of hell," completely forgetting his own founder's attempt to minister to the Muslims in Egypt peaceably.

The first mission in California—San Diego de Alcalá—was basically constructed by medics in their spare time after treating the sick of the ships. They erected little more than tule rushes intertwined over poles on Presidio Hill overlooking the harbor. After the first Mass at this *enramada*, Serra pulled out a bound register that he signed, along with Fathers Parron and Vizcaíno. The fledgling mission took form side by side with the army presidio.

Made suspicious of the intentions of the Spaniards by the unlikely signs in sky and shaking earth, and possessing a language different from any of the Baja interpreters, the Kumeyaay of San Diego withdrew their rather guarded open arms, in favor of quick hands. Cloth was their chief interest. They preyed on the sick sailors, stripping them. Marveling at the flapping sails when the boats first came into harbor, by night they paddled quietly out to the *San Carlos*, climbed over the gunwales, and ripped swatches of sail, as well as the yardarm ropes. Two of the thinned crew of eight were put on watch through the night.

Perhaps Serra saw the interlopers and hid a smile. He wasn't making much progress with the Indians, and even eight months later, he was painfully aware of it: "Until today—what with the few of us who are well, while most were sick; the poor condition both of the countryside around and the houses we live in; and not having an interpreter to communicate in any proper fashion with these poor naked gentiles—little more could be done than to prepare the ground for their eventual conversion and salvation." Crespí, before he had left, was more direct, calling the San Diego Indians "very sharp, smart, greedy . . . and very great thieves."

The pleasurable encounters with northern Baja tribes seemed a distant memory. The land and the people were different, and with them the Spaniards had inadvertently gotten off on the wrong transcendental foot. The Indians stopped offering food, and certainly didn't need any themselves. Crespí noted the abundant sardines, bat rays, and mussels the Kumeyaay pulled in from the rushes and the bay. Spanish food was of no use as a peace offering; the Indians wouldn't touch it, except one boy, who tried out a lump of sugar, which he "spit out as if it were poison."

Just after giving Communion to four soldiers—the entire guard of the Spanish encampment—Serra barely had time to cover the chalice with the paten before he spotted a group of twenty painted Kumeyaay with bows, arrows, and war clubs stripping the sick of their sheets.

"To arms!" one of the soldiers yelled and bolted for his pistol. Three others strapped on their *cueras*, leather jackets of deerskin, and clutched their oval leather *ardagas*, shields copied exactly from the Moors. The Kumeyaay raiders drew back, but nocked and shot their arrows. They raised "wooden sabers which could cut almost like steel." As Serra put it, "The fight was on."

"Long live the faith of our Lord Jesus Christ," cried the blacksmith Chacón, pitching in with his .69-caliber pistol. "May these enemy dogs die!" He was quickly wounded by an arrow. Soon the carpenter joined the fray: six against twenty.

Serra and Vizcaíno moved quickly to the back of the *enramada*, where there was a small living quarters. They both knelt and prayed to the sound of arrows hitting the shields, shouts, the explosions of shot, Kumeyaay whoops. When Vizcaíno tried to straighten the agave mat door to the room as it fluttered in the breeze, an arrow struck his hand. Though it had no flint tip, it shattered, partly paralyzing Vizcaíno's hand for the rest of his life.

Suddenly Serra's servant crashed through the mat door, falling on reeds, blood pouring from the hole in his neck from which he had pulled the arrow.

"*Padre*, absolve me, for the Indians have killed me!" José María Vergerano cried out.

Stunned to see his side companion all the way from Guadalajara with "so much blood streaming from his temples and mouth," Serra blessed him, "helped him to die well," though any oil for Extreme Unction he once had was long drained. In fifteen minutes, his faithful servant died in his arms. Serra's hutch was now "a sea of blood." He prepared to die himself: "There I was with the dead man, thinking it most probable I would soon have to follow him." In a rain of arrows, he clutched a small statue or painting of the Blessed Mother in one hand and a cross in the other. He slipped unconsciously to the logic of his time and people, "begging God to give victory to our Holy Catholic faith," and yet, incredibly, "without the loss of a single soul." At the same time, he thought death by martyrdom might deliver him, "great sinner that I am." It was not the first time, or last, Serra confessed this to a superior. Serra may also have sensed, unconsciously, that the first battle of San Diego presaged the plunder and violence that lay ahead.

By nightfall, though none of the Spanish soldiers was hurt, the casualties numbered one dead and three wounded (Vizcaíno, Chacón the blacksmith, and one leatherjacketed Christian Indian from San Ignacio in Baja). The three recuperated, for the most part. Three Kumeyaay Indians died and were cremated, and though Serra must have heard the wailing of their mourning ceremonies, he either didn't know of or wouldn't acknowledge these deaths. Clearly, though badly outnumbered, the Spaniards' frightful up-close explosions of firearms, something the Indians had neither seen nor heard, tipped the balance. They would continue to do so, with few exceptions.

What was the effect of the first battle of San Diego? Palou indicates things calmed down, the Indians visiting "with frequency," without arms, chastened by Spanish power. Others are not nearly as sanguine and point out the soldiers quickly erected a stockade and guard far out from the settlement.

Shortly after the nerve-racking initial assault, in late August 1769, a fifteen-year-old boy from the nearby village of Cosoy came to the Spanish encampment, speaking a few words of Spanish. Guileless and confident, he had visited the encampment several times since the strangers arrived aboard their booming ships several months earlier. Serra saw a chance to seize back the initiative. He fetched his silver-plated shell, dipped it into the creek, poured out water on his own head, speaking in slow Spanish and broken Kumeyaay to the teenage boy from Cosoy that he would like to baptize an infant. Could someone bring one? He promised clothes to the parents.

In a few days, Serra, "filled with great joy" (Palou's words), welcomed a father at the head of a group of villagers, a baby boy in his arms. Serra asked a corporal among the soldiers to be the sponsor of the child and gathered as many as could fit of both Indians and soldiers into the crude hut he was using as a chapel. Serra took out a cloth, perhaps a purificator, and spread it over the naked baby. Dressing quickly in surplice, he kissed a stole and looped it over his own head. He dipped his thumb and forefinger into holy oil of a mahogany chrismatory he had carried all the way from Loreto for just such moments (he had used it in good measure with forty-four Indians at Juan de Dios in Baja), crossing oil on the baby's forehead and his soft chest. No one raised a fuss when he put spittle to his fingers and blessed the baby's ears and nostrils.

"I baptize thee in the name of the Father, the Son, and—" That's as far as it got. Just as he filled the silver baptismal shell with water and tumbled it over the baby, the father, with a look of astonishment, snatched the child out of the corporal's arms and ran back with him to Cosoy. Serra poured the water over nothing but dirt and the corporal's shoes. He stood there with an empty shell.

Serra was long haunted by this inaugural failure in San Diego, the baptism left "unperformed." He would be brought to tears by its memory many years later in old age at Carmel, recalling that others took baptism "without the least repugnance." Still, to what did he ascribe the failure with the Cosoy boy? He blamed "his own sins." There was Serra's nagging perfectionism again, masking as unworthiness. He would wait a full year for another chance to baptize in San Diego.

The very day Serra mopped up blood in his hut in San Diego, his old Mallorca student, Father Juan Crespí, was being serenaded by the wooden flutes of Chumash Indians along the Santa Barbara Channel. It was August 15, 1769, and Crespí and his companion, Francisco Gómez, concelebrated Mass for the Assumption at La Asumpta (present-day Ventura) among at least four hundred Chumash; they then traveled two leagues (about six miles) to Santa Cunegundis, a little fishing village of about ten houses (at present-day Pitas Point, or Emma Wood State Beach). The Ventureño Chumash struck up flutes and drums, making Portolá wonder if it were a call to arms: "They began piping to us, here at this spot, about eight o'clock at night or later from some distance off; it went on for a great deal of the night, and had our Captain somewhat worried, but plainly it was all done in order to entertain us."

Crespí was in a zone, that rarefied light on water and mountain and island that is the Santa Barbara Channel. He was aware it drank the sun:

"The whole channel here trends east and west, a coast as calm and clear as though it were a pool of oil or a lake." He saw how it benefited trade: "The islanders and the mainland people, with the canoes they all possess, carry out a great deal of transport to and fro, including . . . their own manner of commerce." The day before at a Ventureño town, for the first time in Crespí's journals (and perhaps any Spaniard's to date) the sound of Indian laughter is celebrated: "They greeted us with great noise and laughter. They were all unarmed." Similarly, on July 28, just north of San Pedro, when the Spaniards had encountered a Tongva tribe that "urged us not to go away" but rather gave the travelers bear meat and "refreshing" sage gruel, "offering us all of their land, which the mountain people wanted to take away from them," that they themselves "would build houses for us and protect us" in return for Spanish protection, Crespí records the Tongva chief bursting into "such tears of joy and happiness . . . as greatly touched the hearts of all of us present there." Those have to be the first tears recorded by a white man of "the others" in California.

Crespí and Portolá passed through many of the twenty prosperous, vibrant Chumash towns of Ventura and Santa Barbara, the thickest native population they would encounter and a culturally and socially formidable one. Crespí remarked on their "extremely large" houses: "round like half oranges." The Chumash stone mortars at their graveyards, for example, "might do well for holy water or even baptismal fonts" (one did at San Buenaventura). Around Santa Paula, the Tongva had draped "beadwork around my neck like a rosary." On the Feast of the Assumption (August 15), he waxed more enthusiastic about the site for a future mission (it would be the long-contested Mission San Buenaventura) than any place in California. In short, the Chumash were the anti-Kumeyaay, Ventura–Santa Barbara the anti–San Diego, where Serra's "assumption" had just backfired.

While Serra suffered in isolation, Crespí and Portolá were encountering, bravely, a new world. Crespí's record of the land trip to Monterey is the first by a European through Upper California. Few today know that downtown Los Angeles was first described by Crespí as it lay at the bend of a once mighty river, the Los Angeles (known later as the L.A. Wash and notoriously cemented by the US Army Corps of Engineers). Portolá had also followed the Santa Ana and San Gabriel Rivers (also cemented and dammed in places) spilling out of the mountains to the sea, and parallel and ever closer to the Los Angeles River, converging on a spot near today's First and Grand Streets, then a wide expanse of bottomlands "looking from afar like nothing so much as large cornfields." On that wild rural spot would grow a city of ten million.

On August 2, Crespí crowned it with the best name he could think of—the Porciúncula, the Assisi land on which St. Francis rebuilt a broken-down church, founding his order five hundred years before. Thus was Los Angeles from its very beginning connected to notions of resurrection, and a saint who talked to wild things and took peace to enemies.

As they rode their horses and mules north, the tribes welcomed them, and nature surprised if not delighted. On the same day the expedition named downtown Los Angeles after St. Francis's home ground (*Nuestra Señora de los Angeles del Río de la Porciúncula*), a scouting party stumbled across the La Brea Tar Pits down the future Wilshire Boulevard, then "in a ravine [with] . . . forty springs of pitch boiling in great surges out of the ground . . . enough to caulk many ships with." No doubt this tar caulked the canoes of the Tongva and Chumash. Around San Juan Capistrano (which he named), Crespí compared a rich grove of sycamores to a Mallorcan sight: "nothing so much as a handsome fig orchard." In Santa Margarita (again Crespí's name), natives approached with bear claw necklaces, hinting at bear country nearby. In clear sight of his newly christened San Clemente Island, probably around Huntington Beach, the expedition happened upon a cinnabar mine for red face paint. They saw so many antelopes in Orange County they looked like vast herds of Mallorcan goats.

In the lagoons of Isla Vista near the present-day campus of the University of California at Santa Barbara, on August 21, the Portolá party shot and killed its first bear in a large gathering of twenty bears drinking and splashing in the water. Crespí thought it was the size of a bull, exclaiming, "A fierce sort of beast in every way, and God deliver any living thing from their claws, horrid to behold!"

At especially arduous times during the six-month trek to and from Monterey, Crespí found his faith, life, and the accoutrements of the land intersecting, no more poignantly than on the feast day of St. Francis's stigmata. The expedition was facing the imposingly beautiful pale green wall that hides Big Sur—the Santa Lucia Mountains. Crespí exclaimed: "On merely viewing from below the way by which we must climb, it becomes almost impossible to believe that it can be done." But they ascended "with God's grace, very slowly and bit by bit . . . climbing this extremely tall height. When standing on top and turning around to look back, it was a very fearful thing to see the depth behind us." That sheer drop into the Pacific Crespí, Portolá, and the rest were daring on foot or on wobbly mules in backbreaking climbs. To Crespí, it all recalled Mount Alverna, where Christ "imprinted" his sacred wounds on Francis of Assisi, and he named a Big Sur mission that should be planted there "The Wounds of Our Father."

Crespí's first taste of evangelism was more successful than Serra's. Unbeknownst to him, Crespí supplanted Serra as the first priest to baptize someone in California. This had occurred on July 22, 1769, south of Laguna Beach (as they went up a pass the very next day) around San Onofre, at a stream he named after St. Apollinaris. Two baptisms, actually—of two girls, one sick unto death from body-long burns, whom he named, pouring the creek water over her head while she cried softly, "Margarita Magdalen." The other was an infant too weak to suck at the breast, whom Crespí named similarly: "María Magdalen," thus wedding them (and himself) in this important moment to the memory of the New Testament's most attractive (and compelling) sinner.

Earlier, near Capistrano, both Crespí and his companion, Father Gómez, got a sobering sense of how hard it was going to be to convert such buoyant people to the worship of a man nailed to a cross. When Gómez went into a peroration pointing at the sad man and the nails about how "our Lord Jesus had died for everyone so that we should go to heaven and not be damned," the Acjachemen (later called Juaneños) knitted their brows, and answered with an incomprehensible speech of their own. Gómez made the soldiers cross themselves at the sign of the crucifix, but the Indians didn't follow suit, "making signs with their hands to take it away from them," whirling around like dervishes, finally just plain sighing. Crespí's admission—"They would sometimes sigh when spoken to about these matters"—indicates more than one frustrated response, and probably from more than one tribe. But such a response was not universal. Up the road, perhaps near Dana Point, an ebullient, friendly tribe with some "very fair and red-haired" children kissed the cross and the rosary "without the slightest reluctance." Crespí taught them to say *Amar a Dios* (Love God)—soon to be a California mission standard—and they rattled that off each morning when the Spaniards emerged from their tents, an unconscious one-upsmanship.

In fact, what may have quickened in certain tribes' hearts at the sight of the advancing Spaniards—at least initially—was not threat, but rescue. Like the Tongva in Los Angeles, the coastal Chumash appear to have been raided repeatedly by mountain tribes; in the Santa Barbara area, a man who had lost an eye to an arrow and was still healing approached them. "By what we understood from the good heathens here, they [the mountain people] destroyed five villages," Crespí noted, and the marauders were about to attack the village the Spaniards were visiting at the time. More than once, Portolá declined to involve himself in intertribe squabbles or warfare. Crespí records at least one Chumash village around Gaviota questioning their intentions: "They asked us: had we killed people along the way, and were reassured as to our not having harmed anyone, which very much pleased them." Crespí, of course, did not know about the deaths of three Indians in the San Diego battle three weeks before.

Still, the people Crespí encountered were the real wonder, and he is especially good at portraying them as individuals as opposed to tribes. One tall "very imposing . . . bright and friendly" Indian chief took an eager interest in the Spanish expedition. Added to his "very good features" was a disfigurement. Crespí nicknamed him "the Goiter" (or *El Buchón*) for "a very large tumor that hangs from one side of his neck, large as a well-swollen ox gall." Crespí was enamored of his inexplicable "goodness towards us," and seeing the great respect his own people had for him, felt that if the Goiter "became a Christian, much would be gained on God's account." Another "bright and lively" fellow at Gaviota who followed them up and down the coast was nicknamed *El Loco*.

However, Crespí admits being "disturbed" by the *berdache* (transvestites) at Tajiguas, near Gaviota. (Still, according to Dr. John Johnson, on at least three occasions *joyas*—"jewels," for homosexuals—were baptized, at missions Santa Barbara, La Purísima, and San Fernando.) As for the Portolá expedition's main objective—Monterey—it was literally lost in fog. Getting farther north, on September 8, they encountered the huge "head" of Morro Rock and Morro Bay (after *morro*, knoll, but with a hinto of *moro*, a Moor), and after veering inland following the Salinas River back toward the sea, they emerged on Monterey Bay—but failed to recognize it. The Salinas River deceptively enters the large bay at the center of its curve. Even on clear days, it is hard to tell that you are in an alcove. Also, Portolá and Crespí mistook the Salinas for the Carmel River, while the famed Vizcaíno oak, where Father Ascensión said the first California Mass in 1602 for the explorer, escaped them.

The consolation prize—and what a consolation it was—for Portolá, trudging a bit farther north in despondency, was the discovery of San Francisco Bay. Rather, it was Sergeant Ortega who spotted it from Sweeney's Ridge east of Pacifica, identifying the Farallon Islands at the bay's mouth and Point Reyes (Francis Drake's hideout) in the distance north. This sighting occurred November 1 and was reported to the expedition two days later. A San Francisco force hit the tents that night: "So strong a north wind blew here that it tore down everything that was standing and tossed quite large firebrands into the air."

The way north around the bay repeatedly blocked, Captain Rivera grew cranky. "It should be evident to Your Excellencies that I have already documented my views and I believe that I should have been excused from doing this again." He reminds Portolá that he was never up for the Monterey journey in the first place, feared the troops would starve along the way, and, ever mindful of his mules (it was Rivera's job to put the mule train together in Baja), thought they, too, would break down. He was even fearful of an Indian massacre, pointing out what had happened to Ponce de León in Florida. On December 7, Portolá turned back south.

The return journey was uneventful, except for honking geese heading the same way overhead, which Crespí rather surrealistically compares to "large plains paved with cobblestones." (Nature for Crespí is always imagistically a "road to the Lord.") In the Santa Lucias, it was so cold Crespí "nearly lost the sense of touch and nearly wailed aloud." By December 20, the addled party was killing every third mule to eat, and Portolá gave up his own final store of food to the men. Christmas was spent in exhaustion on the sand at Morro Bay, staring at the Rock of the Moor.

New Year's turned violent: Lieutenant Fages killed a she bear and her two cubs, on the day of the Lord's Circumcision, Crespí noted. But they ate for three days. Soon the Santa Barbara Channel and its rich fishery further relieved the Spaniards of starvation, who gave in exchange for the natives' catch every bit of iron they had, though presumably not the pistols. The channel was Crespí's blessed zone, and he would remember it for the rest of his life. Finally, on January 24, 1770, the exhausted party reached Los Pocitos de San Diego (the Little Wells of San Diego)—probably Mission Bay—and soon were greeted by Father Serra, who served up "a griddle cake such as we had not had for many a day, and in the excitement, all our troubles were forgotten."

Not for long. Although Serra rejoiced at the expedition's return and even joked with Portolá about missing out on Monterey—"You come from Rome without having seen the pope"—what Serra had to tell everyone hardly inflated Portolá's sails. The Indians had attacked; his valet was dead; many more men had succumbed on the beach to scurvy; the Indians were not resupplying the colony. And worst of all—in the six intervening months the *San Antonio* had not returned, nor had the *San José* come up from the south. They feared both were sunk.

Bereft of supplies and food, Portolá arrived back in San Diego with a distinct liability—seventy-four more mouths to feed. Though Portolá immediately sent Rivera down to Velicatá in Baja with a majority of the soldiers not only to seek relief but give relief (a relief for Crespí in real terms, as he had come to dislike the cranky Rivera immensely), Portolá knew the situation was dire. If San Diego were not to be swallowed up by the wild and starve (the English "Lost Colony" in Roanoke had done just this a century before), there was no alternative but abandonment. Whispers of retreat, Crespí wrote, "were very painful to the Reverend Father President and the rest of us."

Finally, Portolá had had enough. He set a deadline, telling Serra that if no ship arrived by March 19, the Feast of St. Joseph, the patron saint of the whole enterprise, he would march everyone the next day back to Loreto in Baja.

Serra, not naïve about their prospects, was nevertheless devastated: "He had staked his life and health on this venture . . . to Christianize California. His whole nature rebelled against giving up." Palou called up an Indian image, saying the announcement was a "sharp arrow" at Serra's heart, implying what the Kumeyaay had started, Portolá would finish.

Nevertheless, after painting a dramatic picture of the highs and lows of the San Diego enterprise, on February 10, 1770, Serra wrote the guardian in Mexico City, "We are not dead yet, thank God" (*no nos muertos hasta aquí, gracias a Dios*). In fact, he was preparing for martyrdom; what he had missed at San Saba with the Apaches, the Kumeyaay might effect. He asked the guardian for permission to stay on the San Diego strand after everyone else left, alone except for Father Crespí, telling Palou they were determined "to hold out to the last gasp." Of course, Serra's request to stay was disingenuous, for "the inevitable refusal would not have been transmitted to San Diego harbor after the rest of the Expedition had abandoned the place."

Histrionics aside, Serra faced the situation with the confidence of the well versed and constitutionally equipped: prayer and bedrock pragmatics. He invited Portolá and the soldiers to join him in a novena to St. Joseph, the "most anxious" days of his life. But he quietly proposed an alternative plan to Captain Vila of the *San Carlos*, exacting a promise that, should Portolá leave, he and Crespí might take up residence in the hold of his ship.

What happened next provides one of the great legends of the founding of California. Portolá had curried and saddled his horses and mules. Everyone was ready to depart. Exactly on March 19, from the prow of Point Loma on Presidio Hill, just as the soldiers were lifting their packs to trudge the thousand miles to Loreto, someone yelled out, "San Antonio *esta aquí!*"

Astonishingly, the *San Antonio was* there, and then it was gone. Serra didn't know whether to thank God, or curse. The whole group—Portolá, Serra, Costanso, Fages, the Christian Cochimí from Baja, the muleteers and the soldiers—crowded to the point, yelling as the masts and sails disappeared in the mist. All began to argue with each other, eyes alive, hands thrust near the temples. "*Qué pasó? Qué pasó?*" they cried. Confused, Portolá delayed departure.

What happened, in fact, was that the *San Antonio* was executing its orders issued at San Blas: meet up and relieve the land expedition in Monterey. José de Gálvez had figured of the two, Portolá's party would be in worse shape than those staying put in San Diego. Besides, Monterey had always been the fixed star in Spain's California sky. (Was Gálvez implicitly devaluing the first mission, and therefore the *conquista espiritual* in San Diego?) In any case, God soon intervened: the *San Antonio* lost an anchor mooring in the Santa Barbara Channel to take fresh water. When asked if they'd seen Portolá passing through north, the Chumash told Captain Pérez yes, they had, but the expedition had turned around and come back, and was heading south now. Ironically, the Chumash Indians of Santa Barbara saved the whole Spanish enterprise in California, procuring in their honesty their own demise. Pérez, who must have returned to a boat spinning on one anchor, got back on ship and followed Portolá south. Four days after first being spotted at Point Loma and disappearing to anguished cries, the *San Antonio* finally put in at San Diego Harbor, to exaltation.

Palou later proclaimed it "a miracle wrought by the Holy Patriarch on this, his own day." Serra, whose pleadings with Portolá to stay *one more day* must have made him hoarse, broke down on sight of the ship growing larger, coming toward them. From now on, he promised, on the nineteenth of every month, he would say a High Mass in honor of St. Joseph, who had fathered a child he fervently believed not his, but His. Serra would go on to sing of unsung St. Joseph 161 times, lighting 990 tall candles, up to his last breath in California.

Serra led a vigorous *Te Deum Laudamus* that day, facing the Pacific. Crespí pronounced "our cares now at an end, since we regarded the survival at least of San Diego Mission as ensured by this arrival." By 1775, the mission had moved to a safer place inland, away from the danger of the ninety-seven Kumeyaay living "within the sound of the bells," bells staggered in a three-rowed tier unlike anything in Europe. The little blue-eyed friend of Serra's youth was perfectly happy to write off Monterey and its chill.

But not Serra. Monterey! This time he was going, and, damn the anchors, he would find it.

CHAPTER THIRTEEN

MISSION SAN CARLOS BORROMEO DE CARMELO: THE DISAPPEARING OAK OF MONTEREY

Start by doing what is necessary, then what is possible,
and suddenly you are doing the impossible.
—ST. FRANCIS OF ASSISI

The "Virgin of Light" pulling a young man
from the jaws of hell while being offered
hearts in a basket. Carmel Mission Collection.

Serra in the *San Antonio* sailing north: the islands going by—San Clemente, Santa Cruz, San Miguel. Home! Ibiza, Mallorca, Minorca.

Watching the land like a hand, its fingers coming at you. Those gouges of the ocean called cliffs, palisades, coves. The long white strips of beach, the bunched green at the points. The gulls following the wake of the ship as he followed the wake of the Lord, the trail of the sun. A daily Pentecost in cobalt blue, a shimmering ladder of light leading at dawn to Monterey and at sundown across the globe to China. How many times did Serra stare at the ladder of the Pacific, how many times did he want to climb it to the horizon?

Winds, bad maps, perhaps too much rum at night down the throat of Don Pino, Captain Pérez's navigator at the wheel, threw the *San Antonio* off course enough that it took Serra a month and a half to go 430 nautical miles from San Diego to Monterey. Typically understated about unsavory events beyond his control, Serra dubbed the voyage "somewhat trying." Nevertheless, on May 31, 1770, addled by the fear that they, too, had overshot Monterey, if not the whole of Alta California (they had—all the way north to the Farallon Islands outside San Francisco Bay and south halfway down Baja), Serra forgot the Pacific winds quickly when the *San Antonio* dropped anchor in a rocky bay "where our ancestors the Spaniards landed in 1603 [*sic*]." There staring at them was the very oak—or so they believed—under which Vizcaíno had ordered a Mass be said 167 years before. Serra prepared for a second Mass under that great live oak, dispelling the confusion wrought by Crespí's and Portolá's first land expedition: "We should definitely put out of our minds all thought, or any lingering fancy, of the port's having disappeared."

In fact, Crespí and Portolá had beaten Serra to Monterey by eight days (thirty-eight days in all), doing better by land (this second time) than Serra by sea. Their new land journey was largely uneventful; the Indians seemed less "at home" than they had been in the fall and winter. It was now spring and time for fresh seed gathering and early hunting. Several smaller villages had disappeared (probably in migration to better food sources). Around Oceanside, some Luiseño Indians motioned the expedition to get its horses out of a hollow filled with seed-bearing trees and bushes; it hadn't been picked yet. The Spaniards complied, rearing their horses.

Crespí was the first to record a daily chronicle of California's beauty, marveling at details like the purple sage in spring bloom, "the fields abloom on all sides" with mustard, wild carrot, blue and purple lupine, lily of the valley, larkspur, *copa de oro*. He enthused about pine nuts, envisioning among pines and oaks what would become Mission San Antonio. He wagged a wild rose twig bearing exactly 141 rosebuds under the noses of Portolá and Fages, who seemed to delight in it as well.

On the second trip to Monterey they once again went right up the Salinas River, which was swollen in spring meltwater and "came up to the mules' bellies." This time, however, they had a clear bearing on the Point of Pines (Punta de los Piños) a few miles to the southern rim of the bay. Hiking up to it, on May 24 they looked northward and saw "thousands of sea lions seeming like a cobblestone pavement," while two whales moved just offshore together like happy mates. This preternatural moment almost converted to Gregorian chant. Crespí has all three of the leaders—Portolá, Fages, and himself—exclaiming "in a single voice":

"This is Monte-Rey Harbor!"

While they awaited the *San Antonio*, the land party searched out one of the crosses Captain Rivera had planted the year before at the Point of Pines. And what they saw, stumbling upon the cross, astonished, mystified, and emboldened Serra and the Franciscans for many years. Costanoan Indians had strung "still somewhat fresh" sardines under one arm of the cross on a stake, a hunk of deer meat under the other, and a neat pile of mussels at the foot of the cross. Encircling the cross, too, were arrows pushed in the ground and small branches topped by feathers. This transparent Costanoan peace offering, if not a free meal, made for "great wonder to all," but "as none could explain it, they suspended judgment."

In fact, the Indians explained what they had been doing; Serra himself recorded what he had learned about it in a detailed memorandum in 1774, partly through a Rumsen Costanoan boy interpreter. Basically, the Costanoans had seen the cross as a kind of odd version of their own prayer pole (they called it *porpor*) and had placed the food as offerings to the god who either planted it or was embodied in it so that he would not be angry.

According to Serra's report, the Indians took in awe the dazzle of gold or silver crosses the Franciscans wore on their chests. Enamored of a sun god, the Indians saw this reflected sunlight as indication of favor, though they accurately saw the chest crosses growing smaller and less reflective the closer they got to them. Serra wrote that at sundown, the Costanoans or Salinans thought the large wooden cross burst with the leaving light, just as the cross on the chest, so much so that it seemed to ascend to the heavens "resplendent with light and beautiful to behold." He grew amazed that "witch doctors danced," while the cross, "not black like a tree trunk," shone "bright as the sun."

Metal, with all its properties, including bouncing light, was not part of the Indians' everyday experience, and so it was imbued with supernatural qualities, as was the cross shape itself. That it "rose high as the heavens" must have astounded Serra. Repeating this story pushed the padres past the "crushing blows to the friars' feelings" when revolts like San Diego occurred, or when baptisms were slow. Here Spanish and Indian mysticism combined, though the revolts never completely disappeared. Perhaps, too, Serra felt the Costanoans were more in sync with the Spanish Christ than the Kumeyaay of San Diego; if so, that would have been one reason he decided to stay in Monterey and Carmel—and not return to Southern California—for the rest of his life.

The Portolá expedition had bivouacked five miles south of the Point of Pines at Carmel, closer to the clear water source of the Carmel River. On May 31, 1770, the *San Antonio* appeared on the horizon; as planned, Portolá's men lit three fires from a cliff, and the *San Antonio* eagerly shot off its cannons in reply. Serra was rowed to shore exhausted but elated, embracing his old pupil Juan Crespí, as well as Portolá and Fages.

"Ascención," Serra pointed to the old live oak, reminding everyone who had said the first Mass in Monterey—Antonio de Ascención, the Carmelite who not only gave his order's name to Carmel but set down emphatically the rules for the conquest of California: that the padres should call the shots and not the military. In picking the old oak of Monterey from Vizcaino's 1602 landing for his first northern mass, Serra was also implicitly underscoring Ascención's hierarchy of power. But Pedro Fages never accepted this. Portolá may have, but he was soon gone forever from California, leaving Fages the sword of the military command.

For the moment, all was union. On June 3, Pentecost Sunday, two choreographed processions—one from the sea, with Serra leading a rowboat choir of seamen, and one silent from land, led by Portolá—waded into each other around the old Vizcaíno oak. Then soldiers and seamen knelt. Serra went to the makeshift altar under oak boughs and called out in his deep voice, always startling from such a small frame, *Veni, Creator Spiritus!,* or "Come, Spirit of the Creator . . . fill the hearts you made," a ninth-century traditional opening to Pentecost (often sung on the eve of a new pope's election). Blessing water in a silver bucket he had brought from Loreto, Serra dipped in his aspergillum, which resembles nothing so much as a microphone, then rifled water in all four directions over the fields, the Monterey cypress shocked into dance, the rollers of the sea uncurling. Breakers hissed in the intermittent sun, sensing beautiful trouble; the sea lions had their say. Then priests and soldiers, cooks, and engineers grasped a cross—probably made of lodgepole pine, for its straightness—and sank it into the earth. Someone (Crespí?) looped the first foundation bells on the oak (there had been no trees near San Diego Harbor) and pulled them briskly.

"*Viva la Fe, Viva el Rey!*" resounded, Faith and King at least for the moment in full rhyme, if different genders (Faith being feminine). Men coughed it out, many from the *San Antonio* stricken with scurvy. Blood flew off some lips, cannons and muskets exploded, the bells of the oak rang feverishly, the sap of the bark oozing. Thus was the second mission in Alta California founded: Mission San Carlos Borromeo. The sour breath of men long at sea mixed with the smell of pine and salt soon blotted by smoky saltpeter, itself now battling Serra's burning incense, acrid and holy. In this founding moment in Monterey, sacred and profane joined.

But no Indians came. They were all out threshing seeds. The few kneeling in the back partly in shadow in a famous 1877 Léon Trousset painting, *The Founding*, are certainly Christian Indian scouts from Baja, including the two who had run away. (Three other presumably local Indians are pictured spying behind boulders below a towering Douglas fir, but there is no evidence of local Costanoan or Esselen Indians being drawn to this monumental event for Spain, or that they were even at home.) In short, as far as the Indians were concerned, it was a play with no audience.

But the tone switched. Marking the dolor of their difficult journey, Serra said a brief funeral service for Alexo Niño, the man in charge of caulking the *San Antonio*'s leaky floorboards, who had died just after the ship dropped anchor at Monterey. The body going down into the earth in a pine box—probably the first European buried in northern California—sent a pall over the celebration.

Still, Mass commenced with Serra's basso profundo *Introibo ad altare Dei* (I will go to the altar of God), the Latin beginning for any Catholic Mass said worldwide for half a millennium (until the Second Vatican Council in 1965 encouraged the use of vernacular languages, such as English, for the Mass). It was Monterey's second Mass in a century and a half. Serra lit the six candles in the silver candelabra he had brought, soldiering on as the sea breeze pulled at the flames.

Serra wrote that the oak was "close to the beach"; Palou later indicated "the branches bathe in the waters of the sea at high tide." But the fate of one of the most important trees in American history is a strange one that includes misidentification, lightning, and death by railroad.

That summer day in 1770 the oak was acorn-full and covered in incense. After ironing his hosts, Serra raised one high, his fiddleback-shaped chasuble lifting at the shoulders. He distributed Communion to all, putting the unleavened disc of God on tongues covered with bloody sores.

Although akin to one hand clapping in the forest (absent of Indians), the service for the beleaguered Spaniards had to be deeply moving in their open-air church with the blue bay rolling as if at their ribs. At Mass's end,

Serra stripped off his chasuble, led everyone in that most rousing of all Latin hymns, *Salve Regina*, no less poignant for men long on the trail without women or those pledged never to touch them carnally. Heaven and earth, archangels Cherubim and Seraphim, resoundingly cry out in this ecstatic praise to Mary, "Mother of mercy and of woe" hailing her, "*Sa-ah-ve, Sa-ah-ve, Sa-ah-ve Regina!*"

On that makeshift altar of pine boughs, Serra had placed an imposing statue of Mary, Our Lady of Bethlehem, called by art scholars "the most remarkable *imagen para vestir* in California." Exquisitely dressed in gold brocade, right hand proffering a rose, her left arm braces the baby Jesus while holding his infant calf. Gálvez had given the Mary statue to Serra at Cabo San Lucas the year before; she was five foot two, exactly Serra's height. And they were going to dance. He had lugged her a thousand miles up Baja on muleback and flung her out in San Diego, where she topped the makeshift chapel for a year before being stowed in the hold of the *San Antonio*, bound for Monterey, where La Conquistadora, as Gálvez called her, like everyone else, got properly lost.

La Conquistadora was now in California. And she would flee Monterey with Serra to Carmel and there spend almost a century in the reredos niche just below San Carlos, getting a silver crown in 1802 from a sea captain grateful for the rescue of his wave-tossed vessel.

After ending the service with a *Te Deum*, the officers, led by Portolá, pulled up grass and cupped dirt and stones, throwing it all in four directions, by tradition claiming the land for the king. The day ended with a feast for the famished under shade of oaks, and then a walk at sunset in the rollers. Like everyone, Serra loved the feel of calm cold water on his aching toes. He walked deeper, numbing the pain of the abscess on his ankle that had been throbbing for twenty years. The Pacific pacified.

The next day the presidio's spot (and the mission next to it) was chosen "about a rifle shot" from the beach (one mile up a steady rise). Soon the soldiers moved supplies over from their temporary encampment at Carmel and off the *San Antonio*; quickly two storehouses were erected, one for the presidio, one for the mission, with a third away from them both to serve as a magazine for gunpowder, close to the estuary in case of fire. As for Serra, he lived on the ship while his abode, apparently attached to the magazine, was built, something that he himself worked on with gusto. In a rare letter to a woman, he wrote briefly to Sister Antonia Valladolid, that he, like everyone else, was putting up with "all the inconveniences that are unavoidable at the beginning of things."

Within a week, this side-by-side arrangement of sacred and profane was already chafing. Serra wrote the guardian, "There is no *ranchería* in this vicinity." He was already keeping his eye on nearby Carmel, "truly a delightful spot," which had not only more Indians, but better and more plentiful water. He did not mention yet troubles with soldiers hungering for a woman, though the hunger flickered. Candles were his biggest need, and they weren't cheap. The relationship between cattle (animal fat for tallow) and candles was an intimate one. To put it crudely, to illuminate God, one needed animals.

In addition to candles, Serra asked Mexico City for blankets, under-clothes (his tunics were falling apart), clothes for the natives, a small bre-viary, and an *Horae Diurnae* (Divine Office for daily prayers) for Crespí, as his prayer books from two journeys up and down California "were old and falling to pieces." The cornmeal and meat that had come in the resupp-ly of the *San Antonio* was spoiled or weevil-infested. The soldiers had taken to hunting geese and harvesting wild herbs. The stores of chocolate had held; that mild stimulant cut the fact that they had no calendars and were "poor hermits cut off from all human society."

It may seem surprising for a man who had removed himself from the world in a cloister, who had lived for eight years high up in some of the most remote mountains of Mexico, and spent several years wandering in equally remote jungles of southern Mexico, to complain about being lonely. But Serra had confessed his need of human companionship and community more than once in Baja; he had seen it stare back at him in the person of Father Basterra, solitary and nearly driven crazy at Mission Santa Gertrudis in the peninsula's empty center. Perhaps two things were churning inside him: age and fear. Fear of the very wilderness that excited him. California was not an island, but it was far from anything he knew. Unlike Mallorca or even the remotest parts of Mexico, there were no Spanish settlements within a day's ride. The days were bearable; but the night was a different story. The call of the hoot owl, a whisper of death for the Indians, must have haunted him, and though he needed less sleep than most, he slept even less than what would be his norm. All through the night the oaks thrashed in the wind off the sea, and when he awoke or just rolled over wide-eyed, he saw the cypresses with their arms out.

Serra made no bones about his fears of being alone in the wilderness, and he anticipated it would get worse when Crespí left to found a new mission: "That, as far as I am concerned, will constitute the greatest of all hardships—to be at a distance of eighty leagues from the nearest priest." He literally begged Palou, who was now in charge of the Baja missions, to send a new priest north to break "this cruel solitude," and suggested Fermín Lasuén. He seemed disoriented by the lack of ordered time and news. He had not received a letter in a year. Who was the new pope? Did two Franciscans he favored make sainthood? Can you corroborate the rumor that a Franciscan priest was slain by Indians in Sonora or Arizona?

Serra had a remedy for "any little demons that might be lurking about this countryside." He told Palou he was going to celebrate a second processional Mass to mark the Monterey founding, on Corpus Christi the very next day (June 14) "in however poor a fashion." But it wasn't poor at all; in fact, it was lit, quite to the surprise of everyone, by brand-new glass lanterns discovered by accident in crates on the *San Antonio* where medicine was supposed to be. "Now on boats there are no processions," Serra joked drily to Gálvez. No one knew how the lanterns were packed away, as they were not in the bill of lading. There were nine "stowaway" lanterns in all—six on tall poles and three hand lanterns, and Serra made good use of them, delighting that "not a breath of air stirred them."

Two curious items of silver facing the sea Serra used that first feast of Corpus Christi, which survive to this day: first, silver prayer plates etched with Latin prayers for a priest to read while washing his fingers at Mass (the lavabo) and the beginning of the Gospel of John, recited at the end of every Mass since the sixteenth century as the priest cleans the chalice: *In principio erat Verbum, & Verbum erat apud Deum, & Deus erat Verbum* (In the beginning was the Word and the Word was with God, and the Word was God).

The second item is Serra's monstrance, spiked with silver rays that made the Host seem to radiate like the sun, having qualities that appealed to people who had so recently worshipped the fiery heart of the universe. Father Toribio Motolinía, an ally of the first critic of Spanish treatment of the Indians, Bartolomé de Las Casas, described an early (1538) Corpus Christi celebration that charmed the Tlaxcalans with a miniature mountain, cliff, and even meadow presented at four turns of the processional road—four little worlds they understood, constructed like some Spanish crèche, but with revered natural symbols. After all, direction was more important than time.

Geiger aptly summed up Corpus Christi in Monterey; for Serra "it was a perfect day." The two Aquinas songs written for Corpus Christi ringing in his ears (*Tantum Ergo* and *O Salutaris Hostia*), Serra wrote Gálvez a month later, his last letter ever to him (unanswered), wishing the visitor-general had been there to "make our happiness complete."

In fact, José de Gálvez was going insane. He would be no good to Serra, who had staked so much of his future on their partnership, certainly no good to the Indians (who loathed him in a newly rebellious Sonora), and hardly to himself. No sooner had Serra left for Alta California than

Gálvez had rushed out of Baja to deal with the new uprisings. On May 7, 1769, he arrived at the bay of Santa Barbara opposite Loreto on the Mexican mainland, debarking from the *San José*, which he immediately sent to resupply the California project. Indeed, his own mind was sinking as he sent the ship to its doom.

Chastened by the Sonora uprising, the king had begun to wonder if Gálvez's brutality was working at all and suggested amnesty. Reluctantly agreeing, Gálvez issued "passports" to those who would surrender, promising "justice beyond what they had hoped"; if not, they would be "convert[ed] . . . into ashes" by God and the king and presumably, himself.

But it was Gálvez whose soul was in ashes. Reeling from the violence he had witnessed and caused—at one point he poured salt, shamanlike, on homes he had flattened—and told to cease and desist, on October 14, 1769, while Serra was stuck in isolation in San Diego, Gálvez's mind snapped completely.

"I am St. Francis of Assisi!" he shouted in the middle of the night. He ordered an aide to secure six hundred gorillas from Guatemala, dress them in Spanish army uniforms, and send them into the fray.

Gálvez was ordered by the viceroy back to Mexico City. During the February 1770 journey, more unhinged than ever, he raved that he was the king of Prussia, the king of Sweden, the protector of the Bourbons, the bishop of Puebla, and finally, "the Eternal Father" himself. He wrote a flurry of letters and declarations; in a sober moment he signed one "José de Gálvez, insane for this world; pray for him, that he may be happy in the next." At Mission Cuquiarachi, a surgeon picked out a burial site for him.

If Serra's ship came in that spring, it hardly did so for Gálvez, who returned to Spain in 1772, where he was essentially put out to pasture, serving as a *regidor perpetual* in Málaga while building a little school for boys and one for girls. He also invested in a company that made playing cards for the Americas, before being dealt a dead hand himself for an *accidente* (a euphemism for insane convulsion) in Aranjuez in 1787; though suffuse with enemies and his ghosts, some thought he had been poisoned, took poison himself, or was strangled. It was an ignominious end for the man who masterminded the takeover of California, which Viceroy de Croix referred to as "the greatest enterprise since the Conquest [under Cortés]."

On August 16, 1770, Viceroy de Croix issued a printed statement distributed throughout Mexico City announcing the fortuitous landing at Monterey "to the great pleasure of the innumerable gentiles who inhabit that country," conveniently omitting the attack on San Diego. As if fanning a tourist fever, Croix assured "that our Spanish people are quite as safe in Monterey as if they were in the streets of this Capital City." With one eye on the Russians, he announced that the garrison had "abundant supplies of war"; with the other, he promised that "the first obligation" of the Crown was "the extension of the faith of Jesus Christ and the happiness of these same gentiles who groan in their ignorance under the tyrannous slavery of a common enemy."

Serra finally recorded his first baptism in Alta California, in Monterey, the day after Christmas 1770—seven months after they arrived in port. It was a five-year-old boy given the name Bernardino de Jesús Fages, echoing Serra's childhood school in Petra. Pedro Fages, now *comandante* of the guard, as Portolá had left for Mexico the year before, was the godfather, soon the longest thorn in Serra's side.

Serra rejoiced when, on April 21, 1771, his pleadings were answered with ten new missionaries arrived on the *San Antonio*. He assured Palou if any more would like to chance California, they would be rewarded with "a wealth of sufferings," the same thing he had promised the Claretian nuns in Palma just before he left home. By May, Monterey chapel side by side with presidio had twenty more Indians come in for baptism, though it is uncertain how many actually stayed, or how many were women out in their newly erected brush huts, close to food, close to the six leatherjacketed men. The going was slow, the learning of Rumsen for Serra painstaking. Fages, a lover of orders, told the friars to build their mission facing the presidio, and not away. He would be the keeper of the keys of their abode, and not them. He reneged on supplying soldier-laborers and kept them for his presidio. He made a mountain out of a molehill over the boundaries of the cemetery. Serra and Crespí took refuge in snuff, and probably became addicted to it; Serra complimented Palou on the quality of the latest shipment, better than the original, which was "pure dirt" (*pura tierra*).

Within a year of its historic founding, Serra abandoned the second mission in Upper California, abandoned it to Fages's own chapel for the military. He moved the real mission five miles south to Carmel near better water, Indian villages, and away from something he must have heard in the brush huts, a calling out, something violent.

On August 5, 1771, Serra walked out of Monterey with seven men— three sailors and four leatherjackets—along the rock-studded, stunning peninsula, where they would cut down trees to build the new mission, saying the first Carmel Mass on August 24. He had never seen such trees as these two-thousand-year-old Monterey cypress, flung to God, flung to the sea in such beautiful desperation.

Among Serra's early marriage officiating was a ceremony for soldier José Espinosa and an Esselen Indian woman, Catalina Islas, from Socorronda, whose descendant Abel Espinosa would one day set the record (66) at Pebble Beach Golf Course. At Carmel, Serra roused José and Catalina to Lenten services not by big bells, but via a small bell wheel, a *matraca*, churned mightily; for confession, the betrothed were asked to enter a jury-rigged structure of packing crates. Serra always had an oxymoronic bent for the practical and mystical. At his hermitage at Carmel, both kinds of items were gathered. A report to the viceroy included in its long list of San Carlos Borromeo holdings a bucksaw, an alarm clock, a rendering of heaven and hell ("the work of a good painter"), two pounds of agave fiber, and a gross of rosaries. Serra also listed a *lignum crucis*, a relic of the "True Cross" to which Christ himself was nailed. How did *that* get from Palestine to California?

One day as Christmas approached, Serra was called to view a strange thing washed ashore at Carmel: a driftwood pole. Captain Juan Pérez turned it carefully, pointing out several nails in a haphazard pattern. Serra wondered if it were from a ship; Pérez said no. "But where did it come from, then?" Serra asked. Perhaps a mill, Pérez thought, but the closest mill north of Carmel was at Sitka, Alaska. "It was anybody's guess," Serra concluded.

The pole with the untoward nails was as fresh as the infant savior. Perhaps Serra's Christmas sermon spoke of how Christ's death was there right at the exclamation of his birth, as nailed beams roll in from the sea.

Out walking in Carmel, Serra would pass a giant slab of island rock, like a gray striated loaf out in the water, thousands of birds making the rock seem to ripple. Sandpipers tiptoed fast on the firm wet sand like waiters for an impatient duke. He watched the pelicans fly in trinity, their sagging jaws spilling sardines. "O grant us days without end in the Homeland," hummed inside him, joining "*Genitori, genitoque/Laus et jubilatio.*"

Was the beauty of this land godly or ungodly? As a Franciscan, he was a follower of a man who called the sun "brother," the moon "sister." How could the Indians be wrong about nature and St. Francis be right? On summer walks, Serra must have felt two voices coming at him—one from nature itself: "You are not the sea, nor redwood nor cypress. You are a man, and not even a man—a priest, part man, part air. You may not even be as reliable as a rock or as refreshing as the sea. You preach pain and distant reward for it. But we preach pleasure now—or death. We are beauty; and you? You are hardly a whimper in time." And then the Indians' rationale spoke inside him: "The sea, the rock, the sequoia are alive.

They have spirits that help us or hurt us. We pray, too, for a warm sun and fertile moon. What do you ask us to pray to? A man; only a man, and a man with a terrible death, nailed like some bad message to a tree." Between these two voices Serra would have to have cried out to God for help.

And then toward sundown, when the wind rose up and the sun dropped like Communion into the trembling water, he must have wandered toward the lone cypress. How did it live? It was planted on rock. And it was alone, like St. Peter, upside down on his cross. The way it danced in the sinking sun.

CHAPTER FOURTEEN

MISSION SAN ANTONIO DE PADUA: A BELL FOR A WOMAN FLYING IN BLUE

These petitions of His Spouse were very sweet to the Lord;
they were the scarlet lace, with which she bound and secured His love.
—MARÍA DE AGREDA

La Mística Ciudad de Dios (1706) by Cristóbal
de Villalpando portrays María de Agreda wielding
a pen with fellow author (and evangelist)
St. John in front of her "mystical city of God."

*L*et us grant Pedro Fages some points that history, for the most part, has not. He served in one of the hottest spots in New Spain—Sonora during the Indian uprisings in 1767—and had to endure orders to decapitate from a feverishly capricious patron, José de Gálvez. He was promoted three times in California by three different commanders, no mean feat even in the worst bureaucracies. Put in charge of the military on the ill-fated, scurvy-ridden *San Carlos* headed to San Diego, he managed to avoid getting infected. Fages was a good bear hunter, and helped keep Carmel from starving; he was affectionately dubbed "L'Os" (or the Bear), perhaps for his nuzzling qualities. He kept a garden. He married a good woman when he was forty-six; she was twenty-two.

Occasionally he was deferential to Indians, noting their "great covetousness and a certain inclination to traffic and barter," referring to the Chumash as "the Chinese of California." He held the door for Anza's crossing at the Colorado River with his historic wagon train to California. In the midst of their worst troubles, at the end of a letter Junípero Serra managed to throw Fages a kiss. Would you do that to an entirely bad man?

There is, however, another side to these attributes. The three-time promotion could have been due to paucity in personnel in the far reaches of California in the last part of the eighteenth century. To have Gálvez as your patron was a decidedly mixed blessing. While he might have been one of the few healthy aboard the *San Carlos* when it anchored in San Diego, there's some evidence he kept the oranges for himself. His bear-hunting skills, good as they were, did not singlehandedly keep Serra and the Spaniards alive in Carmel in those lean first years—the Indians did. The Quechans soon reversed the opening Fages cleared in the desert and effectively shut off the Mojave land route from New Spain for close to a century. As far as Serra's affection, even if it was real it wasn't long lived.

The Serra-Fages clash was an accident waiting to happen. Although they were both men of rules, Serra was always testing the boundaries that circumscribed his life. Fages was nothing of the sort; one Serra biographer called him "a martinet." Though he was born in 1734, twenty-one years after the War of the Spanish Succession was concluded, as a Catalán his family probably had some bitter memories of Barcelona's last stand crushed by the Bourbons. A teenager when England was pronounced victor over Spain in the War of Jenkins' Ear, Fages joined a Spanish army reeling from one defeat after another. He didn't go to the New World to save souls; he signed up specifically to put down the Sonora native rebellion—a war that Spain, at least for a time, could win. Soon he participated in what today we would call war crimes.

Fages was blunt about the Indians of Southern California. They had "homely features and ungainly figures," and according to him, they were "dirty, very slovenly, and withal evil-looking, suspicious, treacherous, and have scant friendship for the Spaniards." This certainly contrasts with Crespí's observations of the natives, so solicitous they "seem to have known us forever," and the words of naval commander and explorer Alejandro Malaspina about the Chumash of the central coast, "free of the ambition that torments cultured Europe."

Though Serra normally had more in common with Catalonians than anyone else in Spain (Barcelona was right across the water from his home island), his relationship with Fages was an edgy one. Both were from outer-rung minorities in the Spanish political solar system, and Mallorca was farther out of the Crown's orbit than Catalonia. The Mallorquín dialect is different though related to Catalán. It's a time-honored practice for minorities to heap abuses heaped on them on the next smallest in line. Serra sustained a flurry of Fages "complaints": "Complaints were made because he wanted us to have the door of our [mission] house on the inside of the presidio; complaints concerning the church, the cemetery, the cross of the cemetery; because I buried a dead man a little farther away than he liked; complaints, too, because he wanted to keep the key of our yard so as to lock us in and out when he pleased."

Clearly, Fages wanted to physically and mentally subordinate the Franciscans not only to his military government, but to his personal will. It's not a long leap from locking in priests to priests locking in Indian women.

Concrete evidence of soldier molestation of women didn't come up until a year later when Serra reported it to his superior, the new guardian at San Fernando, Rafael Verger. Serra noted that among soldiers sent from Carmel to help found a mission at San Luis Obispo were "the most notorious molesters of gentile women."

Whatever the case with this growing storm between the spiritual and temporal leaders of California, for the moment, Serra's solution was to get away from any presidio (that is, from both San Diego and Monterey) and found a third mission where the Indians themselves lived and thrived. He read the Crespí diaries—which he would soon send, edited, to Mexico City, after "suggesting he [Crespí] go light on the minutiae, repetitions, and superlatives"—and put his finger on it: the Valley of the Oaks just east of Big Sur's Santa Lucia Mountains, a glade Crespí had loved.

On the first Portolá expedition, Crespí discovered in the Santa Lucias "a vast heathen population," naming the spot for Saint Lucy of Salerno,

"trusting that with time it will become a very large mission for converting to our holy faith all this throng of gentiles who are contained in all its
surroundings, the kindest, most tractable gentiles one can wish for." They
were the Salinans. Coming up from the coast through the only mountain
pass near Lucia, Crespí encountered two rivers meandering through a
rich pine forest (they were probably today's Nacimiento and San Antonio); soon six hundred Indians "presented us with a great many pine nuts
like those in Spain, and good, well-flavored gruels." Serra noted happily
that it was there that Indians returned a lame Spanish mule, now healthy.
It had been a hard climb up and across to find this golden valley; Crespí
had tagged it *La Cañada de Los Robles de Las Llegas de Nuestro Seráfico
Padre San Francisco*, the White Oak Hollow of the Wounds of St. Francis,
Our Angelic Father, as long a title as the valley itself.

This was Franciscan code to Serra: a place Christ favored, an origin
point, a place of saving wounds. Crespí's final remarks cinched it: "This
spot is one of the most excellent places that have been met with in the
entire journey. . . . It is the one and only spot for the best supply of timber, especially white and live oaks. . . . Of stone I suppose there can be no
lack, as the place lies still in the mountains."

On that rock Serra would build his third church. Mission San Antonio de Padua was born, far off the beaten path then and now (it's still
the most rural of all twenty-one missions, twenty-five miles off Route
101), though at the time it was in the thoroughfare of twenty Salinan villages, including the largest, Quinau. St. Anthony is the patron saint of the
lost—and, no doubt, rattlers, which slither over the roads today. As far as
Serra was concerned, it was a good place to be lost.

On July 8, 1771, even before he finalized the move to Carmel, Serra
departed Monterey with a pack train of mules, six leatherjacket soldiers,
three sailors, and a handful of Baja Indians to find the Valle de Los Robles
that so enamored Crespí. Traveling south with him were two priests from
among the new arrivals—Buenaventura Sitjar and Miguel Pieras, both
Mallorcans in their early thirties. Both priests would go on to the longest
stretches of service at one mission (San Antonio) in early California history, Pieras for twenty-three years, Sitjar for thirty-six. For a turnaround
mission and new model, going inland to warm country, Serra picked right.

Although he complained to the viceroy that he was basically down to
one bell to spare, that bell may have been the brass one he got in exchange
for a cracked bronze version given the *San Antonio*'s captain. It certainly
was lighter, easier to hoist, and with a sharp ring to it. On July 13, Serra
stopped the party near a rushing Mission Creek, sixty-five miles up the
Carmel River, under shade of oaks in a glow of rye grass. He took the

brass bell out from its burlap mule sack, probably patted the animal's rump, checked the clapper to see if it was loose, threaded the rope through the bell head, and swooped it over oak limbs. Soon he pulled in the heat.

"Come, come, you gentiles, come to the Holy Church!" Serra sang out, the brass bell clanging in the empty woods.

"Come, oh come, receive the faith of Jesus Christ!" If Serra smiled, Sitjar had to laugh. His companion's already ruddy face was burned from five days in the wilderness. He looked around: nothing but a hawk's circling shadow.

"Why exhaust yourself?" appealed Pieras, San Antonio's pastor-to-be. "This isn't a church. There's not a pagan anywhere near who can hear it." To him, the bell sounded like a ship in distress.

Serra kept pulling, his tonsured head undoubtedly gleaming with sweat. He called out, *Venis, venis, mes gentiles.*

"What a waste of time." Pieras turned to fetch water from the creek.

"Father, let my heart overflow," Serra chastised him. "Just as María de Agreda would want—let this bell be heard all over the world. Or at least by the gentiles who live in these mountains." He flung his hand out to the Santa Lucias, that wall before the Pacific.

María de Agreda at her writing desk was carved into Palou's Landa mission high in the Sierra Gorda of Mexico. Her book was Serra's constant companion all over the New World. Since leaving Loreto in Baja, this was Serra's third reference to the bilocating nun he believed preceded him to these parts a century earlier (according to her own testimony, five hundred times after 1620, flying with St. Michael, St. Francis, and assorted angels). First, conversion on sight of Franciscans, as Agreda had promised, with the Cochimí chief at Velicatá; then confiding to Gálvez that Agreda had sent a monstrance to New Mexico; and now at the start of Mission San Antonio, invoking Agreda with his fervent brass bell. Yet Serra knew there had been no conversion on sight in San Diego, where his one baptism had grievously flopped, or in Monterey, where all the ministrations of cannon, incense, and Latin hymns brought no one out of the woods. It's hard to believe what Geiger claims—that as late as 1773, when he visited Mexico, Serra shared with the new viceroy, Antonio María de Bucareli y Ursua, María de Agreda's promise of conversion on sight, unless Serra were bringing it up ironically.

Nevertheless, that brass day in the valley over the mountains from Big Sur brought a surprise: "a single Indian who had been attracted by the ringing of the bell or the strangeness of the people gathered there." Serra, overjoyed, gestured to him to come out from the shadow of the oaks. Whatever this intrepid soul received, Serra proclaimed at his inaugural sermon for San Antonio the next day, after a cross was hoisted, that "this mission will come to be a settlement of many Christians because we behold here what has not been seen at any mission so far founded." It was a newcomer's soul, a curious soul he wanted to enflame for Christ, just as he was enflamed that radiating summer day, the ground blond in the sun.

Though Serra only tarried at the new San Antonio mission for two weeks, overseeing the construction of a crude chapel and living quarters for Sitjar and Pieras, he was rejuvenated, greeting the stream of Salinan Indians who seemed to have no fear and couldn't give the Spaniards enough seeds and acorns. He was no longer in Monterey, its dead stop of hunger and outlaw soldiery. At High Mass "He gave full vent to his pent-up emotions."

In two years there were 158 newly baptized Christians (some of whom Serra christened himself), many living in huts around Mission San Antonio. He was concerned about infant mortality, "a number of babies they have sent on their way to God," but he also told the viceroy, "You could not wish for anything more touching than the love that these gentiles have for the good Fathers. Throughout the whole day, they cannot bring themselves to leave them." In Serra's lifetime, San Antonio would have the largest mission population, establishing, through miles of filtering through sand and charcoal, the first irrigation system in California. And its grape vines would last longer than any, the oldest gnarled trunk in the central coast still giving wine (albeit so bitter deer won't eat its fruit).

Certainly the most unusual of the neophytes was a hundred-year-old shrunken woman who walked slowly out of the forest, asking, even demanding, baptism. To the astonishment of Father Pieras, when asked her name, she told him: "Agueda." The old woman smiled. When he asked her to repeat it, she did: "Agueda." With her lisping version of Agreda, the old Salinan woman told a story that reverberated back three hundred years.

Agueda had heard about the San Antonio mission and, remembering childhood stories of men in such robes, she had come forward for eternal life. The two priests were dumbstruck. If Agueda were telling the truth, her kin's "priest" would have to have arrived in California by the seventeenth century. In 1542, Kumeyaay had told Juan Rodríguez Cabrillo at San Diego "they were afraid because Spaniards were killing many Indians in the region." Was this Francisco Vásquez de Coronado on his elusive hunt for the Seven Cities of Cibola? But Coronado was close to one thousand miles southeast of the Valle de los Robles, in Arizona, with no record of leaving priests behind. Manila galleons piloted by Pedro de Unamuno and Sebastian Cermeno barely touched the California coast in 1587 and 1594, respectively, the former logging a few foggy days in Morro Bay and the latter's ship destroyed by storms at Drake's Bay. Cermeno met the Miwok briefly before limping south in a dinghy.

What really floored Pieras was Agueda's next assertion that the missionary of her ancestors "did not walk through the land, but flew." That must have raised Pieras's red eyebrows. When Palou heard the story in 1773 while passing through the Valley of the Oaks, he checked it out with other Indians, and it appears to have been in the common lore of the Salinans. Of course a flying man is not a flying woman. But how did Agueda get a name so close to that of the Blue Nun of the Southwest? Then Palou remembered: María de Agreda, in her 1631 letter to Franciscans grilling her about her astounding claims of bilocation, says that two non-Spanish Franciscan priests were sent directly to the Southwest by St. Francis, and then suffered martyrdom. Again, this is too early for Father Kino (an Italian), but could there have been others who strayed off course?

There were other Indians in California who had similar stories of a flying Blue Nun, among them, the Santa Cruz mission Indians (probably Costanoan), just north of Carmel. And the legend lingered and even expanded to include in one nineteenth-century report, a "padre of the mamas" (with big breasts) who foretold white men coming.

Whether this was man, woman, hermaphrodite, or flying squirrel, the point is that Serra's fixation with María de Agreda was not idiosyncratic among Franciscans, the viceroy, or even the king of Spain deep into the nineteenth century. It helped convince them that their movement into California was divinely ordained, especially in moments when the realpolitik of what they were doing pulled inside them like an iron chain.

If, however, some anonymous priest had wandered long before Serra into the Valley of the Oaks, he may have left a telling mark. One day early in Mission San Antonio's life, Father Sitjar was led by Salinan scouts on a hard hike into the Santa Lucias. At about three thousand feet, they pointed to a cave filled with prehistoric petroglyphs, La Cueva Pintada. On entering, Sitjar marveled at the crude drawings of what looked like a necklace of suns, spiky hands, little stick-figured humans, huge centipedes or waterbugs. But one image was unmistakable and startling: a prayer pole or a Christian cross, perhaps even—because of a small crossbeam above the large one—a papal version. How is this explained? Sitjar certainly didn't carve it, and it is decidedly more carefully geometrical and even older than the glyphs, some of which are painted over it.

The Salinans explained that this was a site of their native religions' rites, and to prove their devotion to Christianity they would destroy it in front of the father. "No, no," he said, preferring to preserve not just their culture, but this strange, perhaps even miraculous symbol of his, a symbol, he insisted on pointing out, that was now *theirs*.

For Junípero Serra, Mission San Antonio was a hedge against early corruption and the slow monotony of the whole *conquista espiritual*. The year 1771 was a critical one for that enterprise; never again would Serra work in such a flurry, as if creation itself would make good in the waking face of evil. That year was the only one in which he founded three missions—San Antonio, San Gabriel, and San Carlos Borromeo (in moving it from Monterey to Carmel, he was for all intents and purposes starting it anew). He also was taking advantage of Fages's five-month absence in search of more food and soldiers to stanch the tide of desertions.

San Antonio was Serra's secret flagship, and he often visited it. An atmosphere of mutual respect and joy can be divined from a few of the items Serra listed in an inventory of San Antonio: a tin cup for shaving, a dozen little guns for celebrations (Salinans were trusted with firearms), twenty-four *varas* of muslin for ornamental curtains (for Indian living quarters), and twelve scythes (the people were very industrious). In 1773, the first Christian marriage in New California took place at San Antonio, of Juan María Ruiz and Margetta de Cortona (over one thousand of their descendants have been identified today). Sitjar, especially adept in learning Salinan and author of the most comprehensive grammar (four hundred pages) of a California Indian language, had begun to teach the Lord's Prayer in the native tongue. He led the couple and all attendants in saying: "*Za tili, mo quixco nepe limaatnil . . . Zo na quisili jom sig zumlayuitec. Amen.*" (Our Father, who are in heaven . . . deliver us from evil. Amen.") Ultimately, the quarters for married couples at San Antonio, two wings each as long as a football field, would become the largest of any California mission.

Among those likely to have witnessed the first marriage and perhaps met Serra were the Yokuts and Salinan grandparents of Perfecta Encinales (1830–1914), who became famous at Mission San Antonio for weaving *vaquero* hats and beautifully beaded baskets with animal designs unlike the unadorned work of her ancestors. Perfecta's grandmother Juana Carabajal had married one of the original Spanish soldiers who accompanied Serra from Carmel. Perfecta's relatives still live in the area today; in fact, a large percentage of Salinan Indians live on their aboriginal land today.

Maybe it was the music. Juan Bautista Sancho was the man who discerned that the Indians not only had the native aural gifts to make the most sophisticated music, the complicated, vast changes in their lives badly needed it. Like Serra, Sancho was a Mallorcan with a great, rich voice. He was only a boy when Serra entered California, but he was enthralled by Serra's example, and determined to follow him to the New World. From a family of music impresarios, Sancho brought music unlike anything anyone had ever heard in California—Indian or Spaniard. As Craig Russell put it, unique in the mission chain at the turn of the nineteenth century, "San Antonio could boast of an orchestra." And to convey Christian dogma utterly strange to the Indian—such as the death by nailing of God himself, who had grown from a baby in the womb of a woman who never touched a man—music was Sancho's last, best chance. He copied the score with a "jaunty tune" he learned as a youth in Arta, an oratorio for the Nicene Creed called *Credo Artanense* that might bring to the Salinan ear things that otherwise made no sense. Even more impressive is a piece very likely authored by Sancho himself, the *Mise en Sol* (Mass in G, but also with that homonymic "sun"), a complex, gorgeous oratorio for four voices and orchestra considered on a par with the great Classical era masses of Ignacio de Jerusalem or Haydn. The Mass radiating from the Sun. And Salinans. In G.

CHAPTER FIFTEEN

MISSION SAN GABRIEL ARCÁNGEL: WONDER AND WAR IN THE CITY OF ANGELS

My soul magnifies the Lord.
—MARY, "THE MAGNIFICAT," LUKE 1:46.

Native American painting of the sixth Station of the Cross,
"Veronica Wipes the Face of Jesus," at Mission San Gabriel.

*W*hen the music stopped, the only commandment you got was not to walk into the Pacific and drown yourself. You were now a Californian; you were at the sheer end of the world. All these shook-up cypresses turned like Lot's wife forever at Gomorrah. Beyond them you swore He (or She) was there atop the ladder of light. But you could not walk on water. You were a man; you would sink.

There were moments for Serra: the knock of the woodpecker at the wound in the oak, the scrub jay fanning his neck to mate (you almost averted your eyes, *almost*), the fiddler spider who seemed to kneel for Matins in the tallow light, Fages's dishes of bear, even Juan Crespí's snores through the wall. God going on empty when nothing else does, flaring a beauty, reminding you. That moment at the founding of Mission San Gabriel Arcángel.

It was the Assumption, August 15, 1771, only weeks after Serra rang the bell to begin Mission San Antonio, only a month after he secured San Carlos Borromeo in a safer spot near clear, plentiful water. The Tongva, upset at the increased presence of Spaniards across their land, the great plain of what became Los Angeles, saw the Spaniards mass along the Santa Ana River. When the two wearing gray robes begin their chanting in a strange language and stinking smoke, the Indians figured it was time to blot them out.

But when they approached, shouting, brandishing their weapons, one of the Gray Robes held up a canvas painting of a beautiful woman—it was Mary, Queen of Sorrows, holding a baby. They breathed in. It plain stopped them. Soon there were about a hundred Spaniards in what would become downtown Los Angeles.

The Tongva thought the painting alive; Palou recounts that in subsequent days people came "in great numbers," with "loads of various grains which they left at the feet of Our Most Holy Lady, supposing that she needed them for food the same as the rest." But Serra wasn't there to witness the moment; Pedro Fages made sure that he wouldn't be.

It appears Fages, who led the mule train of four muleteers, fourteen soldiers, and two padres (Pedro Cambon and Angel Somera, handpicked by Serra) up from San Diego to found San Gabriel, had told a concerned Serra, now alone in Carmel, that he would give him notice when they would actually found the fourth mission. But Fages didn't send the father president word in time to get there, further alienating Serra. It was the first mission founded without Serra's actual presence.

Perhaps sidestepping an earthquake, Fages and the two friars decided to hold San Gabriel Mission's founding ceremony on September 8, 1771, northwest of the miracle spot—in the Montebello hills on the southern border of the San Gabriel Valley. A large Tongva village, Shevaanga, was nearby, one of forty in an area that stretched seventy miles from present-day Santa Monica to San Bernardino. Flash floods that would plague Los Angeles for much of its history forced San Gabriel to be moved in 1775 to a spot five miles north, its location today.

The vast, wide plain of the Los Angeles Basin, with roses, blackberries, and watercress abundant along its plentiful rivers, was caught by Fages himself, who, if the missionaries saw souls, saw something else: "The entire locality is most alluring . . . fertile plains adapted for all kinds of cattle. [Settlers] would live in comfort and with them we might begin to have hopes of a very important settlement." But he did not see what Serra typically saw: The souls irradiating in the body. The drops of the Divine.

The goodwill generated by the sheathing of weapons at the sight of the Blessed Mother painting Fages leveraged to enlist Indian support in building his stockade. It's not clear what, if anything, they were paid (probably beads, as usual). The Indians paid with labor and food for the privilege of fencing themselves out. As soon as the stockade was finished, Fages issued orders that no more than five Indians could enter at any one time, even if they were weaponless. The Indians, who, after all, had built the structure, didn't understand this ostracism, and chafed at waiting in a line outside the gate.

When the priests protested that this was stirring animosity in the Indians, Fages spoke out of two sides of the mouth—one thing to the priests, another to a quivering corporal. (Serra knew what to blame for such equivocation—lying really—"I rather suspect it is the work of the enemy." Meaning: the devil.)

Some women, still enamored of the image of the Mother and Child, "called to the Fathers and thrusting their full breasts between the poles sought to express in this vivid way their desire to give suck" to the radiant child in the painting. At least this is how Palou interpreted the almost pathetic gesture; it may have been a sexual offer concocted by the chiefs, stymied and trying to hold down a population seething with anger, as if to woo the gate open.

After a food raid on the mission and the trampling of a guard, the son of the chief, named Tomear, proclaimed to Father Cambon, "*Pisax taraxatmi kii chuur paytux*" (When the sun comes up, the Indians will come with bows and arrows). In this tinderbox, some soldiers, supposedly out rounding up cattle, seized a young Indian woman, who happened to be the wife of Tomear. One dragged her into the brush and raped her. Palou called it "an outrage . . . a sin against the Lord"; Serra said this and others like it constituted "most heinous crimes." A nineteenth-century writer, married to a Tongva woman who knew chiefs well acquainted with contact days, indicated it may have been a group rape, as "[the soldiers] commenced tying the hands of the adult males behind their backs; and making signs of their wish to procure women. . . . Harsh measures obtained for them what they sought."

Whether it was a single violation or multiple, the fact that it was a chief's wife made the reaction as predictable as it was immediate. On

October 10, the very next day, after canvassing the surrounding villages for volunteers, the aggrieved Tongva chief led an attack force on the one-month-old San Gabriel presidio and mission. They encountered two soldiers out pasturing horses, soon stampeded by the Indians. One of the soldiers, recognized as the rapist, was hit by a hail of arrows, which his leatherjacket repelled. As Tomear came running at him for his revenge, the soldier took aim with his musket and shot and killed the chief. Two more Indians were dropped by gunfire near the gate to the stockade. Never having seen a man killed by something as small as a bullet, at such speed, the Tongva recoiled.

As if that wasn't enough to repel them, the corporal of the guard barked orders for the chief's head to be cut off; it was soon hoisted on a pike at the gate of the mission, "in grim and gory contrast to the beautiful Lady hanging in the church." Cambon compared the bloody thing to "the head of Holofernes."

An eleven-year-old Tongva girl may have witnessed the carnage that day in San Gabriel and in the days ahead birds pecking at the eyes, the mouth hanging open like dead fish, flies and ants devouring the chief's brain as if it were nothing but fat. Her name was Toypurina. She was the daughter of a chief (though it's undetermined if Tomear was her father). At her *ranchería* of Japchivit, she would apprentice herself to a male shaman and learn the arts of life and death: how to suck out a splinter or the venom of a rattler; how to fumigate a sick child with tobacco smoke or place saliva on the brow, injured part, or mouth. She became a good rain dancer. She gave thanks for fruit and seeds to the sun: "The god whom they adore . . . the spirit to which rattlesnake doctors particularly looked."

Toypurina would also learn as a female shaman the darker arts of targeting an enemy for downfall. Part of a shaman's power in this regard was his or her capacity to withstand pain. Ingesting—and surviving—something poisonous, dancing your legs off, purposely infecting yourself with another's illness and overcoming it quickly: all this added to a shaman's power and ability to project it on an opponent (not entirely different from priestly self-flagellation).

Toypurina would build her war against the Spaniards in silence, till she launched it fourteen years after the chief's head was put on a pike.

Serra in that matter was no abetter. When he first broached the subject in his initial letter to the new viceroy in Mexico City, he lamented "it is as though a plague of immorality had broken out." Punishment of Indians had been usurped by the military, with the friars' counsel bypassed, and meted out in extremis; no surprise, he said, that San Gabriel had resulted "in the worst of evils." Livid, he insisted that the viceroy not only remove the offending soldiers, but Fages, too. Two months later, he graphically revealed to Bucareli: "The soldiers, clever as they are at lassoing cows and mules, would catch an Indian woman with their lassos to become prey for their unbridled lust. At times some Indian men would try to defend their wives, only to be shot down with bullets." Was Toypurina one of the lassoed?

This was no longer just a turf battle; to Serra, it was the forfeiture of authority over the host population by the practice of things vehemently preached against—wanton sexual violence and murder. Serra felt early on, and said so to his superiors, that the Indians impressed him as better Christians than the Spaniards. But now it was questionable whether San Gabriel was doing any good at all: "hardships or no hardships, there are many souls sent to heaven from Monterey, San Antonio, and San Diego. Whether there are any from San Gabriel, I could not say for the present."

Serra declared his best judgment would have been to close down the whole Los Angeles project, more or less in shame: "I must confess that had I been present, even the San Gabriel Mission would have been abandoned, because I would have ordered the fathers to return to San Diego mission." He knew what was at stake, not only from the terrible example soldier rape was giving of Christianity, but the whole practice of separating Indian from Spaniard as Fages ordered it: "If we are not allowed to be in touch with these gentiles, what business have we, or what would hold us, in such a place?" Thinking of San Gabriel while saying Mass in Carmel, Serra might take the maniple off his left wrist, but not for tears of joy.

The night of October 11, 1771, fires burned all across the Los Angeles Basin and up into the mountains. Cambon thought the usually bickering tribes had formed an unlikely alliance and would soon swoop down and destroy San Gabriel once and for all. But instead, two chiefs came to the mission with gifts to sue for peace; the padres breathed sighs of relief and gave gifts in return. Perhaps the Tongva had not pulled off an alliance, or simply were cowed by the force of Spanish firearms. The immediate effect of the black mark on the birth of Mission San Gabriel was the request of the two priests Cambon and Somera for transfer; they were sick at heart and body because of what they had seen. Cambon was further traumatized at the sight of a soldier sodomizing an Indian in the mission complex itself. Cambon also either witnessed or was aware of child abuse: "Young boys coming to the mission were likewise molested by soldiers." Soon they were both off to Baja (where Cambon was told to gather up food for the now starving few at San Gabriel, whom the Tongva had stopped feeding). Cambon came back for a time, serving at the founding of San Francisco and San Buenaventura before chronic illness forced him to retire to his native Galicia. Somera disappears from the record. To replace them, Serra sent "the two Antonios," Cruzado and Paterna, who were supposed to found San Buenaventura (put off because of the San Gabriel uprising), directly to San Gabriel.

Another result of the Southland disaster was that Fages dispatched twenty soldier reinforcements from San Diego to San Gabriel. These men were recycled ne'er-do-wells from Baja, certainly not the professional army men Fages had brought with him from Catalonia. If they weren't lassoing Indian women, or taking mortal vengeance on Indians who captured and ate stray Spanish horses, "hanging and butchering some, disemboweling and castrating others," they were deserting en masse. The disintegration at San Gabriel was not aided by Fages's putting in charge, of all people, the corporal who had shot and beheaded the Tongva chief. Paterna, who wore himself out chasing deserters a hundred miles into Sonora, promising them mercy that Fages canceled, lamented, "There is no joy without its accompanying displeasure . . . no joy lasts for a long time."

Governor Barri in Loreto backed up Fages, accusing the missionaries—despite their extraordinary efforts to do for Fages what he would not do for himself—of meddling with military authority. New to the scene, Viceroy Bucareli admonished Serra and his confreres "to stimulate all by example and persuasion to obey and comply with your [Fages's] orders," though this was based on a highly selective, if not false, report of the *comandante*. But over time Bucareli revised his assessment considerably, cautioning Fages to allow the missionaries to "freely work," ultimately lambasting him for the "notoriously bad example" of his soldiers that could "provoke grave and damaging consequences."

Serra's whirlwind "glory year" of 1771 was beginning to come under sharper scrutiny in Mexico City and even Spain. Was he moving too fast, too oblivious to conditions on the ground? In all, the four missions were a mix of success and failure. San Antonio was the win; San Diego and San Gabriel, the southern California missions, were losses, grievous ones, and Monterey-Carmel, a tie at best. Serra was not blind to the sluggishness, but he blamed it on the soldiers preying on the Indians, the ungodly slowness of the resupply ships that made the settlements teeter constantly on the edge of starvation, and the language barrier, for which, typically, he castigates himself: "If, at the present time, they are not as yet all Christians, it is, in my judgment, only for want of a knowledge of their language, a trouble longstanding with me which I have never been granted the grace to overcome, it seems to me, because of my many sins." Some historians interpret this at face value: Serra was bad at language acquisition. But there's plenty of evidence to the contrary: Serra not only knew Spanish, he knew three versions of it (Mallorquín, Catalán, and Castilian), he knew Latin and Greek and probably at least some French, the official language of the Bourbons. He was reasonably fluent in Pame in the Sierra Gorda, and successful because of it. That's five languages. More likely than not, probably as a hedge against intellectual pride, Serra instinctively downgraded himself. With two distinct tribes and languages touching at the Carmel nexus (Rumsen Costanoan and Esselen), responding quickly would have challenged even the most proficient polyglot.

Three years out, despite his own frustrations, he told his superiors, "the gentiles are still, as when we arrived, docile, friendly, and peaceful. For many a league the only salutation you hear is: 'Love God! Hail Jesus, Mary and Joseph! Holy Cross!' When sighing they say, 'Oh Jesus!'" This disregards the two violent uprisings at San Diego and San Gabriel. Was Serra taking the recitations at face value, without detecting the possible rib tickling or calculation? Serra's zeal trumped his sizable brain. His devotion to the Indians produced an irrepressible optimism, if not naïveté. Still, according to what he confided to Palou, Serra was capable of doubt: "And though some claim that these gentle sheep, as they all are, will someday turn into tigers and lions, and it may be so, if God permits it, at any rate, as regards those of Monterey, where we have almost three years of experience, and those of San Antonio, almost two years, with each passing day they improve." In 1773, at San Diego, which Serra admits had a "pitiable start," he exclaimed, "I was deeply moved at the sight of so many Christians, and at seeing how changed the little town was."

When Fages demanded that neophyte homes be moved away from San Diego's presidio, Serra "strongly objected" to the viceroy that if they could not trust the new Christians, they should not be baptizing them. He said he could not refrain from "bursting into laughter" at Fages's paranoia.

The new guardian at San Fernando, Rafael Verger, getting wind of Serra's flurry of mission building and the ongoing atrocities, was having serious reservations. Verger wrote a storm of letters before, during, and after the scandals at San Gabriel to several Spanish leaders, sifting just what he should do with Serra and Fages. He wrote to the *fiscal* in Spain, Manuel de Casafonda, detailing the clashes between the captain of California's military forces and the president of the missions; he wondered aloud if Serra's enthusiasms needed restraint. Verger told Serra to "moderate somewhat his ardent zeal," wondering how on earth he could ask for an absurd one hundred more missionaries (Serra told him he hadn't—the figure had come from the hard-charging Gálvez; Serra had merely said he'd be happy to have them if available). "Command me to do whatever you like," Serra snapped, almost asking to be fired.

Verger's deeper reservations about the whole California project are revealing: "It is easy to deceive the public who will believe that California is a terrestrial paradise, whereas in fact it is a miserable, unfortunate country." He felt lurching from Baja northward made Spain "overextended" and he implicitly rebuked Gálvez's (and Serra's) impetuosity: "This enterprise has been undertaken without that ground work, maturity, and caution which have always been employed in similar circumstances." California, he thought, would require "miracles" to be pulled off. After carefully reading Crespí's and Serra's reports, confessing sleeplessness, Verger laced his own misgivings with black humor: instead of getting food and shelter, the Indians were granted "indulgences." He understood that silver altar ornaments appeared at poor Baja missions because of the generosity of the Jesuits' parents, but to make the Alta California missions go on one thousand pesos each was "a solemn joke." He caustically dropped: "I'd like to meet the extraordinary genius who could do it."

Verger's greatest fear was that Spain was failing to secure the most important element for success—Indian approval. "Our Spaniards ought to be certain about this willingness of the Indians, for if the contrary is true, the enterprise . . . is jeopardized." His reading of reports showed only one out-and-out invitation "to share the land"—among the Acjachemen of Orange County. He concluded his grim prognosis: "They have neither pronounced obedience to our monarch . . . nor have they indicated a desire to receive our holy law."

It's not clear anyone heard what Verger was saying, nor even that Verger understood the implications—namely, that Spain abandon its California operations because the cost in treasure and blood was too high.

Serra admitted to Bucareli the missions "are still tender plants" (which Fages, to his mind, had done his best to trample). But the miracle, he intimated, was not that they were falling apart, but that despite the tragedies and outrages (the seed of which had planted syphilis, whose devastation to the Indian population in particular no one, including Serra, had truly apprehended) any conversions had happened at all. However slow, they had (Verger's "miracle," perhaps). It had helped that Serra insisted that his favorite soldier, the sensitive Corporal Góngora, be reassigned to San Gabriel to help calm things down. And though a flash flood smothered a promising field of wheat the fathers "had sown in low land," Serra pointed out "What succeeded to perfection was a large garden, well-enclosed. When I passed there it was filled with all kinds of vegetables, melons, watermelons." And it drew Indians, despite their well-grounded suspicions and fears. Said the Mallorcan farmer Serra, "Given hands to cultivate the land, I repeat, much may be expected from that fertile soil."

If it is unlikely, as Palou states, the Tongva "little by little, came to forget the deed of the soldier and the death of their chief," the patient kindnesses (and soil tilling and offering of fruits and vegetables) by Fathers Cruzado and Paterna began in part to salve the wound. The first baptism after the atrocities was actually of the son of the chief who had been killed, a peace gesture by his widow that brought others to muffle their suspicions. Serra was overjoyed. With the young boy, Serra saw a chance to bring the "tender plant" of relations with the Tongva back to life. Cruzado added music at Mass; fields of grapes; wheat and corn on higher ground. The first cattle up with Captain Rivera from Baja he steered into corrals. He tried to make the church itself into a thing of beauty, and in 1805 it was christened with a light rain of holy water on its adobe and stone, under the direction of an Indian master mason from Baja, Miguel Blanco, with a Tongva assistant, Remigio. Clearly, San Gabriel's turnaround had a lot to do with Cruzado's and Paterna's giving the Indians leadership roles in its creation. Even Indian children were given jobs—shooing animals out of the brickyard where tiles and adobe were drying, chasing birds and squirrels out of the vegetable gardens and orchards.

The church unveiled was "one of the most distinctive in California," with an unusual fortresslike horizonality designed by Cruzado. San Gabriel's long flank of pillar buttresses topped by *almenas*, or staggered pyramidical finials, made it resemble the Great Mosque (turned cathedral) of Córdoba, Cruzado's native city. The rippled effect of the finials echoes the marvelous *espadaña*, three levels of bells—the most numerous of any mission—that produced a giant, rich sound that would have awed Serra.

In addition to Tongva, the Cahuilla and Serrano tribes from the San Bernardino Mountains and beyond to the interior were drawn to San Gabriel. By 1817, there were 1,700 Indians in San Gabriel, which, at its height, had one of the largest mission populations, five times the size of the largest Tongva *ranchería*. San Gabriel Mission went on to be the richest of all the missions, reaching 16,500 head of cattle, with vast vineyards producing more wine than any other, and a horse farm of 1,200. Its abundant vegetable fields became the chief produce supplier of the whole chain, to Serra's marvel. An *asistencia*, or substation mission that handled the overflow of San Gabriel, was founded nearby along the Los Angeles River in Serra's last years (1781). Called Nuestra Señora la Reina de Los Angeles, it was built by Indian labor for one Spanish real a day

(12.5 cents). A pueblo soon sprang up around it, the actual center of what became two and a half centuries later the largest metropolitan area in the United States.

Throughout much of the nineteenth century, Mission San Gabriel was kept running not just by its priests but by an exceptional woman, Eulalia Pérez, who was under contract to be exhibited at the San Francisco and Philadelphia World Fairs in 1876 as the oldest woman in the world (she was probably 117 at the time). Born prior to the 1768 Portolá expedition in Loreto, Baja (*ca.* 1759), Eulalia came up to San Diego in 1810 with her first husband, the soldier Miguel Guillén, with whom she had twelve children. By 1819, and now a widow, Eulalia became the *llavera*, or "keeper of the keys," at Mission San Gabriel, where she did just about everything, from midwifing the birth of decades of Tongva Indians to serving as chief cook. Eulalia outfitted the *vaqueros*, not just with saddles, but a kerchief and sash of Chinese silk. She concocted a delicious lemonade the priests insisted she take to the Indians working in the fields. She was considered the best dancer in California, an expert at *fandango, la zorrita,* and *jarabe.* Eulalia sang while dancing: "Go, Horse, to the washerwoman who is washing her underwear. Since she is so tiny she does nice little things for herself."

Though there was pleasure to be had, San Gabriel and the other missions hardly had their fairy-tale endings. If the Indians were not forced into the missions—as is sometimes claimed—they were often compelled to stay, or punished for straying back to their native lands beyond time allotted, tied to a status James Sandos calls "spiritual debt peonage." They were given shelter, food, pay (however small), and a place to practice their new faith in return for their work and presence. They were asked to live by what historian Douglas Monroy calls "a communitarian impulse" (not entirely different from their centuries-old mode of living) for a greater good, though that good took a lot of explaining. At the same time, they endured whippings for sexual transgressions, theft, being "away-without-out-leave." Eulalia Pérez herself describes another punishment, the Ley de Bayona, in which a shotgun was placed behind a man's knees and their hands tied to the gun: "It was very painful." The single *monjerío,* the woman's dormitory at San Gabriel—which Pérez administered—a typical, though particularly large, example, crammed fifty to one hundred women into seven hundred square feet, giving each woman, at most, a seven-by-two-foot spot to sleep, with no privacy. Men tripping the lock for sex was the least of it; germs in such a hothouse proliferated and became the invisible bane of the whole mission project.

It is fitting, perhaps, that after their exhibition at the 1893 World's Fair in Chicago and near destruction in the 1971 San Fernando earthquake, the final resting place of an uncanny California Indian–painted fourteen Stations of the Cross is Mission San Gabriel. Some consider them the most exceptional artworks in all the missions. Christ appears as an Indian in them, as do Veronica, soothing his face with a cloth, and Simon of Cyrene (with birdlike eye), helping Christ lift the cross; the Roman soldiers look like Spaniards.

If St. Gabriel the Archangel announced to old Elizabeth she would be pregnant beyond anyone's belief, and later told her cousin Mary something even more astounding—she was pregnant by no man, and would give birth to God—it would appear anything good coming out of San Gabriel was just as unlikely. Jacob's muscle-bound angel, unnamed, had to have been the namesake of the mission that began that most rich, beautiful, violent city named for angels. Like Jacob, Serra had plenty of angel wrestling to go.

CHAPTER SIXTEEN

MISSION SAN LUIS OBISPO DE TOLOSA Y TILINI: A PRAYER FOR BEARS

Warmth, warmth, and more warmth! Man dies of cold, not of darkness.
—MIGUEL DE UNAMUNO

The Bucareli Monstrance, a gift of Viceroy
Antonio María Bucareli to Serra.

Great friendships, like Serra and Crespí's, imply misery without which there'd be no need of friendship. Theirs, too, had its ups and downs, born and raised on the same Spanish island, linked in the classroom, and now out on the edge of the known world. Ultimately, the pressures and frustrations of life on the frontier brought out the differences between the men. Snores, sneezes, nightmare shouts had begun to grate. Crespí was given to face-to-face complaints, unlike Serra, who was a stoic about his own physical disabilities. For Serra, pains of the frontier were part of the landscape, and he enjoined Franciscans who signed up for California to prepare for a "wealth of sufferings." But to Crespí, if suffering were wealth, why, he'd just as soon be poor.

California was taking a toll on Crespí, from the unrelenting chill of Carmel and Monterey to the obstacle-ridden course of the missionary work. He complained of the few miles' walk from Carmel to Monterey to hear the confessions of the soldiers at the presidio—confessions that, no doubt, made him wonder how on earth they would convert Indians preyed on by the very people who were supposed to protect them. He walked back, bones creaking, into the fog.

Serra knew not only what toll Crespí's travel had taken on his body, but what his old student had achieved: "The truth of the matter is the poor Father, as regards explorations, has accomplished more than all of us put together." Crespí had walked and ridden on mule the 1,200-mile journey back and forth from San Diego to San Francisco *twice*; Serra, cajoled by Gálvez into going north by ship, had yet to do the overland route *once*.

Still, Serra's patience with Crespí was fraying: "He told me repeatedly that he could not live in this country, on account of the extreme cold, fogs and bad weather, that I should take him away from here on the first occasion that came up, that he wanted to go to the Santa Barbara Channel and found Mission San Buenaventura, that everything was all right there, etc." There's a lot of burning scalp in that "etc." Serra confessed to Verger, in the same critical letter in which he first lambasted Fages and decried the molestations at San Gabriel, that, peering over the ten new missionaries who had arrived for assignment at Monterey, "I began to think which of them would be my companion." Almost coldly utilitarian, Serra was willing to forge forward at all costs. Serra basically told Crespí he could head south on the next boat, if he wanted; a fey promise, as the ships in 1772 were chronically late, stretching everyone's food to the limit. Struck by how quickly Serra could be done with him, Crespí reconsidered. He put in writing that he would endure the cold and stay. Serra wondered aloud about Crespí's mercurial moods, "Such a sudden and troublesome about-face should not be looked upon as a practical joke or child's play. You can see the cause of my being alone from what I have told you."

While Crespí oscillated, Serra thought he'd rid himself at least temporarily of two problems, and he suggested to Fages, with whom he was barely on speaking terms and who, to Serra's sputtering disbelief, had just been promoted to captain, to take Crespí with him to more closely explore the San Francisco Bay area. The two left Monterey on March 20, 1772. They essentially took the route Fages and his scouts had tried in early 1771, around the shore of the East Bay near present-day Oakland, running into, once again, the swollen Sacramento River and Suisun Bay. Traveling west, from roughly the Berkeley area, they glimpsed the mouth of San Francisco Bay from the east for the first time. Crespí waxed one last time about "a strait reaching up within the land," the mythical Strait of Anian, but "regrettably, by the time the next sentence was written, the scouts had returned and reported 'nothing but [tidal] flats.'"

Near Martínez, just as Fages was loading up the pack mules to mulishly follow the Sacramento River east, hoping to find a crossing, a rider with five accompanying soldiers galloped up with an emergency message from Monterey: the southern missions, especially San Diego, were facing starvation, and without immediate relief would be abandoned. Frustrated, Fages pushed everyone east for one more day's march, stopping abruptly at noon to let Crespí take his latitudinal readings. Father Juan was so rattled by the news and rushed circumstances, he wrote wildly inaccurate figures, generating a map of San Francisco Bay called by the printer "strange, salamanderlike." They camped that night along the nearly mile-wide Sacramento River, dubbing it the Río de San Francisco, and gazed in the sundown eastward at the outline of the snow-capped Sierra Nevada, perhaps the first Europeans to see the great California mountain chain, certainly from the west. On the way south, Crespí entered geographic history by taking a leak—"making water," as Crespí put it—at a little stream near today's Pleasanton (just above Fremont); the soldiers laughed and named it *El Arroyo del Padre Juan*, Father Juan's Creek.

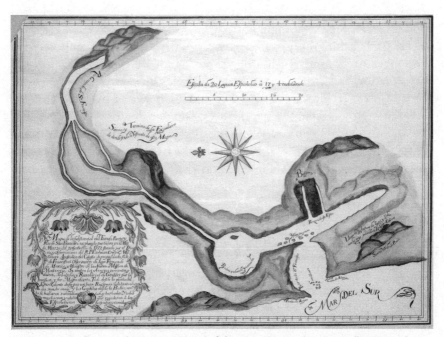

Crespí map of "immense arm of the sea, San Francisco Bay," 1772.

On April 5, within days of his arrival at Monterey, Crespí was immediately sent to address the hunger in San Diego, leaving with a twenty-two-mule train. When Crespí arrived he was stunned to find the cows withered and giving only dribbles of milk, the corn sere, the tallow for candles and wine for Mass long gone. There was only one priest (Luis Jayme), traumatized by soldier misbehavior on a scale even worse than San Gabriel; the other Franciscan had gone off to Baja in desperate search of food. This must have sent Crespí—who suffered, according to a French Serra biographer, from a form of clinical depression (*neurasthénie*)—into a tailspin.

Serra tried to sweeten the bitter pill of giving Crespí exactly what he wanted—more sun—by promising him that this was his chance to found San Buenaventura once and for all. But on arrival in San Diego, Crespí found that Father Dumetz had taken stores intended for San Buenaventura to San Gabriel, where food was also scarce and Indian-Spanish relations were still chilly a year after the rape-and-decapitation incident. The thick population of souls in the central coast was once again spared its saving. Crespí, manic at this point, wrote Serra, begging to return to the fog of Carmel. Exasperated, Serra replied (in a lost letter) that Crespí and Dumetz should both repair to Carmel.

But something changed. Instead of waiting—not the most common word in the Serra vocabulary—Junípero decided to leave for San Diego himself. Even more astounding, he went with his mortal enemy, Pedro Fages. And, having been warned by Verger from San Fernando to put the brakes on his mission founding, he founded a fifth mission on the way. Mission San Luis Obispo de Tolosa was thus a product of a rift in Serra's closest friendship, carried out under the eye of his chief antagonist waiting for a misstep, amid the heaviest concentration of grizzly and brown bear in California. A wealth of sufferings indeed! In despair, Serra wrote Palou just before leaving that what he had described as a plentiful and wondrous garden in California was nothing but "these desert waste lands."

With Crespí darting up and down the coast, and San Buenaventura being once again postponed, for the first time in his missionary life in the New World, Serra found himself alone (at Carmel). For four months he was in his dreaded solitude, without a Franciscan in sight and the soldiers five miles up the road at the presidio in Monterey. He turned out most of the thirty Indian families who lived in their tule homes near the makeshift chapel made of poles and adobe to forage for themselves in the teeth of the famine of 1772. They would be gone for weeks at a time, and when they did return, his heart sank. They were dirty, covered with paint, their Spanish clothes torn off.

Serra knew that if San Diego failed, the rest would wither and die. San Diego was the linchpin, however imperiled, between Old and New California, between Baja and Alta, not to mention between Mexico and California. And with Spain too jittery about the central coast, he saw the opportunity to establish, in today's phrase, a "fact on the ground" in place of San Buenaventura in the midst of the populous Chumash: San Luis Obispo, on the north end of the territory where Chumash languages were spoken, a test case for the channel. Finally, being the quintessential hands-on missionary, Serra probably thought that a land journey to inspect progress (or lack of it) at the first four Alta California missions was long overdue. He wanted to see the land he had only read about through Crespí and to escape from the lonely adobe corner in Carmel into which he had painted himself.

It's not entirely certain that Serra intended the missions to be founded one day's journey apart, as the legend has it. The "proper intervals," he fancied, would be "every twenty-five leagues" (or sixty-five miles), and that "every third day one might sleep in a populated place [*poblado*]." But did Serra mean by foot, mule, or horse? That's certainly an ascending order of speed. Serra rarely rode by horseback, but to make each mission in a day, a horse it would have taken, and only after the twenty-one-mission chain was filled in, long after his death. Another myth is that the Franciscans marked the common six-hundred-mile trail that ultimately ran from San Diego to Sonoma specifically as El Camino Real. In fact, *any* road cut by Spaniards in the New World was technically a highway of the king. Highway 101, the route originally traced by Portolá and Crespí, was not really memorialized until 1892.

For the road south, Serra took on an unlikely buffer between himself and Fages in the form of the ten-year-old Rumsen Costanoan Indian Juan Evangelista José, one of his first baptisms in Carmel the year before. Serra didn't know it, but when he inhaled Monterey pine and waved good-bye to the Indians of that storied bay on August 24, 1772, he wouldn't be back for a year and a half; he was going far beyond his destination of San Diego. Juan Evangelista, too, did not know that soon he would be seeing not just the quaint, hardscrabble little missions like San Carlos Borromeo; he was going to see a great white man's city of the world.

Even under the Aztecs, Mexico City (known then as Tenochtitlán) was four times the size of London. In the time of Serra, Mexico City had 137,000 people, twice as large as California's entire coastal Indian population. Juan Evangelista would be transformed from a boy who thought of the Spaniards as fascinating oddities who may have been the offspring of mules (for being virtually womanless) to seeing them as representative of a sprawling civilization that dwarfed anything in his home country along the Pacific.

The first leg of the journey Serra had traveled before—Monterey to Mission San Antonio, the sixty-mile trek alongside the Salinas River, not yet Steinbeck's lettuce and sugar beet fields, only a vast dry floodplain that dipped past today's King City into the steep Jolon Grade. It was late summer, deep heat. Spring's poppies and wild lupin were gone to straw, though yellow still dotted the shadows. Could this have been where the legend of Franciscan yellow mustard started? Corpulent Father José Cavaller, along with him, munching wild onion, taking a mustardseed shower from a bemused Serra?

The heat planted on their faces, Serra and his companions were covered with wisps of mustard. They descended into a modicum of shade in the Valley of Oaks, following the spine of the Santa Lucias along the sea (the highest point, at 5,844 feet, would later be named Junipero Serra Peak). Fellow Mallorcans Fathers Sitjar and Pieras welcomed the party for a night, giving Serra the traditional two slats of board for a bed with a thin cover in the priests' quarters, under repair since being flooded. Serra slept with the smell of whitewash and wet adobe, if not the onion-and-fennel breath of Cavaller. Up in the morning, they learned that the first year had had its setbacks, but not huge ones. Fages had raided soldiers who were helping with the walls in quadrangle, replacing them with inferior workers, so building had stalled. There were only twelve Indians in residence. They were taken, Sitjar explained, with the spectacle of soldiers confessing their wrongdoings, and inquired a lot about it.

The road grew steeper. From the high point of Cuesta Pass (1,521 feet), the famous Cuesta Grade, down which many a modern semi truck has plummeted only to fly up cutouts, the Serra-Fages party descended into the Valle de los Osos, or Valley of the Bears, where Fages had ravaged the grizzlies earlier that year, bringing nine thousand pounds of bear meat back to Monterey, reason alone for Indians to take up residence around San Carlos Borromeo. Stones were splashed with bear blood. Serra and Cavaller moved on their mules, distributing the soreness of their pelvises, praying in silence for the mules' spines. Low snorts, mule breath coming out in the light from dilating nostrils, sweat dripping from blow holes, the mules' mouths foaming. All was opening as the Cuesta Grade pulled. Even the mountains seemed to move like a woman reclining, the crinks of her legs sliding together as she rose. The hills were golden, breasts sloughed, full of night milk, rising to the day. Under broccoli-like oaks, the padres stopped and took shade, tipping their water casks. Serra threw more mustard over his shoulder. By mid-morning all colors strengthened. Tips of yucca stood tall.

The friars who slept in the gold hills without bedrolls knew that this blonde was dry, with grass itch, flies, ticks. Rattlers. A cougar lying hidden in tall grass. Did they feel prey to the land itself? They flowed, the fathers, downhill like water. They had found home in this golden pain.

Mission San Luis Obispo de Tolosa was founded on September 1, 1772, at the bottom of the Cuesta Grade in an arroyo between two peaks (the closest, Saddle Peak, at 1,819 feet) that resembled to one British writer a bishop's mitre. Serra knew another mission at this time was risky business, even though the northern Chumash showered them with gifts. The cause of this welcome seems exaggerated by Palou: "the land had been rid of those fierce animals, who had killed many Indians, of whom not a few who were still alive showed the terrible scars of their dreadful claws." The grizzlies were hardly exterminated in one or two hunting sprees, and it seems unlikely that many natives had been killed by them, as no bear goes out of his way to encounter man. Many years later, shortly before his death, Serra admitted Obispo's founding "should have been considered rashness." His only rationale? "He who trusts in Him will not be confounded." That was Serra's faith, but also his opportunism.

Perhaps Serra prayed at first Mass at Obispo under his breath for the bears, that they lie down if not with the lambs, at least the crickets. It's telling that Serra chose to name the fifth mission not after the better known St. Louis (the Ninth), who led many Crusades against the Muslims, but rather for the obscure thirteenth-century man from Toulouse who died young (twenty-three) after spurning family wealth and even a crown to join the Franciscans, serving the poor, sick, and hungry of Provence as a young bishop. The next day, Fages put a box of brown sugar in Father Cavaller's hands to exchange for native seeds, about fifty pounds of flour near the altar, and slightly less than a bushel of wheat to feed him, a corporal, and four soldiers. He threw in three of his most flea-bitten mules, "their harness still worse." Otherwise Cavaller was left alone in the Valley of Bears, bewildered. The Chumash, like Indians elsewhere, kept him alive, bringing in a son of a chief for baptism who died three days later, a shock to the parents, and Cavaller, too. Still, no one was drawing conclusions about the uptick of deaths, particularly of the young, in the native population in contact with Spaniards.

Within a few months, despite the resilient and supportive northern Chumash, Serra reported to the viceroy that in San Luis Obispo "the enemy" had begun "to show his tail": "A rascally soldier was caught in sin with an Indian woman and it upset the poor Father considerably," forgetting, of course, the woman.

This inauspicious start took a toll: three times in the first two years, Mission San Luis Obispo's nascent buildings were torched, the first time by a fiery arrow shot into the thatch of the chapel. Another fire was started during midnight Mass on Christmas Eve; it was quickly dampened, since so many were up and about. A third fire did the most damage, though its cause was never quite determined; some thought it was the result of intratribal disputes. It's unclear whether Mission San Antonio or San Luis Obispo hosted the first tiled roof. But mass production of California mission tile did begin in the Valley of the Bears, a response to the early pyrotechnics at San Luis Obispo, which soon supplied the whole chain its curved clay roofs. The notion of Chumash shaping clay around their shins appears romantic; logs, sometimes hollow, were used as molds. With mussel, clam, and abalone middens nearby, San Luis Obispo was also the first California mission to use a lime-based mortar.

Perhaps to cut his loneliness, Cavaller kept his two brass bells ringing in regular patterns daily. Obispo is the only mission to do so, with a distinctive Angeles pattern at noon of twelve slow peals, then twelve fast, a bipolarity of prayer in the anxious surroundings. The bells did their work, as did five hundred beams of cypress for a church roof and local redwood for a confessional. In 1787, Cavaller opened an *asistencia* ten miles north to serve the overflow at San Luis Obispo, called Santa Margarita de Cortona, that patron saint of the homeless. There she was again—María Contreras begging for mercy from Oaxaca all the way to the middle coast of California. Santa Margarita, indeed, became a hospice for those afflicted by syphilis and other diseases ravaging the Indians in California.

Whether from grizzlies or Serra's nervous desire to get to San Diego, Serra and Fages picked up the pace out of San Luis Obispo, trekking southward. Passing through the crowded Santa Barbara villages, just south of Carpinteria around Rincón, southern Chumash rained arrows on the Spaniards and an Indian was killed by shot. What had been friendly to Crespí was not to Serra. Was it fear or wisdom that made Serra refer to the mission as San Luis Obispo *de Tilini*, making it the only mission named both for a Christian saint and an Indian village?

Troubled, before La Asumpta, Serra saw something out on the blue of the calm morning: a wound on the sea, a lambent dark red. The kelp beds like a stigmata on the water. At the hottest point of the sun, he might have climbed off the mule and taken to the sea, the water making his robes heavy but his heart light. Close up, the kelp was golden, its pods upright in the water. The kelp leaf could pass over his face like a hand. God, he loved suffering for this beauty.

Soon his mule clopped slowly down what became Ventura Boulevard through Woodland Hills, Tarzana, and Encino, where like Crespí he rested under the oaks and took fresh water. At San Gabriel, he felt the mission had begun a rebound from its grim start, finding a handful of "lovely children, especially one of them who could express himself beautifully in Spanish." Serra ratified Crespí's feeling for the fertile plain, "undoubtedly the best we have discovered thus far," feeling it would not only feed itself someday, "but all the others." Finally, the father president reached San Diego on September 16, 1772—a record three-week traverse of California north to south.

Almost from the moment they arrived in the windy harbor of the south, Serra began to cross swords again with Fages. The immediate issue was yet again the founding of San Buenaventura, for which Serra was mightily stirred up, having just passed through Chumash territory and La Asumpta for the first time. Fages was incredulous. What about being fired on by Indians at Rincón? Fages agreed to a twenty-man guard. So frigid did the air get between them that the two stopped speaking face-to-face and, though apart by only a few hundred yards, began communicating solely through letters. They battled back and forth about various items: food, servants, status of mules. Though Fages tried to affect reason, what really set Serra off was the officer's imperious tone, which reached its apogee in his insistence that sailors (and by implication everyone else) "must all recognize me as the fount of military justice, Captain of the Infantry Don Pedro Fages, appointed by His Excellency the Marquis de Croix and recently confirmed by the Most Excellent, Lord Viceroy Don Antonio Bucareli y Ursua." *Me.* That was an incendiary pronoun to Serra.

If the Baja Indians, wrenched from their lands, could not be given pay and a steady allotment of food and clothing, Serra felt they should be sent back home. As for "the new Christians," presumably of Upper California, Serra said, "if nothing be given to them, may God bless them. They, at least, are in *their own country*" (my italics).

This was a moment of clarity born of complete exasperation: Serra was saying that the country they were in was borrowed. It was the Indians'. Not Fages's. Not the Franciscans'. Not even Spain's, though Serra was not naïve about the *conquista* being more than *espiritual*. The land was theirs to forage and live in as needed. If you can't even feed them for their labor and as an enticement to Christianity, don't go thinking the Indians are yours by fiat. They are not.

It's not clear Serra understood the import of what he had said. Or if Fages had gotten it. (Fages never answered the letter.) But on a certain level Serra was admitting something inherently indicting to the whole Spanish project in California: the land was theirs, not ours. If you don't act wisely and charitably, you have no right to keep them from returning to their ways. (Verger spoke similarly to Casafonda.) Serra had turned the tables on Fages on the question of charity, but he had also put in stark relief the crisis Spain had brought the Indians.

A month after arriving in San Diego, stymied as to his next move, the day after unburdening himself to four of his confreres (Fathers Crespí, Dumetz, Jayme, and de la Peña) about the impossible tension with Fages, they suggested that either he or someone else go to Mexico City and confront the new viceroy with the problems in California. Unsure, Serra announced he would sing a High Mass on October 13, the feast day of St. Daniel, to "ask God for divine direction as to what might be his will." Observing the sizable number of Kumeyaay baptized at San Diego, Fages had blasted Serra that the missions should baptize no one until they had enough crops to feed the Indians. It was a fair point. Palou himself confided later that on the matter of founding new missions Serra "never seemed to be satisfied" and that this relentlessness "may have had to do with shortening his life."

For the second time, and in San Diego again, the whole mission project lay in the balance. Serra was one month shy of his sixtieth birthday. He had just traversed the whole length of California in three weeks; he was exhausted. His foot and leg had begun to pain him like never before. It's almost as if San Diego intensified the pain. But he knew with Croix resigned and his patron, Gálvez, gone mad, there was no one at the court in Mexico City who really knew him or his holy cause in California. There was no one who could plead his case to Spain. Already Fages was citing the new viceroy to him that he should knuckle under. If he didn't go now, chances were his dream of California was lost.

Right after Mass, Serra told his fellows he was leaving for Mexico City immediately, that Father Paterna would govern the missions in his stead, and furthermore, the baptisms they were holding up for him at San Gabriel should proceed as soon as possible. This was his answer to Fages, who was stunned.

Just before setting sail, José de Cañizares, assistant to the *San Carlos* ship captain, Miguel del Pino, also locked horns with Fages. Cañizares accused Fages of dragging his feet getting mail for the viceroy to the boat.

"If I have the duty of accepting the mail, you do not fulfill your part," Cañizares snapped.

"Control your tongue," Fages snapped back. "I am an officer of the king."

"And whom do you think I am serving, the king or the devil?"

"Lower your voice!" Fages barked.

Cañizares got in a parting shot. "The only way one can speak with you is to put it in writing."

While Serra walked to the rowboat to start his long journey on the *San Carlos*, Luis Jayme ran up and pressed a letter into his hands. It contained perhaps the most damning evidence of soldier depredations that ever came out of the missions, a cry of conscience.

Jayme was young, thirty-two, and a fellow Mallorcan, as were 11 percent of all Franciscans who served in California. (The California frontier drew Spanish "outsiders"—Cataláns, Mallorcans, and even Basques such as Anza and Fermín Lasuén.) Jayme was vigorous, olive-skinned, with a muscular, though wiry frame. In only a year and a half of service, he appears to have won over many wary Kumeyaay, having studied and learned their language. An energetic, unswerving dedication to the Indians earned him his fellow Franciscans' admiration.

Though Santa Clara professors Rose Marie Beebe and Robert Senkewicz caution that Jayme's testimony may not be completely accurate, since it was based on his self-admittedly flawed knowledge of the Kumeyaay tongue, his letter is still deeply disturbing, all the more so for its exceptional detail. Jayme begins simply and pointedly, "With reference to the Indians, I wish to say that great progress would be made if there were anything to eat and the soldiers would set a good example." While giving the nod to some exemplary soldiers, Jayme was unsparing. "Very many of them deserve to be hanged on account of the continuous outrages which they are committing in seizing and raping the women. There is not a single mission where all the gentiles have not been scandalized, and even on the roads." Jayme didn't mince words about the fallout of such attitudes and practices: "The gentiles many times have been on the point of coming here to kill us all." (In fact, on the anniversary of the first attack, on August 15, 1771, eighty Kumeyaay sporting bows, arrows, and clubs had approached the mission, only to mysteriously withdraw.) Other Indians were so afraid of the soldiers, said Jayme, they had taken to the woods, leaving only old people in their villages. Jayme took the *conquista* from the Indians' point of view, an unprecedented admission of colonialism: "They did not know why they [the Spaniards] had come, unless they intended to take their lands away from them." The original sickness of so many Spaniards was also a logical disincentive: "When the vessels came at first, they saw most of the crews died; they were very loathe to pray, and did not want to become Christians at all; instead, they said that it was bad to become a Christian because they would die immediately."

Still, amazingly, "God has converted them from Sauls to Pauls." Jayme found the Kumeyaay and other San Diego tribes to be exemplary, even in their pre-Christian behavior and understanding of "natural law": "They do not have any idols; they do not go on drinking sprees; they do not marry relatives; and they have but one wife." They punished adultery without the sanction of hell, and were bewildered that Spanish soldiers would risk hell to rape Indian women. "When I heard this," said Jayme, "I burst into tears to see how these gentiles were setting an example for us Christians."

Two incidents riveted Father Jayme. The first had occurred only two months before, in August 1772: three soldiers (Hernández, Bravo, and Julián Murillo) had seized a nearly blind woman at Rincónada, about five miles from San Diego Mission, and gang-raped her. In her shame at being impregnated by force, the woman wanted to abort the fetus or kill it at birth. Jayme pleaded with her through an interpreter not to do such a thing. It was to no avail. The woman killed the newborn in mid-August; it was pale, giving "every indication of being a son of the soldiers." In the second case, only a month old, four soldiers (the same Bravo as before, Castelo, Juan María Ruiz, and an unnamed man) on September 11 came upon two women picking prickly pears near their village of El Corral. The soldiers asked for the fruit and the women complied. When they asked for their clay pots, the women refused; they were then pulled into a corral inside the village and raped, red ribbons and tortillas thrown at the women as bribes for silence. Serra must have folded Jayme's letter carefully in his Bible or María de Agreda.

On October 20, 1772, after the sailors shot off four cannon, shouting "Viva el Rey!" Fages saluting, and dropping the mailbags, Serra left San Diego. By November 4, the *San Carlos* had rounded Cabo San Lucas and arrived in San Blas. The die was cast.

Serra and his young companion made it to Tepic, welcomed by their confreres at the hospice of Santa Cruz, where they rested for a week from their two-week boat journey. A hard muleback climb from Tepic through the Sierra Madre Oriental down and up "yawning *barrancas*" took Serra and Juan Evangelista a week before they made it to Guadalajara, Serra's head "burning with fever." In a rare letter back home to his nephew in Mallorca, Serra confessed "the roughness of the road . . . has broken my health." In fact, Serra seems to have exhibited symptoms of malaria, perhaps caught in his years around Veracruz and the jungles of southern

Mexico. So high rose his fever that he was given Extreme Unction, the sacrament of the dying, by an unnamed priest at the Convento de San Francisco. Juan Evangelista also took sick. Serra prayed desperately for the young boy's recovery before his own. The boy rallied, while Serra, in and out of fever, insisted, against his fellow friars' exhortations to stay, that he go on. Two hundred miles east in Querétaro, he collapsed again.

Near-death experiences were not new to Serra. He had had five of them: almost drowned in the violent storm off Veracruz; the death threat at Jalpan; the poisoned altar wine in the Huasteca; dodging the arrows of the Kumeyaay at the birth of the San Diego mission; the skyrocketing fever in Guadalajara. And now in Querétaro, less than a hundred miles shy of his destination, Mexico City, to stave off the death of his life's dream.

An old friend, Father Alejandro Llaneras, who "waited on me with an unusual degree of care and devotion," slowly nursed Serra back to life at Santa Cruz. On a particularly bad day, however, when the Viaticum was prepared (Communion for the dying), his doctor took his pulse, felt his brow, and patted him on the shoulder. "Get up, Father," he said briskly. "You are well and there is nothing the matter with you." Llaneras was overjoyed; Serra smiled with his eyes closed.

In the cold of a new year, January 1773, after a two-month convalescence in Querétaro, Serra and Juan Evangelista left for the capital, arriving in Mexico City on February 6. The father president was emaciated, weak, and soon hit with sad news: the priest who had nursed him back to his feet, Father Llaneras, died three weeks after he had departed, of high fever, in Querétaro. Had he caught, and succumbed, to what Serra had barely escaped?

Despite his condition, Serra immediately thrust himself into midnight choir at San Fernando, elated to be among so many of his old friends from Mallorca, Sierra Gorda, and other days. But the guardian, Verger, counseled Junípero to ease off and recuperate. He was on a deeply important mission and had to prepare himself physically as well as emotionally for the meeting with Viceroy Bucareli.

Mexico City in 1773 was not much different from 1768, the year Serra left it for Baja. But to Juan Evangelista, it may as well have been a colony on the moon. Serra enjoyed ferrying the boy around town, showing him its great streets, cathedrals, parks, and esplanades. There were plenty of sinks and potholes, as Mexico City was largely made of landfill in the old great Aztec lake (Montezuma's revenge for the burning of his causeways). Only spot repairs had been made to the sunken cobblestone streets laid originally in 1712, one year before Serra was born. The boy thrilled at the sight of red-stoned buildings (made of *tezontle*), donkey carts piled high with oranges, the smell of coffee and perfumed ladies. The *zócalo*, the main plaza, left Juan reeling at the incredible richness of food piled above heads—cabbages, squash, melons, dozens of chickens hooked and stripped of feathers, whole carcasses of pigs and cows upended, their blood draining on the sidewalk. He pointed at the Palacio Nacional, which Serra smilingly told him was, indeed, the home of the Spanish chief, though, he told Juan, the chief above this chief was three months away by boat halfway around the world. Juan shook his head. The viceregal palace was a city block long, as large as El Capitán in Yosemite fallen on its side. They walked its patios and came to sit on a fountain with a bronze horse at its center, spewing water from its mouth, eyes, ears, and nose. No doubt Juan stepped in and put his head in this ungodly shower, throwing water up with his hands. In the countless parks and plazas Juan had to roll in the grass and the dust. *That* was a touch of California! As were the colonnades of sycamores, smelling yeasty as his hardworking family. They walked past the nine hundred arches of the *mampostería*, the aqueduct that took fresh water from beyond Chapultepec Park all the way to the Alameda. Juan cupped his hand and drank, marveling at the man-made river. There were at least 107 churches and chapels in Mexico City in 1773. Serra pointed out what a real church was—the pews, the tall candles, the gold-leafed reredos, the stained glass windows—and how he wanted to build churches like them in California. Serra angled the boy into the Royal Hospital, one of twelve in the city, founded especially for Indians. It's doubtful he showed off El Hospital del Amor de Dios, founded early in the sixteenth century for syphilitics.

The sea of humanity that filled the capital's streets dizzied the boy. Half the population was white, and many of these bearded. Some in Mexico City wore white wigs, as strange to Juan Evangelista as Indian headdress had been to Serra or Portolá. Their powdered faces made the boy wonder if this were war paint. Most of the rest of the population were mestizos, as well as mulattoes and blacks, otherwise known to some Indians as "the black white man." There were only about ten thousand pure Indians in Mexico City in 1773, about 8 percent of the population. Juan would have to have noticed they were the workers, hauling cement and wood, nailing boards, driving the rickety coaches.

Eight thousand people worked in Mexico City's cigar factory, and the pungent odor of the hanging leaves joined the sweet smell of roses, honeysuckle, lemony gardenias. Endless vendors of cloth: cotton, velvet, burlap; ticking clocks, especially fascinating to a Rumsen boy. Perhaps on a street of silver, Juan looked at himself in a knife. That would have widened his eyes and closed Junípero's.

The filth. The *zócalo's* central fountain, built in the year of Serra's birth (1713), was stagnant, putrid, filled with dirty clothes and urine from children and drunkards. Chickens shat on the cobbles, along with the city's many stray dogs. The public privies reeked. Serra steered the boy toward the entrance to the viceroy's palace, where the guards at the guardhouse were playing whist, the homeless and legless and *borrachos* keening on the tall steps to the ruler of New Spain. As the city darkened, the only light was from nightwatchmen carrying torches of burning pitch. While the boy played up and down on the steps, Serra must have mused. This was where California would live or die.

Antonio María de Bucareli y Ursua (the last name a reminder he had bear in him) was at first glance not a promising match for the father protector of the Pacific coast. Born in 1717 in Seville, roughly Serra's contemporary, Bucareli, unlike the bounder Gálvez, was an aristocrat and had served as a military officer. In the New World, his first post was as governor of Cuba, a colony that had sustained the worst of Spain's atrocities toward the native population. Bucareli had a severe frown line down the center of a tall forehead, which continued down a long, sharp nose. "Upon this stranger," said one biographer, "Serra had to pin all his hopes."

But there were flecks of spiritual, or at least ecclesiastical, gold in Bucareli, who was of Italian origin. Within his family tree were three popes and six cardinals. He was a knight of Malta and, though a layman, had taken vows of poverty, chastity, and obedience at the age of twenty-four, soon after Serra had taken his own. Made viceroy of New Spain in 1771, he took advantage of a window of peace after the Sonora and Guanajuato uprisings to reverse the troop increases insisted on by Gálvez. Bucareli had a strong humanitarian streak. After meeting with Serra, he later founded hospitals for military veterans, the poor, and the mentally ill in Mexico City. Bucareli was one of the few Spanish New World high officials not audited for corruption, "unprecedented in the history of Spanish royal representation," according to Herbert Bancroft.

That March 1773, Junípero Serra mounted the tall steps of the Palacio Nacional with his good luck charm, the boy Juan Evangelista. In plush quarters of burgundy, velvet-lined chairs with emblems of Spain, the little priest from Mallorca met the chief officer of King Charles III in the New World. Serra introduced the Rumsen Indian to Viceroy Bucareli, and an aide took the boy away.

The meeting went on perhaps half the day. As the "most important remedial measure," Serra asked the viceroy to fire Fages. In addition to Jayme's seething letter, Serra presented Bucareli with two other letters, from the sergeant of the leatherjackets, Mariano Carillo, and the corporal at Monterey, Miguel Periquez, both backing Serra's request, the latter detailing a "torrent of abuse" from Fages that included working the men in literal salt mines without food, even the injured, refusing chickens from his own personal larder for men dying of scurvy that caused Dr. Pedro Prat, who asked for the sustenance to help the men, to burst into tears (and ultimately to run off in a nervous breakdown as far from Monterey as he could get, leaving California without a doctor).

Bucareli asked Serra for a suggestion on a successor to Fages. Serra recommended Sergeant José Francisco Ortega. But Bucareli balked; Ortega as a sergeant was not ranked high enough to take over all military affairs in California. Bucareli calmly suggested Captain Rivera y Moncada, a man who had grated on Crespí on the first Portolá expedition. Serra pointed out Ortega's intrepidness as a scout, side by side with Rivera in exploring the estuaries of San Francisco, while "he is firm without rigidity, and has prudence and common sense."

Leaving the matter of Fages's successor undecided, gathering up his little fellow traveler, Serra took his leave of the leader of New Spain. It had been an animated, emotionally and mentally draining experience. Bucareli had asked for a written document specifying each of Serra's requests that he would take up with other ministers.

Bucareli impressed Serra, who wrote the viceroy soon after that he was "inspired with confidence and edification" at the ruler's "great zeal." So confident he was of the new viceroy's engagement and support, Serra concluded his *Representación*, the report Bucareli required, with the rather forward request for reimbursement of trip expenses, a sly way of eliciting "a sign of your special graciousness and favor towards me." Two months later, even more confident, he wrote Bucareli, nudging him to decision with honey rather than salt, that he felt certain "the outlook [in California] will be totally changed." He was convinced that the viceroy's "good will, added to your great piety and zeal, provides the crowning touch [*pone la corona*] to the success of this great enterprise."

As for Bucareli's impressions of Serra, they were strong and positive. Four years later, he told a governor of the northern territories, "On his [Serra's] arrival I listened to him with the greatest pleasure and I realized the apostolic zeal that animated him." Bucareli "seems to have been one of those rare individuals who can throw themselves wholeheartedly into an enterprise, merely out of a sense of duty, without a thought of self." Serra had met his match.

Within a week or so, Serra completed his thirty-two-point *Representación* to Bucareli, so detailed and thorough it has been called the basis for "the first significant body of laws to govern early California." Given how exhausted and weak Serra still was from his fevers in Guadalajara and Querétaro, the accomplishment was phenomenal.

First and foremost, Serra gave his rationale that the military commander of California be removed from his position (point 6). He asserts both that the "story" of the "damage [Fages's] conduct has continually caused the missions would be a long [one]" but also, in a compassionate spirit, that Fages "should be discharged honorably, and without any humiliation whatsoever."

Beyond that, though related to it, the "most important topic" by far was soldier immorality and sexual violation of Indian women and children (point 9). Serra's remedy was to yank any authority of treatment of the Indians out of the military's hands: "The training, governance, punishment, and education of baptized Indians, or of those who are being prepared for Baptism, belong exclusively to the Missionary Fathers, the only exception being for capital offenses." Not only was giving the missionaries chief responsibility for the "education of the children" the law of Spain, it was "the law of nature."

No doubt his intentions were good—to get the Indians out of soldierly jurisdiction, if not contact completely, to halt the compromising of the Indians' trust. But although the apparently arbitrary punishments and violations—that ran the gamut from whippings, to the stocks, to rape— were largely perpetrated by the military, they were not exclusive to it. Corporal punishment by the whip or cane, for one, was common in most European schools at the time, Catholic or otherwise, and in jurisprudence, too. Some padres allowed and even conducted whippings themselves of Indians for such things as stealing, sexual transgressions, and absenteeism, though there is no record of Serra's having done so. Toward the end of his days, however, Serra seemed wearily resigned to it.

The notion of Indians as "children" was common at the time among Spanish missionaries, and not as pejorative as it seems. There is plenty of evidence of Serra's perception of Indian agency and power and competence in a whole range of areas. But that he and the other padres had a paternal, familial feeling for Indians in their care is axiomatic. Priests often referred to their "flock," even in Spain, as "children." Postcolonialists have been too quick to couch this as a master-slave relationship. Still, as Indians became more attached to the mission and their responsibilities broadened, regarding them as children became less defensible.

Serra insisted that soldiers who "give bad example, especially in the matter of incontinence" be immediately removed (point 8). It's to Serra's credit that he did not prevaricate on this when attitudes toward indigenous people, not to mention women, were decidedly less enlightened. At the same time, Serra does not stipulate how or to where the offending soldiers should be removed, nor, exactly what their punishment should be (one assumes it would have been somewhat less than what Jayme had asked for them all—the gibbet!).

Among other suggestions about the military Serra put forth:

Soldier strength should rise to one hundred in California, over double the current forty. Soldier pay should increase.

Married soldiers coming to California with their wives should be favored in recruitment.

Intermarriage between Spaniards and the Indians should be encouraged and financial incentives given, including two cows, a mule, land, and ultimately relief from military service itself. (This was seized on by many; from 1773 to 1778, 38 percent of all Monterey-Carmel mission marriages were intermarriages.)

Past deserters should be pardoned.

Leave should be immediately granted for soldiers exhausted by duty.

Missionaries should receive free mail privileges (a franking), just as the military: "Who are more soldiers than we, who are continually on the battlefield, and as exposed as any soldier to the arrows of the enemy?"

As for the economic development and practical upkeep of the missions, Serra asked for more skilled laborers, a doctor (one for the whole state) to replace Pedro Prat, two or three Baja Christian Indian families to give good example to Alta California neophytes, and more mules.

Among other miscellaneous items, Serra asked, for the first time, for a salary (*sinodo*), like the other priests. He asked for new vestments and altar furnishings, even a silver salt container for baptisms "so that we may celebrate with some sort of decency"; and, of course, the required two bells for each mission, preferably cast in Mexico City, as those cast at San Blas "are ugly and of poor quality." A forge would be a godsend for workers, for "an ax head flies off the handle, a hoe or some other tool gets broken and all they can do is throw it aside." Serra, as always, thought logistically as a farmer who happened to be a priest. He wanted duplicate invoices of everything shipped to "that far land of exile," tipping some disillusionment.

As for the critical issue of settlers, who had not yet been brought into California en masse, Serra said he was for it. Related to this was the question of whether Spain should prefer land travel (and shut down San Blas and the boat traffic) or improve the San Blas shipyards and build new boats. On this, Serra doubled down—he asked for *both*. A land expedition with settlers to finally open up the long-elusive interior route from Sonora to California should be led by the well-known, charismatic explorer Juan Bautista de Anza from Tubac presidio in Arizona. This did not mean closing up San Blas, which some in the government had been lobbying for. Serra argued the price of hauling supplies the missions needed solely overland would be prohibitive. Two ships could carry what would take 1,500 mules. But there was another reason: excessively large land parties—filled with oversexed soldiers and mule drivers from "the dregs of society"—would inevitably be the cause of "quarrels and disputes with the poor, downtrodden gentiles." Furthermore, strung out on the trail, far from their own women, "the presence of so many [Indian] women there—it would be a great miracle, yes, a whole series of miracles, if it did not provoke so many men of such low character to disorders which we have to lament in all our missions."

Arbitrary and excessive force against the Indians was killing the *conquista espiritual*. Serra gave Bucareli many details of this, and how soldiers misconstrued Indian curiosity in the most violent ways:

> The curiosity and vivacity of the gentiles themselves, especially those living in the Santa Barbara Channel, who want to see everything; and when they get the opportunity of stealing, especially iron, they will not miss it. Now to our men this has been a cause for killing, as has happened many a time.

He cited his own experience: "In a similar way, on my last trip from Monterey to San Diego, in one of the towns along the channel, notwithstanding my presence and remonstrances, a man was killed and another left dying, and all without proper reason."

Serra met with Bucareli and oftentimes separately with his ministers over the next six months to argue the details of his requests. At key meetings, there were no fewer than thirty-six titles for officials gathered to determine California's fate. Serra did not mince words about what was at stake. If things didn't change at the highest level of authority, "It is certain that the poor gentiles, until now as gentle as sheep, will turn on us like tigers." In the long letter to Bucareli detailing the state of each mission—and especially soldier transgressions with Indians—Serra insists that if the better side of Christianity is not shown the Indians on a daily basis, "what business have we . . . in such a place?"

Ultimately, Bucareli gave Serra the lion's share of what he wanted. Fages was sacked (though Rivera, not Ortega, was his replacement).

Predatory soldiers were removed and punished. Deserting soldiers were pardoned. An overland route would be cut, San Blas shipyards would be saved and expanded. A whole host of supplies and practical infrastructure was approved. The Serra reforms, as polished by Bucareli, were signed off on in Madrid on March 8, 1774. King Charles III approved them shortly thereafter.

When Serra bent to kiss the feet of his confreres at San Fernando one last time, asking that "they would all pardon the unworthy example he had given," he knew he was leaving Mexico for good and that he would never see them again. "All were so deeply moved that they shed copious tears," Palou recounted. "They all feared he would die on the road." A cousin of Father Pedro Font was at San Fernando when Serra said good-bye. Font marveled as Serra's insistence at singing at choir "day or night" despite his weakness and felt that "this holy man" was "worthy to be counted among the imitators of the apostles." Font was amazed at Serra's spiritual strength and sense of purpose: "Now he is returning to Monterey, a thousand leagues away by land and sea, as if it were a trifle."

Just before leaving Mexico City in September 1773 with Juan Evangelista for the long trip back to Carmel (or perhaps on a rest stop at Querétaro), Serra may have sat for the only original painting ever made of him, by the famous Mexican artist José de Páez. He had asked Páez for several oils of the saints for the California missions. Serra is pictured with a taciturn, rather lonely expression, a wisp of forehead hair, and a large cross around his neck. The painting has been lost. Serra also wrote his nephew, Father Miguel Ribot de Petra, back in Mallorca, just before leaving for San Blas, where he would board the new frigate *Santiago* at the turn of the new year of 1774, that California "is my life and, I hope to God, where I will die."

Commending himself to his "one and only and dearest sister Juana" (Miguel's mother), Serra grew philosophical, as if he knew his days were numbered: "Let us make good use of time. . . . Let us work out our spiritual salvation with fear and trembling, and with a burning love and zeal for the salvation of our brethren and neighbors." He then ended with a most unusual, and enigmatic statement, that when he left Mallorca so long before as a young man "I made up my mind to leave it not merely in body alone."

"If I was continually to keep before my mind what I had left behind, of what use would it be to leave it at all?" he said to his nephew.

Renewed, having rescued his whole dream of California and just barely spared paying the price of his life, he returned to the scene of the dream.

The Kumeyaay were waiting.

CHAPTER SEVENTEEN

MISSION SAN JUAN CAPISTRANO: THE BURNING SWALLOWS

When you whispered "Farewell" in Capistrano,
'Twas the day the swallows flew out to sea.
—LEON RENÉ

The bell wall at Mission San Juan Capistrano,
a survivor of the massive 1812 earthquake.

On the way back to Carmel that fall of 1773, Serra was lighthearted, despite his years and the long return journey ahead. He had concluded an extraordinary compact with the viceroy of New Spain, feeling an even stronger accord with him than he had had with Gálvez. Bucareli was not only more stable as viceroy rather than special envoy; as a sworn celibate, he was practically a lay priest and in tune with Serra's vision for California. Bucareli seemed to understand Serra: without a *conquista espiritual*, the *conquista actual* was sterile and even condemnable.

"If it rained mules from heaven on Monterey," Serra wrote Verger gingerly from Guadalajara, "the missions would be without any of them, unless they were expressly labeled for the missions." He held the syndic's feet to the fire in Guadalajara for billing errors over flour, iron forges, and other items, declaring, essentially, that little things add up. He joked semiseriously that "God's hand is working in the land of our new conquests" not only because of what he saw as a "great number of people baptized" (it was a modest 491 by the end of 1773, four years in Upper California—mostly children), but because of efficacious "stories" such as that of the *puella centum annorum.*" This was a Latin reference to the tales of Agueda, the hundred-year-old "girl" at Mission San Antonio, of flying padres and/or nuns. Serra promised a sober investigation of such possible miracles, as well as "the story of the foundered boat," a reference no one has been able to deconstruct.

His boat, however, was not foundering, not yet. Serra had brought his full powers to Mexico City—not only of spiritual commitment and theological insight, but political savvy, his acumen as a community builder, organizational psychologist, agrarian, architect, art historian, infrastructure and logistical planner, animal husbandry expert, maritime strategist, boat builder, and diplomat from international to deeply interpersonal levels. A Renaissance man, he also had a gift for articulating a case for a person or a predicament, sculpting an argument, and managing the circles of authorities on whom he was dependent—in short, he had all the abilities needed to keep the California project going despite the assaults it faced from within and without. He was also convinced he walked on beloved if not holy ground: "Can there be a greater happiness than to live in a land which God and our Seraphic father St. Francis have taken so much to their hearts?"

Serra was emboldened as never before to defend the Indians of California, even as he attempted to convert them. Bucareli understood his logic implicitly and explicitly. A hard conversion would not work and would, in fact, boomerang; a soft conversion was the only way. This Serra had learned not only from the two-hundred-year history of post-Cortés rule, but from his own experience in the Sierra Gorda. Repressing someone to believe is a contradiction in terms. Serra was ready to bring his newfound leverage to bear on the "awful outbreaks of debauchery" that Jayme and now Crespí were reporting.

The return trip to California was something of a triumphal march. At San Blas, the shipyard workers mobbed him, showering him with cheers and affection. He had not only saved their jobs, he had literally rescued the half-finished *Santiago* from oblivion.

"My great desire to see a big ship capable of hauling a large quantity of food for those unfortunates made me say what I did," Serra said elatedly. "Now that God has satisfied my desire, let us give Him thanks." Everyone cheered. To Verger, Serra confessed, "the bread is rather hard" in San Blas, "but God is life and with his help everything is possible."

After two weeks on the pitching sea with the newly christened *Santiago*, most everyone became sick, including the captain, Juan Pérez, the boy Juan Evangelista, and even a new doctor, Dávila, who retched nearly the entire trip and swore he would never get on a boat again. As usual, Serra was calm and unaffected, a "good sailor," though for the first time he watched a man thrown overboard who had succumbed to a "violent fever." Betraying his perfectionism, strangely equating sickness with a failure of will, Serra confessed, "Thank God I didn't fall into the temptation."

The *Santiago* pulled into San Diego on March 13, 1774. Father Vicente Fuster and Sergeant Carrillo, accompanied by four soldiers, welcomed the returning father president on the beach. They lifted Serra from his launch and gave *abrazos* all around. Juan Evangelista must have been wide-eyed, exhausted, and happy to make land.

It's emblematic of the power Serra felt at the moment that he commandeered orders to go straight to Monterey and stopped with his abundant store of food on the *Santiago* at his first mission in San Diego, which was near starvation. There, Serra embraced Luis Jayme and Cantabrian Father Gregorio Amurrio. All were overwhelmed at the sight of barrels of wheat, corn, and beans, and cried out at the iron forge.

This was followed by another sign of change. Within a week, the first land expedition directly from Sonora, Mexico—over the Colorado River at Yuma—arrived at Mission San Gabriel, on March 22, 1774. It was led by Lieutenant Colonel Juan Bautista de Anza, along with the then equally well-known Father Francisco Garcés. Clearly, Serra's strong argument with Bucareli to keep up the elusive land probing tipped the scale. Now the route was open and the influx of settlers inevitable. With San Gabriel in as dire need of food as San Diego, Garcés quickly came down to intercept the stores of the *Santiago*, and in the process the two giants of Spanish Franciscan exploration in the New World met. Serra and Garcés concelebrated Easter Mass, and Serra baptized ten Kumeyaay neophytes that weekend, April 2 and 3. Then Serra headed north with Garcés to try to intercept Anza, who had already left for Monterey. At San Gabriel, the padres—including a new arrival from Baja, Fermín Lasuén—rejoiced at the sight of Serra and his gift of a full-sized oil painting of St. Gabriel the Archangel to replace an image on a page torn from a missal that had been propped on the altar. Serra threw in a carpenter.

On April 28, 1774, Junípero Serra and Anza ran into each other past Santa Barbara, about 2.6 miles east of Point Concepcion near the El Cojo *ranchería* and El Cojo creek. Anza, who had looped around San Francisco, was itchy to return south, but Serra pleaded with him to stay for at least one night. When Serra gave him an *arroba* (twenty pounds) of chocolate, Anza relented. A heated discussion followed; Serra wanted to know all about the land trail from Sonora across the Mojave into California, and regaled Anza with his encounter in Mexico City with Bucareli. Anza told Serra he had reassured the padres at Carmel that reinforcements had arrived with the *Santiago* at San Diego.

The next morning both were off in different directions, Anza taking only twenty-three days for the return trip to Tubac (Arizona), Serra heading north to San Luis Obispo, blessing the large cross of the new mission and pressing lightly his thumb in olive oil to the foreheads and breasts of six Chumash Indian children he baptized, bringing the baptisms there to fifty. One child had been brought all the way from the wide, misty beach of Pismo (today's "Clam Capital of the World"). Serra offered a brand new painting of St. Louis of Toulouse for the mission, but Father Cavaller demurred. Serra sang: "Yours is nicely executed, but the one I have with me is still nicer." Finding the priests unmoved, Serra complained, "I was somewhat hurt by their attitude." He didn't even take the wraps off until getting to Mission San Antonio, where Fathers Pieras and Sitjar exulted and swept up a painting of St. Anthony, making a bid for the spurned San Luis de Tolosa. But by now Serra had gotten attached to it; he took San Luis to Carmel, arriving home at May 11, 1774.

Baptisms, under a recondite Crespí and a rejuvenated-from-Baja Francisco Palou, had increased in Serra's year-and-a-half absence at Carmel from twenty-two to 174. Serra's two best friends had united and produced substantial gains. Furthermore, the *Santiago* with its stores had beaten Serra by two days to Monterey.

There was great excitement among the wild cypresses. Serra wrote Bucareli: "Now all the land, heretofore so melancholy and miserable, is rejoicing because of the abundant provisions and most fitting measures with which your Excellency has consoled us." Taken up himself, Serra declared, reflecting on the movement of olive oil, wheat, beeswax for candles, salted meats, flour, wine for mass, even chocolate, "All past sufferings were turned to joy." He felt certain now they could "increase the number of Christians almost at will." So prevalent were the *gaudeamuses* (a favorite Serra exclamation, "We are joyful," in Latin) that Serra immediately put into action one of Bucareli's imperatives in the *Reglamento*, that is, he chose Crespí to forge north with the *Santiago* all the way to Alaska to probe the Russians.

Crespí was none too excited, but bowed his head to the master's will: "Notwithstanding my great fatigue after so many expeditions by land, I sacrificed myself in order to take part in this enterprise." This would be his final journey outward to lands unknown to Spain. His one recompense was that Serra assigned Father de la Peña as a companion chaplain. On June 10, 1774, Serra sang a farewell Mass under the Vizcaíno oak at Monterey, now something of an "outdoor temple." Joining him in song were not only the chaplains for the far north voyage, but the outgoing *comandante* of California, Pedro Fages, and his newly arrived replacement, Fernando Rivera y Moncada. That was a choir with very temporary, if any, harmony. In his sermon, Serra blessed the crew and fathers all the way "to Russia." In fact, the farthest north they could make due to winds and cold was Queen Charlotte Island off the coast of today's British Columbia, where they planted a cross, inscribed: *INRI. Carolus Tertius Rex Hispaniarum. Año de 1774.* (After the so-called Nootka Controversy in 1790, in which Spain transferred its claim to the Northwest to England after English trading vessels were spotted in Nootka Sound on Vancouver Island, Spain never got farther north than Mendocino again.) When the beleaguered *Santiago* returned after a year, Serra was in good humor: "Practically all I hear is 'Southeast,' 'Northeast,' and I understand as much as I do making pottery."

The final parting of Fages from Monterey took place on July 19, 1774, when he embarked on the *San Antonio* to San Diego. Serra was surprisingly conciliatory: "It has caused me much distress, and still does, to see how crestfallen he is. By God's great goodness, I never aimed to do him harm." For Fages's part, he told the father president, who had essentially vanquished him, "mistakes he made originated, not from malice, but from sheer lack of understanding and reflection." When Fages arrived in bad health in Mexico City, on Serra's appeal Bucareli added to the old Catalán's record achievements that were actually Serra's. It was a generous end to an acrimonious relationship.

Serra concentrated with new vigor on Mission San Carlos Borromeo, his home in Carmel. The debarkation from both the *San Antonio* and *Santiago* of Spanish-Mexican women, along with the avid testimony and stories of the Mexican capital told by the boy Juan Evangelista, not to mention the cornucopia of food, sparked an upsurge in Indian interest in the Carmel mission. Serra was certain that the boy's word assured converts that "we did not need them for anything, but that we came only to seek their good." For his part, Juan Evangelista sent to Bucareli from his family a barrel of dried, smoked sardines, in thanksgiving for his days in the Mexican capital. By August 24, 1774, 245 Indians, mostly Rumsen, had been baptized at San Carlos Borromeo, seventy-two of them children over the age of eight who received the water on the forehead directly from Serra since his return. By the turn of 1775, Serra had over one hundred Indian adults under instruction for Christianity; clothing, he wrote, was already running out. He crowed about new supplies shipped in, including a strop "without which we could not have sharpened our razors for shaving."

Serra chided Spanish ignorance of Indian customs, the sailors' mistaking smoking out game for "wisps of fog." He saluted "the remarkable qualities of these people who, until now, were unknown—yet like ourselves cost our beloved redeemer Jesus his blood and his life."

This period of late 1774 through much of 1775 was a halcyon one for many of the California missions, particularly Serra's in Carmel. Serra strongly rejected his critics: "That the peacefulness of this country and the full four years we have spent here should not be of help in Christianizing the entire land . . . I do not approve nor do I agree." He admitted the unlikeliness of it all: "I have never read of enterprises of this description ever succeeding except at the price of sacrifice and peril," and he even granted, good debater that he was, a point of his critics with a curious conclusion. "If there are still those who think the whole affair one huge blunder, they may console themselves with at least the *rectum ab errore* [right can issue from wrong]."

Salinan and Esselen Indians were coming in from as far as thirty-five miles away, in the stretch between Carmel and San Antonio and Soledad. Serra enthused, "They see our church which stands before their eyes so neatly; they see the *milpas* with corn which are pretty to behold; they see so many children as well as people like themselves going about clothed who sing and eat well and who work." He revealed to the viceroy that the Indians put their hands on his shoulders and called him "Padre Viejo!" and admitted, "They stated the truth for I am old." He had the pleasure that summer of baptizing the chief of the *ranchería* of Ichxenta, Tatlun, as well as his four-year-old son, whom the Old Father named Junípero Bucareli for himself and the viceroy. His godfather was the captain of the *San Antonio*, José Cañizares.

Junípero Bucareli lived to be ten. He died before Serra, and Serra insisted that when he should go, he should be buried alongside that boy. (He was.) Even in this period of sudden plenty, a shadow began to creep over the land, what one historian called the "dual revolution" of the loss of Indian arable land and infection by the white man's microbes.

For Serra, this shadow was preceded by the arrival of the new military commander, a man who he had hoped would set everything right. He was mistaken almost from the beginning. It took the grand total of two months to realize that in changing commanders Serra may have jumped from the frying pan into the fire. Serra had traded the arrogant Fages for the hesitant, insecure Rivera.

Rivera was forty-nine when he reluctantly took up the command at Monterey. After thirty years of service on the frontiers of New Spain, most in Baja, and many journeys moving cattle and other beasts of burden to Upper California, he was clearly worn out. A native-born Spaniard in Mexico, he was in fact retired when summoned by Bucareli. With money tight, Rivera answered the call more out of necessity than fealty.

From the first land expedition up from Baja in 1769 when he and the captain had clashed over rations, Crespí had never liked Rivera, and warned Serra. He thought Rivera was anticlerical. But the father president wanted to accentuate an era of renewal in the missions, and he gave Rivera the benefit of the doubt. As Geiger puts it, Serra always saw the missions as rungs of a ladder, and couldn't wait to create another rung. Soon the warm wind of change cooled in the bureaucratic dungeon of Rivera's mind.

Though silos were high, Rivera parceled food out niggardly. "My Mexican blacksmiths are in rags," Serra fulminated. "They have not even been able to get hold of a pair of breeches, nor pots, frying pans, ladles, or grinding stones." Rivera, zealously dedicated to his soldiers, refused to discipline them as Bucareli had wanted. A military majordomo who had inflicted his illicit hungers on Indian women at San Antonio, as well as at San Luis Obispo, and caused the priests affliction "at the mere sight of him" was retained. To add to the problems, barrels of oil and wine arrived from San Blas half full, apparently pilfered, a fact Rivera appropriated for severe conservation. On San Buenaventura, Rivera just plain refused. When Serra pointedly invited Rivera to Mass in Carmel, the *comandante* did not attend.

To Rivera, there weren't enough soldiers to take on the boisterous Chumash of the Santa Barbara Channel. Serra knew the dangers; going south in 1772, he had witnessed firsthand an attack between Goleta and Gaviota near the Mikiw *ranchería*. But how could Spain leave the central fastener for the whole California coast undone?

While Rivera dithered, Serra wrote a scathing report of nondiscipline for a notorious rapist in the San Diego area: "One of the vicious ones who contributed to the death of a young female child in San Diego was a certain Camacho who scandalized and horrified the entire country, so much so that when we pass through the first thing the gentiles ask is, 'Is

Camacho there?' Another is Francisco Cordero, very unworthy of his namesake [St. Francis]." While in Mexico City he had been cautious to preserve the privacy of violators, Serra was now openly naming names.

In spring and into summer, the grunion (or night smelt) began running in the surf up and down California. Serra spoke of "twenty days" of "an abundance of sardines" spawning in the rollers of Carmel, spasming by the thousands. Fish being a key Christian symbol, Serra must have thought it was time to found a sixth mission.

Ironically, Mission San Juan Capistrano, soon born in the wake of extraordinary mercy in the face of violence, was named for a man who demonstrated little forgiveness in his militant life. Giovanni Capistrano was born in 1356 in Abruzzi, Italy, at the height of the bubonic plague, which killed about half the population of Europe and would ultimately kill him. Part French or German, Capistrano was trained in law (in fact, he is the "patron saint of jurists") and married a rich Italian woman. It was on an ambassadorial mission to a rebellious prince—Italy was honeycombed with such princes—that he was thrown into prison by the leader he was trying to mollify. In captivity, he was said to have been visited by St. Francis in a dream, calling him to the priesthood. His young marriage unconsummated, Capistrano entered the seminary when he got out.

As a priest with a spellbinding public presence (he drew a crowd of 126,000 at Breschia), Capistrano gained fame for railing against mankind's propensity for evil that, to him, brought about the Black Death, perhaps scapegoating Jews. His extreme claim to healing simply by the recitation of the Holy Name of Jesus brought both Capistrano and his teacher, St. Bernardine of Siena, investigation by the Inquisition. After the fall of Constantinople to Mehmed II, Pope Callixtus II sent Father Capistrano at the craggy age of seventy to preach a Crusade against the Turks in Frankfurt. Joining victorious Christian forces in Belgrade, Capistrano survived, only to fall victim himself on his journey home to the plague, dying on the border of present-day Croatia and Serbia.

No surprise, then, that Mission San Juan Capistrano was born three hundred years later halfway around the world in a baptism of blood.

In 1775, to found Mission San Juan Capistrano, Serra assigned the young Father Fermén Lasuén, protected by six soldiers and a muleteer named Feliciano, to the confluence of the Trabuco and San Juan creeks. Lasuén had spent five lonely years as the only priest at Mission San Francisco de Borja in northern Baja California and intensely disliked it. Relieved by the Dominicans, he jumped at the opportunity to go north.

Lasuén was something of a dashing Serra rival, though with a pockmarked face and prematurely gray hair. He was thirty-nine at the time (to Serra's sixty-two). At first Serra expressed "a special love for this splendid minister," who was "agreeable company." But Lasuén got entangled in one of the many battles between Serra and the Spanish military.

Having served with him in Baja, Lasuén was friendly with Captain Fernando Rivera y Moncada, Fages's replacement, whom Serra soon determined was far more indecisive than his "martinet" predecessor. When Lasuén requested to be Rivera's personal chaplain at Monterey garrison, Serra balked. He gave an entreating Lasuén a decidedly "cold reception" at Carmel, but finally approved the assignment.

Rivera was worried about a Chumash revolt along the central coast. Instead of approving the sixth mission to be at Santa Barbara or Ventura, he picked a compromise spot halfway between San Diego and Los Angeles near a stream called La Quema (or the burn—grasses around it had sustained a bad fire). It was Lasuén who felt burned, plunked in the middle of nowhere.

"Well, Father Lasuén, now your reverence has a mission," Serra told him. "Had it been San Buenaventura, it would be yours, but this is one that he [Rivera] is in a position to found."

Missions to paradise founder on bureaucracy. Quietly Serra and Rivera clashed on the number of soldiers needed to found Capistrano. Viceroy Bucareli had added in a postscript that the standard "escort" to each mission was to be six soldiers. But Bucareli evidently did not have access to the Palmer Method; his handwriting was "not only illegible to our eyes two centuries later; Serra misread it." Serra saw *seis* (six) as *trece* (thirteen). The ensuing exchange on the matter was almost burlesque.

Serra: "Then we are not agreed on ten[soldiers]?"

Rivera: "No, no. Only six."

Serra: "It may be six later, but when we begin we always have more soldiers."

Silence.

Rivera: "Father, the viceroy has definitely stated six is the limit for a mission."

Serra: "The viceroy does not say that."

Rivera: "He does. I have orders to provide six."

Serra: "There is no such order!"

Rivera: "Sí, there is."

Serra: "No."

Rivera "Sí!"

"Now you see how excited you are?" the voluble Father Murguía called out. "You do not even remember what you said!"

Lasuén actually thought Serra ended the argument: "He and the commander continued their 'no' and 'sí' for some time until the Father President terminated it saying that they would be reciting that litany all night."

When Rivera thrust forward a copy of the Bucareli letter, made by the viceroy's aide, with a clear *seis*, Serra was mortified. He was trapped in his own righteousness. That Sunday saying Mass at the Monterey garrison, Serra read the Gospel of St. Luke (10:27) story about the Good Samaritan and the love of one's downtrodden neighbor, emphasizing the Two Great Commandments: "Love the Lord thy God with thy whole heart, thy whole soul, thy whole strength and thy whole mind; and thy neighbor as thyself." It was Christ's own elucidation of what was most important in life, the two imperatives under which all the others are subsumed. Serra had been stripped bare by Rivera, his pride exposed, and he knew it. "The truth is at core bitter," Serra mused. "A kind of antipathy," Lasuén said of the relationship between Rivera and Serra.

Perhaps it is not inexplicable. Both were idealists facing the reality of the land and its people. No wonder they were reduced to muttering, Serra repeating forever his *razoncitas, razoncitas*, as Rivera bitterly called them ("Explanations, explanations"). Serra chided himself, "since the matter of San Juan Capistrano turned out so sadly, we have gone back to writing . . . an occupation that has been the most repugnant of my life." He concluded, "I am more of a scribe than a missionary."

Serra's mood was black. He had been reduced to begging for more soldiers, all the while knowing what a risk they were to the Indian women and to the whole example of his mission. And he had been found stupidly inaccurate and arrogant. He called himself "ashamed," "a fool." He wrote his Franciscan superior in Mexico City, Father Pangua: "I am full of faults and perform badly in all things. . . . I will say only that I wanted peace and will try to keep peace, with the help of God. And what can be more desirable—even for a man whose only wish is to avoid trouble and above all in such places of exile as these missions?"

Places of exile. The missions were no longer in his mind a place of utopic bliss; the very situation of ministering for God so far from home was now a kind of sentence.

The blood of San Diego and the swallows of Capistrano are inextricably caught up in each other. The Cross and the Resurrection. The Flood and the Dove.

At about the time of Capistrano's soon-to-be aborted founding (1775), there were four hundred baptized Indians living in the San Diego area. Most did not live in the mission, as was the case in the five other missions dotting the coast. The poverty of San Diego Mission—and its picayune harvest of crops—made it even less attractive. Christian and pagan Indians alike lived back in their villages, converts coming warily to Mass on Sunday, to a ritual they hardly understood.

Perhaps the Kumeyaay—living so close to Baja California—had been convinced by the lackluster reaction of the natives of Baja to the Jesuits, Franciscans, and Dominicans that if they just waited it out, it would die. Like their compatriots in the laissez-faire Baja world of two seas teeming with fish surrounding a strip of land, they had an abundance of maritime food and shell money in the bays of San Diego and were less drawn to padres with glass beads and prayer books. In short, they were satisfied.

But there was more than economic self-sufficiency or cultural inertia to the Indians' brewing anger. Differences in everything from faith systems to hygiene were grating. (Historians have pointed out that the Kumeyaay disliked the Spaniards' harsh soap, preferring to bathe daily in water tinctured by soapy plants, and that they bristled at the friars' snatching their soft twigs used as toothbrushes.) In August 1774, concerned about soldier depredations, Father Jayme moved the mission three miles inland from the presidio, closer to the interior *rancherías*, which commenced a fourfold increase in baptisms in only three months (over those baptized in five years) but also "raised native anxiety."

Palou, in the timeworn tradition, cited the devil behind the Kumeyaay unrest. But Jayme, whose sensitivity and love for the Indians was perhaps unmatched in its fervor anywhere in California, wrote to Palou: "I feel deeply about the fact that what the devil does not succeed in accomplishing among the pagans, is accomplished by the Christians." Jayme makes clear the rebellious motive: "The uprisings which have occurred in some of the *rancherías* closest to us were due to the fact that the soldiers had dishonored the wives of some of the Indians." And Jayme insisted native women had honored their own "natural law"; it was the soldiers who had broken the Sixth Commandment (Thou Shalt Not Commit Adultery), not the women.

On the one hand, the padres were truly heroic, protesting angrily against rape or molestation by the soldiers; clearly, they felt it their duty to protect single Indian women. But on the other hand, the very mode of that protection, the *monjerio*, locked in not only virtue, but lethal germs. Enforcing monogamy by the lash was hardly cogent. And taking the lash to those who frequented "naked" fertility dances such as those that occurred at El Corral Ranchería in late October 1775 was going further than had Serra and Crespí themselves.

Granting the Church's at times stiff attitudes toward sex, human love nonetheless remains Christianity's major strength. Christ himself rebuked the Pharisees who were ready to pummel the adulteress, "Let he who is without sin cast the first stone" (John 8:7). And yet how many useless stones have been cast by people charged with Christian doctrine against things which anyone with common sense could not proclaim sinful, such as birth control or masturbation? Still, a decidedly rigid view of human sexuality was consistently at the nexus of the Spaniards' encounter with the Indians. Combined with this was, to the Indian, a violent abrogation of Christianity's own rules of conjugal sexual love, what Geiger calls, too gently, the "bad example" of the soldiers (and sometimes civilians and clergy). In this light, a second attack on San Diego was inevitable.

But something else complicated matters—a theft. Not by a Spaniard, but an Indian, a Christian Indian, one capable of betraying his own culture and his new one simultaneously.

His Kumeyaay name was Chisli; his Christian name, Carlos. To make matters worse, he was the chief of the Christian Indians at the mission. On the road to the *ranchería* of Las Choyas, a few miles from Mission San Diego, he and his brother Canuch (or Francisco) spotted old Indian women carrying seeds and fish and assaulted them, stealing their loads for themselves. The old women reported the theft to the mission fathers. Sensing they were on the brink of a flogging, Chisli and Canuch snuck out of the mission the night of October 3, 1775, with five other Indian leaders, and soon began to rouse the countryside against the mission. It may have not been sufficient cover, given their not-so-petty thefts of the old women's supplies. But the recent history of Spanish rapine and floggings of the Christian Indians for participating in the naked dances at El Corral—and Fuster's supposed threat to burn it if they continued—were more than enough to obliterate their own guilt in a sea of righteousness.

On October 19, Sergeant Ortega set out with Fermín Lasuén and twelve soldiers to found Capistrano, leaving San Diego thinly guarded. Serra's "brambles and thorns in either direction" since returning from Mexico City sprang darkly to life. Mission San Diego was left with only four soldiers to defend it (six more were at the presidio); Ortega had failed to detect the anger gathering in the countryside. A war party of between six hundred and a thousand Indians began to swell. Just before the attack, flummoxed by his encounters with Rivera, agonized about an Indian woman who had run off with her son-in-law and fallen dead on the road "without anyone to say the name of Jesus" over her, Serra seemed to sense, even six hundred miles away, impending disaster: "May the Lord solve our difficulties. I do not have room for more."

Five days later, on November 4, 1775, a Saturday night under a full moon, just after Christian Indians had walked into the mission to sleep over for Mass the next day, two columns each of several hundred Kumeyaay painted for battle split up, one going to the mission and one to the presidio. At about one thirty in the morning, the Indians touched a hot iron to a thatch of the mission guardhouse, and soon it was crackling into flames, awakening the sleeping guards, two priests, and three laborers. Urcelino, the carpenter, was the first to be shot with an arrow. He called out in a deathly gargle, "O, Indian, you have killed me! God forgive you!" One of the blacksmiths, Romero, also was killed by an arrow. The other, Arroyo, saved himself with a pistol, shooting the Indian rushing at him.

Told throughout the month of October that the Indians were fomenting an attack in the surrounding countryside, Father Jayme had chosen not to believe it. Instead, he criticized his own Spaniards as rumormongers. Roused by the commotion that night, Jayme did nothing to protect himself but instead walked straight toward the Indians holding clubs and enflamed arrows.

"*Amar a Dios, mis hijos*," he gave them his customary greeting (Love God, my sons).

The Indians seized him, dragged him to a nearby arroyo, stripped him to his underwear, and proceeded to pound him to death with clubs and stones. They also shot a dozen arrows through his body. When he was later found, his face was so disfigured he was only identified by his tonsure.

Father Fuster took refuge in a storehouse just completed, with two soldiers and the two of Ortega's young boys. They prayed to the Virgin Mary and the patron saint of San Diego (St. Didacus). The dawn attack was ferocious; so many "arrows, stones, chunks of adobe, and firebrands thrown at us that it seemed they intended to bury us," Fuster later wrote. One corporal took nine arrow wounds. Fuster escaped serious harm, though an arrow sank into a pillow he used to cover his face. He also took it as a sign of God's grace that a gunpowder box for the cannon used for celebrations did not ignite from the fiery arrows. Musket and pistol of the soldiers staved off a final Indian charge, felling a Kumeyaay leader. Soon the attackers disbanded, making off with some stolen vestments and statues of the Immaculate Conception and St. Joseph. Some Christian Indians gave pursuit, wounding a few of the rebels, but they didn't go far. On their return, Fuster experienced a clash of disparate feelings: "I cannot adequately describe this action for I do not know if anxiety or joy filled me most." In the wake of the onslaught lay doubt. Led to the body of his mutilated priestly friend Jayme, Fuster fainted. "I do not know what would have happened if a number of Indian women had not taken hold of me as I fell across the body of the dead Father."

On November 6, Fuster said a Requiem Mass at the presidio, which, almost miraculously, had not been assaulted by the contingent of three hundred Indians facing it, because there they felt they had lost the element of surprise due to fires visible at the mission, which somehow had survived the attackers' thirty-to-one edge.

On hearing of the battle, Lieutenant Ortega and Father Lasuén buried the two bells of the barely birthed Mission San Juan Capistrano and rushed down to San Diego. Ortega conducted a twenty-day investigation, sending soldier parties into the hillsides, arresting nine men and women. A contingent of six soldiers set out to report the disaster to Rivera five hundred miles north at the Monterey garrison, and arrived on December 13, almost six weeks after the attack. With a blackened San Diego incensor in his saddlebag, Rivera rode over the hills to Carmel to present it to Serra.

Serra's response to the news that Jayme and two others were killed is legendary and troubling. Echoing a line from the Roman historian Tertullian (*Sanguis, semen Christianorum*) he exclaimed, "Thanks be to God. Now that the earth has been watered by blood, the conversion of the San Diego Indians is inevitable." It's hard to believe Serra's first reaction would be untoward joy instead of grief. It seems insensitive in the extreme. But Serra had a frightful instinct for seeing the positive in the worst situations.

As for Rivera, he is purported to have told Serra—by way of Father Font, now scooping up the news at Monterey presidio—"One thing pleases me greatly, and that is that they did not kill a single soldier, thank God." Turning from this callousness, Serra said a solemn High Mass the very next day in honor of his fellow Mallorcan, who had been born in San Juan, one village away from his home of Petra. Rivera made some excuse not to attend. When Serra appealed to Rivera for a guard so he could rush down to San Diego and help restore order and restart San Juan Capistrano, Rivera refused.

In the wake of the second major Indian uprising in California, Serra sat down December 15, 1775, to write a soul-searching letter to Bucareli in Mexico City. He contemplated the burned, shredded baptismal records, the stolen vestments and utensils of the sacristy. He hovered on giving up. But then he hit on a black spot in the abortive mission to Texas years before: "May God never permit that these antecedents result in what took place at Mission San Saba . . . the soldiers are still in their presidios and the Indians in their paganism." A revolt there had led to a counter-massacre and ultimately a shutdown of the Texas missions. And so Serra dropped his love bomb.

He reminded Bucareli of his insistence "at the beginning of these conquests" that "in case the Indians, whether pagans or Christians, would kill me, they should be pardoned." From the very outset of the Spanish movement into Alta California, Serra seemed to sense violence was inevitable. And he wasn't going to return it, nor did he want the military to return it. Serra's insistent note to Bucareli was not only exceptional in its anticipatory mercy, it seemed to beg the question of the whole enterprise.

This is a stunning position. It's almost as if Serra were asking for forgiveness not only for the Indian, but *from* him, knowing what the Indian was going to have to give up even if he felt he was offering a better way, salvation as he understood it. An intellectual and scholar, Serra would also have known that there had been much debate since the Council of Trent in the sixteenth century ratified "baptism of desire" for those studying to be Christians who die without baptism. A whole speculative tradition developed regarding to what others "baptism of desire" might apply. Of course, such a notion applied to the Indians would have to have been hidden far down in his heart of hearts, or else his whole New World effort would be found hollow. But Serra went further. He asked for clemency for all rebel Indians in prison in San Diego, including those who had murdered Father Jayme. And he asked that, after some "moderate punishment," all be immediately released.

What of Rivera's rejoinder to this astonishing stance? That an exemplary punishment—such as execution—would deter others from such attacks?

Serra tackled it simply and profoundly. "To prevent the Indians from killing others, let the soldiers protect us in better fashion than they did the now deceased padre; and as to the killer, let him live so that he can be saved, for that is the purpose of our coming here and its sole justification."

In short, the Gospel of Love.

Bucareli was deeply moved. On April 3, 1776, he gave orders for the release of all Indians incarcerated at San Diego, including those accused of murder, to effect "tranquillity of souls."

In the months it took for these orders to actually reach Rivera, the *comandante* conducted his own investigation. He faulted the sleepy sentinels, but came down hardest on Ortega for taking precious soldiers sixty miles north to found Capistrano at a time when he knew the Kumeyaay were fomenting an attack on the San Diego mission. The heavy rains of January and February 1776 prevented Rivera from a wholesale counterattack and roundup. Several short forays, however, brought in fifteen more Indians, including Francisco (Canuch), the leader, Carlos's, brother. All were given fifty lashes. (Was this the "moderate punishment" Serra had suggested? It is twice the normal limit.) One was flogged so hard he died. And what happened to the revolt's leader? On March 27, 1776, Carlos (Chisli) did a thing either mad or very shrewd. He stole into the makeshift chapel of Mission San Diego and asked for asylum.

Rivera was incensed. He told Fuster the danger Carlos posed to the whole community; he argued that the church had been burned to the ground by the Indians and that this storehouse serving as chapel was hardly a holy place. Fuster warned him that he was treading on a serious ecclesiastical crime. But Rivera flew into a rage. Over the shouts of Fuster, he seized Carlos with his own hands, dragged him to the guardhouse, and threw him in stocks.

Before the sun set, Fuster pronounced orders of excommunication on the commander of all military forces in California. On April 3, 1776, Fuster wrote his supervisor in Mexico City, Francisco Pangua, that he was suffering his life's "greatest tribulation and sorrow."

Rivera traveled all the way north to Serra at Carmel to plead his case. But Serra firmly backed Fuster. Rivera was now outside the Church for violating sanctuary. Completely beside himself, Rivera returned to San Diego and handed Carlos back to Fuster, who ceremoniously lifted the excommunication. Soon all Indians, including the leader, were released as per the viceroy's orders and Serra's wishes.

Rivera was traumatized by the events in San Diego and wrote to Mexico City to be relieved of his command; he mused openly about retiring or even entering the Franciscan monastery. As for Fuster, he, too, totally spent, sought retirement. Even Lasuén asked from Pangua "permission to retire," as he had seen, at his early age, enough desolation for three lifetimes and did not want to return to San Juan Capistrano and unearth the bells.

That was left to Serra himself, who, on November 1, 1776, pulled the bronze music out of the earth at Capistrano, dusted it off, and angled the heavy bells back and forth on a thick oak till they sang in their earthen way of the glory of the Lord. The California missions, half dead, were breathing again.

At exactly the moment on the West Coast that the Spanish project for California sputtered back to life, two Anglo armies were slaughtering each other. Three days before Serra rang his Capistrano bells, British General William Howe dealt General George Washington his biggest defeat to date in the Battle of White Plains. On December 11, Washington made his famous escape across the Delaware River and set up at Valley Forge, Pennsylvania, for a bitter winter. That very same day, Serra baptized an Indian named Damaso Joseph at Mission San Gabriel. The day was sunny and warm.

There had to have been goodwill engendered—at least for a while—toward the Spaniards, and Serra in particular, after his extraordinary intercession on behalf of the Indian rebels in San Diego. Certainly it affected the peaceful inauguration of San Juan Capistrano and later marked that mission as one of the most serene in the chain of twenty-one. But not before a fearful incident or two. On November 11, on his way back from stocking up provisions from San Gabriel for San Juan Capistrano around what is today Anaheim, with only one soldier and one Indian interpreter in the pack train, Serra was confronted by several dozen howling Indians painted for war, with arrows in the nock of their bows. The Indian interpreter may have saved the day. He shouted at the tribe in their language (Acjachemen) that if they didn't back off, the Spaniards would pursue and kill them. Then Serra came forward, gave each a sign of the cross on his forehead, and then filled their palms with glass beads. He later told Palou he had thought in that moment his life was over. A sixth brush with death, a sort of aftershock of the San Diego uprising, ending in grace Serra had invoked on the road to Anaheim.

On February 27, 1778, following three years of drought during which the ringleader Cinquanto accused the Spaniards of causing "seeds not to grow," the Acjachemen from six *rancherías*, including Ubange near Dana Point and several where Camp Pendleton stands today, rose up. But a preemptive strike led by the Carrillo brothers stopped the uprising before it started. Eighty bows and 150 arrows were confiscated. One village, opting completely out of the new social order, migrated east toward the San Jacinto Valley.

Nevertheless, the earliest close inspection of Indian culture in California before much of it died or was roped off or went into hiding was at San Juan Capistrano—of the Acjachemen Nation (or Juaneños), by Father Gerónimo Boscana. First published in 1846, the book Boscana wrote based on his answers to the Crown's 1812 inquiries about Indian life, *Chinigchinich*, strongly influenced one of the fathers of modern anthropology, Alfred Kroeber. It is as revealing of the prejudices of the Spaniards as it is surprisingly objective.

The famous cliff swallows, which for many years seemed to congregate at the mission on St. Joseph's Feast Day (March 19), were attracted to three things at Capistrano. The seventy-five-foot bell tower of the old stone church, completed in 1805, was the tallest building west of the Mississippi, a perfect place to build their gourd-shaped nests and give their young a high-flying start. Then there was the multitude of insects the birds fed on. But what really drew the birds was the mud. All the land cleared for the mission made it a mud-dauber's paradise, and no cliff swallow builds a nest without a thousand points of mud.

After the one fierce battle of the Mexican–American War in California (at San Diego on December 5, 1846), some of the temporarily victorious Californios (Californian citizens of independent Mexico) took refuge with their wounded at Capistrano. Pio Pico, governor of Mexican California, also retreated to the old mission of the swallows. What the 1812 earthquake didn't take from the great stone church at Capistrano (two domes), army engineers took in 1864, accidentally exploding gunpowder, which felled two more domes. Today, only half a dome (of eight domes of the original church) is left. It got its first retaining rod in 1912, and in 1924 it got actress Mary Pickford, who was married in the Serra Chapel.

In 1939, as Europe descended into hell, composer Leon René wrote a hit song, "When the Swallows Come Back to Capistrano," recorded and sung by artists such as Glenn Miller, Gene Autry, and the Ink Spots. Two decades later, freeway underpasses were as favorable to swallows as any Capistrano mission, but no one sang of that.

The Juaneños, the old Acjachemens, comprise 908 of San Juan Capistrano's 33,826 people today. Split into three factions, the tribe was denied recognition as recently as 2007, short-circuiting its efforts to build a casino. On November 16, 2009, Monsignor Arthur Holquin embraced a sort of nemesis, one of the claimants to Juaneño leadership, David Belardes, who had pestered Holquin to dismantle a barbecue pit constructed on Indian graves. He did. The embrace occurred on the altar, shortly after Holquin said the funeral Mass for Belardes's wife, Cha Cha, who had worked at the mission church for many years. Holquin had also married the two during Cha Cha's decline. For a moment, there was genuine sorrow and peace between native leader and priest, with or without swallows.

The Querétaro portrait of Serra by José Mosqueda is actually a copy of an original that was lost or destroyed during the Mexican Revolution (1910–17). Serra may also have sat in September 1773 for the original in Mexico City after his meetings with Viceroy Bucareli; the artist may have been the well-known José de Páez, from whom Serra secured several paintings for his California missions. The original hung for over a century in three different convents in Querétaro, most often at the Convent of Santa Cruz. There were two copies made later: Mosqueda's, around 1900, and another, which is lost. (The eyes in the Mosqueda copy are hazel; Serra's were brown. And the complexion is somewhat fairer than his olive *Moreno*. But otherwise, with gray robe and large Mallorcan crucifix, it seems an accurate likeness.)

Six Calle Barracar in Petra, Mallorca, Serra's childhood home, photographed by Maynard Geiger in the early 1950s.

Serra's childhood bedroom, shown in 2011. The double bed with posts, canopy, and square halo in the headboard is appropriate to the period but is not the original, which was almost certainly more austere.

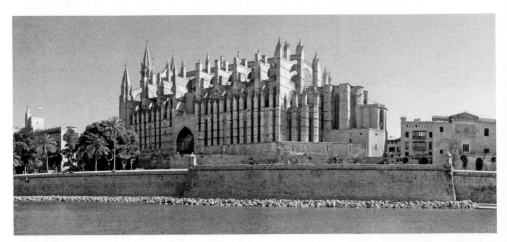

"La Seu" (or "The See" in Catalan)—the great thirteenth-century Cathedral of St. Mary in Palma, Mallorca, among Spanish churches second only in size to the Cathedral of Seville. This was the locus of some of Serra's earliest classes as a teenager preparing for the priesthood. He preached here at least three times, including the favored Corpus Christi sermon in 1743.

The bell tower of St. Peter's, Serra's childhood parish church, in Petra, Mallorca.

The interior of "La Seu," containing one of the largest rose windows in the world, with over 1,200 pieces of glass. The main altar was redesigned in the nineteenth century by the great Spanish architect Antoni Gaudí.

Carlos III of Spain, who ruled over Spanish lands in North and South America and the Indies, at the time of Serra's travels and work in the New World.

The Founding by Leon Trusset (1877), depicting Serra saying the first Mass on the Spanish landing in Monterey on June 3, 1770. The makeshift altar was placed under the so-called Vizcaíno live oak, near where the explorer who discovered Monterey Bay set anchor in 1602 and whose original mass, said by Vizcaíno's chaplain, Father Antonio de Ascensión, Serra commemorated over a century and a half later.

This gruesome scene by Flemish engraver Theodor de Bry illustrated the 1604 edition of Dominican Bartolomé de Las Casas's strong protest of Spanish atrocities in the Columbian era, *A Brief Account of the Destruction of the Indies.* Such images were used by some Protestant European governments to project the so-called Black Legend that attributed to Spain alone cruel treatment of Indians, sidestepping their own reprehensible behavior.

The frontispiece of the *Relación*, the first biography of Serra, published in 1787 by his friend Fray Francisco Palou. Serra clutches a cross in one hand and a stone in the other (with which he was said to beat his chest during sermons to illustrate mortification of the flesh). The snakelike form in the chalice at his feet may refer to the poisoning of his altar wine. The skull brings to mind an image often seen of the Blessed Virgin or Christ himself smashing a skull underfoot—the victory over death.

V. R. DEL V. P. F. JUNIPERO SERRA

Title page of the *Relación* by Palou, "disciple and venerable founder," alongside Palou's map of "The Grand Port of San Francisco."

The title page of the 1573 Italian version, published in Venice, of the immensely popular chivalric novel *The Labors of the Very Brave Knight Esplandián* (*Le Prodezze di Spandiano*) by Garci Rodríguez de Montalvo, first published in Spanish in 1510. This book contained the first-ever reference to "California," which the novelist imagined as an island "on the right hand of the Indies" populated entirely by black Amazon women with gold armor. The image of a Spanish knight on horseback in the original edition is replaced here by Moors about to mount a camel.

The extraordinary facade of Santiago de Jalpan, Serra's home mission in the Sierra Gorda Mountains of central Mexico, which he designed and built with the help of Pame Indian artisans and construction workers between 1752 and 1758. Statues of saints Francis and Dominic flank the St. James scallop-shell canopy over the entry, but the central image is purely Franciscan: the arm of Christ crossing the arm of St. Francis, both of them nailed to the same cross.

Sitting at their writing desks facing each other, two of Serra's favorite writers are carved in bas-relief at Mission Landa (1768): John Duns Scotus (left), who believed art was a way to God, and María de Agreda (right), the famed bilocator to the New World and author of books on Mary, with plume lifted and dress rippling as if to fly. Above the latter are the five bleeding wounds of Christ, and above the former a crossed-arm insignia of Christ and St. Francis—both Franciscan symbols.

A dance of Ohlone Indians at Mission Dolores in San Francisco intertwines native ritual and Christianity in an 1815 drawing by Louis Choris.

Carmel Mission on San Carlos Day, a romantic oil evocation of Mission San Carlos Borromeo, Serra's home mission in Carmel, by Jules Tavernier (*ca.* 1875).

Mission San Luis Rey, founded in 1798 near today's Oceanside, *ca.* 1895. The mission is in better shape than many California missions after secularization, but is still dilapidated. It was the home mission of the popular Father Antonio Peyri, who ministered to the largest mission population (almost three thousand Luiseño Indians).

Mission San Gabriel Arcángel, founded near central Los Angeles in 1771 by *Comandante* Pedro Fages and two priests, leaving Serra out, much to his chagrin. Resembling the Great Mosque at Cordová in its horizontality and pillar buttresses, "one of the most distinctive in California," San Gabriel was plagued by violence in its early years. Though the agitated Tongva Indians were initially calmed by an image of the Blessed Mother, rape and murder by Spanish soldiers inspired an early uprising, followed by a later one in 1785, a year after Serra's death, led by a female shaman, Toypurina. Nevertheless, San Gabriel became the richest of the twenty-one missions, with vast vineyards and cattle herds. This photo, with its lone horse, was taken in worse times, *ca.* 1874.

The ruined church of Mission San Juan Capistrano, photographed *ca.* 1930. Only half of one dome is left today (of eight original domes, two were felled by an earthquake in 1812 and two by an accidental US Army Corps of Engineers explosion in 1864). Restoration is a long, ongoing process. But the Serra Chapel, the only one extant at a mission where Serra said Mass, remains intact.

Sunrise over the Pacific Ocean floods the nave of Mission Santa Barbara at dawn Mass, December 22, 2012. Archeologist Ruben Mendoza believes Serra and others situated the California missions to capture first light at winter and summer solstices, moments of significance to the native population.

MISSION SAN FRANCISCO DE ASÍS (DOLORES) AND MISSION SANTA CLARA DE ASÍS: MICROBES AND THE GREAT FRANCISCAN COUPLE

A no-matter-what-ness.
—FATHER GREGORY BOYLE

Mission Dolores, still standing just after the 1906 San Francisco earthquake and fire.

R *educción.*
When it comes to the policy toward the Indians, no word for the Spanish conquest of California is more charged with meaning. Translated

into English literally as "reduction," it did not constitute that meaning for the Franciscans. Not even the Spanish military had "addition by subtraction" in mind when they embarked on their conquest.

The Spaniards felt that in setting up missions, Indians in their *rancherías*, their villages, would be so drawn to the message of Christian love, they would naturally gather around the altar of a life dictum of loving your neighbor as yourself without suspicion, letting go of their endless intertribal warfare and disputes (not taking into account Spain's own battles with England and both empires' wars against Islam). To reduce the Indians was to increase their numbers in the new faith.

But the tragedy of actual reduction was as inherent in the policy as it was in the reverberations of the thorny word itself. If the slowly accelerating transfer from their *rancherías* (or the "wild and unsettled" places, as Serra called the San Francisco Peninsula) to the missions had merely exchanged one living condition for another, with no lessening of numbers, the tragedy would have been only cultural. While this is tragic enough, it would not be unusual in the annals of conquest, and be mitigated somewhat by the benevolence of the Franciscans (a benevolence the Crown had counted on—sometimes fervently, sometimes cynically—from the very first moments in the New World).

But the fact is that the California Indians' numbers were not kept constant, nor did they increase. They were reduced drastically over time by contact with whites, in which the x factor of deadly germs the Spaniards unwittingly brought played a major part. Though the Spaniards thought their *reducción* spiritual, its obvious effects were catastrophically physical.

It is doubtful Serra ever understood the ramifications of this biological *reducción*. By the early nineteenth century, Franciscans who followed after him, such as Mariano Payeras, understood it all too well, but by then it was too late.

If the year 1776 saw the birth of the American nation in the East, it also saw the extension of the Spanish Empire in the West via Juan Bautista de Anza's second settler expedition and the creation of Mission Dolores in San Francisco. Her "sorrows" seemed to have been launched by the very dampness of that gorgeous northern peninsula (and continue to this day in the Mission District, a bustling area that encompasses a wide spectrum of inhabitants, from gangs, AIDS patients, and the homeless to newly gentrified artist and Latino neighborhoods).

In the aftermath of the debacle of the second battle of San Diego in November 1775, several relationships between (and among) padres and the Spanish state changed. Once his avid admirer, Lasuén found himself cooling toward *Comandante* Rivera. In the wake of Rivera's violation of sanctuary for the rebels at San Diego, his excommunication, as well as Serra's eloquent appeal for mercy for those Rivera wanted brutally punished, if not dead, Lasuén began to see Serra in a warmer light than the man whom he once "felt extraordinarily devoted and attracted to." Lasuén confessed, "When I see his actions and behavior at the present time, I must say I have been deceived."

"The greatest merit," Serra told the Basque Lasuén, "goes to him who overcomes himself the most."

With "neck bowed to the yoke," Lasuén took on what was essentially combat duty in San Diego, endearing him to the father president after a long, silently testy relationship. Lasuén went where others feared to tread, such as Vicente Santa María, who felt Serra "left me at San Diego like a bird in the air," and who basically fled the scene after complaints to both Pangua and Serra. Father Fuster, traumatized, also abandoned San Diego.

For the first and only time on record, Serra considered quitting. Just before Christmas 1775, he had led off a long, dark letter to Bucareli on the second battle of San Diego, "we are in a vale of tears." But something less spiritual had Serra dangling. He knew he was going to be reined in. His first defense was an offense, something, one suspects, he must have later regretted. He complained to Bucareli, "Though they may wish to blame the loss of Mission San Diego on the founding of San Juan Capistrano and the imprudent zeal and desire of the religious to found new missions . . . there is no foundation whatsoever for such an accusation." But that is not true. Serra's pressing for San Juan Capistrano drained San Diego of precious military guards, who went north with Sergeant Ortega to the Capistrano founding.

More immediately, Serra's thoughts of resignation were sparked by restrictions Father Pangua sent from Mexico City regarding changes in the protocols between the missionaries and Spanish authorities. The *patente* arrived on March 11, 1776—a full year after it was sent from Mexico City—and imposed severe restrictions on the father president. Among them were an injunction against moving priests from mission to mission unless they specifically requested it, and placing a sort of gag order on padres in communicating with soldiers and governmental authorities. Serra was specifically told not to write directly to political or military officers about Indian or mission affairs, but rather go through San Fernando. The bureaucratic implications of this were colossal. Imagine the icy correspondence between Serra and Rivera in San Diego—where they would not talk with each other for weeks, if not months—going through Mexico City just to reach a few yards across the street!

"I ask your Paternities not to be surprised that the expression slipped from me 'that it made me somewhat ashamed' on my reading it [the *patente*] and giving it to others to read," Serra wrote the guardian in response. "Despite everything, I read it promptly because I thought that only my bad conduct could have occasioned some of the limitations imposed on the office of the President. Never have such limitations been in place since the foundation of our holy College."

The suggestion in some quarters that he could be profiting from mission hardware, art, or crops he rejected roundly. In not assuming the cost of the San Luis Obispo painting, for example, he semi-joked that his "sin" was not against the Seventh Commandment (against stealing), but forgetfulness. On the other hand, reminded to give Anza hospitality, he went into a long recitation of the cornucopia of food put at Anza's table, including chickens "killed in number," steaks, cakes, and "other delicacies."

"So much for treating [Anza] kindly," Serra said. He later told Pangua that Anza never reimbursed him for the *arroba* of chocolate Serra gave him out on the Lompoc Peninsula.

Serra pointed out his own concerns about the implications of the *patente*. What if two missionaries were at each other's throats but neither asked to be moved? Was Serra to just let that discord fester? What if two priests were living harmoniously "but the conduct of both is irreligious," a veiled reference to homosexuality or concubinage. The new regulations forbade him acting. What if one wanted a change, but another didn't? Who was to break the Gordian knot? Thus Serra flirted with resignation: "I have been very much inclined to ask for my retirement from so angelical an employment." Serraesque, the old man of Carmel doubled down. "But this I am not doing because I think it is better—with the help of God—to work toward amendment." It was vintage Serra. He would tell authorities the logical fallacies of their actions *and* he would assert his obedience.

For seven years, though he did not specifically spell out his method, Serra had established a pattern in his mission chain. He had moved quickly to mark the northernmost and southernmost boundaries (Monterey and San Diego) and steadily he was filling in the space between. Insistent about settling the central coast among the populous and challenging Chumash ("San Buenaventura is an old story in Madrid," he quipped to Pangua), the time had come to expand the frame of reference northward. If they married in spirit in Assisi, Francesco (St. Francis) and Chiara (St. Clare) would marry in stone at San Francisco Dolores and Santa Clara in northern California.

Spain and the Franciscans had been playing a cat-and-mouse game with San Franciscan fog for centuries. In the early sixteenth century, Juan Cabrillo "ran great risks, especially at Cape Mendocino, where the storms were most violent." In 1595, Sebastian Cermeno completely missed San Francisco Bay before wrecking ten miles north at Point Reyes, which he named Bahia de San Francisco. A century and a half later, Ortega and Crespí caught sight of the "immense arm of the sea," though they took it for Cermeno's Point Reyes in today's Drake's Bay. In their 1772 jaunt thrashing around the East Bay, Fages and Crespí couldn't get past a cloud of mosquitoes to cross the Carquinez Strait.

With orders to find a spot for a mission, in 1774 Rivera and Palou followed the western edge of the peninsula north. Past San Francisquito Creek, Rivera noted that Ssalson Indians, apprehensive at this third movement of strange whites in a few years on their land, "keep us always on their left-hand or bow side." Palou erected a cross far up the peninsula with a view of the inlet of the Golden Gate close to where Portolá and Fages and Crespí had been, naming it, once and for all, San Francisco. One red-faced fellow put his head under the priest's habit, declaring "*Me Apam*," or "You are my father."

Anza's second thrust into California with two hundred colonists was directly related to the founding of two missions on the northern peninsula. Serra was overjoyed, declaring "I intend to go with him [Anza] . . . to be an eyewitness of the foundation of these new establishments." This was not to be, partly because Rivera was still dithering about whether to approve a mission in San Francisco, and partly because Serra chose to repair to San Diego and help bring it (and Capistrano) back to life. So Serra sent Palou ahead to be in place when official orders finally arrived to found Dolores, "a small step for future conversions in higher latitudes" where men of "stouter frame may ascend . . . those rungs."

To Serra, the metaphor was implicitly and mystically mixed: the missions were steps to heaven. Those steps became a ladder. They were inherently transcendent.

One last foray before Anza and Palou founded the San Francisco presidio and mission was that of the *San Carlos*, piloted by Captain Juan Manuel de Ayala, which explored the inner bays of Richardson, San Pablo, and Suisun after being the first to pass through the Golden Gate on August 9, 1775. Chaplain Vicente Santa María (who in one year refused to go near the cinders of San Diego, preferring his northern encounters with the "lords of these coasts, quite weaponless and obedient to our least sign to them to sit down") compared shell wampum to a Catholic rosary. Members of the Huimen Coast Miwok tribe were especially taken with the all-hands-on-deck bell, "which was purposely ordered to be struck so they could see what effect it had on ears that had never heard it. It pleased the Indians so much that while on board they went up to it from time to time to sound it themselves." This upper-bay experience was one of the last encounters of the Spanish with pre-contact Indians in California. On San Francisco, Captain Ayala reported back that "It is not a port, but a whole pocketful of ports into which a great many squadrons could enter without one being discovered by the other." The military advantages of these harbors within harbors were obvious and highly unusual.

As for Mission San Francisco, the actual mission site was chosen by Pedro Font, who arrived in late March 1776 with Lieutenant Colonel Anza, resting at two lakes—called Laguna de los Dolores—and a creek, all three dry or earth-filled today. As they approached a village on horse and mule, an old Huchuin woman danced a greeting, "making motions very indicative of pleasure." In this northern region, clothing against the cold seemed to be preferred to beads, so Anza handed out plenty of shirts and blankets. Later, with an "impudent" Indian who showed no shame in stealing, Anza, "half-angry, took from the Indian a stick which he had in his hands, gave him a light blow with it and then threw the stick away." Anza soon left for Mexico, leaving his two hundred settlers at Monterey. The stick smoldered in place.

On the way back the Anza party dropped an old bear too slow to get away; its teeth were either missing or worn to the gums—a cipher of the incipient loss of old native ways. Soon Anza spotted a huge California redwood (*palo alto*) past San Mateo in the southern peninsula along San Francisquito Creek. Father Font took out a graphometer; it was 140 feet high (50 *varas*) and 15.5 feet in circumference. He did all this "while savage Indians stood gaping at the proceedings."

Finally, Lieutenant José Joaquin Moraga, head of the guard at Monterey, essentially countermanded Rivera on a San Francisco presidio and mission. Just before he left to tend to a San Diego in cinders, Serra told Palou to found Mission Dolores in San Francisco, along with Moraga and Father Pedro Cambon. As he prepared his knapsacks and bags, candlesticks pressing out the burlap in ways that would hurt the flanks of the mules, Palou was alarmed to hear that a tribe called the Zanjones, emboldened by the attack on San Diego, were themselves threatening to attack Carmel. Hardly deterred, Serra "was full of joy, for apparently he believed for certain that that night they would take his life." All the priests went to confession to each other, and slept that night behind the blacksmith's forge. Serra talked incessantly throughout the night, hyperactive with excitement, keeping everyone up. But by morning a heavy rain fell, and all fell asleep, the Zanjones having spared Serra more joy.

The peninsula itself was less threatening, and so on June 29, 1776 (the very day Serra left by ship for the south), Palou and Cambon said the first "founding" Mass north under a leafy *enramada*, surrounded by fourteen soldiers, seven settlers with their wives and children, one Carmel Indian translator, five Indian muleteers, two servants from Baja, and two hundred lowing, snorting, and pissing cattle. At the *Salve Regina*, the cattle kicked up dust.

The setting was, in fact, lovely: to the west loomed the Twin Peaks and Buena Vista Heights. The mission-to-be would face east, toward San Francisco Bay, the bird-fed Lake of Dolores between the two. Geiger put it aptly, "The padres chose their sites with very practical ideas in mind but they never overlooked the element of beauty." The mission today faces a wide palm-lined esplanade at Sixteenth and Dolores streets.

Over time, the great Spanish (and Arab) love, a quadrangle with fountain, was placed in Dolores. The Yelamu Costanoan tribe gave significant labor, astonished at a vision of finely sawn and planed timbers and the beginnings of a phenomenon few Californian Indians knew—hard walls. Redwood logs supported much of the church structure, and rawhide undergirded the tiled roof. With a facade carved with four Doric columns, at completion in 1791, the church on the bay measured 114 feet long by twenty-two feet wide; Mission San Francisco still stands today, the most enduring of the original mission churches in the twenty-one-mission chain.

In time, Cambon would go on a shopping spree in Manila, bringing back to San Francisco fifty-five palm hats, two thousand cigars, 280 pounds of candle wax, and a two-century-old porcelain dish from the Ming Dynasty that even today serves as a holy water font, having survived the 1906 San Francisco earthquake. But Dolores's durability was hardly presaged. In fact, Palou admits that none of the foundation ceremonies was witnessed by natives because in August "they all left this peninsula and went in their rush canoes, some to the uninhabited islands within the port and others to the farthest shores of the strait [east of Oakland]." It wasn't the Spaniards who made them flee: "This sudden move was caused by the coming unexpectedly upon them of their great enemies, the Ssalson nation," who lived along San Mateo Creek farther south. It was quite a massacre, "not a minor feud," as the Ssalsons set fire to the major Yelamu town of Sitlintac on Mission Creek, as well as most of their other villages. The Spaniards were "unable to restrain them, even though we let them know by signs that they should have no fear, for the soldiers would defend them." Nevertheless, anthropologist Randall Milliken muses: "The timing of the Ssalson attack leaves many unanswered questions." He considers that the Ssalsons "may have been trying to do the Spanish a favor by securing for them complete control of the Yelamu lands" or "they may have been removing an impediment to their own easy access to the Spaniards." The Yelamu didn't creep back to their lands until eight months later—March 1777.

Serra built on the momentum of San Francisco and launched the founding of Mission Santa Clara forty miles southeast at the lower tip of the bay. On January 12, 1777, Father Tomás de la Peña raised the cross and said the first Mass in a laurel grove the natives called Sociostraka ("The Laurel"). He was soon joined by José Murguía, an old Serra confrere from the Sierra Gorda days, leading cattle and pack mules laden with church vestments and chalices. Nine days before Santa Clara's joyous beginning, George Washington waved his hat and rallied his American revolutionary forces to a critical victory against the British at Princeton, New Jersey.

If Washington "stole" Princeton that week, the Franciscans stole northern California. Santa Clara was founded on the Feast Day of the Lost Boy (a week after Epiphany); in Spain, the Christ Child is "stolen" from crèches, and symbolically returned to the crib, with much dancing, singing, and eating. Within weeks of the Feast of the Lost Boy at Santa Clara, not a boy, or even the statue of the Savior, but mules were stolen. Local Indians (perhaps Tamien Costanoans) butchered them and prepared to roast the meat. A detachment of soldiers from the new San Francisco presidio, however, surprised the celebrants and chased them into high brush where, arrows expended, three were shot to death. "They took some of the leaders to the mission and flogged them," Palou relates, an inauspicious early legacy of Santa Clara.

When Rivera finally shipped out, Felipe de Neve was named the new governor for both Californias. On his journey north from Baja, Neve selected two sites for farming communities with the broadest, best-watered, most fertile lands in the territory: the lands around the Río de Porciúncula and the Río de Guadalupe of Santa Clara. This is the origin of the rivalry between Los Angeles and San Francisco—not in freeways or microchips or movie stars, and certainly not baseball—but in agriculture. And fresh water, not the ocean.

This same abundant water was soon raised by Father Peña in feverish silver shells over the heads of infants dying in bushels around Santa Clara. The first (Spanish) recorded epidemic of the San Francisco Bay area swept through lower bay Costanoan (Ohlone) villages—three of which had at least 120 inhabitants—during May and June of 1777. The exact cause of it is uncertain; because most who died were infants one to two years old, Milliken thinks it was from a bacterium in bad water that was either drunk by infants being weaned, or from baths. The children suffered from diarrhea, vomiting, high fever, and finally convulsions typical of dysentery. Peña and Murguía baptized almost nonstop, "going through the villages" and pouring blessed water over the heads of fifty-four children, twenty-five of whom, according to Palou, "died almost as soon as they were baptized." The near 50 percent survival rate, however, may have played into the missionaries' hands: "The Tamien families must have thought the missionaries were attempting to heal by exorcising malevolent forces."

Marriages at the missions, often a neutral ground between warring parties, sometimes effected peace, as between the Ssalsons of Santa Clara and the Yelamu of San Francisco: "They [the Ssalsons] have married among those of this place. . . . With these conversions the continuous warfare in which they lived has ceased, with which both nations show themselves to be well pleased." But they were also used to shape natives into the Spanish connubial custom of monogamy (honored more often than not in the breach) and "a means of controlling and channeling the sexual behavior of young people."

The first marriage at Mission San Francisco took place on April 24, 1778, between a fourteen-year-old Indian girl named Paszem who had been a Christian for a month, and a twenty-one-year-old groom, Francisco Moraga (or Chamis), who was the first convert at Dolores. Perhaps one of the witnesses was newly baptized Miwok chief Whimoosa, who became "Marino," then Chief Marin, naming today's county across the Golden Gate. Just as the new couple settled into a tule-covered house near the mission, the Iroquois, egged on by the British, attacked and burned the western New York settlement of Cobleskill, massacring twenty-two American settlers. Soon after, the first couple at Mission Santa Clara was married in Catholic tradition, a renewal ceremony for the middle-aged Alson Indian pair named Riguis and Juinite (who had been baptized the day before as Pasqual and Barbara). If an eagle could have gazed across the entire continent, perhaps he would have seen the Alsons of Santa Clara as having a somewhat more promising future than the Iroquois.

In late 1776 and early 1777, Serra made his way up from Southern California after ministering to a prostrate San Diego and refounding Capistrano, taking six months of casual baptizing along the way at San Gabriel, San Luis Obispo, and San Antonio. He took his time, not only to rest his always aching foot and leg, but no doubt to treasure the land and the sea. Resting the reins of his animal, getting off, feeding him grain, Serra regarded the crags of the San Gabriels; one peak (Mount Wilson) limned in triangular shape the Trinity; the spine of Los Angeles was beautiful. Serra was greeted by the Chumash on this third journey through his cherished channel. A fierce rainstorm forced him off the beach up into higher ground of the coastal foothills (perhaps today's Alameda Padre Serra, but more likely slightly north of La Conchita at Rincón). There, slipping and sliding, he was literally given arms and legs by the Indians:

> Despite my lukewarmness, tears welled up into my eyes when I saw with what good will they came to my assistance, linking me on both sides by the arm to get me over the muddy steep hills, which I could not negotiate on foot or on horseback.

Serra was rarely moved to tears. There was the rare moment saying Mass when he would use the maniple, the thin silk handkerchief looped over the left wrist expressly for that purpose. We know he burst into tears at the sight of Father Basterra out in the middle of nowhere in Baja. That he was brought to tears by the Chumash who lifted him out of the mud and floodwaters shows they were as dear to him as priests. They were, in some ways, concelebrators: "It was sad to think that I had not been able — nor do I yet know if I will be enabled — to repay them as I would for all their sympathy and trouble."

Was word of Serra's springing free the condemned in San Diego sent up the California coast? Was that responsible for this magnetic joy between the Chumash and Serra?

When the storm cleared, the luminous blue Santa Barbara Channel would have to have taken his eye. That ladder of afternoon light to Santa Cruz Island. Chumash stroking in the silver. He pulled up on the reins; the mule snorted, the dust of his mane blessing the path.

Serra was getting old. The massed weight of his years and achievements and sorrows bent his shoulders; the fall sun, too, was like a weight. But before he flipped up his cowl, he perhaps let himself take the one luxury he would ever take (other than chocolate and snuff) — the drinking in of that vision of mountain, sea, and island. That greater Mallorca of Santa Barbara.

One Pacific rung after another. Like bells. Could a priest ring bells so well they would enliven the sea? *Las campanas doblan como el mar dobla.*

Arriving back at Carmel on January 15, 1777, exhausted, Serra was pleased that in his absence Dolores and Santa Clara were finally founded. He revealed, "I am having a little trouble with my chest," hastening to add, "but it does not amount to much, thank God." It was probably his childhood asthma coming back to haunt him at sixty-four in the wintry mists of Monterey Bay.

The advent of the new governor came with the movement of the capital of California from Loreto in Baja to Monterey, immediately elevating Upper California over Lower and twinning political power with the spiritual seat of the president of the missions right down the road in Carmel. Serra was ebullient: "The pleasure I have experienced, and still feel, at seeing our own Monterey, whose birth I witnessed, now made the capital of so large a province and that the King, our lord, should choose so distinguished an Officer in charge, is hard for me to describe." Serra went even further, praising Neve as the better man in Monterey: "I am under the impression that, in zeal and desire to assure, to prosper and to spread this Christianity, and in being in a position to formulate plans to carry out so commendable a purpose, he has many advantages over me. Thanks be to God." Finally, Serra went so far as to see the advent of Neve as his own personal deliverance, even "the coming of that peace of mind we have all so longed for."

In fact, Neve was taking over a decidedly wobbly California in the wake of the burning of two missions (San Diego and San Luis Obispo), the sacking of two military commanders, the influx of settlers, and the onset of epidemics. It was a difficult assignment, even without the transfer of the capital north, side by side with the military's chief antagonist, old Junípero.

Felipe de Neve was born in 1727 near Seville of an ancient family line that traced its name to the Roman conquest of Spain. A veteran of the Portugal campaign, Neve may have parlayed royal favor at this "zenith of [Spain's] territorial expansion." Charles III was half Italian.

Neve was a proponent of the Enlightenment and suspicious of the religious orders. That he and his wife could not bear children may have helped thrust them overseas. One of his first assignments in the New World was arresting all the Jesuits in Zacatecas, seizing their property, and deporting them through Veracruz. Neve was run out of town by a mob in Pátzcuaro when he tried to recruit militia.

In his twenty-seven-point Christmas 1776 message to Neve (making his way north to the new assignment), Bucareli was devoted to detail (another quality that the viceroy and Serra shared). Point six supported Serra's vision for two missions in the central coast ("for which [Serra] has always clamored"): "Then a ladder can be formed from mission to mission and this will strengthen communications." Bucareli envisioned a monthly mail service unimpeded from San Francisco to Loreto to Mexico City. Above all he instructed the new governor, "The peninsula of the Californias has suffered from confusions which need to be uprooted."

Perhaps the most important and difficult order Bucareli gave Neve was shaped by Serra's radical mercy at San Diego. It was Point 25 of the *carta instructiva*: "The good treatment of the Indians and the kindness, love, and gifts showered upon them are the only means, all taken together, to win them over; and may Your Grace prefer those means to others that stem from rigor. By the latter we have never been able to win good will from anyone." Insistent words, impressed on someone who had participated in the physical suppression of an Indian uprising in Guanajuato.

Neve arrived in Monterey on February 3, 1777. Unlike so many travelers through early California who were stunned by the coast's beauty, Neve said nothing about it, though he noted the "21 populous *rancherías*" hugging the cliff of the Santa Barbara Channel making for a "difficult passage." Neve thought Serra's favored spot would require a presidio and twenty-six soldiers. He also spotted the close roll of waves to cliffs (perhaps Rincón or Summerland or Isla Vista) so that "one has to pass through water for a way."

After inspecting the leatherjackets, Neve's first meeting was with Serra. In contrast to Rivera, Neve assured Serra he would not need a Lasuén or anyone for a chaplain. Still, Serra's optimism flared to new heights. He told Pangua that, unlike Rivera's bundle of nerves, here was a man "who listens to what is said to him," who "showed himself to be a gentleman in his manners," and with whom "we will live in peace."

But that was not to be. On January 14, 1778, Serra lost his anchor—Bucareli. California and most of Spain's northern provinces were pulled out of the purview of Mexico City, to a second viceroy called a "commandancy general," the nephew of an earlier viceroy, Teodoro de Croix. The area Teodoro would govern was called Provincias Internas. With this appointment, the twenty-seven-point plan negotiated with Bucareli went up in dust. And the Neve honeymoon—lasting less than a year—was over.

The first clash was over confirmations. In lieu of a bishop on the California frontier, in 1777 the Vatican, via the College of San Fernando in Mexico City, gave Serra the power to administer the sacrament of confirmation, usually reserved for a bishop in ceremony. After his August 1778 sailing down to San Diego, Serra began a confirmation tour, confirming 610 at the chain's first embattled mission, including the pardoned murderers of Father Jayme. By the time he got back to Carmel a year later, he had confirmed 1,897 Indians.

But Neve gave him halt. Serra was confirming under a *patente* from religious authorities that, by Spanish law, had to be accepted by the Council of the Indies in Madrid. The royal *pase* had not been given. Serra had to stop confirming, said Neve on April 20, 1780, after securing Teodoro de Croix's stringent agreement. Furthermore, Neve told Serra that the adobe structures were no longer to be referred to as missions, but rather as *doctrinas*, or parishes, places subject to movement of personnel by a bishop in an actual diocese. The closest bishop was a thousand miles away in Guadalajara. Thinking this all "preposterous," Serra wrote the guardian, "I began to wonder if I had passed my whole life in a dream."

Neve was cannily asserting the Crown's political authority over the frontier missionaries, and slowly wresting them from the Franciscans. Neve was also going for the jugular of Serra's utopic dream in California, to live in salvific community with the Indians with as little interference from the Crown and the military as possible.

Serra tried to tone down the growing disagreement; it was "the little grain of pepper which the governor has placed in the condiment." But with Neve insisting he see Serra's original document from San Fernando getting the *pase* to confirm, and with Serra (perhaps cagily) sending it back to San Fernando for safekeeping instead of to Neve directly, the friction between the two mounted. At one point, Neve accused Serra of "unspeakable artifice and cleverness," and of the Franciscans in general of "boundless unbelievable pride."

Serra ached to continue confirming, especially in the two new northern missions. He first visited and said a High Mass at Santa Clara on the Feast Day of St. Michael the Archangel, September 28, 1778, and moving on to San Francisco, gazing out from the presidio on the slim, flickering golden entry to San Francisco Bay, he proclaimed, "Now Our Father St. Francis, the crossbearer in the procession of missions, has come to the final point of the mainland of California. To go farther, ships will be necessary."

Serra said his first Mass at Mission Dolores on October 4, 1778, and was "a source of joy" to the seventeen Yelamu Ohlones who had come under the grassy roof of the mission in its first year. Said at dawn, the Mass plucked secret chords in the Ohlones' cosmology: "The closest parallel might have been Bay Area Californians' relationship to the sun, which they regarded as one of the most powerful beings in the universe." The notion of the Mass as sacrifice touched the Ohlone and other natives, who typically surrendered gifts of food, slaughtered game, and prized shells at dawn "to appease a violent deity." The awe was visceral. One early visitor to Mission Dolores was struck when, at the sound of drums and trumpets at Mass, Ohlones "fall to the ground as if half dead," remaining there for most of the service.

By the next year, 1779, Serra fended off repeated requests of both San Francisco and Santa Clara that he come to confirm, saying his leg pained him too much. The legalistic clamps Neve had put on him not to confirm probably pained him more. By October, Serra, his leg still severely inflamed, set out on foot from Carmel to Santa Clara, making the seventy-one miles in two days (the one actual case of his walking in Upper California that Palou documents). In fact, according to Palou, "he arrived in such a condition that he could hardly stand."

As Neve's fall deadline approached, Serra got up the nerve and strength to continue to confirm. Throughout October and November 1779, he confirmed 189 in San Francisco and 167 in Santa Clara. His doctors insisted he rest his leg, but Serra only answered that since the cure would have to be a long one, and that his time left on earth was probably short, he would keep moving, putting his fate in the hands "of the Divine Physician."

Finally, the Vatican's original orders to Serra were transferred back to California from Mexico City with the royal *pase*, and Serra was vindicated. On May 19, 1781, Neve approved Serra's confirming powers five years after the father president had first gotten them; as Neve's biographer put it, "Serra, vastly weaker than his opponent, had won not only the game but every hand."

But Neve struck back, canceling the double rations for the new missions of San Juan Capistrano, San Francisco, and Santa Clara on the grounds that they did not exist when José Echeveste, in charge of California supplies, had approved extra food (in 1773). Serra and his confreres were furious; double rations had been essential for attracting new Indian converts and feeding the ones who had come in. Even Rivera had approved them for the northern peninsular missions; Neve reversed this as illegal and levied a fine on the Franciscans. Ultimately Serra had to bow to a compromise that favored the state—the fine was lifted, but double rations were stopped.

The guardian Rafael Verger had warned Serra not to expect much of civil authorities, that Bucareli may have been an exception: "According to what we know here, these gentlemen direct their projects not so much to conquer souls as territory." Serra was not unaware of such realities, but he was getting older and losing focus, being outmaneuvered at times by someone even cannier with rhetoric than he: "This gentleman takes advantage of words not being absolutely concise and explicit to refuse to accept them." He called Neve "cunning," and confessed the governor had "an unusual knack of stripping me of any self-love—if any yet remains in me."

Another point of contention between Serra and Neve was the growth of the first town (separate from a mission) in California—San José, adjacent to Mission Santa Clara. Founded on November 29, 1777, the pueblo of San José was created by a Spanish version of the Homestead Act: around a central plaza, settlers were given plots of land for homes (*solares*) and for farming (*suertes*). They could not be subdivided. Pueblos covered about 3.2 square miles (four leagues); they were to be placed in a healthy, nonswampy area, though not on crags. Still, the sun should strike the town before a nearby river. On the relation to the Indian population, the Laws of the Indies were clear: the pueblo was to be in an unoccupied area in a place not prejudicial to the Indians; animals could not graze on Indian land, for example. The pueblos were not supposed to butt up to the mission, but San José did to Santa Clara. Serra caustically noted that Neve referred to colonists as *gente de razón*, "as if the Indians did not have any reason." Serra met with Neve, asserting that San José violated the law in being too close to the mission, which was still getting its legs; it also drained off water and grazing land from the Indians, both of the mission and the villages. But with Neve, said Serra, "neither reasoning, laws, nor complaints have any value." Ultimately, Neve admitted the violation, but did nothing about it.

Exacerbating Serra's frustration, in 1782 Neve was kicked upstairs to an advisory role to the viceroy, prompting the return of Pedro Fages, now to the post of governor. Still, the Santa Clara padres quickly decided to make a case against the encroachment of San José by citing the *Recopilación*, or Laws of the Indies. The second iteration of the Laws (1580), no doubt influenced by the protests of Bartolomé de Las Casas, who had watched the massacres in Cuba firsthand, was aimed right at civil and military authorities:

> It is our will to charge the viceroys, presidents, and *audiencias* with the duty of protecting the Indians and of issuing corresponding orders so that they may be protected, favored and alleviated. . . . Transgressors are to be punished with particular and vigorous demonstration.

Needless to say, there was nothing in colonial British American or even early law even close to the tolerance and cooperation Spain promulgated legally for the Indian. But on the frontier, the best of laws suffered from remoteness, lack of police to enforce them, and paucity of authorities—excepting the missionaries—to police the police. The missionaries' leverage was not often strong. And now there was no Bucareli to appeal to. Still, the *Recopilación* was clear: new pueblos and estates could not prejudice the rights of Indians whatsoever; settler cattle could not come within twelve miles of Indian land, and sheep, goats, and pigs not within five miles. Violation risked forfeiture of an estate and half the cattle on it.

Just as he was about to relay the Santa Clara fathers' appeal to Neve to stop San José's encroachment on mission and Indian lands, Serra was hit by a royal war tax on all the missions. He was repelled by it, and several fathers (including Lasuén of San Diego and Mugartegui of San Juan Capistrano) implored the father president to intercede to exempt them from a tax to fund Spain's wars. Essentially, the San José–Santa Clara battle got waylaid in the war tax fight. Serra was being pummeled on all fronts by civil and military authorities. Lieutenant Moraga, made a commissioner to San José, handed out branding irons and land titles to nine families, the first Spanish citizens. Moraga bungled the area's mapping, compromising Santa Clara's and the Indians' lands. Few Indians benefited, though later an Ohlone named Lope Inigo received three thousand acres.

On October 24, 1779, Serra's great friend and patron, Antonio María de Bucareli y Ursua, died in Mexico City. Only the year before, in the spirit Bucareli had applauded, Serra had successfully gotten death sentences commuted against four chiefs who had planned yet another attack on Mission San Diego. But now the companion of that spirit was gone.

Heartbroken, Serra kept on. On December 9, 1779, he married at Carmel one of his favorite leatherjacket soldiers, (now) Sergeant José María Góngora, to Rosalia Verdugo. When one of the two witnesses (Juan María Olivera) forgot to sign the marriage certificate, Serra took up the pen for him and, with a bit of relish, wrote "I did it myself."

Soon after, yet another war broke out between Spain and England, which again cued the war tax, a peso expected from each Indian. For such, a basket would be passed at Mass for collection. Serra opposed it strenuously:

> And this is a land where pesos have never existed and do not now exist, from Indians who do not know what a peso is. Nor could they understand why pesos are necessary to wage a war for they have had frequent wars among themselves and for them no pesos were necessary. Much less could they understand why the king of Spain, our master, must ask them to give him a peso apiece.

He thought Neve was forcing the missions to "prove the adage that 'those who have nothing, contribute.'" The missions sent 4,216 pesos for the war. "I really believe that our naked Indians here have given more . . . than the Governor himself," he flatly concluded. "The affair really calls for a melody but we are not in a mood to sing." Serra refused to pay the fifteen pesos he was charged for the war tax on San Carlos Borromeo while the war was on. He paid it when the war was over.

On October 7, 1781, at 7 P.M., just after Vespers, Serra stood in his Carmel room, shaking. At first he may have thought it was a heart attack, but then he saw the cross trembling on its nail in the adobe wall. The room pitched briefly. He heard the bells of the church ring in an odd timbre. It was an earthquake. He remembered the quake the year they arrived in San Diego—twelve long years before. The Kumeyaay had taken it as a sign the gods were angry. Now, old in his bones, he did not take it as a sign of God's or the earth's pleasure. This time he reacted like the Indians.

Two weeks after the quake, he did something he had never done before, or perhaps never had to—comfort a doomed man before his execution, a soldier at the Monterey presidio named Juan Antonio Labra, whom Neve condemned to death by firing squad for stealing. (The poor private must have stolen half of California.)

By noon on October 23, 1781—the execution ringing in their ears— Serra and Crespí hoisted themselves on their mules and left for Santa Clara. Serra confirmed for three days; on November 9, he dedicated the completed adobe church of Santa Clara de Asís. (The first one had been destroyed by floods in 1779.) On hand was Father Murguía, who had designed and built a sturdy church at Conca in the Sierra Gorda that still stands today. Santa Clara was not so fortunate; five times the church had to be rebuilt after floods, earthquakes, and a consuming fire in 1926. But Serra did his all with this second version, reading from Psalm 183, "My soul longeth and fainteth for the courts of the Lord." The sixty-eight-year-old friar bent down and cut a cross into the cornerstone before calling on Christ "who are the cornerstone cut from the mountains, and the unchangeable foundation," to "strengthen this stone." Serra then knelt and helped the workmen roll and rope the mammoth round stone in its hole in the altar, together with a cross and some Spanish coins.

Leaving immediately after laying the stone, referring to himself as "this burden," Serra was thrown by his mule. He was covered with a blanket on the ground and a bonesetter in San José sought. Though shaken, Serra had sustained only a "badly sprained hand and bruised ribs," and was happy to discover "all my bones were sound and in place . . . and now it is a matter of the past. Blessed be God."

Crespí had touched the cornerstone, marveling at Serra's strength rekindled for the moment: dust clung to their palms. Before they had made it back to Carmel, Crespí's lungs swelled so that he could barely breathe. His legs and feet swelled, too, as in phlebitis. There was no doctor at Monterey or Carmel at that moment. Dr. Dávila had been cashiered in 1777 for "a troublesome and captious character" and for "giving scandal." He was also, apparently, not a good doctor. Serra and the fathers feverishly consulted a 1712 medical book, to no avail.

Juan Crespí died on New Year's Day 1782. The Esselen and Rumsen Indians of Carmel cried into the night. Having made his greatest mark as an explorer and diarist on the first thrust into Alta California, the friar with eyes as blue as the sea was beloved and admired for his humility and devotion to Serra, to whose Quixote Crespí played Sancho Panza for forty years. Serra ordered his old friend a coffin of California redwood, and Serra himself lowered Crespí into his grave in the sanctuary of San Carlos Borromeo, reciting, as he had promised to do if he should outlive any student, the *Requiescat in Pace*.

Serra was reeling. He had sustained a double inner earthquake—the loss of his closest friend and chief benefactor in the halls of power. His power to shape the missions with a vision of comity between Indian and Spaniard was being diminished by the day. Of all people, Pedro Fages was back to taunt him.

And then came the sores. It is bewildering, to put it mildly, that not once does Serra in all four volumes of letters mention the epidemic deaths of masses of Indians, particularly from syphilis, measles, and smallpox. Though it is true that the population of his own mission San Carlos Borromeo in Carmel steadily increased until its peak at 1795—eleven years after he died—Serra would have to have known and witnessed that in the last five years of his life, the number of Indian deaths at San Carlos was between twice and three times that of those born at the mission. Indians at Mission San Carlos Borromeo were simply not having children, and the children they did have were dying early. Many of the missions followed this agonizing record.

For the period over which we have figures (1784 to 1831), the crude death rate at San Carlos Borromeo was seventy-nine deaths per thousand. As historian Steven Hackel notes, this extremely high rate maintained itself while the crude death rate was going significantly down in England. From 1730 to 1820, the British rate went from thirty-one to twenty-four deaths per thousand. That means that at San Carlos Borromeo in Carmel, the Indians were dying at two to three times the rate in England. However, though the infant mortality rate at San Carlos was high (396 per thousand), it was apparently consistent with most European countries, which had large urban poor populations living in unsanitary conditions. Where San Carlos was four times that of England and twice that of Spain was in *childhood* mortality rate: 43 percent of those California Indian children who survived the first year died before they were five. Less than 25 percent of Indians born at San Carlos lived to be fifteen years old. That's the tragedy and the shame.

The Indian death rates at Mission Santa Clara reached twice that of the aboriginal community in their villages. Some of this may have been fanned by a mass migration in the winter of 1794 and 1795, when 360 more Indians were baptized at Santa Clara. Arriving at this time, Father Magín Catalá tried out exorcism as a way of driving out sickness and "a legion of evil spirits." With cures attributed to his activities, Catalá was considered for sainthood for a time long before Serra; he also was a steadfast voice against the swallowing of Indian lands by settlers and the Crown.

Neophytes were flooding into Santa Clara from the south around Los Gatos and the Santa Cruz Mountains, from the east in the Fremont area, even from up the San Francisco Peninsula. Similar mass conversions occurred at Mission Dolores in San Francisco, where the population jumped from 628 in October 1794 to 1,095 in May 1795 (even as 280 Indians fled Dolores): "The level of religious instruction that could have been provided for so many new people must have been absolutely minimal." Severe droughts had struck the Indian population with hunger they felt could only be relieved by stores at the mission and row crops; when their own desiccated crops did grow they were often trampled by settler cattle. In any event, the close quarters women especially were forced to live in (the *monjerio*) spread the undetected germs; at Dolores in San Francisco, 1795 saw a severe typhus epidemic followed on the heels of the mass migration, crowded living, and feverish conversion.

There were other microbial destroyers. The worst of the nonvenereal diseases was measles, taking one-third of the Indian children under five years old in 1806 alone. At the peak of communicable disease among California Indians (1800), the natives were dying at a rate 70 percent higher than that of pre-contact with Europeans. (It was 50 percent higher in Serra's era, 1770–80).

Though we know the Indians were not helping themselves by fleeing *into* the missions, they may have thought they had little choice and had to try anything to survive. Milliken cogently describes the complex mind-set:

Events in the Bay Area were unfolding for which the traditional culture had not prepared people. . . . Traditional rituals did not prevent the increased deaths, the military defeats, or the crop losses of 1794, nor did they bring the skills and goods associated with Spanish culture. Native peoples scrambled to find stable points, but the world no longer fit within their complex cultural template. They were left in a state of disorganization and confusion.

What was for Serra and his confreres a "religious conversion movement" was for many Indians—though not all—"a psychological disintegration movement."

For the chief bane—syphilis—the friars, often absent a real doctor, tried several homemade remedies, including poultices and salves; neither worked. Shamans, or "sucking doctors," as the friars ridiculed them, tried a sight gag, putting a stone or piece of wood in their mouths and sucking one of the syphilitic sores, then spitting out the object as if it were the culprit. This sleight of hand only spread the disease.

The Franciscans were not ignorant about who brought in the syphilis; Fathers Miguel and Zalvidea reported in 1818 that "the putrid and contagious disease had its beginnings with the time Don Juan Bautista de Anza stopped at Mission San Gabriel with his expedition [in 1776]." The contagious diseases spread from mission Indians back to the villages quickly. Father Ramón Abella at Mission Dolores observed that "Young [gentile] women never bring children," and few had more than two or three children, hardly the size of large Spanish families (or their own pre-contact broods). In fact, half of the couples at San Carlos Borromeo, Serra's home base, were childless. The great paradox of the mission system: missions were both protection *and* exposure.

The Franciscans may have known, or at least sensed, the trouble started with Spain (Las Casas describes syphilis, as did Columbus's son Ferdinand, as early as the sixteenth century), but they didn't know exactly how. (It wasn't until the mid-nineteenth century that scientists such as Pasteur described the theory of microbial pathogens spread through blood, water, and other hosts.) Though it has been a subject of much controversy over the past century, it is now a prevailing theory that Columbus and the early conquistadors actually brought syphilis *to* Europe *from* the Caribbean, after which it broke out in microbial riots all over the continent around 1560. Spain and other Europeans then brought this heartier strain *back* to the New World. The catch is this: unlike other North American and South American tribes who had a resistance to syphilis, the California Indian didn't. Hence the California Indian tribes were more devastated by the venereal disease than anyone else.

Syphilis, as Sandos puts it, is "baffling," even to modern diagnostics, requiring long observation. The spirochete bacterium (*Treponema pal-*

lidum) enters through a cut or lesion or in mucus, producing an initial chancre at site of infection for ten to forty days, which then disappears. In the second stage, painful sores appear in areas like the mouth and rectum. The third stage, which unleashes itself five to fifteen years after the original infection, is deadly, causing everything from a breakdown of the central nervous system to blindness, insanity, or a burst aorta. An incoherent babbling can occur just before death. It is not a pretty illness, and it's hard to believe Serra did not see it.

In the 1812 survey the mission fathers answered for Spanish officials, 72 percent put syphilis and venereal disease at the top of their list of Indian ailments. (One of only three who didn't—an astringent fellow at Soledad—cited "laziness.") The priests at San Antonio put it plainly: "Unchastity is the prevailing vice in both sexes and this it is that is carrying them to the grave. They know this well enough and realize it but lack understanding."

Another devastation of venereal disease is to childbearing, as well as children. In a word, it sterilizes. Father Abella at Mission Santa Barbara wrote with tragic poignancy that "all are infected with it for they see no objection to marrying another infected with it. As a result, births are few and deaths are many." As for gonorrhea, about 20 percent of women infected with it develop inflammation of the fallopian tubes and uterus; this sterilizes most of them. Couldn't Serra have seen gonorrhea's painful red eye in the newborn?

His final successor, the last president of the California missions, Father Mariano Payeras, did, to great revulsion and guilt. In 1820, Payeras wrote that in their half century effort, the Franciscans had succeeded in baptizing nearly all the California coastal Indians from San Diego to what is now Marin County. Serra and his confreres had wanted to fashion "a beautiful and flourishing church and some beautiful towns which could be the joy of the sovereign majesties of heaven and earth." But missions had become a place of "people miserable and sick" and in the countryside "rapid depopulation of the *rancherías* which with profound horror fills the cemeteries."

Serra did not share the pessimism of that assessment. Perhaps if he had lived longer, he would have. Dolores has the only statue of Junípero Serra with his head down.

CHAPTER NINETEEN

MISSION SAN BUENAVENTURA AND THE DEATH OF SERRA

O death, where is thy victory?
—PAUL TO THE CORINTHIANS 15:55

The *Great Fear* painting by Andres Caimari (1790),
depicting Serra's last night, with Palou and aspergill
of water (right), an Indian peering over his shoulder,
and possibly Fages (left) over Serra's.

*T*he last day of his life he spent sitting on a stool. It was August 28, 1784.
"I have come under the shadow of fear."
Junípero Serra's last words, or almost last, were not like him. A man

300

who feared little, he left his island home and an adoring flock to sail halfway around the world, ultimately to walk into a land where no Spaniard, no European, had settled before him. Where many were killed, fled, or threw themselves on a ship back to Mexico or Spain—half delirious with sickness, exhaustion, or revulsion over violence—he remained. He kept on walking despite the spider bite that gnawed on his foot and leg for a quarter century, he kept consecrating after nearly succumbing to the poison served in his altar wine. Watching a man bleed to death from an arrow intended for him, he blessed the man who shot it. When told priests were killed at San Saba, he said he was excited to go.

But now he was afraid. "Can fear and hope exist together?" the despairing shepherd Grisostomo asks in *Don Quixote*, concluding that "fear is forever more likely. More things bring it blazing to life."

It was the feast day of St. Augustine, August 28. He was as afraid as Augustine had once been, loath to leave that beautiful, faithful woman of North Africa. How strange for fear to flood into a soul who had laughed in death's face, who seemed to relish suffering itself. For Serra, woes were blessings, ways to store up and kindle the goodwill of the Lord. Hadn't he said to the nuns back in Mallorca forty years before and a life and world away, "Start congratulating yourselves!" They were getting a nosegay of troubles! What did he tell the guardian? Prepare for a "wealth of sufferings."

It would be hard to find a Spaniard then who believed more in the transformative act of suffering than Junípero Serra. No Franciscan of his time—and few people of any time—appreciated the mystery of God becoming man, of suffering like a man to rescue man, than Serra. He well knew that for nearly two thousand years atheists had posed a strong challenge to the incarnation: If God was Almighty, and man needed saving, why not just save him in the quickest, most efficient way? Why suffer? Lift him by the hairs of his head. Or make man perfect, unable to be anything but good. In short, a wonderful automaton. No need to descend into the earth, through a woman. No need to bear the arrogance of the Pharisees or the whips of the soldiers or Pilate's tomfoolery or the accusations of the bad thief while on the cross.

Except that Serra knew what Christ knew: love was of the earth. It was a function of the desire for the earth and for human beings created in his image and likeness. If man was like God, then God was like man. He had this hankering for existence. If the earth was created, it was created out of love. And to create out of love was to give up control. It was to give the creation choice.

• • •

Serra knew that Christ's coming had not only posed a great, blistering challenge to the old Hebrews, it had also done so to the ancient Greeks and Romans. The life of an eye for an eye was no life; it was not what God had in mind when he created the world. (This was as big a challenge to the Indians of California as the ancients, and, for that matter, most Spaniards.) God was not getting back at the universe for its emptiness; he was not inflicting man on the void. Mankind's spot of the divine was this strange freedom; just as God chose to create, mankind could choose like Icarus to fly up and challenge the sun. It was choice that had crippled even Edenic California. And Serra had to wonder, on his last night, if he and the Spaniards had brought, not salvation, but a shiny, worm-bored Apple.

Up till now, Serra had banked his life on it: man had come to need saving. And he wasn't saved by a Christ solo concert on the ram's horn, or handfuls of fishes and bread loaves festooning over a crowd of thousands, one great magician's trick! He was saved not from hunger or incredulity or dullness; he was saved from death—a rather larger thing. And though the Greeks, Romans, and Hebrews did not do that, one Old Testament prophet had an inkling: "All you who thirst, come to the waters. . . . Why do you spend money for that which is not bread, and your labor for that which doth not satisfy you? . . . For you shall go out with joy and be led forth with peace." This was Isaiah, whose philosophy finds its startling fulfillment in the Sermon on the Mount: "Love your enemies, do good to those who hate you" (Luke 6:25–29). This is the most radical spiritual notion in human history, certainly up until its birthing, and in many ways it still is. Much in human nature struggles against it.

Love and suffer. Suffer and love. Christianity was one big oxymoron, and Serra felt it in his bones, ever since childhood on one suffering beautiful island. Was there another one like it in the world? Yes, halfway around the world. California. The people of California whom no one knew—he had brought them love and suffering on a scale they had not known before. Could he have questioned it that last Augustine night in Carmel?

Throughout the last day and night, and into his last morning, Serra sat "in profoundest silence and deep recollection." After his authority to perform confirmations had expired (on July 16, 1784), he had announced, echoing the great farewell of St. Paul imprisoned in Rome, "I have fought the good fight, I have finished the course, I have kept the faith." Then he withdrew from most human contact. And now, on that last night, instead of lying down, he propped himself on the rush stool, meditating, perhaps, on the most difficult encounters and realizations of his final years. If, in the final hour, you admit "great fear," you are hardly at rest. Great wakefulness must have meant great inner pain. But what was Serra afraid of? It seems doubtful that it was death; eternal life was his life's goal as a Christian, not to mention as a priest. It certainly wasn't physical suffering; he'd shown himself nearly superhuman in that regard. It must have been, based on his earlier calibration of a "happy death," fear that his life had not mattered, or worse, had no meaning, or that he would be judged poorly by history, or that, in fact, he had failed to measure up to his own profoundest beliefs.

So it seems likely some shred of five important encounters of his last years crossed his tortured conscience those final twenty-four hours: the explosive argument with Governor Neve about Indian *alcáldes* and the question of flogging (1779–80); the martyrdom of Father Garcés out in the desert (1781); the founding of Buenaventura and the "unfounding" of Santa Barbara (1782); the return of Pedro Fages (1783); and the nightmarish advent of a Franciscan bishop named Reyes, a sort of betrayer to Serra for trying to get California's missions shut down (1783).

On Palm Sunday 1779, Serra had an incendiary argument with Governor Neve in which the father president completely lost his temper. The subject was the prospect of Indian *alcáldes*, sort of mission mayors. As another method in his relentless campaign to remove the missions from Franciscan control and secularize them, Neve felt two Indians should be elected as mayors at each mission, and two as *regidors* (aldermen). Furthermore, the Indian *alcáldes* could not be disciplined by the padres or given orders by them. Presumably they would answer to Spain directly.

At one point Neve had said something deeply offensive to Serra that hasn't been documented verbatim but sounds like it was worse than *mierda*—some challenge to Serra's sensibility and nature, perhaps, as Junípero called it "a statement so alien to the truth that I changed my attitude, raised my voice to a shout."

It's possible Neve made a provocative assertion along the lines of: *So you want to whip the Indian* alcáldes? *You don't trust the government to do it?* Or: *Are you afraid an Indian could be as wise as you?*

"Nobody has ever said that to me because they could not say that to me!" Serra yelled, shocking Juan Crespí and the soldier watching guard outside the room at the Monterey presidio. No one had ever heard Serra shout like that.

So shaken he stopped dead preparing for Palm Sunday Mass, Serra later stood at the altar, "for a prolonged period trying to compose my interior self." That night he could not sleep, writing a letter to Neve in his head, "struggling with that wretched letter almost to midnight, attributing my failure to compose it properly to my agitated interior." Unable to take on Neve, he tried to calm his nerves with a letter to Father Sánchez at San Gabriel Mission. But it didn't work.

"What is this all about, Lord?" he called out in the night, the Monterey cypress tossing on the cliffs.

In his moment of despair Serra said he heard an urgent, rescuing voice, not unlike that Augustine heard in his hour of great crisis, but different: "Be prudent as serpents and simple as doves." It was Matthew 10:16, the outset of a great, complicated, troubling, yet ultimately calming parable about how the disciples should go out and tell people what they had seen and heard.

Having told them, at first, to be careful, Christ does a 180-degree turn and counsels bravery: "What I tell you in darkness, speak it in the light, and what you hear whispered, preach it on the housetops. And do not be afraid of those who kill the body, but cannot kill the soul." Suddenly, in one of the great free associational sermons in the Gospel, Christ speaks of sparrows "sold for a farthing," each watched over by God: "As for you, the very hairs of your head are all numbered. Therefore do not be afraid; you are of more value than many sparrows."

The Matthew passage, the very ignition point of Christianity, would have spoken profoundly to a missionary priest out on the peripheries such as Serra. Watch out; be brave; I've got your back. It is as contrary, as risky, as Christianity itself. And the startling union of dove and serpent at the outset calmed Serra. "I felt like a new man," he wrote Lasuén.

"Yes, Lord, yes, Lord," Serra had said. And he fell asleep.

But the matter of floggings would not go away, not then in 1779, nor on Serra's last night on the stool. He did manage to finish his letter to Lasuén about his essential belief in purposeful pain: "In the midst of all my troubles I am happy because children are born amidst pain." Life, his life, was the life of a birthing mother, one given no painkiller in the act. In a letter the very next day to Father Figuer, also in San Diego with Lasuén, he gave an even more graphic analogy for the usefulness of suffering: "Whither does the ox go that does not plow except to Campeche? . . . If I should have to speak of the value of hardships, it would not be proof of my ability to say much and say it well, for much has been written about them. Let it be enough to read a little in St. Bonaventure's book or library, namely *Christ Crucified*."

Still, the issue of the Indian *alcáldes*—and the extremely thorny matter of punishment in the missions, especially flogging—reared its Hydra head. Neve's motives, "professedly to train the Indians in the procedures of civil life, and thus prepare them for their role as citizens after the secularization of the missions," was to his biographer "undoubtedly genuine." But there was a subtext that Serra caught: if Indians were free of the missions, they could be quickly thrown into essentially slave labor in the newly sprouting *ranchos*, or private ranches, in California. In the missions they were paid, meagerly perhaps, but paid, and also given clothes, food, and shelter. This was not assured in the "outside world." Serra was being paternal, in both the good and bad senses of the term. He also wondered what license they would take if not subject to the padres' discipline; thus he worried for their souls and their very lives among the *gente de razón*—as Neve gratingly (to Serra) referred to Spaniards. Reluctantly, Serra struck a compromise and agreed to the election of *alcáldes* (mayors) and *regidores* (town councilmen) in the first five missions, though he gave a graphic example of the downside of exempting *alcáldes* from punishment:

> Balthasar, while in office [at San Carlos Borromeo] as *alcalde*, once aware of his privileges and exemption from correction by the Fathers, began to do just as he pleased. He had a son by one of his relatives, and had an Indian flogged because he carried out an order from the Father missionary. . . . There is no need to speak of his neglect of duty while in office. And now, everyone sees and knows in what circumstances he is living— deserter, adulterer, inciting people here.

Here was an elected Indian exempt from flogging who nevertheless flogged at will his fellows. Serra called for Balthasar's arrest before new elections took place.

The question of whipping a fellow human being you are trying to bring into Christ's fold remains. Serra believed in it, if that is the word, and not just because he whipped himself, as we have seen, to imitate Christ's passion. He felt it necessary to instill order in a working community that relied on one another for sustenance, and more importantly, as Monroy notes, to teach work as a "crucial mark of civilization" so that "work . . . had importance and dignity beyond the merely instrumental." As well, the priests were inculcating a Christian morality of personal possession and monogamy for those for whom it was strange.

Corporal punishment was consistent with the times, to an extent, particularly for disciplining schoolchildren and teenagers. Indians were often referred to by Serra and other missionaries as their "children," whose very souls hung in the balance. Flogging, however perverse it is to our contemporary sensibilities, had not only a societal purpose on a frontier, it had a spiritual purpose. Souls were at stake in that bloody mess.

We know that in England, flogging the young to bring them in line was common and favored by such luminaries as the Enlightenment's John Locke and poet Samuel Taylor Coleridge. At Eton, four lashes was a "scrubbing," six was a "bibling," and parents actually paid half a guinea at the beginning of the school year for such disciplining. The birch rod was not birch but the much denser applewood. And there were excesses; in 1699, a Scottish schoolmaster named Carmichael was banished for whipping and punching a schoolboy so severely he died. There's no evidence that eighteenth-century Spanish life in these sordid matters was any different from England's.

Serra was not naïve about excesses: "I am willing to admit that in the infliction of the punishment we are now discussing, there may have been inequities and excesses on the part of some Fathers and that we are all exposed to err in that regard." The record does not show Serra personally flogging anyone other than himself, though he may be suggesting that he had done so or consented to it. But when he tried to defend the practice in a long 1780 letter to Neve he cited no less an authority than St. Francis Solano, the South American missionary for whom the last (twenty-first) California mission is named. Serra noted that Solano "has been solemnly canonized [and] had a special gift from God to soften the ferocity of the most barbarous by the sweetness of his presence and his words; nevertheless, in the running of his mission in the Province of Tucuman in Peru . . . when they failed to carry out his orders, he gave directions for the Indians to be whipped by his *fiscales.*"

Serra went even further and cited Cortés himself, who famously had himself flogged, presumably for concubinage, "in full sight of the Indians . . . to set an example to all." No one was above the law of God, at least in sexual matters (whether Cortés made himself "subject to his humiliating treatment" because of his genocidal massacres of the Aztecs is rather doubtful).

Serra makes it clear that the practice of corporal punishment should be a function of love: "We, every one of us, came here for the single purpose of doing them [the Indians] good and for their eternal salvation; and I feel sure that everyone knows that we love them." Serra was not being coy. His affection, protectiveness, and even wonder over the Indians was consistent from the day on his historic journey northward in 1769 when he saw the naked Cochimí man in Baja to interceding a second time to save the rebel Carlos (Chisli). Banished to an endless sea voyage by Neve, Carlos would have no chance of amendment, as there were no priests on that kind of ship, and Serra pleaded with Neve to let him go to a fixed place on land, where "we might not persuade them [Carlos and Bernardino] to repent and win them over to a better life?" He even regarded the recidivists as kin: "I ask you to give them my warmest greetings, since they are members of my family." Neve relented.

Neve heard Serra on Carlos but never answered Serra's passionate—perhaps too passionate—defense of floggings of *alcáldes*. Perhaps there was no answer to it. Spain was involved in an impossible double bind. On the one hand, it wanted to convert the Indians to Christianity, partly because it was felt more Christian to do so, and partly because this was seen as a more humane and useful way to effect the *Conquista*. At the same time, Spain, like every other European invader of the Americas, wanted land, harbors, raw materials, and most especially, precious metals. Floggings truly confused the mission, for the native population had shown in San Diego and San Gabriel, and in many other less spectacular ways, that they could and would resist the *Conquista*.

Was flogging making a better Christian or Spaniard? (Likely neither.) If Neve seems more humane, to an extent, on floggings, Serra certainly knew the people he was dealing with on the ground—respecting them, loving them, fearing them, too. He knew the angers in the human heart, knew them as far back as his Palma classrooms from which students were snatched for war (and his own choler at Neve). And he knew the passions of the body, as far back as that headless officer and his runaway nun on Mallorca (if not María Contreras). Conquest of land meant conquest of body; and so did conquest of spirit, every Christian's challenge throughout the world, but not something easily appropriated by people whose shame level and attitudes toward the body were very different. Nevertheless, most adjusted, or felt they had to, fleeing the disorientation of their shaken world. As anthropologist Randall Milliken observes, mission life in its "colorful dress, esoteric prayer, and ostentatious architecture, provided them with a sense of contentment and longing." If some certainly resisted the floggings, more appropriated the punishment for a guilt they were beginning to feel.

Guilt: Serra must have wondered that last night on the rush stool what was worth guilt and what wasn't, staring up at his books, his holy texts, their covers as torn as men's backs. It may have crossed his mind that the songs, the raising of the monstrance, the Communion were better instigants to God than the flog. What good was humiliation, stirring the pot of Indian anger? There is a big difference, truly, between Christ acceding to whippings and someone ordering them. Had Serra forgotten the Fifth Commandment?

Thou Shalt Not Kill. A second recent episode Serra may have contemplated, pressing hand to forehead that last night in Carmel, was the 1781 disaster in the Mojave desert in which the Quechans had killed celebrated brother explorer Father Francisco Garcés along with many others, the worst loss of Spanish life in New Spain in a century. Serra, who envied martyrdom, no doubt had survivor's guilt. He may also have wondered at what terrible cost he had won an argument.

Garcés was a legend before he ever got to the Mojave. Born 1738 in Aragon, like Serra, Garcés joined the Franciscan order early, at fifteen. In 1766, as Serra encountered what he took to be the Holy Family in the Huasteca, Garcés joined the college of Santa Cruz de Querétaro. Soon he asked for and got the northernmost—and therefore most risky—post in the Pimeria (Arizona), that is, at Mission San Xavier del Bac, south of Tucson. There he gained great respect among the O'odham (Pima), Hopi, and Quechan peoples for his enthusiasm and willingness to mix in the circle of Indian councils. The year before Serra entered San Diego, in 1768, Garcés set out on his own into Apache territory around the Gila River. After joining Anza's 1776 expedition, he traveled 2,500 miles across the Mojave and back, a "far western Daniel Boone in Franciscan garb." Garcés was the first white man coming from the west to see the Grand Canyon, which he named.

Two missions Garcés helped found on the Colorado River separating California and Arizona—Puerto de la Purísima Concepción (present-day Fort Yuma) and, ten miles northeast, San Pedro y San Pablo de Bicuner (present-day Bard)—were built on a different model than Serra's. In fact, they were the brainchildren of Neve and Teodoro Croix; the Quechans were allowed to stay in their villages. But over time, construction-bound settlers had brought too few gifts of clothing and food and their cattle was chewing up the Indian grasses. Garcés warned that the foundings could be doomed.

On July 17–19, 1781, the Quechan Indians attacked the Spanish contingent in force, as well as the two missions. Chief Palma had ordered that Garcés be spared, but he wasn't. All four missionaries were clubbed to death, forty-six Spaniards in all (thirty of them soldiers, including the ill-fated lieutenant governor Fernando Rivera y Moncada, Serra's old nemesis, who was leading settlers to found Los Angeles). Both missions were burned to the ground.

The 1781 Quechan attack along the Colorado was New Spain's worst loss of life since the 1680 Pueblo Revolt in New Mexico, and it was certainly the bloodiest resistance ever in California. Anza's land-bridge from Sonora was effectively shut off; it wasn't opened again for a century, when it was forced open by the American cavalry.

"Our poor Don Fernando, who was so cautious in the matter of Indians, such a strong person, alert, and so many soldiers, and that they should be wiped out so completely!" Serra exclaimed when he heard. The pathos of the moment overcame old bad blood, and there was no gloating over the summary failure of Neve's and Croix's notion of how to found a mission: "As to what happened on the Colorado River—both as regards to the new experiment in mission management as well as the frightful disaster which followed—what can one say?" It was left to "the inscrutable decrees of God."

Why am I afraid, when Garcés met his Maker so readily? Serra may have pondered on his rush stool.

Serra's burden may have lightened briefly, adjusting his hurting back on the stool, conjuring Los Angeles, whose founding is directly tied to the conflagration out in the desert. Essentially founded by war refugees, tiny Los Angeles had welcomed a solitary Serra on March 18, 1782, a moment that was witnessed in writing by no one. Two days after Serra's arrival in the Southland, Lord North resigned as British prime minister in the wake of the British surrender to the American rebels. (Though Serra called for "public prayers" against "perfidious heretics" in Spain's 1779 war against England, there is no hard evidence that he directly supported the American Revolution.)

That night in Los Angeles pueblo, Serra may have seen late snow dusted on the San Gabriels. The site Crespí had named Neve expanded to El Pueblo de Nuestra Señora la Reina de Los Angeles del Río de Porciúncula. A mouthful, about which Geiger aptly comments: "The roots of the name stretched across the world: Palma, Assisi, Palestine."

The night Serra camped in L.A., the population of the new city was forty-eight. The average age of the men was thirty-six; there were four Mexican Indians, two blacks, two mulattoes, and two mestizos. Six women were Indians from Mexico, five of those mulattas. L.A., multi-ethnic from the start, slept with the tolerance of necessity.

Only seven hundred under independent Mexican rule in 1831, only 1,610 at the first American census in 1850, nowhere near the population of San Francisco or San Jose or San Diego, about 100,000 at the turn of the twentieth century—today Los Angeles, at ten million souls, is the largest metropolitan area in the United States, and at 453 square miles is the largest city in area in the world. A vision that would have brought Serra a wonderful headache: the five freeways that knot their gridlock within walking distance of his Porciúncula. No, Serra saw antelopes bedding down for the night. He did not see the demise of the mission system in a tide of government of people for whom God would not be at the center.

The thought of the 1782 founding of Mission San Buenaventura in the Santa Barbara Channel, too, may have provided Serra brief relief from tortured thoughts that last night. The Chumash peoples, some twenty-five thousand strong, had always been his favorites. After his fourth land journey south, he still could say "I saw the Channel inhabitants, and, as always, they were charming and attractive, waiting silently for the Gospel." There were at least twenty towns, from three to four hundred people at La Asumpta (Shisholop) in Ventura, the eastern rim of the channel, to 1,500 in the four clustered towns of Mescaltitan in the Goleta Slough at the western rim (near present-day Isla Vista and the Santa Barbara Airport).

Serra had left his brief stay at the new settlement in Los Angeles to rendezvous with Neve at Mission San Gabriel from which the two-hundred-mile procession to found San Buenaventura began. They spent the first night in the San Fernando Valley, where Neve received a courier at midnight with an insistent message from Fages that the governor return to San Gabriel to join him for a punitive march on the Quechans. Taking some soldiers with him, Neve withdrew. Serra wrote rather coyly, playing on the words *santo patrón*, "These people danced for joy, not so much out of devotion toward their saint but from a lack of devotion toward their patron."

On March 31, 1782, Easter Sunday, two days after arriving at La Asumpta, Serra sang the first High Mass of Mission San Buenaventura under an *enramada* of brushwood, the ninth bead in place of his California rosary. It was to be his last. The cross was planted on the beach at La Playa de la Canal de Santa Bárbara. Serra gave a sermon on the resurrection as he stared out at the silvery ladder on the Pacific. He had gone to the center of his dream, where the mountains and the sea embraced, where the ladder climbed high on the water. Could you walk alongside death all your life? This maybe seeped into his first San Buenaventura sermon, that death could be in the wine cup, in the high note at Matins, in the ink of the first letter, in ears of corn, behind your ears as you wash, just missing your fingers. Was death just missing you your whole life? Be ready. Love and be ready. To fall and to ascend. Now he was neither north nor south, but in the busy, wild, loving, pregnant middle. Naming the mission for the "Seraphic Doctor," St. Bonaventure, Serra quoted a saying about his long-delayed canonization, "The longer you have had to wait for it, the more impressive it is." Serra was in tune with Bonaventure's philosophy, more mystical and heart-driven than the scholastic logic of his medieval classmate, Thomas Aquinas. He may have subscribed to the legend that Bonaventure's name derived from an exclamation made by St. Francis, holding the infant in his arms: "*O buena fortuna!*" (Oh great fortune!).

Among exclamations on the beach at Ventura, Serra ordered both a bull and sheep slaughtered (the latter was Mallorcan custom at Easter). Neve later disapproved; the cattlemaster was upset, too. Serra cheerfully took the blame. "How glad the gentiles all around were and what outward show they gave of their pleasure," he recounted. Buenaventura, he felt, "in a short time . . . will surpass all the others." He wasn't far off. The quick plotting by Serra and Cambon for an irrigation ditch that first week would, over time, become a seven-mile stone-and-mortar canal to the sea from a reservoir and aqueduct off the Ventura River. By 1816, San Buenaventura had reached its peak Indian population of 1,328; it was surrounded by stables, corrals, wallows, and fields for 41,000 animals, including 4,493 horses—among the largest figures in the final twenty-one-mission chain. The padres would carry on a lucrative, illicit trade for "Yankee dollars" with the British and Americans for tallow and hides. With its vineyards, figs, coconuts, bananas, corn and grain fields, excepting Mission Santa Inés to come, San Buenaventura was the most successful agricultural producer per capita of all the missions.

Serra felt especially close to Buenaventura. It had been long in the making and he may have sensed it might be his last. He apologized to Lasuén for grasping it too close: "May God pardon me that I said 'my mission' when I meant that of San Buenaventura, our Father. I am sorry. I am sorry. Please forgive me, Your Reverence. There is nothing good I can claim for my own in this world. But I dearly love that mission, and with a gladsome heart would be its minister."

Eleven industrious days after its founding, San Buenaventura was surprised, however, by the appearance of Neve, after which "the aspect of everything took a change." Neve had decided not to accompany Fages to the incipient revenge on the Quechans, against which Serra had spoken. Perhaps this is why of all the twenty-one missions, San Buenaventura was the only one to possess, in addition to its bronze bells, bells made of wood. An enterprising Cambon (and Serra briefly) also heard confessions in a shipping crate stood on its side and used a Chumash stone mortar as a baptismal font.

In 1821, Ventureña Chumash Juana Basilia's complex basket with the king's arms and cross at its center and repeated seven times on the circumference was given as a "farewell" to Spanish authorities when Mexico broke free. Among other Ventureño Chumash traceable to Serra's founding of the mission was the son of apricot laborers, Vincent Tumamait, a middleweight boxer in the 1930s who later sang at the Hollywood Bowl.

And what of Santa Barbara, the next stop up the road? It should have brought Serra great joy, both at its creation and in memory that last night. But either is very unlikely. On April 15, 1782, Neve yanked Serra from San Buenaventura prematurely to lead a pack train of soldiers, settlers, and animals to the center of the rose. Strangely, Serra thought the first site selected in the populous central coast "not a good place." For this sacred zone of silvery waters of the channel, islands in a Monet-like bluish outline, and majestic mountains, it would seem any spot in Santa Barbara would suffice. Even Geiger called Serra's pique "surprising from our point of view." Palou called it "a gloomy spot." Was it the boggy, mosquito-rich area around present-day Stearns Wharf, or the many lagoons where today's Laguna Street ends? Serra may have thought Goleta a better, higher stretch of land, or freshwater pools near Mescaltitan (Isla Vista today); Carpinteria (Crespí's favorite) and Montecito were considered. Nevertheless, moving about a mile to higher ground, on April 21, 1782, Serra raised the cross and sang out a High Mass, leading all in the "Alabado" at the end of the service. He raised the small silver-plated chalice, his left hand gripping the grooved joiner, his right balancing lightly the rippled stand, drinking the wine that was now Christ's blood, to the amazement of the Chumash at the translation. He signed the church registers, *"Esta Nueva Misión y Presidio Real"* (This new mission and the king's presidio). He met the Siytún chief Yanonalit, who, suspicious at first, by the end of the year was convinced the Spaniards' intentions were good; the chief even banished a belligerent rival, Citu, who spoke of fomenting a rebellion.

Serra thought he was founding both the tenth mission *and* presidio simultaneously; he waited three weeks at Santa Barbara to begin construction of the church, but Neve broke his heart. The whole Channel Island mission project would be suspended, the governor announced, until the presidio was finished. On his death night, Serra must have recalled Neve's anger that the Franciscans' College of San Fernando had rejected his idea of one priest per mission, Serra's attempts to stall, if not refuse, the war tax (offering prayers instead!), and his insistent plunge into the thickly populated channel before a garrison was in place. What an irony. To be denied founding the church and given instead a holy water sprinkling for a fort.

"The governor has become a missionary!" Serra exclaimed to Pangua. "He says we do not have the gift for it and he promised to give Father Cambon the formula for it." Serra's great hopes for a glorious final act, securing the tenth bead in his California rosary in the holy zone of Santa Barbara, had become only "a dismal foundation."

• • •

Serra must have felt his lower back fuse to the stool in pain, thinking how, after all he had suffered, they had forbidden him Santa Barbara. Still, Serra had labeled his next year, 1783, his second to last, "the happiest year of the mission" [Carmel], and he had concluded, with not total exaggeration, "Those . . . pointed to us as such enemies are almost all Christians today." Serra congratulated Pangua on his second ascent to the guardianship: "I know that the Cross is not light, but Your Reverence knows better than *this manager of farms*, how priceless it is for one to carry it whom God has called to do so." The emphasis was unmistakable: he was a farmer, a farmer from Mallorca. That was it.

But those stupid franks! It might have killed a smile, contemplating that after Neve was finally kicked upstairs, Pedro Fages had returned as governor, a walking cactus if there ever was one. They had clashed immediately over who would pay for postage to submit mission annual reports. "Having to pay for our letters by mail, they skin me alive!" Serra fulminated. What a waste of breath for something so small. And then, he had prattled to Fages for paper to write on, as the missionaries were now reduced to "writing me regularly on pages torn out of their baptismal records." Imagine. You can barely breathe and what comes back to haunt you? Stamps and stationery!

Is this how the Enemy pulls us toward him? Through these little cracks of self-importance?

Fixating on minutiae was the last hardening sign of age; it had been coming on a while. It's in the last letters, too, not just the fixations, but the speechlessness, the ellipses, the forgetting, the rigidity. Quibbling with Lasuén over fees for Masses—six pesos for High, and six more for a vigil. The slippages of thought: "I do not know if I have forgotten anything." Asking for war prayers suddenly when he had been opposing the war tax for years, sending letters not to a person but a place. The excessive use of etc., as if the wonderful specifics of the world had become tedious. Missing lines.

There were, toward the end, glimpses of redemption. Serra opened a letter to Lasuén, "God give your Reverence and to all 'that peace which the world cannot give.'"

Fages called him "a great despotic spirit" who "walks roughshod over the measures of government." He had even gone further, accusing Serra of overusing the stocks and forced labor as punishment, while at the same time complaining of Serra's letting Indians ride horseback, warning they were more skilled at it than soldiers.

Yet it appears the two old warhorses softened toward the end. Serra had sympathy (if not mirth) for Fages's marital plight. Fages had married late, to Eulalia Callis in Mexico City, a woman many years his junior. Pregnant in San Francisco with their second child (after Pedrito), Eulalia constantly harped, Crespí-like, on the cold of the Bay Area (where she had been carried in a litter), and insisted she be taken in at sunnier, drier Mission Santa Clara. But the friars there in their prudery thought it unseemly, and María del Carmen was born in San Francisco, August 8, 1784, even as death began his slow crawl into El Viejo Padre.

Reyes! Betrayed by a Franciscan! To recall this man would have thrown Serra into near despair.

On September 15, 1782, a new bishop for the provinces of Sonora, Sinaloa, and Upper and Lower California was consecrated at Tacubaya, outside Mexico City. He was Antonio de los Reyes, and he was close to the king. The Franciscans should have exulted; Reyes was one of them and had served as a missionary in Sonora out of the College of Santa Cruz in Querétaro. But it wasn't long before Bishop Reyes was on the warpath not only with San Fernando, but the entire California mission project of Serra.

Reyes was scathing in his indictments, accusing the Franciscans in the northern frontier missions of depopulating "entire provinces" with a method that was simply "fatal."

In discussing Texas (where he hadn't served), Reyes took on the sharpest thorn in Serra's soul, floggings: "Who will believe and who will be convinced that the Indians will be reduced and live willingly in their [mission] towns when they are forced to their daily labors which are called community enterprises through force and by use of the whip?"

Was Reyes a humane reformer? Or was he settling scores? Geiger thinks the latter. But Serra, puzzled, infirm, ignored the threats and Reyes himself, or appeared to, a failure of judgment to Geiger. In a long, joint *representación*, the Franciscan colleges rejected Reyes's ideas for a new custody and transfer of authority to the Dominicans and they refuted his criticism of their rule, point by point. Pangua wrote Serra directly about Reyes's claims, calling them "a marvel of falsehoods and impossibilities."

Toward the end, Serra weighed in, with no small note of pride: "Concerning the matter of our expulsion from these lands, we who were the first and only ones who announced the name of the true God, of Jesus Christ and his holy gospel . . . I hope to give them a good account of more than five thousand baptized in these lands, and they will have much to think about." He went on, excoriating Gálvez, who favored the Reyes plan, and "only yesterday was adamant that the Fathers who are now in

[Baja] California should get out and those of San Fernando return there!" His sum of Gálvez: "much evil."

Fool, Junípero. Condemning the man who launched you.

While in Southern California for the last time in 1783, he took to musing about childhood. His early island life off Spain imprinted on the place that had become home, with no relatives but the Indians:

> Once I realized that I came from a province made up of eleven friaries, including those in Minorca, now again part of Spain. And I could see a tiny replica among these gentiles, made up of the same number of houses, with two friars in each of them. But who pays attention to such foolishness?

Fool of fools! He had hoped for a blessed eleven, to add two to the nine he had founded—Santa Barbara and La Purisima (soon to be founded near Lompoc). "We already have the vestments and the bells," he had said, forlornly. "I will have to die without seeing them."

On October 4, 1783, his only sibling, Juana María Serra Ribot, died. Why had he never written her? And yet he could write about Teodoro Croix, disparaging his sign-offs "with the 'God keep's' thrown in"?

Judge not, Junípero.

He had confessed to black moods: "feelings of heaviness and depression." The thoughts pummeled him on that stool, some questions of conscience, taunts, but to Serra they may have seemed the temptations of the Enemy:

> *Croix and Neve have no business saving souls. That is your job!*
> *You were right to flog them.*
> *You should have been bishop, not Reyes!*
> *María Contreras was yours for the taking.*
> *The Indians were better without you. Your touch brought them hell. So enter hell!*

He slid off the stool to the floor and married the side of the bed with his chest. Some Esselen and Rumsen Indians began to enter his bedroom, crying out softly, trying to hold him up. And perhaps with their aid over the late self-hate, his own wisdoms came back:

"This is the hour to look within and amend my ways."

"We will put an end to envy, which, while it can be holy, it may also not be."

And from the last letter of his life: "God is everywhere."

Morning came. He may have gone to the casement window and looked out on the Carmel fog, but in his mind's eye, it had to be the channel, with its old kelp beds moving, so slowly, dark as old blood, and then a glint on the sea, the first rung of the silver ladder.

At noon and twelve bells he called out: Palou!

Ten days before the end, Palou had rushed south. Arriving at San Carlos Borromeo on August 18, Palou found Serra's legs ballooned and the father president hard of breath. But the two repaired to the church, where with the Indians they sang *"Suba, suba, suba/La Virgen al cielo!"* Palou thought Serra's resonant bass strong.

"It doesn't seem the Father is so sick," Palou said to a soldier after Mass.

"Father, this saintly priest is always well when it comes to praying and singing, but he is nearly finished," the soldier said.

The next day, August 19, Serra deferred to Palou to say the Mass. Instead, Junípero mingled with the Indian choir and sang with them. Palou blessed the Host, amazed.

On August 22, the packet boat *San Carlos* sailed into Monterey; the royal surgeon, Dr. Juan García, alighted and hurried to Carmel. He was alarmed at Serra's heavy coughing and labored breathing. To force phlegm out of the lungs, the doctor cauterized the old priest's chest, but it only burned him and added to his pain.

Serra, distracting himself, took up a bolt of cloth that had come off the ship and cut it into sections for clothes, handing them out to the Indians who approached. Two days later, an old Indian lady said she hadn't gotten hers yet, and Serra went and brought out his own wide blanket, cut it in half, and gave half to her.

Palou recognized her and cracked to Serra: "Is she going to pay you for the chickens?"

It was the same old woman who, many years before when San Carlos was first founded, had taught her nephew how to shoot a bow and arrow by killing the only hen Serra had.

On August 25, Serra worsened. He lamented that the priests he sought out for a farewell from San Antonio and San Luis Obispo had not arrived. The next day, he was exhausted after a night tossing and turning. That evening he made his confession to Palou, in tears. The maniple did not wipe them.

Palou had found him in his chamber at the crack of dawn on August 27 with his breviary, saying Matins. Serra asked Palou to administer to him the Holy Viaticum, the Communion given to a dying man, but added that he wanted to receive it in the church. Palou was taken aback. Serra was too weak to make it the hundred yards. "If I can walk, there is no reason for the Lord to come to me," Junípero wheezed.

So the process was reversed. But as Serra moved slowly toward the church at Carmel, white stole over his gray habit, Indians and soldiers both gathered around him. At San Carlos, Serra knelt and began singing *Tantum Ergo* with his deep voice suddenly clear:

> *Tantum ergo, Sacramentum*
> *Veneremur cernui.*
> *Et antiquum documentum,*
> *Novo cedat ritui.*

From Palou, Serra received Communion for the last time.

On the way back to his room, the Indians accompanied him: "Some of them were weeping from devotion and tenderness, and others from grief and sorrow, because they feared they were to be deprived of their beloved Father." Serra sat on his rush stool "and fell into a deep abstraction." He never lay down all day, taking only a little soup. Palou let no one visit, trying to conserve Junípero's strength. But that night the father president suffered badly and asked for the holy oils of Extreme Unction. He prayed not for rain but to pry open heaven. Or let loose his fears.

Serra would not lie down on the wooden slats, but rather sat on the rush stool before sinking to the floor, where the surgeon found him, telling Palou he thought Serra wanted to die on the floor, as had St. Francis.

The next morning, August 28, 1784, sleepless, he rallied. He told newly arrived José de Cañizares, *San Carlos* captain and an old friend, "Throw a little earth on my body and I shall be greatly indebted to you." He asked Palou to bury him next to Crespí.

Palou asked, "Be not unmindful of me."

Serra said he did not deserve eternal happiness, but that if he got it, he would pray for Palou and for the conversion of the rest of the Indians of California. He asked Palou to sprinkle the room with holy water. Then he was quiet on his rush stool.

The quiet broke: "I have come under the shadow of fear." Palou left, alarmed.

After Serra battled for the last time alone with the Enemy identified more than ever with the self, Palou lurched in at Serra's call. Serra said, "Read from the Commendation for a Departing Soul and say it loudly so that I can hear it."

"Depart, O Christian soul, out of this sinful world," Palou intoned.

"Amen," said Serra. After every invocation Palou recited, Serra answered "as if he were well"—Amen.

The twelfth bell reverberated. The sun was on the wall.

"Thanks be to God, thanks be to God. All fear has left me now. Let us go outside."

After sitting a while reading Sext and Nones in the anteroom, he whispered, "Let us go to rest." It was one in the afternoon, siesta time. Serra went back to his bedroom and, after thirty hours of not sleeping, he fell fast asleep on two boards, holding to his chest the large cross of Caravaca with the Blessed Mary at its base and tiny relics of Raymond Lull cut into its back. In the end, he slept with Mallorca and the Lady.

Perhaps he dreamt of mounting Campanilla, the mule, now fat and healed, ready for the road. And that they set out together. But looking over the water, Serra slid off the mule, careened down the chalky cliff right into the Pacific, climbing that silvery ladder till he sank in the sun.

Around two in the afternoon, Palou closed his teacher's eyelids. Then, as in Petra, he ordered a double tolling of the bells.

In many ways, death was a key theme of Serra's life. It had ever been at the center of his vision. When he wrote that good-bye letter to his parents in 1749, he said, "A happy death is the most important thing in this life. For if we reach that goal, it matters little if we lose all the rest. But if we do not reach it, nothing else will have mattered." Though hardly unperturbed, his death was happy. Though shy of Santa Barbara, he had reached his ultimate goal, the one he felt we are born for from the moment of first breath.

In 1770, Serra had inscribed these scriptural references in the Book of the Dead and Burials at the founding of his own Mission San Carlos Borromeo: "We all die, and like waters that return no more, we fall down into the earth." He also wrote, "Though he be dead, he that believes in me shall live." One was earthen, organic, and Indian; one was Christian. These visions and these people were joined at Carmel. More than anything else, that is what he wanted to give the Indian—eternal life through the Gospel of Love. Some were quite happy without it; but some were not, not after Serra had sung to them.

It seemed as if the entire population of the surrounding Esselen and Costanoan villages soon gathered at the mission, drawn by the death bells, and when they saw it was Father Serra, there was a great crying, for he was "more esteemed by them than if he had been their natural father." Soldiers and sailors and laborers, as well as the Indians, crowded toward the room where Serra's body was being prepared for burial in a redwood coffin. At first, Palou had to bar the door. Palou and Father Matias de Noriega took the sandals from Serra's hardened feet and gave one each to Cañizares and Dr. García. And then the door was opened for a mourning line of the crowd.

"*Santo Padre*," "*Bendito Padre*," the mourners murmured, touching his face and hands with their rosaries and medals. Wildflowers crowded into the room and soon covered the body like an earthen blanket.

That night, Palou ordered two soldiers to stand guard while Serra's body lay in state in the sanctuary. But both guards and Indians cut off snippets of Serra's hair, swatches of his robe, and his stole, stealing them away as relics.

Father Sitjar arrived just in time to direct the Indian choir at the solemn Requiem Mass on Sunday morning, August 29. The mourners included candle-holding soldiers from the presidio and crew of the *San Carlos*, all the Spanish craftsmen and artisans and laborers, and six hundred Indians, including Bernardino de Jesús Fages, the first child Serra had baptized in Monterey and now a *fiscal* of the mission. The singing of the *Responsorio* was almost drowned out by the "tears and sobs and wailing of those present." Palou brought out the under tunic Serra had eschewed in the final moment, dividing it in small parts for the sailors to use as scapulars (worn like cloth medals under garments on the chest). He did the same with Serra's handkerchiefs. A complete handkerchief he gave to Dr. García for his troubles.

"With this little cloth I expect to cure more people than with all my books and bottles," the doctor said. A few days later, he tied it around the head of a sailor with migraine headaches; the relief was striking.

A week later, Palou held another memorial Mass, with an even larger choir of Indians, and Fathers Paterna and Sitjar, who had arrived too late for the moment of death, joined the singing, too. Told that the army were feeling spurned (as the sailors had their Serra cloth scapulars), Palou later gave each soldier either one of Serra's books or one of his personal collection of medals.

As if sparked by a fiery sadness, the annual reports for the Spanish governor Serra had dodged were completed by Palou by the end of 1784. They showed that the total number of baptisms in the nine missions went from 5,800 at Serra's death to 6,736, an amazing increase of 20 percent in four months. Palou thought it was Serra working in heaven.

On hearing of Serra's death, Serra's last superior—and his acolyte in Baja—Juan Sancho, the guardian at the College of San Fernando in Mexico City, took up the difficult duty of telling the world a great man was gone:

So great was his charity which he manifested toward those poor Indians that not only the ordinary people, but likewise persons of higher condition were struck with admiration. All men said openly that that man was a saint and that his actions were those of an apostle. . . . This opinion has been constant and without interruption.

Sancho promised a second letter "to write in more detail concerning the virtues of this deceased missionary."

The second letter, if it was written, is lost.

PART FOUR

IN THE SHADOW OF SERRA

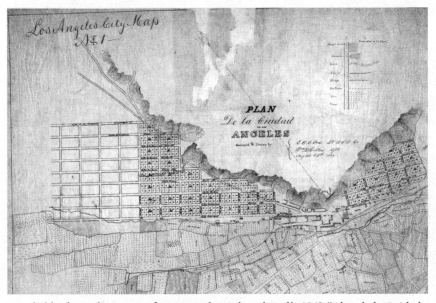

Probably the earliest map of Los Angeles: Edward Ord's 1849 "Plan de la Cuidad de Los Angeles," depicting what became the downtown garment district (left grid) and the Los Angeles pueblo and *asistencia* mission (center grid), which Serra visited in 1782. Streets are noted in Spanish (e.g., *Calle Esperanza*, or Hope Street, which still exists, and *Calle Caridad*, or Charity Street, which is no more).

CHAPTER TWENTY

LASUÉN COMPLETES THE MISSION

A palm tree stands in the middle of Rusafa,
Born in the West, far from the land of palms.
—ABD AL-RAHMAN, POET AND ARCHITECT
OF THE GREAT MOSQUE OF CÓRDOBA

Patwin or Yokuts celebrating surviving the measles epidemic
at Mission San José, 1806.

From the moment Father Fermín Lasuén crossed out Serra's own handwriting—*Misión y*—from the would-be Santa Barbara founding documents (restricting Serra's blessing to the presidio and *not* the mission), the new president of the California missions asserted himself. Lasuén, no mystic or follower of mystics, a far more pragmatic, urbane man, simply scratched out Serra's irrational hope for a final mission in the land of light. And then he rode north, toward the mountains. Two years after Serra's death, on December 4, 1786, on a knoll overlooking the sea, Fermín Lasuén planted the cross a mile uphill from where Serra had said his presidio Mass alongside a bog. Thus the "Queen of the Missions" was born, the elusive monument to St. Barbara that Serra had promised since the day nearly forty years before when the lady of the tower had saved the Franciscans offshore at Veracruz.

Serra last saw Lasuén in San Diego in 1783, on his final confirmation tour, but he wrote his Basque confrere to the end, clearly handpicking his successor. Months before his death, Serra saluted Lasuén post-Christmas: "Words fail me to tell you all that I feel." God would, he assured, support San Diego long past the old father president, who seemed to be dissolving: "He who can do all things loves them [the Kumeyaay] more and in His court no good deed is ever lost. May God reward your Reverence and the new Christian chief and all his people. May He give them great faith and abundant grace in this life and eternal glory in the next. Amen. I am very, very, very happy." Only a Serra close to death would have allowed himself such emphatics.

Lasuén's views of the Indians were at once less tolerant (rather racist, actually) than Serra's, and more understanding—a paradox. Stirred to write an extraordinary forty-page "Refutation of Charges" defending the Franciscan cause in California against accusations of a priest cashiered from the new Mission San Miguel who showed signs of severe mental disorder, Lasuén fumed, "Here are aborigines whom we are teaching to be men, people of vicious and ferocious habits who know no law but force, no superior but their own free will, and no reason but their own caprice." (Serra would have been bothered by much of this, especially that "no reason"; he had castigated Neve for saying essentially the same thing.)

Unlike Serra, Lasuén was under no illusions about mass conversion of California Indians. Lasuén understood the psychology of a people under conquest, and he didn't delude himself into thinking that, caught in what Serra always called "the spiritual net," they would feel the catch benign, like a hammock. More like a shackle. "The majority of our neophytes have not acquired much love for our way of life," he confided to a colleague, when notified that the governor was thinking of lessening forces at the presidios. Lasuén insisted they were "addicted" to the pull of the natural world.

On October 25, 1785, the warrior population of six *rancherías* (the exact number of attackers is unknown) descended on Mission San Gabriel, with a woman shaman of nearby Japchivit *ranchería* in the lead as some native victress, a Tongva Joan of Arc, who had "encouraged them to be brave and fight." It was Toypurina. As a girl, she had probably witnessed her chief's head hanging on a pike for his challenge to a soldier guilty of raping the chief's wife. Toypurina had waited fourteen years for revenge. She had joined forces with San Gabriel's native *alcalde*, Nicolás José, a complex and conflicted man, who had procured women for Spanish soldiers and also lost two wives and a son to the mysterious pox.

The San Gabriel missionaries had been tipped off to the rebellion, and no sooner had the war party arrived than they were surrounded by the Spanish guard; those who did not escape were arrested. Twenty-five Tongva were lashed up to twenty-five times and released. Four, including Nicolás José and Toypurina, stood trial. When asked during the legal proceedings, "Have they [the Tongva] been harmed in any way at the hands of the soldiers, priests, or other Christians which would make them want to kill them?" Toypurina responded, "the only harm she had experienced was that we [the Spaniards] were living on their land." There is no more succinct expression of Indian motive to revolt in California, or anywhere else on the continent. Imprisoned "as much for her own protection as punishment" (some rebels blamed her for inciting them to a battle lost before it started), Toypurina was impregnated in prison. She ended up marrying a Spanish soldier—Manuel Montero—turning Christian (taking the name Regina Josefa), and raising three children at Carmel before her death in 1799 at Mission San Juan Bautista. (In 1821, one of her daughters, Clementina, was accused by a priest at Mission Santa Cruz— himself accused of "immoral conduct"—of having "mother's milk like snake venom.")

Some version of Toypurina's story runs through much of the Indian population of the California coast. In fact, against all likelihood of trends at Serra's death, when the missions seemed on the verge of either secularization, closure, or loss to the Dominicans, their numbers and their population began to wax. Ironically, they did so under a father president skeptical of the whole conversion process. Despite Lasuén's withering attitudes about the attraction of mission life to Indians or about their capacities to adapt to Spanish ways, the eighteen-year period of Lasuén's presidency (1785–1803) was truly the golden age of the California missions. During that time, the number of missions doubled (from nine to eighteen) and the number of missionaries did, too (from eighteen to forty), prompting one commentator to note that if Lasuén's challenges with his rank-and-file padres increased, it did so because their numbers did.

The abundance of the missions—no doubt the chief attraction for the Indians, and one they themselves helped bring about by the sweat of their brow—reached extraordinary levels in the early nineteenth century. By 1803, the wheat, barley, and corn crops were five times those at

Serra's death, mission cattle twelve times greater, and the number of converted Indians themselves in threefold increase—from 5,125 under Serra to 15,562 under Lasuén. Disease in the villages, as we have seen, spurred not a little of this. Nevertheless, the seeds Serra had sown in the toughest ground—an uncertain people with plenty of questions if not fear of Spaniards and their ways—had not only sprouted, they were suffused with fruit. Soon the villages along the coast were emptying, and then villages farther inland—from a combination of disease, hunger, desperation, and hope.

The first of Lasuén's contributions to the exponential growth was Mission Santa Barbara. The conversion of the charismatic Chumash chief Yananoli (named Pedro at baptism) and his family went a long way to signaling favor for the padres in the Chumash communities at large. Santa Barbara reignited San Fernando's hesitance to send new missionaries, and soon they sent six. The first building, little more than logs strapped together with reed covering, gave way to an adobe church, completed in 1794, which collapsed in the devastating 1812 earthquake. The church visitors see today, set stunningly above a sprawling grassy knoll and rose garden facing the Pacific, essentially dates from the rebuilt church of 1820, the product of master stonecutter José Antonio Ramírez.

A young Chumash girl who ran alongside ditches and workmen in 1820 as the Santa Barbara mission came back to life, María Ignacio, spoke of "running along the edge where they were digging." According to her present-day ancestor, a female shaman and nurse who participates in cross-cultural services at Mission Santa Barbara, María was "very, very happy to see the mission resurrected." Santa Barbara's signature eighty-seven-foot double steeple—the only such steeple in the entire chain—and pink facade could be seen by boats for miles. Its beauty became world-famous in the nineteenth century. The most neoclassical of all the missions, Santa Barbara's design, with its six half columns on which rest statues of Faith, Hope, and Charity, was based on the writings of the ancient Roman architect Vitruvius Pollio in 27 BC. At the same time, the mission has decidedly Chumash features, including an altar of inlaid abalone (so often vandalized it had to be removed for safekeeping), a *lavandería* where clothes were washed and tallow melted, sporting an 1808 gargoyle spigot sculpted with the head of a cougar, considered the oldest public sculpture in California; and "winged lightning" settings for chandeliers in the church's ceiling.

Santa Barbara was marked by sizable affordable housing. Though they could live in their half-orange-shaped tule huts, over time Indians were offered single-unit individual homes—252 of them by 1807—eighteen-foot-by-twelve-foot adobes with tiled roofs, a movable window, and a door. To build them it was not unusual to have forty Indian laborers a day out in the mountain ranges forty miles off cutting timber.

A remarkable grammar and personal memoir has come down to us of the last native speaker of Chumash, Mary Yee, in care of her daughter Ernestine de Soto, who charted the family back through six generations of exceptional Chumash women in Santa Barbara. The progenitor of this lineage, María Paula (María Ignacio's mother), was born the year Serra entered California and Portolá and Crespí first came through the Santa Barbara Channel—1769. Mary Yee recounts how her ancestors loved "taking a bath" in an icy stream or cold sea, letting the wind dry them off as they ate breakfast.

Everyone at Mission Santa Barbara, including the Chumash, ate extraordinarily well; no surprise Santa Barbara is to this day an epicure's delight. Santa Barbara was the only mission the Franciscans never abandoned; they are still there.

In 1787, Lasuén founded his next mission (number 11) on the Lompoc Peninsula, completing the threesome contemplated by Serra for the central coast Chumash. It was La Purísima Concepción, founded on what became the Feast of the Immaculate Conception (December 8), near the Indian village of Algascupi. Idyllically set in a sweeping area surrounded on three sides by the sea, La Purísima was devastated in the 1812 earthquake, not just by the shake, but also by a flood that crashed down from the hill behind and collapsed it. The mission was rebuilt by 1818 in a form unique in the entire mission system, not a quadrangle, but a "shotgun" line of twenty buildings in file. When it fell to ruin after secularization, it was sold at auction for $1,100 to an L.A. man. However, beginning in 1933, President Franklin Roosevelt's CCC—Civilian Conservation Corps—took on the project of restoring La Purísima, and it is today the most fully restored of all the missions, uniquely comprising a California state park on two thousand acres of land.

Not nearly as driven as Serra to establish missions, Lasuén waited four years to found one of his own (i.e., not in the Santa Barbara Channel pipeline that Serra had sketched)—the hard-luck mission of Santa Cruz. Founded on August 28, 1791, on a lovely site on the northern rim of Monterey Bay along the strategic San Lorenzo River, Santa Cruz began auspiciously, with an abundance of coastal redwood nearby for building and trade. But soon it was hit by everything from earthquakes and floods to the pugnacious civilian settlement, the Villa Branciforte, begun nearby in 1797 with a number of ex-convicts from Guadalajara. In fact, when the French pirate Hippolyte de Bouchard threatened the Santa Cruz coast and the mission personnel retreated to the hills, Branciforte residents looted the mission, leaving Bouchard with little to do.

Lasuén soon moved to fill in another gap—Nuestra Señora de la Soledad ("solitude" in Spanish), plunked halfway between Mission San Antonio and Serra's own Carmel, in a windy, dusty plain surrounded by bare hills. It was haunting to Serra, who thought he heard the word *soledad* spill from an old Salinan woman's lips when the Spaniards first came through; it was haunting at its founding on October 9, 1791 by Lasuén, who, strangely, wrote virtually nothing about the event. It was Soledad's misfortune to be the assignment of two of the most bizarre priests who ever came to California—the thick-black-bearded Mariano Rubí and Bartolomé Gilí, with his red beard and "honey-colored eyes," both from Serra's own Mallorca. The two of them would break into wine storehouses, bang on kettles like Indians, and throw wooden balls around—at two in the morning. Rubí contracted syphilis; Gilí brandished pistols; both of them disappeared, the former on the Mexican coast, the latter on the docks of Cádiz. Geiger's assessment of the two: "psychopaths."

The trouble at Santa Cruz and Soledad may have soured Lasuén on new missions. Six years passed without one, but the increasing level of resistance to the Spanish by tribes east of San Francisco Bay led Serra's successor to found La Misión del Gloriosísimo Patriarca Señor San José (Mission San José) the first of four near the Camino Real in one whirlwind year, 1797. San José drew Yokuts, Miwok, and Ohlone from the Lodi and Stockton areas. The mission of San José actually was placed twelve miles north of the pueblo of San José, near today's Fremont. Ultimately, Mission San José prospered, with the second highest amount of grain and produce of all twenty-one missions (289,000 bushels); with its rich soil, San José was also known for its exquisite pear orchards (six hundred trees), as well as groves of olive, peach, and apple. Its Indian population swelled to the third largest in the chain (1,886 in 1831), just behind San Antonio and the king of all, San Luis Rey. Over a span of twenty-seven years, Father Narciso Durán directed a thirty-person Indian orchestra with flutes, violins, trumpets, and drums. For six years, while he was father president, Durán "whose *aguardiente* was double distilled and as strong as the revered father's faith," made San José the mission capital. American trappers Kit Carson and Jedediah Smith took refuge at Mission San José, Father Durán giving Carson horses and provisions for his return trip over the Sierras to the United States. Nevertheless, where there was prosperity there was pain, an old mission theme. The year 1806 saw a horrific measles and smallpox epidemic that killed 150 Indians at San José (1806–10 was the worst epidemic period for Spanish California). In 1828, a favorite Yokuts of Durán's, Estanislao Cucunuchi, twenty-eight, failed to return to the mission while visiting his home village and instead led a one-thousand-warrior rebellion against the Spanish, repelling two Spanish campaigns and declaring himself king of the central valley. A third military effort of 157 men (including fifty Indian auxiliaries), led by (soon to be general) Lieutenant Mariano Vallejo, taking advantage of a cannon barrage, captured and executed many rebelling Yokuts.

Ironically, the next mission, San Juan Bautista, planted right on the San Andreas Fault east of the central Monterey Bay by Lasuén on June 24, 1797, was one of the few missions not harmed by the 1812 earthquake. Called "the Mission of Music" due to an Indian youth choir expertly trained by Estevan Tapis with four-color music sheet parchments, Bautista drew Miwok from as far away as the Sierra Nevada foothills. Yokuts and Mutsun Costanoan also crowded into what became the largest mission church in Alta California: 188 by 72 feet, containing side aisles through grand arches, a feature unique in the mission chain (perhaps modeled on Roman ruins at Segovia). Its romantic setting and fervent Mexican-American community have drawn Hollywood: Alfred Hitchcock filmed *Vertigo* at San Juan Bautista in 1957; and novelist Joan Didion married her screenwriter husband, John Gregory Dunne, at its altar.

The third of Lasuén's sudden ring of "protective" inland missions was Mission San Miguel Arcángel, the sixteenth mission, founded by Serra's successor one month and a day after San Juan Bautista (July 25, 1797), in honor of "the Prince of the Celestial Militia." San Miguel was equidistant from San Antonio and San Luis Obispo, in the golden foothills of the central coast along the Salinas River. The Indians revered a medicinal hot springs nearby (in present-day Paso Robles). Rather small, San Miguel nevertheless was granted extensive lands sixty-five miles east deep into the San Joaquin Valley (and the Tulare Indians), and thirty-five miles from the Pacific Ocean. It was the farthest of all the missions from the sea, and though modest in its agricultural output, it soon developed a hefty hide-and-tallow trade following an old Indian trail to the ocean at San Simeon (passing over hills that would 150 years later see the construction of the gaudy Hearst Castle). In 1831, when the newly independent Mexico announced the secularization of the mission system and Commissioner Juan Alvarado told the neophytes at San Miguel that "No tyrannical priest could compel them to work," gesturing that those who wanted freedom could move to the right, those who chose "hideous bondage" should go left, nearly the entire congregation went to the left. Still, San Miguel eventually deteriorated into a saloon and dance hall.

The San Fernando Valley was the site of the last of Lasuén's 1797 three-month flurry of missions, brought into being at a fertile confluence of four streams as San Fernando Rey de España, named after the thirteenth-century Spanish King Ferdinand. Not far from it, the Porciúncula (or Los Angeles Wash) flooded into the valley, until it was stopped up centuries later by the Sepulveda Dam. The 1806 church was destroyed in the latter-day Sylmar earthquake (1971), and the 1994 Northridge quake badly hurt the uniquely detached *convento* section with its nineteen exceptional Roman arches.

San Fernando was the birthplace of perhaps the most important and mysterious works of art in early California: the fourteen Stations of the Cross (*Via Crucis*) painted on canvas, almost certainly by several Indians, including Juan Antonio, baptized from Ranchería de Topanga (in today's Topanga Canyon) in 1798, San Fernando's first year of existence. Ironically, these paintings are referred to in an 1849 inventory as *cuadros muy ordinarios*, very ordinary pictures. They were anything but. Clearly, the Indian artists projected themselves and their plight (as well as their need for a Savior) onto the dramatic scenes of Christ's final suffering journey from Pilate's headquarters to judgment to Crucifixion, Golgotha, and the Cross. At Station 6, an Indian-like Veronica wipes Jesus's face while two clear Indians help Christ carry the cross, one looking sideways at the viewer like a knowing bird.

Lasuén saved the best for last (as had Serra with Buenaventura). On June 13, 1798, he founded "the King of the Missions" (to Santa Barbara's "Queen") between San Diego and San Juan Capistrano—Mission San Luis Rey de Francia. Thus did Lasuén play a politically ecumenical role, honoring royalty of *both* Spain and France. Though founded late in mission history as the eighteenth mission, San Luis Rey became in short order the most prosperous, most populous, and healthiest of all the missions. At its peak year (1826), San Luis Rey had 2,869 Indians (Luiseño, Cupeño, and Cahuilla mostly); this was three times the mission average. It had over 57,000 head of livestock, half cattle, half sheep, far beyond any other mission. And, at a time when most of the missions were rapidly losing population to disease, San Luis Rey was growing. How did this happen? "Recent studies have attributed this to Father Antonio Peyri's unusual decision to allow nearly half of his baptized neophytes to remain in their traditional villages instead of requiring them to move to the mission community."

Father Peyri was essentially a joyous man, full of energy and acumen; he was a great builder and architect, designing the cruciform church of San Luis Rey, the only one like it in California, and creating an *asistencia* twenty-five miles east of the mission at Pala so durable and beloved it is the only surviving mission structure that serves primarily an Indian population (on the Pala Reservation today). (On the bell tower at Pala grows an unlikely old cactus just below the cross, planted, according to legend, by Peyri as a reminder of Christ's enduring a crown of thorns.)

Still, as he aged, and the demands of the new state pressed on him—including the expulsion of most of the Spanish-born priests—Peyri decided it was time to go, slipping away one night to San Diego to board a ship. His flock, however, had other ideas; when they got wind that Peyri had gone, five hundred Indians of San Luis Rey rushed down to San Diego, begging him to stay, walking into the surf with their sorrow. Peyri blessed them and left, though he took with him a Luiseño Indian who would be the first native to study for the priesthood from California—Pablo Tac.

In 1803, at sixty-seven, Lasuén died in Carmel, to the end retaining "a low estimate of himself." There he was buried on one side of Serra (Crespí on the other). Lasuén had matched Serra's nine missions with nine of his own, however, and doubled if not tripled their agricultural output.

The last three missions were each founded by a different priest. Mission Santa Inés, Virgen y Martir, named for the third-century thirteen-year-old girl (Agnes) martyred in Rome, was established by the new mission president, Esteban Tapis, on September 17, 1804. Despite its short life (thirty years), the rich soil of the valley over the Santa Inés Mountains from Santa Barbara brought Santa Inés high wheat harvests. Its inaccessible, rural area sidestepped the vandalism that plagued other missions; Santa Inés has some of the best-preserved original buildings and surrounding land, including olive groves and fields of lavender. It also maintains some of the most striking early art, especially native art, in California, including the famous Chumash artist rendering of the Archangel Rafael as an unmistakable Chumash warrior, clutching a large channel rockfish. Santa Inés was also the site in 1824 of the ignition by Ineseño Chumash of perhaps the most effective (though short-lived) uprising of Indians in California. The Chumash Revolt began as a response to the flogging of a young neophyte by a Spanish soldier at Santa Inés, where the Indian workshops and soldiers' quarters were burned down, and it quickly spread to Santa Barbara and La Purísima, which were both seized for a month.

In 1816, Russian visitor Otto von Kotzebue (whose botanist named the California poppy), noted poignantly that the Indians, on mission "leave" twice a year to visit their native villages, felt it "the happiest period of their existence," but they would sit for days, stunned, "without taking any food, so much does the sight of their lost home affect these new Christians." Soon the social earthquake that would lead to independence from Spain shook the natives so that that melancholic gaze was then turned back at the mission.

The last two of the Alta California missions—the only two north of San Francisco—were put in place as a last-gasp effort of Spain to extend its influence northward and confront the Russians in Bodega Bay. On December 14, 1817, Mission San Rafael Arcángel was founded by Father Vicente de Sarria fifteen miles north of San Francisco, at first as an *asistencia* for Mission Dolores's sick population. San Rafael became California's first sanitarium and hospital, with two hundred initial patients. One of the smallest missions, San Rafael was also atypical in that it had no quadrangle, no bell tower, and no accommodations for the Indians, outside of sickbeds. It did have the children of one rogue priest running around— Father Mercado. San Rafael was the first mission to be secularized, and it soon fell into ruin. John Frémont housed his soldiers in the lost rooms of San Rafael during the Mexican–American War, and soon after Gypsies took up residence. By the early twentieth century, all that was left of San Rafael was one pear tree.

The trail that Serra had begun fifty-four years before finally came to rest with Mission San Francisco Solano de Sonoma, the twenty-first and last California mission, begun by a priest who started it without permission on July 4, 1823, the only mission begun under an independent Mexico and the most short-lived. Number 21 was named for one of Serra's favorite saints, Francisco Solano, who served in Peru and Paraguay with both flute and flog. Solano's large moment in history—and a telling one for the new rulers coming from the East—took place on June 14, 1846, when Lieutenant Colonel John C. Frémont captured General Vallejo of Mexican California and, across from the mission, ran up the Bear Flag on which a grizzly padded, proclaiming California an independent country, at least for a month. Its first and last president was William Ide. In July, the US Marines landed in Monterey, and that was that. The great guns of the East—and gold in them thar hills—soon drowned out what was left of Serra's mission bells. The missions, and Serra's dream, fell apart.

CHAPTER TWENTY-ONE

SECULARIZATION, GOLD, AND THE DESTRUCTION OF THE MISSIONS

There is no real way to deal with everything we lose.
—JOAN DIDION

Edward Vischer's 1865 drawing of General Don Andrés Pico at his *hacienda* made from old Mission San Fernando.

*I*n 1821, after eleven years of armed conflict, Mexico was declared independent of Spain. Fanned by an anticlerical strain in the Enlightenment, Mexican independence was the death knell of the California mission. By mid-century, most of the twenty-one missions had fallen into ruin and most of the priests gone back, heartbroken, to Spain—if they weren't dead, or, like Gilí and Rubí, *loco*. By 1824, Mexico embraced a secular constitution, and California came under a liberated Mexico's umbrella.

Secular leanings were no stranger by then to California. The pueblos

333

of San José and Los Angeles had already begun to challenge the missions' authority and its land and water. *Ranchos* outside the mission's orbit, where old soldiers were rewarded for their service to Spain, as well as Spanish noblemen, had grown to seventeen even before the missions were secularized, though the *ranchos* greatly proliferated after secularization in 1834 (an astonishing eight hundred *ranchos* were created in the fourteen years before the coming of the Americans and gold).

Shortly after Serra died in 1784, Pedro Fages assigned one of the first huge land grants, Rancho San Pedro, to Juan José Domínguez, a soldier who had weathered the uprisings in San Diego; the nearly fifty square miles covered present-day Long Beach, San Pedro Harbor, the Palos Verdes Peninsula, Culver City, and Inglewood (including the area of present-day Los Angeles International Airport). Domínguez was so lax in developing the land that thousands of his horses became feral, interbreeding with horses from Mission San Gabriel, so that they, too, became wild. Another *invalido* (as these old and sometimes not so old veterans of military service were called) who struck it rich at this time was José María Verdugo, whose name is on streets, a town, a set of hills, and a hospital in present-day Los Angeles. The largest land grant of all was Rancho La Puente, comprising much of East Los Angeles, Orange County, and beaches south of Palos Verdes to Newport Beach, given to José Manuel Nieto, who promised "not to harm a living soul," though soon his animals were overgrazing Mission San Gabriel land, his harvests of corn three times that of San Gabriel. At the time of his death in 1804, Nieto was wealthy beyond just about anyone in California, Alta or Baja. As if to assert the rule of money over Indian, as well as Christian deities, one of Nieto's sons built a large adobe house near the decrepit Mission San Gabriel right on the site of Povuu'nga, where the Tongva and Juaneño believed their god Chinigchinich had once appeared.

For a quarter century, Mexican California enjoyed a sort of independence within the independence. The Californios, as they called themselves, Spaniards, most actually mestizo and nominally pledged as citizens of Mexico, lived a leisurely life and developed a strong sense of their own culture of cattle and wine along the Pacific coast. In 1832, four thousand Californios existed. A handful of families dominated the landscape, passing the governorship back and forth, absorbing early *ranchos*, and handing out *ranchos* in a flurry as the missions were taken apart. Mariano Vallejo strode across Rancho Petaluma and the area north of San Francisco; Juan Bautista Alvarado dominated the politics of Monterey; Santa Barbara was led by Pablo de la Guerra; Los Angeles split between the Pico brothers, Andrés and Pio; Orange County by José Andrés

Sepulveda; and San Diego by José Antonio Carrillo and Juan Bandini, whose descendants attached the Bandini name to a fertilizer that fueled the growth of L.A. suburbs after World War II. The life the Californios lived—made possible by Indian labor that was suddenly turned out of the missions, to both relief and vertigo—was one of abundance:

> It was a prodigal existence, generous and unheeding. Innumerable long-horn cattle roamed the hills. Families were large and extended. It was common for more than twenty relatives, near-relatives, and retainers to sit down to plentiful meals of beef, tortillas, chili peppers, tomatoes, garbanzo and green beans, pumpkins, onions, oranges, apples, pears, and imported chocolates and spices, all of it prepared by Indian cooks under the supervision of the mistress of the house. . . . In a society challenged by a paucity of civil institutions . . . family was everything.

The *rancho* had supplanted the mission as the center of life, though the religious life was still somewhat important, especially to the señoras, memorialized by Señora Moreno, the matron of the hacienda in Helen Hunt Jackson's *Ramona*. With the few priests left in the state, religious festivals led with the cross, trailed by a procession of fine lace, brocaded dresses, top hats, sombreros, black satin *chaleco* waistcoats, and silver-clad saddles, finally ending in an evening of rodeo, Indian *vaqueros* doing the honors of roping. Was it so strange that those who were roped were great ropers? Freedom had brought them a life primarily as cowpunchers, entertainers, and servants, at least for those who had forgotten—if they ever knew them—the ways of the woods.

Then there were the bull-and-bear fights, where Californios and Indians both spent several days and nights drinking *aguardiente* (a brandy, literally "firewater," but also called mule kick), betting on whether or not the bull's upending horns would disembowel a bear before the bear's teeth and claws would bleed the bull to death. (More often than not, the old bull prevailed.) Imbued with a fascination with the wild, with the largeness and power of nature, California had fostered a soul of drama from the beginning; bell-ringing Junípero Serra had seen to that.

And California had welcomed wealth, something Serra and Crespí neither experienced nor valued, but foretold when they beheld those vast lands and rivers and roses. Strangely enough, it wasn't the meat of cattle that drew customers from all over the world—meat spoiled quickly unless it was cooked or made into jerky—it was the hides and the tallow. Clothes and soap. There was something Protestants and Catholics could agree on. And the Californios, often glutted with cattle, were not concerned about strays or even thieves: "If an occasional cow was killed mysteriously it was of no consequence as long as the 'California dollar' [the hide] was left behind. The poor had a ready source of food."

Freedom for the Indian, however, was hardly invigorating. Despite punitive excesses, for decades he had had a deeply ordered, communal life under the paternal watchfulness and care of the padres. To suddenly be thrown into a private enterprise system with little or no money, vying for properties with rich *alcáldes* from Mexico was disorienting, to say the least. The memoirist-voyager Richard Henry Dana (*Two Years Before the Mast*) went ashore and stayed in Santa Barbara during the early years of secularization, contrasting the dedication of the mission priests to "*administradores* [who] are strangers sent from Mexico, having no interest in the country; not identified in any way with their charge, and, for the most part, men of desperate fortunes, broken-down politicians and soldiers—whose only object is to retrieve their condition in as short a time as possible."

The government of Mexican California, to Dana, was "arbitrary democracy," and that was probably a generous assessment. Some Indians left for work in Los Angeles, some hired for slave wages onto the lands of the *rancheros*, and some sank back into the woods. With none of the hardihood of days before the white man showed his face, life in the woods was a rainy, muddy, dusty hell.

In fact, the new "liberating" laws were, for the Indian, not very liberating. Governor José Figueroa issued twenty-three articles in his 1835 *Reglamento* that transferred mission land and property to *ranchos* and others: "As the articles clearly state, the secularization of the missions did not free the neophytes but placed them under different management. Title to land was denied them. True ownership of animals and equipment placed in their care also was denied." Even the compulsion to work, which stood among many republican Mexicans as a sore point in mission life, did not disappear; the *mayordomos* "could compel the Indians to work at their respective tasks and to chastise them moderately for any misdemeanors they might commit." Randall Milliken is a dissenting voice on the *Reglamento*: "If enacted as written, the Indians of California would have had pueblos like New Mexico. But the government didn't keep to it." Some tribes took advantage of the changeover to assert themselves; the Cahuillas, for example, seized the *asistencia* at San Bernardino, and made off with sacred vessels of the chapel, grain, and even Father Tomás Estenaga, who had come from San Gabriel to negotiate return of property. Some Indians managed to survive the turmoil by intermarriage with those building *ranchos*.

Between 1827 and 1829, the new Mexican government expelled most royalist Spaniards living in California, including priests. Replacing them were Zacatecan Franciscans, homegrown in Mexico, and "less inclined to a *reducción*-style of missioning." They were greeted in 1833 on the eve of secularization by a fractious system already coming apart, "with mission finances greatly reduced, then cut off."

Some Indians simply refused to work, or became itinerant workers. In 1839, when Estenaga asked a "freed" Indian to make stirrups and saddles for *vaqueros*, he ignored him, taking up two dead carpenters' tools and making off. Estenaga asked new visitor-general William Hartnell (an Englishman), charged by Mexico with inspecting the secularization, "If only the most useful were emancipated, who and how will one-half of the community maintain itself, composed as it is of aged, infirm, children, etc.?" Californio squatters flooded into the mission space, overwhelming the remaining padres. Meanwhile, Indians were reverting to nakedness, as *ranchos* did not supply them with clothes as had the padres. If they could labor naked, fine. In 1840, Estenaga (whom Hugo Reid called "a truly good man . . . and despiser of hypocrisy") spent his entire salary of nine hundred pesos plus savings of a thousand pesos on clothing for Indians who would not or could not leave the crumbling mission.

And then came the houses of firewater. Taverns started up, not just in pueblos, but also in what was left of Indian *rancherías* or in their "new" shantytown settlements. In 1840, one *rancho* owner "sold *aguardiente* to all the Indians who could afford it and then punished most severely those who got drunk."

In fact, the onset of Indian alcoholism in California—only a small portion of a disease that ravages Indian reservations across the country today—was spawned in an era of Californio license. Juan Bautista Alvarado, the first native-born Californio governor, was quite a libertine. Alvarado kept a mistress at an adobe down the street in Monterey from his governor's mansion, had five daughters with her, and for good measure had a son out of wedlock in Los Angeles for whom Pio Pico stood as godparent. Described as "sober, taciturn, without affection" when he got liquored up, Alvarado "destroyed everything he could lay his hands on."

If anything, for all the bugaboo about nakedness, miscegenation was *less* feared under the padres than after secularization. For a five-year period in the 1770s, Monterey, for instance, recorded 37 percent of marriages as interracial, no doubt due to "Spanish priests' famous disregard of Indian phenotype—usually attributed to the Iberian Peninsula's history with the Moors." But over time and into secularization, that rate was cut in half, at least intermarriages with Indians. With increasing visitations by Colorado and Appalachian trappers like Jedediah Smith (who made an early penetration from the east in 1826), Bostonian whalers, traders, and land speculators, intermarriage between Californios and Yankees was favored—and politically astute for those *rancheros* who sensed the inexorable tide of empire coming from the east as stronger than that of the Mexican south. When José Antonio Carrillo of Santa Barbara sought husbands for his five daughters, every one of them was American.

Onto this stage strode John Sutter, a German-Swiss immigrant, who made a pact with Governor Alvarado in 1839 to guard the northern frontier against the Russians, building a fort on the site of what became Sacramento to brandish a totally self-fabricated myth of his prowess with the Royal Swiss Guards. Something of a megalomaniac, Sutter called his 48,000-acre spread New Helvetia. He provisioned at his huge general store or employed in his sawmills everyone from Mormon irregulars in an American battalion to some of the ill-fated Donner Party, eighty-seven people from Missouri snowbound in the High Sierras in the winter of 1846–47, most of whom froze to death, only seven surviving after cannibalizing the dead.

If silver had seduced Spain, riveting its interest in Mexico, gold in the Far West was about to do that to the eastern Americans. On January 24, 1848, a carpenter named James Wilson Marshall spotted some golden pebbles in a tailrace of the Sutter sawmill, thinking them quartz. Soon what he found out the world found out, and the die was cast on what Josiah Royce, the California-born Harvard philosopher, was to call "the original sin" of Californian history—the forcible seizure of Serra's dream coast by the United States after the discovery of massive seams of gold in the Sierra Nevadas.

Following the 1848 Treaty of Guadalupe Hidalgo between the United States and Mexico, California became a territory of the United States, and shortly after the Gold Rush that year, in 1850 America declared the Golden State the thirty-first of the union. In 1865, three weeks before he was assassinated, President Abraham Lincoln restored the missions of California to the Catholic Church. Perhaps in giving the missions of California back to God, Lincoln sensed he would soon be following.

But in fact the missions were already gone. Lincoln gave them back to ghosts. The effect of the Gold Rush on California was total, and can be divined by the following facts: within two years the number of ships in San Francisco Bay went from a few dozen to 635, most of them abandoned while the miners from all over the world rushed to Sutter's Mill; in a decade the equivalent of $10 billion in ingots left the goldfields for the East; the rate of homicide in one of the larger mines (Sonora) was fifty times the US rate in 1999, while the homicide rate in 1850–51 in Los Angeles was the all-time highest in US history (literally 1.2 percent of the city were murdered). No surprise that in this violent paroxysm of greed the missions—and the Indians loosed of them—were barely footnotes in the burgeoning life of the new Golden State. The American state of California, sanctioning indenturing of Indians to whites as early as April 1850, "fostered the rise of a slave trade, with slave traders being especially interested in kidnapping Indian children," while clearing the mining areas of Indians became nothing short of genocide. The Clear Lake Massacre alone, in May 1850, saw the slaughtering of hundreds of Pomos by the US Army. The first American governor of California, Peter Hardeman Burnett, put it bluntly: "It is inevitable that the Indian must go."

Gold miners turned Mission Dolores in San Francisco into a hotel and tavern, featuring a spiked "milk punch." San Juan Capistrano, sold by Pio Pico to his brother-in-law, spent most of the nineteenth century in complete ruin. Protesting the theft of twenty-three violins at Mission Santa Clara, the breakage of its choir door, and arsonists burning the wooden walls, for his troubles in 1851 Father José Real was told to leave California. Before taking off, he managed to intercede with John Burton, the *alcalde* of Pueblo San José, for the release of an Indian couple forcibly seized by the American authorities. Real took to gambling and womanizing, finally leaving the priesthood, ending up alone in Baja.

The mission Indian population, about eighteen thousand at the moment of secularization, went down to one thousand by 1839. The value of the mission holdings went from 548,100 pesos (in 1834) to 73,755 (in 1845)—a drop of 86 percent. Flocks of sheep and cattle herds fell 74 percent at thirteen of the twenty-one missions, and most of what was left transferred to the *rancheros*.

The destruction of the California Indian limned that of the missions; though indeed the mission system had begun that destruction, it was greatly accelerated by the Gold Rush, the rapaciousness if not unconscionable cruelty of the American settlers and armies, as well as diseases. "We were begging on our land to the American pioneers," said one Ohlone descendant. "My father was furious that he had to pay for a hunting license on our own land." A California Indian population of 150,000 in 1845 dropped to 30,000 by 1870, 60 percent of the loss due to disease, but 40 percent due to murder. The last stand of the California Indians took place in 1873 with the Modoc War, pitting fifty-three Modoc Indians in a remote northeastern corner of the state against a one-thousand-strong US Army regiment. For a while, the brave Modocs held out in lava beds, before the few survivors escaped to Oregon, where there were no missions or gold.

CHAPTER TWENTY-TWO

THE SERRA LEGEND AND THE QUESTION OF SAINTHOOD

I am quite aware of the enormous difference
there is between reading about it and actually going through it.
Here indeed Deo Gratias *is the thing to say.*
—JUNÍPERO SERRA

Be strong. Be brave. Do the work.
—CHRONICLES (2 PARALIPOMENON) 15:7

The Glory of Heaven by Jose de Páez (1771–72),
Mission San Carlos Borromeo de Carmelo.

*T*he case for Junípero Serra's sainthood dates back to the days immediately following his death. But one of the more startling revelations
about the man came about in 1943, in conjunction with the formaliza-
tion of sainthood investigations, when his corpse was exhumed in Carmel. It turns out that indeed he was short, had a "well-vaulted" head,
long straight nose, and pointed chin—no surprises there. The physical
anthropologist Dr. Theodore McCown thought the subject "gives every
indication of a sound body and a strong constitution." That, too, was predictable. But something else gave the scientific team pause: "the absence
of any marked manifestations of changes to the bones usually accompanying old age." It seems that Serra was forever young.

We live in a cynical age. Nothing of import is asserted that isn't pillo-
ried from ten directions—the electronic age's death by a thousand cuts.
There's nonstop consciousness, excruciating self-consciousness played to
the masses on Facebook and YouTube, which might be better termed
"MeTube." Logorrhea is considered artful. Blogging is publishing; everyone is published by everyone, or self publishes self and distributes self to
the universe. Just about everything claimed about media speech is a mis-
nomer: social media is often antisocial if not sociopathic; adult websites
are made for people who never grew up.

In such a world, what could a saint possibly mean? Or a possible saint,
a man from the eighteenth century yet? In an age of wholesale suspicion,
what use openhearted belief?

The growth of the Serra legend began when Francisco Palou noted
the frenzy with which mourners right after his death snatched parts of
his clothing, belongings, and even his hair. Within three years, Palou had
written the first biography, the *Relación Historica de la Vida y Apostolicas Tareas del Venerable Padre Fray Junípero Serra*, published in 1787
in Mexico City, without which, for all its flaws, nothing else happens.
One feels that, in addition to three motives a historian caught for Palou's
work—a recruiting tool for missionaries, an answer to the secularization push by the Bourbons, an homage to his master—there may have
been other spurs. Certainly the sheer magnitude of the story of entering
"virgin" territory with Spain and the challenge of getting it down was
an additional motive; perhaps earning a closeness to the subject he could
never be certain of in life was another. Finally, though he demurred ("I
declare and affirm that in none of these things . . . should be given more
credence than they may deserve as in a simple human history"), Palou
began a case for Serra veneration and even sainthood.

341

So large a shadow did Palou's *Relación* cast that no biography in English was attempted for 130 years, until Abigail Fitch published a romantic one on the eve of the First World War. But the legend of the California missions had been growing toward the end of the nineteenth century, with the 1884 publication of the bestselling novel *Ramona* by Helen Hunt Jackson. A tireless defender of Indian rights and a New England mandarin who was childhood friends with Emily Dickinson, Jackson had gone west—as so many did—from family tragedy. She had lost her husband to a freak accident in an experimental American submarine during the Civil War, and then her two children to childhood disease. Her anger generated *A Century of Dishonor* (1881), Jackson's jeremiad against the US government for its treatment of Indians, but her love loss took itself to the beauty and loneliness of the West, and a novel in which she married the plight of the California Indian with the goodness of the Franciscans. When the beautiful mulatta heroine Ramona first appears, she emerges from a "golden snow-storm" of wild mustard, which "in Southern California is like that spoken of in the New Testament." In an essay at the time, Jackson asserted that Serra was "the most foremost, grandest figure" in California's history, and that none of his successors were even close to him.

Soon Jackson was joining forces with the irrepressible Charles Fletcher Lummis, the Harvard-educated city editor of the *Los Angeles Times* who had walked, Serra-like, three thousand miles from Cincinnati, Ohio, to Los Angeles in 1885. By the 1890s, armed with his own magazine, *The Land of Sunshine/Out West*, Lummis made land and health appeals to easterners, who, by World War I, were already eating twenty million crates of oranges from California. "The lands of sunshine expand the soul" was Lummis's cheerful motto. (The California model, "widely known in Palestine" among early twentieth century Jewish immigrants, brought citriculture full circle from its Levantine and Spanish origins. Zionist land purchase and later seizure took away the "Moors'" ownership of most ancient Jaffa orange groves.)

In 1891, Mrs. Leland Stanford, wife of the railroad robber baron and founder of Stanford University, unveiled the Serra statue in Monterey. In 1895, Lummis began the Landmarks Club, declaring "the Missions are, next to our climate and its consequences, the best capital Southern California has." By 1902, Lummis had published the first English translation of Serra's Baja diary. Commemorative mission bells began to appear along Highway 101 (the old El Camino Real, or at least part of it, proposed today as a World Heritage Site).

Part of this groundswell, historian Theodore Hittell said, was that "Serra was very much a man as St. Francis might have been if he lived in the 18th century," and "If any man were ever deserving canonization, it seems Junípero was."

There are yawning errors in the encomiums of Serra, such as Walter Hawley's assertion in 1910 that Serra was "tall" (in *Early Days of Santa Barbara*). Early versions of what might be called the "pejorative view" of Serra (as opposed to the honorific) also made themselves felt. French explorer Jean-François de la Pérouse, on a visit to California in 1786, caught a "heavy depression" hanging over Carmel and roundly criticized the whippings for "sins, which in Europe are left to Divine Justice," though he found the Franciscans in general "pious and prudent." The author of the seminal seven-volume history of California, Herbert Bancroft, though he saw Serra as "a great and remarkable man," "a brilliant exception" to other missionaries, excoriated him for accepting "an absolute right to flog his neophytes for any slight negligence." But an indefatigable champion of Serra who wrote detailed singular volumes on several missions, Father Zephyrin Engelhardt—with a few prejudicial blind spots of his own—took on Bancroft for "a willful mistranslation for the purpose of rendering Catholic religious practices ridiculous." In one instance, Engelhardt blasts Bancroft for describing the feast day of St. Francis's stigmata as "The Day of the *Sores* of our seraphic father."

Still, momentum for recognition was growing. In 1927, Willa Cather published the novel *Death Comes for the Archbishop*, whose climactic scene is an expansion of the encounter Serra thought he had with the Holy Family in the Huasteca. Cather retells the story to her amazed, fictional archbishop, adding three cottonwoods (for Joseph, Mary, Jesus) shedding a Christmas-like cotton, while the Infant "with his tiny finger made the cross upon Father Junípero's forehead." In 1931, a Serra statue was placed in the US Capitol, one of two representing the state of California. In 1934, the Serra Cause for Canonization, pushed by prominent Catholic laymen such as Isidore Dockweiler of Los Angeles, was formally submitted to the Vatican's Congregation for the Causes of Saints. In 1937, *Time* magazine asked, "Sainthood for Serra?"

Sainthood in the Church's early days was largely one of folk veneration for zealous Christians "who suffered in that neighborhood." In the earliest centuries, those who died for the faith were known as "red martyrs." As Tertullian (cited by Serra after the second battle of San Diego) famously remarked, "If the Tiber overflowed its banks . . . your cry immediately is 'Christians to the lions!'" But with the conversion of Emperor Constantine in AD 313, so-called white martyrdom become more widespread—a martyr who didn't need to be killed for his beliefs, but simply lived a life of "heroic virtue" and exhibited *charismata*, signs of holiness.

Over time, the Vatican began to assert its authority. The first significant move was in the eleventh century, when Pope Urban II introduced the necessity of multiple eyewitnesses for miracles, without which no canonization could take place. Finally, in 1634, in the wake of the Protestant Reformation's attack on Catholic sainthood as idolatrous, Pope Urban VIII set down detailed procedures for both beatification (which required at least one miracle) and canonization (at least two to five miracles). For the first time, the Vatican had "final control over the saintly narrative." Soon these procedures were codified in Canon Law, and for the most part define the process today.

Included in these codifications was the use of a "devil's advocate," a lawyer appointed by the Holy See to poke holes in the arguments for sainthood. Over a hundred questions in fourteen separate areas are typically directed to all witnesses, including whether a reputation for holiness (*fama sanctitatis*) "was continuous or interrupted?" and "Was there anything said or done or heard contrary to this reputation?" Most importantly, the "Servant of God," as the candidate for sainthood was called, had to exemplify in heroic degree the four cardinal virtues (prudence, justice, fortitude, and temperance) and the three theological virtues (faith, hope, and charity). Martyrdom was not required, nor did it assure sainthood.

There are six thousand saints, most listed in the perennially updated *Lives of the Saints* by Alban Butler, first published in 1756, and perhaps read by Serra in Spanish translation. Not all of these, either, have secured papal sanction, and several from antiquity have actually been scratched from the list upon closer examination. St. Barbara, a Serra favorite, is one of these. Another was St. Vibiana, an early Christian martyr, whom my father and I used to pray to as she appeared to lie supposedly undecomposed after 1,700 years above an altar in downtown Los Angeles (this was, however, a wax effigy shaped around relics).

Today the process for canonization is an extremely rigorous and exhaustive one (five to ten years required in preliminaries alone before any serious investigation begins). Who qualifies and ultimately gets through? One thing can be dispelled right off: a saint need not have a perfect life, inasmuch as none exists. A whole host of saints sinned in epic fashion. One need only think of St. Augustine and his libidinous twenties, Bonaventure (who apparently had a habit of filing his nails and leaping from trees to attack people), and of course, Paul, who spent much of his early life as Saul of Damascus putting Christians to death.

Falling into severe official disfavor, too, does not necessarily disqualify one from sainthood. One woman, executed as a heretic in 1431, was rehabilitated twenty-five years later, and finally, five hundred years on, in 1920 was made a saint. Her name is Joan of Arc.

An especially dramatic spiritual life (combined with friends in high places who actively push for sainthood) does not hurt. A close friend of St. Francis of Assisi became Pope Gregory IX, who commissioned his first biography. One can also divine these trends: many wounded or imprisoned soldiers have become saints (St. Martin of Tours is a primary example, known for his healing power throughout France, where over four thousand churches are named in his honor; the founder of the Jesuits, Ignatius Loyola, is another example). Being a man seems to help (75 percent of saints are men) and noblemen or notable male witnesses seem to outpace commoners and women. Miracles that are "connected" versus those "unconnected" through time are favored. Being a religious (priest, brother, or nun) or just single helps; married saints are extremely rare; the first married saint of the modern era was named in 2004 by Pope John Paul II—St. Gianna Beretta Molla, a mother and pediatrician who died in childbirth.

In the 1960s, the Second Vatican Council homed in on the reason to revere saints, "To look on the life of those who have faithfully followed Christ is to be inspired with a new reason for seeking the city which is to come . . . we will be able to arrive at perfect union with Christ, that is, holiness." Among the current saints-in-waiting are Dorothy Day, the great minister to New York's poor, Cardinal John Joseph O'Conner's "Saint of the Lonely"; Archbishop Oscar Romero, slain by Salvadoran death squads while saying Mass; and Mother Teresa, the legendary Albanian woman who devoted her life to lepers in India. These candidates are often governed by complex, and sometimes controversial, considerations. Included among these is Blessed Junípero Serra.

Serra's case has been through most of the necessary steps. After prodding from members of the Serra Cause in Los Angeles and San Francisco, in the 1940s the bishop of Monterey-Fresno opened a tribunal to investigate Serra's worthiness for sainthood. A vice-postulator was appointed as point man for the effort (the first full-time vice-postulator was Eric O'Brien, who served from 1941 to 1958). In 1942, Father O'Brien distributed several hundred thousand Serra leaflets to California parishes and newspapers. As Serra had long been deceased, a historical commission of experts was formed in 1943, made of Santa Barbara Mission archivist Maynard Geiger, OFM, Monsignor James Culleton of Fresno, and Herbert Bolton, a Berkeley professor and translator of Crespí and Palou, as well as author of many books on the Spanish settlement and missions.

Astoundingly, the commission assembled in one place 905 documents from 125 locations on two continents, which totaled 7,440 pages. Geiger turned a lifelong obsession and his participation on this commission into his magnum opus, the two-volume biography *The Life and Times of Fray Junípero Serra, O.F.M.* (1959), rightfully called "magisterial."

In addition to the commission's gathered documentation, O'Brien personally interviewed at least two hundred descendants of mission days, none of whom, of course, would have known Serra, but some of whose ancestors did, including many Indians. In all, 350 descendants of old California families were interviewed, including fifty at diocesan hearings in 1949, taped in Monterey, San Francisco, and Los Angeles.

Finally, three volumes of the *Positio* (also known as the *Summarium*), comprising over six hundred pages, were painstakingly and sometimes haltingly assembled and written in the so-called Roman Process, to be presented to the cardinals and pope for a decision. Five different people labored to complete the huge document—one took ill and left (Father Francis Guest) and another had a nervous breakdown but finally managed to produce it in 1981 (Father Jacinto Fernandez Largo); all told, the *Positio* had taken thirty-one years to write. It seems several researchers have suffered some physical, emotional, or mental ordeal considering the life of Serra.

The *Positio*, accessed with difficulty by the public, contains some very interesting and revealing material. Several witnesses from the 1949 hearings describe Serra granting "concessions" to those who prayed to him, and even miracles. Clotilde González, whose great-grandfather Serra had urged the governor to make the recipient of the first land grant in California, spoke to one witness (Harry Downie, the curator of Carmel Mission) about "a long-standing tradition of Serra's sanctity and mercy" and that "these narrations of miraculous events attributed to Serra are still present among direct descendants of this family." A member of the Guerrero family spoke of praying to a book "because Serra's hands touched it." María Antonio Field of Monterey (b. 1886) said Serra was commonly "venerated" in her family and community: "We would talk about him often, just like the Americans tend to talk about their national figures." Emma Butler Ambrosia (b. 1850), also of Monterey, said she was taught a prayer in Spanish as a child, "Father Junípero Serra, help me in all my needs," and that her prayers were "satisfied many times," including healing her husband, who was told by a doctor "he had no hope," as well as her own lameness. An Irish priest at Carmel (Michael O'Connell) noted pilgrimages from San Francisco around 1880. A non-Catholic, in fact, unattached to any church, Herbert Bolton (one of the three commissioners), testified, "I am deeply convinced that Father Serra was constantly considered throughout his life as a holy man and that his fame of sanctity is corroborated from certain facts." Nathaniel Soberanes (b. 1884), a Salinas farmworker, said a grandfather who knew Serra spoke of him as "a very holy man and that he had done a lot for the Indians ... he would always bless the Indians for the many jobs they used to do at the mission." (This would probably have been Mission San Antonio.) The editor and publisher of the *Oakland Tribune*, a Methodist named Joe Knowland (b. 1871), declared, "I do not know anyone in the history of California who deserves the title of saint more than him." A housewife from Los Angeles, Rosa Santa Cruz de Logan (b. 1867), noted that her grandmother knew people who had met Serra and "talked" about him (what if anything they talked about is not disclosed).

An important part of the *Positio* is the discussion of Serra's practice of the four cardinal and three theological virtues, grounded by Palou's discussion of them in the last chapter of the *Relación*. First, Palou inspected Serra's "deep humility." Like St. Bernard, self-knowledge to Serra made him conclude that he himself was "despicable." Often he closed a letter "unworthy priest," or even "most unworthy priest." Palou's point is well taken: "The greater the honor which came to him, the greater was his repugnance for it." He confessed to his superior, "By good fortune, completely unmerited by my count, our college counts me among its workers. My shortcomings, my lack of judgment, and still worse, my sins, are, without doubt, manifold." Serra never spared himself because in a sense he was embarrassed—and perhaps even afraid—of the power of his own intellect.

Prudence? Serra often consulted others (as he did the night before he decided to go to Mexico and get Fages cashiered). Rash decisions did not seem to be his modus operandi, though he founded Mission San Luis Obispo in the teeth of a sharp reassessment by his superiors. On the other hand, throwing his whole life prior to age thirty-six away to go to a New World might seem a little rash. "Perhaps Serra's dark side was [lack of] obedience," said John Vaughn, the current vice-postulator, referring to the way Serra surged forward with confirming before the government gave its official approval.

As for justice, we have two seemingly disparate pieces of evidence. On the one hand, we know Serra tipped way over on the side of mercy for the prisoners at San Diego, risking his own standing, not to mention his life, as well as the lives of the mission personnel in ordering the release of murderers, going over the head of Rivera all the way to the viceroy. Rivera certainly didn't see that as just; to him it was crazy, and it led to his resignation. Such tensions, however, propelled Serra into a vision of comity between white man and Indian that had virtually no parallel in three centuries of colonization of the New World by Europe. On the other hand, there's the use of flogging against Indians. What to make of this? Was it just? It's important to register that by 1813—only twenty-nine years after Serra's death—the Spanish government outlawed the use of the whip as a form of punishment throughout the entire empire, not just by priests, but in prisons, schools, chain gangs—everywhere. About this difficult, painful matter, Father Guest makes four points: first, there is overwhelming evidence that the Indians were considered theologically and pedagogically to be children; second, the discipline given was tempered both in number and kind, so that the *azotes* ("blows" in Spanish, and a term often used to describe corporal punishment to children) were rarely more than twelve (half the limit of twenty-five); third, that these were meted out not as punishment, but as penance, that there was a religious expiation element that the natives were quite aware of ("Father, you do not punish me; my offense punishes me," Indians repeatedly told a priest in Sonora); and fourth, several pastoral manuals insisted that discipline whippings be done with dispassion, not anger, and not excessively, and those who did so "committed a mortal sin." Guest concludes, "For the clergy of the Spanish empire, then, restricting physical punishment of an Indian adult to what normally would be given to a boy of nine or ten was a matter of justice."

Still, we may well ask why Indians were considered children at all, why Serra, who freely acknowledged "excesses" in whippings but accepted them, couldn't go further to abolish them before the state did (interestingly, Neve—who wanted the Indians secularized—still did not remove floggings from the docket of punishment meted by civil authorities). But the fact remains that to Serra, the purpose of the whippings was spiritual improvement.

Palou points to Serra's exercise of "justice" in other, less troublesome ways; for example, whenever someone in conversation criticized an individual or "something was said which might lessen the warmth of his charity toward his fellow," Serra "would always try to change the conversation." For the most part, this seems true, though we see in the letters places where Serra's patience with the civil authorities spilled over to criticism, if not outright anger. At the same time, even with adversaries, he could show remarkable tenderness and *apologia*, such as the letter of reference he wrote for Fages after the man lost his job (on Serra's account), going so far as to impute to Fages his own achievements.

As for fortitude, Serra's almost superhuman tolerance for pain, especially that badly infected foot and lower leg, the gift of the spider on his first leg in the New World, was marked. Palou notes that the only medicine he ever took for it—and only once—on his arrival in San Diego was salve given to mules. He consistently resisted relief for two decades. Even granting Geiger's corrections of the myth, we can corroborate that Serra walked at least one thousand of his nine thousand miles of land journeys in the New World. His bravery was legendary, and deservedly so. When everyone else was turning tail in San Diego—including a brave man, Portolá—Serra insisted he was staying and would munch on grass if he had to. He often traveled with little or no guard, running into Indians on his way to Capistrano with only one soldier by his side, and somehow quelling what appeared to be a war party. Temperance? Palou has a bit of a joke on this one, noting Serra's lavish call from all quarters to build and adorn the missions. *"This Father Junípero is a holy man,"* Palou paraphrases about the general complaint, *"but in this matter of asking for help for the founding of Missions he is a very burdensome saint."* Bells, chasubles, altar cloths, artwork, statues, cruets, monstrances—anything that could decorate the church and inspire the Indians was not to be spared. So in this sense, he was intemperate. By our standards, flogging and his own self-flogging were not intemperate, they were sinful. But in most every other sense, Serra was abstemious and prayerful in the extreme; some confreres thought he never slept, keeping prayer vigils, often till 4 A.M. His big indulgence was a siesta at noon, an occasional cup of chocolate or pinch of snuff when things got really exciting. Oftentimes, Serra's fey sense of humor tempered an otherwise nervous situation.

As for the theological virtues—faith, hope, and charity—Serra had them all in healthy abundance. It would be hard to find anyone with a stronger faith in God than Junípero Serra, with one huge caveat—the Dark Night of the Soul in the fear he expressed on the last day of his life. During his service in California, six thousand natives were baptized (577 by Serra personally), and Serra himself confirmed over five thousand; for the entire mission period, 100,000 were baptized. For the toughest days— the killing of Father Jayme in San Diego, the slaughter out on the Colorado River by the Quechan tribe, the rape by Spanish soldiers—Serra shook his head. "The ways of God are inscrutable." His faith endured, even when he didn't understand it. "When he spoke of the Holy Scriptures, it seemed as though he knew them by heart," Palou says, and that Serra was given to a kind of mystical reverie at times, which amazed some and repelled others: "In these holy conversations and homilies he seemed almost beside himself, as they were often prolonged more than the ordinary, and to those who were little given to piety and the Divine Word, they seemed tiresome, and there were not lacking those who said they were not at all in accord with the teachings of our father, St. Francis." Palou heard him "on many occasions" talk in his sleep, muttering, "*Gloria Patri, et Filio, et Spiritu Sancto,*" the prayer for the Sign of the Cross.

Hope followed from faith; Palou conflates St. Bernard and Gregory the Great in this matter: "The more one believes, the greater is his hope." Serra created ciphers of hope and perseverance. When an Indian named for St. Bernardine was crushed under a pine at Carmel and yet miraculously survived, Serra had a painting done and hung of the saint at San Carlos Borromeo. It was Serra, not anyone else, who had hope that missions in the Santa Barbara Channel among the Chumash would bear fruit (they did). It was Serra who hoped for a relief ship at San Diego when everyone else had given up on (it came). It was Serra who prayed to St. Barbara for abatement of a storm that everyone else thought would kill them all (saint or not, she calmed it).

As for charity, love, is, of course, the undergirding of the entire Christian faith, or should be. Paul plainly said so to the Corinthians. It is certainly what Christ ordained when, asked to prioritize the Ten Commandments, instead he squeezed them all into two, one of which is not even in the Ten Commandments: Love the Lord thy God with thy whole mind, soul, and heart. And number two, the new Commandment, Love your neighbor as yourself. Everything else was subordinate to those two ironclad imperatives for living a good life. Serra certainly loved his Indian neighbors beyond the norm, even for a missionary. Time and again, he defended them, even with his own life, against the Spanish authorities.

Despite the fervent testimonies of 1949, as far as miracles went, it was hearsay. But in the spring of 1960, a Franciscan nun in St. Louis, Mother Boniface Dyrda, took ill with an enlarged spleen (removed surgically), rashes, and high fever that eluded diagnosis, and she dropped to eighty-five pounds and stopped eating. When her kidneys began to fail, she was given the Last Rites on Palm Sunday. Her doctors said there was no hope for recovery. The good sister's chaplain, Marion Habig, was from California and a devotee of Serra; he suggested her fellow nuns begin a novena to Serra. By Good Friday, Mother Boniface said she felt better. In a month, she was fully recuperated and released from the hospital, the mysterious illness having passed. Normally, the Vatican doctors take no more than two months examining a possible miracle; this took six months. The final report of the doctors (*Positio Super Miraculo*) was an extraordinary 445 pages and came to an "unusual but not unprecedented decision," that Mother Boniface's recovery could not be explained by science, and that she should have died; at the same time, it was not possible to say definitively just what she had had. The swiftness of the recovery—important throughout the history of miracles—had made a difference. The full five-doctor Vatican board concurred.

As the movement for Serra sainthood intensified, so did the pejorative assessments. In 1984, an extraordinary "face-off" occurred, between the American Catholic Historical Association and the Conference of Latin American Historians at a conference in Chicago on the two hundredth anniversary of Serra's death. While Father Louis Luzbetak discussed the dramatic differences in Church evangelical methods from the eighteenth century to today, Dr. Florence Shipek bemoaned the treatment of the Kumeyaay in San Diego, while others shouted "Genocide." (Two respected California mission historians subsequently rejected this claim.)

In any case, as of 2013, a second miracle—the minimum requirement for sainthood—is still outstanding, though a Miami Panamanian woman who has prayed to Serra for successful recuperation from each of her fourteen brain surgeries insists that it has. Father Vaughn, who believes the Church is being particularly tough on a second miracle ("We have to be. Otherwise we'd lose credibility.") admits that he prays to Serra: "I had a stroke and a bad heart attack and lost one-third of my heart. You can't prove it's a miracle, but I'm still kicking!"

During a 2011 interview, a key figure in the Serra Cause, the pastor of Mission San Juan Capistrano Basilica, Monsignor Arthur Holquin, refused to dodge the tough issues. "Line up the arguments one after the other," he said. "The detractors are not just foolish individuals. They are not. The historic rape of the American Indians antecedent [and subsequent] to that of the Spanish government has led to the perceived collusion of it with the Church, bringing some to the conclusion that Serra was part of the Spanish machine or apparatus that suppressed the Californian Indian. But Serra did everything he could to protect the Indians from sexually abusive soldiers. Serra had many fights with various *comandantes*. It was always a tense relationship."

When asked why Serra didn't resign in protest over the soldier molestations and rape, Holquin paused. Two things prevented it, he thought: Serra's vow of obedience, and his devotion to protect the Indians' body and soul.

And were whippings the actions of a saint? To apply standards of three centuries ago to today was "a little disingenuous" to Holquin. Granting that schoolboy discipline was not the same as flogging, he smiled faintly when the interviewer admitted being belted by the Carmelites in the 1960s. "Weren't we all?" he offered.

Asked to discuss how Indians in the relative ease of California would have responded to a gospel filled with a suffering God, he called it, "an intriguing question, the whole area of evangelization in the post-Reformation world." More than reciting the Catechism, the elements of Baroque Catholicism—the incense and paintings and vestments and chantings, as well as references to the Holy Family in a family-oriented society, may have worked, at least with some.

But why did Indians need saving at all? Aren't we in a more pluralistic, accepting world? "You are speaking of soteriology, the study of salvation," Holquin responded. "Vatican II changed everything" with its encyclical *Ad Gentes* (On the Mission Activity of the Church), which expanded the doctrine of "invincible ignorance," in which people can be saved by Jesus Christ before they even know about him. *Ad Gentes* eloquently speaks of a pre-Catholic, perhaps even pre-Christian faith "secretly in the soul of man" following "the leading strings towards God." A good life essentially wins out, said Holquin, pointing out that theologian Karl Rahner talks about "the anonymous Christian," a theistic notion that a loving God is hardwired into human nature. "We are better now at working with the culture and religion of the people we are serving," Holquin thought.

About Serra being worthy of sainthood, he didn't think there was any question for a man who left everything as a university professor to minister to Indians on a remote frontier: "Here is a man who obviously heard 'the Call,' who limped and suffered a great deal. Yet he pushed on."

Still, I am left with three haunting, critical questions about the life of the Franciscan founder of California, whose population today is 37 million people: First, was Serra as a missionary—and the California missions themselves—a success, or were they and he cruel? Second, what if the Spaniards and Serra had never come to California? Would the Indians have been better off? Third, are there positive lessons for living we can take today from Serra's three-hundred-year-old life, and are they enough to warrant canonization?

As James Sandos intimates, the first question may pose a false choice, for, ironically perhaps, the height of the missions' economic success—and swollen Indian population—occurred at the worst onslaught of epidemics. Some were succeeding even as they failed. As for spiritual success, consider that as late as 1879, Robert Louis Stevenson, the celebrated novelist, could say of the holdover Indians in the obviously deteriorated Carmel mission, "You may hear God served with perhaps more touching circumstances than in any other temple under heaven," including an elderly, blind man who served as music conductor for a choir that had "Gregorian music at their finger ends, [who] pronounce the Gregorian chant so correctly I could follow the meaning as they sang. I have never seen faces more vividly lit up with joy than the faces of these Indian singers." Such faith, a century after Serra's death, cannot simply be ignored. For all that was done wrong, the stirring of that was done right.

Yes, it is shamefully true that the pre-contact population of California Indians (225,000) had decreased by a sizable 28 percent within sixty years (by 1830, just prior to secularization), due mostly to the tyranny of microbes. But the tyranny of the American army and the gold-inspired settlers and *their* microbes (and weapons) took a far higher toll by the end of the century. At its height, the number of California Indians, mostly coastal, who actually lived at the missions (under 22,000 in the early 1830s) was little more than one-third of the pre-contact coastal population (sixty thousand). But studies done as late as 1980 of the descendants of mission Indians at San Luis Rey, Chumash on the Santa Ynez Reservation (near where the last great revolt sparked), and even among the aggressive and proud Quechan Indians, have shown that the vast majority of California Indians are still Catholic. I myself have witnessed this phenomenon of faith at several of the missions today, such as the *asistencia* on the Pala Reservation, at Mission San Luis Rey, and Mission Santa Barbara. If Serra and his confreres were guilty of unmitigated cruelty, spiritual bankruptcy, or even, as some claim, genocide, it is hard to fathom how Indian warriors could voluntarily join Spanish soldiers to repel the pirate Hippolyte de Bouchard, who invaded California, as they did eagerly and successfully in 1818; several hundred could run into the water begging Father Peyri not to leave San Luis Rey; former rebels (such as Canuch/Francisco in San Diego) could become spiritual leaders of their missions; and the surrounding population of Rumsens, Esselens, and Salinans could break down for days in sorrow at Carmel when Serra died. Something went right, despite the misery, and despite the violation of Indian sovereignty that the whole colonial regime entailed. Though the California Indians were not cannibals like the Aztecs, nor did they have similar bloodthirsty habits as the cult of Huitzipochtli, some tribes' practice of violent vendetta, intertribal skirmishes, and possession status of women may have made the Gospel of Love and the peace Christ promised attractive alternatives—or at least pragmatic ones—to what was, for them, a crumbling world. I realize there is an irreducible, even terrible, irony in that, but there's absolute value, too. And the effect was in two directions. As historian Richard Pointer reminds us, spiritual encounters between Europeans and Native Americans "were fundamentally reciprocal and often mutually transformational."

Sandos notes "success" (material, spiritual, social) varied greatly mission to mission. Santa Cruz and Soledad were ultimately disasters; San Antonio, Santa Barbara, and San Luis Rey thrived. Santa Clara, San Carlos Borromeo, and San Gabriel waned and waxed, and then waned again. And San Gabriel's great material prosperity followed an abysmal, violent start. Spiritual success was longer in coming and harder won. Toypurina no doubt felt she was lost before she was found, if she was found.

As for Serra himself, it should be evident by now that he was not a cruel man, quite the contrary. To the Indian, he was loving, enthusiastic, and spiritually and physically devoted. At his best, he avoided a head-on clash with evil, preferring "the act of seeking a workaround, which is loving." Nevertheless, at times he butted heads with evil as he knew it too harshly. Though a product of its time and mitigated by fewer repetitions for "children," whipping had no real counterpart in Indian culture (with the exception of the gauntlet run by prisoners of war). It was all too subject to excess, and ultimately repelled the Franciscans themselves (Francisco Diego at Santa Clara applauded in 1833 that "such punishment as revolts my soul is being abolished.") It was cruel, a violation of the Fifth Commandment; Christ accepted the Roman soldiers' whipping his body, but he certainly didn't recommend it. Serra's and Lasuén's arguments for flogging ultimately ring hollow. They should have had the wisdom and foresight to stop it.

One wonders if Serra was brutalized by things he witnessed or suffered in Mallorca or, in fact, by the suicides, apparent or actual, in Mexico City, Tancoyol, and Oaxaca to which his extra-scrupulosity contributed. Or, as Sandos sees it, punishments may have resulted from the austere "way he was trained." Serra's humility could slide into self-loathing. In always coming up short to himself, "in hiding his own self-torture, Serra takes on the suffering of Christ," but he also may have shifted the sufferings and their "value" on others: "There's a transference, no doubt, a weird psychology that saw all flaws as essentially evil. But, of course, this is wrong, even arrogant. Perfectionism is, alas, at the root of much suffering in human history."

Second, would the Indians have been better off if the Spaniards had never come to California? This is the question to which all critiques of colonialism ultimately move. Such a question is impossible to answer. Time marches inexorably. And sooner or later, the aborigines of California, the last on the continent untouched by the Europeans, were going to meet them. With their "guns, germs, and steel," as MacArthur Fellow and Pulitzer Prize–winning author Jared Diamond reminds us, the Europeans were the most powerful, rapacious force on the globe, and there was very little that was going to stop them. (Diamond calls these "proximate causes" of Europe's dominance; for "ultimate causes"—the reason why Native Americans didn't invade Europe—Diamond emphasizes food: "Advanced technology, centralized political organization, and other features of complex societies could emerge only in dense sedentary populations capable of accumulating food surpluses.") If invasion from across the water was inevitable, the question then becomes: Who were the California Indians going to meet? Any Europeans would have unleashed the microbe war on the first Californians. But the English—and the Americans—were far more violent and racist to the Indians they met across the North American continent. As we know from their treatment of the Aleuts, the Russians would have been little better, and perhaps worse. The French had a more enlightened contact with the Indians of the upper Midwest and Canada, but under Robespierre and then Napoleon, they turned as bloody and destructive of other cultures as Cortés or the Aztecs.

No conqueror can be lauded by the victims, and Spain was the conqueror, though Spanish California lasted only fifty-two years. Nevertheless, after two hundred years of conquest in Spanish America, half the population was still Indian, whereas east of the Mississippi in English America, only 6 percent remained Indian. Whatever the excesses that plagued Serra, historian David Weber of Southern Methodist University explained, "Throughout the Spanish-American mainland by the 1790s, numerous indigenous peoples had been incorporated rather than eliminated." Because of the presence of followers of St. Francis, because of a Spanish mind-set that evolved from seeing the Indians as barbarous to recognizing them as gentiles, men and women with an inviolable soul, and particularly because of the life of service embodied by Junípero Serra—who saw the Indians as *gente de razón* when even others such as Neve didn't—the toll of that conquest, terribly high, was less under the late-eighteenth-century Spaniards, with something of a better legacy, or at least hope for one, than other colonial powers. Something had been learned.

And continues to be. On December 15, 2007, Bishop Frances Quinn of Sacramento offered an unusual public apology at Mass to Coast Miwok Indians at Mission San Rafael, for mistreatment and communicable diseases that took them close to extinction (fifty thousand on contact to fourteen people in 1852, though now the Coast Miwok number around a thousand). Though early Pomo baskets are plentiful, only two original Coast Miwok baskets are extant.

Granting the severe blow to a whole culture over time, the fact is, the California Indian did not disappear. From the low point at the turn of the century (25,000 remained), the Indian population has grown to well over 600,000 today, twice what it was at pre-contact. Unlike the East and

Southeast, where Indian life is severly diminished if not gone, there are 109 federally recognized California tribes with tribal lands, while seventy-eight more seek recognition. As James Luna of the La Jolla Reservation has said, "We are still living on the land of our ancestors, from ocean to mountain. The cross for me represents four directions. It's a small miracle that we are here, but we are here." In fact, in 2011, the Coast Miwok held their first acorn festival on ancestral ground in their own language in many years.

Mel Vernon, a captain of the Luiseño tribe, bewailed that "our history got smudged over by everyone else's agenda." Wondering "How do you find happiness in such a situation," he also took a strange pride in being part of a people who built the beautiful, and painful, houses of spirit that the missions, especially San Luis Rey, embodied: "If we weren't here, who would have put the bricks on top of each other?" David Belardes, one of the leaders of the Capistrano community and at times a critic of Monsignor Holquin, emphasizes, "When things declined [during secularization] we took care of the church here. We took care of the vestments and the chalices. The mission we see today being rebuilt is the result of that work. You had to have historical ties to do this work. What I've seen over the years, what has rocked my faith, they want to hear our stories, and that's it." He hoped the *Our Father* in Juaneño and drums could be added to the Mass. He also gave me a qualified encouragement, "If you tell the whole story."

Belardes's cousin, Jerry Nieblas, a Juaneño, has some fascinating insights into Serra:

I think Serra's politics changed over the years. He was angry about the treatment of the Indians. He was almost turning into an activist for the rights of the native community. But many Franciscans didn't want to ruffle feathers. Nothing Serra was saying was mattering. . . . Serra does deserve something within the Church, in a very cautious, slow process, as long as there is a solid history presenting Serra, a listing of Franciscan wrongs and rights. I get a sense that in the end Serra almost gave up—this brilliant frontiersman was being shot down by his own people. I had a sense they wanted him gone.

Nieblas concluded with a knowing look. "If you take a look at the accomplishments of Serra, there has to be a recognition. But I don't want Franciscans to be too proud."

And then there is the witness of the only Indian curator of a California mission (Dolores), Andrew Galvan, a Bay Area Indian who grew up near

Mission San José and whose family's favorite vacation was visiting other missions. "I fell in love with St. Francis," Galvan said with a smile during an interview conducted at Mission Dolores's small but lovely cemetery and garden, while he watered the marigolds three months before they would be needed for Day of the Dead ceremonies.

"I don't think Serra should be a saint," Galvan exclaimed. "He *is* a saint." He admits, however, that Serra "was hooked on the discipline" and "was very tough to live with," recalling that when Palou asked for Serra's blessing in the father president's last hours, Serra told him, "Not just for you, but for everyone." Palou wanted to be a favorite and Serra would not have it. Galvan descends from East Bay Indians—Bay Miwok, Ohlone, and Patwin—and specifically from a man named Polyemja, baptized as Faustino in 1794, and a woman named Jocbocme, baptized in 1802. They were both alive during Serra's life. A puckish, brilliant, unsparing man, Andy Galvan carefully asserted, still watering, "Junípero Serra is not being considered for canonization as a builder of missions, but for his life as a saint. He meets all the criteria spelled out by Palou and the Church today. Dominicans saw evil and guilt in the Indians, but not Serra. When he saw the Indians in northern Baja naked, he kissed the ground. He was entering paradise in San Diego, and in a sense contaminating the garden. But he said, 'If I baptize the Indians, I rescue them to a greater good.'" Galvan kept his hose going, over the primroses on graves, on the marigolds. "You walk up a hill to get to Dolores, and chances are, you are walking on somebody." He smiled slightly, squinting in the sunlight of an afternoon. Galvan's mentor was Father Noel Moholy, a recent vice-postulator for the Serra Cause. Moholy felt on his last day in 1998 he had failed, calling out to Galvan, "This is how I turned out—dusting altars! Serra, where is the spot I missed?" Galvan gets misty, reliving his mentor's own deathbed scene, saying that he asked Moholy, "Let me play Palou to your Serra, and ask for your blessing."

"Not only for you!" Moholy whispered.

"I burst into tears. 'You're supposed to be dead,' I told him."

"It's difficult work giving birth to a new man," Moholy said. Four days later, two heart attacks took him down.

There is always a lot at stake in examining Junípero Serra's life. But what of the meritorious from that life can be brought to our lives today? Serra can enrich us in several ways. Perhaps most important, as revolutionary two thousand years ago as it is today, Serra's notion and practice of love beyond justice was the crown of his life. His radical mercy to insist that those who assassinated Father Jayme in San Diego be released and even rehabilitated was as moving as Christ's invocation to the Good Thief. As theologian and California Lutheran University professor Jarvis Streeter reveals, "I find it highly significant that Jesus rarely, according to the gospels, used the metaphor of God as Judge, but instead consistently spoke of a loving and merciful Father."

Serra's sense of the noumenal—something he derived not just from Spanish mysticism but from California Indians—can brighten a world dominated by the often invisible tyranny of technology. His simplicity can inform a world at the mercy of multitasking and the distractions and complexities of systems no one can even explain, even when they collapse (such as the plunge of mortgage-backed securities in 2008 that brought on the Great Recession). Serra's evangelical methods in the Sierra Gorda that emphasized language accession of the native peoples and opened a two-way street with godly artistic expression (recall how he carried the Pame statue Cachum in his pocket), these methods were two hundred years ahead of their time, and were far more galvanizing than the lash. Consider the Serra ripples in the observations of a contemporary Franciscan missionary who has spent half a century in today's Muslim-dominated island of Mindanao in the Philippines: "Others see dialogue as a first step towards evangelization, but there are people now who are beginning to see dialogue and evangelization as one."

In a country unable to endure pain or find meaning in it, with a skyrocketing substance abuse problem, the notion that pain transforms oneself to a higher plane, to an imitation of the great spirit we harbor, if not Christ himself, is one that Serra embodied from his first steps in the New World. The courage to speak truth to power; the healing aspects of nature—the mountain and the sea that mesmerized him in Mallorca and California—and the natural world's "intimations of immortality"; intimations, too, of a new, more equal role for women in the Catholic Church—all of these have echoes in Serra. His love and respect for his mother, his sister, Juana, his great devotion to the Blessed Mother and María de Agreda (whose words were hoisted in his satchel wherever he went, as closely carried as the Bible), not to mention his submerged but unmistakable love for María Contreras of Oaxaca and his special designation as a confessor of nuns: Who is to say Junípero Serra would oppose something long overdue in the Catholic Church? That is, women priests and a married priesthood.

Serra brings an appreciation of the "physical" faith and fervency of Latinos to our culture and a "taking down the wall" that separates Mexico from California and the United States, welcoming immigrants with open arms, a practice this country has always exercised when true to its roots, or ignored to its shame. Indeed, the walls and barbed wire, the dogs and the manhunts, represent a kind of disunion and inhospitality Serra not only could not have stomached, he could hardly have envisioned it.

Could the Serra story help us, in a paradoxical way, reconsider the hyper-focus on sexuality in Christian notions of sin—notions that often crippled and haunted the missions—in a realignment of attitudes more in line with what Christ himself revealed and taught, not to mention plain reason? If Christ's Two Great Commandments supersede the others, and I take him on his own authority—they do—love wins out on judgment or ostracism or fear or delineation. And besides, God does not make junk. That principle should apply to those whose sexual orientation was set at birth.

Perhaps Serra took the Two Great Commandments in deeper, that "endlessly hazardous ethic," according to Reynolds Price, a translator of the New Testament and novelist. As Pope Francis I recently said, "Who am I to judge?" Take the Church out of the bedroom. Take it to the streets of the poor and the voiceless and the suffering, as Christ did. Serra would and should have rung his bell for that. And that a woman could raise the Host as sure as he could open her book.

Does Serra deserve sainthood? Clearly, there are those both less and more worthy who have achieved it. Perhaps, as Father John Vaughn puts it, "The goodness of Serra overcomes the flogging." Or as Berkeley theologian Father Kenan Osborne wonders, "Can we see him as a little inspiring without necessarily making him a saint? Twenty-one missions are monuments, after all." What's more important than what was reprehensible and long died out is that we recognize what was exemplary, even holy, in him, a voice from the past that informs our changing world. The man, after all, created a world. It was utopic, it was tragic. But it was a world whose eye was ultimately on the Creator. Despite our mooring in the material, we're still in Serra's other, yearning world. We can still see its hopes flicker on that ladder of light, trying to draw the island back to the land, trying to see Chinigchinich and Christ embrace in that sun, before it goes down.

WINTER SOLSTICE AT MISSION SANTA BARBARA

I, John, your brother,
who share with you the distress, the kingdom,
and the endurance we have in Jesus, found myself
on the island called Patmos.
—REVELATION, 1:9

Dawn light at Mission Santa Barbara.

*D*ecember 22, 2012. 7:30 A.M. The doors to Mission Santa Barbara are open in the back. The priest says, before Mass starts, "Take a look." There are only a few of us. Something will be seen today at the winter solstice that is unusual.

Soon, the winter dawn begins. The sun comes up over Santa Cruz Island and the water, moving blue as Mary's robes, flooding through the door of the church. We are where Father Serra wanted the mission to be, though its founding was snatched from him. We are watching the sea, and the sun breasting it.

The light hits the old stone baptismal font. It floods down the nave of the church and pounces left of the altar on the face of the statue of the Blessed Mother. And then the light grows soft and ripples, like that that comes from water.

This is the theory of Ruben Mendoza, archaeologist of California State University at Monterey Bay: that Serra and Lasuén positioned several of the mission churches to face the rising sun on the winter solstice and that it would strike the altar. "For many Native American groups," Mendoza has said, "the solstice was the most dreaded day of the year. They believed the sun was dying and only its rebirth could ensure their survival." Hence December 22 as the first day of a sun "growth" cycle. Mendoza first saw the phenomenon at Mission San Juan Bautista in 2000: "I was smitten by the most unusual sensation that I was soon to share two centuries of a most esoteric and spiritual experience."

Mendoza thinks the Franciscans "precisely oriented at least 13 missions and an old Spanish chapel to capture illuminations—some on days that would have been sacred in Native American faiths." At Mission San Carlos Borromeo, it takes place on the summer solstice; at San Miguel, statues of saints are illuminated on their feast days in October; at Mission San José, at the spring and fall equinoxes.

Above the light of the morning sun shimmering on Mary at Santa Barbara, a sparrow flits near the ceiling in the rafters.

"*Ave Regina!*" sings the threadbare choir.

The sun is coming up now, stronger. It begins to move off Mary's face eastward toward the altar. The sparrow flies down the ceiling of the nave, toward the light streaming, alighting on the chandelier hanging down from an image of the cross painted by the Indians with spokes of lightning. A cross of Christ and Chinigchinich.

Father Larry Gosselin reads from the Gospel of Luke, the Magnificat, Mary saying, "My soul magnifies the Lord." "Some governments," he says, "banned the prayer as too powerful. Maybe it was the beginning of a new era—yesterday. Maybe we are bright to the beginning of new circumstances. The people who built this church, the Chumash, had great wisdom, they revered the changing of the seasons. Not the images themselves, but we are illuminated by the light of Christ. Truly this brings

361

us to a new day. Even in our calendar we are turning after a loss of light toward the light. Easter is the people who look east."

The sunlight pouring through the door is now dropping from the high altar to the tabernacle as the sun rises. Sun has completely filled the baptismal font so that the water is light and light is the water.

8:04 A.M. The light now is directly striking the tabernacle. Two Chumash women begin drumming on the altar, a quick, haunting beat. Not loud, but strong. Tina Fosse, curator of the museum at Santa Barbara Mission, is hitting two sticks in rhythm in the front pew as the gifts are brought up for consecration. What is the Chumash Indian singer singing now? I helped her up the knoll outside the mission when it was dark. She grasped my two fingers with two of hers and I had strength I did not know. And now she is drumming.

The drumming stops at the lifting of the chalice at the Offertory. Father Larry is blessing the wine and bread with a large eagle's wing. Now he is circling the altar with incense and moving it with the wing toward the drummers, and then us in the pews, and then the water and wine and bread that will become God. Ernestine de Soto reads the "Our Father" in Chumash. We hold hands across the aisles, a human lattice.

All during Communion, the drummers drum like humming bees.

And later, when the Mass is over, when the trembling light is off Mary's face and the altar, I dip my hands into the giant water basin of the baptismal font and see reflected there the cross, the spiked cross of the Chumash twined in lightning on the ceiling, now in the water. I bless myself, go out on the stones.

The sun is complete now, the ladder Serra climbed to Santa Cruz, and I know this is what he wanted—the people risen together like the sun, the island drawn into the mainland, the ladder put away in our hearts.

AFTERWORD

Remember that when you leave this earth,
you can take with you nothing that you have received—
only what you have given.
—ST. FRANCIS OF ASSISI

Author's three sons
at Mission Santa Barbara, *ca*. 1995.

$\mathcal{T}$he origin for this book goes far back in my childhood, when I was
four or so, peering into the murky water of Mission San Juan Capistrano's fountain, watching the garibaldi move like a submerged sun under
the lily pads. We were living in downtown Los Angeles then, with my
paternal grandparents, but we had met my Anaheim-dwelling favorites,

Aunt Bette and Uncle Jerry Unrein—who hailed from Hays, Kansas—at the fountain. I have a vague recollection that it was March 19, St. Joseph's feast day, my father's feast day, as Joseph was his middle name, his first name, Aref, being distinctly Arab, connected to no Christian feast but with meaning of its own—*A'arif*, the knowing one.

Memory for Californians implies the missions. They are part of our early emotional geography. I recall a bird lighting near me on the fountain, Uncle Jerry pouring some seed into my palm, the bird climbing onto my forearm, probably thinking it a branch. It was a little creepy, his prickled feet slowly moving toward the seed, and then the sharp bill as it pecked and ate. Such pain and pleasure had to have a name, and when I heard the story of the swallows coming back to Capistrano on St. Joseph's Day, I believed for many years I had been visited by a swallow.

It was a common pigeon.

You can't write this story without being captured long ago. The story begins in glowing myth and somewhere along the line, perhaps when you lose an early love, you begin looking at the seams of the myth for a tear.

When I was twenty-two, unsure of what to do with my life, having spent four years at college in the East, I returned to my hometown of Los Angeles and met a Mexican girl from La Paz in Baja who was studying to be a nurse at Santa Monica City College. Her name was Fabiola López Ponce. She was quite a beauty and had barely survived a car wreck in which most of her family died. We took a trip together along that sacramental California road that roughly follows the old El Camino Real on Highway 101 and Route 1, and we visited several missions. Fabiola prayed in every one of them; and what did I do? I saw her calves bathed in light coming through stained glass windows. At Buenaventura, she was the real thing; I was, alas, a facsimile, too young and American rosy to understand what Fabiola understood too well: life was short, rough, and meant to take you.

Going east from the West Coast for college was rare in those days—I think our class at Crespí Carmelite High School was the first to have students venture east of the Mississippi. But once there, it was a recurrent notion that I hailed from a part of the country that was not substantial, that was somehow wild or unstable, or worse, frivolous. As crazy as this sounds, I had a running argument with a Brooklyn uncle of mine about the relative merits of apples versus oranges. Much of this was good-natured East Coast–West Coast rivalry (the hardihood of snow versus the lassitude of sun; the convenience of the subways versus the chaos of the freeways; the Yankees versus the Dodgers; the historic New York World's Fair versus the antihistorical Disneyland). I had my own way of bending these arguments (the imperious East versus the egalitarian West; eastern groupthink versus western rugged individualism; the team that money bought versus the team that birthed Jackie Robinson). Times change; now it's the Dodgers who seem the team that money bought. But underneath all these essentially innocent arguments was something deeper and more serious: a sense that the West, and the Far West especially, came from a culture that was not quite up to ruling substance, that was polluted by Hispanics and Asians, a culture that was not quite American. This underlying racism, if not sense of pure evil, in the East–West debate can be seen very early on in our history. The Puritan poet Michael Wigglesworth thought the western stretch of the continent was filled with only "waste and howling wilderness." In his otherwise fascinating memoir, *Two Years Before the Mast*, Richard Henry Dana declares, "Californians are an idle, thriftless people and can make nothing for themselves." Too, Dana claimed, "Grapes are a drug here." So we were lazy and debauched. But in 1840, who was the we? Well, it had to be Mexicans and Indians. There was hardly anyone else there.

It is true that the suburb mania (whose emergence is blamed for some reason on California) of the postwar 1950s plowed under a lot of our history. And it is also true that many of those who came to California for a better life, by the wooing of the railroad robber barons and Charles Lummis, the push of the winds of the Dust Bowl (my Uncle Jerry's family were Dust Bowl Kansans), or post–World War II traumatized vets such as my own father, were antihistorical, doing everything they could to escape the past. Still, those of us born Californian are obsessed with the history denied us (note Joan Didion) and will dig, scrape, and claw to find out what our life born in such sun near gorgeous water we cannot drink means.

The Spanish Franciscan missions play into this. We know, because their battered clay and melting adobe tell us so, that there is a whole other profound layer to American life that has been kept from us, one that begins before the Liberty Bell. One might call it the Bell of Beautiful Suffering, the toll of the mission bell that tells of the cost of liberty, colonialism, and the sacrificial love of the other.

Perhaps coming from a family that traces its roots to the earliest sites of Christendom in the Levant imbued this child of immigrants to California with more than the normal burden of history, and hankering for it. The minaret-like steeples of the missions clanged in me an old, haunting music. It took me a while, but over time I began to think, history-weighed as I was, I was not an entirely hopeless searcher for the life of Junípero Serra. When I began to uncover that he was likely to have had Jewish *and* Arab blood, well, this was not only a man for all seasons, he was a man for mine.

We took our boys through the missions on vacations west. I have a great picture of the three of them sulking with burned faces in front of a giant cactus at Mission San Miguel, another of them half asleep, chins in hands, on the cascading steps at Mission Santa Barbara, my wife trying her best to give the scene a smile while the Santa Inez range loomed behind. Yet something must have taken: one of them makes his living working in Hollywood as a film editor, another as manager of a popular restaurant in Santa Barbara. The third comes back and forth with me, California perhaps his favorite place on earth. Will I be a poor Moses, always shy of the Promised Land?

Somewhere deep in the deadness of a government job in Washington, I began to question people about Junípero Serra. Virtually no one had heard of him. This was true of just about anyone I spoke to east of the Rocky Mountains. Some thought I might be referring to a borderlands bandit or the bibical Sarah. Did Serra fight with Pancho Villa? Was he an actor from the 1930s?

Serra left home to go home; could I do the same? Ultimately, the search for Junípero Serra's real life became a search for final things, for home.

About twelve years ago, sometime either before or just after September 11, 2001, I began to outline this book. For some years, I informally researched *Journey to the Sun*, reading the literature surrounding the Spaniards' entry into New Spain and California in particular. I was surprised, at first, at how little there was of any authority on Serra himself, and how sentimental, romantic, essentially self-marginalizing such books were. But one by one I followed the stepping-stones back to Francisco Palou, Serra's not-quite-celebrated friend, and then forward to Maynard Geiger, the man who would make him a saint with a book so large and rare few had read it. Most amazing to me was the fact that there had not been a major biography of Junípero Serra in half a century, and whatever Geiger's brilliance and devotion, *The Life and Times* had been long out of print.

Still, at first editors in New York saw it as a regional story. But this is a way of dismissing California—and all the jealosies that surround it—placing it outside the founding of our country, with a laggard history full of plausible deniability. But why couldn't California's history present another paradigm? The Golden State was already the ninth largest economy *on its own* in the world. For all its problems—and they were not few (the fires, the reliance on aqueduct water coming from hundreds of miles away, a broken education system, a failure to integrate completely the Mexican who keeps the economy rolling), California was producing history. You can't continue producing what you don't originally have.

My agent, a dear man from Bakersfield who loved Serra and understood implicitly what I was after, did not give up. And one day he turned up the best editor at the best publisher. When I asked Colin Harrison why he had chosen the book, he said, "Because I am interested in alternate foundation stories for this country." Colin was raised a Quaker. For this Catholic, it was better than the Liberty Bell, an earthen music of multiple iron, a music meant to be, and perhaps *for being*.

The original Spanish conquest of the West stands in contrast to the founding story of the East—that of the Anglo Puritan and Protestant—upon which a two-hundred-year civilization has rested. That prevalent story looked upon material wealth as a sign of faith and down on the body in favor of the mind. In religious matters it elevated pure spirit over the sullied and often artistic flesh. But the foundation story of the West—that is, Spanish Catholic—is distinctly antimaterialistic, unabashedly colorful and sensual, mystical in its approach to the natural world, and more complicated by and interlaced (by virtue of its blood ties) with aboriginal peoples.

All of this began to emerge from the complex life of Junípero Serra. The chief challenge was to scrape away the shellac of complete reverence, or, on the other hand, the pitch. It doesn't take long to realize that Serra has been used as a symbol of all that is good or bad with the Catholic Church. With the exception of Geiger, most treatments are either honorific or pejorative; there is no middle, no real man. He is either a priest to elevate or one to revile.

Above all, I wanted to present Miguel Junípero Serra as a man, a person with flaws, some great ones, but with great gifts, too. Stripping off the paint, I wanted to make him come alive. The reader will find I have taken some liberties in reconstructing Serra's thoughts and feelings. These are clearly indicated as such—for example, by the spare use of italics or exploratory suppositions grounded entirely in the real.

Research was arduous: trips to Spain twice, Mexico twice, up and down California countless times, the Southwest, archives in the East, too. It involved broken bones, stolen wallets, fear of drug lords. It was almost as if Serra would say to any would-be biographer: *If you want to know me, you have to lose a lot, not the least your strength.*

The deeper I went, the deeper the contradictions: here was a proud Mallorcan who left Mallorca forever; a celibate priest who loved women, and carried the book of a woman alongside his Bible; a man who preached peace yet used the lash; a man sworn to obedience who clashed with authority; a man filled with rectitude who chose mercy in the toughest moments; a writer who hated writing; a teacher who eschewed all knowledge but that which leads to God.

Serra was complicated, and I delighted in the complication. But he was also unnerving, elusive, something of a mystery. I propped a sign on my desk, the one part of the Mass not a complete sentence, but utterly central: *The Mystery of Faith*. For some time, that was an alternate title to the book, at least in my head.

If, as Aquinas tells us, *Bonum diffisuvium*, "Goodness spreads," how do you help spread it, especially when others have their own concept of what is good and bad? Questions pummeled me throughout my Serra journey, and I hoped they would the reader: What does goodness cost? How do we devote ourselves without destroying? Can the Gospel of Love turn to the practice of degradation? Can a Crucified Man heal? What would you give your life for? How can we leave those we love, and they us, to be taken to love others? How does one love the Unknown?

My faith grew as part of this journey. But there was disillusion too, as there is for all these realms under heaven. For all its beauty, California became a place of exile for Serra. And there were acts and policies of his and the missions that could simply not be seen as anything but wrong. He was, in short, a man. *Ecce homo*. A man whom the world drew from initial beauty to great pain, doubt, trial. And back to beauty. And the Lord.

Can unflinching history become in itself devotion?

At one point, the manuscript was 1,300 pages. My editor and agent were shocked and pulled out the carving knives.

Paradise, always elusive, has a brief shelf life here. It is always being lost, always being sought.

Isn't this what we all want? Whether our beginnings are cruel or wonderful, that we end in love? That we at least apprehend an approach? Serra was born in paradise, lost it, and sought it again. It cost him everything.

I finished the book exhausted. Paradise gained, paradise lost, paradise flickering on the Channel.

SOURCES AND ACKNOWLEDGMENTS

Serra's 1737 notebook for his last seminary class, "On Angels,"
with singular funnel script, signed "faithfully writing."

*U*nearthing the reality of Serra's life is a challenge to the biographer in two directions: on the one hand, up to his entry into Alta California there is precious little primary material to go on. For the first thirty-six years of his life—that is, his life in Spain—we have a grand total of one letter (the good-bye letter to his parents sent from Cádiz in 1749). For the next eighteen years—his life in Mexico (or New Spain)—we have five letters. That means for the period up to when he was fifty-four, when he entered San Diego Harbor—with two-thirds of his life over—until now only six letters (of 270 in the four volumes edited by Antonine Tibesar) have been available to try to construct a pre-California life for Junípero Serra.

Most biographers simply dismiss it. The author of the lodestone

Relación Historica de la Vida, Serra's first biographer, friend, and former student on Mallorca, Father Francisco Palou, devoted a mere three paragraphs to his boyhood prior to entering seminary. For Serra's life prior to 1749 and the decision to leave for New Spain, Palou gives us only three pages—thus four pages for thirty-six years. Abigail Fitch, who wrote the first Serra biography in English (in 1914) managed six pages for this crucial Old World life—half of the Franciscan founder of California's life, after all.

I was especially concerned to look closely at Serra's young years, which, as we know, set the blueprint for the person who walks out into the world. I was also determined to somehow defray the paucity of information on Serra's early life and managed, to my surprise and that of my spirited archivists, to discover two letters no one had previously seen, both from the Sierra Gorda period in Mexico. One was lost in a "Miscellaneous file" in the Riggs Family collection at the Georgetown University Lauinger Library (in care of intrepid archivist Scott Taylor), and the other I found at the bottom of a Sierra Gorda mountain gorge in the tiny village of San Pedro Escanela.

Another major find occurred in Oaxaca, where, after a week of frustrations walking to and from five archives and coming up empty, archivist Berenice Ibarra at the Archivo de Archdiocese de Oaxaca put an old spindle of microfilm on the one tired machine that stood by the dusty door to the entrance, which revealed eleven dead in Oaxaca in 1764, and by process of elimination, led me to the stunning triangle of Serra–María Contreras–Don Mathías Cortabarría.

There are reasons for the dearth of information on Serra's pre-California life: the closing of his university in Palma in 1835 (when we may have lost his many lectures and sermons); the fact that he never returned from California to secure his records; the downgrading of Franciscan mission work in New Spain when the missions were secularized and dismantled; the closing of the College of San Fernando in Mexico City around 1860; the general anticlericalism in Mexico after independence from Spain; poor record keeping on the remote island of Mallorca, exacerbated by the attacks by Franco on Catalonia in the 1930s and his ongoing campaign to obliterate Catalán culture, society, and even language; the difficulty Catalán and Mallorquín Spanish presented to scholars and archivists; the remoteness of Serra's work in Mexican mountains and southern hinterlands; and of course the sheer passage of time over three centuries.

The two pillars of Serra research remain Francisco Palou and Maynard Geiger—Franciscans separated by two centuries. Palou returned to Mexico City within a year of Serra's death in 1784, with the manuscript already in hand, the one eyewitness report we have in book form of Serra's life—the essential *Relación Historica de la Vida y Apostolicas Tareas del Venerable Padre Fray Junípero Serra* (*Historical Account of the Life and Apostolic Labors of the Venerable Father Junípero Serra*). Written in one feverish, grief- and fervor-filled year, it was published in 1787 by the Mexico City publisher Don Felipe de Zuñiga y Ontiveros. It has its exaggerations. When Palou finds the Indians "are groaning" for conversion and release from "the tyrannous slavery of the enemy of their souls" (p. 192), we must groan; not Serra, with all his "evil" awareness, and certainly not Fermín Lasuén, were this blind. Still, a writer of a biography of Serra simply cannot avoid Palou, nor would want to.

The other pillar is Geiger. His extraordinary two-volume, nearly one-thousand-page biography, *The Life and Times of Fray Junípero Serra, O.F.M., or The Man Who Never Turned Back, 1713–1784* (1959), remains in a class by itself, an achievement against which everything else must be compared. Geiger's bibliography alone is eighty pages, a treasure trove for those of us who followed. For about fifteen years, Geiger retraced Serra's steps in Spain, Mexico, Puerto Rico, Baja and Alta California. Being chief archivist and historian at the Santa Barbara Mission Archives and Library greatly informed his work; his tone is dispassionate, scholarly, and he does not sentimentalize his subject. He famously corrected Palou, who inflated Serra's walking mileage tenfold, noting that about Serra's burning himself in the pulpit, Palou "is really supposing." But Geiger himself is not perfect; he can get badly out of sequence and sidetracked (the tour of Mexico City, though interesting, is twelve pages, and the excruciatingly inbred detail on the confirmation controversy is thirty pages).

A third pillar is Antonine Tibesar's four-volume bilingual collection of Serra's letters, *Writings of Junípero Serra*, published by the same Franciscan press as Geiger's work, between 1955 and 1966. Some have taken issue with Tibesar's translations as too loose; sometimes they are, but sometimes they are also too literal (and Geiger more daring). For the great Serra good-bye letter to his parents, I relied heavily on Geiger's version, though some of Tibesar is in there, too. (I have indicated in the endnotes where I have relied on Geiger's or Tibesar's version of the letters, or, for that matter, Geiger's 1955 or Scott Williams's 1913 translation of Palou's *Relación,* indicated by MG or SW. At times, I also have ventured my own translations.) The Serra letters are invaluable and rich; I make the claim of being one of the few alive who has read every one of them—900 pages.

In the wake of the early Serra sainthood tribunals, other biographies appeared in the 1950s, such as the inflated, almost unreadable Omer Englebert's *The Last of the Conquistadors* (1956), blasted by Eric O'Brien, and

Theodore Maynard's *The Long Road of Father Serra* (1954), which, though also marred by racial attitudes (Englebert speaks of "Redskins") and written in under a year, has some interesting insights into Serra's thinking. A flawed but spirited American bicentennial (1976) walk-through of the missions is Kenneth King's *Mission to Paradise*. After half a century of silence on the subject, in the tricentennial of Serra's birth (2013) other works appeared, such as Tomàs Vibot's *El Viaje de Junípero Serra (de Mallorca a Calfornia)* (in Catalán Spanish); Andrés Garrido del Toral's *Los Caminos de Fray Junípero Serra en Querétaro* (in Querétaro, Mexico); and Steven Hackel's *Junípero Serra: California's Founding Father*, which appeared just before my own book went to press. Our Serras, though similar at times, are essentially different, and our approaches are vastly different.

Of the many coffee-table versions of Serra's life entwined with the missions, the best by far is *Junípero Serra: A Pictorial Biography* (1991) by Martin Morgado. *The California Missions*, by Edna Kimbro and Julia Costello, with Tevya Ball, published by the Getty Museum in 2009, is simply beautiful *and* informative.

Among several Spanish historians who have shed light on Father Serra are the Franciscans Lino Gómez Canedo (on the Sierra Gorda period) and José Luis Soto Pérez (on Baja and Palou). An early Spanish biographer who discovered the Serra sermons to the Claretian nuns was Francisco Torrens y Nicholau, *Bosquero histórico del insigne franciscano v.p.f. Junípero Serra* (1913), or *Historical Sketch of the Famous v.p.f. Junípero Serra*. An excellent bilingual treatment, *The Missions of the Sierra Gorda*, edited by Francisco Gaiton and Jaime Lajous, appeared in 1985. A recent (2010) sweeping review of Serra's work in California is *Orígenes Hispanicos de California* by Jaume Sobrequés i Callicó. The chief Spanish authority on Serra, however, has been Bartolomé Font Obrador, a fellow Mallorcan. Obrador's drawing on contemporaneous sources, such as the diary of Nicolás Ferrer, for the troubled island of Mallorca in the eighteenth century in his *El apóstol de California, sus albores* (1989) or *The Apostle of California: His Youth*, was extremely useful. I had to rework some of the awkward, if not outright poor, translations in this bilingual edition, however, especially of the Claretian sermons. Llorenc Gari Jaume's recent *Iglesia y Claustro de San Francisco: Memoria del Beato Fray Junípero Serra* (1990) gives a close look at Serra's life in Palma.

One of the great challenges of writing Serra's life is that the controversies surrounding it span three centuries across three continents in at least five disciplines: history; anthropology; theology-philosophy; geography and the environment; and literature and the arts. The following list is only a short selection of the massive literature in these fields that cross-hatch the subject of Serra and the missions. It isn't even inclusive of the works that mattered to me, but simply those that have been most useful.

One of the more entertaining, and instructive, face-offs occurred early in the twentieth century between the first titan of California history, Herbert Bancroft (who gave his name to the great library at the University of California at Berkeley) and a feisty early exponent of the missions, the Franciscan Zephryin Engelhardt. Written in the 1920s and 1930s, Engelhardt's sixteen separate volumes on individual missions are detailed, at times marred by racialist attitudes, but often revelatory, though his vision is heavily skewed toward the Franciscans.

Among authors of general histories of California that shed light on this subject, there is no finer successor to Bancroft than Kevin Starr; his *California: A History* (2005) and *Inventing the Dream: California Through the Progressive Era* (1985) helped me interpret the secularization period. *Major Problems in California History* (1997), edited by Sucheng Chan and Spencer Olin, sheds light on differences and similarities between Indian and Hispanic families (Albert Hurtado) as well as various takes on the question of whippings and other violence in and around the missions (by Jayme, Serra, Malaspina, Lorenzo Asisara, Guest, and Antonio Casteñeda). Other useful texts on the nineteenth century are *California Conquered: The Annexation of a Mexican Province, 1846–1850* (1982) by Neil Harlow, and *Competing Visions: A History of California* (2005) by Robert Cerny, Gretchen Lemke-Santangelo, and Richard Griswold del Castillo.

The controversy over Serra's treatment of the Indians could separate brother from brother, as it did the two Hittell historians, Theodore and John. The former's four-volume *History of California* (1885) took the honorific road, the latter's *History of San Francisco and Incidentally the State of California* (1878) the pejorative. Responding to the groundswell of interest in Serra during the sainthood considerations begun in the late 1940s and into the 1950s (and culminated in Geiger's work), historians began to register serious doubts about Spanish treatment of the California Indian in general, and Serra's in particular. Key among these is the work by Sherbourne Cook on the destruction wrought by germs in *The Conflict Between the California Indian and White Civilization* (1976). Among these "Christophobic" historians (as James Sandos calls them, versus their opposite—those who are "Christophilic") are *Nation* editor Carey McWilliams, who first lodged the "genocide" canard in his otherwise excellent *Southern California: An Island on the Land* (1946); Florence Shipek's *Pushed Into the Rocks: Southern California Land Tenure, 1769–1986* (1987); Robert Jackson and Edward Castillo's *Indians, Franciscans, and Spanish Civilization: The Impact of the Mission System on*

California Indians (1995); and perhaps most strident of all, Rupert and Jeannette Costo's *The Missions of California: A Legacy of Genocide* (1987). Dan Fogel also used Serra to level a broadside attack on church attitudes toward homesexuality, Third World revolutions, and women in his *Junípero Serra, the Vatican, and Enslavement Theology* (1988). To Fogel, Serra was a "serene fanatic" and Christ himself "resigned" to be a martyr.

One of the fairest of these critics of the missions is George Harwood Phillips. I gained much from his detailed study of Spanish-Indian economic interactions, *Vineyards and Vaqueros: Indian Labor and the Economic Expansion of Southern California, 1771–1877* (2010).

Perhaps of most value was the work of three synthesizing and innovative historians of the missions: James Sandos (*Converting California*, 2004); Francis Guest (*Hispanic California Revisited*, 1996); and Douglas Monroy (*The Borders Within: Encounters Between Mexico and the U.S.*, 2008).

I must acknowledge, too, my indebtedness to the tireless work of the Spanish linguist Rose Marie Beebe and her husband, former priest and Santa Clara University historian Robert Senkewicz. Most valuable for my purposes are their translations into English of important documents in *Lands of Promise and Despair: Chronicles of Early California, 1535–1846* (2001); *Testimonios: Early California Through the Eyes of Women, 1815–1848* (2006); and *"To Toil in That Vineyard of the Lord": Contemporary Scholarship on Junípero Serra* (2010). Indeed, Beebe and Senkewicz are the chief historiographers of this subject.

I have taken much from the progenitor of the entire field of anthropology, Alfred Kroeber, whose salient writings appear in *The California Indians: A Source Book* (1971), edited by R. F. Heizer and M. A. Whipple. For the northern tribes, nothing matches Randall Milliken's *A Time of Little Choice: The Disintegration of Tribal Culture in the San Francisco Bay Area, 1769–1810* (1995/2009). I also gained immeasurably from a spirited correspondence with Milliken and a long interview. For the central coast, Dr. John Johnson of the Santa Barbara Museum of Natural History has been a dear friend (and reader of this manuscript); he is always fair-minded and deeply informed. Finally, for the southern coast, Richard Carrico's *Strangers in a Stolen Land: Indians of San Diego County from Prehistory to the New Deal* (2008) is compelling. For an overview of Indian life in North America that helped me construct the "New World Others" chapter, Jake Page's *In the Hands of the Great Spirit: The 20,000-Year History of American Indians* (2003) was critical.

To sample early Franciscan takes on their charges, the Indians, a good place to start is Maynard Geiger and Clement W. Meighan's *As the Padres*

Saw Them: California Indian Life and Customs as Reported by the Franciscan Missionaries, 1813–1815 (1976). Gerónimo Boscana's *Chinigchinich* (1846/1978), despite its biases, is revealing, as are the writings of Pablo Tac, the first California Indian seminarian. For an overview of Spanish attitudes toward the Indian population of the New World, *Bárbaros: Spaniards and Their Savages in the Age of Enlightenment* (2005) by David Weber is brilliant, a word that also applies to *Brown: The Last Discovery of America* (2002) by Richard Rodríguez.

In addition to the Cahuilla-Luiseño historian Edward Castillo, the Kumeyaay anthropologist Florence Shipek, and the early seminal work of Jack Forbes, the close treatment *Kumeyaay: A History Text Book* (2007), by Kumeyaay scholar Michael Connolly Miskwish, is valuable.

Among the many books that informed my evocation of Spain and Mexico in the eighteenth and nineteenth centuries, the most helpful (for Spain) were *Daily Life of Spain in the Golden Age* by the French traveler and historian Marcelin Defourneaux, and the incomparable *The Buried Mirror: Reflections on Spain and the New World*, by Carlos Fuentes. Henry Kamen's work on the Spanish Inquisition is seminal, along with the more recent work on the subject by Joseph Pérez. For the phenomenon of Andalusia, I learned a lot from and fully enjoyed *The Ornament of the World: How Muslims, Jews, and Christians Created a Culture of Tolerance in Medieval Spain* (2002) by María Rosa Menocal. As for Mexico, the classic remains Octavio Paz's *The Labyrinth of Solitude* (1961). The well-known works of Hugh Thomas on Cortés and the Spanish Conquest were important, as was the fascinating study by Maurice Collis, *Cortéz and Montezuma* (1954/1999).

Of great use in framing the "New World Others" chapter were David Hackett Fischer's *Champlain's Dream: The European Founding of North America* (2008), Henry Warner Bowden's *American Indians and Christian Missions: Studies in Cultural Conflict* (1981), *Missions, Missionaries, and Native Americans: Long-Term Processes and Daily Practices* by Maria Wade (2008), Colin Calloway's *New Worlds for All: Indians, Europeans, and the Remaking of Early America* (1997), and the revelatory *Encounters of the Spirit: Native Americans and European Colonial Religion* by Richard W. Pointer.

Sister Mary Beth Ingham of Loyola-Marymount University provided me with a good interview that helped me penetrate Serra's chief philosophical influence, Duns Scotus; her *Scotus for Dunces: An Introduction to the Subtle Doctor* (2003) is the standard in the field. In addition to the timeless *Fioretti*, G. K. Chesterton and Valerie Martin opened up St. Francis to me. I usually rely on a few books at my bedstand throughout a book's writing; one of these was *The Mystical City of God* (1686) by María de Agreda. I cannot claim to understand it, but I have tried and will continue to. A fine tool in this effort was Clark Colahan's *The Visions of Sor María de Agreda: Writing, Knowledge, and Power* (1994). (The other trusty companions on the nightstand, besides the Bible, were *Don Quixote* and Lauren Hillenbrand's *Unbroken*.) I found something of a key to Serra's vision of the missions as a "ladder" to God—inexorably "mixed" in metaphor with the cross—in St. Bonaventure's mystical work, *The Journey of the Mind to God*, originally written in 1259. This led me to a wonderful work on the medieval philosopher, *Crucified Love: Bonaventure's Mysticism of the Crucified Christ* (1998) by Ilia Delio. (I recommend the blessed ladder-on-the-water of the Santa Barbara Channel to all who pass there.)

The works of Hans Kung, Teilhard de Chardin, Denis de Rougemont, Reynolds Price, and Garry Wills helped reinforce my faith during difficult times; I still draw on the lectures on mysticism I was lucky enough to hear by Dr. Louis Dupre at Georgetown University (later of Yale University). I took every class I could get from him (three). Diarmaid MacCullough's massive *Christianity* was a bulwark.

Many of the early diarists and memoirists were explorers who were mapping California and the New World. Chief among these was Juan Crespí, Serra's long-standing companion in Carmel, whose diaries are meticulously rendered in the lifelong project of editor and translator Alan K. Brown, *A Description of Distant Roads: Original Journals of the First Expedition into California, 1769–1770* (2001), with its mind-boggling 146-page introduction. Serra's own invaluable diary of the 1769 expedition up through Baja is in Tibesar's first volume of letters. The diaries, journals, and memoirs of Pedro Font, Pedro Fages, Gaspar de Portolá, Juan Bautista de Anza, Fernando Rivera y Moncada, Alejandro Malaspina, Hugo Reid, Otto von Kotzebue, Miguel Costanso, George Vancouver, Rafael González, Vincente Santa María, and Alfred Robinson, among others, have been crucial to this study. One of the great sea journeys ever recorded as a memoir, *Two Years Before the Mast and Other Voyages* (1869/2005), by Richard Henry Dana, treats a great deal more than two years in Mexican and early American California. Also, a fascinating travelogue of Mallorcan towns and topography is in Dina Moore Bowden's *Junípero Serra in His Native Isle (1713–1749)* (1976).

The letters of Serra's Franciscan confreres, as well as Spanish officials of the time, such as Neve and Gálvez, are scattered in several archives, though many are captured at the Santa Barbara Mission Archive and Library. Most important is the two-volume set edited by Finbar Kenneally, *Writings of*

Fermín Francisco de Lasuén (1965), supplemented by *Fermín Francisco de Lasuén: A Biography* (1973) by Francis Guest. I was pleased to have had translated for the first time several letters of Gálvez, Neve, Grimaldi, Croix, Barri, Rafael Verger, Luis Jayme, and Palou himself.

The Serra story, or some aspect of it, has entered into literature in many ways. I've made use of the appearance (and distortion) of Serra's encounter with the Holy Family in the Huasteca in Willa Cather's *Death Comes for the Archbishop,* as well as Helen Hunt Jackson's evocative if sentimental portrayals of Serra in the violent secularization period in *Ramona* (1884). But other figures come into play in novels as diverse as *Zorro* (2006) by Isabel Allende (who draws on Fages for a character) and William Gaddis's *The Recognitions* (1955), which has a gloss on Raymond Lull. Serra appears in many poems throughout the past three centuries, most of them bad; however, I would recommend to any reader the American poet Paul Willis's "On the 225th Year of Mission Santa Barbara." There are plays (*Father Junípero Serra: A New and Original Historical Drama in Four Acts* by Chester Gore Miller); symphonies (*Symphony No. 2 in E Minor* by Meredith Wilson); and many works of art and statuary that represent Serra. My friend Craig Russell's extraordinary *From Serra to Sancho: Music and Pageantry in the California Missions* (2009) is the result of original scholarship and is an illumination. In addition to the Getty survey of all twenty-one missions, *Art from the Carmel Mission* (2011), by Gail Sheridan and Mary Pat McCormick, is beautifully rendered and expertly written.

I relied on two major anthologies for the literature of California Indians: *Surviving Through the Days: Translations of Native California Stories and Songs* (2002), edited by Herbert Luthin; and *The Literature of California: Writings from the Golden State* (2000), edited by Jack Hicks, James Houston, Maxine Hong Kingston, and Al Young. Among other valuable books in this vein were *Mulu'Wetam: The First People* (1973), edited by Jane Hill and Rosinda Nolasquez, and *First Families: A Photographic History of California Indians* (2007), edited by L. Frank and Kim Hogeland. Many thanks, too, to Lisa Woodward, anthropologist and student of the Juaneño and Luiseño peoples, and the work of John Harrington, for guidance throughout.

This turns me from actual books (and I mean *actual*; anyone who knows me knows what books have done to my back) to individuals. This is the moment most authors wait for. As Serra said we must say, *Deo gratias.* My thanks to people who helped me in everything from lodging to knowledgeable tours to the manuscript research and photo hunt will be missing some. To do this by place:

In Spain, on Mallorca, a special thanks to Mateu Ferrer, a seminarian living on the very corridors that a young Serra did at the Convento de San Francisco in the old city of Palma. Also thanks to dear Llorenc Vich Sancho, Joan Vives, Mosen Gili y Ferrer, Isabel Salom Galmes, Catalina Font, Juan Marti Gandia, Fausto Roldan, Salvador Cabot Rossello, Bartomeo Bestard, Toni Amoros, and María Castillo Adrover.

In Barcelona, Father Augusti Boadas Llavat, director of the Franciscan archives, granted me a useful interview and also took me up the street to Arxiver Provincial; and Fra Valenti Serra de Manresa kindly opened up the treasures of the Caputxins de Catalunya. When my stupid chase of a pickpocket in the Barcelona subway ended in a fall that left me with "the terrible triad" (an elbow with two broken bones, dislocation, and rupture of a tendon), Dr. Oscar Ares and Dr. Raquel García of the Barnaclinic of the University of Barcelona reassembled the elbow after three hours of surgery. *Muchas gracias por todo, también, a los ángeles de Gregory!*

In Mexico, Querétaro is the place to start. I wish to heartily thank Araceli Ardon Martínez, accomplished Mexican short story writer and my colleague at Westmont College, where she taught Spanish; her knowledge of Querétaro history is unparalleled. Araceli and her dear husband, Eduardo Zárate, shepherded me everywhere, including the ancestral home of José Escandón. Thanks, also, to Professor José Andrés Landaverde Rivera, Francisco Javier Félix Hernández, José Martín Hurtado Gálvez, María Louis Sagoz, Antonio Arelle, and Pepe Homs.

In Celaya, Ana María Ruiz Marun, Pedro Gil Munoz, Father Eulalia Gomez, and Freida Elizidar.

In Zacatecas, Violeta Tavizon Mondragon at the Museo de Guadalupe.

In San Miguel de Allende, many thanks to my cousin Marlene Orfalea Johansing; Susan Page, director of the San Miguel Writers Sala and Conference; dear Fran Mahoney; and David Rico Olalde.

In Jalpan and the Sierra Gordas: Osiris Olvera of Adventurate Sierra Gorda and her husband, Marcelo Trejos, whose work as my driver and companion on the hike to the Cascada de Echuve finally led to the exceptional find of sixteen undiscovered items, including letters of Serra and Palou, in the village of San Pedro Escanela; Arnoldo Montés Rodríguez, Teo Vázquez Alvarado, Rafael Sanchez, and Aquileo Hernandez.

In Mexico City, Fernando Amezcua, Clara Bargellini, Teresita Hernandez, and Jorge Juarez Paredes, Instituto Nacional de Antropología de Histórica (INAH).

In Oaxaca, for the discovery of the tragic triangle of Serra-Contreras-Cortabarría, it all begins and ends with Berenice Ibarra, archivist at the

Archidiocesis de Oaxaca-Antequera (her director is Francisco Reyes Ochoa) and the extraordinary Penelope Orozco Sánchez and her assistant, "Coco" (Burgoa Library); also the president of the Burgoa Library, María Isabel Granen Porrúa; Manuel Esparza (INAH); Jesús Mendoza, Gloria Ima Méndez, and Nora Olivia Sedeño Torres (Archivo Histórico Municipal); Israel Garrido Esquivel, chief (Archivo General del H. Tribunal Superior de Justica del Estado); Carlo Magno Ochoa Arellano, director (Archivo General del Poder Ejecutivo del Estado); Francisco José Ruiz, or "Paco Pepe" (Instituto de Humanidades, as well as director of the Burgoa Library); Elizabeth Polak (Welte Institute); and Leticia Martínez Rosas (Universidad Autónoma Benito Juárez de Oaxaca). Mariana Arroyo and her family at Casa Bugambilias were my family in Oaxaca, along with art historian Richard Perry.

In California, at Mission Santa Barbara, thanks to: Monica Orozco, Kristina Foss, and Sister Susan Blomstad. Fathers Kenan Osborne, John Vaughn, Larry Gosselin, and Charles Talley afforded me insightful interviews and discussion. Father Richard McManus granted me a monthlong stay at the mission to carefully comb the vast Serra holdings. Thanks to my supportive colleagues at Westmont College, especially Randy VanderMey, our provost Mark Sargent, Rick Pointer, Telford Work, the remarkable Richard Burnweit, Ruth Angelos, and Debra Quast. Heather Keaney and Jim Wright gave generously of their home—wonderful friends. Our chaplain, Ben Patterson, dug out several scriptural references with no complaint and neat insight. English colleagues Steve Cook, Paul Delaney, Cheri Larsen Hoeckley, and Randy bravely donated their offices for four semesters, as did my old friend and colleague from Claremont days, Kathryn Stelmach Artuso. Others among my English and Spanish language colleagues provided friendship and encouragement, including Paul Willis, Jamie Friedman, Sarah Skripsky and her fine parents, Mike and Carolyn Yoder, Mary Docter, Leonor Elias, and Dinora Cardoso. How often the book gained a note from the sound of the Westmont choir, practicing right down the road with Michael Shasberger. My Westmont students pitched in with enthusiasm: Elise Kimball, Karly Dowling, Keaton Hudson, Lidiya Markova, Frances Rozkho, Lauren Henslin, Emily Keach, and dear Kylie Miller. Also in Santa Barbara, thanks to Michael Imwalle, Anne Petersen, Scott Love, Father Mario Prietto at Our Lady of Sorrows Church, Brenda Murrow, Ernestine de Soto, and the good crew at Casa de Maria, including Teresa Fanucchi, Catherine Collis, Taran Collis, and Joanne Conners.

At Mission San Juan Capistrano: Lee Goode, Don Tryon, Father William Kreckleberg, and Monsignor Arthur Holquin.

At Mission San Carlos Borromeo: Maureen Bianchini and Pam Tanous.

At Mission San Antonio: Joan Kathryn Steele and Judy Grindstaff.

At Mission San Buenaventura: Father Tom Elewaut, historian John Engler, and Julie Tumamait-Stenslie.

At Mission San José: Margaret Menke McCarthy (my old childhood classmate at St. Boniface in Anaheim), the Dominican Sisters, and historian Charlene Duval of San Jose State University.

At Mission San Miguel: Father Larry Gosselin (who later became associate pastor at Mission Santa Barbara), inspired poet and friend.

At Mission San Gabriel: Roberta Martínez for her lecture on the Hispanic community's evolution from mission days, and in particular Doña Eulalia's story; Jennifer Perry, Pomona College anthropologist, and her lecture on peoples of the Channel Islands.

At Mission San Rafael: archivist Teresa Brunner; at Petaluma Adobe State Park, Phil McCulley.

At Mission San Luis Rey: Father Garrett Galvin, who gave the California Mission Studies Association (CMSA) a Mass inside the old church still undergoing restoration.

At Mission Dolores de San Francisco: curator Andrew Galvan, Vincent Medina, Father Arturo Albano, and Paul Seliga.

At Mission Santa Clara: Rebecca Schapp, director of the De Saisset Museum.

I wish to thank my former colleague at California Lutheran University and special friend, theologian Dr. Jarvis Streeter, whose heroic battle with pancreatic cancer has inspired so many of us. Others at California Lutheran who were supportive: Dean Joan Griffin, Dan Geeting, Randy Toland, Joan Wines, and Judy Larsen. At the Claremont Colleges: Wendy Martin (Claremont Graduate University); close friend Greta Schyler (Claremont-McKenna); Frank Cioffi and Kimberly Drake (Scripps); Albert Wachtel, Lissa Petersen, and dear Caitlin Sanders (Pitzer); Samuel Yamashita (Pomona); and Dan Petersen (Harvey Mudd). At Georgetown University: President John DeGioia, Judith Tucker, Michael Hudson, Nicholas Sheets, Scott Taylor, John Buchtel, Zeina Seikaly, Ricardo Ortiz, and Jennifer Long.

Among many other California institutions, archivists, and researchers to thank: the Getty Research Center (Kathleen Saloman and Lois White); the Huntington Library (Bill Frank); the Bancroft Library (Susan Snyder); the Honnold Library of the Claremont Colleges (Carrie Marsh); the San Diego History Center (Cris Travers and Carol Myers); the Natural History Museum of Los Angeles County (John Cahoon and Richard Hulser); UCLA (Amy Wong); the University of Southern California

Special Collections (Dace Taub); Stanford University (Jane Ingalls and Salim Mohammed); and the Anza Society (Phil Valdez, Jr.).

Two others besides John Johnson graced me with a close reading of the manuscript: Dr. Daniel Krieger, professor emeritus of history at California Polytechnic University, San Luis Obispo; and Father Alan Deck, S. J., professor of theology at Loyola-Marymount University. Deep thanks.

Several translators have helped this project immensely, especially Professor Cristina Gonzalez-Huix Wray (from Barcelona, a master with Catalán), UCSB doctoral candidate Michael Grafals, Araceli Ardon and her husband, Eduardo Zarate, Georgetown University doctoral candidate Francesco Sinatora (with Italian), Emma Garroute, Pablo Medina, and Dr. Mary Docter.

Others who have helped along the way are Mayer Nudell, Ruben Mendoza, Stephen O'Neill, Father Fred Tillotson, Dr. Daniel Young, Vladimir Guerrero, Joe and Sharon Myers, Hale Sargent, Jim and Peggy Jo Clark, Dana Gioia, David McLaughlin, Jane Hill, and especially Christine Kettmer.

I have dedicated this book to Sister Mary Mark Schoenstein, O.P., who taught me both second and third grade at St. Boniface in Anaheim, and has, in one way or the other, taught me ever since. It was a complete joy to be reunited with her after many decades, and to share with her a most meaningful milestone at Mission San José and the Dominican Mother House: her sixtieth anniversary as a nun. If there is any doubt in anyone's mind what a great priest a woman would make, let them meet Mary Mark. Also, the writings of Sister Mary Mark's fifty-year missionary brother to the Muslims of Mindanao, Father Irwin Schoenstein, have been a complete revelation. Dialogue, yes! I also included in the dedication Father John Columba Fogarty, O. Carm., who first fired my love of writing and literature at Crespí Carmelite High School in Encino, California, and who went on to publish an important work, *The Catholic Priest* (1988). There was a time when Father John wanted to leave the priesthood to marry, but when the woman he loved told him, "You are a priest in your bones. You cannot do this," they parted ways and he remained a priest of priests till the end. I miss him.

Other priests who have touched my life and the lives of our family in special ways, as well as contributing to this work: first and foremost, Albert Koppes, O. Carm., associate provost of Loyola-Marymount University, who has known me since I was a child; Percival D'Silva of Blessed Sacrament Parish in Washington, DC; Gregory Boyle, S.J. (*mí tocayó!*); and Tom Schrader, O. Carm.

My writer friends gave emotional sustenance at just the right times, especially Garrett Hongo, Pablo Medina, John Hildebrand, Gary Paul

SOURCES AND ACKNOWLEDGMENTS

Nabhan, Naomi Shihab Nye, Max Holland, and Sharif Elmusa. Jason Berry must be singled out for his persistent belief in the book and for introducing me to his agent, who became mine.

John Moore, fellow writer, professor of kinesiology at Westmont, and inspired men's basketball coach, listened to my Serra obsession with great patience and has been, with his wife, Rachel, and daughters, Jackie and Jessie, a great and steadfast friend.

John Millsfield was incredible, as always, picking me up from various journeys at LAX and from many doubts. Other old friends who continued their faith in me and this labor beyond the evidence: Marco Pardo, Ed Siegler, Barbara Aquino, Marty Martínez, Joe Chiu, the Roarks, Alan Moin and Sabrina Ousmaal, Harry Kettmer, Terry Noeltner Snadzjer, and Kirsten and Frank Ellsworth.

My agent, Stephen Hanselman of LevelFiveMedia, understood this book from its inception, having grown up outside Bakersfield in Shafter. His wife, Julia Serebrinsky, a gifted editor in her own right, gave selflessly to the cause, helping cut the mammoth manuscript and bearing my shouts of agony and the blood on the floor.

There was no better luck and grace than having Colin Harrison as my editor at Scribner. Having a writer as an editor is a total blessing; we have become good friends. Katrina Diaz, his assistant, was indefatigable. Others at Scribner who ferried our monstrosity merrily along included Kate Lloyd, Kelsey Smith, Fred Chase, Tal Goretsky, Erich Hobbing, and Benjamin Holmes.

Finally, my family: thanks to my brother Mark for lending me his cars and sympathy for being who I am; Gary and Georgette Awad, as always, for love, understanding, judicious advice; my cousins Dennis, John, and Teresa Awad; Roger Edwards; Karen Awad; Eddie and Lila Awad; Joe and Carmen Awad, *requiescat in pace*; Natalie Orfalea; Keenan Orfalea; Teresa Johansing; Bonnie Orfalea Allison and her husband, Gene; George and Nora Hanna; Garrett and Sarah Awad; Father George and Janine Ajalat; Lily and Norm Barakat; Michael, Jimmy, and Paul Malouf and their great families; Al and Nancy Malouf; and my pals Daniel, Peter, and David Malouf. My mother, Rose, has been an inspiration from birth; in a real sense, everything I have ever written is dedicated to her.

Our boys, who are now young men, have my love and gratitude for being who they are: Matt (always getting me to or from the Van Nuys flyaway, with his feisty heart and mind); Andy (getting the books back on time, our hikes, his own amazing heart); and Luke (my "strong and tender" companion, the very glue of this family). And to Eileen, for listening and love. As D. H. Lawrence said, "Look! We have come through!"

NOTES

Abbreviations and Short Titles Frequently Used in Notes

Geiger, *Life and Times*: Maynard Geiger, O.F.M. *The Life and Times of Fray Junípero Serra, O.F.M., or The Man Who Never Turned Back*. Vols. I and II. Washington, DC: Academy of American Franciscan History, 1959.

GO: Gregory Orfalea translation.

MG: Maynard Geiger translation of *Palou's Life of Fray Junípero Serra*. Washington, DC: Academy of American Franciscan History, 1955.

Palou, *Relación*: Francisco Palou. *Relación Histórica de la Vida del Venerable Padre Fray Junípero Serra (Life and Apostolic Labors of the Venerable Father Junípero Serra)*. Edited by George Wharton James. Translated by C. Scott Williams. Pasadena, CA: George Wharton James, 1913.

SW: C. Scott Williams translation.

Tibesar: Antonine Tibesar, ed. *Writings of Junípero Serra*. Vols I–IV. Washington, DC: Academy of American Franciscan History, 1955, 1956, 1966.

Prologue

1 *María de la Soledad*: Serra to Bucareli, in Mexico City from Carmel, August 24, 1774. In Tibesar, II, 141.

Chapter One: Island Son

5 *At the darkest point of night*: "Miguel Serra" later replaced the old Mallorquín that appeared on his baptismal certificate (Miquel Serre). His parents also went by the name Serra-Dalmau.

6 *he is close to the savage*: George Sand, *Winter in Mallorca*, Valdemosa Edition, Mallorca, 1885, p. 146. Sand also noted, however, a xenophobic strain in the Mallorcans, and saw the island "as one of the most technologically retarded places in Europe."

6 *a boyhood friend*: Perhaps this childhood friend across the alley was Amon Rafael Moragues Casta, whom Serra singled out for "very special greetings" at the top of a list of friends he signed off to in his August 20, 1749, farewell letter to his parents. See Tibesar, I, 3–9.

6 *a workman's saw*: Sierra is Castilian Spanish for "saw," and thus the high

mountains of California recall the shape of mountains on Serra's home island.

7 *with shrewd allowance by James I*: Angus Mackay, "The Late Middle Ages, 1250–1500," in Raymond Carr, ed., *Spain: A History*, 2000, 95.

7 *some of Serra's ancestors*: According to historian James Sandos, Serra's application to enter the seminary at sixteen to become a priest was delayed and scrutinized more carefully "in order to ensure that he was not a backslider, a closet Judaizer" (*Converting California*, 33). A close look at *cuetas* in Mallorcan history is in Miguel Forteza's *Els Descendents dels Jueus Conversos de Mallorca*, 1966.

7 *Serra descended in part*: Bartolomé Font Obrador, Serra's primary biographer in Spanish and a fellow Mallorcan, calls it a "distant indication." See *El Apóstol de California: Sus Albores*, Palma de Mallorca, 1989, 164.

7 *the preciousness of life*: Author interview with Sister Mary Beth Ingham, Loyola-Marymount University, Los Angeles, March 21, 2011.

7 *A procession of relatives and neighbors*: Dina Moore Bowden, *Junípero Serra in His Native Isle*, Gráficas Miramar, 1976, 14.

8 *withholding a kiss*: "We return to you a Christian," (*J'al vos tornam Crista*), the midwife would have said to Margarita, in Mallorquín.

8 *Francophobia had deep roots*: Linda Frey and Marsha Frey, *Societies in Upheaval*, Greenwood Press, 1987, 94.

9 *Margarita sternly oversaw*: Francisco Torrens y Nicholau, *El Bosquejo Histórico*, 1913, 6.

9 *he probably awoke early*: The original Petra home at 48 Carrer Botellas where Serra was born no longer exists; the street was later changed—probably honorifically—to Calle California, but the wall of homes there was bulldozed in 1930. From the age of six till he entered the seminary at sixteen, Serra lived three blocks away at 6 Calle Barracar.

10 *This homage to the Immaculate Conception*: Geiger, *Life and Times*, I, 14.

12 *the greatest Christian missionary*: Francis DuBose, *Classics of Christian Missions*, 1979.

13 *Men are wont, O Lord*: In G. S. M. Walker, *The Growing Storm: Sketches of Church History from AD 600 to AD 1350*, Paternoster Press, 1961, 223.

13 *mania for martyrdom*: DuBose, *Classics of Christian Missions*, 125.

13 *deep tide driving out*: G. K. Chesterton, *St. Francis of Assisi*, Doubleday, 1924/1957, 31, 38, 50, 66.

13 *He ordered the friars served*: Valerie Martin, *Salvation: Scenes from the Life of St. Francis*, Vintage, 2001, 139. In paintings of the era, St. Francis is often shown juggling three balls (faith, hope, and charity) like a "clown of God."

14 *it is better to create Christians*: Chesterton, *Saint Francis of Assisi*, 114.

14 *Canticle of the Sun*: Though Francis also praises "sister water and brother wind," "mother earth and brother fire," the sun is especially honored by Francis: "O Lord, he [the sun] signifies to us Thee!" See Dina Moore Bowden, *Junípero Serra in His Native Isle*, 24.

15 *young boy with a bell-like voice*: Geiger, *Life and Times*, I, 15.

Chapter Two: The Call

17 *priestly status*: One study found nearly half of American priests did not see celibacy as crucial to their priesthood. See Rev. John Columba Fogarty, O. Carm.,

The Catholic Priest: His Identity and Values, Sheed & Ward, 1988, p. 58. Fogarty also found that 66 percent of the priests in the diocese of Joliet, Illinois (the basis of his landmark study), were in favor of women priests.

18 *an itch that longs to be scratched*: Rev. John P. Mack Jr., *Priests: An Inside Look*, St. Mary's Press, 2001, 13–17.

18 *One acclaimed poet*: Roland Flint, "Follow," *And Morning*, Dryad Press, 1975, 11.

18 *To the young Serra*: Palma today has a population of roughly half a million.

18 *sensations of light*: *Mallorca, A Pearl in the Mediterranean*, Cofiba, 5.

18 *The Cathedral of Palma*: Santiago Rusiñol, in Dina Moore Bowden, *Junípero Serra in His Native Isle*, 40.

19 *if you had the surname "Serre"*: Rose Marie Beebe and Robert Senkewicz, "The Alta California Franciscans Before 1769," in Stephen Hackel, ed., *Alta California: Peoples in Motion, Identities in Formation, 1769–1850*, University of California Press, 2010.

19 *in all its parts consonant*: Fray Francisco Bordoy's 1814 description, in Geiger, *Life and Times*, I, 18.

19 *When I was a novice*: Palou, *Relación*, 4 (SW).

20 *All good things came to me*: Ibid. The phrase comes from Wisdom 7:11, "*Venerunt mihi Omnia bona partier cum illa,*" wherein "this" refers to the spirit of wisdom. The anonymous author of the book of Wisdom was part of the Jewish community of Alexandria and was concerned about intra-Jewish fratricide and war.

20 *patches of cactus*: See Luis Jeronimo Oré, *Relacíon de la Vida y Milagros de San Francisco Solano*, Fondo Editorial, 1998, 398.

21 *He worked against slave traders*: Author interview with Father Agusti Boadas Llavat, Barcelona, June 11, 2011.

21 *Augustine scoffs*: Augustine, *The Confessions*, VI, vii, 22.

21 *I prated as if I was well-instructed*: Ibid., VII, xx, 26.

21 *one of the greatest pages*: Radoslav Tsanoff, *Autobiographies of Ten Religious Leaders: Alternatives in Christian Experience*, Trinity University Press, 1968, 14.

22 *But put on the Lord Jesus Christ*: Romans 13:13.

22 *There was infused in my heart*: Augustine, *The Confessions*, 145–46.

22 *Lay aside the works of darkness*: Romans 13:12.

22 *he will be destroyed by the power*: Martin, *Salvation*, 82.

23 *Would to God, my brethren*: All passages quoted are from *The Little Flowers of Saint Francis*, edited and translated by Raphael Brown, 1958.

23 *An editor of Palou's writings*: Palou, *Relación*, 335 (SW).

24 *He even carved a Brother Juniper woodblock*: Junípero is pictured holding a lily, the hand of God extending to him from a cloud, and the devil fleeing. See Morgado, *Junípero Serra*, Figure 26.

24 *the greatest exemplar*: Geiger, *Life and Times*, I, 21.

24 *I, Fray Junípero Serra*: Ibid., 21–22.

25 *Touching the banner*: See Morgado, *Junípero Serra*, Figure 19.

25 *the way of Thomas Aquinas*: Author interview with Father Kenan Osborne, Mission Santa Barbara, Santa Barbara, California, May 26, 2012.

25 *It's a political view*: Author interview with Father Agusti Llavat.

NOTES

26 *Majorca's prize ecclesiastical structure*: Geiger, *Life and Times*, I, 23.

26 *the visual accompaniment*: The trefoil, or three-petaled tip, to the arches bears a close resemblance to the Rose Cross of the Rosicrucians, a secretive Christian society begun in the fourteenth century about the same time as the 114 trefoiled arches were carved in the San Francisco courtyard. The Rosicrucians questioned the arbitrary and often political authority assumed by popes during this period, two hundred years before the Protestant Reformation. Would Serra have known he was walking through colonnades of such a symbol?

27 *it may also have been*: By 1687, the Copernican model that the sun was the center of the solar system was generally accepted in Europe, long before Serra was born. The model, however, was not taken off the Catholic Index until 1758. See Morgado, *Junípero Serra*, Figure 20.

27 *Serra was not medieval*: Author interview with Father Kenan Osborne.

27 *amazement in the face of beauty*: Clark Colahon, *The Visions of Sor María de Agreda: Writing, Knowledge, and Power*, University of Arizona Press, 1994, 26.

28 *early enrapt witness*: Lope de Vega, *The Discovery of the New World by Christopher Columbus: A Comedy in Verse*, Gillick Press, 1590/1950.

28 *María certainly developed*: See Colahan, *The Visions of Sor María de Agreda*, 102–3, 108, 115–16. Also Venerable Maria de Agreda, *The Mystical City of God*, Tan Books, 1686/1978 (abridged edition), 13.

28 *her magnum opus*: Considered for sainthood, María de Agreda's cause, like Serra's, has long been stalled. In her case, the problem, beyond the bilocation stories, may be theological; her interpretation of Mary is both more deeply human and more "God-like" than that of official Catholicism.

29 *an unsolved mystery*: Geiger, *Life and Times*, I, 25.

29 *collected with discretion*: And Serra was not alone. A fellow pupil, Michael Verd (Verdugo?), had similar problems. Documents turned over on "these or similar topics are not to be allowed." His offensive "conclusions" began with *Christum deme* (Christ removes) and *Christi effuses Sanguis* (Christ's blood flows). These judgments came down on September 2, 1739—more than a year and a half after the offending material was written. At the same time or around it, Serra had also told students taking a theology test not to claim that Mary's Immaculate Conception was a fraud (*captiunculis*) or deceptive (*captiosa*) at the top of their exams. So he was publicly bucking the official taboo about the Immaculate Conception. In 1734–35, the Holy Tribunal had circulated a decree that all references to such a status in prayer books be eliminated. See Order of the Inquisition, Vol. 1085, 132–33, Biblioteca Provincial de Palma de Mallorca. The translations of this complicated material were masterfully done by Professor Cristina Huix-González Wray, Newport News, Virginia, April 2013.

Chapter Three: A Professor, Wanting

30 *the last of the conquistadors*: See Omer Englebert, *The Last of the Conquistadors: Junípero Serra, 1713–1784*, Kessinger, 1956.

31 *even on another continent*: Juan Crespí, *A Description of Distant Roads: Original Journals of the First Expedition into California, 1769–1770*, edited and translated by Alan K. Brown, San Diego State University Press, 2001, 5.

31 *We grew up together*: Francisco Palou, *Noticias (Historical Memoirs of New California)*, edited and translated by Herbert Bolton, Berkeley, 1926, 312.

31 *made up in industry*: Geiger, *Life and Times*, I, 26.

31 *one scholar thought he suffered*: See Fray Salustiano Vicedo, *El Mallorquín Fray Juan Crespí, O.F.M., Misionero y Explorador, Sus Diarios*, Valencia, Spain, 1994, in Crespí, 7. Crespí's writing lacked the Castilian *jota*; he left off entirely unstressed vowels, as well as the *l* in the initial use of *ll* (such as for Raymond Llull); he often wrote two ends for a sentence, leaving the reader wondering which one he meant.

32 *I was the object*: Geiger, *Life and Times*, I, 27.

32 *Walk in that light worthily*: Ibid.

33 *the divine ear*: Mary Beth Ingham, *Scotus for Dunces: An Introduction to the Subtle Doctor*, Franciscan Institute, 2003, 31.

33 *Every morally good act*: Author interview with Sister Mary Beth Ingham.

33 *Devotion to her as a Scotist*: Geiger, *Life and Times*, I, 27. The doctrine of Immaculate Conception, that is, that Mary conceived Christ without sexual intercourse, was announced by Pope Pius IX in 1854, but Serra and Franciscans in general were early proponents.

33 *Individualism is very big*: Author interview with Father Kenan Osborne.

33 *Jove will soon dispose*: Geiger, *Life and Times*, I, 28. The Virgil quote is from *The Aeneid*, I:199.

33 *eleven who were brought*: Gustav Henningsen and John Tedeschi, *The Inquisition in Modern Europe: Studies on Sources and Methods*, Yale University Press, 1997. That late forty-six-year period saw an average of two people executed a year (111 total) in all of Spain under Inquisition tribunals.

34 *Was [Serra] aware*: Steven Hackel, "Father Junípero Serra: Agent of the Inquisition," Brown American Seminar, Oregon State University, April 24, 2007, 11.

34 *these people found themselves*: Beebe and Senkewicz, "What They Brought," 25.

34 *The seizure of property*: Henry Kamen, *The Spanish Inquisition: A Historical Revision*, Yale University Press, 1998. Three people were burned alive after several auto-da-fés in 1691. Serra was not born for another twenty-two years.

34 *the "medieval Catholicism"*: Kenneth Moore, *Those of the Street: The Catholic-Jews of Mallorca*, University of Notre Dame Press, 1976, 14.

34 *In Serra's time*: Hackel, "Father Junípero Serra," 11–12.

34 *Serra was chosen*: Author interview with Father Kenan Osborne.

35 *three hundred years of relative tranquillity*: Some speak of a seven-hundred-year reign of tolerance until the final expulsion of the Moors in 1492, but when two fundamentalist Berber armies defeated Alfonso VI in 1086, bringing in the fanatical Almoravids and later Almohads, the intolerance of the Christian Alfonso was equally met by that of the Muslims.

35 *The mystery of its very name*: Some say its origin lies in the name of the Roman legend of Atlantis; others see Vandal or Visigoth origins.

35 *At the hub of Andalusia*: María Rosa Menocal, *The Ornament of the World: How Muslims, Jews and Christians Created a Culture of Tolerance in Medieval Spain*, Back Bay Books, 2002, 32.

35 *recapitulates the artistic history*: John Crow, *Spain: The Root and the Flower*, University of California Press, 3rd edition, 1985, 53.

35 *all things have to be reimagined*: Carlos Fuentes, *The Buried Mirror: Reflections on Spain and the New World*, Houghton Mifflin, 1999, 53–54.

36 *hygienic apartheid*: Richard Fletcher, "The Early Middle Ages, 700–1250," in Raymond Carr, ed., *Spain: A History*, Oxford University Press, 2001, 85.

36 *the tiled fountain*: Crow, *Spain*, 61.

36 *hallmarks of modern thought*: Fuentes, *The Buried Mirror*, 56.

36 *thoroughly dismissive attitudes*: Fletcher, "The Early Middle Ages," 84.

37 *her head on a magenta pillow*: Ibid., 86.

38 *five thousand killed in total*: The life of Arab and Jew in Spain, however, was never really extinguished. A 2008 study showed 30 percent of the current Spanish population to have genetic Arab and Jewish ancestry (10 and 20 percent, respectively).

38 *The Holy Office had come*: Antonio Elorza, *La Inquisición y El Pensamiento Illustrado*, Historia 16, Especial 100 Aniversario La Inquisición, n.d., 88.

38 *Thomas More was not*: In this regard, it is revealing to note that Teresa of Avila, one of the great saints in two thousand years of Christendom, was of *converso* stock; her grandfather was penanced under the Inquisition in 1485.

38 *The ban apparently stimulated*: David J. Weber, *Bárbaros: Spaniards and Their Savages in the Age of Enlightenment*, Yale University Press, 2005, 35.

40 *shooting the head*: Obrador, *El Apóstol de California: Sus Albores*.

40 *These were hardly celebrations*: In November–December 1732, the Moor was burned at the stake for his capital crime, not under the Inquisition. It's hard to imagine Serra not having seen that gruesome hand or the captain's lost head publicly displayed in Palma.

41 *He [Ramonell] protested*: *Actes de Bachille y Graus de Theoa de la Univd Littra t Estudi Genl Lulliano desde 1738 fins en 1751*, Vol. 33. In Geiger, *Life and Times*, I, 32.

41 *Serra also grew up*: Beebe and Senkewicz, "What They Brought," 20. See also Carlos Manera, "Manufactura textile y comercio en Mallorca, 1700–1830," *Revista de historia económica* 6, no. 3 (1988): 523–55.

41 *they were not translated*: In Obrador, *El Apóstol de California*. Maynard Geiger refers only to Serra's epigraph taken from the Psalms ("Taste and see the goodness of the Lord") and does not examine any of the four sermons—an astounding omission for a one-thousand-page biography of a priest.

41 *I suffer in loving*: Sor Juana Inés de la Cruz, *Sor Juana's Love Poems*, translated by Jaime Manrique and Joan Larkin, University of Wisconsin Press, 2003.

42 *Their men set siege*: Fuentes, *Buried Mirror*, 211.

42 *What a difference*: All quotes from the four sermons are from the bilingual edition of Obrador's *El Apóstol de California, Sus Albores*, 1989, or a retranslation of mine, including some of the Latin passages.

42 *They were guaranteed possession*: Richard Fletcher, *Moorish Spain*, Henry Holt, 1992, 137.

47 *Our Lady of Snows*: The deeply revered, life-size statue of Our Lady of Snows, carved of white Carrara alabaster, holding Christ in one hand and a pomegranate in the other (to which Christ reaches) is thought to be from early Christendom, mentioned specifically by Pope Innocent IV in 1248. Serra spoke in Bunyola in 1740, just as the church was being built and the statue put in place.

47 *one witness thought the snow*: Nicolás Ferrer de Sant Jordi, in Obrador, *El Apóstol de California*, 143.

48 *no priest holding his hand*: Ibid., 144–48.

48 *You won't live to see Easter*: Geiger, *Life and Times*, I, 34.

49 *Our heart spontaneously cried out*: *Aeneid*, II:3. Dido has asked Aeneas to recount his bloody campaign at Troy.

50 *Since you found out the news*: Palou, *Relación*, 7 (SW); 9 (MG).

50 *some of the hesitation was due*: Ibid., 10–11, 329 (MG).

51 *too inconstant and fickle*: Geiger, *Life and Times*, I, 40.

51 *there was a high dropout rate*: See Maynard Geiger, "The Mallorcan Contribution to Franciscan California," *The Americas*, October 1947, 141–50. As it turned out, sixteen of 128 Franciscans who served in California were Mallorcans.

51 *When he finished the sermon*: Palou, *Relación*, 6 (MG).

51 *As the needle naturally turns*: DuBose, *Classics of Christian Missions*, 125.

51 *This is a personal God*: Mary Beth Ingham, *Scotus for Dunces*, 120.

52 *Thou hast lighted up*: Agreda, *The Mystical City of God*, 18.

52 *were lost between the doorway*: Palou, *Relación*, 9 (SW).

53 *These longings had become*: Ibid., 36. Sister Mary Beth Ingham has a unique take on Serra's motive for leaving: "Maybe he wanted to know what that extreme experience of love was like—without a people, place, or language you know." (Author interview.)

54 *May their souls rest in peace*: Francisco Noguera, *Compendium Scotium*, Santa Barbara Mission Archive and Library, JSC 34, Palma, April 13, 1749.

54 *Serra may have handed*: It is the only Bible we have with Serra's signature, with a note that it was for his "simple use" (at the Diocese of Mallorca).

54 *I call you Francisco*: Geiger, *Life and Times*, I, 48; Palou, *Relación*, 263 (MG) (GO).

Chapter Four: To the Spanish Mainland

56 *the packet boat was built*: See www.thepirateking.com/ships/ship_types, 21–22.

56 *packet rats*: The origin of the phrase "pack rat" may derive in part from the less-than-stellar reputation of packet boat captains.

56 *stiff-necked heretic*: Palou, *Relación*, 10 (MG); Geiger, *Life and Times*, I, 50.

56 *arose on deck*: Geiger, *Life and Times*, I, 50.

57 *Our king will demand*: Palou, *Relación*, 11 (SW), 12 (MG).

57 *they had to be quoting*: Serra's was either a Spanish or Catalán version of the Douay-Rheims Bible completed in 1609 and the standard Catholic Bible until the Second Vatican Council in 1962 introduced others.

57 *Our Father Junípero*: Palou, *Relación*, 10 (SW), 12 (MG).

57 *John Wyclif, an Oxford don*: Diarmaid MacCullough, *Christianity: The First Three Thousand Years*, Penguin, 2011, 568–69.

57 *For this is my body*: Mark 14:22.

57 *it sent Aquinas into all sorts*: Poisoned blood is encased in a vessel and deposited in the tabernacle. The fly was to be "daintily" washed, burned, and the ashes and even the "dishwater" of the washing put in the tabernacle, as well. Ditto the vomit. See Garry Wills, *Why Priests? A Failed Tradition*, Viking, 2013, 48.

58 *one author counted two hundred*: Christopher Rasperger, *Two Hundred Interpretations of the Words, "This Is My Body,"* Ingolstadt, Germany, 1577.

58 *it's tougher for the rich*: Luke 18:25.

58 *My yoke is easy*: Matthew 11:30.

59 *But in conscience*: Geiger, *Life and Times*, I, 51. Palou, *Relación*, 11 (SW), 13 (MG).

62 *caution . . . accommodating*: Pedro José Parras, *Diario y derrotero de sus viajes, 1749–1753. España—Río de la Plata—Cordoba—Paraguay*, 61.

62 *a lector of theology*: Geiger, *Life and Times*, I, 57.

64 *I saw such terrible cruelties*: Bartolomé de Las Casas, *The Devastation of the Indies: A Brief Account*, originally published in Spain in 1552, translated by Herma Briffault, Johns Hopkins University Press, 1992, 46.

64 *was a condition that commissaries*: Geiger, *Life and Times*, I, 57.

64 *Built in 1260*: The Cathedral of Cádiz was finally rebuilt in 1776, the year Serra announced the rebuilding of Mission San Juan Capistrano with a bell ringing halfway around the world.

65 *The public* putería: The first quote on Valencia is from a social critic of the time, Barthelemy Joly, and the notary is Enrique Cock; both are in Marcelin Defourneaux, *Daily Life of Spain in the Golden Age*, translated by George Allen, Praeger, 1966, 223–25. Many details of prostitution in Spain in this era are also taken from this source.

65 *When he was in the presence*: Palou, *Relación*, 279 (MG).

65 *Women never saw*: Abigail Fitch, *Junípero Serra*, A. C. McClung, 1914, 36.

66 *the magna carta*: Geiger, *Life and Times*, I, 59.

66 *the only surviving letter*: Palou quotes a fragment from a Serra Mallorca letter to him, but the original has never been found. In 1749, Serra wrote three other letters (besides the one for his parents) to his cousin Francesch Serra in Petra: one before he left Cádiz, one en route across the Atlantic, and one on arrival at Veracruz, Mexico. Only the last has been found.

67 *We had thought*: The letter referred to is lost.

67 *St. Bonaventure's day*: St. Bonaventure's feast day is celebrated on July 14, so the *Villasota*'s launch was delayed by at least a month.

67 *move forward and never turn back*: Maynard Geiger took as his subtitle for his 1959 magnum opus on Serra, "The Man Who Never Turned Back." Some have seen in this famous Serra passage echoes of St. Paul to the Philippians, 3:12–13: "Forgetting what is behind, I strain forward to what is before." However, many, including Geiger, have distorted what Serra actually said for the aphorism *Siempre adalante, nunca atras* (Always go forward, never back). What Serra actually wrote was: *a passer avant, y nunca retroceder*.

70 All you are my letter: This echoes Paul's Epistle to the Corinthians: "Do I need letters of recommendation to you or from you as others might? You are my letter, known and read by all men, written in our hearts" (3:1–3).

Chapter Five: The Sea of Darkness

73 *On August 30, 1749*: There are some discrepancies as to the exact date of departure. In a second letter to his namesake priest cousin in Petra, Francesch Serra, written at Veracruz (December 14, 1769) about the sea crossing, Serra says he

boarded the *Villasota* on August 29 and left the next day. Palou—whose memory is probably not as reliable as Serra's—put the departure at August 28. Government records indicate a third date: August 31.

74 *I was so thirsty*: Letter to Francesch Serra (Petra), December 14, 1749, from Veracruz, Mexico. In Tibesar, I, 11.

75 *From that eminence*: Agreda, *The Mystical City of God*, 87.

75 *Talk less*: Palou, *Relación*, 13 (SW), 15 (MG, GO).

75 *the restoration of the ladder*: The symbol of the ladder is a key one for Bonaventure, one of Serra's favorite saints: "The sin of humankind had broken the first ladder but Christ restored the broken ladder linking humankind with God in his crucifixion." Ilia Delio, O.S.F., *Crucified Love: Bonaventure's Mysticism of the Crucified Christ*, Franciscan Press, 1998, 50.

75 *I was made to see*: Agreda, *The Mystical City of God*, 5. In her reference to a woman (Mary) with stars around her head and "clothed in sun," Agreda echoed the Book of Revelation, 12:1.

75 *he was a godsend*: Serra to Serra, in Tibesar, I, 11. Also see Geiger, *Life and Times*, I, 64.

76 *what may be considered*: Geiger, *Life and Times*, 66.

77 *the visiting friars*: Palou, *Relación*, 15 (MG).

77 *Serra had gone over*: Geiger, *Life and Times*, I, 67.

77 *Cardona "rejoiced"*: Palou, *Relación*, 13 (SW), 15 (MG).

77 *in accordance with*: Serra to Serra, in Tibesar, I, 13.

77 *an assault, or spiritual attack*: Geiger, *Life and Times*, I, 69.

78 *unable to find the right words*: Tibesar, I, 13.

78 *during his first hours*: Geiger, *Life and Times*, I, 70.

78 *chocolate, pipe tobacco*: Serra to Serra, in Tibesar, I, 15.

79 *disproportionately long*: Ibid.

79 *we gave ourselves up*: Palou, *Relación*, 14 (SW).

80 *we recited the prayer*: Tibesar, I, 17.

80 *Whether Ferrer knew it or not*: St. Barbara's story is a rather spectacular one; in 1969, Pope Paul VI removed her feast day from the liturgical calendar, the Church finally questioning the historicity of her legend. Barbara was said to be the third-century daughter of a rich pagan, Dioscorus, who locked her up in a tower where she secretly studied Christianity and converted. Among the many myths swirling around Barbara is that to escape from her enraged father, she melted through the tower wall. Her father finally chopped her head off and received his own due, a lightning bolt that fried him. No surprise, perhaps, that this explosive saint is the patron saint of those guarding explosives, artillerymen, or anyone risking violent death in their work, such as missionaries in a sea storm.

80 *the storm ceased*: Palou, *Relación*, 15 (SW).

80 *And that is a fact*: Tibesar, I, 17.

80 *of such perfection*: Palou, *Relación*, 16 (SW).

81 *Cortés had been told specifically*: A soldier-memoirist of the Cortés conquest, Bernal Díaz del Castillo, disputes this, insisting that the two men parted amicably when Cortés sailed. See *The Conquest of New Spain*, or *Historia Verdadera*, 1569/1973. In either case, Velázquez soon suspected Cortés's motives, and wanted him detained. It didn't happen.

81 *straws dipped in his own blood*: Hugh Thomas, *Conquest: Montezuma, Cortéz, and the Fall of Old Mexico*, Simon & Schuster, 1993, 176.

81 *Las Casas thought*: Bartolomé de Las Casas, *Historia de las Indias, 1527–66*, Book II, in Thomas, *Conquest*, 177, and translated as "excrement." The Spanish *estiercol* may also mean "dung," but the sarcasm of Las Casas—who knew Cortés—can't be mistaken.

81 *when they mounted their deer*: in Maurice Collis, *Cortéz and Montezuma*, New Directions, 1954, 65.

Chapter Six: The Long Walk to Mexico City

84 *This journey started*: According to Maynard Geiger, there are two hundred land travels of Serra mentioned in Palou's *Relación*, but only five are described as his actually walking. Geiger reports, "We know definitely from documentary evidence that he did not walk" on many journeys.

85 *if not in this world*: Tibesar, I, 17.

85 *Serra set off on December 15*: The only two possibilities—both from Jerez—were friars Francisco Patino or Pedro Pérez.

85 *they must surely have perished*: Palou, *Relación*, 17.

86 *unusually savory quality*: Ibid., 18–19 (CW); 19 (MG). Geiger upbraids Palou for not locating these incidents in exact time or place: "Palou's statements stand thin and weak." He wrote, however, thirty-five years after the fact.

87 *destroying the soft tissue*: Serra thought he was bitten by a mosquito (*zancudo*), but medical experts I have consulted feel a wound lasting decades would have been a more serious insect bite, probably from a spider.

87 *It was a dangerous place*: More innocents were killed in a twenty-day Aztec ritual (twenty thousand) than during three centuries of the Spanish Inquisition (five thousand). See Collis, *Cortéz and Montezuma*, 137.

88 *intelligent as Moslems*: Collis, *Cortéz and Montezuma*, 102.

89 *the Blessed Mother ablaze*: This original image of Our Lady of Guadalupe on Diego's cloth—*ayote* made of coarse *agave*—is framed and hangs in the largest of five churches at the miraculous site in northeastern Mexico City.

89 *the temple at San Hipólito*: Still a hospital for the insane when Geiger visited it in 1952, today St. Hippolito is a church dedicated to St. Judas Tadeo, the patron saint of the unemployed.

90 *Our Seraphic Patriarch*: Palou, *Relación*, 20 (SW), 21 (MG, GO).

90 *His humility was admirable*: Geiger, *Life and Times*, I, 98.

90 *Except for five priests*: One, Father Melchor Velasco, was written off by Geiger as a "disturbing character whose only contribution in six days was scandal." *Life and Times*, I, 99.

92 *the crowd was ecstatic*: Unfortunately, printed or not, neither landmark Serra sermon, leaving Spain or arriving in Mexico, has ever been found.

92 *A university professor*: Geiger, *Life and Times*, I, 101.

Chapter Seven: New World Others

94 *Hispanics made room*: Albert L. Hurtado, *Indian Survival on the California Frontier*, Yale University Press, 1988, 3.

94 *Captain John Smith claims*: Jake Page, *In the Hands of the Great Spirit: The 20,000-Year History of American Indians*, Free Press, 2003, 159.

94 *We are cautioned by anthropologists*: Even Page, though, notes the likelihood of cannibalism among tribes other than the Aztecs, such as the Anasazi of 1100 BC in Colorado and the Chippewa on the Michigan frontier in the 1760s.

95 *What will avail you*: Page, *In the Hands of the Great Spirit*, 161.

95 *The creation of the Iroquois Confederacy*: The Iroquois Confederacy was composed of the Senecas, Mohawks, Onondagas, Cayugas, and Oneidas.

96 *The idea of someone's claiming*: Henry Warner Bowden, *American Indians and Christian Missions: Studies in Cultural Conflict*, University of Chicago Press, 1981, 103.

96 *As a persecuted minority*: Ibid., 114.

97 *the hated Papists*: Kristin Brass, *Dry Bones and Indian Sermons: Praying Indians in Colonial America*, Cornell University Press, 2004, 110.

97 *that irony seems to have escaped*: Richard Pointer, *Encounters of the Spirit*, Indiana University Press, 2007, 64, 65, 67.

97 *because it was too difficult*: Thomas Shepard, *The Day-Breaking, If Not the Sun Rising of the Gospel: With the Indians in New England*, in *The Eliot Tracts*, edited by Michael Cook, Praeger, 2003, 89–90.

97 *worrisome people*: Pointer, *Encounters of the Spirit*, 67.

98 *Not one in a thousand*: Ibid., 153.

98 *In the end, however*: Jonathan Edwards, *The Life of David Brainerd*, Vol. 7 of *The Works of Jonathan Edwards*, Yale University Press, 1985, 380.

98 *I am a blazed pine*: James Fenimore Cooper, *The Last of the Mohicans: A Narrative of 1757*, 1826/1962, Signet, 414.

98 *He held up for a time*: Serra, another syncretic figure, would die the same year as Occom.

99 *clubbed, scalped and burned*: Edmund A. Schewinitz, *The Life and Times of David Zeisberger: The Western Pioneer and Apostle of the Indians*, Lippincott, 1870/1971, 551–52.

99 *It was the English*: Bowden, *American Indians and Christian Missions*, 113.

99 *stressed the importance of converting*: David Hackett Fischer, *Champlain's Dream: The European Founding of North America*, Simon & Schuster, 2008, 434.

99 *This war weary soldier*: Ibid., 528–31.

100 *The Jesuits gained immeasurable credibility*: Bowden, *American Indians and Christian Missions*, 78.

100 *("Jesus Ahatonia")*: Written in 1642 by Jean de Brébeuf in the Huron tongue, this was a sort of Huron Christmas carol (meaning "Jesus, he is born").

101 *sensible and confident*: Bowden, *American Indians and Christian Missions*, 75.

101 *Christ's atoning death*: Ibid., 82.

101 *the principal God of the Hurons*: Colin Calloway, *New Worlds for All: Indians, Europeans, and the Remaking of Early America*, Johns Hopkins University Press, 1997, 68.

101 *dramatically rendered*: Starring Robert De Niro (the guilty bounty hunter) and Jeremy Irons (as the leading Jesuit), *The Mission* was rated by Catholic critics the number one film (out of two hundred) of all time.

101 *As for what concerns me*: Calloway, *New Worlds for All*, 89.

102 *rarely a one-way street*: Page, *In the Hands of the Great Spirit*, 201. See also

Daniel Usner, *Indians, Settlers, and Slaves in a Frontier Exchange Economy*, University of North Carolina Press, 1992, on gumbo-cultured New Orleans.

102 *[It] encourages me*: Richard Rodriguez, *Brown: The Last Discovery of America*, Penguin, 2002, xv.

103 *we consider it something*: Octavio Paz, *The Labyrinth of Solitude*, Grove Press, 1985, 20, 24.

103 *Spain abolished the African slave trade*: The caveat to this is that Spain did not free the slaves in Cuba and Puerto Rico, where they toiled in sugarcane plantations, until 1866 and 1873, respectively.

104 *knowledge as a form of possession*: Jacques le Goff, *Saint Francis of Assisi*, Routledge, 2004, 84.

104 *Ignatius's practice of reading signs*: Maria F. Wade, *Missions, Missionaries, and Native Americans: Long-Term Processes and Daily Practices*, University Press of Florida, 2008, 45.

104 *Ignatius smiled*: Antonio de Nicolás, *Powers of Imagining: Ignatius Loyola*, State University of New York Press, 1986, 49–50.

104 *an overt indictment*: Wade, *Missions, Missionaries, and Native Americans*, 38.

105 *evangelism around the world*: Pointer, *Encounters of the Spirit*, 16–17, 39–40.

106 *I see no impediment*: John Hann, *The Indians of Central and South Florida*, University Press of Florida, 2003, 246.

106 *The Calusa neither mellowed*: Wade, *Missions, Missionaries, and Native Americans*, 60.

107 *One historian spoke*: Page, *In the Hands of the Great Spirit*, 133–34.

107 *The sense of a vanishing future*: Quoted in ibid., 134.

107 *All these people*: In Tony Horowitz, *A Voyage Long and Strange: On the Trail of the Vikings, Conquistadors, Lost Colonists, and Other Adventurers in Early America*, Picador, 2008, 128.

108 *a statue of Oñate*: In fact, Franciscans had often defended the Pueblo Indian against the Oñates of the world. See Page, *In the Hands of the Great Spirit*, 145.

108 *[Kino] was, in the Jesuit manner*: Alan Knight, *Mexico: The Colonial Era*, Cambridge University Press, 2002, 131.

109 *American silver came to play*: Ibid., 175.

109 *Moved by their desperation*: The Jumanos were the same tribe that claimed to have been visited by the Lady in Blue—María de Agreda.

109 *The Christian aspect*: Vito Alessio Robles, *Coahuila y Texas en la Época Colonial*, Mexico City, Editorial Porrúa, 1978, 191–92.

109 *for no motive whatsoever*: Cequia del Rey, an announcement of King Philip V on September 15, 1713, of his intention to amend the *Recopilación*, translated by Maynard Geiger, in the Santa Barbara Mission Archives and Library.

Chapter Eight: The Fat Mountains

112 *the miraculous cross trees*: A predecessor of Serra, Antonio Margil, who ministered in Guatemala and Zacatecas, planted his walking stick in the graveyard at Santa Cruz and, legend has it, bushes with thorns shaped like small crosses sprang up. Pilgrims still pray in front of an iron fence protecting them.

112 *Serra's eight years*: On November 2, 2011, accompanied by Jalpan guide

Marcelo Benítez Trejo, I discovered sixteen eighteenth-century documents, including previously unknown letters of Serra and Palou, that had rested with *campesinos* near San Pedro Escanela, Rafael Sánchez and Aquilio Hernandez and their families, for at least a century.

113 *at least four Indian revolts*: In 1727, the Pames erupted in Celaya west of the city; in 1732, Indian workers at mines in Guanajuato and Irapuato revolted; and in 1734, a large uprising of ten thousand Indians took place at San Miguel el Grande.

114 *capable and fair-minded*: Armando Alonzo, *Tejano Legacy: Rancheros and Settlers in South Texas, 1734–1900*, University of New Mexico Press, 1998, 27.

114 *one that Spain never repeated*: David Weber, *Bárbaros*, Yale University Press, 105.

114 *If only one [Indian]*: María del Carmen Velásquez, *El Estado de Guerra en Nueva España, 1760–1808*, Colegio de Mexico, 1976, 43, in ibid., 106.

114 *There is little doubt*: The History Museum of Jalpan has permanent exhibitions about the destruction of the Jonace tribe. General Gabriel Guerrero (1713–15) dealt the Jonaces crippling blows, which Escandón completed at the Battle of Media Luna.

114 *denounced the use*: Beebe and Senkewicz, "What They Brought," 35.

115 *To persuasion he added example*: Geiger, *Life and Times*, I, 112.

115 *the little worship structure*: The church at Jalpan, the presidio in Santa Barbara, and the Serra chapel at San Juan Capistrano are the only original structures still standing where we know Serra said Mass.

116 *interchanges between priest and penitent*: Lu Ana Homza, *Religious Authority in the Spanish Renaissance*, Johns Hopkins University Press, 2000, 150.

116 *the greatest colonial grammarian*: Ibid. Granting that the confessions of Aztecs predate the Pames and Serra by a century, Sell's translations reveal notions of sin being absorbed, as well as priestly prompts.

116 *Perhaps our Lord God*: Ibid.

117 *he was able to instruct them*: Palou, *Relación*, 28 (SW).

117 *so large and heavy*: Ibid., 30 (MG).

117 *Whoever loves this death*: Ewert Cousins, trans., *Bonaventure: The Soul's Journey to God*, Paulist Press, 1978, 6–7, in Delio, *Crucified Love*, Franciscan Press, 1988, 65.

117 *the whole Trinity cries out*: Jose de Vinch, trans., *St. Bonaventure: Opuscula Second Series*, Vol. III, *The Works of Bonaventure*, St. Anthony Guild Press, 1966, 69, in Delio, *Crucified Love*, 65.

117 *Greater love*: John 15:13, "Greater love hath no man than this, that a man lays down his life for his friends."

117 *yet the soul is supremely flooded*: Delio, *Crucified Love*, 61.

117 *Bonaventure illuminates*: Delio, *Crucified Love*, 59.

118 *Serra's deliberate use of Pame*: Dr. Craig Russell, *From Serra to Sancho: Music and Pageantry in the California Missions*, Oxford University Press, 2009, 170. The translation of Palou's commentary in the previous sentence is Russell's.

118 *with great solemnity*: Palou, *Relación*, 31 (SW).

118 *there is no mention*: Geiger, *Life and Times*, I, 115. A rare dig at Palou.

118 *For Godsake*: Palou, *Relación*, 35 (MG, SW, GO).

118 *the College of San Fernando*: San Fernando was destroyed around 1860 and the statue of Cachum lost.

119 *soldiers complained to him*: Geiger, *Life and Times*, I, 125–26.

119 *You are bound*: Pumeda to Escandón, in the Sierra Gorda from Mexico City, June 29, 1751, in Geiger, *Life and Times*, 128.

119 *more hurt than angry*: Geiger, *Life and Times*, I, 128–29.

120 *some distance of the mission compound*: Hackel, *Junípero Serra*, 100.

120 *Serra sided with the Indians*: Geiger, *Life and Times*, I, 120.

121 *If such evil is not attacked*: Serra, "Report to the Inquisition of Mexico City," from Mexico City, September 1, 1752. In Tibesar, I, 19–20.

122 *a shiny violin*: These items purchased in the capital are in a document titled, "Partial expense account for Mission Santiago de Jalpan," dated September 30, 1758, in the Santa Barbara Mission Archive and Library, Junípero Serra Collection, #69. The *saylete* was noted as bought on December 11, 1752.

122 *morphed from pelican to eagle*: Perry spoke to me one day in early February 2012 at Mission Santa Barbara about this fascinating blur of symbolic translation that could occur between the drawer of plans and the executor of design.

123 *Many of the motifs*: Mission San Carlos Borromeo uses Jalpan's sea scallop motif around the choir window, Santa Barbara employs its interior Moorish arches, the large cruciform nave with octagonal dome finds a copy at Mission San Luis Rey in Oceanside, and the pink-and-green washes repeat themselves in Mission San Miguel just north of San Luis Obispo.

123 *We are not safe here*: Palou, *Relación*, 276 (MG).

124 *The smallest of the five*: Conca may also derive from the Chichimeca for "the place where frogs are found."

124 *movement-enfused*: Julianne Burton-Carvajal, *In the Footsteps of Father Junípero Serra, 1750–1758: The Five Folk-Baroque Mission Churches of Mexico's Sierra Gorda*, Anthony's Gate Publications, 2009, 21.

124 *proof of the syncretism*: UNESCO 2003 Report establishing the Sierra Gorda missions as a World Historic Site; cited in ibid., 21.

127 *There is nothing else new*: Serra letter to Father Joseph Campos, in Landa from Jalpan, June 8, 1755. Because Serra gives his "regards" to Palou and Molina, both of whom were stationed for a time at Jalpan, it's possible this letter was written by Serra on the road at one of the other Sierra Gorda missions back to Jalpan. Campos's main station, however, was at Landa. From the archives of the Museum of San Pedro Escanela, Sierra Gorda, Mexico.

127 *I am waiting*: Letter of Francisco Palou (possibly to Hermano Salvador) from either Landa or Jalpan, October 6, 1755. At the Museum of San Pedro Escanela, Sierra Gorda, Mexico. Palou also wrote a fragment of a letter on the same topic two days before (October 4) to Antonio Castenada, so it is possible Castenada was once more the recipient.

Chapter Nine: Lost

129 *a stunning defeat*: S. C. Gwynne, *Empire of the Summer Moon: Quanah Parker and the Rise and Fall of the Comanches, the Most Powerful Indian Tribe in American History*, Scribner, 2010, 69.

129 *a "mystical dream"*: Ibid., 62–63.

129 *two thousand Comanches*: Geiger makes one of his occasional racial slips, calling the Comanche war party "barbarians" facing "the almost helpless mission" (*Life and Times*, I, 137). Perhaps he had in mind not what they were but what they were about to do.

130 *took off his purple Lent chasuble*: Palou says Santiestevan "retired to a little room with his holy crucifix in hand," while Geiger identifies the place of his killing specifically as an "altar" at which he was praying. Perhaps it was a side altar, or sacristy.

130 *playing that comedy*: Serra to Fray Miguel de Petra in Palma de Mallorca, from Mexico City, September 29, 1758. In Tibesar, I, 22–25.

130 *suddenly extinguished*: Palou, *Relación*, 39. Whether or not this is one of Palou's exaggerations, he heard the story of the massacre from Father Molina some months later at San Fernando in Mexico City, as did Serra.

130 *bleeding and fainting*: Ibid., 40.

130 *amounted to a sort*: Gwynne, *Empire of the Summer Moon*, 67.

131 *he was headed to the Apaches*: Serra to Miguel de Petra. In Tibesar, I, 23.

132 *these miserable ones*: Tibesar translates "de aquellos miserables" as "miserable pagans." But that is not what Serra said. In Tibesar, I, 25.

132 *stars fell from heaven*: "And the stars of heaven fell upon the earth" (Apocalypse 6:13). This could be a reference to the fallen angels who defy God and follow Lucifer, but some scholars have seen it as a reference to corrupt priests.

133 *Some of his confreres*: Geiger, *Life and Times*, I, 145.

133 *He had the reputation*: Ibid., 147.

133 *Serra was not safe*: Author interview with Father John Vaughn, O.F.M., Mission Santa Barbara, March 2, 2012.

134 *I am the sinner*: Palou, *Relación*, 42–43 (SW); 41, 236 (MG).

134 *Until you have done*: See Aumann Jordan, *Spiritual Theology*, Sheed & Ward, 1993, 172.

134 *Even the current advocate*: John Vaughn, a Franciscan of Mission Santa Barbara, used the *disciplina* in the late 1940s in California, flogging and being flogged by another novice. He hasn't done it since. Though I never saw a Carmelite priest self-flagellate, as late as 1967, corporal punishment—thrashings with a thick leather belt—was common at our Carmelite high school in the San Fernando Valley. I myself was put "on the pan" twice, and probably deserved it. One priest, in theology class no less, went overboard; he had a habit of conducting the opening prayer while randomly but forcefully hitting a row of teenage boys on the head with his leather strap.

134 *lighting four wicks*: Asserting that Palou does not actually admit witnessing any of this himself, Geiger thinks Palou might have "turned novelist" with his descriptions of Serra self-mutilation; see *Life and Times*, I, 173; and Palou, *Relación*, 257 (SW), 236 (MG). Palou never mentions self-flagellation in California; he only says Serra did it at night (308, SW). Geiger notes that the College of San Fernando did not condemn the practice, though it was to be "rare" and done with "great modesty, prudence, and judgment" (*Life and Times*, I, 173).

135 *the soul descends*: Richard of St. Victor, "Four Degrees of Passionate Charity," *Selected Writings on Contemplation*, translated by Clare Kirchberger, Faber & Faber, 1957, 224. A fascinating twelfth-century Augustinian Scotsman who

died young, Richard of St. Victor is known for an unusually early psychogical treatment of the path to God, one Bonaventure (and Serra) studied.

135 *though the orders were "discreet"*: Jean Louis de Holme, *The History of the Flagellants, or The Advantages of the Discipline*, Fielding & Walker, 1777, 113.

135 *a sword of compassionate sorrow*: Bonaventure, *Legenda Maior*, in *Bonaventure: The Soul's Journey to God*, translated by Ewert Cousins, Paulist Press, 1978, 305.

135 Domine, non sum dignus: A phrase uttered by both priest and congregation just before Communion at Mass.

136 *Yet he kept on*: Palou thought the cause of Serra's difficulty breathing as he walked the paths of southern Mexico was due to thumping of his chest with a stone during sermons because "those in the audience often feared he would break his chest and die in the pulpit" (*Relación*, 257). Geiger, having consulted doctors, is correct in questioning this interpretation. Asthma is not caused by external laceration but by an inflammation of the airways that can be brought on by a variety of stimuli, such as allergens, severe exertion, and emotional duress. Such duress may have accompanied the self-beating with a stone.

136 *a most fateful journey*: Serra was accompanied to Oaxaca by Juan Andrés, Antonio Martínez, Francisco Samaniego, Joaquín Ossorio, and that secret sharer of many of his solitudinous moments, Dionosio Basterra.

136 *Twelve Apostles*: The rest of the group of twelve Franciscans, who arrived from Spain in 1524 to evangelize the indigenous population, were García de Cisneros, Andrés de Córdoba, Luis de Fuensalida, Martín de Jesus, Francisco Jiménez, Juan Juárez, Juan de Palos, Juan de Ribas, Antonio de Ciudad Rodrigo, Francisco de Soto, and Martín de Valencia (the group's leader).

136 *So Herod is*: Louise M. Burkhart, "Moteuczoma and Cortés, Herod and the Magi," in *Invasion and Transformation: Interdisciplinary Perspectives on the Conquest of Mexico,* edited by Rebecca Brienen and Margaret A. Jackson, University of Colorado Press, 2008, 17.

136 *they would state the truth*: Ethelia Ruiz Mendoza, *Mexico's Indigenous Communities: Their Lands and Histories, 1500–2010,* translated by Russ Davidson, University of Colorado Press, 2010, 15.

137 *Río de Los Mijes*: Palou gives no dates or names to Serra's southern river trip, only that it took eight days to arrive at Villa Alta. Most likely, Serra took rivers (not a backtracking footpath) to Acayucan—the Papaloapan and the San Juan—and circled on the large and strong-flowing Río de Lana, with its wide channels to Villa Alta.

137 *tigers and lions and snakes*: Palou, *Relación*, 43.

138 *a spiritual* coup d'état: Geiger, *Life and Times*, I, 162.

138 *fair and beautiful city*: In Richard D. Perry, *Exploring Colonial Oaxaca: The Art and Architecture*, Espadaña Press, 2006, 15.

138 *the "spiritual assault"*: Geiger's phrase, *Life and Times*, I, 162.

139 *causing significant deaths*: Luis Rodrigo Alvarez, *Historia General del Estado de Oaxaca*, Mexico, 2008, 104.

139 *The province of Villa Alta*: María de Los Angeles Romero Frizzi, "La Historia Colonial," in *Oaxaca: Historia Breve*, edited by Alicia Hernández Chávez, Fideicomiso Historia de las Americas, El Colegio de Mexico, 2011, 76.

139 *creating a shimmering tapestry*: Perry, *Exploring Colonial Oaxaca*, 23.

139 *authentic feeling*: Ibid., 24.

139 *a member of the city council*: Palou says only that he was a "rich and powerful man" (*Relación*, 50).

139 *such a dangerous relationship*: Ibid., 51. Palou—though he spends two striking pages on this story in the *Relación*—mentions no names, and Geiger is even more tight-lipped—three sentences and no names.

140 *delivering his soul*: Ibid., 51.

140 *the city was shaken*: Ibid. Though I could not corroborate an earthquake in Oaxaca in 1764, a book surveying earthquakes over the centuries there showed the eighteenth century to have the most (forty-seven), versus the seventeenth century (sixteen) and sixteenth century (eight). It also reveals that "earthquake season" in Oaxaca was clearly spring, and two large temblors occurred in 1768 in April, for which a 1764 quake could have been a precursor. See Genaro D. Vásquez, *Para la Historia del Terreno*, Casa Editorial "Sorta," 1931.

141 *in serious debt*: Cortabarría writes about imposing a *Ramo de la Sisa* (or Royal Tax) on missions in New Spain, or perhaps on cattle, soap, and other items whose proceeds were used to protect borders "that was my responsibility" for at least a decade. He appeared to have been profiting from this venture. Cortabarría letter in Oaxaca, 1757, Archivo Histórico Municipal de Oaxaca, Tomo 17, Actas de Cabildo.

141 *the body of Don Mathías Cortabarría*: After fruitlessly walking all over Oaxaca for a week to five different archives, the first break in the dike occurred at the Archivo de Arquidiócesis de Antequerra-Oaxaca, where an analysis of eighteenth-century death records for the months of March and April 1764 turned up eleven names. Process of elimination cut the list to two, one of whom (José Antonio) died on the very first day of the mission (March 1). Since the events described could not have occurred in one day, I eliminated Antonio and arrived at Cortabarría, the details of whose life clearly fit what Palou revealed in 1787. With the critical name apparently discovered, several relevant commercial and *testimonio* records at the grand Burgoa Library and Archive attached to the Iglesia de Santo Domingo emerged, including: the August 3, 1764, will drawn up by José Bonifacio Mexia (#319) and signed by Josefa Cortabarría, a much shorter version of the original March 22, 1764, will with detailed property holdings and debts signed by José de Pinos and Cortabarría himself (#399); and his commercial dealings, which included the debts paid at the convent for the widow. The name of María Contreras y Burgoa as the widow and possibly Cortabarría's lover is less certain, but the correspondences are compelling and I think the connection likely.

141 *a general feeling of horror*: Palou, *Relación*, 51 (SW), 47–49 (MG).

141 *She was said to imitate*: An interesting allusion by Palou. St. Margaret of Cortona is also the patron saint of the homeless and insane. She lived with a man in Italy for ten years, unwed, and bore him a son (he would not marry her). After the man was found murdered on the road, Margaret joined the Franciscans (to some dissension among the men) and wandered as a beggar, finally founding a hospital for the homeless and poor. The allusion may have indicated that María Contreras had been living under a cloud of accusation long before Serra came to town and also that she became homeless.

141 *that unfortunate man*: Palou, *Relación*, 49 (MG).

143 *Was she María Contreras*: On April 16, 1765, the woman was discovered in

front of La Defensa. See homicide records of El Archivo Histórico General, Oaxaca.

143 *Some heavy weight*: Palou, *Relación*, 48 (SW), 46 (MG).

143 *How could you ask me*: Ibid., 47 (MG).

143 *Ordered there as a commissary*: Documents corroborating this incident (unmentioned by Palou) did not come to light until their discovery in the 1940s in the Archivo General in Mexico City by Eric O'Brien, the first vice-postulator of the Serra Cause, along with Maynard Geiger.

145 *She also clarified*: The source of this incident and quotes are from the declaration of María Pasquala de Nava, April 9, 1766, signed by Melchor de Media Villa y Ascona, Theniente de este Partido, and two witnesses, Joseph Joachim Campos and C. Romero, and also "The Inquisition Case Against María Pasquala Nava" in the Archivo General de la Nación, Mexico City, Mexico, 196 pp. A photocopy of these materials is at the Santa Barbara Mission Archives, Santa Barbara, California, where I reviewed it and made notes and my own copied selections in February 2012. I am also indebted to the interesting treatment of the Pasquala case, "Father Junípero Serra: Agent of the Inquisition" by Dr. Steven Hackel, given as a presentation at the Brown American Seminar, Oregon State University, April 24, 2007, and posted online. Hackel devoted a sizable fourteen pages (122–36) to Serra and the Inquisition in *Junípero Serra*, 2013.

145 *Serra was convinced*: Palou, *Relación*, 46 (MG).

Chapter Ten: Baja

148 *energetic bodies*: Rodríguez de Montalvo Garci, *The Labors of the Very Brave Knight Esplandián*, Chapter 157, translated by William Thomas Little, Center for Medieval and Early Renaissance Studies, 1510/1992, in *Lands of Promise and Despair: Chronicles of Early California, 1535–1846*, edited by Rose Marie Beebe and Robert Senkewicz, Santa Clara University and Heyday Books, 2001, 11.

148 *she did not know*: "The Queen of California," in *The Literature of California: Writings from the Golden State*, edited by Jack Hicks et al., University of California Press, 2000, 77; translated by Edward Everett Hale in an article of the same name in *Atlantic Monthly*, March 1864.

148 *dried out his brain*: Miguel Cervantes, *Don Quixote*, translated by Dawn Raffel, Norton, 1605/1999, 14. *Don Quixote*, considered by many one of the greatest—if not *the* greatest—novels ever written, was devoured by the public over a century before *Joseph Andrews* and *Pamela*. The British "founding" novelists certainly knew their predecessor, many (such as Henry Fielding and Laurence Sterne) praising Cervantes.

148 *a huge dagger-shaped island*: See Larry Gordon, "A Collection That Identifies California as a World Apart," *Los Angeles Times*, December 17, 2012, A1–A13; also Dora Beale Polk, *The Island of California: A History of the Myth*, University of Nebraska Press, 1991.

149 *Coronado's failure*: Wallace Stegner, *Where the Bluebird Sings to the Lemonade Springs: Living and Writing in the West*, Modern Library, 2002, 57–58.

149 *They indicated that they were afraid*: Urdaneta, in Beebe and Senkewicz, eds., *Lands of Promise and Despair*, 37.

150 *a series of unsuccessful attempts*: In 1587, Pedro de Unamuno made it across the Pacific from the Philippines to discover Morro Bay, but fog prevented harboring. In 1594, the Portuguese captain Sebastián Cermeno sailed Manila–California, but Northern Pacific winds and rains wrecked his main galleon. Going east–west seemed a bridge too far.

150 *quite amenable*: Letter from Vizcaíno, March 23, 1603, to Felipe III of Spain. From *Colección de Documentos Inéditos Relativos al Descubrimiento, Conquista, y Organización de las Antiguas Posesiones Españolas de America y Oceania*, Vol. 8, Luis Torres de Mendoza, ed., Madrid, 1867, 560–70, translated by Rose Marie Beebe in *Lands of Promise and Despair*, 45.

151 *How much the residents understood*: Beebe and Senkewicz, *Lands of Promise and Despair*, 42.

152 *They should be treated*: Report by Antonio de la Ascension, ibid.

152 *set in the midst*: Fernando Boneu Companys, *Gaspar de Portolá: Explorer and Founder of California*, Instituto de Estudios Ilerenses, 1983, 119.

152 *no Jesuit . . . ever sat*: MacCullough, *Christianity*, 665.

152 *It was not surprising*: Ibid., 666.

153 *a considerable sum*: Croix letter, in Herbert Ingram Priestley, *José de Gálvez: Visitor-General of New Spain (1765–1771)*, University of California, 1916, reprint edition, Porcupine Press, 1980, 230–31.

153 *It never rains in California*: "A Letter by Juan María de Salvatierra," in Beebe and Senkewicz, eds., *Lands of Promise and Despair*, 79.

153 *vigilance and attention*: Marqués de Grimaldi letter to Viceroy Carlos de Croix, January 23, 1768. From the Geiger papers at Mission Santa Barbara, translated by Michael Grafals, University of California, Santa Barbara, 2012.

153 *Fort Ross's establishment*: The Russian fort was, not long after, bought outright by the American gold striker John Sutter.

154 *Russian Alaska's capital at Sitka*: Sitka was 2,100 miles from Kamchatka, Siberia, and Fort Ross was one thousand miles farther.

154 *a beautiful lady*: Adele Ogden, *The California Sea Otter Trade, 1784–1848*, University of California Press, 1941, 4.

154 *the Aleuts rose up in rebellion*: By the time twenty-four Aleuts were arrested and thrown in prison in Los Angeles (1815), nearly the entire sea otter population was destroyed.

154 *the most able representative*: Priestley, *José de Gálvez*, vii–viii. This revolt in northwestern Mexico lasted ten years.

155 *the true nature of the commotions*: Ibid., 214.

155 *one thousand Indians*: Of these, eighty-five were executed, seventy-three lashed up to two hundred times, 673 given life or long imprisonment, and 117 banished.

155 *this peculiar minister*: Priestley, *José de Gálvez*, 223.

156 *a bloody rehearsal*: The Father of Mexican Independence, Miguel Hidalgo, was a teenager at the time in Valladolid and saw Gálvez's grisly punishments.

156 *Gálvez now focused*: Beebe and Senkewicz call Gálvez's collaboration with Serra a "considerable irony" (*Lands of Promise and Despair*, p. 112) because they deem the visitor-general "genuinely a man of the Enlightenment" and Serra and in fact all Franciscans "especially unaffected by the intellectual changes wrought by the Enlightenment." My own reading of this is: if Gálvez

was a man of the Enlightenment, he was a pretty brutal one. Serra's attitude toward the Indians, especially in California, was positively Rousseauian.

156 *You go, beloved Fathers*: Palou, *Relación*, 53 (SW).

156 *the Sea of Cortez*: The Sea of Cortez and Gulf of California are used interchangeably for the same narrow body of water separating the Mexican mainland from Baja.

156 *goodbye was for eternity*: Palou, *Relación*, 53 (SW).

156 *as far as the Golden Gate*: Geiger, *Life and Times*, I, 184.

156 *they rested at Santa Cruz*: Twenty-two years later, Palou would be buried at Santa Cruz in Querétaro, alongside Garcés, martyred in the desert.

157 *astonished at its contents*: Geiger, *Life and Times*, I, 185.

157 *We favor the first decision*: Serra to Father García, in Mexico City from Tepic, October 17, 1767. In Tibesar, I, 31–33.

157 *spiritual expedition*: Serra letter to the viceroy, Francisco Carlos de Croix, March 2, 1768. In Tibesar, I, 35.

157 *Tribes were thick*: Statistics for Baja in 2010 show it with a population of 3.1 million; in 1768, the population was probably less than 200,000—most of whom were indigenous.

158 *For so long we had lived*: Juan Crespí, *A Description of Distant Roads: Original Journals of the First Expedition into California, 1769–1770*, translated and edited by Alan K. Brown, San Diego State University Press, 161.

158 *to erect the holy standard*: Geiger, *Life and Times*, I, 201. Strangely, Geiger does not cite the date of this "first" letter to Gálvez, and it is not in his exhaustive collection at the Santa Barbara Mission Archives, nor in Tibesar. With the exception of this mysterious "first" letter, the bulk of Serra's letters to the visitor-general have been lost.

158 *documents and the insight*: Gálvez omnibus letter to Junípero Serra (and other friars in Baja), from Santa Ana, July 12, 1768. Unless otherwise noted, letters from Gálvez are translated for the first time by Michael Grafals, Department of Spanish, University of California, Santa Barbara, April 2012.

158 *All of them became*: Gálvez letter to Julián de Arriaga, Spain's secretary of seas and Indies, in Madrid from Santa Ana, September 8, 1769.

158 *keeping shoddy records*: In a July 3, 1771, letter to Manuel Lanza de Casafonda, Rafael Verger reveals that by "the accounts the commissioners handed in" they slaughtered nine hundred head of cattle in six months.

158 *commissioners were born to obey*: Gálvez letter to Serra, in Loreto from Santa Ana, August 13, 1768, in the Santa Barbara Mission Archive and Library.

159 *slipshod if not renegade soldiers*: Strange, too, that Geiger does not name what the soldiers fanned out in Baja did—he talks about the "damage" they caused, "the chaos," their "near ruination" of communities (*Life and Times*, I, 202). But given what happened later in Alta California with these same soldiers isolated on an even more severe frontier, rape and theft are not unlikely.

159 *took to the fields*: Gálvez public declaration in La Paz, November 21, 1768.

159 *the wild abandon*: Gálvez letter to Miguel de la Campa, in Baja from Santa Ana, September 14, 1769.

159 *It's not necessary*: Gálvez letter to Serra, in Loreto from Santa Ana, August 13, 1768.

159 *to have myself bled*: Harry Crosby, *Gateway to Alta California: The Expedition to San Diego, 1769*, Sunbelt, 2003, 42.

159 *one day's horse journey*: Geiger makes the claim (*Life and Times*, I, 204) that Serra cooked up the legendary one-day ride between missions at this time, but there's no direct evidence of it, no Serra letters quoted from, nothing in Palou. Gálvez may have made an indirect reference to it in his letter to Serra, September 24, 1768, but the letter is missing.

159 *Let him find the port*: Palou, *Relacíon*, 80 (MG).

159 *my labors are sufficiently bad*: Gálvez letter to Serra, in Loreto from Santa Ana, September 15, 1768, in Geiger, *Life and Times*, I, 205.

159 *I second the fervor*: Gálvez letter to Palou, in San Javier de Borja from Santa Ana, July 26, 1768.

160 *stew in abundance*: Gálvez letter to Serra, in Loreto from Santa Ana, October 22, 1769. If it ever existed, a written record of the historic Gálvez-Serra meeting in Baja is lost.

160 whenever you ask for an Indian: Gálvez in May 14, 1769, Curimpo notice, from La Paz, responding to letter of Juan Gutiérrez of Loreto, May 14, 1769. The emphasis, an underline in the original, was Gutiérrez's.

161 *the wretched heathens' daily bread*: Crespí, *A Description of Distant Roads*, 153–253. Further Crespí references are from this diary.

162 *With much sorrow:* This and other Serra comments in chapter 10 from here on are from the *Diary of the Expedition from Loreto to San Diego, March 28 to July 1, 1769*. In Tibesar, I, 38–123.

162 *I see myself tied*: Palou to Juan Andrés, in Mexico City from Baja, March 15, 1769.

163 *encourage me to move forward*: Geiger certainly felt this was a key, if not the key, to Serra's character (one that implies not just an indomitable spirit, but also the treachery of the past and perhaps an inability to deal with the complexities of failure and tragedy).

163 *he kicked his mule*: This dialogue is derived by three different translations (including my own) of Palou's account in the *Relación*.

164 *paid, in generous measure*: Serra's original diary entry reads "*pagado largo rato este tributo licito a la naturaleza.*" Crespí, who had been through Gertrudis a month or so before, did not receive this emotional outburst, though Basterra had given him "a hearty clasp."

164 *The Most Holy Cross of the Pools*: The pools of fresh water he dubbed "The Pools of Santa Monica," after the long-suffering mother of that perennially rebellious son, Augustine.

165 *gained sight*: In his diary Crespí capitalizes "HARBOR OF SAN DIEGO" and centers it on his page. There's nothing like that anywhere else in his text.

167 *They were going to lie*: *Diary of Gaspar de Portolá During the California Expedition of 1769–1770*, edited by Donald Smith and Frederick Teggart, University of California Press, 1909, 41. All statements by Portolá throughout chapter 10 are from his diary of the expedition.

167 *hostile Indians*: Serra relates explorer Gonzalez Cabrera Bueno's encounter with warlike Indians at just this spot (Bay of San Quintín), noted in the *Navegación Especulativa y Práctica*, the admiral's classic pilot manual of the time,

published in 1734. Serra had done his homework, carrying not only the Bible and María de Agreda, but Bueno's manual and the diary of Jesuit Wenceslaus Linck.

170 *Barrabas, the Indian*: The thief had been nicknamed Barrabas earlier by Crespí. Geiger cracks one of his few jokes about this heist, saying that if the spectacles hadn't been recovered, Serra was in trouble—the nearest "oculist" was in Guadalajara, 1,500 miles away.

171 O taste and see: Psalm 34:8.

Chapter Eleven: Who They Were, What They Did,
What They Believed

175 *Pacific coast of California*: From this point on in the text, reference to "California" means "Upper" or "Alta" or "New" California, unless otherwise specified. That is, it refers to the present boundaries of the state of California of the United States.

175 *The California Indian*: A. L. Kroeber, "Elements of Culture in Native California," in R. F. Heizer and M. A. Whipple, *The California Indians: A Sourcebook*, University of California Press, 1971, 59.

175 *most tribes did not have*: Ibid.

176 *Extensive early treatments*: Alfred Kroeber's *Handbook of the Indians of California* (1925, reprinted in 1953) and *The California Indians, A Sourcebook*, edited by R. F. Heizer and M. A. Whipple (1971) are the lodestones. Archaeological activity has been on an upswing for the past several decades, uncovered in Brian Fagan's *Before California: An Archaeologist Looks at Our Earliest Inhabitants*, Altamira Press, 2003.

177 *you will be doing*: In Herbert Luthin, ed., *Surviving Through the Days: Translations of Native California Stories and Songs*, University of California Press, 2002, 506.

177 *At contact in 1769*: This population of 225,000 is anthropologist John Johnson's compromise 2013 estimate, based on the 300,000 figure of Sherburne Cook's in 1962, itself a revision of his and Kroeber's earlier lower estimates (around 130,000).

177 *seventy-eight mutually unintelligible languages*: Victor Golla, *California Indian Languages*, University of California Press, 2011, 1–3. The five hundred to six hundred tribes and tribelets figure is Kroeber's in "The Nature of Land Holding Groups in Aboriginal California," *University of California Archaeological Survey Reports* 56 (1962): 19–58.

179 *Smaller beds for children*: See Geiger and Johnson, *The Indians of Mission Santa Barbara*, 6.

179 *fairly good looking*: Ibid., 5.

180 *industriousness of making arrows*: See "A Story of Lizard" in Luthin, ed., *Surviving Through the Days*, 156. The arrows of the storyteller Ishi are among the best of the few that survive from pre-contact days.

180 *perhaps the most omnivorous*: A. L. Kroeber, "The Food Problem in California," in Heizer and Whipple, eds., *The California Indians*, 298.

180 *acorn leaching was unique*: See E. W. Gifford, "Californian Balanophagy," in Heizer and Whipple, eds., *The California Indians*, 301–5.

181 *It may have been smoke*: William McCawley, *The First Angelinos: The Gabrielino Indians of Los Angeles*, Malki Museum/Ballena Press, 1996, 4.

181 *a kind of popcorn*: E. O. Essig, "The Value of Insects to the California Indians," in Heizer and Whipple, eds., *The California Indians*, 315–18.

181 *pulpy, sweet and nutritious*: David Prescott Barrows, "Desert Plant Foods of the Coahuilla," in Heizer and Whipple, eds., *The California Indians*, 307.

182 *triggered by trespass*: Robert Heizer, "Village Shifts and Tribal Spreads in California Prehistory," in Heizer and Whipple, eds., *The California Indians*, 482.

183 *a string of very large shells*: Kroeber estimated the Yurok's sizable eleven-shell string to be worth $50 (in 1959 dollars—about four times that in today's money).

183 *The persistence*: A. L. Kroeber, "Yurok Law and Custom," in Heizer and Whipple, eds., *The California Indians*, 412.

183 *people of such and such*: Kroeber, "Elements of Culture in Native California," 27.

186 *When the waters recede*: "The Tidal Wave, *Test-ch'as*," in Luthin, ed., *Surviving Through the Days*, 71–76.

186 *to the rim of the world*: "The Creation," in Hicks, et al., eds., *The Literature of California*, 23–25.

187 *difficult to manage*: Raymond White, "Religion and Its Role Among the Luiseño," in *Native Californians: A Theoretical Retrospective*, edited by Lowell Bean and Thomas C. Blackburn, Ballena Press, 1976, 361–77.

187 *a prudent Luiseño*: Sandos, *Converting California*, 21.

187 *Four religious cults*: See A. L. Kroeber, "The Religion of the Indians of California," *University of California Publications in American Archaeology and Ethnology* 4, no. 6 (1907).

188 *such ceremonies*: Some anthropologists saw a "death obsession" in the prevalence of mourning ceremonies in some southern California tribes.

188 *shocking (to Franciscan sensibilities)*: Father Boscana called a similar routine where the naked woman sang a song invoking the man's penis and the woman's vagina "an infamous thing and a diabolical invention." See Gerónimo Boscana, *Chinigchinich: Historical Account of the Belief, Usage, Customs and Extravagancies of the Indians of This Mission of San Juan Capistrano Called the Acagchemem Tribe*, translated by Alfred Robinson and John P. Harrington, Malki Museum Press, 1978.

189 *they had seen men*: From "The Official Account of the Rodríguez Cabrillo Expedition," in Beebe and Senkewicz, eds., *Lands of Promise and Despair*, 33.

189 *Let us have a dance*: R. L. Oswalt, *Kashaya Texts*, University of California Press, 1964, 245–47, in *The California Missions: History, Art, and Preservation*, Kimbro, Costello, and Ball, Getty Conservation Institute, 2010, 7.

Chapter Twelve: Mission San Diego de Alcalá:
The Solace of Unfortunates

196 *profound indications*: The Kumeyaay leaders, the *kuseyaay*, often "explained why some natural occurences affected food sources." Richard Carrico, *Strangers in a Stolen Land*, Sunbelt, 2008, 14.

196 *On that day*: Serra letter to Viceroy Antonio María de Bucareli, in Mexico City from Mexico City, May 21, 1773. In Tibesar, I, 367.

196 *The expedition by sea*: Serra letter to Father Juan Andrés, in Mexico City from San Diego, July 3, 1769. In Tibesar, I, 133.

197 *It was torture*: Kenneth King, *Mission to Paradise: The Story of Junípero Serra and the Missions of California*, Franciscan Herald Press, 1975, 36.

197 *an infirmary*: Geiger, *Life and Times*, I, 231.

197 *falling to pieces*: Serra to Guardian Juan Andrés. In Tibesar, I, 137.

197 *bottom of the sea*: Marla Daley and diver Jim Luche have found wreckage off Catalina Island that might be the *San José*.

198 *not only impolite*: James Sandos and Patricia Sandos, "Chisli, Canuch, and Junípero Serra: Indian Responses to Mission San Diego, 1769–1788," in Rose Marie Beebe and Robert Senkewicz, eds., *"To Toil in That Vineyard of the Lord": Contemporary Scholarship on Junípero Serra*, Academy of American Franciscan History, 2010, 56.

198 *the army of hell*: Palou, *Relación*, 75 (MG).

199 *little more could be done*: Serra letter to Guardian Juan Andrés, in Mexico City from San Diego, February 10, 1770. In Tibesar, I, 150–51.

199 *very great thieves*: Crespí, *A Description of Distant Roads*, 253.

199 *spit out*: Palou, *Relación*, 80 (SW), 76 (MG).

199 *wooden sabers*: Ibid.

200 *without the loss*: Serra letter to Guardian Juan Andrés, San Diego, February 10, 1770. In Tibesar, I, 151. Some of the descriptions in this passage come from Palou, *Relación*, 80–82, and Geiger, *Life and Times*, I, 234–35.

200 *chastened by Spanish power*: Palou, *Relación*, 82.

201 *without the least repugnance*: Palou, quoting Serra, *Relación*, 83 (SW), 787 (MG).

202 *manner of commerce*: Crespí, *A Description of Distant Roads*, 399–401. All quotes from Crespí in this chapter, unless otherwise noted, are from his travel journals of 1769–1770.

203 *took peace to enemies*: One might, viewing L.A.'s crosses—the race riots, the earthquakes, the violence of gangs, the pedophilia scandal—extend the analogy further to Francis's stigmata. No saint had ever felt Christ's suffering more acutely, and no American city—with the possible exception of New Orleans—better understood the costs of freedom.

203 *Wounds of Our Father*: No one was ever going to pitch mortar for a mission on the precipice of the Santa Lucias. There was never any "Wounds of Our Father" mission along the Big Sur coast. The closest mission would be on the east side of the mountains—San Antonio de Padua.

204 *body-long burns*: The child may have caught fire during grass burns of the Luiseño or perhaps around the typical firepit in a Acjachemen (Juaneño) home.

204 *"very fair and red-haired" children*: These Juaneño children may have resulted from brief sexual liaisons with sailors of the Cabrillo (1542) or Vizcaíno (1602) expeditions, or Spaniards or northern European Jesuits in Baja. Pedro Font thought Crespí was unconsciously comparing them to "so many angels" seen with "blue-eyed blondness" in Baroque paintings. See Font's *Complete Diary*, translated by Herbert Bolton, University of California Press, 1931, 345. See also Brown's introduction to Crespí's *Description of Distant Roads*, 63.

206 *You come from Rome*: The source for the little joke is Portolá's letter to a friend, September 17, 1773, in Charles E. Chapman, *A History of California: The Spanish Period*, New York, 1921, 227. Cited in Geiger, *Life and Times*, I, 237.

206 *were very painful*: Crespí, *A Description of Distant Roads*, 677.

207 *His whole nature rebelled*: Geiger, *Life and Times*, I, 240.

207 *Portolá would finish*: Palou, *Relación*, 87 (SW).

207 *to the last gasp*: Brown's translation of the Serra letter to Palou, San Diego, February 10, 1770, in Crespí, *A Description of Distant Roads*, 79. Tibesar translates *para aguantar hasta el último esfuerzo* as "to hang on to the limit of our endurance."

207 *the inevitable refusal*: Ibid., 79.

207 *most anxious*: Geiger's phrase, *Life and Times*, I, 241.

208 *up to his last breath*: Palou actually said the last High Mass in honor of the saint who saved California, on August 19, 1784, in Carmel, when Serra was too weak to lead it.

208 *our cares now at an end*: Crespí, *A Description of Distant Roads*, 677.

208 *within the sound of the bells*: Serra to Bucareli, in Mexico City from Carmel, February 5, 1775. In Tibesar, I, 229.

Chapter Thirteen: Mission San Carlos Borromeo de Carmelo: The Disappearing Oak of Monterey

210 *shimmering ladder of light*: In his masterpiece, *The Soul's Journey into God* (*Itinerarium Mentis in Deum*), Bonaventure introduces the metaphor of Christ as the restorative ladder: "Just as when one has fallen he must lie unless someone join him and lend him a hand, so our soul could not be perfectly lifted up out of those things of sense to see itself and the eternal Truth, had not Truth, taking on human form in Christ, become a ladder restoring the first ladder that had been broken in Adam." Philotheus Boehner, O.F.M., trans., *The Journey of the Mind to God*, Hackett, 1993, 23.

210 *How many times*: Though Serra would often refer to his California missions as "rungs of a ladder" that would lead to God, and in that his direct influence is certainly St. Bonaventure, St. Francis's first substantive biographer, he would probably also have known that the image of the ladder was as ancient as Homer's *catena aurea* (Golden Chain) or Aristotle's *scala naturae*. The metaphor of the ladder is fused in both its "Greek cosmic sense" with the ascension of Christ by two twelfth-century mystics: Richard of St. Victor, who said, "We who are men and cannot fly are accustomed to use a ladder," and Isaac of Stella. Bernard McGinn comments about the ladder, "The symbol is important not for what it said but for what it did. In enabling man to feel at home in the world, in giving him a sense of the unity of all being with God, in inviting him to the arduous ascent to which his nature called him." See Bernard McGinn, *The Golden Chain: A Study in the Theological Anthropology of Isaac of Stella*, Cistercian Publications, 1972, 4–5, 93–102, 179.

210 *where our ancestors*: Serra was off by a year. Vizcaíno landed in Monterey on December 16, 1602, and left for Mendocino on December 29, before winds turned him southward, arriving in Acapulco in March 1603.

210 *the port's having disappeared*: Serra letter to Guardian Juan Andrés, in Mexico City from Monterey, June 12, 1770. In Tibesar, I, 167.

211 *still somewhat fresh*: Palou, *Relación*, 101 (SW), 95 (MG).

211 *bright as the sun*: Serra memoranda to Guardian Pangua, Monterey, June 22, 1774, and July 18, 1774. In Tibesar, II, 89, 113.

211 *crushing blows*: Wade, *Missions, Missionaries, and Native Americans*, 168.

212 *gave his order's name*: Carmel may be the oldest place name given by a European to what became the United States. It certainly predates anything in Virginia or Massachusetts.

212 *ninth-century traditional opening*: Attributed originally to Rabanus Marius, the song has been the basis of a Mahler symphony, a Martin Luther prayer, and a John Dryden poem.

213 *Three other presumably local Indians*: See description of *The Founding* in Gail Sheridan and Mary Pat McCormick, *Art from the Carmel Mission*, Fine Arts, 2011, 92. Born and raised in France, Trousset arrived in Monterey in 1875, where he painted his classic rendering of the founding of Monterey (a more romantic "beginning" for California than earlier at San Diego).

213 *the branches bathe*: Palou, *Historical Memoirs of New California (Noticias)*. Cited in exhibit at the Monterey San Carlos Heritage Center, Monterey, California.

213 *death by railroad*: The Vizcaíno-Serra oak was hit repeatedly by lightning in the 1840s, and in 1889, while an embankment for a railroad line was being built, a culvert collapsed and seawater invaded the oak, killing it. On July 6, 1904, when a utility crew finally cut its roots and threw it into the bay, the *Monterey New Era* wrote, "The oak tree under which Serra said Monterey's founding Mass on June 3, 1770, is declared dead." Worm-eaten pieces rest today at Carmel Mission, the presidio museum, and at the Vatican.

213 *fiddleback-shaped chasuble*: From the Latin *casula*, or "little house." Chasubles are the poncholike overgarment used by priests at Mass by decree starting in the eighth century. One left today at Carmel might have fit the diminutive Serra, with its image of the Lamb surrounded by sunlike gold rays.

214 *the most remarkable*: Kimbro and Costello, *The California Missions*, 121.

214 *And she would flee*: Ibid. See also M. J. Morgado, *Junípero Serra's Legacy*, Pacific Grove, 1987, 44–48. When the missions were secularized and fell apart, the last Indian at Carmel Mission (named Cantu) rescued La Conquistadora, though later the infant Jesus figure was stolen, then returned in 1945.

214 *all the inconveniences*: Serra letter to Sister Antonia Valladolid, in Mexico City (?) from Monterey, June 30, 1770. Was Sister Antonia a special friend? It seems so. He told no one else about constructing the place where he would sleep, "a small cabin of wood, for my abode." See Tibesar, I, 181.

215 *they weren't cheap*: Craig Russell called it "exorbitantly expensive" during the mission period "to provide man-made light." See *From Serra to Sancho*, 175.

215 *poor hermits cut off*: Serra letter to Francisco Palou, in Baja from Monterey, June 13, 1770. In Tibesar, I, 179. Like the twelfth-century hermit Isaac of Stella on his small French island, the monk who revealed the ladder to God?

215 *eighty leagues from the nearest priest*: Ibid.

216 *slain by Indians in Sonora*: The new pope was Clement XIV, who had been elected while Serra was journeying north in Baja the year before—in May 1769.

The two beatified Italian Franciscans (Joseph of Cupertino and Seraphim) indeed had been canonized by Clement XIII in 1767. Serra named a town in present-day Silicon Valley, California, in 1775 after Cupertino, the patron saint of the mentally handicapped.

216 *any little demons*: Serra letter to Palou. In Tibesar, I, 179.

216 *not a breath of air*: Serra letter to Gálvez, in Mexico City from Monterey, July 2, 1770. In Tibesar, I, 185–87.

216 *fiery heart of the universe*: See Samuel Edgerton, in *Theatres of Conversion*, 64, who refers to the monstrance "replicating the sun" in Corpus Christi celebrations, in Russell, *From Serra to Sancho*, 172.

216 *revered natural symbols*: See Fray Toribio Motolinía, *History of the Indians of Spain*, edited by Elizabeth Andros Foster, Cortés Society of the Bancroft Library, 1950, 103, in Russell, *From Serra to Sancho*, 178, 230.

217 *convert[ed] . . . into ashes*: Gálvez to Col. Juan Piñeda, Alamos, May 23, 1769, in Priestley, *José de Gálvez*, 274.

217 *some thought he had been poisoned*: Priestley, *José de Gálvez*, 10–11, 275–80.

217 *the greatest enterprise*: Croix letter to Gálvez, Mexico City, February 29, 1769.

218 *the extension of the faith*: Croix's declaration is reproduced in Palou, *Relación*, 104–6 (SW), 100 (MG).

218 *Serra's childhood school*: Serra literally recast his Mallorcan childhood in the baptism of Indians. Another example: on September 3, 1782, he christened at Carmel a thirteen-year-old Esselen girl, María de Buen Año—a reference to the Shrine of Bon Any in Petra.

218 *a wealth of sufferings*: Serra letter to Palou, in Baja from Carmel, August 18, 1772. In Tibesar, I, 269.

218 *pure dirt*: See Serra letter to Palou, in Baja from Monterey, June 21, 1771. In Tibesar, I, 237–45.

218 *something violent*: Serra soon called Fages "a molester" (Geiger, *Life and Times*, 279). A cautionary note: in both English and Spanish (*molestar, inquietar*), the verb "to molest" has a primary meaning without sexual content, that is "to disturb, interfere with, or annoy." Its second meaning is more commonly assumed today, "to accost and harass sexually." It's not certain which Serra meant (Geiger cites no source), but as early as Serra's August 8, 1772, letter to Verger he leaves no doubt that he thought the soldiers were violating the Indian women sexually, jeopardizing the evangelical enterprise.

219 *Pebble Beach Golf Course*: Testifying in 1949 for Serra sainthood, Abel Espinosa insisted that prayers to Serra had helped him, although one can't help wondering if he were praying for par. See Pamela Tanous, "The Espinosa Brothers: Monterey County Golf Legends," n.d. See also *The Positio of Fray Junípero Serra*, The Vatican, 1981, 569; and author's interview with Pamela Tanous, Carmel, CA, March 4, 2013. Socorranda was a Rumsen village.

219 *O grant us days*: One of the last lines of *O Salutaris Hostia* (whose title means "O Saving Victim").

219 Genitori, genitoque: "To the Begetter and the Begotten, praise and joy" (from *Tantum Ergo,* or "So Great a Sacrament").

220 *The way it danced*: This is the path of today's breathtaking toll road 17-Mile Drive, which goes in and out of Pebble Beach Golf Course, including the "Lone Cypress." For Serra, it was sculpted by God and perfectly free—of

golfers, as well as tolls. The reference is to Peter, leader of the twelve apostles, who just before his execution said he was unworthy to be crucified as the savior, and so was crucified upside down.

Chapter Fourteen: Mission San Antonio de Padua:
A Bell for a Woman Flying in Blue

222 *the Chinese of California*: Pedro Fages, *A Historical, Political and Natural Description of California*, translated by Herbert Priestley, University of California Press, 1937 (originally published in 1775), 31.

222 *a martinet*: Theodore Maynard, *The Long Road of Father Serra*, Appleton-Century-Crofts, 1954, 158.

223 *dirty, very slovenly*: Fages, *A Historical, Political, and Natural Description of California*, 11.

223 *free of the ambition*: David Weber, *Bárbaros*, 30.

223 *Complaints were made*: Serra letter to Palou, in Baja from Monterey, June 21, 1771. In Tibesar, I, 241.

223 *the most notorious molesters*: Serra letter to Rafael Verger, in Mexico City from Carmel, August 8, 1772. In Tibesar, I, 261. Serra's original phrase is *muy notados de inquietadores. Inquietar*, like *molestar*, invites double entendres, both in the English and in the Spanish of then and today.

223 *the Valley of the Oaks*: Begun as a retreat from the military, Mission San Antonio today is surrounded by Fort Hunter Liggett, some of whose soldiers returned from Afghanistan without limbs to pray in its church.

224 *trusting that with time*: Crespí, *A Description of Distant Roads*, 513–21.

224 *the only mountain pass near Lucia*: Crespí probably took the route of today's Nacimiento–Fergusson road through the mountains, seventeen miles southwest of Mission San Antonio.

224 *rattlers, which slither*: On May 26, 2012, the director of Mission San Antonio, Joan Steele, showed this visitor a boxful of rattlesnake tails she had cut off after killing the rattlers, who live in the melted old adobe walls.

225 *hawk's circling shadow*: My descriptions of Pieras and Sitjar derive from Maynard Geiger, *Franciscan Missionaries in Hispanic California*, Huntington Library, 1969, 196–97, 245–47. The dialogue from this marvelous exchange comes from Palou, *Relación*, 117–18, Geiger's translation in *Life and Times*, I, 280, and my own.

225 *fervent brass bell*: Serra diary. In Tibesar, I, 65. Serra letter to Gálvez, in New Spain from Monterey, July 2, 1770. In Tibesar, I, 185.

225 *bringing it up ironically*: Geiger, *Life and Times*, I, 292.

225 *a single Indian*: Palou, *Relación*, 118 (SW), 111 (MG).

226 *this mission will come to be*: Ibid.

226 *He gave full vent*: Geiger, *Life and Times*, I, 281.

226 *cannot bring themselves to leave them*: Serra letter to Bucareli, in Mexico City from Mexico City, May 21, 1773. In Tibesar, I, 355.

226 *its grape vines would last longer*: The landmark grape vine at San Antonio dates from 1860.

226 *they were afraid*: "Official Account of the Rodriguez Cabrillo Expedition," in Beebe and Senkewicz, eds., *Lands of Promise and Despair*, 37.

227 *did not walk*: Palou, *Relación*, 119.

227 *foretold white men coming*: Fathers Marcelino Marquinez and Jayme Escude, in Geiger, *Life and Times*, I, 295–96. This astounding claim rested in the 1814 report of the missionaries of Mission Santa Cruz to Spain, and was amplified for an American correspondent in 1856 by Father Juan Comellas, who thought the "woman priest" was indeed María de Agreda. *Alta California*, San Francisco, April 5, 1860.

228 *that was now* theirs: See photographic images of the caves inside and out in Susan Raycraft and Ann Keenan Beckett, *San Antonio Valley*, Arcadia, 2006, 10–11; and Beatrice (Tid) Casey, *Padres and People of Old Mission San Antonio*, Casey Printing, 1957/2006, 7–8.

228 *a large percentage of Salinan Indians*: The talent of "shaping and weaving" has come down two and a half centuries from pre-contact time through the Ensinales family. A current descendant is Judy Grindstaff of nearby Jolon.

229 *Even more impressive*: Russell, *From Serra to Sancho*, 256, 259, 263. The *Mise en Sol* is one of only two Sancho works not stolen or vanished from Stanford University's holdings.

Chapter Fifteen: Mission San Gabriel Arcángel:
Wonder and War in the City of Angels

231 *It was the Assumption*: On November 1, 1950, Pope Pius XII declared August 15 the Feast Day of the Assumption of the Blessed Mother bodily into heaven, without her actually dying, the last *ex cathedra* papal pronouncement. But the date had been cherished by custom in the Church since the seventh century, when John of Damascus first discussed the Assumption, influenced, according to some commentators, by the Muslim doctrine, then all around him, of the bodily ride on horse to heaven of Muhammad.

231 *downtown Los Angeles*: The same image hangs at Mission San Gabriel today to the left of the altar, surrounded by ten million Angelenos. Who sees the Lady of Sorrows today?

231 *loads of various grains*: Palou, *Relación*, 127.

232 *a very important settlement*: Fages, *A Historical, Political, and Natural Description of California*, 20.

232 *I rather suspect*: Serra letter to Pedro Fages, in San Diego from San Diego, October 13, 1772. In Tibesar, I, 289.

232 *called to the Fathers*: Palou, *Relación*, 127.

232 *with bows and arrows*: Geiger, *Life and Times*, I, 305. Cambon (or Palou) thought he heard "Tomorrow all of us will come and shoot you with arrows" from a badly misheard or mistranslated *Pisag Farafat Migich Tux*. Dr. Jane Hill of the University of Arizona provided the more likely transliteration and translation.

232 *an outrage*: Palou, *Relación*, 128.

232 *most heinous crimes*: Serra letter to Rafael Verger, in Mexico City from Monterey, August 8, 1772. In Tibesar, I, 259.

232 *what they sought*: Robert Heizer, ed., *The Indians of Los Angeles County: Hugo Reid's Letters of 1852*, Southwest Museum, 1968, 70. Hugo Reid was the first to translate Boscaná's *Chinigchinich* into English.

233 *in grim and gory contrast*: Geiger, *Life and Times*, I, 303.

233 *the head of Holofernes*: See Cambon's account of the battle in Palou, *Historical Memoirs of New California (Noticias)*, 321–28. In the Book of Deuteronomy, Holofernes was the Babylonian general seduced before he attacked the Hebrews by Judith, who cut his head off.

233 *The god whom they adore*: Fages, *A Historical, Political, and Natural Description of California*, 48, was referring to the Chumash of San Luis Obispo, but the first quote on the sun appears to hold for most of the Indians of southern California; the second reference is from Kroeber, *The California Indians*, 42, particularly pronounced among the Yokuts of the Joaquin Valley, but common to many California tribes.

234 *shot down with bullets*: Serra letter to Bucareli, in Mexico City from San Fernando, May 21, 1773. In Tibesar, I, 361.

234 *I could not say for the present*: Serra letter to Palou, in Baja from Monterey, August 18, 1772. In Tibesar, I, 267. This is the "wealth of sufferings" letter (Tibesar, I, 269).

234 *If we are not allowed*: Serra letter to Bucareli, May 21, 1773.

234 *molested by soldiers*: Geiger, *Life and Times*, I, 307.

235 *disemboweling and castrating others*: M. N. L. Couve de Murville, *The Man Who Founded California: The Life of Blessed Junípero Serra*, Ignatius Press, 2000, 74.

235 *There is no joy*: Father Antonio Paterna to Governor Barri, in Loreto from San Diego, included in the *Expediente* on California affairs sent by Verger to Viceroy Bucareli, Mexico City, December 23, 1771, in Geiger, *Life and Times*, I, 341.

235 *grave and damaging consequences*: Bucareli's first admonishing letter to Serra in Carmel from Mexico City is dated November 30, 1771; his beginning of a change of heart, the second quote here, is from his letter to Verger at San Fernando in Mexico City, March 1, 1772. The lambasting letter is Bucareli to Fages, December 2, 1772, Santa Barbara Mission Archive and Library, JSC 311, translated by Cristina Wray, Newport News, VA.

235 *because of my many sins*: Serra letter to Palou, in Baja from Monterey, August 18, 1772. In Tibesar, I, 267.

236 *When sighing they say*: Ibid., 257.

236 *each passing day they improve*: Serra letter to Palou, in Baja from Carmel, August 18, 1772, In Tibesar, I, 267.

236 *bursting into laughter*: Serra letter to Bucareli, in Mexico City from Mexico City, May 21, 1773. In Tibesar, I, 371.

236 *his ardent zeal*: Rafael Verger to Don Manuel Lanz de Casfonda, August 3, 1771, Santa Barbara Mission Archive and Library, JSC 264; also Serra to Verger, in Mexico City from Carmel, June 20, 1772. In Tibesar, I, 219.

237 *would require "miracles"*: Verger to Casafonda, in Madrid from Mexico City, June 30, 1771, in the Santa Barbara Mission Archive and Library, JSC 258.

237 *still tender plants*: Serra to Bucareli, in Mexico City from Mexico City, May 21, 1773. In Tibesar, I, 371, 359.

237 *planted syphilis*: Sherbourne Cook thought the first cases of venereal disease must have been triggered by the original Portolá expedition in 1769, as the Baja soldiers were riddled with it. Other historians think the sexual transmission

was isolated or ephemeral until 1777, when the first settlers of the Anza expedition entered California. In either case, once it started, it was, among many, the greatest plague of all.

238 *Given hands to cultivate*: Serra to Bucareli, May 21, 1773.

238 *death of their chief*: Palou, *Relación*, 129 (SW).

238 *chasing birds and squirrels*: See William McCawley, *The First Angelinos*, 194.

238 *one of the most distinctive*: Kimbro and Costello, *The California Missions*, 182.

238 *staggered pyramidical finials*: There was a similarity to the finials in the Sierra Gorda mission, "Turk's caps" at Tancoyol.

239 *nice little things for herself*: Rose Marie Beebe and Robert Senkewicz, eds., *Testimonios: Early California Through the Eyes of Women, 1815–1848*, Heydey Books and the Bancroft Library, 2006, 94–117. Eulalia Pérez also midwifed the future governor of Mexican California, Pio Pico, witnessing, too, the tragic deaths during the War of Independence of fathers Sanchez and Zaldivea, the former with burst eardrums, the latter thrown into a *carreta* on top of hides. Much of early California is encapsulated in her life.

239 *spiritual debt peonage*: See Sandos, *Converting California*, 108.

239 *a communitarian impulse*: Douglas Monroy, *The Borders Within: Encounters Between Mexico and the U.S.*, University of Arizona Press, 2008, 156.

239 *It was very painful*: Beebe and Senkewicz, eds., *Testimonios*, 109.

239 *with no privacy*: McCawley, *The First Angelinos*, 196.

240 *Jacob's muscle-bound angel*: See Genesis 35:1–7. For the annunciation of Gabriel to Mary, see Luke 1:26–38; and to Elizabeth, Luke 1:5–25.

Chapter Sixteen: Mission San Luis Obispo de Tolosa y Tilini:
A Prayer for Bears

242 *I began to think which*: Serra to Verger, in Mexico City from Carmel, August 8, 1772. In Tibesar, I, 251–53.

243 *'nothing but [tidal] flats'*: Stanger and Brown, *Who Discovered the Golden Gate?*, 125; also Crespí, *A Description of Distant Roads*, 92.

243 *strange, salamanderlike*: See Neil Harlow, *Maps of San Francisco Bay from the Spanish Discovery in 1769 to the American Occupation*, Book Club of California, 1950, Map 2, in Stanger and Brown, *Who Discovered the Golden Gate?*, 93.

244 *into a tailspin*: Charles J. G. Maximin Piette, *Evocation de Junípero Serra, Fondateur de la Californie*, Academy of American Franciscan History, 1946, 109.

244 *brown bear in California*: The California golden bear, or brown bear, featured on the state's flag, is now considered extinct, the last shot in 1922.

244 *these desert waste lands*: Serra letter to Palou, in Baja from Carmel, August 18, 1772. In Tibesar, I, 271.

245 *a populated place* [poblado]: See Serra letter to Pangua, in Mexico City from Carmel, August 24, 1774. In Tibesar, II, 143. At the time of this letter, there were only five missions. The huge gap between San Luis Obispo and San Gabriel alone (two hundred miles) would have taken even a sleepless rider at least two days.

245 *Highway 101*: The route from San Jose to San Francisco is actually State Highway 82, which closely parallels US 101. The El Camino Real that Portolá and Crespí took, which Serra also followed, going from downtown Los Angeles

to Anaheim, is today a series of surface streets, including Anaheim Boulevard, Harbor Boulevard, State Route 72, and Whittier Boulevard. This means Portolá, Crespí, and Serra all walked or rode their slow mules or horses on ground that became Disneyland.

246 *legend of Franciscan yellow mustard*: Mediterranean hoary mustard (*Hirschfeldia incana*) or field mustard (*Brassica rapa*) are the gorgeous yellow flowers backdropped by the sea in California. Neither is native to the coast, but almost certainly came with the Spaniards. Most of this mustard appears outside San Diego, between San Francisco and San Jose, and between Santa Barbara and San Luis Obispo—Franciscan beaten paths. Mustard is the most privileged herb in the Bible. To Matthew, even a tiny mustard seed of faith can move mountains, and is directly equivalent to "the kingdom of heaven" (13:31; 17:20). Luke goes even further: if you are as faithful as a mustard seed, you can tell a sycamore to plant itself in the sea, and it will (17:6).

247 *a bishop's mitre*: This was the British fiction writer and memoirist Horace Annesley Vachell, who came to California around 1883, marrying the daughter of a land speculator, his employer. In King, *Mission to Paradise*, 77.

247 *scars of their dreadful claws*: Palou, *Relación*, 137 (SW).

247 *considered rashness*: Serra Report on the Missions, to Mathias Noriega, in Mexico City from Carmel, July 1, 1784. In Tibesar, IV, 261.

248 *upset the poor Father considerably*: Serra to Bucareli, in Mexico City from Mexico City, May 21, 1773. In Tibesar, I, 357.

248 *were used as molds*: "The molds for tiles were made out of sections of logs into pieces 15" to 18" long . . . the tiles were not made by using the naked thighs of Indian women lying out in the hot sun as moulds, as some storytellers have stated." George Tays, "Ranch and Mission Industries in Spanish California," PhD dissertation, 1941, University of California, Berkeley.

248 *became a hospice*: The Santa Margarita de Cortona *asistencia* has a storied history. It sits at exactly the geologic midpoint of California, and was once flooded by the sea; several prehistoric oyster beds have been found on the property. The oldest continually working cattle ranch in California dates to the seventeen-thousand-acre property, to 1774. Its brand was a Christian cross.

248 *a Christian saint and an Indian village*: Serra used "de Tixlini" in his report to Bucareli, February 5, 1775. In Tibesar, II, 233.

249 *but all the others*: Serra report to Bucareli, in Mexico City from Mexico City, May 21, 1773. In Tibesar, I, 363–65, 359.

249 *Don Antonio Bucareli y Ursua*: Fages to Serra, in San Diego from San Diego, September 30, 1772. In Tibesar, I, 400.

249 *in their own country*: Serra to Fages, in San Diego from San Diego, October 2, 1772. In Tibesar, I, 285.

250 *shortening his life*: Palou, *Relación*, 139 (SW).

251 *put it in writing*: This dialogue is derived from Geiger's account in *Life and Times* (I, 336–37), itself based on Fages's letter to the viceroy, in Mexico City from San Diego, October 17, 1772, and Cañizares's *Diario de Navegación*, November 1772.

251 *11 percent of all Franciscans*: Sixteen of 142 Franciscan missionaries in California were from Mallorca.

NOTES

251 *flawed knowledge*: See Beebe and Senkewicz, eds., *Lands of Promise and Despair*, 155.

252 *bribes for silence*: Letter of Luis Jayme, O.F.M., to Serra, in San Diego from San Diego, October 17, 1772, translated and edited by Maynard Geiger as *Letter of Luis Jayme*, San Diego Public Library, Dawson's Bookshop, 1970, 38–49. Apparently penitent, Ruiz married an Indian woman at San Antonio the next year.

252 *yawning* barrancas: Geiger, *Life and Times*, I, 345.

252 *broken my health*: Serra to Miguel de Petra, in Palma, Mallorca, from Mexico City, August 4, 1773. In Tibesar, I, 393.

252 *symptoms of malaria*: Palou thought Serra was stricken by typhus (*Relación*, 145).

253 *care and devotion*: Serra to Miguel de Petra, August 4, 1773, p. 393.

253 *nothing the matter with you*: Palou, *Relación*, 146 (SW).

254 *El Hospital del Amor de Dios*: Today the San Carlos Academy for Fine Arts.

255 *the ruler of New Spain*: According to Geiger (*Life and Times*, I, 367), the city's homeless population was not expelled by the viceroy until 1790.

255 *pin all his hopes*: Theodore Maynard, *The Long Road of Father Serra*, 167.

255 *unprecedented in the history*: Cited in Maynard, ibid.

256 *torrent of abuse*: Report of Corporal Miguel Periquez to Captain Augustín Callis via Serra in Mexico City, March 1773. In Tibesar, I, 403.

256 *prudence and common sense*: *Representación* of Junípero Serra to Bucareli, in Mexico City from Mexico City, March 13, 1773. In Tibesar, I, 303–5.

256 *great zeal*: Ibid., 295, 327.

256 *success of this great enterprise*: Serra to Bucareli, in Mexico City from Mexico City, May 21, 1773. In Tibesar, I, 371–73.

256 *zeal that animated him*: Bucareli to Croix, in Mexico City from Mexico City, March 20, 1777. In Geiger, *Life and Times*, I, 378.

256 *without a thought of self*: Charles Chapman, *The Founding of Spanish California*, Macmillan, 1916, in Maynard, *The Long Road of Father Serra*, 167.

256 *govern early California*: Geiger, *Life and Times*, I, 378. On Mount Ribidoux outside Riverside, a cross refers specifically to Serra as a "legislator."

257 *the law of nature*: *Representación* of Serra to Bucareli, 301.

258 *intermarriages*: When land incentives were taken away, in 1790, intermarriage rates dropped dramatically; after 1798, they virtually ceased at San Carlos Borromeo. See Virginia Bouvier, *Codes of Silence: Women and the Conquest of California, 1542–1840*, University of Arizona Press, 2001, 115. Serra himself came to lament the inauthenticity of such liaisons: "When, without tying them up, they can be made to follow their husbands, it must be with great disgust."

258 *exhausted by duty*: Most frontier soldiers in California did not have leave for four years; one, Domino Clua, had been nonstop in service for six years.

258 *that far land of exile*: For all citations concerning the *Representación*, see the complete document, Serra to Bucareli, in Mexico City from Mexico City, March 13, 1773. In Tibesar, I, 295–329.

259 *lament in all our missions*: Serra to Bucareli, in Mexico City from Mexico City, April 22, 1773. In Tibesar, I, 341.

259 *turn on us like tigers*: Serra to Bucareli, April 22, 1773.

259 *in such a place*: Ibid., 361.

260 *die on the road*: Palou, *Relación*, 153 (SW).

260 *as if it were a trifle*: Letter of Pablo Font to Jayme Alaxo, from Mexico City to Catalonia, August 26, 1773, in Geiger, *Life and Times*, I, 399.

260 *The painting has been lost*: Zephyrin Engelhardt received a letter in 1924 that indicated an original painting of Serra was destroyed in 1910–12 during the Mexican Revolution; an eyewitness ratified this in 1945. According to Monica Orozco, archivist at the Santa Barbara Mission Archive and Library, two copies of the Querétaro painting were made by a Father Mosqueda, one at the Santa Barbara Mission Archive, and the other lost. If an original exists, and could be authenticated as such, it would be worth millions.

260 *to leave it at all*: Serra to Fr. Miguel de Petra in Palma, Mallorca, from Mexico City, August 4, 1773. In Tibesar, I, 389–91.

Chapter Seventeen: Mission San Juan Capistrano:
The Burning Swallows

262 *little things add up*: *Muchas pocas hazen un*, Serra wrote, which Tibesar oddly translates, "Many a mickle makes a muckle." Serra to Verger, in Mexico City from Tepic, January 16, 1774. In Tibesar, II, 21.

262 *so much to their hearts*: Serra to Verger, in Mexico City from Guadalajara, November 11, 1773. In Tibesar, II, 15.

262 *awful outbreaks of debauchery*: Ibid., 3–7. Crespí had sent a critical letter to Serra that arrived too late in Guadalajara to take to the viceroy.

263 *let us give Him thanks*: Palou, *Relación*, 144 (MG). Serra had earlier promised the shipyard workers at San Blas work even before he met the viceroy.

263 *everything is possible*: Serra to Verger, in Mexico City from San Blas, January 24, 1774. In Tibesar, II, 25.

263 *good sailor*: Geiger's phrase, *Life and Times*, I, 409.

263 *fall into the temptation*: Serra to Antonio Zamudio, in Tepic from San Diego, March 26, 1774. In Tibesar, II, 37.

264 *2.6 miles east*: This figure is a 2013 calculation of Phil Valdez, Jr., president of the Anza Society, made after a strenuous hike and consultation with Joe and Sharon Myers.

264 *hurt by their attitude*: Serra to Guardian Francisco Pangua, in Mexico City from Carmel, April 13, 1776. In Tibesar, II, 431.

264 *has consoled us*: Serra to Bucareli, in Mexico City from Carmel, May 29, 1774. In Tibesar, II, 81–83. Geiger's translation, in *Life and Times*, I, 416.

264 *were turned to joy*: Serra to the Guardian [Pangua] and Discretorium, in Mexico City from Carmel, July 18, 1774. In Tibesar, II, 97.

264 *almost at will*: Serra to Bucareli, in Mexico City from Carmel, June 21, 1774. In Tibesar, II, 79.

265 *take part in this enterprise*: Crespí's diary of the Pérez-led 1774 *Santiago* sea voyage to the northwest.

265 *outdoor temple*: Geiger, *Life and Times*, I, 420.

265 *Nootka Controversy*: See Warren Cook, *Flood Tide of Empire: Spain and the Pacific Northwest, 1543–1819*, Yale University Press, 1973.

265 *making pottery*: Serra to Pangua, in Mexico City from Carmel, October 10, 1775. In Tibesar, II, 329.

265 *lack of understanding and reflection*: Serra to Bucareli, in Mexico City from Carmel, July 19, 1774. In Tibesar, II, 127.

266 *to seek their good*: Serra to Pangua, in Mexico City from Carmel, July 18, 1774. In Tibesar, II, 115.

266 *razors for shaving*: Ibid., 117.

266 *his blood and his life*: Serra to Bucareli, in Mexico City from Carmel, August 30, 1774. In Tibesar, II, 159.

266 *[right can issue from wrong]*: Serra to Pangua, July 18, 1774, 98–99. (Tibesar's tortured translation of the Latin is "the sum is wrong, but the answer is right.")

266 *and who work*: Serra to Bucareli, in Mexico City from Carmel, August 24, 1774. In Tibesar, II, 141.

266 *white man's microbes*: See Steven W. Hackel, *Children of Coyote, Missionaries of Saint Francis: Indian-Spanish Relations in Colonial California, 1769–1850*, University of North Carolina Press, 2005, 65–123.

267 *to create another rung*: Geiger, *Life and Times*, I, 432. Serra often referred to the missions as *escalas*, which Tibesar translates as "stepping-stones" but more literally is a ladder or "rungs" of a ladder (*escala de cuerda* was a common term for a "rope ladder" hung off a ship). See Serra to Bucareli, Mexico City from Carmel, January 8, 1775. In Tibesar, II, 197.

268 *his namesake [St. Francis]*: Serra to Bucareli, in Mexico City from Carmel, August 24, 1774. In Tibesar, II, 143. My own translation as well.

268 *an abundance of sardines*: Serra to Bucareli, in Mexico City from Carmel, September 9, 1774. In Tibesar, II, 177.

269 *agreeable company*: Serra diary, April 28, 1769, in Baja (San Francisco de Borja). In Tibesar, I, 55.

269 *cold reception*: William Kreckelberg, *Mission San Juan Capistrano*, Diocese of Orange, 2004, ii.

269 *in a position to found*: Serra to Pangua, in Mexico City from Carmel, October 29, 1775. In Tibesar, II, 393.

269 *Serra misread it*: Geiger, *Life and Times*, II, 35.

269 *remember what you said*: For this exchange I have combined and condensed material from Geiger (*Life and Times*, II, 37–38); a letter from Lasuén to Pangua, in Mexico City from Monterey, August 17, 1775 (in Kenneally, ed., *Writings of Fermín Francisco de Lasuén*, I, 56–58); and finally Serra to Pangua, in Mexico City from Carmel, October 29, 1775 (Tibesar, II, 395).

270 *The truth is at core bitter*: In Tibesar, II, 395. Tibesar translates *La verdad suele amargar* as "Truth never makes friends." But I have recast Geiger's version ("The truth is ordinarily bitter"—in *Life and Times*, II, 44), as *suele* means "at bottom," or "at the core."

270 *between Rivera and Serra*: Lasuén to Pangua, in Mexico City from Monterey, August 3, 1775. In Kenneally, *Writings of Fermín Francisco de Lasuén*, I, 55.

270 *I am more of a scribe*: Serra also said, "Yet I am fully aware that I do not write as much as I should." See also Serra to Pangua, October 29, 1775. In Tibesar, II, 395.

270 *exile as these missions*: Ibid., 385, 397. Also see Geiger's version, *Life and Times*, II, 42.

271 *used as toothbrushes*: Sandos, *Converting California*, 61. See also Florence Shipek, "California Indian Reactions to the Franciscans," *The Americas* 41 (April 1, 1985): 480–92.

271 *raised native anxiety*: Carrico, *Strangers in a Stolen Land*, 32. In June 1774 there were one hundred baptized Kumeyaay; by the end of September, there were five hundred.

271 *wives of some of the Indians*: Geiger, *Life and Times*, II, 60. This August 22, 1772, Jayme letter to Palou in Loreto, Baja, was also forwarded to San Fernando and ultimately to the viceroy.

272 *cast the first stone*: What makes this passage deeply interesting, besides Christ's deft rebuke of the Pharisees' hypocrisy in sexual matters, is Christ's drawing in the dust before his reply and after. One pastor I listened to in Kansas City, Kansas (on March 17, 2013), said, "He's writing charity, mercy, forgiveness."

272 *stealing their loads*: Geiger, *Life and Times*, II, 59.

272 *thorns in either direction*: Serra to the Guardian (Pangua), in Mexico City from Carmel, August 31, 1774. In Tibesar, II, 167.

272 *I do not have room for more*: Serra to Pangua, in Mexico City from Carmel, October 29, 1775. In Tibesar, II, 397.

273 *one to the presidio*: The Ipai Kumeyaay of North San Diego County did not participate (and neither did the Tipai of Las Choyas). See the breakdown by village of the battle in Michael Connolly Miskwish, *Kumeyaay: A History Textbook, Vol. I, Precontact to 1893*, Sycuan Press, 2007, 46.

273 *God forgive you*: Palou, *Relación*, 174 (SW), 162 (MG).

273 *Love God, my sons*: Ibid., 173 (SW), 163 (MG). See also Geiger, *Life and Times*, II, 62.

274 *body of the dead Father*: Fuster to Serra, in Carmel from San Diego, November 28, 1775. In Tibesar, II, 449–58. See also Beebe and Senkewicz's translation in *Lands of Promise and Despair*, 191.

276 *"baptism of desire" might apply*: Pius IX in his 1863 encyclical "On False Doctrines" spoke of "invincible ignorance" of those who "observe the natural law and its precepts inscribed by God on all hearts. . . . They live honest lives and are able to attain eternal life." This fit aborigines outside Western culture.

276 *its sole justification*: Serra to Bucareli, in Mexico City from Carmel, December 15, 1775. In Tibesar, II, 407. See also Geiger's version, *Life and Times*, II, 71. I have added my own. A lot hangs on the word *título* in "*el título que la justifica*."

276 *greatest tribulation and sorrow*: Geiger, *Life and Times*, II, 92.

276 *breathing again*: On October 23, 1778, Serra christened what became known as the Serra Chapel at San Juan Capistrano, one of only two remaining original mission-era churches in California in which Serra said Mass. Earthquakes felled most of the others. (A personal note: on October 23, 1948, my parents were wed at the Church of the Precious Blood in Los Angeles.)

277 *San Jacinto Valley*: See Stephen O'Neil, "The Chiefs Saw What Was Happening: Intratribal Politics of an Acjachemen Uprising Against Mission San Juan Capistrano, AD 1778," a paper presented at the California Indian Conference, Irvine, California, October 15, 2010.

Chapter Eighteen: Mission San Francisco de Asís (Dolores) and
Mission Santa Clara de Asís: Microbes and the Great Franciscan Couple

280 *wild and unsettled*: Serra to Bucareli, in Mexico City from Carmel, July 2, 1775. In Tibesar, II, 265.

281 *I have been deceived*: Lasuén to Pangua, in Mexico City from San Diego, September 13, 1776, in Kenneally, *Writings of Fermín Francisco de Lasuén*, I, 66.

281 *overcomes himself*: Serra to Pangua, February 26, 1777. In Tibesar, III, 105.

281 *neck bowed to the yoke*: Serra to Pangua, in Mexico City from Carmel, June 6, 1777. In Tibesar, III, 155.

281 *like a bird in the air*: Diary of Santa María, in Geiger, *Life and Times*, II, 115.

281 *vale of tears*: Serra to Bucareli, in Mexico City from Carmel, December 15, 1775. In Tibesar, II, 401.

281 *for such an accusation*: Serra to Bucareli, March 12, 1776. In Tibesar, II, 413.

282 *foundation of our holy College*: Serra to Pangua, in Carmel to Mexico City, April 13, 1776. In Tibesar, II, 425.

282 *treating [Anza] kindly*: Ibid., 435.

282 *an old story in Madrid*: Serra to Pangua, in Mexico City from Carmel, July 24, 1775. In Tibesar, II, 295.

283 *storms were most violent*: Juan Torquemada, *Monarquia Indiana*, 1595, 694, in Zephyrin Englehardt, *San Francisco or Mission Dolores*, Franciscan Herald Press, 1924, 4.

283 *cloud of mosquitoes*: Fages, *A Historical, Political, and Natural Description of California*, 119.

283 *left-hand or bow side*: Stanger and Brown, *Who Discovered the Golden Gate?*, 138.

283 *once and for all, San Francisco*: Bancroft makes of this a humorous decision: "When the Spaniards found they could not go to San Francisco, they decided that San Francisco must come to them, and accordingly transferred the name southward to the peninsula and bay." See *History of California*, I, 152.

283 *You are my father*: Palou, *Historical Memoirs of New California (Noticias)*, 271–72.

283 *those rungs*: Serra to Bucareli, in Mexico City from Carmel, July 2, 1775. In Tibesar, II, 263–67. Tibesar translates *escalancito* as "stepping-stone." I use the literal "small step," and for *los ideas succesivas*—"rungs."

283 *to sit down*: John Galvin, ed., *The Journal of Father Vicente Santa María*, Howell Books, 1775/1971, 29.

284 *sound it themselves*: Ibid., 59.

284 *discovered by the other*: In Palou, *Relación*, 197 (SW).

284 *indicative of pleasure*: Pedro Font, *With Anza to California*, 368.

284 *gaping at the proceedings*: Englehardt, *San Francisco or Mission Dolores*, 41. Giant redwoods in San Francisco would disappear sooner than the Indians in California.

284 *the Zanjones*: Zanjones in Spanish meant "the ditches." They were native to the arroyos around Salinas, and were probably Rumsen Ohlone.

284 *they would take his life*: Palou, *Historical Memoirs of New California (Noticias)*, in Geiger, *Life and Times*, II, 137–38.

285 *the element of beauty*: Geiger, *Life and Times*, II, 136.

285 *twenty-one-mission chain*: Miraculously, Mission Dolores withstood the great San Francisco earthquake and fire of 1906. Nearly everything around it was destroyed. A matter of local lore, the one fire hydrant functioning in that part of the city stood right in front of Dolores and was used to quench fires.

285 *the Ssalson nation*: Palou, *Relación*, 208 (SW).

285 *not a minor feud*: Milliken, *A Time of Little Choice*, 63.

286 *flogged them*: Palou, *Relación*, 161 (SW).

287 *exorcising malevolent forces*: Milliken, *A Time of Little Choice*, 68.

287 *to be well pleased*: Palou and Cambon, in ibid., 79.

287 *twenty-two American settlers*: The Battle of Cobleskill took place May 30, 1778. In retribution, the 1779 expedition of American revolutionary forces gave a final blow to the Iroquois, destroying many of their ancestral homes across New York.

288 *on foot or on horseback*: Serra letter to Bucareli, to Mexico City from Carmel, March 1, 1777. In Tibesar, III, 114–15.

288 *como el mar dobla*: "The bells toll like the sea folds" (Pablo Medina translation).

289 *amount to much, thank God*: Serra to Pangua, in Mexico City from Carmel, February 26, 1777. In Tibesar, III, 105.

289 *all so longed for*: Serra to Bucareli, in Mexico City from Carmel, March 1, 1777. In Tibesar, III, 111–13.

289 *territorial expansion*: Edwin Beilharz, *Felipe de Neve: First Governor of California*, California Historical Society, 1971, 9.

290 *need to be uprooted*: Ibid., 20.

290 *good will from anyone*: Bucareli to Neve, in Monterey from Mexico City, December 25, 1776, in Geiger, *Life and Times*, II, 146.

290 *through water for a way*: Neve to Bucareli, in Mexico City from Monterey, June 3, 1777, in Geiger, *Life and Times*, II, 150.

290 *we will live in peace*: Serra to Pangua, in Mexico City from Carmel, February 26, 1777. In Tibesar, III, 93.

291 *my whole life in a dream*: Serra to Verger, in Mexico City from Carmel, August 13, 1778. In Tibesar, III, 219, and in Geiger, *Life and Times*, II, 160. "Preposterous" is Geiger's word.

292 *placed in the condiment*: Serra to Verger, in Mexico City from Carmel, August 19, 1778. In Tibesar, III, 235.

292 *boundless unbelievable pride*: Neve letter to Teodoro de Croix, in Arizpe from Monterey, March 26, 1781, in Beilharz, *Felipe de Neve*, 60.

292 *ships will be necessary*: Palou, *Relación*, 201 (MG, GO).

292 *a violent deity*: Quincy D. Newell, *Constructing Lives at Mission San Francisco: Native Colonists and Hispanic Colonists, 1776–1821,* University of New Mexico Press, 2009, 38. The Spanish Catechism used by Palou (Repalda's) defined the Mass as "a sacrifice that is made of Christ."

292 *as if half dead*: Louis Choris, *The Visit of the "Rurik" to San Francisco in 1816*, translated by August Mahr, Stanford University Press, 1932, 91–102.

292 *he could hardly stand*: Palou, *Relación*, 224 (SW).

292 *the Divine Physician*: Geiger, *Life and Times*, II, 213.

292 *every hand*: Beilharz, *Felipe de Neve*, 61.

293 *if any yet remains in me*: Serra to Verger, in Mexico City from Carmel, August 15, 1779. In Tibesar, III, 347–49.

293 *did not have any reason*: Serra to Pangua, in Mexico City from Carmel, December 8, 1782. In Tibesar, IV, 169.

293 *vigorous demonstration*: From 1580 law: Law 1, Title 1, Book 6.

294 *half the cattle on it*: Law 20, Title 3, Book 6.

294 *three thousand acres*: Russell Skowronek, *Situating Mission Santa Clara*, Academy of American Franciscan History, 2006, 304. Born during Serra's time in present-day Palo Alto and resident at Mission Santa Clara for half a century, Inigo filled Rancho Polsomi with fruit orchards and lived in a tule reed house.

294 *attack on Mission San Diego*: Serra told Lasuén that if a beefed-up guard at San Diego wasn't sufficient to deter another attack, "I should accept such a death with a cheerful heart, with grace, and as a favor from God" (April 22, 1778).

294 *I did it myself*: Marriage of José María, Soldier Sergeant of the Company of Monte Rey, December 9, 1779, a certificate written and signed by Junípero Serra (with two witnesses—Juan José Robles and Juan María Olivera), at the Lauinger Library, Georgetown University Rare Books and Manuscript section.

295 *not in a mood to sing*: Serra to Pangua, in Mexico City from Carmel, July 17, 1782. In Tibesar, IV, 147–48. Tibesar's stiffer version: "The story should be set forth in song. But at present we feel little inclined to sing." I prefer Geiger's, *Life and Times*, II, 242.

295 *strengthen this stone*: Geiger, *Life and Times*, II, 236.

295 *a cross and Spanish coins*: This cornerstone was discovered in 1911 by workers laying a gas main.

295 *Blessed be God*: Serra to Pangua, in Mexico City from Carmel, July 17, 1782. In Tibesar, IV, 145–47.

296 *giving scandal*: Neve letter to Croix, in Arizpe from Monterey, November 19, 1781. In Geiger, *Life and Times*, II, 240. Dávila left California for good sometime in 1782 or 1783.

296 *halls of power*: Also close to Serra, Father Jose Murguía died on May 11, 1784, at Mission Santa Clara.

296 *those born at the mission*: For example, in 1799 there were forty deaths at San Carlos versus twenty-four births.

296 *the rate in England*: Hackel, *Children of Coyote, Missionaries of St. Francis*, 98–101.

297 *evil spirits*: Zephyrin Englehardt, *The Holy Man of Santa Clara or Life, Virtues and Miracles of Fr. Magin Catalá*, San Francisco, 1909, 153; also Magin Catalá and José Viader, *Informe al Gobernador Diego de Borica*, Santa Clara Mission, August 6, 1797, in Milliken, *A Time of Little Choice*, 125–26.

297 *absolutely minimal*: Milliken, *A Time of Little Choice*, 134.

297 *Serra's era, 1770–80*: The pre-contact crude death rate was 50 per 1,000 Indians; from 1770 to 1780, the first decade of missionization, it rose to 70 per 1,000. By 1800, the peak, the CDR was 85 per 1,000. These figures are cited in Sherburne Cook and Cesare Marino, "Roman Catholic Missions in California and the Southwest," in *History of Indian-White Relations*, edited by Wilcomb E. Washburn, Smithsonian Institution, 1988, 472–80.

298 *disorganization and confusion*: Milliken, *A Time of Little Choice*, 136.

298 *neither worked*: Only in 1910 did an arsenic-based compound, Salvarsan, become the first effective cure for syphilis.

298 *his expedition [in 1776]*: Sherburne Cook, *The Conflict Between the California Indian and White Civilization*, 23. Cook has Anza at San Gabriel in 1777, which I have corrected.

298 *never bring children*: Abella to Sola, in Mexico City from San Francisco, July 31, 1817, in Hackel, *Children of Coyote, Missionaries of St. Francis*, 118.

298 *than anyone else*: An excellent examination of the devastation of syphilis and germs on California Indians is in James Sandos's *Converting California*, chapter 8: "The Only Heritage Their Parents Gave Them: Syphilis, Gonorrhea and Other Diseases," 111–27.

299 *but lack understanding*: Maynard Geiger and Clement W. Meighan, *As the Padres Saw Them: California Indian Life and Customs as Reported by the Franciscan Missionaries, 1813–1815*, Santa Barbara Mission Archive and Library, 1976, 105–6.

299 *red eye in the newborn*: Gonorrhea is typically contracted by a third of men and over half of women after one or two instances of sexual intercourse with someone infected.

299 *fills the cemeteries*: Payeras to Baldomero López, in Mexico City from La Purísima Mission in the Lompoc Peninsula, February 2, 1820, in Donald Cutter, ed. and trans., *Writings of Mariano Payeras*, Bellerophon Press, 1995, 225.

Chapter Nineteen: Mission San Buenaventura and the Death of Serra

300 *sitting on a stool*: Palou calls it *una equipal* (*humilde silla de canas*), which Geiger translates as a "rush stool," literally "a humble chair of cane." See *Relación*, 246 (MG). I have slightly adjusted the Williams version.

300 *the shadow of fear*: Palou, *Relación*, 271 (SW). Palou reports Serra saying "*Mucho miedo me entrada, mucho miedo tengo*" (literally, "Much fear has entered me; I have much fear"). I have slightly adjusted the Williams version.

301 *blazing to life*: Cervantes, *Don Quixote*, translated by Burton Raffel, W. W. Norton, 1605/1999, I:14, 75.

302 *This was Isaiah*: Isaiah 55:1–2, 12–13. Inspired by this passage, St. Louis University's director of Liturgy Studies, Father John Foley, S. J., wrote the powerful song "Come to the Water" (1978), given new life by young singer-songwriter Matthew Maher on YouTube.

302 *deep recollection*: Palou, *Relación*, 245 (MG).

302 *kept the faith*: Palou had Serra quoting Latin (*Cursum consumavi* [sic] *fidem servavi* (Timothy 4:7)). Palou comments, "It appears that on that very day the announcement of his approaching death arrived." *Relación*, 241 (MG).

304 *What is this all about*: Serra to Lasuén, in San Diego from Carmel, Monday of Holy Week (May 28, 1779). In Tibesar, III, 293–95, and Geiger, *Life and Times*, II, 245, with my own translations in part.

304 *hour of great crisis*: The Latin *Tolle. Lege.* (Pick it up; read it) spoken by a child, which caused Augustine to flip feverishly in his Bible to Romans 13:13: "Put on the Lord Jesus Christ and make no provision for the flesh."

304 *Yes, Lord, yes, Lord*: Serra to Lasuén, May 28, 1779. In Tibesar, III, 295.

304 *namely Christ Crucified*: Serra to Father Figuer, in San Diego from Carmel, March 30, 1779. In Tibesar, III, 307; also quoted in Geiger, *Life and Times*, II, 248. Campeche was a slaughtering site in Mexico's Yucatán; its Mayan-derived name meant "place of snakes and ticks." Bonaventure's mystical understanding of "crucified love" is the central notion of all his writings. As he counseled a Poor Clare nun, "Your heart is to be on the altar of God. It is here that the fact of intense love must burn always. You are to feed it every day with the wood of the Cross." Delio, *Crucified Love*, 102. Delio comments incisively, "The world

moves toward its completion not because God stands 'over' the world with almighty power but because God is humble and, in the poverty of the cross, stands 'with' the world" (123).

305 *undoubtedly genuine*: Beilhartz, *Felipe de Neve*, 64.

305 *inciting people here*: Serra to Neve, in Monterey from Carmel, January 7, 1780. In Tibesar, III, 407–9.

305 *merely instrumental*: Monroy, *The Borders Within*, 157.

305 *it was strange*: Though not entirely strange, as we have seen. Monogamy, at least serial monogamy, held for most of the Indians, unless they were chiefs. And encroachment, if not theft, of hunting and fishing grounds could be grounds for war. The Ten Commandments were probably stranger in their details (and enforcement) to the Indians than in their general thrust.

306 *in that regard*: Serra to Neve, in Monterey from Carmel, January 7, 1780. In Tibesar, III, 413–15.

307 *members of my family*: Serra to Lasuén, in San Diego from Carmel, January 12, 1780. In Tibesar, III, 423–25.

307 *Neve relented*: Ultimately, and somewhat ironically, Carlos and his wife and children ended up at Serra's own Mission San Carlos Borromeo, where he died in 1809, receiving Last Rites, including Communion, from Lasuén, though Sandos wondered if Carlos "died as a Christian renouncing his old Indian ways or as a Digueño adding the Christian power to his own." "Chisli, Canuch, and Junípero Serra," in Beebe and Senkewicz, eds., *"To Toil in That Vineyard of the Lord,"* 71–72.

307 *resist the* Conquista: During the 1824 uprising of the Chumash at Santa Barbara, an Indian rebel placed a crucifix under his shirt to protect himself from shot, speaking the whole time to the Christ figure on it as *"tu,"* the familiar you, and not the polite *usted* taught by the fathers. All the while the Indian shot his arrows at the Spanish soldiers. When he came out alive, he worked as a sacristan at the mission until his death. See Sandos's "Indian Resistance to Missionization" in *Converting California*, 154–73.

307 *contentment and longing*: Milliken, *A Time of Little Choice*, 224.

308 *in Franciscan garb*: Herbert Bolton, in Velez Silvestre, *Pageant in the Wilderness*, 1950, 3; also in Geiger, *Franciscan Missionaries in Hispanic California*, 95.

309 *inscrutable decrees of God*: Serra to Lasuén, in San Diego from Carmel, December 7, 1781. In Tibesar, IV, 103.

309 *American Revolution*: Quotations from Serra to Missionaries of Mission San Antonio and Elsewhere, from Carmel, June 15, 1780. In Tibesar, IV, 17. Engelbert makes the unsubstantiated claim that the Los Angeles pueblo contributed fifteen pesos to the "American War of Independence" and that Serra "had taken his humble part" in the American victory, implying this happened in part because of such donations. (See *The Last of the Conquistadores*, 296, 300.) The Internet is rife with claims from the Serra Club and others that Serra raised $137 for George Washington—a spurious assertion with no apparent evidential support. Also, a supposed correspondence between Serra and Thomas Jefferson was a hoax fomented by *Westways* magazine. See Msgr. Francis J. Weber, *Blessed Fray Junípero Serra: An Outstanding California Hero*, Editions du Signe, 2007, 113.

309 *Palma, Assisi, Palestine*: Geiger, *Life and Times*, II, 268.

310 *waiting silently for the Gospel*: Serra to Teodoro de Croix, in Arizpe from Carmel, March 30, 1779. In Tibesar, III, 311.

310 *devotion toward their patron*: Serra to Pangua, in Mexico City from Carmel, July 17, 1782. In Tibesar, IV, 151, and in Geiger, *Life and Times*, II, 286.

310 *more impressive it is*: Serra to Lasuén, in San Diego from San Buenaventura, March 31, 1782. In Tibesar, IV, 113.

311 *would be its minister*: Serra to Lasuén, in San Diego from Carmel, July 20, 1782. In Tibesar, IV, 161.

311 *took a change*: Serra to Pangua, July 17, 1782. In Tibesar, IV, 151.

311 *bells made of wood*: Engelhardt thinks the wooden bells were brought by ship by J. M. Rosales, a Mexican priest, around 1848, though John Engler has evidence it was closer to 1865. The Mexican practice of "silent bells" from Holy Thursday through Holy Saturday "proved far more ingenious than practical." *San Buenaventura: The Mission by the Sea*, Mission Santa Barbara, 1930, 141.

311 *Hollywood Bowl*: Julie Tumamait-Stensley, in L. Frank Hogeland and Kim Hogeland, *First Families: A Photographic History of Caliornia Indians*, Heydey Books, 2007, 99, 121.

312 *from our point of view*: Geiger, *Life and Times*, II, 288.

312 *the "Alabado"*: The "Alabado," written by the legendary Father Antonio Margil, who ministered in Mexico and the northern provinces, begins, "Lift up your heart in joy and praise Him!" It became the earliest song of California, one of Serra's favorites.

312 *silver-plated chalice*: This silver-plated gold chalice was small because only the priest drank the wine turned to blood in those days; Communion under "two forms" did not occur in Western Catholicism until after Vatican II. This rare chalice is said to be the only one still in existence with which Serra said Mass. It resides today at Our Lady of Sorrows parish in Santa Barbara, a Jesuit church, much to the chagrin of Franciscans.

312 *Siytún chief Yanonalit*: Chief Yanonali took his time becoming a Christian; he was not baptized until 1797, when he was sixty, accepting the Christian name Pedro. Yanonali Street runs into lower State Street today.

312 *a dismal foundation*: Serra to Pangua, July 17, 1782. In Tibesar, IV, 153.

313 *all Christians today*: Serra to Mathias Noriega, Report on the Missions, from Carmel, July 7, 1873. In Tibesar, IV, 267, 271.

313 *called to do so*: Serra to Pangua, July 17, 1782. In Tibear, IV, 143. See Geiger's version, *Life and Times*, II.

313 *they skin me alive*: Serra to Sancho, in Mexico City from Carmel, August 6, 1784. In Tibesar, IV, 289.

313 *their baptismal records*: Serra to Fages, in Monterey from Carmel, February 25, 1783. In Tibesar, IV, 181–83.

313 *which the world cannot give*: Serra to Lasuén, in San Diego from Carmel, September 5, 1780. In Tibesar, IV, 39.

313 *the measures of government*: Fages to Neve, in Arizpe from Monterey, September 15, 1783, in Geiger, *Life and Times*, II, 330.

313 *more skilled at it than soldiers*: Fages to Neve, in Arizpe from Monterey, March 1, 1783, in Geiger, *Life and Times*, II, 330. These contrary accusations—too permissive and too punitive—are difficult to assess. Geiger found "no documents are available" on stocks or forced labor, or at least the frequency of

practice. I have found nothing to counter Geiger, at least insofar as Serra is concerned.

314 *use of the whip*: Bishop Antonio de los Reyes to Viceroy Mayorga, in Mexico City from Alamos, Sonora, June 20, 1783, in Geiger, *Life and Times*, II, 359–60.

314 *falsehoods and impossibilities*: Pangua to Serra, in Carmel from Mexico City, January 8, 1783, in Geiger, *Life and Times*, II, 349. Among other things, in their *representación*, the colleges saw no evidence of forcible Indian labor or missionary destruction of Indian lands — quite the contrary.

315 *San Fernando return there*: Serra to Lasuén, in San Diego from Carmel, April 17, 1784. In Tibesar, IV, 229. Also in Geiger, *Life and Times*, II, 372. Actually, Gálvez did not back the Dominican takeover of Upper California.

316 *die without seeing them*: Serra to Juan Sancho, the new guardian, in Mexico City from San Gabriel, October 27, 1783. In Tibesar, IV, 193. Minorca had recently been won back to Spain from England in war.

316 *'God keep's' thrown in*: Serra to Sancho, in Mexico City from San Gabriel, October 29, 1783. In Tibesar, IV, 205.

316 *heaviness and depression*: Serra to Lasuén, in San Diego from San Gabriel, November 9, 1783. In Tibesar, IV, 217

316 *amend my ways*: Serra to Lasuén, in San Diego from Carmel, April 17, 1784. In Tibesar, IV, 231.

316 *it may also not be*: Serra to Sancho, in Mexico City from Carmel, Feast of the Sacred Heart, 1784. In Tibesar, IV, 245.

316 *God is everywhere*: Serra to Sancho, in Mexico City from Carmel, August 6, 1784. In Tibesar, IV, 289.

316 La Virgen al cielo: A hymn in honor of the Feast of the Assumption of the Blessed Virgin three days before on August 16, composed by Antonio Margil.

316 *he is nearly finished*: Palou, *Relación*, 266 (SW).

317 Novo cedat ritui: From the medieval hymn written by St. Thomas Aquinas: "Hence so great a sacrament / Let us venerate with heads bowed / And let the old practice / Give way to the new rite / Let faith provide supplement / For the failure of the senses."

317 *a deep abstraction*: Palou, *Relación*, 268 (SW).

318 *as if he were well*: Ibid., 271.

318 *cross of Caravaca*: The Cruz de Caravaca, with its signature extra cross beam, was credited with converting Moors after its design was revealed in 1232 to Ginés Pérez, a priest imprisoned by the Arabs in south Spanish town of Caravaca.

318 *ready for the road*: Serra mentioned Campanilla by name only once: "Campanilla the mule is now fat and well and will take to the road at once." Serra to Lasuén, in San Diego from San Gabriel, November 9, 1783. In Tibesar, IV, 219.

318 *will have mattered*: Serra to Francesch Serra, in Palma from Cádiz, August 20, 1749. In Tibesar, I, 5. Also in Geiger, *Life and Times*, II, 375.

318 *believes in me shall live*: Geiger, *Life and Times*, II, 375.

318 *their natural father*: Palou, *Relación*, 272 (SW); in Geiger, *Life and Times*, II, 384.

319 *stealing them away as relics*: When his body was exhumed in the twentieth century, Serra's original gold stole was discovered in the casket, now browned and holey from the swatches taken as relics.

319 *wailing of those present*: Palou, *Relación*, 277 (SW).

319 *all my books and bottles*: Ibid., 277–78.
320 *this deceased missionary*: In Geiger, *Life and Times*, II, 392.

Chapter Twenty: Lasuén Completes the Mission

324 *lady of the tower*: According to legend, locked in a tower by her father, St. Barbara is often represented in paintings near a tower.
324 *very, very, very happy*: Serra to Lasuén, in San Diego from Carmel, April 17, 1784. In Tibesar, IV, 221. Also in Geiger, *Life and Times*, II, 320.
324 *their own caprice*: Lasuén, "Refutation of Charges," June 19, 1801, in Kenneally, *The Writings of Fermín Francisco de Lasuén*, II, 220. The priest, Concepción Horra, was so given to screaming that he scared Indians out of the mission. Both Sitjar and the governor at the time (Diego de Borica) found Horra insane, and he was sent back to Mexico City after only seven wild months in California.
324 *they were "addicted"*: Lasuén to Fray Antonio Noguerya, January 21, 1797, in Kenneally, *The Writings of Fermín Francisco de Lasuén*, II, 6.
325 *the mysterious pox*: See Hackel, "Sources of Rebellion," 655, in George Harwood Phillips, *Chiefs and Challenges: Indian Resistance and Cooperation in Southern California*, University of California Press, 1975, 75.
325 *living on their land*: "Investigation of Occurrences at Mission San Gabriel on the Night of October 25, 1785," in Beebe and Senkewicz, eds., *Lands of Promise and Despair*, 248.
325 *protection as punishment*: George Harwood Phillips, *Vineyards and Vaqueros: Indian Labor and the Economic Expansion of Southern California, 1771–1877*, University of Oklahoma Press, 2010, 76.
325 *milk like snake venom*: John R. Johnson and William W. Williams, "Toypurina's Descendants: Three Generations of an Alta California Family," *Boletin* 24, no. 2 (2007): 42.
325 *their numbers did*: Sandos, *Converting California*, 84.
326 *15,562 under Lasuén*: Ibid., 85.
326 *devastating 1812 earthquake*: No mission suffered so badly from the 1812 quake as Mission San Juan Capistrano, which saw its roof collapse on an Acjachemen Indian crowd attending Feast of the Immaculate Conception services, killing forty. Eulalia Pérez, visiting from San Gabriel and pregnant, was trampled in the melee that ensued, but spared.
326 *to see the mission resurrected*: Author interview with Ernestine de Soto, Santa Barbara, California, May 6, 2011.
326 *Vitruvius Pollio in 27 BC*: The Latin text had been translated into Spanish in 1797, and thus was a "new" text for Santa Barbara architects.
327 *as they ate breakfast*: The remarkable 250-year story of Ernestine de Soto's Chumash family in Santa Barbara, dating back to Serra's first coming, she narrates in the 2009 documentary film *Six Generations*, by Paul Goldsmith.
328 *nothing about the event*: Lasuén only mentions in passing that the week before "eleven Indians set out from here with a supply of implements to build a hut at Soledad." Lasuén to Don José Antonio de Romeu, in Monterey from Carmel, September 29, 1791, in Kenneally, *The Writings of Fermín Francisco de Lasuén*, I, 236.
328 *honey-colored eyes*: Geiger, *Life and Times*, 106–8, 210–12.
328 *psychopaths*: Ibid., 106.

328 *olive, peach, and apple*: See Michael Hardwick, *Changes in Landscape: The Beginnings of Horticulture in the California Missions*, Paragon, 2005, 83–84.

328 *revered father's faith*: Dr. Russ Skowonek, presentation at Mission San Rafael, Calfifornia Missions Studies Association, February 18, 2012.

329 *many rebelling Yokuts*: See Sandos, *Converting California*, 170–71; Sherbourne Cook, "Expeditions to the Interior of California: Central Valley, 1820–1840," *Anthropological Records*, 1962, 168–80, 205–6; and also Richard Orsi, "Estanislao's Rebellion, 1829," in *The Elusive Eden: A New History of California*, edited by William Burrough, Richard Orsi, and Richard Rice, Alfred A. Knopf, 1996, 53–68.

329 *Celestial Militia*: Lasuén, in Janice Stevens and Pat Hunter, *Remembering the California Missions*, Craven Street Books, 2010, 84.

329 *went to the left*: See "Secularization of the Missions," 1922, in Stevens and Hunter, *Remembering the California Missions*, 86.

329 *saloon and dance hall*: In 1848, San Miguel also sustained the murder by roving vagabonds of eleven members and friends of the Reid family, who had bought the place in secularization.

330 *a knowing bird*: Due to San Fernando's deteriorating state, the extraordinary Indian Stations of the Cross are now at Mission San Gabriel. (Buried at Mission San Fernando is American comedian Bob Hope, who died July 27, 2003. When asked by his wife where he would like to be buried, Hope responded, "Surprise me.")

330 *Spain and France*: The new southern mission five miles east of present-day Oceanside, San Luis Rey, was named for Louis IX, though its most famous priest, Antonio Peyri, became an avid supporter of the Mexican Revolution ("Dios y Libertad!") and the French Revolution, as well.

330 *healthiest of all the missions*: Englehardt claimed more: "Father Peyri erected and successfully managed the largest and most populous Indian mission in both Americas." See Engelhardt, *San Luis Rey Mission*, 205.

330 *to the mission community*: Kimbro, Costello, and Ball, *The California Missions*, 238.

331 *Pablo Tac*: Antonio Peyri to Don Estevan Anderson, in Scotland from Barcelona, Spain, June 1834, in Englehardt, *San Luis Rey Mission*, 84.

331 *a low estimate of himself*: Kenneally, *The Writings of Fermín Francisco de Lasuén*, I, xxxix.

332 *these new Christians*: Kotzebue diary, from *The Visit of the Rurik to San Francisco in 1816*, 321–35, in Milliken, *A Time of Little Choice*, 219.

332 *one pear tree*: The sorry fate continued. In 1966, three of San Rafael's bells were stolen by fraternity brothers; one is still missing.

332 *the Bear Flag*: The original Bear Flag, which sported the words "California Republic," was burned in the great San Francisco earthquake and fire of 1906. But the state's official flag is quite similar to it.

Chapter Twenty-one: Secularization, Gold,
and the Destruction of the Missions

335 *family was everything*: Kevin Starr, *California: A History*, Modern Library, 2005, 50.

335 *Helen Hunt Jackson's* Ramona: The fictitious Moreno hacienda was modeled on Rancho Camulos, part of a huge (48,000-acre) Rancho San Francisco deeded in 1836 to the de Valle family. Camulos sat between Santa Clarita and Piru, and encompassed a large part of Ventura County and the San Fernando Valley.

336 *ready source of food*: Robert Chernyu, Gretchen Lemke-Santangelo, and Richard Griswold del Castillo, *Competing Visions: A History of California*, Houghton Mifflin, 2005, 76.

336 *arbitrary democracy*: Richard Henry Dana, *Two Years Before the Mast and Other Voyages*, Modern Library, 1840/2005, 162–63.

336 *also was denied*: Phillips, *Vineyards and Vaqueros*, 165.

336 *misdemeanors they might commit*: Ibid., 170.

336 *didn't keep to it*: Author interview with Randall Milliken, September 2013.

337 *then cut off*: Damien Bacich, "Zacatecan Franciscans in Alta California," paper presented at the California Missions Studies Association conference, Mission San Rafael, February 18, 2012.

337 *aged, infirm, children, etc.*: Englehardt, *San Gabriel Mission*, 194–95.

337 *despiser of hypocrisy*: Hugo Reid, "Los Angeles County Indians," *Los Angeles Star*, July 17, 1852.

337 *the crumbling mission*: Engelhardt, *San Gabriel Mission*, 192.

337 *those who got drunk*: Phillips, *Vineyards and Vaqueros*, 172.

337 *across the country today*: According to a recent report of the National Institute for Alcohol Abuse and Alcoholism, the Native American population on reservations in San Diego County (also known as "Mission Indians") have a 60 percent lifetime prevalence rate of alcohol abuse and disorder. This is six times greater than the abuse rate for the general population ("Risk Factors for Alcoholism and Native Americans"). The Native American rate of death nationally from alcoholism is almost six times the national average, too.

337 *lay his hands on*: Robert Ryal Miller, *Juan Alvarado: Governor of California, 1836–1842*, University of Oklahoma Press, 1998, 32–34.

337 *history with the Moors*: Douglas Monroy, "Zorro, Cows, Indians, and Dons: Re-creating California Rancho Society," in *The Borders Within*, 77.

339 *kidnapping Indian children*: Starr, *California*, 99.

339 *milk punch*: Stevens and Hunter, *Remembering the California Missions*, 38.

339 *transferred to the* rancheros: Sandos, *Converting California*, 110.

339 *on our own land*: Author interview with Greg Castro, California Indian Conference, Irvine, California, October 10, 2010.

Chapter Twenty-two: The Serra Legend
and the Question of Sainthood

341 *accompanying old age*: From "Where Is Serra Buried?" Chapter V, Section I of Series 4: Serra Burial, in the Serra Cause collection, Santa Barbara Mission Archive and Library.

341 *may have been other spurs*: See Robert Senkewicz, "The Representation of Junípero Serra in California History," in Beebe and Senkewicz, eds., *"To Toil in that Vineyard of the Lord,"* 20.

341 *simple human history*: Palou, *Relación*, xxvi (SW).

342 *golden snow-storm*: Helen Hunt Jackson, *Ramona*, Modern Library, 1884/2005, 37–38.

342 *foremost, grandest figure*: H.H. (Helen Hunt Jackson), "Father Junípero Serra and His Work," *Century Magazine* 26, I & II (1883): 11, 18.

342 *most ancient Jaffa orange groves*: See Nahum Karlinsky, *California Dreaming: Ideology, Society, and Technology in the Citrus Industry of Palestine, 1890–1939*, State University of New York Press, 2005.

342 *Southern California has*: Starr, *California*, 85.

343 *it seems Junípero was*: Theodore Hittell, *History of California*, Vol. I, 1885, 300, 448.

343 *pious and prudent*: Jean-François de la Pérouse, *Life in a California Mission: Monterey in 1786*, Heydey Books, 1789/1989, 57, 70. Pérouse even compares Mission San Carlos "to a plantation at Santo Domingo or any other West Indian Island"—i.e., where there was slavery.

343 *any slight negligence*: Herbert Bancroft, *History of California*, Vol. I, San Francisco, 1884–1890, 414–16.

343 *our seraphic father*: Engelhardt, *San Francisco or Mission Dolores*, 52.

343 *Father Junípero's forehead*: Willa Cather, *Death Comes for the Archbishop*, Modern Library, 1927, 284.

343 *suffered in that neighborhood*: Beatification and Canonization, *Catholic Encyclopedia*, www.newadvent.org/cathen/o2364b.htm, 3.

343 *Christians to the lions*: Lawrence Cunningham, *A Brief History of the Saints*, Blackwell, 2005, 12.

344 *the saintly narrative*: June Macklin, "Saints and Near-Saints in Transition: The Sacred, the Secular, the Popular," in *The Making of the Saints*, edited by James Hopgood, University of Alabama Press, 2005, 4.

344 *contrary to this reputation*: See Sacra Congregatio Pro Causa Sanctorum, *Super Vita et Virtutibus Positio Iuniperi Serra*, The Vatican, 1981.

345 *that is, holiness*: "*Lumen gentium*," Vatican Council II, *The Conciliar and Post-Conciliar Documents*, edited by Austin Flannery, O. P., St. Paul Editions, 1988, 411, in Michael Higgins, *Stalking the Holy: The Pursuit of Saint Making*, Simon & Schuster, 2006, 27.

346 *totaled 7,440 pages*: Brother Lawrence Scrivani, "Seeing the Serra Documents Through the Eyes of an Archivist," in *"To Toil in that Vineyard of the Lord,"* Beebe and Senkewicz, eds., 124–44.

346 *magisterial*: "Magisterial" is the assessment of Robert Senkewicz.

346 *descendants of this family*: For these interviews, see the *Positio*, 566–88. González's great-uncle was Manuel Patrón, corporal of the guard during Serra's time at Mission San Carlos Borromeo and husband of a Rumsen Ohlone woman, Margarita Amarillo.

347 *three theological virtues*: The *Positio* also discusses the "gifts of grace" as exemplified by Serra: wisdom, understanding, knowledge, courage, counsel, piety, and fear of the Lord. Serra had most, if not all, of these in abundance before he left Mallorca; they only increased in the New World. The *Positio* also deals with the three vows of a Franciscan (and any priest): poverty, chastity, and obedience. Serra was a prime exponent of the first two; "obedience" to his San Fernando superiors he practiced, though not easily, and obedience to the civil and military leaders of New Spain was a rocky thing.

NOTES

347 *his repugnance for it*: Palou, *Relación*, 293 (SW).

347 *without doubt, manifold*: Serra to Pangua, in Mexico City from Carmel, August 22, 1775. In Tibesar II, 325.

347 *[lack of] obedience*: Author interview with Father John Vaughn, Mission Santa Barbara, March 2, 2012.

348 *New World by Europe*: Among the few others with such a vision is Samuel Champlain of France. The difference is Champlain led a large punitive campaign and army of French and Huron against the Iroquois. Serra led with the imperative of mercy.

348 *my offense punishes me*: Theodore E. Treutlein, trans., *Missionary in Sonora: The Travels of Joseph Och, S.J., 1755–1767*, California Historical Society, 1965, 168, in Francis Guest, "Discipline in California Mission Life," in *Hispanic California Revisited*, Santa Barbara Mission Archive and Library, 1996, 269.

348 *committed a mortal sin*: Alfonso de la Peña Montenegro, *El Itinerario para Parochos de Indios*, Hermanos de Tournes, 1754, 180–81, in Guest, *Hispanic California Revisited*, 272.

348 *a matter of justice*: Guest, *Hispanic California Revisited*, 271.

348 *change the conversation*: Palou, *Relación*, 298 (SW).

349 *journeys in the New World*: Geiger counts 5,525 miles in thirty-three Serra land trips in Alta California alone. Adding excursions around Mexico and Baja brings the total to about nine thousand. Geiger found only five Serra trips (of two hundred) specifically noted by Palou done on foot, and only one of these in Alta California. My calculations of these five amount to one thousand miles on foot. See *Life and Times*, I, 83. This does not take into consideration his considerable travel around Mallorca nor his several sea voyages.

349 *a very burdensome saint*: Palou, *Relación*, 306 (SW).

349 *100,000 were baptized*: The six thousand figure is Geiger's (*Life and Times*, II, 373); Sandos has a smaller figure ("at least 4,600") in *Converting California*, 33. Hackel noted the 577 personal baptisms by Serra in "Junípero Serra's California Sacramental Community," in Beebe and Senkewicz, eds., *"To Toil in That Vineyard of the Lord,"* 77; he also assesses 100,000 mission baptisms for the period 1769–1850 (*Alta California*, 3).

350 *our father, St. Francis*: Geiger, *Life and Times*, II, 311.

350 *greater is his hope*: Palou, *Relación*, 316 (SW).

351 *Vatican board concurred*: Kenneth Woodward, *Making Saints: How the Catholic Church Determines Who Becomes a Saint, Who Doesn't, and Why*, Simon & Schuster, 1990, 202–3.

351 *Genocide*: Canonizing Serra, when he had "helped in the genocide of Native American peoples . . . is a contradiction of the words the religion preaches," suggested one critic. See Rupert Costo and Jeannette Henry Costo, eds., *The Missions of California: A Legacy of Genocide*, Indian Historian Press, 1987.

351 *rejected this claim*: James Sandos, who holds a chair in history at the University of Redlands, said, "Comparison [of Franciscan acts] to genocide is totally false. The U.S. Government paying people to slaughter others, that's genocide." George Harwood Phillips noted, "I don't think you can see Franciscan missionaries committing genocide [in California]." Both historians spoke at the California Indian Conference, Irvine, California, October 15, 2010.

NOTES

351 *I'm still kicking*: Author interviews with Father John Vaughn, Mission Santa Barbara, January 1 and March 2, 2012.

351 *a tense relationship*: Author interview with Monsignor Arthur Holquin, San Juan Capistrano Basilica, San Juan Capistrano, California, December 2010.

353 *these Indian singers*: Robert Louis Stevenson, "The Old Pacific Capital," in *Across the Plains*, 106–7.

353 *are still Catholic*: See William Sturtevant, gen. ed., *Handbook of North American Indians*, Vol. 8, *California*, edited by Robert Heizer, Smithsonian Institution Press, 1978, 561, 595; also Nadia Powers, "The Chumash," unpublished bachelors thesis, University of California, Los Angeles, 1980, 19-20, in Guest, *Hispanic California Revisited*, 235.

354 *a workaround, which is loving*: Author interviews with Dr. Daniel Young, Washington, DC, 2011–13. Dr. Young elaborated: "Serra transferred through the floggings his anger not only at Indian behavior marring his utopian dream, but also at his own human imperfection. Serra, being an intellectual, could not have escaped the realization of the trap he'd fallen into by the end, despite his best intentions, and therein lies his personal tragedy."

354 *my soul is being abolished*: Sandos, *Converting California*, 178.

354 *foresight to stop it*: Guest judged the whipping unsparingly: "It was a form of degradation that violated human dignity." Guest, *Hispanic California Revisited*, 282.

354 *way he was trained*: Author interview with Dr. James Sandos, California Missions Studies Association conference, November 2010.

354 *wrong, even arrogant*: Author interview with Dr. Daniel Young.

355 *accumulating food surpluses*: Jared Diamond, *Guns, Germs, and Steel: The Fate of Human Societies*, W. W. Norton, 1999/2003, 426.

355 *rather than eliminated*: David Weber, *Bárbaros*, 4.

355 *close to extinction*: Julie Sly, "Retired Bishop Apologizes to Indians for Church's Treatment," *Catholic News Service*, January 21, 2008.

355 *at pre-contact*: An Indian by federal designation, however, is defined as one-quarter Indian by blood; thus the "Indians" of today are much different from the pre-contact ones. The actual 2005 US Census figure is 696,000, the largest total of Native Americans for any state.

356 *on top of each other*: Author interview with James Luna and Mel Vernon, California Missions Studies Association Conference, Oceanside, California, February 27, 2010.

356 *to be too proud*: Author interview with David Belardes and Jerry Nieblas, California Mission Studies Association conference, Oceanside, California, February 27, 2010.

357 *I don't think Serra*: All quotations here to break from author interview with Andrew Galvan, San Francisco, California, 2012.

358 *loving and merciful Father*: Dr. Jarvis Streeter, "God and the History of the Universe," unpublished manuscript, 38.

358 *evangelization as one*: Father Irwin Schoenstein, "How I Have Been Enriched by Dialogue," unpublished manuscript, 57–58.

359 *hardly have envisioned it*: Many observers lay the second presidential victory of Barack Obama at the feet of the Latino vote, the growing number of Latino campaign donors, and the importance of Latinos in the US economy.

NOTES

359 *endlessly hazardous ethic*: Reynolds Price, *A Serious Way of Wondering: The Ethics of Jesus Imagined*, Scribner, 2003, 125.

359 *Who am I to judge*: Rachel Donadio, "On Gay Priests, Pope Francis Asks, 'Who Am I to Judge?'" *New York Times*, July 29, 2013.

359 *monuments, after all*: Author interviews with Fathers Vaughn and Osborne.

Epilogue: Winter Solstice at Mission Santa Barbara

361 *esoteric and spiritual experience*: See Steve Chawkins, "A Light Show and a Mystery," *Los Angeles Times*, December 22, 2011.

BIBLIOGRAPHY

The Visitation by Mariotto Albertinelli
(1503) depicts the meeting between cousins
Mary and St. Elizabeth in the New Testament.
Displayed as a copy of the Uffizi Gallery
original at Carmel Mission once a year.

Agreda, Venerable Mary of. *The Mystical City of God*. Charlotte, NC: Tan Books, 1686/1978 (abridged edition).

Alonzo, Armando. *Tejano Legacy: Rancheros and Settlers in South Texas, 1734–1900*. Albuquerque: University of New Mexico Press, 1998.

Augustine. *The Confessions*. Translated by Albert Outler. Mineola, NY: Dover Publications, 2003.

Bancroft, Herbert Howe. *History of California*. 4 vols. San Francisco: various publishers, 1884–86.

Bargellini, Clara and Michael Komanecky. *The Arts of the Missions of Northern New Spain, 1600–1821*. Mexico City: Mondato Antiguo Colegio de San Ildefonso, 2009.

Beebe, Rose Marie, and Robert Senkewicz, eds. and trans. *Lands of Promise and Despair: Chronicles of Early California, 1535–1846*. Berkeley, CA: Heyday Books, 2001.

———, eds. *Testimonios: Early California Through the Eyes of Women, 1815–1848*. Berkeley: University of California Press and Heyday Books, 2006.

———, eds. *"To Toil in That Vineyard of the Lord": Contemporary Scholarship on Junípero Serra*. Berkeley, CA: Academy of American Franciscan History, 2010.

Beilharz, Edwin. *Felipe Neve: First Governor of California*. San Francisco: California Historical Society, 1971.

Blackhawk, Ned. *Violence over the Land: Indians and Empires in the Early American West*. Cambridge, MA: Harvard University Press, 2006.

Bolton, Herbert, ed. *Pedro Font's Complete Diary of the Second Anza Expedition*. New York: Russell & Russell, 1966 (reprint).

Bonaventure. *The Journey of the Mind to God*. Translated by Philotheus Boehner. Indianapolis: Hackett Publishing Company, 1993.

Boneu Companys, Ferando. *Gaspar de Portolá: Explorer and Founder of California*. Lerida: Instituto de Estudios Ilerenses, 1983.

Bonner, Anthony. *Doctor Illuminatus: A Raymond Lull Reader*. Princeton, NJ: Princeton University Press, 1993.

Boscaná, Gerónimo. *Chinigchinich: Historical Account of the Belief, Usage, Customs, and Extravagancies of the Indians of This Mission of San Juan Capistrano Called the Acagchemen Tribe*. Translated by Alfred Robinson and John P. Harrington. Banning, CA: Malki Museum Press, 1978.

Bowden, Dina Moore. *Junípero Serra in His Native Isle (1713–1749)*. Palma de Mallorca: Gráficas Miramar, 1976.

Bowden, Henry Warner. *American Indians and Christian Missions: Studies in Cultural Conflict*. Chicago: University of Chicago Press, 1981.

Brass, Kristin. *Dry Bones and Indian Sermons: Praying Indians in Colonial America*. Ithaca, NY: Cornell University Press, 2004.

Brienen, Rebecca and Margaret A. Jackson. *Invasion and Transformation: Interdisciplinary Perspectives on the Conquest of Mexico*. Boulder: University of Colorado Press, 2008.

Brown, Raphael, ed. and trans. *The Little Flowers of St. Francis of Assisi*. New York: Image Books, 1971.

Burton-Carvajal, Julianne. *In the Footsteps of Father Junípero Serra, 1750–1758: The Five Folk-Baroque Mission Churches of Mexico's Sierra Gorda*. Monterey, CA: Anthony's Gate Publications, 2009.

Cabrera Bueno, Gonzalez. *Navegación Especulativa y Practica*. Edited by Michael Mathes. Madrid: Ediciónes José Francisco Turanzas, 1970.

Calloway, Colin. *New Worlds for All: Indians, Europeans, and the Remaking of Early America*. Baltimore: Johns Hopkins University Press, 1997.

Carr, Raymond, ed. *Spain: A History*. New York: Oxford University Press, 2001.

Carrico, Richard. *Strangers in a Stolen Land: Indians of San Diego County from Prehistory to the New Deal*. San Diego: Sunbelt, 2008.

Casey, Beatrice (Tid). *Padres and People of Old Mission San Antonio*. King City, CA: Casey Printing, 1957/2006.

Cather, Willa. *Death Comes for the Archbishop*. New York: Vintage, 1927/1990.

Cerny, Robert, Gretchen Lemke-Santangelo, and Richard Griswold del Castillo. *Competing Visions: A History of California*. Boston: Houghton Mifflin, 2005.

Cervantes, Miguel de. *Don Quixote*. Translated by Burton Raffel. New York: W. W. Norton, 1605/1999.

Chan, Sucheng and Spencer Olin, eds. *Major Problems in California History*. Boston: Houghton Mifflin, 1997.

Cheetham, Nicholas. *New Spain: The Birth of Modern Mexico*. London: Victor Gollancz, Ltd., 1974.

Chesterton, G. K. *Saint Francis of Assisi*. New York: Doubleday, 1957.

Colahan, Clark. *The Visions of Sor María de Agreda*: *Writing, Knowledge, and Power*. Tucson: University of Arizona Press, 1994.

Collis, Maurice. *Cortéz and Montezuma*. New York: New Directions, 1954.

Cook, Michael, ed. *The Eliot Tracts*. Westport, CT: Praeger, 2003.

Cook, Sherburne. *The Conflict Between the California Indian and White Civilization*. Berkeley: University of California Press, 1976.

Cooper, James Fenimore. *The Last of the Mohicans: A Narrative of 1757*. New York: Signet, 1826/1962.

Couve de Murville, M. N. L. *The Man Who Founded California: The Life of Blessed Junípero Serra*. San Francisco: Ignatius Press, 2000.

Crespí, Juan. *A Description of Distant Roads: Original Journals of the First Expedition into California, 1769–1770*. Translated and edited by Alan K. Brown. San Diego: San Diego State University Press, 2000.

Crosby, Harry. *Gateway to Alta California: The Expedition to San Diego, 1769*. San Diego: Sunbelt, 2003.

Crow, John. *Spain: The Root and the Flower*. Berkeley: University of California Press, 1985.

Cunningham, Lawrence. *A Brief History of the Saints*. Oxford: Blackwell, 2005.

Dana, Richard Henry. *Two Years Before the Mast and Other Voyages*. New York: Library of America, 1869/2005.

Defourneaux, Marcelin. *Daily Life of Spain in the Golden Age*. Translated by George Allen. New York: Praeger, 1971.

Delio, Ilia, O.S.F. *Crucified Love: Bonaventure's Mysticism of the Crucified Christ*. Quincy, IL: Franciscan Press, 1998.

DeNevi, Don and Noel Frances Moholy. *Junípero Serra: The Illustrated Story of the Franciscan Founder of California's Missions*. San Francisco: Harper & Row, 1985.

DeVinck, José, trans. *Works of Bonaventure*. 5 vols. Paterson, NJ: St. Anthony Guild Press, 1966–70.

Didion, Joan. *Where I Was From*. New York: Vintage, 2003.

DuBose, Francis. *Classics of Christian Missions*. Nashville: Broadman Press, 1979.

Edwards, Jonathan. *The Life of David Brainerd*. Vol. 7 of *The Works of Jonathan Edwards*. Edited by Norman Pettit. New Haven, CT: Yale University Press, 1985.

———. *Original Sin*. Vol. 3 of *The Works of Jonathan Edwards*. Edited by Clyde Holbrook. New Haven, CT: Yale University Press, 1970.

Engelbert, Omer. *The Last of the Conquistadors: Junípero Serra, 1713–1784*. New York: Harcourt, Brace, 1956.

Engelhardt, Zephyrin. *Mission San Carlos Borromeo: The Father of the Missions.* Ramona, CA: Ballena Press, 1973.

———. *Mission San Luis Obispo: In the Valley of the Bears.* Santa Barbara, CA: W. T. Gens, 1933/1963.

———.*The Missions and Missionaries of California.* San Francisco: James H. Barny, 1908–15.

———. *San Buenaventura: The Mission by the Sea.* Santa Barbara, CA: Mission Santa Barbara, 1930.

———. *San Francisco, or Mission Dolores.* Chicago: Franciscan Herald Press, 1924.

———. *San Gabriel Mission and the Beginnings of Los Angeles.* Chicago: Franciscan Herald, 1927.

———. *San Luis Rey Mission.* San Francisco: James H. Barry, 1921.

Espinosa, Isidor Felix, O.F.M. *Crónica Apostólica y Seráfica de Todos los Colegios de Propaganda Fide de Esta Nueva España.* Mexico: 1746.

Fagan, Brian. *Before California: An Archaeologist Looks at Our Earliest Inhabitants.* Lanham, MD: Altamira Press, 2003.

Fages, Pedro. *An Historical, Political, and Natural Description of California.* Translated by Herbert Priestley. Berkeley: University of California Press, 1775/1937.

Ferrer de Sant Jordi y Figuera, Nicolás. *Libro de las Cosas Memorables que han Acontecido en Mallorca, Desde Ano 1730 a 1739.*

Fischer, David Hackett. *Champlain's Dream: The European Founding of North America.* New York: Simon & Schuster, 2008.

Fitch, Abigail. *Junípero Serra, The Man and His Work.* New York: A. C. McClung, 1914.

Flannery, Austin, O.P., ed. *Vatican Council II: The Concilar and Post-Concilar Documents.* Boston: St. Paul Editions, 1988.

Fletcher, Richard. *Moorish Spain.* New York: Henry Holt, 1992.

Flint, Roland. *And Morning.* Washington, DC: Dryad Press, 1975.

Fogarty, John Columba. *The Catholic Priest: His Identity and Values.* Kansas City, MO: Sheed and Ward, 1988.

Fogel, Daniel. *Junípero Serra, the Vatican, and Enslavement Theology.* San Francisco: Ism Press, 1988.

Font, Pedro. *With Anza to California, 1775–1776: The Journal of Pedro Font, O.F.M.* Translated by Alan K. Brown. Norman: University of Oklahoma Press, 2011.

Forbes, Jack D. *Native Americans of California and Nevada.* Healdsburg, CA: Naturegraph Publishers, 1968.

Forteza, Miguel. *Els Decendents dels Jueus Conversos de Mallorca.* Palma de Mallorca: Gráficas Miramar, 1966.

Frey, Linda and Marsha Frey. *Societies in Upheaval: Insurrection in France, Hungary, and Spain in the Early Eighteenth Century.* Westport, CT: Greenwood Press, 1987.

Fuentes, Alvaro Campaner y. *Croninicon Majoricense. Palma de Mallorca: Estable Cimiento Tipográfico de Juan Colomar y Salas.* 1881.

Fuentes, Carlos. *The Buried Mirror: Reflections on Spain and the New World.* Boston: Houghton Mifflin, 1992.

Gaitan, Francisco and Jaime Lajous, eds. *The Missions of the Sierra Gorda.* Mexico City: Elzevir Editores, 1985.

Galvin, John, ed. *The Journal of Father Vicente Santa María*. San Francisco: Howell Books, 1775/1971.

Garate, Donald. *Juan Bautista de Anza, Basque Explorer in the New World*. Reno: University of Nevada Press, 2003.

Geiger, Maynard, O.F.M. *Franciscan Missionaries in Hispanic California, 1769–1848*. San Marino, CA: Huntington Library, 1969.

———. *God's Acre at Mission Santa Barbara: The History of the Mission Cemetery and Its Famous Dead*. China: CKI, 2008.

———. *The Life and Times of Fray Junípero Serra, O.F.M., or The Man Who Never Turned Back, 1713–1784*. Vols. I and II. Washington, DC: Academy of American Franciscan History, 1959.

———, trans. *Palou's Life of Fray Junípero Serra*. Washington, DC: Academy of American Franciscan History, 1955.

Geiger, Maynard and Clement W. Meighan. *As the Padres Saw Them: California Indian Life and Customs as Reported by the Franciscan Missionaries, 1813–1815*. Santa Barbara, CA: Santa Barbara Mission Archive and Library, 1976.

Geiger, Maynard and John Johnson. *The Indians of Mission Santa Barbara*. Santa Barbara, CA: Old Mission, 2010.

Gomez Canedo, Lino. *Sierra Gorda, un Tipico Enclave Missional en el Centro de Mexico (siglos XVII–XVIII)*. Querétaro: Ediciones del Gobierno del Estado de Querétaro, 1988.

Gorracz, José de and José de Escandón. *Papeles sobre la reducción del Seno Mexicano y Sierra Gorda (1748–1792)*. 1700–1770.

Guest, Francis. *Hispanic California Revisited*. Santa Barbara, CA: Santa Barbara Mission Archive Library, 1996.

Hackel, Steven W., ed. *Alta California: Peoples in Motion, Identities in Formation, 1769–1850*. San Marino, CA: The Huntington Library and the University of California Press, 2010.

———. *Children of Coyote, Missionaries of Saint Francis: Indian-Spanish Relations in Colonial California, 1769–1850*. Williamsburg, VA: University of North Carolina Press, 2005.

———. "Father Junípero Serra: Agent of the Inquisition." Paper presented at the Brown America Seminar, Oregon State University, April 24, 2007.

———. *Junípero Serra: California's Founding Father*. New York: Hill & Wang, 2013.

Hann, John. *The Indians of Central South Florida*. Gainesville: University Press of Florida, 2003.

Hardwick, Michael R. *Changes in Landscape: The Beginnings of Horticulture in the California Missions*. Orange, CA: Paragon, 2005.

Harlow, Neil. *California Conquered: The Annexation of a Mexican Province, 1846–1850*. Berkeley: University of California Press, 1982.

Heizer, Robert, ed. *The Indians of Los Angeles County: Hugo Reid's Letters of 1852*. Southwest Museum: 1968.

Heizer, Robert and M. A. Whipple, eds. *The California Indians: A Sourcebook*. Berkeley: University of California Press, 1971.

Hennigsen, Gustav and John Tedeschi. *The Inquisition in Modern Europe: Studies in Sources and Methods*. New Haven, CT: Yale University Press, 1997.

Hicks, Jack, James D. Houston, Maxine Hong Kingston, and Al Young, eds. *The

BIBLIOGRAPHY

Literature of California: Writings from the Golden State. Berkeley: University of California Press, 2000.

Hittel, John. *A History of the City of San Francisco and Incidentally of the State of California.* San Francisco: A. L. Bancroft, 1878.

Hittel, Theodore. *History of California.* San Francisco: Pacific Press, 1885.

Hogeland, L. Frank and Kim Hogeland. *First Families: A Photographic History of California Indians.* Berkeley, CA: Heyday Books, 2007.

Homza, LuAna. *Religious Authority in the Spanish Renaissance.* Baltimore: Johns Hopkins University Press, 2000.

Hopgood, James. *The Making of Saints.* Mobile: University of Alabama Press, 2005.

Horowitz, Tony. *A Voyage Long and Strange: On the Trail of the Vikings, Conquistadors, Lost Colonists, and Other Adventurers in Early America.* New York: Picador, 2008.

Hurtado, Albert L. *Indian Survival on the California Frontier.* New Haven, CT: Yale University Press, 1988.

———. *Intimate Frontiers: Sex, Gender, and Culture in Old California.* Albuquerque: University of New Mexico Press, 1999.

Imágenes del Convento Franciscano Santiago. Querétaro: Museo Regional de Querétaro, 2002.

Inés de la Cruz, Sor Juana. *Sor Juana's Love Poems.* Translated by Jaime Manrique and Joan Larkin. Madison: University of Wisconsin Press, 2003.

Ingham, Mary Beth. *Scotus for Dunces: An Introduction to the Subtle Doctor.* St. Bonaventure, NY: Franciscan Institute, 2003.

Jackson, Helen Hunt. *Ramona.* New York: The Modern Library, 1884/2005.

Jackson, Robert H. and Edward Castillo. *Indians, Franciscans, and Spanish Colonization: The Impact of the Mission System on California Indians.* Albuquerque: University of New Mexico Press, 1995.

Jaume, Llorenc Gari. *Iglesia y Claustro de San Francisco, Memoria del Beato Fray Junípero Serra.* Palma: Taller Gràfic Ramon, 1990.

Jones, Terry and Kathryn Klar. *California Prehistory: Colonization, Culture, and Complexity.* Plymouth (UK): AltaMira Press, 2007.

Kamen, Henry. "Vicissitudes of a World Power, 1500–1700," in *Spain: A History*, edited by Raymond Carr. New York: Oxford University Press, 2000.

———. *The Spanish Inquisition: A Historical Revision.* New Haven, CT: Yale University Press, 1998.

Karlinsky, Nahum. *California Dreaming: Ideology, Society, and Technology in the Citrus Industry of Palestine, 1890–1939.* Albany: State University of New York Press, 2005.

Kenneally, Finbar, ed. and trans. *Writings of Fermín Francisco de Lasuén*, Vols. I and II. Washington, DC: Academy of American Franciscan History, 1965.

Kimbro, Edna and Julia Costello, with Tevvy Ball. *The California Missions: History, Art, and Preservation.* Los Angeles: Getty Conservation Institute, 2009.

King, Kenneth. *Mission to Paradise: The Life and Times of Junípero Serra.* London: Burns & Oates, 1956; Chicago: Franciscan Herald Press, 1975.

Knight, Alan. *Mexico: The Colonial Era.* New York: Cambridge University Press, 2002.

Krekelberg, William. *Mission San Juan Capistrano.* Orange County, CA: Diocese of Orange, 2004.

Kroeber, Alfred. *Handbook of the Indians of California*. Bureau of American Ethnology, Bulletin 18, 1925.

Larkin, Brian. *The Very Nature of God: Baroque Catholicism and Religious Reform in Bourbon Mexico City*. Albuquerque: University of New Mexico Press, 2010.

Las Casas, Bartolomé de. *The Devastation of the Indies: A Brief Account*. Translated by Herman Briffault. Baltimore: Johns Hopkins University Press, 1992.

Luthin, Herbert, ed. *Surviving Through the Days: Translations of Native California Stories and Songs*. Berkeley: University of California Press, 2002.

MacCullough, Diarmaid. *Christianity: The First Three Thousand Years*. New York: Penguin, 2010.

Mack, John P., Jr. *Priests: An Inside Look*. Winona, MN: St. Mary's Press, 2001.

Manera, Carlos. "Manufactura texile y comercio en Mallorca, 1700–1830." *Revista de Historia Economica* 6, no. 3 (1988): 523–55.

Marino, Cesare. "Roman Catholic Missions in California and the Southwest." In *History of Indian-White Relations*, edited by Wiolcomb E. Washburn. Washington, DC: Smithsonian Institution, 1988.

Martin, Valerie. *Salvation: Scenes from the Life of St. Francis*. New York: Vintage, 2001.

Mathes, W. Michael. *The Land of Calafia: A Brief History of Peninsular California, 1533–1848*. Tecate: CAREM, 2009.

Maynard, Theodore. *The Long Road of Father Serra*. New York: Appleton-Century-Crofts, 1954.

McCawley, William. *The First Angelinos: The Gabrielino Indians of Los Angeles*. Menlo Park, CA: Ballena Press and Malki Museum, 1996.

McGinn, Bernard. *The Golden Chain: A Study in the Theological Anthropology of Isaac of Stella*. Washington, DC: Cistercian Publications, 1972.

McLaughlin, David J., with Rubén Mendoza. *The California Missions Source Book*. Albuquerque, NM: Pentacle Press, 2009.

McWilliams, Carey. *Southern California: An Island on the Land*. Salt Lake City: Peregrine Smith, 1946/1973.

Medrano, Ethelia Ruiz. *Mexico's Indigenous Communities: Their Lands and Histories, 1500–2010*. Boulder: University of Colorado Press, 2010.

Menocal, Maria Rosa. *The Ornament of the World: How Muslims, Jews, and Christians Created a Culture of Tolerance in Medieval Spain*. New York: Back Bay Books, 2002.

Miller, Chester Gore. *Father Junípero Serra: A New and Original Historical Drama in Four Acts*. Chicago: Press of Skeen, Baker & Co., 1894.

Miller, Robert Ryal. *Juan Alvarado: Governor of California, 1836–1842*. Norman: University of Oklahoma Press, 1998.

Milliken, Randall. *A Time of Little Choice: The Disintegration of Tribal Culture in the San Francisco Bay Area, 1769–1810*. Menlo Park, CA: Ballena Press, 1995.

Miskwish, Michael Connolly. *Kumeyaay: A History Textbook*. El Cajon, CA: Sycuan Press, 2007.

Monroy, Douglas. *The Borders Within: Encounters Between Mexico and the U.S.* Tucson: University of Arizona Press, 2008.

Montalvo, Garci Rodriguez de. *The Labors of the Very Brave Knight Esplandian*. Translated by William Little. Binghamton, NY: Medieval and Renaissance Texts and Studies, 1510/1992.

BIBLIOGRAPHY

Moore, Kenneth. *Those of the Street: The Catholic-Jews of Mallorca.* South Bend, IN: University of Notre Dame Press, 1976.

Morgado, Martin. *Junípero Serra, A Pictorial Biography.* Monterey, CA: Siempre Adelante Publishing, 1991.

Newell, Quincy D. *Constructing Lives at Mission San Francisco: Native Californians and Hispanic Colonists, 1776–1821.* Albuquerque: University of New Mexico, 2009.

Nicolas, Antonio. *Powers of Imagining: Ignatius Loyola.* Albany: State University of New York Press, 1986.

Obrador, Bartolomé Font. *El Apóstol de California, sus Albores.* Palma: Direccio General de Cultura, 1989.

Obrador, Bartolomé Font and Norman Neuerburg. *Junípero Serra: Mallorca, Mexico, Sierra Gorda, Californias.* Palma: Comissio de Cultura, Consell Insular de Mallorca, 1992.

Ogden, Adele. *The California Sea Otter Trade, 1784–1848.* Berkeley: University of California Press, 1941.

Osio, Antonio María. *The History of Alta California: A Memoir of Mexican California.* Madison: University of Wisconsin Press, 1996.

Page, Jake. *In the Hands of the Great Spirit: The 20,000-Year History of the American Indians.* New York: Free Press, 2003.

Palou, Francisco, O.F.M. *Apostólicas Tareas Noticias de la Nueva California (Historical Memoirs of of New California).* 4 Vols. Edited and translated by Herbert Bolton. Berkeley: University of California Press, 1926.

———. *Relación Histórica de la Vida del Venerable Padre Fray Junípero Serra (Life and Apostolic Labors of the Venerable Father Junípero Serra).* Edited by George Wharton James. Translated by C. Scott Williams. Pasadena, CA: George Wharton James, 1913.

Parras, Pedro Josaé. *Diario y Defretero de Sus Viajes, 1749–1753.* Buenos Aires: Ediciones Argentianas "Solar," 1943.

Paz, Octavio. *The Labyrinth of Solitude.* New York: Grove Press, 1985.

Pérouse, François de la. *Life in a California Mission: Monterey in 1786.* Berkeley, CA: Heyday Books, 1989.

Perry, Richard. *Exploring Colonial Oaxaca: The Art and Architecture.* Santa Barbara, CA: Espadaña Press, 2006.

Phillips, George Harwood. *Chiefs and Challenges: Indian Resistance and Cooperation in Southern California.* Berkeley: University of California Press, 1975.

———. *Vineyards and Vaqueros: Indian Labor and the Economic Expansion of Southern California, 1771–1877.* Norman: University of Oklahoma Press, 2010.

Piette, Charles J. G. *Evocation de Junípero Serra, fondateur de la Californie.* Washington, DC: Academy of American Franciscan History, 1976.

Pointer, Richard W. *Encounters of the Spirit: Native Americans and European Colonial Religion.* Bloomington: Indiana University Press, 2007.

Polk, Dora Beale. *The Island of California: A History of the Myth.* Lincoln: University of Nebraska Press, 1991.

Prescott, William H. *History of the Conquest of Mexico.* New York: Modern Library, 1843/2001.

Price, Reynolds. *A Serious Way of Wondering: The Ethics of Jesus Imagined.* New York: Scribner, 2003.

BIBLIOGRAPHY

Priestley, Herbert Ingram. *José de Gálvez: Visitor-General of New Spain, 1765–1771.* Berkeley: University of California Press, 1916/1980.

Rasperger, Christopher. *Two Hundred Interpretations of the Words "This Is My Body."* Ingolstadt: 1577.

Raycraft, Susan and Ann Keenan Beckett. *San Antonio Valley.* Charleston, SC: Arcadia, 2006.

Rivera y Moncada, Fernando de. *Diario del Capitán Comandante Fernando de Rivera y Moncada.* Madrid: Ediciones José Parrua Tuvanzas, 1967.

Robles, Vito Alessio. *Coahuila y Texas en la Época Colonial.* Mexico City: Editorial Porrua, 1978.

Rodriguez, Richard. *Brown: The Last Discovery of America.* New York: Penguin, 2002.

Rougement, Denis de. *Love in the Western World.* New York: Harper Colophon, 1956.

Russell, Craig H. *From Serra to Sancho: Music and Pageantry in the California Missions.* New York: Oxford University Press, 2009.

Sandos, James A. *Converting California: Indians and Franciscans in the Missions.* New Haven, CT: Yale University Press, 2004.

Schewinitz, Edmund. *The Life and Times of David Zeisberger: The Western Pioneer and Apostle of the Indians.* New York: Lippincott, 1870/1971.

Schoenstein, Irwin. "How I Have Been Enriched by Dialogue." Unpublished manuscript, 2013.

Schroeder, Susan, ed. *The Conquest All Over Again: Nahuas and Zapotecs Thinking, Writing, and Painting Spanish Colonialism.* Eastbourne, UK: Sussex Press, 2010.

Scott, George Ryley. *The History of Corporal Punishment.* London: Senate, 1996.

Sheridan, Gail and Mary Pat McCormick. *Art from the Carmel Mission.* Carmel, CA: Fine Arts Press, 2011.

Shipek, Florence. *Pushed into the Rocks: Southern California Land Tenure, 1769–1986.* San Diego: Viejas Band of Kumeyaay Indians, 1987.

Shoup, Laurence H. and Randall T. Milliken. *Inigo of Rancho Posolmi.* Novato, CA: Ballena Press, 1999.

Skowronek, Russell. *Situating Mission Santa Clara.* Washington, DC: Academy of American Franciscan History, 2006.

Smith, David and Frederick Taggart, eds. *Diary of Gaspar de Portolá During the California Expedition of 1769–1770.* Berkeley: University of California Press, 1909.

Sobreques i Callicó, Jaume. *Orígenes Hispanos de California: De la Expedición de Portolá a la Independencia de Mexico.* Barcelona: Editorial Base, 2010.

Solnit, Rebecca. *River of Shadows: Eadweard Muybridge and the Technological Wild West.* New York: Viking, 2003.

Starr, Kevin. *California: A History.* New York: Modern Library, 2005.

———. *Inventing the Dream: California Through the Progressive Era.* New York: Oxford University Press, 1985.

Stegner, Wallace. *Where the Bluebird Sings to the Lemonade Springs: Living and Writing in the West.* New York: Modern Library, 2002.

Stevens, Janice and Pat Hunter. *Remembering the California Missions.* Fresno, CA: Craven Street Books, 2010.

Stevenson, Robert Louis. *Across the Plains.* New York: Scribner, 1898.

Streeter, Jarvis. *God and the History of the Universe.* Unpublished manuscript, 2013.

Sturdevant, William. *Handbook of North American Indians.* Washington, DC: Smithsonian Institution, 1978.

Suntree, Susan. *Sacred Sites: The Secret History of California.* Lincoln: University of Nebraska Press, 2010.

Taraval, Sigismundo. *The Indian Uprising in Lower California, 1734–1737.* Translated by Marguerite Ayer Wilbur. Los Angeles: The Quivira Society, 1931.

Thomas, Hugh. *Conquest: Montezuma, Cortéz, and the Fall of Old Mexico.* New York: Simon & Schuster, 1995.

———. *Rivers of Gold: The Rise of the Spanish Empire, from Columbus to Magellan.* New York: Random House, 2005.

Tibesar, Antonine, ed. *Writings of Junípero Serra.* Vols I–IV. Washington, DC: Academy of American Franciscan History, 1955, 1956, 1966.

Torrens y Nicolau, Francisco. *Bosquejo Histórico del Insigne Franciscano, V. P. F. Junípero Serra, Fundador y Apóstol de la California Septentrional.* Felanix, Mallorca: B. Reus, 1913.

Trevino, Robert and Richard Francaviglia. *Catholicism in the American West: A Rosary of Hidden Voices.* Arlington, TX: A & M Press, 2007.

Tsanoff, Radoslav. *Autobiographies of Ten Religious Leaders: Alternatives in Christian Experience.* San Antonio, TX: Trinity University Press, 1968.

Velasquez, María del Carmen. *El Estado de Guerra en Nueva España, 1760–1808.* Mexico City: Colegio de Mexico, 1976.

Vega, Lope de. *The Discovery of the New World by Christopher Columbus: A Comedy in Verse.* Berkeley, CA: Gillick Press, 1590/1950.

Wade, Maria F. *Missions, Missionaries, and Native Americans: Long-Term Processes and Daily Practices.* Gainesville: University Press of Florida, 2008.

Walker, G. S. M. *The Growing Storm: Sketches of Church History from AD 600 to AD 1300.* London: Paternoster Press, 1961.

Weber, David J. *Bárbaros: Spaniards and Their Savages in the Age of Enlightenment.* New Haven, CT: Yale University Press, 2005.

Weber, Msgr. Francis J. *Blessed Fray Junípero Serra: An Outstanding California Hero.* Strasbourg: Editions du Signe, 2007.

Williams, Walter L. *The Spirit and the Flesh: Sexual Diversity in American Indian Culture.* Boston: Beacon Press, 1986.

Wills, Garry. *Why Priests? A Failed Tradition.* New York: Viking, 2013.

Wolff, Catherine. *Not Less than Everything: Catholic Writers on Heroes of Conscience from Joan of Arc to Oscar Romero.* New York: HarperCollins, 2013.

Zaehner, R. C. *Mysticism: Sacred and Profane.* London: Oxford University Press, 1961.

INDEX

INDEX

PHOTO AND MAP CREDITS

Text

p. ix   Image from the Glen McLaughlin Map Collection, courtesy Stanford University Libraries.

p. 3   Courtesy of The Bancroft Library, University of California, Berkeley.

p. 5   Gregory Orfalea.

p. 17   Gregory Orfalea.

p. 30   Gregory Orfalea.

p. 55   Father Valentí Serra, Archivo Provincial de los Capuchinos de Cataluña, Barcelona.

p. 73   The Granger Collection, New York.

p. 84   Drawing by Fernando Brambilia, Malaspina Expedition, 1790. Courtesy of Superstock/Museo Naval, Madrid.

p. 93   Courtesy of The Bancroft Library, University of California, Berkeley.

p. 111   Museo Comunitario San Pedro Escanela.

p. 128   Biblioteca Francisco de Burgoa, Oaxaca.

p. 146   Bill Dewey.

p. 173   Map image courtesy of Barry Lawrence Ruderman Antique Maps, www.RareMaps.com.

p. 175   Courtesy of The Bancroft Library, University of California, Berkeley.

p. 191   Courtesy of The Bancroft Library, University of California, Berkeley.

p. 195   San Diego History Center.

p. 209   Dennis Wysynski.

p. 221   Museo Regional de Guadalupe, Zacatecas, Mexico.

p. 230   Bill Dewey.

p. 241   Dennis Wysynski.

p. 243   Courtesy of The Bancroft Library, University of California, Berkeley.

p. 261   © Mark Rightmire/The Orange County Register/ZUMAPRESS.com.

p. 279   Photograph by C. C. Pierce. Courtesy of the University of Southern California, on behalf of the USC Special Collection.

p. 300   Ayuntamiento de Palma, Mallorca.

p. 321   Reproduced by permission of The Huntington Library, San Marino, California.

p. 323   Courtesy of The Bancroft Library, University of California, Berkeley.

p. 333   Courtesy of The Bancroft Library, University of California, Berkeley.

p. 340   Dennis Wysynski.

p. 360   Gregory Orfalea.

p. 363   Gregory Orfalea.

p. 369   Patrick Tregenza.

p. 433   Dennis Wysynski.

p. 465   Eileen Orfalea.

Insert

1. Santa Barbara Mission Archive and Library.
2. Santa Barbara Mission Archive and Library.
3. Gregory Orfalea.
4. Andreas Bischof.
5. Dina Moore Bowden.
6. Andreas Bischof.
7. © Museo Nacional del Prado, Madrid.
8. Dennis Wysynski.
9. Courtesy of The Bancroft Library, University of California, Berkeley.
10. Courtesy of The Bancroft Library, University of California, Berkeley.
11. Courtesy of The Bancroft Library, University of California, Berkeley.
12. The Seaver Library, Natural History Museum of Los Angeles.
13. © Jeffrey Becom 2014.
14. © Jeffrey Becom 2014.
15. Courtesy of The Bancroft Library, University of California, Berkeley.
16. William A. Karges.
17. San Diego History Center.
18. San Diego History Center.
19. San Diego History Center.
20. Gregory Orfalea.

ABOUT THE AUTHOR

Looking out Serra's childhood window, Petra, 2011.

Gregory Orfalea was born and raised in Los Angeles, California, and educated at Georgetown University and the University of Alaska. He has taught at Georgetown University, the Claremont Colleges, and Westmont College. Orfalea is the author and editor of eight previous books, the most recent of which are the short story collection *The Man Who Guarded the Bomb* (2010) and *Angeleno Days* (2009). The recipient of many awards for his writing, Orfalea won the 2010 Arab American Book Award and was named a Finalist for the PEN USA Award in Creative Nonfiction for *Angeleno Days*.